Arabic and Hebrew Love P(
in Al-Andalus

CW01024966

Arabic and Hebrew Love Poems in Al-Andalus investigates a largely overlooked subset of Muslim and Jewish love poetry in medieval Spain: hetero- and homoerotic love poems written by Muslim and Jewish religious scholars, in which the lover and his sensual experience of the beloved are compared to scriptural characters and storylines.

This book examines the ways in which the scriptural referents fit in with, or differ from, the traditional Andalusian poetic conventions. The study then proceeds to compare the scriptural stories and characters as presented in the poems with their scriptural and exegetical sources. This new intertextual analysis reveals that the Jewish and Muslim scholar-poets utilized their sacred literature in their poems of desire as more than poetic ornamentation; the Muslim poets employ Qur'ānic heroes in order to justify profane love and sanctify erotic human passions. In the Hebrew lust poems, which utilize biblical heroes, we can detect subtle, subversive, and surprisingly placed interpretations of biblical accounts.

Moving beyond the concern with literary history to challenge the traditional boundaries between secular and religious poetry, this book provides a new, multidisciplinary, approach to existing materials and will be of interest to students, scholars, and researchers of Islamic and Jewish Studies as well as to those with an interest in Hebrew and Arabic poetry of Islamic Spain.

Shari L. Lowin is Associate Professor in the Religious Studies Department at Stonehill College, USA, teaching Islamic and Jewish Studies. Her research focuses on early Islamic intellectual thought, and its interplay with midrashic texts.

Culture and civilization in the Middle East
General Editor: Ian Richard Netton
Professor of Islamic Studies, University of Exeter

This series studies the Middle East through the twin foci of its diverse cultures and civilisations. Comprising original monographs as well as scholarly surveys, it covers topics in the fields of Middle Eastern literature, archaeology, law, history, philosophy, science, folklore, art, architecture and language. While there is a plurality of views, the series presents serious scholarship in a lucid and stimulating fashion.

PREVIOUSLY PUBLISHED BY CURZON

The Origins of Islamic Law
The Qur'an, the Muwatta' and Madinan Amal
Yasin Dutton

A Jewish Archive from Old Cairo
The History of Cambridge University's Genizah Collection
Stefan Reif

The Formative Period of Twelver Shi'ism
Hadith as Discourse Between Qum and Baghdad
Andrew J. Newman

Qur'an Translation
Discourse, Texture and Exegesis
Hussein Abdul-Raof

Christians in Al-Andalus 711–1000
Ann Rosemary Christys

Folklore and Folklife in the United Arab Emirates
Sayyid Hamid Hurriez

The Formation of Hanbalism
Piety into Power
Nimrod Hurvitz

Arabic Literature
An Overview
Pierre Cachia

Structure and Meaning in Medieval Arabic and Persian Lyric Poetry
Orient Pearls
Julie Scott Meisami

Muslims and Christians in Norman Sicily
Arabic-Speakers and the End of Islam
Alexander Metcalfe

Modern Arab Historiography
Historical Discourse and the Nation-State
Youssef Choueiri

The Philosophical Poetics of Alfarabi, Avicenna and Averroes
The Aristotelian Reception
Salim Kemal

PUBLISHED BY ROUTLEDGE

1. **The Epistemology of Ibn Khaldun**
   Zaid Ahmad

2. **The Hanbali School of Law and Ibn Taymiyyah**
   Conflict or Concilation
   Abdul Hakim I Al-Matroudi

3. **Arabic Rhetoric**
   A Pragmatic Analysis
   Hussein Abdul-Raof

4. **Arab Representations of the Occident**
   East–West Encounters in Arabic Fiction
   Rasheed El-Enany

5. **God and Humans in Islamic Thought**
   Abd al-Jabbār, Ibn Sīnā and al-Ghazālī
   Maha Elkaisy-Friemuth

6. **Original Islam**
   Malik and the madhhab of Madina
   Yasin Dutton

7. **Al-Ghazali and the Qur'an**
   One Book, Many Meanings
   Martin Whittingham

8. **Birth of The Prophet Muhammad**
   Devotional Piety in Sunni Islam
   Marion Holmes Katz

9. **Space and Muslim Urban Life**
   At the Limits of the Labyrinth of Fez
   Simon O'Meara

10. **Islam and Science**
    The Intellectual Career of Nizam al-Din al-Nizaburi
    Robert G. Morrison

11. **Ibn 'Arabî – Time and Cosmology**
    Mohamed Haj Yousef

12. **The Status of Women in Islamic Law and Society**
    Annotated translation of al-Ṭāhir al-Ḥaddād's *Imra'tunā fi'l-sharī'a wa 'l-mujtama'*, with an introduction
    Ronak Husni and Daniel L. Newman

13. **Islam and the Baha'i Faith**
    A Comparative Study of Muhammad 'Abduh and 'Abdul-Baha 'Abbas
    Oliver Scharbrodt

14. **Comte de Gobineau and Orientalism**
    Selected Eastern Writings
    Translated by Daniel O'Donoghue
    Edited by Geoffrey Nash

15. **Early Islamic Spain**
    The History of Ibn al-Qūṭīya
    David James

16. **German Orientalism**
    The Study of the Middle East and Islam from 1800 to 1945
    Ursula Wokoeck

17. **Mullā Ṣadrā and Metaphysics**
    Modulation of Being
    Sajjad H. Rizvi

18. **Schools of Qur'anic Exegesis**
    Genesis and Development
    Hussein Abdul-Raof

19. **Al-Ghazali, Averroes and the Interpretation of the Qur'an**
    Common Sense and Philosophy in Islam
    Avital Wohlman, translated by David Burrell

20. **Eastern Christianity in the Modern Middle East**
    Edited by Anthony O'Mahony and Emma Loosley

21. **Islamic Reform and Arab Nationalism**
Expanding the Crescent from the Mediterranean to the Indian Ocean (1880s–1930s)
Amal N. Ghazal

22. **Islamic Ethics**
Divine Command Theory in Arabo-Islamic Thought
Mariam al-Attar

23. **Muslim Fortresses in the Levant**
Between Crusaders and Mongols
Kate Raphael

24. **Being Human in Islam**
The Impact of the Evolutionary Worldview
Damian Howard

25. **The UAE and Foreign Policy**
Foreign Aid, Identities and Interests
Khalid S. Almezaini

26. **A History of Early al-Andalus**
The Akhbar Majmu'a
David James

27. **Inspired Knowledge in Islamic Thought**
Al-Ghazali's Theory of Mystical Cognition and its Avicennian Foundation
Alexander Treiger

28. **Shi'i Theology in Iran**
The Challenge of Religious Experience
Ori Goldberg

29. **Founding Figures and Commentators in Arabic Mathematics**
A History of Arabic Sciences and Mathematics, Volume 1
Roshdi Rashed, translated and edited by Nader El-Bizri

30. **The Muslim Conquest of Iberia**
Medieval Arabic Narratives
Nicola Clarke

31. **Angels in Islam**
Jalal al-Din al-Suyuti's *al-Haba'ik fi akhbar al-mala'ik*
Stephen Burge

32. **Theological Approaches to Qur'anic Exegesis**
A Practical Comparative-Contrastive Analysis
Hussein Abdul-Raof

33. **Ibn al-Haytham and Analytical Mathematics**
A History of Arabic Sciences and Mathematics, Volume 2
Roshdi Rashed, translated and edited by Nader El-Bizri

34. **Ghazali's Politics in Context**
Yazeed Said

35. **Orientalism Revisited**
Art, Land and Voyage
Edited by Ian Richard Netton

36. **Ibn al-Haytham's Theory of Conics, Geometrical Constructions and Practical Geometry**
A History of Arabic Sciences and Mathematics, Volume 3
Roshdi Rashed, translated by J. V. Field

37. **Science and Religion in Mamluk Egypt**
Ibn al-Nafis, Pulmonary Transit and Bodily Resurrection
Nahyan Fancy

38. **The Qur'an in Christian–Muslim Dialogue**
Historical and Modern Interpretations
C. Jonn Block

39. **Arabic and Hebrew Love Poems in Al-Andalus**
Shari L. Lowin

Arabic and Hebrew Love Poems in Al-Andalus

Shari L. Lowin

Routledge
Taylor & Francis Group
LONDON AND NEW YORK

First published 2014 by Routledge

2 Park Square, Milton Park, Abingdon, Oxfordshire OX14 4RN
52 Vanderbilt Avenue, New York, NY 10017

Routledge is an imprint of the Taylor & Francis Group, an informa business

First issued in paperback 2019

Copyright © 2014 Shari L. Lowin

The right of Shari L. Lowin to be identified as author of this work has been asserted by her in accordance with sections 77 and 78 of the Copyright, Designs and Patents Act 1988.

All rights reserved. No part of this book may be reprinted or reproduced or utilised in any form or by any electronic, mechanical, or other means, now known or hereafter invented, including photocopying and recording, or in any information storage or retrieval system, without permission in writing from the publishers.

Notice:
Product or corporate names may be trademarks or registered trademarks, and are used only for identification and explanation without intent to infringe.

British Library Cataloguing in Publication Data
A catalogue record for this book is available from the British Library

Library of Congress Cataloging in Publication Data
A catalog record for this book has been requested

ISBN: 978-0-415-82416-3 (hbk)
ISBN: 978-0-367-86756-0 (pbk)

Typeset in Times New Roman
by Graphicraft Limited, Hong Kong

If you wish to make some matter well known, put it in a poem. If you put it in a book, never on your life will it spread abroad.

Jedaiah ben Abraham Bedersi (1270–1340)

If you read something in God's book that you do not understand, then look for it in the poetry of the Arabs, for poetry is the register of the Arabs.

Ibn `Abbās (d. 687)

Poetry is a more hidden kind of philosophy, of higher worth and not for the profane.

Morton W. Bloomfield, "Allegory as Interpretation"

Contents

7 The cloak of Joseph: Ibn Ḥazm and the therapeutic power of romantic love 218

PART IV
The hermeneutics of desire 255

8 Surprise kisses and the burning bush: Ibn al-Milḥ and the metaphysics of passion 257

Summary 274

Bibliography 277
Index 296
Index of complete poems (by title) 304

Preface

This book offers an analysis of secular poems of desire produced in Islamic Spain of the tenth to thirteenth centuries. Specifically, it presents an intertextual and multidisciplinary study of a largely overlooked category of Arabic and Hebrew poetry: eros poems produced by religious scholars, in which the lover's passion for the beloved is compared to scriptural characters and storylines.

Although other examples supporting my claim exist, the current analysis limits itself to a digestible number of poems, three in Hebrew and four in Arabic. The three Hebrew poems come from two different Jewish scholar-poets: the tenth-century Hebrew grammarian, religious scholar, and *piyyut* (religious poetry) author, Isaac ibn Mar Shaul of Lucena, and the slightly later master poet and virtuoso of biblical *remizah* (hinting), Solomon ibn Gabirol (*c.* 1021–*c.* 1058). Of the four Arabic poems, three belong to the Muslim theologian and author of a treatise on love and passion, Abū Muḥammad ʿAlī b. Aḥmad b. Saʿīd b. Ḥazm (Cordoba, 994–1064). The fourth comes from Abū al-Qāsim b. al-Milḥ, known for his poetry and works of belles-lettres compositions and who also served as the *khaṭīb* of his mosque, preparing and delivering the religious sermons there. While he thus was not of the religious status or level of scholarship as Ibn Ḥazm, he proves a respectable complement to Ibn Ḥazm.

These seven poems are arranged in three parts composed of two poems each, one in Hebrew and one in Arabic. Part I examines poems in which the lovers are compared to scriptural characters to whom Scripture attributes no romantic affiliation. Importantly, these characters are scripturally outsider, rather than heroic, characters. The poems of Part II similarly present scriptural referents with no connection to love; here the scriptural characters and accounts, heroes in major narratives, employ the imagery of opposites, emphasizing the fickle nature of romantic love. Part III differs from the previous two in that the scriptural characters come from narratives in which love does play a role. However, these accounts concern familial rather than romantic love. Nonetheless, the poets utilize these accounts and characters as the scriptural parallels for their romantic lovers. Part IV consists of a single chapter, an Arabic poem which emphasizes a lover's surprise at having attained the actualization of passion rather than fires of passion itself.

All seven chapters point to the same two conclusions. Namely, the chapters on the Hebrew poems show that Ibn Mar Shaul and Ibn Gabirol employed scriptural allusions in eros poems, not only as poetic ornament, but also as embedded and potentially unpopular scriptural exegesis. The chapters on the Arabic poems show the opposite to be at work. Rather than using the eros poems as a vehicle for teaching about Scripture, Ibn Ḥazm and Ibn al-Milḥ here employ Scripture as a vehicle for teaching about human love and passion.

Acknowledgements

In *Winnie the Pooh*, a children's story laced with mature philosophical lessons, A. A. Milne wrote of Piglet that though his heart was physically very small, it could contain copious amounts of gratitude. Like Piglet, I feel a great deal of gratitude for the many people and institutions whose input made the writing of this book possible.

Practically speaking, I could never have taken the time to research and write had I not been the recipient of a number of generous grants. Therefore, I would like to express my sincerest thanks to the American Council of Learned Societies, the Memorial Foundation for Jewish Culture, the Yad Hanadiv/Beracha Fellowship, the Albright Institute, the Stonehill College Professional Development Grant Fund, and the Conboy Fund at Stonehill College. Their support made this project financially feasible.

These grants would have been ineffective without the generosity of my colleagues and the administration at Stonehill College, my professional home for the past ten years. The major work on this project was done during a consecutive two-year period in which I buried myself in the Middle East Reading Room of the National Library of Israel. This was possible only because my chairman Chris Ives, my colleagues in the Religious Studies department, and Provost and Vice President for Academic Affairs Katie Conboy allowed me to take a leave of absence on the heels of my sabbatical year, freeing me from teaching for a second year in a row and allowing me to take advantage of a subsequent fellowship I had been awarded. Their generosity also enabled me to become a film star in Jerusalem; I spent so much time in the library during that period that I appear in not one but two films shot there, and am onscreen for at least four seconds.

I owe a great debt to the many individuals who allowed me to talk through my ideas with them, who gave me crucial feedback, who argued with me and forced me to hone my arguments, who smiled when I described my topic, and who encouraged me to turn it from the spark of an idea into a full-fledged research project. Among the many such individuals, I would like to single out Alanna Cooper, Pearl Kaplan, Nancy Khalek, Raquel Ukeles, Avi Shmidman, and Jonathan Sarna. At points, each also talked me down from the various emotional ledges that solitary academic research combined with intense academic skirmishing can lead one toward. Additionally, Pearl Kaplan, a model of hospitality and generosity, opened her home to me in Jerusalem and, as she has for the past fifteen years, blessed me with the power of her friendship. Alanna Cooper and Moshe Shapiro's home has become one of my favorite places in Cambridge, MA; it is filled with love, warmth, intellectual sustenance, and emotional support. It also has three little girls who shout with joy when I enter the room, and that too helps a book get written.

Because this book began life as a presentation on Islamic Spain in an Islamic historiography class in my first year of graduate school, I wish to thank the man who assigned that topic to me. Fred M. Donner has been my professor and advisor for close to twenty years now. I hope this work makes him proud.

Finally, I would like to thank my father, Dr. Joseph Lowin, for all of his help, and input, and encouragement, for always dropping whatever he was doing to work out a point with me, or to read something that required a second set of eyes, and for believing in the value of the project in those moments when I faltered. I am a fortunate daughter to have learned to love the life of the mind from him. He is my first reader and the one whose pleasure in my work I take most pleasure in. A special debt of thanks goes also to my mother Judith, whose quiet support and faith in me I have never questioned. And to Sophie and Eitan Lowin, who were born during the writing of this book and who have brought crucially needed comedic interludes, a fact that is even more impressive considering they did so from 250 miles away and are completely unaware of the good they were doing.

Permission has been granted to reproduce poems, or translations of poems, or portions of poems in and by the following:

A. J. Arberry, *The Ring of the Dove* (London: Luzac and Company, Ltd. 1953). Reprinted with permission of Mrs. Anna Evans.

James A. Bellamy and Patricia Owen Steiner, *The Banners of the Champions: An Anthology of Medieval Hebrew Poetry from Andalusia and Beyond*. Madison, WI: The Hispanic Seminary of Medieval Studies, 1989: 171, 194, 199.

Judah al-Ḥarizi, *The Book of the Taḥkemoni: Jewish Tales from Medieval Spain*. Translated, explicated, and annotated by David Simha Segal. London: Littman Library of Jewish Civilization, 2001: 402.

Solomon Ibn Gabirol, *Shirei ha-Ḥol le-Rabbi Shelomo ibn Gabirol*. Edited by Ḥ. Brody and Ḥ. Schirmann. Jerusalem: Machon Schocken, 5735 [1974].

Jewish Prince in Moslem Spain: Selected Poems of Samuel Ibn Nagrela. Introduced, translated, and notes by Leon J. Weinberger. Tuscaloosa: University of Alabama Press, 1973.

Norman Roth, " 'Deal Gently with the Young Man': Love of Boys in Medieval Hebrew Poetry of Spain." *Speculum* 57:1 (January 1982): 20–51. Copyright © 1982 Medieval Academy of America. Reprinted with the permission of Cambridge University Press.

Raymond Scheindlin, "Ibn Gabirol's Religious and Sufi Poetry," *Sefarad* 54:1 (1994): 113–14.

Ḥaim (Jefim) Schirmann, *Ha-Shirah ha-`Ivrit be-Sefarad u-ve-Provans*. Jerusalem: Mossad Bialik, 1954. Reprinted with the permission of Mossad Bialik and Dvir Publishing House.

Jefim (Ḥaim) Schirmann, *New Hebrew Poems from the Genizah*. Jerusalem: The Israel Academy of Sciences and Humanities, 1965, p. 158. © The Israel Academy of Sciences and Humanities. Reproduced by permission.

Shirei ha-Ḥol le-Rabbi Shelomo ibn Gabirol. Edited by Ḥaim Brody and Ḥaim Schirmann. Jerusalem: Machon Schocken, 5735 [1974]: 61.

Wine, Women and Death: Medieval Hebrew Poems on the Good Life. Edited and translated by Raymond Scheindlin. Philadelphia: Jewish Publication Society, 1986. Reprinted with the permission of the University of Nebraska Press. Copyright 1986 by the Jewish Publication Society.

Transliterations and notations

The transliteration of Arabic words follows the style of the *Encyclopedia of Islam*, new edition, with a modification in the case of the letter ج (*jīm*), which appears as "j" rather than "dj," in accordance with current scholarly practice. Arabic words that have been transliterated in non-Arabic book and article titles have been left as they appear there.

The transliteration of Hebrew words follows the style set in the *Encyclopedia Judaica*. The style of the transliteration of titles and commonly used words follows common scholarly practice. Hebrew words and names that have been transliterated in non-Hebrew titles have been left as they appear there. The exception to this is Jefim Schirmann, who publishes in English as Jefim and in Hebrew as Ḥaim Schirmann. In order to make clear that this is the same individual, I have included both of his names even when he does not.

References to *EJ* refer to the 2007 edition of the *Encyclopedia Judaica*, unless otherwise noted.

As much as possible, Judeo-Arabic words have been transliterated in accordance with the rules of Arabic transliteration. The exception to this rule is the word דיואן. In the titles of Hebrew books about Hebrew poets and poems, it appears as *Diwan* (not *Dīwān*).

In order to allow readers of Hebrew to follow the Arabic chapters and readers of Arabic to follow the Hebrew chapters, I have included references to English translations of the Arabic and Hebrew poems, when available. For example, references to the Arabic version of Ibn Ḥazm's *Ṭawq al-ḥamama* are followed by the corresponding pages in the translations of A. J. Arberry and A. R. Nykl. Similarly, Ibn Sa'īd's *Rāyāt al-mubarrizīn* is followed by the page/poem numbers in Bellamy and Steiner's *The Banners of the Champions*.

In order to use one uniform dating system, I have employed the Common Era designation. For aesthetic reasons, I have not, however, used the letters CE.

Abbreviations

BDB	Brown, Driver, and Briggs, eds, *A Hebrew and English Lexicon of the Old Testament*
BT	*Babylonian Talmud*
EI[2]	*New Encyclopedia of Islam*
EJ	*Encyclopedia Judaica.* 2007 Edition.
EQ	*Encyclopedia of the Qur'ān*
IOS	*Israel Oriental Society*
JAOS	*Journal of the American Oriental Society*
JJS	*Journal of Jewish Studies*
JNES	*Journal of Near Eastern Studies*
JQR	*Jewish Quarterly Review*
JSAI	*Jerusalem Studies in Arabic and Islam*
JSS	*Jewish Social Studies*

1 Introduction

It is told that an aristocratic Muslim gentleman fell in love at first sight with a certain woman while they were at the Ka`ba, Islam's most holy site. Overcome with love, the man approached the lady and recited:

> I have great passion for my religion while I like pleasures.
> How can I have passion for pleasures as well as Islam?

The lady replied, "Leave the one and you will have the other."[1]

It has become almost axiomatic to note that many religious traditions teach that to be closer to God, one must distance oneself from the pull of the sensual world. It is thus puzzling to the modern mind to find Muslim and Jewish scholars of religion, authority figures in their faiths, standing proudly among the greatest composers of erotic secular love poetry in Muslim Spain of the tenth to thirteenth centuries. After all, we do not generally find imams or rabbis among the prime proponents of indulgence in physical pleasures. Yet, in Muslim Spain, rather than separating the spiritual world from the physical world, distinguishing between what the modern world deems the secular and the religious realms,[2] these Muslim and Jewish religious authority figures fused the two. Many of the men who composed influential works of scriptural exegesis, theological compositions, and religious legal tomes very often are the very same scholars who authored works on science, literature, and nature. Indeed, while Christian Europe found itself in an intellectual slumber, the educated leaders of Muslim Spain produced literature on almost every subject then known to man: theology, language, history and historiography, belles-lettres, geography, medicine, mathematics, astronomy, philosophy, and religious studies.[3]

But perhaps the literary product most wide-ranging in appeal are the poems, composed in both Arabic and Hebrew, touching on almost every sentiment and topic under the sun. Just as they involved themselves in composing "secular" and "religious" prose works, so too Muslim and Jewish religious scholars saw fit to write religious as well as secular verse.[4] They composed poems that praised God and yearned for His presence, while simultaneously extolling the drinking of wine, the beauty of gardens, of animals, and of beauty itself. They wrote poems bemoaning death, illness, and poverty. They contemplated the role of man in the world, the forces exerted by fate on the life of the individual, the circle of life. They complained in meter and rhyme of slights committed against them by friends or employers,[5] praised comrades and politicians, or wrote commissioned works of praise. Some later found themselves with the task of eulogizing these same people after their deaths. We find verses encouraging ethical behavior, warning against earthly seductions, or providing guidance in all matters. We find even witty epigrams, riddles, and language puns.[6] But perhaps the most enchanting of these secular poems composed by Muslim and Jewish poets, and the ones that form the basis of the current study, are the powerful, beautiful, and somewhat surprising (to the modern reader, at least) poems that speak of romantic desire, eros, between two people. These poems are known in Arabic as poems of عشق (*`ishq*) and in Hebrew as שירת חשק (*shirat ḥesheq*).

The current study addresses one particularly intriguing category of these secular *`ishq/ḥesheq* poems: poems written by religious scholars in which the lover and his sensual experience of the beloved are compared to scriptural characters and storylines. As any library catalog search will show, the Arabic and Hebrew love poetry of Andalusia serves as the subject of many a modern scholarly work. Yet, in engaging the scriptural allusions found in the love poetry, scholars have very generally restricted themselves to a two-pronged approach. Most commonly, scholars have approached such scriptural references and allusions in these poems largely to identify them, to show readers the scriptural sources from which the poets drew. Additionally, scholarly attention to the scriptural references has focused on demonstrating that the themes and imagery used by religious scholar-poets in their secular verses form part of the stock imagery current in the poetry of the Andalusian period.[7] In other words, modern scholars have shown that the medieval poets used Scripture largely as poetic ornament in service of the Andalusian poetic conventions of the day.

The current study challenges the notion of Scripture as ornament alone and what Ross Brann has termed the "rigorously formulaic approach to the study of literature"[8] of studies that insist on this as the only path. To be sure, the religious scholar-poets conformed to the "poetic vogue" in composing their secular poems. However, that religious authority figures turned to decidedly scriptural/exegetical characters and storylines in otherwise secular compositions begs our further attention. Indeed, it can be no accident that those most concerned with upholding the sacredness of religion, most involved in its texts, and promulgating its ideals, culled sacred imagery from the Bible, Qur'ān, *ḥadīth* (Islamic oral traditions), and *midrash aggadah* (rabbinic exegetical texts) to flesh out their heterosexually and homosexually charged poems of eros. As the current study shows, while both the Muslim and Hebrew poets eroticized their forebears in their poems of desire, they did so with differing results. As we shall see, when Arabic religious scholar-poets allude to their Scripture, drawing parallels between their lovers and their scriptural forefathers, they do so to sanctify earthly love. While Hebrew scholar-poets employ their own Scripture to the same effect, to be sure, some of the Hebrew poems appear to take the allusion a step further. In some of the hetero- and homoerotic Hebrew love poetry, we can detect subtle, subversive, and surprisingly placed biblical exegesis.

Brief history of Andalusian poetry

The Iberian Peninsula first came into contact with both Islam and Muslim Arabic culture in a significant way when the scion of the crushed Umayyad dynasty, `Abd al-Raḥmān I (r. 756–88), escaped the hands of the Abbasid defeaters, raced across the Strait of Gibraltar,[9] and established an independent Umayyad kingdom on Spanish soil, based out of Cordoba. While `Abd al-Raḥmān I brought with him from Damascus Eastern traditions and literary sensibilities, which he promoted in his new kingdom, it was not until the reign of `Abd al-Raḥmān III (912–61) that Arabic culture truly began to flourish in Andalusia. A patron of the arts, `Abd al-Raḥmān III built mosques, palaces, and libraries, turning Cordoba into one of the greatest intellectual centers of Western Europe at the time. Under his encouragement, Cordoba became renowned as a hub for learning in medicine, mathematics, astronomy, jurisprudence, philosophy, and literature.[10] Cultivation of culture and education continued under al-Ḥakam II (r. 961/2–976/7) who founded twenty-seven free elementary schools for Cordoba's children, ensuring literacy for almost all of his subjects. Al-Ḥakam II also founded a library whose catalog alone came to twenty-four volumes. To be sure, Cordoba did not remain the only seat of learning and education in Muslim-conquered Spain. Schools of higher education and of theology were founded and flourished in Seville, Toledo, Valencia, Almeria, Granada, Jaen, and Malaga.[11]

When the Umayyads fell from power in 1031 and were replaced by the smaller dynasties known as the Party Kings[12] over the course of the eleventh century, the flourishing of Arab culture in Spain grew even stronger. Vying with one another in monetary and cultural splendor, the Party Kings set aside many of the religious restrictions of Islam to more grandiosely foster both material and intellectual cultural development. Despite the political instability that reigned, they built sumptuous palaces and villas, saw to the establishment of magnificent gardens, indulged in wine-drinking, and reveled in literary parties to which they drew scholars, poets, and musicians.[13] Under the Party Kings, Arabic poetry flourished as princely patronage of the poets continued in stride. Indeed, each principality became a center of literature and art.

It was sometime during this period that two new forms of Arabic poetry were born, both of them native to Muslim Spain: the *zajal* (زجل) and the *muwashshaḥ* (موشح). These accompanied the *qaṣīda* (قصيدة), a pre-Islamic form of long, formulaic, mono-rhymed desert poetry with a rigid tripartite structure.[14] The *zajal* poems, the longer of the two new formats, constitute vernacular Arabic strophic poems with varying meter, beginning with a rhyming couplet that then serves as the refrain; evidence from the Arabic sources indicates that although not every *zajal* came with a musical score, the *zajal* was intended to be sung rather than read. Since poetry was the product of literate men, often these "vernacular" poems tilt toward classical Arabic. The greatest of the *zajal* poets of Andalusia was Ibn Quzmān (Cordoba, 1078–1160), whose longest *zajal* stretched to forty-two stanzas.[15] Like the *zajal*, the *muwashshaḥ* also constitutes a strophic poem with varying rhyme scheme, but the *muwashshaḥ* rarely extends beyond five or six stanzas. The main body of the poem is composed in classical Arabic, while the final couplet, the *kharja* (خرجة), appears in non-classical vernacular Arabic, in a Romance language, or in Romance mixed with vernacular Arabic. Frequently, the *kharja* was taken from a popular song or poem and was often spoken by a female voice.[16] The themes of the *muwashshaḥ* did not differ much from the *qaṣīda*, the earlier Arabic poetic form; these concerned love (mostly unrequited or blocked), panegyric, and wine. Like the *zajal*, the *muwashshaḥ* was intended to be sung, although, also like the *zajal*, a musical score was not necessarily composed with each poem. One of the great composers of Arabic *muwashshaḥ* poems in the later period was Ibn Sahl al-Isrā'īlī (d. *c.* 1251), a Jewish convert to Islam.[17]

With the crumbling of the kingdoms of the Party Kings and their conquest by the Almoravids, Muslim Berbers who seized control in *c.* 1086 and established their capital in Seville, it initially appeared as if Andalusian poetry had met its end. After all, the Almoravids initiated a period of religious stringency in which they restricted liberal thinking and which initially appeared to strangle poetic expression. But poetry was not, in fact, abandoned. Instead, the *fuqahā'* (religious legal authorities) and the poets clashed head on, and while as a result many of the poets simply left Seville, they continued to write poetry about their city and other topics. Those poets who remained and those who fell under the control of the Almoravids in other cities were given leave to write as scandalous verses as they deemed fit; in return, they were to publicly renounce independent thinking in other realms and refrain from attempting to influence the flow of politics. One of the more famous of such court-supported poets who composed sexually suggestive (and not so "suggestive") verse was the previously mentioned Ibn Quzmān.[18] Furthermore, since the Almoravid courts had little familiarity with classical Arabic and classical Arabic poetry, the poets now found themselves entertaining less-refined audiences and composing poems based on lighter forms than those of classical Arabic. James T. Monroe notes that one result of this was that the *kharja* became openly obscene.[19]

Less than a century after the Almoravids invaded Andalusia, they were themselves conquered by a Berber dynasty, the Almohads. Combining Sunnī and Shī`ī concepts regarding the role and nature of the caliph, the Almohads maintained that the key to salvation depended on obedience to their caliphs, whose word and rule was associated with the word and rule of Allāh. With their conquest of the Iberian Peninsula in 1145, the Almohads initiated a period of reform in almost every aspect of life, from the economy to religion, to art, architecture, and literature. Additionally, the Almohads rejected the earlier practices of religious tolerance toward non-Muslims that had reigned in Andalusia. As a result, the Mozarabs (Arabic-speaking Christians in Spain) and Jews were persecuted and either were expelled, converted to save their lives, or left Almohad-ruled Spain.[20]

Many of the fleeing Jews traveled north to Christian Spain, where they found safer haven, albeit one they felt was culturally inferior to the homeland from which they had taken flight.[21]

While the religious stringency of the Almohads might have signaled the end of poetry, the very opposite took place. Just as the Almohads "reformed" other types of expression in Andalusia, so too they reformed poetry.[22] Love poetry of the courtly type, considered to be a dignified format, saw a resurgence and became court-protected. Additionally, because the Almohads rejected the idea of narrow legalism, mystical love poetry (i.e., Ṣūfī poetry) – which celebrated spirituality and divine love – found support and a place in the Almohad environment.[23] Hebrew poetry also experienced a shift rather than a demise during this period. With the transplantation of the Andalusian poetic tradition to the Christian realm, Hebrew poetry faced a new set of challenges and cultural mores, sometimes perceived as a "decline" and earning the period the title of "Silver Age."[24] Unfortunately for the Almohads, their reign was to last only 100 years. In 1248, an alliance of Christian rulers effectively ended the Almohad dominance of Iberia, and with it came the final end of the prolific production, the Golden Age, of both Andalusian Arabic and Hebrew poetry.[25]

Despite the extensive breadth and high quality of the poems produced on Andalusian Muslim soil, one should understand that poetry was not an invention of the Muslim Spanish milieu but owes much to the poetic traditions that preceded it. Scholars have put forth two main theses regarding the influences that helped to create the poetic forms of this era. One theory, articulated by Henri Pérès, maintained that Arabic poetry of medieval Spain was the continuation of the native Iberian poetic tradition that had first been written in Latin.[26] Modern scholars have noted, for example, that Ibn Ḥazm (994–1064) and al-Raḍī, the son of the Sevillian caliph al-Mu`tamid (r. 1069–91), both include in their poems a comparison (admittedly rare) of the beloved to an angel, an image commonly found in Christian rather than Muslim imagery.[27]

Others insist that the poetry was a transplant of Eastern Arabic poetic forms; the intellectual Muslim elite of Spain were known to have looked consistently to the East, to have mined the East for cultural guidance until at least the eleventh century. The earliest traceable Arabic poetic form appears among the pre-Islamic Bedouins who, although largely thought to have been illiterate, composed long mono-rhymed poems of elaborate meter known as *qaṣīdas*,[28] compositions that frequently extolled Arab bravery in war, Arab generosity of spirit, or described Bedouin battlefield or pastoral scenes.[29] With the Islamization of the Arabian Peninsula that began in the seventh century with the Umayyad caliphate, this early form of Arabic poetry was preserved and underwent Islamization as well. Pagan ideas and values were replaced by Muslim ideals and values;[30] satirical poems that had earlier served to deride competing tribes were now used as political tools in the various skirmishes among the Muslim groups vying for power and control; poems of tribal boasting were reformulated to praise deeds done in the service of Islam. Themes from `Udhrite love began to work their way into the poems as well. Also known as pessimistic love poetry, `Udhrite love spoke of a lover's passionate desire for an unattainable beloved, a chaste desire that often led to the poet-lover's death from lovesickness.[31] With the rise of the Abbasid caliphate in 750 and its urbanization of Muslim Arab culture, Arabic poetry began to reflect this "new" lifestyle. Poems now spoke of gardens rather than deserts and of urban concerns rather than of desert nomad issues. Additionally, poems about wine and love of boys arose and flowered. As scholars have noted, a sense of sexual permissiveness pervades this period, with the poets and their compositions playing a large role in this arena.[32] All of these themes can be found in the poems of the "Golden Age" in Spain.

Taking the middle road, James Monroe convincingly points out that the truth lies in a combination of the two theories. On the one hand, he writes, there is no doubt that native Iberian elements appear in the strophic forms of poetry that arose in Muslim Spain. However, Monroe insists, Hispano-Arabic poetry is without a doubt of Eastern and Arab origin. It constitutes a branch of the Arabic literary tradition, rather than the Spanish. As a branch of the Arabic literary tradition, it reflects a far greater number of the Arabic elements and stylistic waves than are found in the native Spanish tradition.[33]

Love poetry and its conventions in medieval Spain

Like the other categories of poetry, *`ishq* poetry in Muslim Spain drew from the Arabic forms that predated it and was highly conventionalized. Indeed, so strong are the conventions used to describe the beloved that the reader often finds himself hard-pressed to figure out the gender of the beloved in question. The love-object rarely bears a name or any other identifying characteristics and poets describe male and female beloveds with almost identical terminology and imagery. Even the use of a gender-specific pronoun, when it appears, does not always solve the riddle; the poets were known to employ the masculine forms even when a feminine subject was intended, out of modesty.[34] Even more problematically, as Raymond Scheindlin notes, the poetic use of the masculine gender is often intended to create an atmosphere of indefinite sexuality which celebrates beauty as an ideal, rather than the beauty of any particular person or form.[35] While these poems of desire were intended to express the particular experience of the lover, they also echo the common experience of every human who loves.[36]

Among the many conventions of beauty that we find in Andalusian descriptions of the beloved, the most frequent present the beloved's hair as a mass of dark tresses, amid which a white, or bright, face shines through like the sun or the moon.[37] The shape of the beloved is compared to the branches of date palms. The beloved's beauty frequently causes the lover physical pain; the beloved's eyes tear the lover's heart to pieces, ensnare or capture him. When the beloved is identified outright as female, her breasts act as arrows, piercing the heart of the lover. If the beloved appears as a male, the early sprouting of his beard acts as thorns that prick the lover.[38] Not only is the beloved physically dangerous, but she or he is emotionally abusive as well. The beloved is hardhearted, abandoning the lover and leaving the lover pining, physically stricken from lovesickness. If the beloved appears to the lover in a dream, the beloved will not speak with him.[39] Or, if the beloved once graced the lover with his or her love, the beloved now cruelly betrays him.

As did their `Udhrite models, for the most part Andalusian lovers find themselves frustrated by involuntary and unwanted sexual chasteness. External obstacles or situations beyond their control impede the actualization of union with the beloved. Thus the lover remains alone, pining painfully and loyally for his beloved. Love burns in the heart of the lover as fire, threatening to consume him. It rages within him as a disease, an illness from which no true lover desires to be cured. This disease appears not only as a physical ailment, but results in psychological madness, which burns the lover painfully.[40] After all, as Norman Roth notes, the chief purpose of secular love/desire poetry is to express not the Joy of Love but the Pain of Love, pain which causes both spiritual and physical damage.[41] A lover who does not suffer, it was assumed, does not have a reason to write *`ishq* poetry, since *`ishq* poetry derives from the experience in which emotions and reality clash with one another.[42]

One should not understand, however, that because of this generally enforced poetic chastity, the poems make little reference to sexual interactions altogether. Some of the poems do in fact speak of stolen kisses and caresses. And while reference to complete physical union is somewhat rare, such descriptions do appear. More importantly, almost all the poems express a *desire* for sexual activity of some sort. The very title by which scholars refer to this category of poetry affirms that they speak of a clearly sexualized framework: عشق/חשק (*`ishq*/*ḥesheq*), rather than حب/אהבה (*ḥubb*/*ahavah*, love).[43] Even a brief survey of the Andalusian poems reveals that the Arabic and Hebrew poets rarely, if ever, spoke of spiritual love between human beings. Instead, the Hebrew and Arabic poets, secular and religious alike, restricted themselves to descriptions of the physical person and of physical desire, describing a longing for sexual interactions once experienced, or sexual experiences to which they were looking forward.

Modern scholars have pointed out that the Hebrew poetic expressions appear to have been somewhat less physically explicit than the Arabic compositions. Norman Roth, for example, insists that while Hebrew poetic love is "sensual, purely physical, and frankly erotic,"[44] in none of the Hebrew poems discovered does one detect references to any sexual activity other than kissing.[45] This, he maintains, is a far cry from the sexually explicit Arabic poetry of the same genre and age.[46] Roth's statement strikes the reader of the Hebrew poems as somewhat of an overgeneralization. While the Hebrew poems are less physically explicit than the Arabic, and while kissing remains the predominant activity in Hebrew, the Hebrew poems do not restrict themselves to kissing alone. In one poem, for example, Moses ibn Ezra exhorts his readers to "Caress the breasts of a lovely girl at night and kiss the lips of the beautiful girl all day long!"[47] In a reverse move, Judah Halevi presents a female beloved who asks her lover to *cease* fondling her breasts; although the lover's intentions appear to have been well placed, his hands lack the necessary skill, and thus his ministrations cause her physical discomfort, which she is keen to end.[48]

The popularity and prevalence of Arabic and Hebrew poetry of desire in medieval Andalusia should not mislead us into thinking that Muslim and Jewish religious authorities in Spain and its environs universally and without complaint accepted or supported the dissemination and publication of such sexually expressive poetry. Rather, criticism of the poems and their authors did take place. James Monroe brings numerous examples of poets who were told, under caliphal threat, to cease and desist from writing *`ishq* poems about their womenfolk.[49] The existence of religious criticism of the poets can be detected also in the self-justification of various Muslim poets who appear to be defending themselves against such accusations. One of the more famous examples appears in the writings of Ibn Ḥazm (994–1064), himself a jurist and author of numerous lines of *`ishq* poetry. At the end of his treatise on love and lovers (*Ṭawq al-ḥamāma*), he makes a point of defending himself against possible charges of impropriety or of violating religious prohibitions, stating that he is "a man of spotless innocence, pure, clean and undefiled." More dramatically, he swears in Allāh's name that he has never, in all his adult life, removed his trousers in order to commit an unlawful act.[50] Similarly, when the orthodoxy of the Ṣūfī poet Ibn `Arabī (1165–1240) was questioned because of his love poetry, he composed an exegesis of his poetry in self-defense (the *Tarjumān al-ashwāq*).[51]

The Hebrew *shirat ḥesheq* did not go uncriticized by contemporary religious Jewish authorities either. As in the Arabic case, the existence of such criticism can be detected in the self-defensive stances evident in the love poems. In the midst of a poem that begins as a typical poetic description of a boy beloved, Samuel ha-Nagid detours to remind his readers that his righteousness should not be doubted. "My soul," he writes, "as you know, is bound close to the fear of God." In the next line, he insists that readers understand his poems allegorically, just as rabbinic readers understood the erotica of the Song of Songs as religious allegory.[52] In the introduction to the edited volume of Samuel's secular poems, his son Joseph similarly insists on his father's abiding righteousness; the poems of desire, Joseph explains, should be understood as allegories for God's love of Israel.[53]

Another Jewish tactic of self-defense concerned aging poets' renunciation of their secular poems as "youthful folly." Most famously, Judah Halevi is said to have vowed at the end of his life never to write poetry again.[54] Similarly, Moses ibn Ezra wrote, "I, too, when a boy and a youth, considered poetry as something to be proud of ... However, I gave it up later, because I longed to fill my days with worthier things."[55] One should approach Ibn Ezra's statement, and perhaps similar statements by other scholar-poets, with a measure of suspicion. After all, later in the same work, Ibn Ezra writes, "Despite this, I did not withdraw completely from creating poetry, *when it was needed*"[56] (italics mine). Indeed, Ḥaim [Jefim] Schirmann maintains that the poets wrote their apologetic words only in order to pacify their more conservative critics.[57]

Condemnation of the Hebrew secular *ḥesheq* poetry centered not only on the content, but also on the format. In the course of a discussion in his *Perush `al ha-Mishnah* regarding the problem of listening to poetry, the philosopher/physician/

rabbinic scholar and authority Moses Maimonides (1138–1204) writes that pious men mistakenly think that Hebrew poems written on the model of "Ishmaelite" *muwashshaḥāt*, whose content is problematically lascivious, are permissible because they are written in Hebrew.[58] Not so, corrects Maimonides; Hebrew *muwashshaḥāt* rank as even more problematic. The Holy Tongue does not purify the lascivious content, as people might think; rather, he insists, it has thereby itself been defiled.

Charges of improper behavior continued to plague the Andalusian poets well beyond the Muslim Spanish period. In the seventeenth century, al-Maqqarī, an Algerian historian of Muslim Spain, defends the earlier *`ishq* poets in his *Nafḥ al-ṭīb*, saying, "حاكي الكفر ليس بكافر" (*ḥākī al-kufr laysa bi-kāfir*), "to speak of unbelief is not itself unbelief."[59] Some poems attracted the attention and condemnation not only of the religious authorities, but also of the caliphs, the political rulers who were ultimately responsible for the religious well-being of their republics. Importantly, however, in spite of the apparent religious criticism levied against both the Arabic and Hebrew poets for their secular *`ishq* poems, to our knowledge, none was ever charged with religious sedition.[60]

Poetry and scriptural references

Criticism of the *`ishq* poems of Andalusia concerned not only the possibly suspect behavior of the people who composed such verses, or the effects it might have on those hearing them, but also the fact that one of the conventions of *`ishq* poetry was its use of scriptural references and allusions. In the Hebrew realm, this issue perturbed Maimonides in particular. Already negatively predisposed to the use of Hebrew for bawdy poems, Maimonides declares that the use of scriptural verses does little to help the matter. Instead, he writes, in using a biblical verse in a Hebrew *muwashshaḥ*, the poet has violated Jewish law, employing the words of prophecy (i.e., the Hebrew Bible) for vice and vileness.[61] Geert Jan van Gelder points out that Muslim critics took a similar stance vis-à-vis the Arabic poems. Like Maimonides, they objected to what they considered "frivolous" usage of the sacred Qur'ān or the *ḥadīth* in poems that were of objectionable content.[62]

The Muslim and Jewish poets involved in the creation of such poems clearly disagreed. Not only did the less religious or a-religious poets incorporate their sacred Scripture into their secular compositions, but the religious scholar-poets, those whom one might presume to share more conservative religious sensibilities, did so as well.[63] It seems that citing Scripture or otherwise alluding to it or other religious texts constituted a convention of both Arabic and Hebrew poetry, one that religious scholar-poets saw little need to do without. In fact, the Hebrew poets rejoiced in such scriptural allusions, making a point of referencing extremely obscure biblical references, which their audience then had to figure out. In some cases, the references and allusions to the sacred text served as clues for the audience to use in figuring out a riddle that formed the main purpose of the poem.[64]

Like many other conventions of Spanish-era poetry, the use of religious ideas or texts in secular poems traces back to the very early days of production of Arabic poetry. Even before the Islamic period, Arabic poets had incorporated into their poems references to Arab literature and history, and also to religion.[65] With the rise of Islam, the Muslim Arab poets carried on this practice, but altered it to fit the new reality. Although they continued to refer to Arab history and Arabic literature, the Muslim Arabic poets as early as the Umayyad period were known to draw ideas, images, diction, and narratives from the Qur'ān for use in their poetry.[66] According to Wadād al-Qāḍī, even those poems that do not initially appear to be Qur'ānically charged frequently reveal themselves to be so on second glance.[67] At times the Qur'ānic ideas and elements that appear in Umayyad love poetry materialize as direct citations and at times as modified Qur'ānic references. For the Umayyads, such incorporation of the religious materials into the poetic compositions served not only a literary function. Umayyad Arabic poets employed their religiously infused and scripturally influenced verses as weapons in the political battles and in the religious disputes of the period.[68]

The Abbasid period saw the influence of the Qur'ān and *ḥadīth* in an even wider array of poems, especially love poetry.[69] Although the Abbasids did not invent love poetry, the Abbasid poet, writes A. M. Zubaidi, "exploited" everything in the Qur'ān and the traditions in which he found even the slightest semblance to his love theme. Beginning in the ninth century, we find also an increased use, not only of the Qur'ān itself, but of the entirety of the Islamic religious traditions (*ḥadīth*). Thus, Abbasid poets wrote of love as a holy war or of death and revivification taking place at the hands of a beloved (instead of God's hands); they wrote of the beloved as a *houri* of Paradise or as beautiful as the Qur'ānic Queen of Sheba (Bilqīs).[70]

Iqtibās *and* Talmīḥ

While allusions to the Qur'ān and religious texts appear in a variety of formats in the Arabic poetry of Andalusia, two of these prove of particular importance in the current study: *iqtibās* and *talmīḥ*.[71] The first, *iqtibās*, was used to indicate quotations from the words of the Qur'ān or *ḥadīth* without indicating that one was quoting.[72] *Iqtibās* usages generally take two forms. In one, the passage bears the same meaning in the poem as it does in the original text from which it is taken. In the second format, the Qur'ānic passage is used to transmit a new meaning that goes beyond the original sense of the sacred text.[73] In his masterful work on rhetoric and poetry, *Kitāb al-muḥāḍara wa-al-mudhākara*, comparing Arabic poetics to Hebrew poetics, Moses ibn Ezra notes this poetic convention as commonly occurring in Arabic poetry.[74] He also notes that in the majority of poetic cases where such quoting appears, the citation's meaning moves beyond that of its original (scriptural) context.

The second method of poetic incorporation of the Qur'ānic and *ḥadīth* materials relevant to our discussion concerns *talmīḥ*. In *talmīḥ*, Muslim poets employed themes or allusions from their sacred literature without quoting the religious texts directly.[75] Indeed, Wadād al-Qāḍī has noted that Arabic poetry tends to reformulate the Qur'ānic materials more than it quotes them directly.[76] So strong and pervasive was the Qur'ānic influence that sometimes, as Arie Schippers notes, the Arabic poets blurred the lines between thematic and textual citation, simultaneously employing both in the same poem.[77] In these references, adds David Yellin, the Arabic poets hinted not only to their sacred Scripture and other religious materials, but to the whole history of Arabic poetry as well.[78]

Shibbutz *and* Remizah

In the Hebrew context, the references and allusions to Scripture generally took one of two forms, not coincidentally reflecting characteristics of *iqtibās* and *talmīḥ*. Scholars have termed these two forms שיבוץ (*shibbutz*, integration) and רמיזה or רמז (*remizah* or *remez*, hints). As Dan Pagis writes, while *shibbutz* (integration) depended upon the format of the biblical verse used, *remizah* (hinting) depended on the situation described in the biblical text.[79] More specifically, *shibbutz* entailed utilizing a usually recognizable verse or part of a verse from the Bible, a direct citation. *Shibbutz* differs from a "regular" citation in that, while a "regular" citation can stand independently, a *shibbutz* cannot. Rather, the *shibbutz* constitutes an integral part of the context's continuity and cannot stand alone.[80] In *remizah/remez*, as in *talmīḥ*, poets hinted to biblical events or personalities without citing them directly, and then returned immediately to the context of the poem. As with the Islamic allusions in Arabic, this type of poetic ornament depended on scriptural content, and on the reader's familiarity with the Bible and its players, for the full meaning of the line to be made clear.[81] In some cases, the *remez* demanded familiarity with the extra-biblical rabbinic materials as well in order to figure it out.[82]

Function of the scriptural reference in secular poetry

Scholars have noted that, for the most part, the Hebrew and Muslim Andalusian poets engaged in utilization of their Scriptures to a number of ends. On the most basic level, as already mentioned, in introducing scriptural characters into an otherwise completely secular poem of desire the authors were engaging in typical play with their audience, for Andalusian poets, religious and nonreligious alike, delighted in the art of entertainment.[83] As Schippers writes, "When a Koranic passage is inserted, additional solemnity, or, in the case of obscenities, humor, had been conveyed."[84] So too the appearance of a biblical *remez* (hint) in a Hebrew poem often brings a sense of humor to the poem.[85] As Ross Brann has written, "The Andalusian poet-rabbis never tired of a chance to affect an insolent, if conventional, poetic attitude and flirt with literary impiety."[86] One of the functions of the biblical referent in the secular poetry of both the Muslims and the Jews, he adds elsewhere, "is to create the false impression of irreverence, and thereby to entertain the audience (or reader)."[87] And what could have been more entertaining, more surprisingly titillating, than the sudden appearance of a recognizable scriptural forefather or storyline in a sexually charged poem of yearning?[88]

On the Jewish side, such scriptural references to the forefathers served an additional purpose, one that went beyond literary entertainment. With the flowering of Arabic literary production in the ninth to eleventh centuries, a controversy known as the *ʿarabiyya-shuʿūbiyya* controversy came into full force. The *ʿarabiyya* side of the argument maintained that the best of all languages, and hence the one most suited for poetry, was Arabic, the language of the Qur'ān. By extension, *ʿarabiyya* proponents insisted on the overriding excellence of Arabic culture, of Arab land, and even of the Arab race.[89] Given the ethnic variation of the Muslim world, it was not long before non-Arab Muslims, led by the Persians, formulated a reaction spurred by their refusal to submit to such cultural and racial denigration. Known as the *shuʿūbiyya*, this movement acknowledged that while Arabic, the language of the Qur'ān, was the most superior language, the Arabs were not, by extension, the greatest of all peoples. Instead, the *shuʿūbī*s argued, Persians and other non-Arab Muslims surpassed them.[90] The *shuʿūbī* ideology quickly spread among the Muslims of Spain, who supported the claim of Arabic's excellence over all other languages while denying the predominance of Arab culture and ethnicity over their own. In the realm of poetry writing, the *shuʿūbī* ideology encouraged a return to earlier motifs, promoting the themes of love and wine, and encouraging the rejection of classical Arab forms of poetry in favor of markedly simpler and shorter poems.[91] It also encouraged the use of far more blunt, or everyday, language and allowed for poetry composed not only by professional poets but by court secretaries and dabbling rulers as well.[92]

When it came to the *arabiyya-shuʿūbiyya* divide, the Jews of Muslim Spain found themselves in a unique position. Although they were not themselves Muslims or Arabs, they had nonetheless become Arabized to the point that literary Hebrew had become somewhat of a rarity. Indeed, many of the most important Jewish works of the medieval period were written in Arabic, not Hebrew.[93] Similarly, many Jewish writers used Arabic as the language of composition for works on Hebrew grammar and on the Hebrew Bible.[94] Arabization, which had begun with Saadiah Gaon in Iraq in the tenth century, reached such an extent that in their religious writings, medieval Jews used even Islamic terminology. Hava Lazarus-Yafeh points out that they referred to the Torah as "*al-Kitāb*," "*Umm al-Kitāb*," and even "*al-Qur'ān*"; chapters of the Bible were called *sūras*; the Oral Law appears as the *sunna*, and Jerusalem, the holy city, by the Muslim epithet "*dār al-salām*" (the realm of peace). Similarly, medieval Jewish religious literature is filled with quotes from the Qur'ān, the *ḥadīth*, and later Muslim religious literature.[95]

Despite, or perhaps because of, this extensive Arabization, the Jews of Muslim Spain found themselves drawn to the ranks of the *shuʿūbī*s. The flourishing of poetry composed in biblically influenced Hebrew, as well as the use of biblical citations, narratives, and characters, formed part of this. In composing Hebrew poetry, the Jews of Muslim Spain aimed to prove that they too possessed a language which was used to transmit divine revelation, and one that predated the Qur'ān. Moreover, they strove to show that, like Arabic, the Jewish Holy Tongue was appropriate for the composition of excellent poetry.[96] Thus, as Carmi has pointed out, while not all the Hebrew grammarians came to compose Hebrew poetry, all the Hebrew poets were, of necessity, accomplished philologists.[97] The emphasis on Hebrew's primacy reached such a state that Hebrew writers even began to claim that the Arabic culture that appeared to influence them was actually the descendant of a previous Hebrew culture that had been lost due to the exile and the dispersion of the Jews from their homeland. In composing Hebrew poems and other literary forms, the Jews were thus "recovering" their culture rather than inventing it.[98] In replacing Arabic historical or folk characters with the biblical, the Hebrew authors presented the Bible as a valid and fitting Jewish national and cultural alternate for the Arabic, demonstrating that Jewish culture could compete with, and win, in the same sphere and on the same terms as Arabic literature.[99] Pagis maintains that this burst of national pride in which the poets strove to revive Hebrew language and culture through the composition of secular poems helped the Hebrew authors come to see themselves in a prophetic light, an attitude expressed in their poems.[100]

Muslim and Jewish scholar-poets of Spain

But who were these scholar-poets of whom we speak? What role did they play in the societies in which they lived? What was the intellectual context in which they composed their poems?

Andalusia's Arabic-writing Muslim poets hailed from all different levels of society. After all, since Arabic was the language of the realm, all Spain's residents learned and spoke Arabic, from the highest to the lowest classes. Since Arabic poetry was held out as the highest register of culture, men (and some women) from all levels of society tried their hands, many successfully, at composing Arabic verse. Thus we find that some Arabic Muslim poets were highly educated and served in positions of government, among them caliphs such as al-Mu`tamid (r. 1069–91). Others worked in agriculture or as laborers and had not experienced the luxury of a formal education.

Not only did their religious and economic levels differ, but so did their religious obedience. Many of the Arabic Muslim poets were not particularly religiously observant or compliant, a fact they frequently showcased in their writings.[101] Indeed, in their poems they often mock religion, purposely satirizing it in often startling ways. Ibn Shuhayd (Cordoba, 992–1035), for example, writes that he and a friend would attend the mosque, not in search of prayer, but in search of prey.[102] Similarly, the Muslim al-Ramādī al-Qurṭubī (Cordoba, b. *c.* 926, d. *c.* 1013) sacrilegiously writes that he was so in love with a Christian boy, named Yaḥya or Nuṣair, that he began making the sign of the cross over wine before drinking it.[103]

Other Arabic poets of secular verse were quite pious; indeed, not a few were themselves religious authority figures. The most famous of these is perhaps Ibn

Ḥazm (994–1064), the Cordoban Ẓāhirī theologian and philosopher who also wrote a treatise on love, *Ṭawq al-ḥamāma*, in which he cites many of his own love poems freely.[104] But Ibn Ḥazm is not alone in his intellectual dualism. In his anthology of Andalusian poets, which lists poetry-writing kings, viziers, secretaries, scholars of Arabic literature, scholars of grammar, and professional poets, the author Ibn Sa`īd (d. 1286) includes also a small but significant number of men whom he identifies as holding various official and unofficial religious positions in the different cities and caliphates. Among them we find the Santamarian *qāḍī* and jurisconsult (*faqīh*) Abū al-Faḍl Ja`far b. Muḥammad b. Abū al-Ḥajjāj al-A`lam (*c.* 1085–1151); the religious scholar, ascetic, and jurisconsult Abū Muḥammad `Abdāllah al-`Assāl of Toledo (d. *c.* 1182, Granada); and the Malagan legal scholar `Iyyād b. Mūsā b. `Iyyād (*c.* 1083–1149). From Granada alone we find three scholars of Islamic law: Abū Muḥammad `Abd al-Ḥaqq b. Ghālib b. `Iṭiyya (*c.* 1068–1141), who also wrote a Qur'ān commentary; Abū Muḥammad `Abd al-Mun`im b. al-Fars (*c.* 1129–1200), the *qāḍī* of Granada, who was also a prominent transmitter of *ḥadīth*, and the master of various religiously significant realms, Abū al-Ḥasan Sahl b. Mālik (*c.* 1163–1241).[105]

This emphasis on fluency in Arabic and Arabic poetry did not escape the Jewish community of Muslim Spain. Understanding that the precondition for being considered educated hinged on one's Arabic education, aristocratic Jews saw to educating their children accordingly. Samuel ha-Nagid, the Jewish philosopher and military leader of Granada, would send Arabic poems to his sons for study so that they would thereby obtain proficiency in poetic Arabic.[106] Of his own intellectual prowess, Samuel wrote, "My mouth speaks correctly to Qedar's heart and captures it."[107] According to Norman Roth, "There is not one of the outstanding Jewish figures of al-Andalus about whom we have any information at all who did not complete several years of schooling under Muslim scholars." Roth notes that the curriculum studied included not only Arabic grammar and literature, but also sciences, metaphysics, and medicine.[108] Somewhat surprisingly, given the Islamic ruling against non-Muslims studying their sacred Scripture, the subjects studied by Jews appear to have included also the Qur'ān and the fundamentals of Islamic law.[109]

Thanks to this Arabic-centered education, educated Jews not only studied Arabic poetry but composed poems in Arabic themselves. Samuel ha-Nagid is known to have composed many a poem in Arabic while on the battlefield awaiting battle.[110] At least one collection of Arabic poetry maintains that Samuel's son Joseph also wrote poems in Arabic, which became well known.[111] The Saragossan Jewish Abū al-Faḍl Ḥisdai ibn Ḥisdai (b. *c.* 1050) wrote poetry almost exclusively in Arabic, some of which appears in collections made by Spanish Muslim collectors of Arabic poetry.[112] So too Abū Ayyūb Solomon ibn al-Mu'allim of Seville (mid-twelfth century), a physician, philosopher, and friend of Judah Halevi, composed poems in both Hebrew and Arabic; while only one of his Hebrew poems has survived, two of his Arabic poems, or lines thereof, remain.[113] The Toledan Ibrāhīm ibn al-Fakhār (d. *c.* 1240) composed Arabic poems of such beauty that al-Maqqarī, in his *Nafḥ al-ṭīb*, reports that it boggles the mind to think that God had given such intelligence and sublime control over the Arabic language to a Jew.[114] Al-Maqqarī also singles out the Sevillian Ibrāhīm ibn Sahl al-Isrā'īlī (d. 1259/60) for the wide-ranging wisdom and good taste he exhibits in his Arabic poetry.[115] Among the Jewish poets of Arabic, al-Maqqarī also mentions and cites a few lines from Nissim al-Isrā'īlī, a poet of *muwashshaḥāt* from Seville; Ilyās (Elijah) b. al-Madūr al-Yahūdī, and the doctor Bassām b. Sham`ūn al-Yahūdī al-Washqī.[116] Importantly, we find not only Jewish men composing Arabic poems in this period, but also at least one Jewish woman. Known as Qasmūna bint Ismā`īl al-Yahūdī, or Ismā`īl ibn Baghdāla, she has been identified as the probable daughter of Samuel ha-Nagid.[117]

It would be a mistake to think that the Jewish education in Muslim Spain concentrated only on Arabic culture and language. Jewish education focused first and foremost on the topics and sacred texts most important to Jews: Bible, Mishna, Talmud, and Hebrew grammar (though Hebrew was a language they did not actually speak).[118] Because Hebrew poetry was considered to be a tool that aided a student in learning Hebrew grammar and lexicology, and thus the Bible itself, young students studied Hebrew poetry quite intensely.[119] Since students as young as 10 years of age were already connoisseurs of Hebrew poetry, it comes as little surprise to learn that many of the greatest of the Hebrew poets began composing poems of their own at ages that today would seem quite precocious. For example, Ibn Gabirol's earliest poem gives his age as only 16 at its composition; according to Schirmann, Isaac ibn Ghayyat, the rival of Ibn Shabbetai, and Todros Abulafia had already composed impressive verse by age 10; and, with the help of his father, Joseph the son of Samuel ha-Nagid had already produced Hebrew poems by the age of 9.[120]

Thanks to the emphasis on a rigorous Jewish education, and the difficulties of earning a living as a full-time poet, almost all of the Hebrew poets of Spain were also scholars of renown in different intellectual, mainly religious, fields. These include grammar, dictionary-making, biblical and talmudic exegesis, philosophy, sciences, ritual poetry writing, etc.[121] Many also held positions in the political, spiritual, or religious-legal leadership of the Jewish community. For example, the poet Abū Ayyūb Solomon ibn al-Mu'allim (mid-twelfth century) served not only as the only Jewish courtier in the Seville court, but also as one of the chief scholars of Jewish law and as a physician (along with Judah Halevi and Joseph ibn Zabara). Joseph ibn Tzaddiq (d. 1149) not only wrote poetry but also served as a highly regarded Talmudist and as the chief authority on ritual law (*dayyan*) in Cordoba. Levi ibn al-Tabbān worked as a poet and also as a preacher, as did Abū al-Ḥassan ben Batat. The master poets Judah Halevi, Samuel ha-Nagid, and Solomon ibn Gabirol all wrote works of philosophical theology, and Abraham ibn Ezra (1092/3–*c.* 1164) composed a Bible commentary still studied in the Jewish curricula today.[122]

Jewish scriptural exegesis in Muslim Spain

Since many Hebrew poets of this age also composed commentaries and exegeses of the Bible, a final issue of importance concerns the attitude toward the reading of the Bible, scriptural exegesis, among the Jews of Muslim Spain. The earlier classical rabbinic attitude toward the Bible insisted on what James Kugel has termed the Bible's "omnisignificance." Namely, the pre-medieval rabbinic exegetes believed that all biblical details were significant. Every word, every letter, had a message to send the reader about the text's meaning or intent. Thus they regularly endeavored to differentiate among synonymous or repeated phrases, insisting that each and every word in Scripture served an exegetical purpose.[123] This often led to exegetical interpretations known as *derash*, homiletical or metaphorical readings of the text that often departed widely from the context and the text's plain meaning. Partially under the influence of the medieval Spanish Muslim dogmatic emphasis on the *style* of Scripture as the key to its worth, the Spanish Jewish exegetes began moving away from such a *derash*-heavy approach to the Bible.[124] Instead, the Spanish Jewish exegetes insisted that since the Bible spoke in human terms and in human language,[125] one could apply literary techniques used for understanding and analyzing human speech to the sacred text. Thus not all details in the biblical text bear significance for the Andalusian exegetes; some serve simply as literary ornamentation. Uriel Simon has written that the Spanish Jewish biblical exegetes employed a "philological-rational interpretation of the Bible, divorced from midrashic exposition,"[126] an approach known as *peshat*, or "simple" reading of the text. Despite the moniker "simple," this methodology did not require that only the surface meaning of a text was correct, as some may incorrectly understand. Instead, at the core of the *peshat* approach was a focus on an intensive study of the text, reading the words of the Bible in context.

In addition to their insistence on reading the Bible through the eyes of the *peshat* approach, the Spanish exegetes also believed that the Bible represented the "best of poetry." They maintained that poetic analysis of Scripture enriches a reader's understanding of it. Thus, almost all the Hebrew poets devoted themselves not only to composing Hebrew poetry that mined the biblical text for imagery and language[127] but also to composing works of biblical exegesis, a sacred task aimed at elucidating the word of God.[128] The idea that familiarity with poetry enriches one's understanding of Scripture appears in the Islamic context as well, especially since Muslim tradition holds the Qur'ān up as the most perfect example of poetry. Abū `Abbās, for example, when asked to explain something in the Qur'ān that was not understood would recite a verse of poetry to elucidate it. Centuries later, the Qur'ānic exegete and historian Abū Ja`far Muḥammad b. Jarīr al-Ṭabarī (d. 923) continued in Abū `Abbās's footsteps, using Arabic poetry to support or make an exegetical point by quoting Arabic poetry to support grammatical points or vocabulary definitions.[129] Unfortunately in the Jewish case, as Uriel Simon points out, most of the exegetical works by the scholar-poets have been lost, either because the works were composed in Arabic (rather than Hebrew) or because later exegetes overshadowed them.[130]

What little that remains of the exegetical materials written by the Hebrew scholar-poets of Muslim Spain can be found largely as references in the works of others. For example, we know that the tenth-century secular poet, grammarian, and *payyetan* (composer of liturgical poetry) Isaac ben Levi ibn Mar Shaul composed a work of biblical exegesis (now lost) because both his student Ibn Janaḥ and the later commentator Abraham ibn Ezra reference it. Ibn Ezra's references to biblical exegesis provided by Samuel ha-Nagid and Solomon ibn Gabirol have led scholars to believe that they both composed longer works of biblical commentary, now lost. Others said to have written Bible commentaries, or at least portions thereof, that did not survive include the liturgical poet and Talmudist Isaac b. Samuel al-Kanzi (*c.* 1050–*c.* 1130),[131] as well as grammarians Moses ha-Cohen ibn Gikatilla (eleventh century, Cordoba/Saragossa) and Judah ibn Bal`am (Toledo, *c.* 1070–90), and the head of the Lucenan yeshiva, Isaac b. Judah ibn Ghayyat (b. Lucena 1038, d. Cordoba 1089).[132]

Methodology

The methodology used in analyzing the poems that constitute the body of this work derives from a combination of two methods of literary analysis drawing from the fields of both comparative religious thought and poetic analysis. The first consists of a close reading of both the poems themselves and the scriptural or extra-scriptural materials from which they draw. This close reading is joined by applied principles drawn from the literary theory of intertextuality.

Close reading

On the most basic level, the close reading of the poems included here strives to understand the plain meaning of the text by paying attention to the nuances and shades of meaning one can detect in the word choice used by the author.[133] This method includes understanding the words themselves, as they would have been understood by the medieval reader of Arabic, the Islamic tradition, biblical Hebrew, and the Hebrew Bible and its attendant traditions. It also requires paying attention to the ways in which the poem uses the tropes of medieval Andalusian poetry. No less important are the ways in which the poets break these tropes in creating compositions of lasting beauty and literary pleasure.[134] In both their adherence to and their breaking from poetic convention, the poets displayed their individuality and mastery. But it is in the deviations from the conventions that we see hints to possible alternate or hidden readings of the poems. In the cases brought here, those deviations concern the scriptural references or allusions woven through the poem's text. These scriptural references, both in the Arabic and in the Hebrew, should be read not just for their philological value but for their thematic value as well. Otherwise, as Aviva Doron writes, each poem becomes simply a collection of ideas rather than an integrated thematic unity.[135]

Indeed, one can hardly read the medieval Hebrew and Arabic poetry for its philological value alone but *must* engage with it on a deeper level, enabled by a close reading. In his early work on the Hebrew poetry and poetics of medieval Spain, Dan Pagis stresses this need, insisting that while New Criticism dismisses the relevance of authorial intention or intended meaning when it comes to modern poems, the poems of medieval Spain require such an investigation.[136] In analyzing the poems, therefore, we need not restrict ourselves to parsing them only in terms of their structure, syntax, or identification of scriptural language and phraseology. Rather, our close reading should lead us to investigate the ways in which these are used and the ways in which the scriptural materials are engaged.

Theory of intertextuality

The second methodological approach employed in analyzing the poems sits squarely within the realm of intertextual studies. The first use of the term "intertextuality" occurred in the writings of Julia Kristeva in 1966, which she defined as signifying that "every text is constructed as a mosaic of citations; every text is an absorption and transformation of other texts."[137] Building on this definition, Daniel Boyarin wrote that "every text is constrained by the literary system of which it is a part and ... every text is ultimately dialogical in that it cannot but record the traces of its contentions and doubling of earlier discourses."[138] In other words, according to the theory of literary intertexuality, every text not only operates within the context of its literary system but, as part of a system, it receives the imprint of those texts that preceded it. Indeed, this imprint occurs as a matter of course and is not necessarily intentional on the part of the author. As Norman Calder has since pointed out, texts in isolation are meaningless.[139]

The intertextual nature of poetry in particular appears in the writings of the French literary critic Michael Riffaterre. While Calder insists on the meaninglessness of *prose* texts taken in isolation, Riffaterre maintains that the meanings of *poems* arise not through mimesis or internal patterning, but through the derivation from and reference to an intertext. As Riffaterre writes, "The poem carries meaning only by referring from text to text."[140] Although Riffaterre's pronouncement emphasizes the existence of intertextual references in poetry and the deeper significance of such references, his assertion seems somewhat extremely stated; after all, one can derive meaning from a beautifully and sensitively written poem even if one does not understand all the cultural, textual, and intertextual references it contains. Indeed, such is the beauty of poetry, it stirs up emotions or reactions in its readers even when some elements remain unclear.

Perhaps recognizing the somewhat extreme nature of Riffaterre's declaration, Ḥaviva Ishay presents a more moderated explanation of the importance of the intertextual approach to reading poetry. In her study of Hebrew love poems of Muslim Spain and their possible relationship with Arabic love prose, Ishay maintains that recognizing the varying fields of reference through which the poem sends the reader helps the reader to understand both the meaning of the poem and its significance. One can never be aware of all the fields of reference of a given text, she warns. However, the more expansive a reader's intertextual orientation, the more successfully will he solve the puzzle of language, make connections between its parts, and understand the situation that the poem often only subtly sets up.[141] The reader himself, she notes, is the junction between all the (inter)texts that he reads, and it is the reader, perhaps even more than the writer, who is responsible for the actualization of the text and giving meaning to its parts.[142]

In his study of the secular poetry of Judah Halevi, Ross Brann too encourages an intertexual approach that appears to be a modification of Riffattere and is useful to the current study. Brann maintains that because the Hebrew poets freely appropriated from the Arab Muslim and Jewish worlds around them, "the reader of the medieval Hebrew verse may forge between texts significant connections perhaps never contemplated by the poet but which nevertheless arise out of the nature of the discourse and the manner of its production."[143] In other words, although the poets may not have consciously intended their readers to see intertextual connections between their poems and other texts of the period, given the multicultural and multitextual culture of the time, these ties can, in fact, be detected and are worthy of study. Indeed, Brann notes, such connections point to various struggles over religious and cultural identity present in the environment at the time. Though Brann speaks of this effect primarily regarding the poetry and personality of Judah Halevi, the same can be said of the poetry of other religious-scholar poets of his day, both Muslim and Jewish.

Under the influence of Kristeva, Riffattere, Doron, Ishay, and Brann, the current study investigates the intertextual references to and usages of religious texts appearing in seven poems – four in Arabic and three in Hebrew. In the case of the Arabic poems, this study investigates their intertextual references to the Qur'ān, while the Hebrew poems are studied for their intertextual utilization of the Hebrew Bible. Since the scriptural references tend to appear in a modified format in their poetic milieu, understanding the Islamic exegetical traditions (in the case of the Arabic poems) and the biblical exegetical traditions (in the case of the Hebrew poems) from which the poems draw proves vitally important. Thus, the analysis here consults both classical scriptural commentaries and the contemporaneous exegetical texts. Where possible, the contemporaneous texts will include the exegeses written by the poets themselves. However, since much has not survived to the modern period, especially among the Jewish exegetes, this will not be possible in all cases. Indeed, practically speaking, only one commentary from a Spanish poet-exegete has endured, that of Abraham ibn Ezra (b. Toledo, 1092/3–1167). Thus, Ibn Ezra's commentary will provide the lion's share of exegetical materials regarding the Hebrew poems, when possible. Since the commentary of R. David Qimḥi (Radaq, 1160–1235, b. Narbonne) exemplifies the Spanish exegetical tradition, despite the fact that Qimḥi himself was not a Spaniard, his work will serve the same purpose.[144] Ibn Ezra and Qimḥi will be supplemented by other medieval commentators, most notably Don Isaac Abrabanel (1437–1508). Although Abrabanel officially belongs to the ranks of Jewish scholars from Christian Spain, his Bible commentary reflects the *peshat*-focused methodology of the exegetes of Muslim Spain and will provide some insight into the exegetical environment in which our poems were composed.

As noted earlier, some scholars have insisted that the biblical and Qur'ānic images in the secular poems find their worth generally as poetic ornament, often one which is clear and simple to break down.[145] While scriptural imagery is understood to have been of the most important imagery included by the Andalusians, modern scholars often insist that its appearance in a poem has few ramifications for the significance or messages of the poem.[146] In the case of the religious scholars who incorporated religious texts into their poems of desire, this position is one with which I strongly disagree. After all, in the Jewish case, the Hebrew Bible and rabbinic traditions were an inseparable part of the education, worldview, and daily experience of the Jewish writers of Hebrew poetry. Biblical *remizot* in the scholars' poetry testify to the fact that the Bible, its verses, and its people "filled the minds" of the poets, as Yellin phrases it.[147] Neal Kozodoy echoes Yellin when he writes that the Hebrew "courtier-poet" was "bibliocentric at his spiritual core."[148] Similarly, Brann later writes that the poets' literary consciousness was "informed by an ideology of biblical saturation."[149] So, too, the Qur'ān and the Islamic religious tradition formed the very fabric of daily life for the religious scholar-poets writing in Arabic. As Suzanne Pinckney Stetkeyvich insists, Arabic poetic imagery and its role in Arabo-Islamic culture in general can be fully understood only with reference to the Qur'ān.[150] The Qur'ān's role in and influence on Arabic poetry becomes especially strong in the Arab-Islamic culture in Andalusia, as discussed above.

Given this influence, when the Muslim and Jewish scholar-poets included in this study refer to their Scripture in their *`ishq* poems, through either allusion or allegory or the like, one ought to look at such references in depth. When we pay close attention to the intertextual connections that link the poems with their religious source materials, and to the ways in which the sacred materials are modified in the poems, we see that in many cases these references serve as more than mere literary ornamentation. In some cases, the intertextual references in the secular *`ishq* poems can open a small window for our understanding more deeply the religious world of Muslim Spain and its literary products.

In restricting the intertextual scope here to the scriptural texts to which they refer, I do not intend to imply that this is the only intertextual connection the reader can find in the poems. Andalusian poetry unabashedly referenced earlier poetry, history, and literature. What's more, poets often wrote poems to one another in which they played off of and made clear references to one another's compositions. We find such references in Arabic poems responding to Arabic poems, such as the love poems that flew back and forth between the eleventh-century Cordoban Ibn Zaydūn and his beloved poetry-writing princess Wallāda bint al-Mustakfī.[151] Similarly, Hebrew poems respond to and reference other Hebrew poems, such as the three-way poetic "conversation" that took place between Joseph ibn Tzaddiq, Judah Halevi, and Moses ibn Ezra.[152] In one poem, so frustrated is Ibn Gabirol by another poet who keeps referring to or "borrowing" his poems that he writes a poem in which he accuses the other man of stealing.[153] Additionally, as many scholars have pointed out, the Arabic poets knew of the Hebrew poets' existence, and the Hebrew poems clearly knew of and played off of the Arabic poems; in one example, A. Ehrlich has shown that a certain poem by Judah Halevi is understandable only if we recognize it as a response to a rare and befuddling form of riddle poem written to him by Abū ‘Omar b. Māthqa.[154] More commonly, Hebrew *muwashshaḥ* poems often employed Arabic *kharja*s taken from well-known Arabic poems or prose.[155] The Hebrew poems did not invent this practice; rather it was the custom of Arabic *muwashshaḥ* compositions to do the same. S. M. Stern has shown that the Hebrew "ליל מחשבות לב אעירה" (*Leyl maḥshavot lev a'ira*) was a Hebrew imitation (*mu'āraḍa*) of an Arabic poem by Ibn Bakr al-Abyaḍ.[156] Judah Halevi subsequently composed "אחר גלות סוד" (*Aḥar galot sod*) using the same rhyme scheme, rhyme sound, and *kharja* as the Hebrew version to showcase his own poetic mastery.[157] Halevi was also known to translate poems from the Arabic into the Hebrew, altering them as he did so.[158]

Why these particular poems?

That the current study focuses on analyzing the intertextual connections of seven medieval Hebrew and Arabic poems to religious texts is certainly not intended to denigrate any of these other connections. I recognize, as Neal Kozodoy has written, the "multiple and simultaneous meanings hovering over, or arising from, the plain meaning" of the poets' words.[159] Rather I have chosen the scriptural intertextual references because their very nature – religious references in eroticized secular poems written by religious/spiritual authority figures – fascinates me. Instead of separating the two parts of their beings and culture – the secular/ sexual from the spiritual/religious – these scholar-poets seamlessly fused them together in works of supreme beauty, sensitivity, and wisdom, in secular and religious poems alike.[160] Even more intriguing, in the poems chosen here the poets incorporate into their love/desire poems references to scriptural couples who are decidedly *not* romantically involved with one another. Indeed, the biblical narratives alluded to in the Hebrew poems all revolve around issues of deception resulting in physical cruelty. And the heroes whose names are mentioned by our poets are those responsible. Similarly, the Islamic accounts speak not of romantic love in the slightest. Rather, the Arabic poems incorporate the accounts of men whose supreme faith in and loyalty to Allāh defies logic and reason. This faith and loyalty prove to be their spiritual and physical deliverance.

I strive to gain insight into what the poets were doing in using such seemingly unsuitable sacred characters in their desire poems. Why choose *these* of all the possible scriptural heroes? And why place them in poems of desire? What messages can we glean from such verses as they speak to us through time and space?

Notes

1 Ibn al-Jawzī, *Dhamm al-hawwā* [The Condemnation of Passionate Love], ed. Muṣṭafa 'Abdelwāḥid (Cairo: 1381/1962), 24f. Cited by Franz Rosenthal in "Fiction and Reality: Sources for the Role of Sex in Medieval Muslim Society," in *Society and the Sexes in Medieval Islam* (Giorgio Levi Della Vida Conference), ed. Afaf Lufti al-Sayyid-Marsot (Malibu: Undena Publications, 1979), 5, n. 7. In Ibn al-Jawzī's version, he names the nobleman: 'Abdallāh b. Ḥasan b. Ḥasan (according to Rosenthal,

likely the great-grandson of `Ali, who perished during the reign of al-Manṣūr, in 763). Rosenthal notes that in other versions of this account, the roles are reversed, with the woman propositioning the nobleman.

2 One should be aware that in the medieval religious world there was no real sense of the "secular." The term and concept belong to the modern world-view. In the medieval world, since the world was created by God, all in it belonged to Him. Thus, science was the study of God's world, not the world of Nature; philosophy, as the study of existence, knowledge, values, and reason (among other elements), likewise related to God's creation.

3 Anwar G. Chejne, *Muslim Spain: Its History and Culture* (Minneapolis: University of Minnesota Press, 1974), 162ff; *The Legacy of Muslim Spain*, ed. Salma Khadra Jayyusi (Leiden, Boston, New York, and Köln: E. J. Brill, 1992), especially Pierre Cachia, "Andalusi Belle Lettres," 307–16.

4 Religious poems are those intended for ritual purpose, to be incorporated into the prayer service, used at a religious function, or whose content deals with explicitly religious themes. Frequently these poems express a person's or a nation's yearning for God and an adherence to His covenant. Secular poems – those that can be mainly characterized as containing non-religious content – speak of everything else, as discussed above.

5 Two particularly humorous Hebrew examples: Ibn Khalfun, railing against a man who promised to pay him and instead sent him cheese, compared his patron's behavior to Elkanah's giving Peninah food when she really desired a child (1 Sam. 1). See Aharon Mirsky, ed., *Shirei Yitzḥaq ibn Khalfun* (Jerusalem: Bialik Institute, 1961), 95–6. An English translation appears in *The Dream of the Poem: Hebrew Poetry from Muslim and Christian Spain 950–1492*, ed. and trans. Peter Cole (Princeton, NJ: Princeton University Press, 2007), 36. Todros Abulafia (Toledo, 1247–after 1298) accuses a man named Ben Shoshan, who refuses to share figs with him, of being fit to be a judge in Sodom, in T. Carmi, ed. and trans., *The Penguin Book of Hebrew Verse* (New York and London: Penguin Books, 1981), 414–15. On the evil nature of the Sodomite judges, see *BT Sanhedrin* 109b.

6 Two pleasant riddles extolling wine can be found among the poems of Moses ibn Ezra (1070–*c.* 1138) and Ibn Gikatilla (late eleventh century). For Ibn Ezra, see Moses ibn Ezra, *Shirei ha-Ḥol*, ed. Ḥaim Brody (Berlin: Schocken, 5695 [1935]), 1:72, l. 7b. For Ibn Gikatilla, see "Moshe ha-Cohen Ibn Gikatilla," in *Ha-Shirah ha-`Ivrit be-Sefarad u-ve-Provans*, ed. Ḥaim [Jefim] Schirmann (Jerusalem: Mossad Bialik, 1954), 1:296 (lines 13–15). Both also appear in Ross Brann, "Andalusian Hebrew Poetry and the Hebrew Bible: Cultural Nationalism or Cultural Ambiguity?" in *Approaches to Judaism in Medieval Times*, ed. David R. Blumenthal (Atlanta: Scholars Press, 1988), 3:101–31.

Todros Abulafia uses similar wording to compose a riddle of a different sort, in which he vows never to be disloyal to his love. See *Gan ha-Meshalim ve-ha-Ḥidot: Osef Shirei Todros ben Yehuda Abu al-`Afia*, ed. David Yellin (Jerusalem: [s.n.], 5692–6 [1932–6]), 1:87 (#272). Abū Muḥammad `Abdullah ibn al-Ṭallā' (Mahdia [Tunisia], eleventh century) composed a riddle poem in which he speaks of the heart of an artichoke as a virgin in a bed surrounded by a warrior's spears. See Abū al-Ḥasan `Alī b. Mūsā b. Sa`īd al-Andalusī, *Rāyāt al-mubarrizīn wa-ghāyāt al-mumayyazīn*, ed. Muḥammad Riḍwān al-Dāya (Dimashq: Dār Ṭalās, 1987), 268–9. An English translation can be found in James A. Bellamy and Patricia Owen Steiner, *The Banners of the Champions: An Anthology of Medieval Arabic Poetry from Andalusia and Beyond* (Madison, WI: The Hispanic Seminary of Medieval Studies, 1989), 25 (#23).

7 One should not understand this as implying that these poems constitute wooden or boring compositions, slavishly reusing stock characters and sentiments. On the contrary, the ways in which the poets manipulated or played with the conventions testify not only to their poetic mastery, but also to their individual visions and personalities,

imbuing their poems with vigor and life. Their individuality, as Raymond Scheindlin notes, can be seen *only* against the backdrop of the conventions that reigned. See Raymond Scheindlin, *Wine, Women and Death: Medieval Hebrew Poems on the Good Life* (Philadelphia: Jewish Publication Society, 1986), 11. See also Andreas Hamori, "Examples of Convention in the Poetry of Abū Nuwās," *Studia Islamica* 30 (1969): 5–26; Dan Pagis, *Hebrew Poetry of the Middle Ages and the Renaissance* (Berkeley, Los Angeles, and Oxford: University of California Press, 1991), lecture three; G. E. von Grunebaum, "The Concept of Plagiarism in Arabic Theory," *JNES* 3 (1944): 234–53.

8 Ross Brann, *The Compunctious Poet: Cultural Ambiguity and Hebrew Poetry in Muslim Spain* (Baltimore: Johns Hopkins University Press, 1991), 18. Brann himself studies the way Samuel ha-Nagid incorporated and alluded to the Bible in his poems in order, says Brann in chapter 2, to sacralize his literary, military, and political activities. Brann laments the fact that the majority of scholars on Hebrew do not seem to take this more wide-ranging view of the scriptural materials. He points out there have been some exceptions. For example, Tova Rosen read the "demonization" of women in medieval Hebrew poetry by reading the poems against the medieval background from which the poems drew: the Bible, rabbinic literature, traditions of chivalry and misogyny in Islamic and Christian culture. See Tova Rosen, *Unveiling Eve: Reading Gender in Medieval Hebrew Literature* (Philadelphia: University of Pennsylvania Press, 2003). Rina Drory also insisted that research in the field of fictionality in classical Arabic literature requires the breaking down of the divisions between poetry, prose literature, Qur'ānic exegesis, historical texts and the like. See Rina Drory, *Models and Contacts: Arabic Literature and its Impact on Medieval Jewish Culture* (Leiden and Boston: E. J. Brill, 2000), 6. Ḥaviva Ishay echoed this attitude when she proposed that we see the scriptural references as a poetic zoom lens, widening and limiting our focus to events beyond the poem itself. See Ḥaviva Ishay, "Mechaniqat ha-'Miqud' be-Shirei Ḥesheq shel Shelomo ibn Gabirol: ha-Mesamen ha-Miqra'i ba-Shir ke-`Adasha Memaqedet ba-Matzleima," *Revue Européenne des Études Hébraïques* (2001), 39–51. Perhaps the most well known of the works to move beyond Scripture-as-ornament alone is Raymond Scheindlin's *Wine, Women and Death*; here he translates the Hebrew poems into English and explains briefly the biblical scenarios utilized and how they affect the reading of the poem.

9 Gibraltar, in Arabic *jabal ṭāriq*, was named for Ṭāriq ibn Ziyād, the Muslim Berber general of the Umayyad caliph al-Walīd I (r. 705–15). In 711, Ṭāriq led the Muslim troops across the strait, defeating King Roderic and, over the next seven years, conquering Hispania from the Christian Visigoths in the name of the Umayyad caliphate in Damascus.

10 See Bellamy and Steiner, *Banners of the Champions*, xix; Chejne, *Muslim Spain*, 31–8; Robert Hillenbrand, "'The Ornament of the World': Medieval Córdoba as a Cultural Center," in *The Legacy of Muslim Spain*, 112–35; David J. Wasserstein, *The Rise and Fall of the Party Kings: Politics and Society in Islamic Spain 1002–1086* (Princeton, NJ: Princeton University Press, 1985), 15–51.

11 Ignác Goldziher, *A Short History of Classical Arabic Literature*, trans. Joseph Desomogyi (Hildesheim: Georg Olms, 1966), 131.

12 Reyes de Taifas (*mulūk al-ṭawā'if*), also known as the Factional Kings. When the Umayyad caliphate fell, the territory was divided into many smaller kingdoms (as many as twenty-three). These were known as *taifas*. For more on these mini-states, see Wasserstein, *The Rise and Fall of the Party Kings*.

13 Bellamy and Steiner, *Banners of the Champions*, xix; A. R. Nykl, *Hispano-Arabic Poetry and its Relations with the Old Provençal Troubadours* (Baltimore: Johns Hopkins University Press, 1946), 69–71; Arie Schippers, *Spanish Hebrew Poetry and the Arabic Literary Tradition: Arabic Themes in Hebrew Andalusian Poetry* (Leiden: E. J. Brill, 1994), 13–35.

14 In these verses the Bedouins praised their own tribes, or denigrated the members of other tribes, spoke of the exploits of heroic characters, of Arab bravery in war and generosity of spirit, or of battlefield or pastoral scenes. David Tzvi Baneth maintains that while scholars previously assumed that the Bedouins were illiterate, transmitting their verses orally rather than in print, this was not the case. See Baneth, "Ha-Shirah ha-`Aravit ha-Qeduma," in *Peraqim be-Toledot ha-`Aravim ve-ha-Islam* ([Tel Aviv]: Hotza'at Reshafim, [1967]), 23–37. D. S. Margoliouth maintains that there is evidence indicating that pre-Islamic poetry was not only preserved in writing, but that it also versified *about* writing. See D. S. Margoliouth, "The Origins of Arabic Poetry," *Journal of the Royal Asiatic Society* (1925): 417–49; James A. Bellamy, "The Impact of Islam on Early Arabic Poetry," in *Islam: Past Influence and Present Challenge*, ed. Alford T. Welch and Pierre Cachia (Albany, NY: SUNY Press, 1979), 141–67.

The *qaṣīda*'s three parts begin with a nostalgic opening known as the *nasīb*, in which the lover bemoans his absent beloved. This is followed by the *raḥīl*, a travel section in which the poet contemplates the harshness of nature and life away from the tribe. The final portion of the poem can be either *fakhr* (praise of the tribe, hero, benefactor), *hijā'* (satire about other tribes), or moral maxims, *ḥikam*. It is in the final portion that we find the point of the poem. These three parts are described in detail in the ninth-century Ibn Qutayba's *Kitāb al-shi'r wa-al-shu'arā'* (Book of Poetry and Poets). *Qaṣīda* format is quite rigid, a fact that led to resentment on the part of the poets, and to often fragmentary poems that took a very long time to compose. See *EI*[2], s.v. "ḳaṣīda," by F. Krenkow and G. Lecomte, 4:713–14. With the rise of Islam and later the rise of the Hebrew poets, the *qaṣīda* format underwent change, as befitting a people no longer living in the desert, with desert values. See Miriam Goldstein, "Adaptations of the Arabic Qaṣīda in Andalusian Hebrew Poetry," in *Ben `Ever la-`Arav*, ed. Yosef Tobi (Tel Aviv: Afikim Publishers, 2004), 3:vii–xxxviii; Raymond Scheindlin, "The Hebrew Qasida in Spain," in *Qasida Poetry in Islamic Asia and Africa*, ed. Stefan Sperl and Christopher Shackle (Leiden: E. J. Brill, 1996), 1:121–35; Nehemiah Allony, "Ha-Tzvi ve-ha-Gamal be-Shirat Sefarad," *Otzar Yehudei Sefarad* 4 (1961): 20; Goldziher, *A Short History of Classical Arabic Literature*, 10ff.

Love poems were found outside of the *qaṣīda*'s *nasīb* as well, in a shorter format known as a *ghazal*. See Schippers, *Spanish Hebrew Poetry*, 144–51; Mahmoud A. Mazalaoui, "'I Follow the Religion of Love': The Erotic Surrogate in the Arabic Tradition," in *Poetics of Love in the Middle Ages: Texts and Contexts*, ed. Moshe Lazar and Norris J. Lacy (Fairfax, VA: George Mason University Press, 1989), 119–21; James T. Monroe, "Hispano-Arabic Poetry During the Caliphate of Cordoba," in *Arabic Poetry: Theory and Development*, ed. G. E. von Grunebaum (Wiesbaden: Otto Harrassowitz, 1973), 134ff.

15 See *EI*[2], s.v. "Zadjal," by W. Stoetzer (9:373–7). According to Nykl, Ibn Quzmān inclined toward drinking, adultery, and sodomy, and was accused of being a hypocrite in religion. When his economic fortunes turned against him toward the end of his life, he became an *imām* in a mosque. See Nykl, *Hispano-Arabic Poetry*, 268.

16 For more on the *kharja*, see Ann Brener, *Judah Halevi and His Circle of Hebrew Poets in Granada* (Leiden: E. J. Brill, 2005), 35ff; James T. Monroe, "Kharjas in Arabic and Romance: Popular Poetry in Muslim Spain?," in *Islam: Past Influence and Present Challenge*, 168–87; Raymond Scheindlin, "Hebrew Poetry in Medieval Iberia," in *Convivencia: Jews, Muslims, and Christians in Medieval Spain*, ed. Vivian B. Mann, Thomas F. Glick, and Jerrilynn D. Dodds (New York: George Braziller, Inc., 1992), 39–60; *EI*[2], s.v. "Muwashshaḥ," by G. Schoeler (7:809–12); S. M. Stern, "Ḥiquei Muwashshaḥot `Aravi'im be-Shirat Sefarad ha-`Ivrit," *Tarbiz* 18:3–4 (1957): 166–86. Monroe and David Swiatlo collected and analyzed all the known Arabic *kharjas* in Hebrew *muwashshaḥāt* in "Ninety-Three Arabic Ḥarǧas in Hebrew

Muwaššaḥs: Their Hispano-Romance Prosody and Thematic Features," *JAOS* 97:2 (Apr.–Jun. 1997): 141–64.

17 Schoeler, 811.

18 See above, p. 4 and nn. 15, 46, 48, 63.

19 James T. Monroe, *Hispano-Arabic Poetry: A Student Anthology* (Berkeley: University of California Press, 1974), 33–45.

20 See Monroe, *Hispano-Arabic Poetry: A Student Anthology*, 48–9; EI^2, s.v. "Al-Muwaḥḥidūn," by M. Shatzmiller (7:801–7); Mercedes Garcia-Arenal, *Messianism and Puritanical Reform: Mahdīs of the Muslim West*, trans. Martin Beagles (Leiden and Boston: E. J. Brill, 2006), 157–216. On those who converted to Islam and maintained a crypto-Jewish life, see especially Norman Roth, *Jews, Visigoths and Muslims in Medieval Spain: Cooperation and Conflict* (Leiden and New York: E. J. Brill, 1994), 113ff; and Mercedes Garcia-Arenal, "Jewish Converts to Islam in the Muslim West," *IOS* XVII (1997): 227–48. See n. 115, on the discussion of the conversion of Ibn Sahl in this context. For a discussion of Abraham ibn Ezra's poem on the Almohad destruction of the Jewish communities of Muslim Spain, see Ross Brann, *Power in the Portrayal* (Princeton and Oxford: Princeton University Press, 2002), 120–6 and Roth, *Jews, Visigoths and Muslims*, 125–7.

21 The exodus of Jewish intellectuals from Muslim Spain did not actually begin with the Almohad period. Rather, a number of prominent people had moved northward to Christian Spanish kingdoms after the Almoravid conquest, such as Moses ibn Ezra (emigrated after conquest of Granada in 1090), Abraham ibn Ezra (emigrated, 1137), and Judah Halevi (emigrated, 1140). With the arrival of the Almohads, the numbers of emigrants increased greatly. See Jonathan P. Decter, *Iberian Jewish Literature: Between al-Andalus and Christian Europe* (Bloomington and Indianapolis: Indiana University Press, 2007), 3–7.

22 The Almohad intellectual program was particularly encouraging of philosophy; the Aristotelian Muslim philosopher Averroes/Ibn Rushd (1126–98) composed his entire oeuvre under the patronage of the Almohad caliphs. Maribel Fierro suggests that the intended audience of such works were the religious elites recruited by the caliphs in order to aid them in imposing the new Almohad doctrines. For more on the Almohad intellectual program of reform, see Maribel Fierro, "Alfonso X 'The Wise': The Last Almohad Caliph?," *Medieval Encounters* 15 (2009): 175–98.

23 On the Almohad attitude toward Andalusian poetry, see Fawzī Sa`d `Īsā, *al-Shi`r al-andalusī fī `aṣr al-muwaḥḥidīn* (Beirut, 1991). For more on Ṣūfī poetry, both in the Andalusian environment and beyond, and its themes, see Simon Kuntze, "Love and God: The Influence of the Ghazal on Mystic Poetry," in *Ghazal as World Literature*, ed. Thomas Bauer and Angelika Neuwirth (Beirut: Ergon Verlag Würzburg in Kommission, 2005), I:157–80; As`ad E. Khairallah, *Love, Madness and Poetry: An Interpretation of the Magnun Legend* (Beirut: Orient-Institut der Deutschen Morgenländischen Gesellschaft, 1980), 4; Mazalaoui, "'I Follow the Religion of Love,'" 119–36; Norman Roth, "'My Beloved Is Like a Gazelle': Imagery of the Beloved Boy in Religious Hebrew Poetry," *Hebrew Annual Review* 8 (1984): 143–65; Raymond Scheindlin, "Ibn Gabirol's Religious and Sufi Poetry," *Sefarad* 54:1 (1994), 109–42; Annemarie Schimmel, "Eros – Heavenly and not so Heavenly – in Sufi Literature and Life," in *Society and the Sexes in Medieval Islam*, 119–41; Jim Wafer, "Vision and Passion: The Symbolism of Male Love in Islamic Mystical Literature," in *Islamic Homosexualities: Culture, History and Literature*, ed. Stephen O. Murray and Will Roscoe (New York and London: New York University Press, 1997), 107–31.

The most famous of the Andalusian Ṣūfī love poets is Ibn `Arabī (Abū `Abdullāh Muḥammad b. `Alī b. Muḥammad b. `Arabī, born in Murcia in 1165, died in Damascus in 1240), who composed the *Tarjumān al-ashwāq*, a collection of his love poems accompanied by a commentary explaining the mystical reading of almost every line. See Reynold A. Nicholson, trans., *The Tarjumán al-Ashwáq: A Collection of Mystical Odes by Muḥyi'ddín ibn al-'Arabí* (London: Royal Asiatic Society, 1911). The later Persian mystic Jalāl al-Dīn al-Rūmī (d. 1273) likewise employed explicit sexual images and tales in his mystical compositions to convey mystical knowledge. See Mahdi Tourage, *Rūmī and the Hermeneutics of Eroticism* (Leiden and Boston: E. J. Brill, 2007). On the influence of Ṣūfī ideas and poetry on the Hebrew poets, see Scheindlin, "Ibn Gabirol's Religious and Sufi Poetry," 109–42; and S. D. Goitein, "A Jewish Addict to Sufism," *JQR* 64, (1954–5), 37–49.

24 Scheindlin and Aviva Doron insist that it was not so much a decline as a shift in which the poets retained many of the elements of Arabic culture, while incorporating elements of the Romance literatures. This period gave rise to the *maqāma* form (narrative rhymed prose studded with short poems, a pattern derived from Arabic literature). Among the famous Hebrew poets from this period are Todros Abulafia and Judah al-Ḥarizi. See Carmi, *The Penguin Book of Hebrew Verse*, 32–3; Decter, *Iberian Jewish Literature*; Aviva Doron, "New Trends in the Conception of Hebrew Poetry in the 13th and 14th Century in Spain in Relation to Spanish Literature," in *Encuentros and Desencuentros: Spanish Jewish Cultural Interaction Throughout History*, ed. Carlos Carrete Parrondo *et al.* (Tel Aviv: University Publication Projects, 2000), 213–39; Scheindlin, "Hebrew Poetry in Medieval Iberia," 39–60; idem, "The Influence of Muslim Arabic Cultural Elements on the Literature of the Hebrew Golden Age," *Conservative Judaism* 35:4 (1982): 63–72; idem, "Secular Hebrew Poetry in Fifteenth Century Spain," in *Crisis and Creativity in the Sephardic World, 1391–1648*, ed. Benjamin R. Gampel (New York: Columbia University Press, 1997), 25–37; Arie Schippers, "The Hebrew Poets of Christian Spain and the Arabic Literary Heritage," in *Jewish Studies at the Turn of the 20th Century*, ed. Judit Targarona Borás and Angel Sáenz-Badillos (Boston, Leiden, and Köln: E. J. Brill, 1999), 521–9.

25 Monroe, *Hispano-Arabic Poetry: A Student Anthology*, 45–60. Muslim control in Andalusia did not end completely with the fall of the Almohads in 1230. In that same year, Muḥammad ibn al-Aḥmar seized control of Granada and established a Muslim empire – known as the Naṣrid empire – there. The Naṣrid dynasty managed to stay alive until the final blow of the Christian Reconquest brought it to an end in 1492.

26 Henri Pérès, *La Poésie andalouse en arabe classique au XIe siècle* (Paris, 1937; reprint, Paris: Adrien-Maisonneuve, 1953).

27 Pierre Cachia, *Arabic Literature: An Overview* (London: RoutledgeCurzon, 2002), 90.

28 As noted earlier (n. 14), David Tzvi Baneth maintains that the Bedouins were not illiterate, as had been previously assumed. So too D. S. Margoliouth maintains that there is physical evidence demonstrating the written nature of pre-Islamic poetry. See Margoliouth, "The Origins of Arabic Poetry," 417–49. Not all of the pre-Islamic poets who wrote in Arabic were pagan Arabs; the Christians and Jews of Arabia were also known to have composed Arabic poetry in the pre-Islamic period. Goldziher singles out the Christian `Adī ibn Zayd (d. 604) and the Jewish Samau'al ibn `Ādiyā, whose son and grandson continued in his poetic footsteps. See Goldziher, *A Short History of Classical Arabic Literature*, 20.

On the form of the *qaṣīda*, see n. 14.

29 See Baneth, "Ha-Shirah ha-`Aravit ha-Qeduma," 23–37; Bellamy, "The Impact of Islam on Early Arabic Poetry," 141–67.

30 Francesco Gabrieli maintains these values do not include a religious element, which was almost entirely absent from pagan Arabic poetry. "An Arabic religious poetry was born with Islam," he writes. According to Gabrieli, the poetry of Umayya ibn Abī Ṣalṭ, generally held up as the prime example of pre-Islamic pagan Arabic religious poetry, forms the exception to the rule. See Francesco Gabrieli, "Religious Poetry

in Early Islam," in *Arabic Poetry: Theory and Development*, 5–17. For more on the religious element of Umayya ibn Abī Salṭ, see Gert Borg, "The Divine in the Works of Umayya b. Abī al-Ṣalt," in *Representations of the Divine in Arabic Poetry*, ed. Gert Borg and Ed de Moor (Amsterdam-Atlanta, GA: Rodopi, 2001), 9–23. Michael Zwettler discusses the fact that pre-Islamic poets were themselves understood to have been semi-prophets. See Michael Zwettler, "A Mantic Manifesto: The Sūra of 'The Poets' and the Qur'ānic Foundations of Prophetic Authority," in *Poetry and Prophecy: The Beginnings of a Literary Tradition*, ed. James L. Kugel (Ithaca, NY and London: Cornell University Press, 1990), 75–120.

31 For more on `Udhrite love poetry, see *EI*[2], s.v. "`Udhrī," by Renate Jacobi (10:774–6). Bürgel notes that in some cases, the chastity of the `Udhrite couple was only temporary, a transitory phase that led to eventual union. This is not the case in the poems under discussion in the current project. See J. C. Bürgel, "Love, Lust, and Longing: Eroticism in Early Islam as Reflected in Literary Sources," in *Society and the Sexes in Medieval Islam*, 92.

32 Such poems appear to have served as a form of protest against the current political situation; the Abbasid government saw itself as the religious, righteous replacement for the Umayyads. See J. W. Wright, Jt., "Masculine Allusion and the Structure of Satire in Early `Abbāsid Poetry," in *Homoeroticism in Classical Arabic Literature*, ed. J. W. Wright, Jr. and Everett K. Rowson (New York: Columbia University Press, 1997), 1–23. Baneth maintains that early on in the Abbasid period, it appeared as if Islam might be replaced. See David Tzvi Baneth, "Ha-Shirah ve-ha-Proza ha-Omanutit ba-Tequfa ha-`Abbasit," in *Peraqim be-Toledot ha-`Aravim ve-ha-Islam*, ed. Lazarus-Yafeh, 333. Similarly, G. E. von Grunebaum writes that the first decades of the Abbasid Empire proved practically devoid of even casual religious poetry. Only with the generation that grew up under the officially pious Abbasid government do we begin to see the idea that God, or His will, stands behind everything and poems in honor of religion appear. See von Grunebaum, "The Early Development of Islamic Religious Poetry," *JAOS* 60 (1940) 23–9.

33 Monroe, *Hispano-Arabic Poetry: A Student Anthology*, 5–6.

34 See Charles Pellat, "Liwāṭ," in *Sexuality and Eroticism among Males in Moslem Societies*, ed. Arno Schmitt and Jehoeda Sofer (New York, London, and Norwood (Australia): Haworth Press, 1992), 157; Norman Roth, " 'Fawn of My Delights': Boy-Love in Hebrew and Arabic Verse," in *Sex in the Middle Ages*, ed. Joyce E. Salisbury (New York and London: Garland Publishing, 1991), 157–72; Bellamy and Steiner, *Banners of the Champions*, xxix; Dan Pagis, *Shirat ha-Ḥol ve-Torat ha-Shir le-Moshe ibn Ezra u-venei Doro* (Jerusalem: Mossad Bialik, 1970), 271; Khaled El-Rouayheb, *Before Homosexuality in the Arab-Islamic World 1500–1800* (Chicago: University of Chicago Press, 2005), 65ff; Jefim [Ḥaim] Schirmann, "The Ephebe in Medieval Hebrew Poetry," *Sefarad* 15 (1955): 55–68; Vern L. Bullough, *Sexual Variance in Society and History* (Chicago: University of Chicago Press, 1976), 235. A good example of this use of the masculine gender for a female subject appears in Ibn Zaydūn's *Nūniyya*, a long poem composed to persuade his beloved Wallāda (994–1091) to return to him after breaking off their affair. Although Wallāda was female, the princess daughter of the Cordoban caliph al-Mustakfī, the poem refers to her with masculine pronouns. See Monroe, *Hispano-Arabic Poetry: A Student Anthology*, 178–83; Monroe, "Zajal and Muwashshaḥ a: Hispano-Arabic Poetry and the Romance Tradition," in *The Legacy of Muslim Spain*, 400.

Norman Roth maintains that love poetry was divided into two categories, *ghazāliyyāt*, love poems about boys, and *mujūniyyāt*, love poems about women. The two categories were not mutually exclusive, however, and the same poet could write of both boys and girls. See Roth, "Religious Constraints on Erotic Poetry among Muslims and Jews in al-Andalus," *Maghreb Review* 19:3–4 (1994): 197. The

Hanbalite jurisconsult Ibn al-Jawzī (d. 1200) once wrote, "He who claims that he experiences no desire [when looking at beautiful boys or youths] is a liar and if we could believe him, he would be an animal and not a human being." Cited in James A. Bellamy, "Sex and Society in Islamic Popular Literature," in *Society and the Sexes in Medieval Islam*, 37.

Early scholars often revealed discomfort with the male pronouns and translated clearly homoerotic poems as hetero-erotic. For example, al-Mu`tamid's ode to a boy cup-bearer named Sayf (Sword) whom he received as a gift from al-Ma`mūn of Toledo is transformed by Dulcie Lawrence Smith into a poem about a girl, by the same name, in *The Poems of al-Mu`tamid King of Seville* (London: John Murray, 1915), 36. The Arabic can be found in *Mukhtārāt min al-shi`r al-Andalusī,* ed. A. R. Nykl (Beirut: Dar al-`ilm lil-malāyīn, 1949), 87 (#22) and in *Dīwān al-Mu`tamid ibn `Abbād*, ed. Aḥmad Aḥmad Badawī and Ḥāmid `Abd al-Majīd (Cairo: Al-Maṭba`a al-amīrīyya, 1951), 67. An accurate (male) English translation appears in Nykl's *Hispano-Arabic Poetry*, 143.

35 Raymond Scheindlin, "A Miniature Anthology of Medieval Hebrew Love Poems," *Prooftexts* 5:2 (1985): 110.

A story told in the *Kitāb al-aghānī* illustrates this idea nicely: Ramla, an Umayyad princess, once asked `Umar ibn Abū Rabī`a, the greatest Arab Muslim poet of the seventh century, who the women mentioned in certain lines in his poems were. He replied that the poems were dedicated "[T]o no particular one. I am a poet, who likes to make gallant songs and to praise female beauty." See Abū al-Faraj al-Iṣbahānī [al-Iṣfahēnī], *Kitāb al-aghāni* (Cairo: Dār al-kutub, 1383/1963), I, 75, and cited by Bürgel, *Love, Lust, and Longing*, 83.

36 Zvi Malachi and Chana David, eds, *Meḥqarim be-Yetzirat Shelomo Ibn Gabirol* ([Tel Aviv]: Machon Katz le-Ḥeqer ha-Sifrut ha-`Ivrit, Tel Aviv University, 1985), 113. Whether or not the poems reflected anyone's actual experience will be discussed further on.

37 While convention praised brunettes, degrading light hair as ugly, in time light hair came into fashion as well. This will be discussed at greater length in Chapter 2 (n. 24).

38 As Rowson notes, the beard is the only factor that definitively marks the description of a male as male. The sprouting of the beard signifies the demise of a relationship, for it serves as the marker of manliness. Since boys, not men, were the acceptable object of desire, the arrival of the beard constituted a cause for mourning. See Everett Rowson, "The Categorization of Gender and Sexual Irregularity in Medieval Arabic Vice Lists," in *Body Guards: The Cultural Politics of Gender Ambiguity*, ed. Julia Epstein and Kristina Straub (New York and London: Routledge, 1991), 58, and Roth, "Fawn," 157. El-Rouayheb posits that the age of "beloved" boys ranged from 7/8 to 20/21, the age at which a beard would have come in fully. The peak of their attractiveness would have been at 14–15 years of age. See his *Before Homosexuality*, 31. Examples of poems that speak of beards and beard-fear can be found in *Rāyāt al-mubarrizīn*: Abū Ja`far ibn al-Ḥājj of Lorca (twelfth century), 202–3; Abū `Abdāllah b. `Ā'isha of Valencia (fl. 1087–1106), 204–5; Abū Muḥammad `Abdāllah b. Sāra of Santarén (d. 1123), 106–8; Abū Isḥāq Ibrāhīm b. `Alī al-Ḥuṣrī of Qairaoun (d. 1061), 259–60; Ibn `Abd Rabbihi of Cordoba (d. 960), 133–4; and Abū `Alī al-Ḥasan b. Rashīq of Masila (1000–64), 249–51. English translations can be found in Bellamy and Steiner, *Banners of the Champions*, 63–7.

39 Schippers, *Spanish Hebrew Poetry*, 149–54.

40 This is in line with the definition of *`ishq* as provided by al-Jāḥiẓ (781–869). See *The Life and Works of Jāḥiẓ,* trans. and ed. Charles Pellat; trans. from French by D. M. Hawke (London: Routledge and Kegan Paul, 1969), 263. Al-Jāḥiẓ's definition will appear in more detail in the coming chapters.

41 Roth, "My Beloved Is Like a Gazelle," 148.

42 Malachi and David, eds, *Meḥqarim be-Yetzirat Shelomo ibn Gabirol*, 113.

43 As Shulamit Elizur has pointed out, the Hebrew term חשק (*ḥesheq*) appears already in the Bible in connection with a man's desire for a woman (Gen. 34:8 and Deut. 21:11). However, the use of the word in medieval Hebrew poetry in Spain was not an independent creation of the Hebrew writers but was influenced by the Arabic term عشق (*`ishq*). See Elizur, *Shirat ha-Ḥol ha-`Ivrit be-Sefarad ha-Muslemit* (Ramat Aviv: The Open University, 2004), 2:70.

44 Roth, "My Beloved is Like a Gazelle," 145.

45 Norman Roth, " 'Deal Gently with the Young Man': Love of Boys in Medieval Hebrew Poetry of Spain," *Speculum* 57:1 (1982): 24. Roth suggests that perhaps this is because kissing between males does not constitute a violation of the Jewish laws against homosexuality, which are concerned primarily with seminal emissions and actual intercourse..

46 A particularly vivid example comes from the pen of the great *zajal* poet Ibn Quzmān (Cordoba, b. 1078–80, d. 1160), when he describes an adulterous event in which he participated. Among the explicitly sexual acts of which he speaks, we find: "I, by God, immediately set to work: / Either it came out, or it went in, / while I thrust away sweetly, sweet as honey, / and [my] breath came out hotly between her legs." In Monroe, *Hispano-Arabic Poetry: A Student Anthology*, 260–72, ll. 51–4. The complete Arabic poem and an English translation can be found there.

47 In Hebrew: "דדי יפת תואר ליל חבוק / ושפת יפת מראה יומם נשוק!" These are the first two lines of a longer poem that appears in Moses ibn Ezra, *Shirei ha-Ḥol*, ed. Ḥaim Brody, 1:263 (#250). In another poem Moses ibn Ezra writes, "אפשט בגדיו ויפשיטיני" (I removed his clothes and he removed mine). See Moses ibn Ezra, *Shirei ha-Ḥol*, 262 ("תאוות לבבי ומחמד עיני," #249). English translations of the poems appear in Carmi, *The Penguin Book of Hebrew Verse*, 324–5 and 325–6. Peter Cole notes that scholars have disagreed about the gender of the beloved in this poem, despite the fact that the poem uses the masculine term, *tzvi* (male gazelle). Scholars have also disagreed as to the meaning of the poem, whether it is to be taken at face value (as describing an erotic interaction) or as a discussion of the Platonic ideal of pleasure. See *The Dream of the Poem*, 429 ("Heart's Desire").

48 Judah Halevi, *Diwan. Shirei ha-Ḥol*, ed. Ḥaim Brody (Berlin 1909), 2:6 (יעלת חן רחמי לבב שכנתיו מעודך). An English translation can be found in Carmi, *The Penguin Book of Hebrew Verse*, 342–3. Sexually explicit verses become even more pronounced in the poems of the later Todros Abulafia (d. after 1298), who, though a product of Christian Spain, was trained in the Muslim Spanish style. For more on Todros, see, among others, *EJ*, s.v. "Abulafia, Todros b. Judah," by Ḥaim [Jefim] Schirmann and Angel Saénz-Badillos, 1:344–5; Schirmann, *Ha-Shirah ha-`Ivrit be-Sefarad u-ve-Provans*, 2:413–48; idem, *Toledot ha-Shirah ha-`Ivrit be-Sefarad ha-Notzerit u-ve-Drom Tzarefat*, edited and notes by Ezra Fleischer (Jerusalem: Magnes Press, 1997), 366–424. See n. 88.

Whether the Muslim and Jewish literary openness regarding sexual matters had practical ramifications remains a matter of scholarly debate. According to Yom Tov Assis, medieval Spain *was* a sexually permissive place; he brings historical evidence in support of this contention saying, "We are struck at times by the laxity in the sexual conduct of some Jewish couples" of the era. See his "Sexual Behavior in Mediaeval Hispano-Jewish Society," in *Jewish History: Essays in Honor of Chimen Abramsky*, ed. Ada Rapoport-Alpert and Steven J. Zipperstein (London: Peter Halban, 1988), 25–59 (quote from p. 33). Schirmann, on the other hand, maintains that one can learn little from the behavior of people based on the literature produced; the homoerotic poems, for instance, can testify only to *literary* fashions of the day. After all, as Moses ibn Ezra writes in his *Kitāb al-muḥāḍara*, one does not *have* to have experienced love to write exquisite love poetry. See *Kitāb al-muḥāḍara wa-al-mudhākara.*

Liber Discussionis et Commenmorationis, ed. and trans. A. S. Halkin (Jerusalem: Mekitze Nirdamim, 5735 [1975]), 275. See this idea in a poem by Samuel ha-Nagid, in *Diwan Shemuel ha-Nagid. Ben Tehillim*, ed. Dov Jarden (Jerusalem: Hebrew Union College, 5726 [1966]), #75 (צבי נעים נתנו אל), ll. 12–13; and in one by Todros Abulafia, *Gan ha-Meshalim*, 1:173–4 (משורר לא ידבר רק התולים). Similarly, Joseph ha-Nagid, editing his father Samuel's secular poetry, wrote in his introduction that, "Although some of these include erotic themes, he [Samuel] believed these to be metaphors for the community of Israel and the like ... Anyone who interprets them in a way contrary to his intention will bear his own guilt." As translated by R. Scheindlin in "Rabbi Moshe Ibn Ezra on the Legitimacy of Poetry," in *Medievalia et Humanistica*, n.s. 7 (1976): 113. The Judeo-Arabic and a Hebrew translation appears on the first page of Jarden's edition of Samuel ha-Nagid, *Diwan Shemuel ha-Nagid. Ben Tehillim*. Nehemiah Allony tries to explain the sexuality away altogether. See his "Ha-Tzvi ve-ha-Gamal." Franz Rosenthal disagrees. According to Rosenthal, "It would be nonsensical to argue that there is anything the poets say about sexual behavior that did not have its large role in reality." He continues, "Poetry allows some glimpses at a reality very different from the official ideal, a small and in its total significance minor slice of reality." See his "Fiction and Reality: Sources for the Role of Sex in Medieval Muslim Society," 12. For more on this debate, see Bürgel, "Love, Lust, and Longing"; Louis Crompton, "Male Love and Islamic Law in Arab Spain," in *Islamic Homosexualities: Culture, History and Literature*, 142–57; Daniel Eisenberg, "Judaism, Sephardic," in *Encyclopedia of Homosexuality*, ed. Wayne R. Dynes (New York: Garland, 1990), 1:644–8; James T. Monroe, "The Striptease that was Blamed on Abū Bakr's Naughty Son: Was Father Being Shamed or Was the Poet Having Fun? (Ibn Quzmān's Zajal no. 133)," in *Homoeroticism in Classical Arabic Literature*, 94–139; Pagis, *Shirat ha-Ḥol ve-Torat ha-Shir le-Moshe ibn Ezra u-venei Doro*, 46ff; Pagis, *Hebrew Poetry of the Middle Ages and the Renaissance*, 63–6; Elizur, *Shirat ha-Ḥol*, 2:85 and various; Pellat, "Liwāṭ," 157; Norman Roth, "The Care and Feeding of Gazelles: Medieval Arabic and Hebrew Love Poetry," in *Poetics of Love in the Middle Ages*, 114; idem, "Deal Gently"; idem, "Fawn"; idem, "My Beloved is Like a Gazelle"; idem, "A Note on Research into Jewish Sexuality in the Medieval Period," in *Handbook of Medieval Sexuality*, ed. Vern L. Bullough and James A. Brundage (New York and London: Garland Publishing, 1996), 309–17; idem, "Religious Constraints"; Rowson, "The Categorization of Gender," 52; Scheindlin, "A Miniature Anthology," 106–16; Schirmann, "The Ephebe," 55–68; Yosef Tobi, *Proximity and Distance: Medieval Hebrew and Arabic Poetry* (Leiden and Boston: E. J. Brill, 2004), 198; Yosef Tobi, "*Shirat ha-Ḥol ha-`Iivrit be-Sefarad ke-Shirah Ḥazranit – ha-Omnam*?," in *Ben `Ever le-`arav*, Volume IV (*Prof. Amnon Shiloah Jubilee Volume*): 46–62 (Haifa: Center for the Study of Jewish Culture in Spain and Islamic Countries, 2008); Helen Leneman, "Reclaiming Jewish History: Homo-erotic Poetry of the Middle Ages," *Changing Men* 18 (Summer/Fall 1987): 22–3.

The debate regarding the ability of writers to convincingly portray something they have not personally experienced appears in the work of the modern American writer Philip Roth. Although Roth insisted that his 1969 novel *Portnoy's Complaint* was a work of fiction, readers and reviewers often assumed that the hero, Alexander Portnoy, was none other than Roth himself and insisted that the work was semi-autobiographical. Playing on this controversy, in his 1981 *Zuckerman Unbound*, Roth created the character Nathan Zuckerman, a writer who finds himself too often confused for his (Zuckerman's) character Carnovsky. Roth writes, "They had mistaken impersonation for confession and were calling out to a character who lived in a book. Zuckerman tried taking it as praise – he had made real people believe Carnovsky real too – but in the end he pretended he was only himself, and with his quick, small steps hurried on." See *Zuckerman Unbound* (London: J. Cape, 1981), 10–11. In 1993 Roth revisited this theme in *Operation Shylock: A Confession* (London: J. Cape, 1993), in which he claims to have discovered a Philip Roth impersonator who has appropriated his identity, leading the "real" Philip Roth on a series of adventures in an attempt to stop him. In the book, Roth simultaneously claims the story is both absolute truth and a complete fabrication.

49 Monroe notes that oftentimes poets composed *`ishq* poems about particular people, especially women, in order to irritate the family members. As the evidence from the caliphal threats demonstrates, in this they proved successful. See Monroe, "The Striptease that was Blamed on Abū Bakr's Naughty Son," 105ff.

50 Abū Muḥammad `Alī ibn Ḥazm al-Andalusī, *Ṭauḳ al-ḥamâma*, ed. D. K. Pétrof (St. Pétersbourg-Leide: E. J. Brill, 1914), 118; A. J. Arberry, trans., *The Ring of the Dove* (London: Luzac and Company, Ltd., 1953), 235 and A. R. Nykl, trans., *A Book Containing the Risāla known as The Dove's Neck-Ring about Love and Lovers composed by Abū Muḥammad `Alī ibn Ḥazm al-Andalusī* (Paris: Libraire Orientaliste Paul Geuthner, 1931), 181. References to both English translations will appear throughout this work.

51 It is perhaps with this same religious criticism in mind that the earlier Ibn `Abd Rabbihi (860–940) composed what he referred to as "sin-effacer" poems (*mumaḥḥiṣāt*). Each of these balanced against one of his erotic poems, imitating it in form, meter, and rhyme. See Mazalaoui, "I Follow the Religion of Love," 123–7.

52 See Song of Songs 5:10 and 7:5, and n. 160. In Hebrew the line reads: "ידידי תשמעו שירי ונפשי / כמו תדעו ליראת אל סמוכה / ולו פשר כפשר שלמה / ב'דודי צח' ו'עין כברכה'." In *Diwan Shemuel ha-Nagid. Ben Tehillim*, ed. Jarden, 221, #75 (צבי נעים נתנו אל ברכה). In her comments on these lines, Shulamit Elizur points out that while Samuel ha-Nagid wrote other, more daring, erotic poems, this is the only one in which he "apologizes." She also notes that the poem here is not an independent love poem, but a praise poem with an erotic introduction, something common among the Arabic poems but not, at the time, among the Hebrew. She thus suggests a second possible reason for his apology here. It is possible, she writes, that Samuel thought that opening a praise poem with an erotic introduction was exceptionally daring, and thus he felt he should include an apology along with the introduction. See Elizur, *Shirat ha-Ḥol*, 2:72–3.

53 *Diwan Shemuel ha-Nagid. Ben Tehillim*, ed. Jarden, 1; also, Aharon Mirsky, "Hebrew Literary Creation," in *Moreshet Sepharad: The Sephardi Legacy*, ed. Haim Beinart (Jerusalem: Magnes Press, 1992). 1:161. Approximately 200–250 years later, Meshullam b. Shelomo DePiera (b. Gerona, mid-late thirteenth century) echoed this sentiment, writing, "מיודעי אני הוא אני הוא המשורר המשקר" ("My friends, I am he, I am the lying poet"). In *Ha-Shirah ha-`Ivrit be-Sefarad u-ve-Provans*, 2:303 (#344).

54 Schirmann maintains that the authenticity of this statement has been contested. See Schirmann, "The Function of the Hebrew Poet in Medieval Spain," *JSS* 16 (1954): 251.

55 As cited by Schirmann in "The Function of the Hebrew Poet," 252. For Ibn Ezra's original Judeo-Arabic, see *Kitāb al-muḥāḍara*, 90 (49a).

56 *Kitāb al-muḥāḍara*, 102 (55a). Moses ibn Ezra's ambivalent repudiation of poetry did not stand alone. Allony, citing Schirmann, notes that Joseph ha-Nagid also wrote wine and love poetry for which he later apologized. See Allony, "Ha-Tzvi ve-ha-Gamal," 33. For more on Ibn Ezra's ambiguous disavowal of poetry writing, see Brann, *The Compunctious Poet*, 64ff. Brann's book discusses the concept of the remorseful poet as a poetic typology of the period, beyond Ibn Ezra.

57 Schirmann, "The Function of the Hebrew Poet," 262. Allony insists we understand that the vast majority of homoerotic Hebrew poems express not physical human love, but the love between God and Israel; only rarely do the poems speak of actual boy-love

and then it is only to prove the power of Hebrew vis-à-vis Arabic. See "Ha-Tzvi ve-ha-Gamal," 41–2. Similarly, Yosef Tobi insists that one should take the poets' declarations at face value and not understand any of the Hebrew poems of desire as speaking of actual sexual desire. Instead, he maintains that they are all praise poems written in honor of friends or patrons but in an allegorical format, using the imagery of love poetry. See his *Between Hebrew and Arabic Poetry*, 116–47. Despite Tobi's persuasively crafted argument, I am more inclined to agree with Schirmann, that the descriptions of desire in the poems of desire are intended as poetic descriptions of desire, rather than friendship.

58 Because of its objectionable content, Maimonides considered the *Kitāb al-aghānī*, an encyclopedic collection of poems and songs compiled by the Muslim Abū al-Faraj al-Iṣfahānī (897–967), to be a heretical book. See Norman Roth, "Maimonides on Hebrew Language and Poetry," *Hebrew Studies* 26:1 (1985): 93–101; Tova Cohen, "Veils and Wiles: Poetry as Woman in Andalusian Hebrew Poetry," in *Israel and Ishmael*, ed. Tudor Parfitt (Richmond, Surrey: Curzon Press, 2000), 84. Maimonides objected not only to secular poetry but also to liturgical tunes, which he felt undermined the solemnity of prayer by adding a sense of frivolity. See Maimonides, *Perush le-Massekhet Avot*, ed. Mordechai Dov Rabinovitz (Jerusalem: Mossad Harav Kook, 5721/1961), 1:16, 30; Schirmann, *Toledot ha-Shirah ha-`Ivrit be-Sefarad ha-Notzerit*, 281–2, n. 10.

A similar criticism of Hebrew poetry appears in the later sixteenth-century code of Jewish law written by R. Joseph Caro (Toledo, 1488–Safed, 1575), the *Shulḥan Arukh*. There R. Caro writes, "Secular flowery writing and parables and writings of desire (*ḥesheq*), such as the books of Immanuel [Immanuel of Rome, *c*. 1261–1328, Italian Jewish scholar and satirical poet], are prohibited to be read from on the Sabbath. And the prohibition remains even on weekdays, because of the issue of idle chatter (מושב ליצים, *moshav leitzim*)." See R. Joseph Caro, *Shulḥan Arukh, Oraḥ Hayyim*, ed. Shamma Friedman (Jerusalem: Mif`al Shulḥan Arukh ha-Shalem, 5768 [*c*. 2007]), *siman* 16:703.

59 As cited by J. C. Bürgel in his "Love, Lust, and Longing," 84, fn. 12. Bürgel cites from al-Maqqarī's *Kitāb nafḥ al-ṭīb min ghuṣn al-andalus al-raṭīb wa-dhikr wazīrihā Lisān al-Dīn ibn al-Khaṭīb* [*Analectes sur l'Histoire et la Littérature des Arabes d'Espagne*], ed. R. Dozy, G. Dugat, L. Krehl, and W. Wright (Leiden: E. J. Brill, 1858), vol. 2, pt. 1, 343. Bürgel cites an earlier defense of the poetic right to speak in verse of things at odds with high moral standards: In the *Naqd al-shi`r*, Qudāma ibn Ja`far (d. 922 or later) wrote: نقل الكفر ليس بالكفر (*naql al-kufr laysa bi-al-kufr*, the transmission of unbelief is not itself unbelief). See Bürgel, 84.

60 Michael Sells adds that even the *mujūn* (profligacy) poets, whose compositions strike the modern reader, and likely the contemporary reader, as not only debauched but at times blasphemous, were never charged with the crime of blasphemy. See his "Love," in *The Literature of al-Andalus*, ed. Maria Rosa Menocal, Raymond P. Scheindlin, and Michael Sells (Cambridge: Cambridge University Press, 2000), 126–58. See also Pagis, *Hebrew Poetry*, 68. Maarten Schild attempts to explain this curious fact by noting that as long as such writing did not present a practical challenge to societal morality or lead to "publicly unlawful behavior," it was not understood to pose a serious threat to the social order. Most of the objections revolve around the potential of the poems to cause problems, rather than problems themselves. See Maarten Schild, "Islam," in *Sexuality and Eroticism among Males in Moslem Societies*, 183. W. Montgomery Watt and Pierre Cachia have written that in the poets' search for increasingly more exaggerated ways of expressing themselves in the *mujūn* poems "neither artificiality nor bad taste were always avoided." See Watt and Cachia, *A History of Islamic Spain* (Edinburgh: Edinburgh University Press, 1967), 117. Rowson has noted that "even the most respectable or sanctimonious

individual was expected to compose *mujūn* (profligacy)" poems; they were similarly expected to compose stories depicting the most outrageous behavior, even attributing it (falsely, Rowson points out) to themselves. See Rowson, "The Categorization of Gender," 52. See also Julie Scott Meisami, "Arabic Mujūn Poetry: The Literary Dimension," in *Verse and the Fair Sex: Studies in Arabic Poetry and in the Representation of Women in Arabic Literature*, ed. Frederick de Jong (Utrecht: M. Th. Houtsma Stichting, 1993), 8–30.

61 According to Roth, despite Maimonides's general disdain for poets and poetry influenced by the Arabic styles, he was known to have been on familiar terms with the compositions of his time, quoting lines of poetry by Judah Halevi. See Roth, "Maimonides on Hebrew Language and Poetry," 97.

62 Geert Jan van Gelder, "Forbidden Firebrands: Frivolous *Iqtibās* (Quotation from the Qur'ān) according to Medieval Arab Critics," *Quaderni di Studi Arabi* 20–1 (2002–3): 3–16.

63 For reasons discussed further on, the differences between the religious scholar-poets and the less or non-religious poets are more visible in the Arabic realm than in the Hebrew. That some of the Arabic "secular" poets were well versed in the religious texts we see in other ways as well. A prime example concerns Ibn Quzmān, a poet known for having led a life of licentiousness resembling Abū Nuwās's, about which he remained unabashed in his poetry. Finding himself poverty-stricken and in need of a non-poetic job at the end of his life, he served as an *imām* teaching in a mosque. See Crompton, "Male Love and Islamic Law," 154; Nykl, *Hispano-Arabic Poetry*, 266–301; Monroe, *Hispano-Arabic Poetry: A Student Anthology*, 260–79.

64 A later example of a biblical reference serving to solve a riddle occurs in Todros's love poem, צביה היא (*tzviya hi*), and in an earlier wine poem by Moses ibn Ezra. For Todros's poem, see *Gan ha-Meshalim*, 1:87. For Moses ibn Ezra's, see his *Shirei ha-Ḥol*, 1:72, l. 7. Both are mentioned by Brann in his "Andalusian Hebrew Poetry."

At times, it almost appears as if the Hebrew scholar-poets adopted the motto: The more obscure the scriptural reference, the better. See, for example, Samuel ha-Nagid's use of the obscure biblical name "Jerimoth" (ירימות), in his "ידידי כל שנותיך תנומות" in his *Diwan Shemuel ha-Nagid. Ben Tehillim*, 297. An English translation appears in Scheindlin, *Wine, Women and Death*, 54–5. Scheindlin explains that while "Jerimoth" appears eight times in the Bible, Samuel ha-Nagid appears to be referring to the one who is the fifth of the fourteen named sons of Heman, Levites who "prophesied to the accompaniment of lyres, harps, and cymbals" in 1 Chron. 24; none of these sons is singled out by the Bible for any special mention, aside from their names. See also Judah al-Ḥarizi's poetic use of the name Ḥelem (חלם) in his *Taḥkemoni*, ed. Y. Toporovsky (Tel Aviv: Hotza'at Maḥbarot le-Sifrut, 1952), 395. Another version of this poem appears in the version of the *Taḥkemoni* edited by A. Kaminka (Warsaw, 1899), 402. Toporovsky's rendering appears to be more correct, as it makes more sense.

65 Goldziher maintains that pagan poetry in northern Arabia contained no mention of religion *per se*, with the exception of ritualistic customs. The pagan Arabs, he maintains, did not engage in ritual out of any religious sentiment, but out of an adherence to traditions inherited from their forefathers. Northern Arabs mention no names of deities in their poems nor do they attribute the conditions of human life to any Higher Power. Southern Arabs, on the other hand, attributed all the elements of existence to the gods, whom they serve and revere. See Goldziher, *A Short History of Classical Arabic Literature*, 25.

66 A. M. Zubaidi, "The Impact of the Qur'ān and Ḥadīth on Medieval Arabic Literature," in *The Cambridge History of Arabic Literature*, ed. A. F. L. Beeston, T. M. Johnstone, R. B. Serjeant, and G. R. Smith (Cambridge: Cambridge University Press, 1983), I:322–43.

67 Wadād al-Qāḍī, "The Limitations of Qur'ānic Usage in Early Arabic Poetry: The Example of a Khārijite Poem," in *Festschrift Ewald Wagner zum 65. Geburtstag* (Beirut, 1994), 162–81. Al-Qāḍī presents as a case in point her analysis of a poem by the Khārijī poet 'Amr b. al-Ḥusayn al-`Anbarī (d. after 130/749) composed on the occasion of a Khārijī battle against the Umayyads, a battle in which many Khārijī leaders were killed.

68 Zubaidi (p. 323) notes that one can see this in any of the poems of Jarīr and Farazdaq, both of whom died *c.* 730. Al-Qāḍī discusses a poem used as a "weapon" in an eighth-century controversy between the Khārijīs and the Umayyads. See n. 67, above.

69 The poetry of Abū Nuwās frequently entailed such religious references, often as satire. In one example, the poet wishes to become a variety of Christian ritual objects, including the Eucharist and the communion wine, so that he could be closer to, would be able to enter, the Christian boy with whom he has fallen in love. According to Philip Kennedy, the poem is laced with discrete references to the Qur'ān as well as to Christianity. In another, Abū Nuwās writes of a failed tryst with an unwilling boy who throws an apple at him, breaking his tooth. He compares this to Muḥammad's breaking his teeth at the Battle of Uhud. See Philip Kennedy, *Abu Nuwas: A Genius of Poetry* (Oxford: Oneworld Publications, 2005), 49, 56. See also Paul Sprachman, "Le beau garçon sans merci: The Homoerotic Tale in Arabic and Persian," in *Homoeroticism in Classical Arabic Literature*, 192–209; Wright, "Masculine Allusion," 1–23.

Many of the famed wine poems (*khamriyyāt*) of Abū Nuwās reflect Qur'ānic ideas and influence in both obvious and less obvious fashions. See Philip Kennedy, "Abū Nuwās, Samuel and Levi," in *Medieval and Modern Perspectives on Muslim–Jewish Relations*, ed. Ronald Nettler (Luxembourg: Harwood Academic Publishers, 1995), 113; Zubaidi, "The Impact of the Qur'ān," 327.

70 Zubaidi, "The Impact of the Qur'ān," 332.

71 So too in *tashbīh* (simile), poets compared two dissimilar things to one another (one Qur'ānic and one not). In *isti`āra* (metaphor), a poet engages in "imaginary ascriptions," borrowing A for B, though B has no A in it. In *mathal*, the poet uses the Qur'ān or another text as an allegory. These terms, and others, are discussed by Wolfhart Heinrichs in his "Contacts between scriptural Hermeneutics and Literary Theory in Islam: The Case of *majāz*," in *Zeitschrift für Geschichte der arabisch-Islamischen wissenschaften* (Frankfurt am Main: Institut für Geschichte der Arabisch-Islamischen Wissenschaften an der Johann Wolfgang Goethe-Universität, 1984), 253–84; idem, "*Isti`ārah* and *badī`* and their Terminological Relationship in Early Arabic Literary Criticism," in *Zeitschrift für Geschichte der arabisch-Islamischen wissenschafte* I (1984), 180–211; and idem, *The Hand of the Northwind: Opinions on Metaphor and the Early Meaning of isti'ara in Arabic Poetics* (Mainz: Deutsche Morgenländische Gesellschadt, 1977). See also Mordechai Z. Cohen, *Three Approaches to Biblical Metaphor: From Ibn Ezra and Maimonides to David Kimhi* (Leiden: E. J. Brill, 2003), 7, 52–62.

72 *EI*^{2}, s.v. "Iḳtibās," by D. B. Macdonald and S. A. Bonebakker (3:1091–2). According to Macdonald and Bonebakker, *iqtibās* means "to take a live coal (*qabas*) from another's fire," as used in Q 20:10, 27:7, and 57:13. It thus came to mean seeking knowledge from some other place. *Iqtibās*, scholars agree, appears in both poetry and prose.

73 Arie Schippers, "Biblical and Koranic Quotations in Hebrew and Arabic Andalusian Poetry," in *Ben `Ever le-`Arav*, ed. Yosef Tobi and Yitzhak Avishur (Tel Aviv: Afikim Publishers, 2001), 2:xvi. See also von Grunebaum, "The Concept of Plagiarism in Arabic Theory," *JNES* 3 (1944): 245. *Iqtibās* resembles another poetic technique, *taḍmīn* (inclusion or incorporation). In the latter a poet incorporated into his poem a line, or part of a line, from another poet by way of quotation. Van Gelder writes that it was "particularly appreciated if a different twist was given to the quoted part

in its new context." See *EI*[2], "Taḍmīn," by Geert van Gelder (10:78–9). For a longer discussion of *taḍmīn*, see Adrian Gully, "Taḍmīn, 'Implication of Meaning' in Medieval Arabic," *JAOS* 113:3 (July–Sept. 1997): 466–80.

74 Interestingly, Ibn Ezra does not himself use the term *iqtibās*, though he describes the phenomenon.

75 See Moses ibn Ezra, *Kitāb al-muḥāḍara*, 296–301 (155a and ff). Ibn Ezra does not himself use the term *talmīḥ*.

76 Al-Qāḍī, "The Limitations of Qur'ānic Usage," 179.

77 As an example, Schippers refers to the Arabic Mūsāwiyya poems of the Jewish convert to Islam Abū Isḥāq Ibrāhīm ibn Sahl al-Isrā'īlī of Seville (d. *c.* 1251); the Mūsāwiyya constitute love poems largely devoted to a boy named Mūsā. Ibn Sahl's love poems are so full of references to the Qur'ān, *ḥadīth*, and even the Bible, it almost seems as if he were incapable of composing a love poem *without* getting involved in the sacred texts. See Arie Schippers, "Humorous Approach of the Divine in the Poetry of al-Andalus: The Case of Ibn Sahl," in *Representations of the Divine in Arabic Poetry*, 119–35. For more on Ibn Sahl, see n. 115.

78 David Yellin, *Torat ha-Shir ha-Sefaradit*, 2nd edition (Jerusalem: Magnes Press, 5732 [1972/3]), 3:103.

79 Dan Pagis, *Ḥiddush u-Masoret be-Shirat ha-Ḥol ha-`Ivrit: Sefarad ve-Italia* (Jerusalem: Keter, 1976), 75.

80 Pagis discusses the three types of שיבוץ (*shibbutz*), from "colorful" to "neutral" to "loaded," in detail in his *Ḥiddush u-Masoret*, 71ff. A similar discussion can be found in Elizur, *Shirat ha-Ḥol*, 3:349–55, 366–400. David Yellin discusses the use of biblical names as a form of *shibbutz/remizah*. See his *Leḥeqer ha-Shirah ha-`Ivrit be-Sefarad*, ed. A. M. Habermann (Jerusalem: Reuben Mas, 5735 [1975]) v. 3 in *Kitvei David Yellin*, 42–3.

81 For more on *remizah/remez*, see Yellin, *Torat ha-Shir ha-Sefaradit*, 103–17; idem, *Kitvei David Yellin*, 3:30–43; Brann, "Andalusian Hebrew Poetry," 101–31; Elizur, *Shirat ha-Ḥol*, 3:413ff.

82 Thus we find a poem by Samuel ha-Nagid in which he writes of Nadab crying after flames shot out from the sanctuary when he and Abihu (sons of Aaron) brought a forbidden foreign fire there (Lev. 10:1–6). Since the Bible states that Nadab and Abihu were instantly incinerated by the Divine flames, Samuel ha-Nagid's poem initially appears to have incorrectly cited the Bible. Yellin points out that Samuel ha-Nagid's poem actually refers to a passage in *BT Sanhedrin* 52a, which teaches that although the souls of Nadab and Abihu were thus burned, their bodies remained alive. See Yellin, *Torat ha-Shir ha-Sefaradit*, 103. The complete poem appears in Samuel ha-Nagid's *Diwan Shemuel ha-Nagid. Ben Tehillim*, 171–2 (לכל זמן ולכל נדוד).

83 Brann, "Andalusian Hebrew Poetry," 3:116; Elizur, *Shirat ha-Ḥol*, 3:349–52; Yellin, *Torat ha-Shir he-Sefaradit*, 103–17. Many modern readers do not appear to find such imagery as entertaining. In an article on the *c.* tenth-century Bedouin Baghdadi Mudrik al-Shaybānī's love poem to a Christian boy, Manfred Ullman discusses the poet's use of religious imagery. At one point, al-Shaybānī's lover declares that he wishes he were the Eucharist so that he could thereby enter his beloved Christian boy's body. This combination of sacred and profane imagery leads Ullman to declare the poem "*besonders geschmacklos*" (particularly tasteless). See a discussion of this poem and Ullman's reaction in Geert Jan van Gelder, "Mudrik al-Shaybānī's Poem on a Christian Boy: Bad Taste or Harmless Wit?," in *Representations of the Divine in Arabic Poetry*, 49–70. Note the similarity between the Eucharist imagery in this poem and the one written by the earlier Abū Nuwās. See above, n. 69.

84 Schippers, "Biblical and Koranic Quotations," xiii.

85 In one short example by Abraham ibn Ezra (1092/3–*c.* 1164), the poet compares the whitening of his black hair (caused by age) to Aḥimaatz's impressive overtaking of

the Cushite (i.e., African) runner in 2 Sam. 18. See David Kahana, ed., *Kovetz Ḥokhmat R. Abraham ibn Ezra* (Warsaw, 1894; reprint, Jerusalem: Hotza'at Kedem, 1971), 1:35 [#20]; also in Yellin, *Torat ha-Shir ha-Sefaradit*, 115. In English: "The hair on my head has changed to white (*lavan*) / Therefore I call out: My head, My head! / Behold, white (*lavan*) has set out in pursuit of me, / it ran and bypassed the Cushite." While the most obvious biblical reference is to Aḥimaatz, each line of the poem riffs on a different biblical verse; for example, *lavan* (white) refers both to the color and to the name of Jacob's father-in-law (Laban; in Hebrew, Lavan), who chased Jacob down in Gen. 31. See Yellin, ibid. and Elizur, *Shirat ha-Ḥol*, 3:399. Another humorous application of the Bible appears in a poem by Solomon ibn Gabirol in which he describes the quiet and security of a particular place as resembling the quiet and security that reigned when Og slept (Deut. 3:11); clearly no person who valued his life would be interested in waking the famed giant-king of the Bashan. Yellin, *Torat ha-Shir ha-Sefaradit*, 107. See also Carmi, ed., *The Penguin Book of Hebrew Verse*, 27; van Gelder, "Forbidden Firebrands," 4.

86 Brann, "Andalusian Hebrew Poetry," 116.

87 Ross Brann, " 'How Can My Heart Be in the East?' Intertextual Irony in Judah Ha-Levi," in *Judaism and Islam: Boundaries, Communication, and Interaction*, ed. B. H. Hary, J. L. Hayes, and F. Astren (Leiden: E. J. Brill, 2000), 374.

88 In one such example, Moses ibn Ezra exhorts his readers to enjoy the material pleasures that life has to offer, saying, "You too deserve a portion of the Ram / of Consecration (איל מילואים, *eil milu`im*) ... do not be shy / But take what's rightly yours – the breast and thigh!" See Scheindlin, *Wine, Women and Death*, 91. The sacrificial Ram of Consecration formed part of the ceremony through which Aaron and his sons were consecrated as priests in Exodus 29 and Leviticus 8. Special rituals involved the breast and thigh of the sacrifice and references to these body parts litter the biblical sections in which the ceremony appears. An even more daring example of the use of the "literarily impious" but humorous use of Scripture appears among the poems of the later Todros Abulafia (d. after 1298). In a poetic response to the criticism levied against him by his uncle, R. Joseph ben Efraim ben ha-Saraqasti, for conducting an affair with a servant girl, Todros replied that since the girl's beauty reflected the might of the Creator, when he made love to her he was worshiping God. See Todros's "ידיד אל תחשביני העבודה" in his *Gan ha-Meshalim*, v. 2, pt. 1, 50–1 [#542]; and Pagis, *Hebrew Poetry*, 54.

89 Allony enumerates the other five principles: a) the Arabian Peninsula is the best because of its climate, b) the Arabs are the best people, c) the best of the Arab tribes is the Quraysh, d) the best of the Quraysh was Muḥammad, who is also the best and last prophet, and e) the best of all the revealed Scriptures is the Qur'ān (revealed in Arabic). See Nehemiah Allony, "The Reaction of Moses Ibn Ezra to `Arabiyya," *Bulletin of the Institute of Jewish Studies* 3 (1975): 20. See also Norman Roth, "Jewish Reactions to the *`Arabiyya* and the Renaissance of Hebrew in Spain," *Journal of Semitic Studies* 28:I (Spring 1983): 63–84; idem, "A Research Note on Sexuality and Muslim Civilization," in *Handbook of Medieval Sexuality*, 321.

90 They referred to Q 49:13 as their proof. See also Roth, "Religious Constraints," 194.

91 Roth, "Religious Constraints," 194.

92 Roth, "A Research Note on Sexuality and Muslim Civilization," 321.

93 These include, among others, Moses ibn Ezra's *Kitāb al-ḥadīqa*, a philosophical work that devotes much attention to the Bible and its use of metaphor, and his *Kitāb al-muḥāḍara wa-al-mudhākara*, a treatise on Hebrew poetics composed in Arabic; Judah Halevi's *Sefer ha-Kuzari* (original title: *Kitāb al-ḥujja wa-al-dalīl fi naṣr al-dīn dhalīl* [The Book of the Argument and Proof in Defense of the Despised Faith]); the history written by Abraham ibn Daud (d. *c.* 1180), a work that traces the development of Jewish tradition and fuses Jewish doctrines with Aristotelian philosophy;

most of Maimonides's works, with the exception of the *Mishnah Torah*; and, the ethical works of Joseph ibn Judah ibn `Aknin (*c.* 1150–1220), as well as his commentary on Song of Songs. Ibn Gabirol appears to complain about this phenomenon in his *`Anaq*, lamenting the almost complete absence of Hebrew from the mouths of his fellow Jews, accusing half of them of speaking the language of the Christians (אדומית, *edomit*) and the other half the language of the Arabs (לשון בני קידר, *leshon benei qedar*), a cold language (קודרת, *qoderet*). See his *Shirei ha-Ḥol le-Rabbi Shelomo ibn Gabirol*, ed. Ḥaim Brody and Ḥaim [Jefim] Schirmann (Jerusalem: Machon Schocken, 5735 [1974]), 169, lines 6–9.

94 This includes even the "greats" such as the eleventh-century Moses b. Samuel ha-Cohen ibn Gikatilla and his critic Judah ibn Bal`am (*c.* 1070–90). See *EJ*, s.v. "Judeo-Arabic Literature," by Hava Lazarus-Yafeh and Abraham Solomon Halkin (11:532–6, Halkin section). As Halkin records, the Jewish use of Arabic for "Jewish" materials began before the Andalusian period. Saadiah Gaon (d. 942) translated the Bible into Arabic and wrote works of theosophy and theology in Arabic. The geonim Hai and Sherira Gaon composed legal works and responsa in Arabic. Ḥefeẓ b. Yaẓliaḥ (late tenth century) composed his *Sefer ha-Mitzvot* in Arabic. And the Karaites used both Hebrew and Arabic in their writings.

95 Some of this borrowing occurred, maintains Yafeh, without the authors being aware of what it was they were actually quoting. See Hava Lazarus-Yafeh, *Intertwined Worlds: Medieval Islam and Bible Criticism* (Princeton: Princeton University Press, 1992), 143–60. See also Jonathan Decter, "The Rendering of Qur'ānic Quotations in Hebrew Translations of Islamic Texts," *JQR* 96 (2006): 336–58. Moses ibn Ezra refers to the Qur'ān explicitly in his *Kitāb al-muḥāḍara*, esp. p. 226 (119b). On the Arabic education and proficiency of Andalusian Jewry, see below, 14ff.

96 This appears to be the reason behind Solomon ibn Gabirol's composition of his *`Anaq* poem, in his *Shirei ha-Ḥol*, ed. Brody and Schirmann, 169, lines 6–8 and 170, l. 24. Discussed in Roth, "Jewish Reactions," 71–2. Al-Ḥarizī, perhaps the last of the "Andalusian" Hebrew poets, echoes this sentiment in his *Taḥkemoni*, ed. Toporovsky, 12, 21.

This phenomenon reappears in the Enlightenment period. In the eighteenth century, Judah Leib Ben-Ze'ev (1764–1811), Hebrew grammarian and lexicographer and active member in the Berlin Haskalah movement, originally from Krakow, wrote what appears to be the earliest Hebrew pornographic poem in the modern era. Like the Andalusian poets before him, Ben-Ze'ev was not interested in describing the emotional dimension of love, favoring instead descriptions of the physical. According to David Biale, the composition of the poem, which relied heavily on adaptations of the imagery and language of the Song of Songs, was the fruit of Ben-Ze'ev's desire to "explore the full capacities of the Hebrew language." It was published as *Shir `Agavim*, ed. G. Kressel (Tel Aviv, 5737 [1977]). Kressel notes that although people were horrified by the poem, they nonetheless read and copied it and passed it around. The poet Ḥaim Naḥman Bialik (1873–1934), later Israel's national poet, is said to have known portions by heart. The scholar of Hebrew literature Yosef Klausner (1874–1958) wrote of this poem that, although Ben-Ze'ev appears to have composed it to show the nations of the world the beauty of the Hebrew language, ancient yet adaptable to modern usage, it is "so pornographic that it is impossible to set it in print." See Klausner, *Historia shel ha-Sifrut ha-`Ivrit ha-Ḥadashah* (Jerusalem: Aḥiasaf, 5712–19 [1951–8]), 1:179–80. See also David Biale, *Eros and the Jews: From Biblical Israel to Contemporary America* (New York: Basic Books, 1992), 161–2.

97 Carmi, *The Penguin Book of Hebrew Verse*, 26–7.

98 Brann, "Andalusian Hebrew Poetry," 108. Norman Roth records that Maimonides, in a letter to his Hebrew translator Ibn Tibbon, writes that Arabic is Hebrew that has

been corrupted a little. The tenth-century grammarian Menaḥem ibn Saruq taught similarly that Hebrew was the original language on earth (an idea championed by Sa`adia Gaon as well) and that Arabic and Aramaic constitute but derivatives. Roth also refers to Judah Halevi's section in the *Kuzari* in which he discusses Arabic vs. Hebrew. Halevi there writes that the Jews knew all about poetic meter before the Arabs did, but refrained from employing it in poetry until they deemed the time right. Ibn Ghayyat (1038–89) opines that King Solomon composed *qaṣīdas* that are now lost. Ibn Ghayyat's student, Moses ibn Ezra, rejects this view. Mordechai Z. Cohen, "The Best of Poetry: Literary Approaches to the Bible in the Spanish Peshat Tradition," *Torah U-Madda Journal* 6 (1995–6): 23; Yosef Tobi, "The Reaction of Rav Sa`adia Gaon to Arabic Poetry and Poetics," *Hebrew Studies* 36 (1995): 35–53.

In a similar pro-Hebrew vein, the grammarian Ibn Gikatilla wrote that the Jews had lost their eloquence by living among and under "a people of a strange/stammering language," by which he appears to mean the Arabic-speaking Muslims. Roth points to a *piyyut* by Joseph ibn Abitur (d. after 1024), in which the poet derides the Muslims for having no language of their own, having taken everything from the Arabs. The full Hebrew poem can be found in Ḥaim [Jefim] Schirmann, *Shirim Ḥadashim min ha-Genizah* [New Hebrew Poems from the Genizah] (Jerusalem: ha-Akademya ha-Le'umit ha-Yisra'elit le-Mada'im, 5726 [1965]), 152. See Roth, "Jewish Reactions," 70–81; idem, "Maimonides on Hebrew Language," 95. Later, Judah al-Ḥarizī (1165–1225) claimed that he composed his poetic *Taḥkemoni* to showcase the power of the Holy Tongue to the Holy Nation, who needed to be so reminded. See *Taḥkemoni*, ed. Toporovsky, 12–19.

Brann rejects the idea that the return to biblical Hebrew arose only as a reactive response to the *`arabiyya* movement. He maintains that we ought to understand the "new" Hebrew poetry as representing "an adaptive subculture under stress," rather than as apologetics or as competition with the *`arabiyya*. He provides an internal Jewish reason – answering the charge of the Karaites that the Rabbinites had paid too little attention to Scripture itself, ignoring it in favor of the Oral Torah. See Brann, "Andalusian Hebrew Poetry," 103–6.

99 Allony points out that Moses ibn Ezra, the prime source on the subject, took a moderate position here. On the one hand, Ibn Ezra maintained that many of the principles of the *`arabiyya* were true (Arab climate, language, and poetry were all superior, he writes). On the other hand, Ibn Ezra insisted that biblical Hebrew was not only excellent but divine, although he maintains that not much of the Bible can truly be considered poetry. See Allony, "The Reaction of Moses Ibn Ezra to `Arabiyya," 19–31; Roth, "Jewish Reactions," 79.

On the different registers of language (Hebrew and Arabic) used by the Jews of Muslim Spain, see David J. Wasserstein, "The Language Situation in al-Andalus," in *The Formation of al-Andalus*, ed. Lawrence I. Conrad (Ashgate: Variorum, 1998), 2:3–18.

100 Dan Pagis, "Ha-Meshorer ke-Navi ba-Shirah ha-`Ivrit bi-Yemei ha-Beinayim," in *Ha-Shir Davur al-`Ofanav*, ed. Ezra Fleischer (Jerusalem: Magnes Press, 1993), 281. Pagis brings another reason for the association between prophecy and poetry: the fact that the poems were so closely based on the Bible itself.

101 Schippers, "Biblical and Koranic Quotations," 9–22. This tendency to showcase one's violation of religious observance in sacrilegious terms finds a precedent in earlier Arabic poetry as well, with Abū Nuwās the most famous among such poets. Similarly, Walīd b. Yazīd (d. 744) called upon God, angels, and righteous men as his witnesses that all he wished to do was enjoy music, drink wine, and "bite the cheeks of nubile youths." See Philip Kennedy, *The Wine Song in Classical Arabic Poetry: Abū Nuwās and the Literary Tradition* (Oxford: Clarendon Press, 1997), 26; on Abū Nuwās's sacrilegious poems, see also Wright, "Masculine Allusion," 1–23.

Francesco Gabrieli very poetically wrote, "The sacred fire burns in craftsmen of poetry not so high as in pious men of action." See his "Religious Poetry in Early Islam," 7.

102 Sells, "Love," 138. Abū Nuwās, Ibn Shuhayd's model, had earlier written that the perfected form of religion has not five daily prayers, as in Islam, but five daily fornications, as noted by Wright in "Masculine Allusion," 10–13.

103 Nykl, *Hispano-Arabic Poetry*, 58–60; and in Roth, "Religious Constraints," 198.

104 It has not escaped scholarly notice that elsewhere Ibn Ḥazm writes of poetry as dangerous and deplorable. See, for example, Uthmān Amīn, ed., *Iḥṣā' al-`ulūm*, 2nd edition (Cairo: Dār al-fikr al-`arabī, 1949), 67–8; Ibn Ḥazm, *al-Taqrīb li-ḥadd al-manṭiq wa-al-madhkhal ilaihi*, ed. Iḥsān `Abbās (Beirut, n.d.), 206–7; and the discussion of this in Scheindlin, "Rabbi Moshe Ibn Ezra on the Legitimacy of Poetry," 107. Ibn Ḥazm's Ẓāhirism will be discussed more in Chapter 3.

105 Poems by these men can be found in *Rāyāt al-mubarrizīn*, 104–5, 140–1, 192, 147–50. Regarding the various expertise of Abū al-Ḥasan Sahl ibn Mālik, the editor of *Rāyāt al-mubarrizīn*, Muḥammad Riḍwān al-Dāya, tells us in n. 133 that he was the head of the legal scholars (رأس الفقهاء, *ra's al-fuqahā'*), the most eloquent of the *khuṭabā'* (official sermon-deliverers), and, according to al-Dāya, the last of the great men of Andalusia of his time.

106 Roth, "Jewish Reactions," 70–1.

107 "ופי דיבר בצחות על / לבב קידר וצדהו." In Samuel ha-Nagid, *Diwan Shemuel ha-Nagid. Ben Tehillim*, #52 (אהוב ליבי), l. 9. English translation by Esperanza Alfonso, *Islamic Culture through Jewish Eyes: Al-Andalus from the tenth to twelfth century* (London and New York: Routledge, 2008), 38. This line is but one of a number of boasts Samuel makes regarding his intellectual mastery, which includes biblical exegesis, Talmudic understanding, and Greek philosophy (lines 7–10). According to the *dīwān*'s editor, Samuel wrote this poem to a friend of his, a jurist named Joseph ben Samuel.

108 Roth, "Jewish Reactions," 65; Elizur, *Shirat ha-Ḥol*, 1:45. Scheindlin points out that, by contrast, the Muslims showed no interest in learning from Jews about Hebrew culture. The Jews were thus the recipients of Arabic culture but not, he insists, partners to it. As far as modern scholars can tell, contemporary Muslim intellectuals were completely unaware of the entire Hebrew Golden Age and its poetry, though they did note that some Jews wrote *Arabic* poetry. Wasserstein supports this contention by noting that in the *Ṭabaqāt al-umam* of Ṣā`id al-Andalusī (1029–70), a classification of the world's nations according to their contribution to the development of the sciences; none of the Jews he mentions are identified for their participation in the production of poetry, though many of them *were* Hebrew poets. See Scheindlin, "Hebrew Poetry in Medieval Iberia," 50; David J. Wasserstein, "The Muslims and the Golden Age of the Jews in al-Andalus," *IOS* 17, ed. Uri Rubin and David J. Wasserstein (Tel Aviv: Eisenbrauns, Inc. 1997), 188–92. Roth disagrees, maintaining that the presence of Jewish students in the classrooms of the Muslim scholars "certainly produced more than a curiosity" about one another's traditions; it produced, he claims, mutual understanding and respect. However, he does not bring any concrete evidence to counter Scheindlin's claim. See Norman Roth, "Muslim Knowledge of the Hebrew Bible and Jewish Traditions in the Middle Ages," *Maghreb Review* 16:1–2 (1991): 74–83. See also Brener, *Judah Halevi and His Circle*, ix. According to Abraham ibn Daud in his *Sefer ha-Qabbalah*, Joseph ibn Abitur interpreted (פירש, *piresh*) the Talmud for the Cordoban caliph al-Ḥakam II al-Mustanṣir (r. 961–76). See Abraham ibn Daud, *Sefer ha-Qabbalah*, ed. and trans. Gerson D. Cohen (Philadelphia: Jewish Publication Society, 1967), Hebrew pages 48–9. David Wasserstein posits that this text may have been in al-Ḥakam's extensive library, and available to Muslim scholars. See David Wasserstein, "An Arabic Version of *Abot* 1:3 from Umayyad Spain," *Arabica* 34 (1987): 370–4.

109 Roth, "Muslim Knowledge," 74. Brann similarly maintains that Jews had primary knowledge of the sacred texts of Islam. See Ross Brann, "The Arabized Jews," in *The Literature of al-Andalus*, ed. Maria Rosa Menocal, Raymond P. Scheindlin, and Michael Sells (Cambridge: Cambridge University Press, 2000), 442. Scheindlin insists that, in line with Islamic law, the Jews could not have been directly Qur'ānically educated. See his "Hebrew Poetry in Medieval Iberia," 44. As noted above (n. 95), Moses ibn Ezra both refers to and quotes from the Qur'ān in *Kitāb al-muḥāḍara*, esp. 226 (119b).

110 Yosef Tobi, "Ha-Yesod ha-Dati be-Shirei ha-Milḥamah shel Shemuel ha-Nagid u-ve-Shirei ha-Shevaḥ ha-`Aravi'im bi-al-Andalus," *Te`udah – Meḥqarim ba-Safrut ha-`Ivrit be-Yimei ha-Beinayim* 19 (2003): 3–25; Ross Brann, "Force of Character: Three Eleventh Century Andalusi-Muslim Views of Ismā`īl ibn Naghrīla (Samuel the Nagid)," in his *Power in the Portrayal*, 24–53; Brann, "Signs of Ambivalence in Islamic Spain: Arabic Representations of Samuel the Nagid," in *Ki Baruch Hu: Ancient Near Eastern, Biblical, and Judaic Studies in Honor of Baruch A. Levine*, ed. Robert Chazan, William W. Hallo, and Lawrence Schiffman (Winona Lake, IN: Eisenbrauns, 1999), 443–65.

111 S. M. Stern, "Arabic Poems by Spanish-Hebrew Poets," in *Romanica et Occidentalia: études dédiées à la mémoire de Hiram Peri (Pflaum)*, ed. Moshe Lazar (Jerusalem: Magnes Press, 1963), 254–63. Stern discusses the entries on both Samuel and his son Joseph that appear in the thirteenth-century Ibn Sa`īd's *Al-Mughrib fī ḥulā al-maghrib*. There the author claims that Samuel mocked Muslims and swore that he would versify the entire Qur'ān, setting it in poems and *muwashshaḥāt*, which he would then set to music to be sung. Ibn Sa`īd includes an "example" of this. See `Alī b. Mūsā b. Sa`īd, *Al-Mughrib fī ḥulā al-maghrib*, ed. Shawqi Ḍayf (Cairo: Dār al-ma`ārif, 1955–64), 2:114–15.

112 Like Ibn al-Fakhār, Abū al-Faḍl also served in the Muslim court, first as vizier to the Saragossan al-Muqtadir (d. 1082), then to al-Muqtadir's son, al-Mu`min (r. 1082–5), and eventually to al-Mu`min's son, al-Musta`īn. The Arab claim that Abū al-Faḍl converted to Islam appears to have been current during his lifetime and appears to have been a complete fabrication. See *EJ*, s.v. "Hisdai ibn Hisdai, Abu al-Fadl," by Eliyahu Ashtor and Angel Saénz-Badillos (9:145); A. S. Yahuda, *`Ever ve-`Arav* (Hotza'at Ogen, [1946]), 113–18. Roth maintains that if Abū al-Faḍl did convert to Islam, which might never have happened, he did so with the intent of salvaging his career. See Norman Roth, "Some Aspects of Muslim–Jewish Relations in Spain," in *Estudios en Homenaje a Don Claudio Sanchez Albornoz en sus 90 años*, ed. Maria del Carmen Carlé, Hilda Grassotti, and Germán Orduna (Buenos Aires: Instituto de Historia de España, 1983), II:195. Al-Maqqarī apparently believed Abū al-Faḍl had converted to Islam; he does not include Abū al-Faḍl on the list of Andalusian Jewish composers of Arabic poetry but lists him simply as Abū al-Faḍl ibn Ḥasdā`ī al-Islāmī al-Saraqasṭī. Aḥmad b. Muḥamad al-Maqqarī, *Nafḥ al-ṭīb min ghuṣn al-andalus al-raṭīb*, ed. Iḥsān `Abbās (Beirut: Dār al-ṣādir, 1388 AH [1968]), 3:401–2.

113 See *Rāyāt al-mubarrizīn*, 242; Brann, "The Arabized Jews," 436; Brener, *Judah Halevi and His Circle*, 4, 93–6; Norman Roth, "Jewish and Muslim Physicians of `Ali ibn Tashufīn," *Korot* 10 (1993–4), 83–91; Stern, "Arabic Poems by Spanish-Hebrew Poets," 254–63.

The Hebrew poem was preserved in Judah Halevi's *dīwān* because it was written for and sent to him. Since Halevi was out of town when the poem arrived, it appears Moses ibn Ezra took it upon himself to reply in kind. When Halevi returned, he composed a poetic reply. It can be found in Schirmann's *Ha-Shirah ha-`Ivrit be-Sefarad u-ve-Provans*, 2:542–3.

114 Al-Maqqarī, *Nafḥ al-ṭīb*, 3:527; and in *al-Mughrib*, 2:23. Among the Arabic poems al-Fakhār composed is a eulogy in honor of the Christian Spanish ruler Alfonso VIII

of Castille (1158–1214), for whom Ibn al-Fakhār served as diplomatic messenger to the Almohad ruler of Morocco, al-Mustanṣir. See Yahuda, *`Ever ve-`Arav*, 106–11.

115 *Nafḥ al-ṭīb*, 3:522–7 and 2:307; Yahuda, *`Ever va-`Arav*, 106. See also *Rāyāt al-mubarrizīn*, 76–7 and *al-Mughrib*, 1:264–5. The inclusion of Ibn Sahl among the Jewish composers of Arabic poems poses somewhat of a conundrum for, according to most accounts, Ibn Sahl converted to Islam at a relatively young age. While the Muslim biographers/collectors express little doubt regarding the sincerity of his conversion, modern Jewish scholars express a measure of suspicion. For example, Hartwig Hirschfeld, Yosef Tobi, and Shmuel Moreh maintain that Ibn Sahl converted due to pressure from the Almohads. Hirschfeld adds that it was said in Spain that Ibn Sahl recanted before his death. It should be noted that Ibn Sahl died at sea, unexpectedly, at the age of 40. Yahuda writes that Ibn Sahl's poetry was so magnificent, Muslims "thought him one of their exalted poets," though Yahuda does admit that Ibn Sahl converted to Islam in his youth. While Tobi maintains that Ibrāhīm descended from the same Ibn Sahl family that produced the Cordoban poet and *dayyan* (religious judge) Joseph ibn Sahl (d. 1123/4), Scheindlin insists that there is no reason to assume this to be true. See "Abu Isḥaḳ Ibrahim Ibn Sahl al-Israili of Seville," by H. Hirschfeld, http://www.jewishencyclopedia.com/view.jsp?artid=669&letter=A&search=Ibn%20Sahl, accessed July 15, 2010; *EJ*, s.v. "Ibrahim ibn Sahl al-Andalusī al-Isra'īlī," by Shmuel Moreh (9:701); Yahuda, *`Ever ve-`Arav*, 106, fn. 4; Scheindlin, "Hebrew Poetry in Medieval Iberia," fn. 9; Schippers, "Humorous Approach of the Divine," 119–35; *EI²*, s.v. "Al-Isrā'ilī al-Ishbīlī, Abū Isḥāq Ibrāhīm," by H. Monés (3:925); Tobi, *Proximity and Distance*, 364–7. A collection of Ibn Sahl's Arabic poems appears in his *Dīwān Ibn Sahl al-Andalusī*, ed. Aḥmad Ḥusayn al-Qarnī (Egypt: al-Maktaba al-`arabiyya, 1926).

116 See al-Maqqarī, *Nafḥ al-ṭīb*, 3:522, 528, 529–30. Ilyās b. al-Madūr al-Yahūdī appears also in *al-Mughrib*, 1:336. Bassām b. Sham`ūn al-Yahūdī al-Washqī also appears in *al-Mughrib*, 1:127, where he is named Isḥāq b. Sham`ūn al-Yahūdī al-Qurṭubī.

117 While al-Maqqarī singles her out and cites her poems, in *Nafḥ al-ṭīb* (3:530), he does not identify her father aside from listing his name as Ismā`īl al-Yahūdī and the fact that he too was a poet, known to have composed *muwashshaḥāt* with her. Qasmūna was not the only female to compose poetry in Muslim Spain. The poems of a number of Muslim women, writing in Arabic, have been preserved. These include the poems of Wallāda bint al-Mustakfī, caliph of Cordoba (994–1091), Ḥafṣa bint al-Ḥajj al-Rukūniyya [Requena, a city in the province of Valencia] (*c.* 1135–91), and Ḥamda bint Ziyād (twelfth century, Gaudix). For Wallāda, see *Nafḥ al-ṭīb*, 4:205–11 and Nykl, *Hispano-Arabic Poetry*, 107–8. For Ḥafṣa, see *Rāyāt al-mubarrizīn*, 161; *Nafḥ al-ṭīb*, 4:171; *al-Mughrib*, 2:138, and Nykl, *Hispano-Arabic Poetry*, 317. For Ḥamda, see *Rāyāt al-mubarrizīn*, 167; *Nafḥ al-ṭīb*, 4:287; and *al-Mughrib*, 2:145. An earlier example of a woman writing poetry in Islamic Spain, and a love poem at that, is the wife of Dunash ibn Labrat, and her poem, היזכור יעלת החן ידידה. Unlike Qasmūna, Dunash's wife wrote in Hebrew. Her poem has been preserved in Ezra Fleischer, "`Al Dunash ben Labrat, ve-Ishto, u-Veno," in *Meḥqarei Yerushalayim be-Sifrut `Ivrit*, ed. Dan Pagis (Jerusalem: Magnes Press, 5744 [1984]), 5:189–202. An English translation can be found in Cole, *The Dream of the Poem*, 27.

For more on Qasmūna, see James A. Bellamy, "Qasmuna the Poetess: Who Was She?," *JAOS* 103 (1983): 423–4; J. M. Nichols, "The Arabic Verses of Qasmuna bint Ismail Ibn Bagdalah," *International Journal for Middle East Studies* 13 (1981): 155–8; and Yahuda, *`Ever va-`Arav*, 111–12.

118 So highly valued was education among the Jews in Muslim Spain that treatises on education appear for the first time in Jewish literature, most notably one by Joseph ben Judah ibn `Aknin (*c.* 1150–1220). See *EJ*, s.v. "Education, Jewish," section "In

the Middle Ages," by Elijah Bortniker (6:172–7). Discourse on the value of educating children traces back to the Talmud, where the rabbis discussed both educational theory and curricula. For example, *BT Baba Batra* 21a records that Rav advised teachers to seat a slow/inattentive child next to a quick/attentive one; it also credits R. Joshua ben Gamla with having established schools in every town in the Land of Israel and instituting compulsory education for children beginning at age 6/7 (in the first century). In *Pirqei Avot* 5:21, R. Judah ben Teima delineates a general curriculum, advising what topics should be studied at what age. See Pinḥas Kehati, ed., *Mishnayot Mevo`arot* (Jerusalem: Keter, 1976), 7th edition, *Nezikin*, vol. 2, *Avot* 5:21. Whole treatises on the topic, however, began to appear only much later, in Spain.

119 Brener, *Judah Halevi and His Circle*, 63.

120 Schirmann, "The Function of the Hebrew Poet," 239. Despite the many names included here, David J. Wasserstein insists that the true numbers of the Jewish elites, the class to which these intellectuals would have belonged, are likely relatively low. He points out that while we may think we know a good deal about the Jewish community of Muslim Spain, and its assimilation into the majority culture, in fact we know less than we would like to. See David J. Wasserstein, "Jewish Élites in al-Andalus," in *The Jews of Medieval Islam: Community, Society, and Identity*, ed. Daniel Frank (Leiden, New York, and Köln: E. J. Brill, 1995), 101–10.

121 Tobi, "*Shirat ha-Ḥol*," 59. See also Elizur, *Shirat ha-Ḥol*, 1:76; Roth, "My Beloved is Like a Gazelle," 146. Judah Halevi, Solomon ibn Gabirol, Moses ibn Ezra, and Samuel ha-Nagid all composed works of Jewish philosophy or theology or biblical exegesis. Schirmann notes that it was rare for a man to be able to support himself or his family as a professional poet (the first to do so was Ibn Khalfun); thus many of the Hebrew poets worked in jobs that would provide an alternate source of income. Some worked as Talmud teachers (Joseph ibn Abitur, Ibn Ghayyat, Meir Abulafia, Isaac bar Sheshet, Simon Duran), others as judges in rabbinical courts (Baḥya, Joseph ibn Sahl, Joseph ibn Tzaddiq), others as physicians (Ibn al-Mu`allim, Judah Halevi, Joseph ibn Zabara), and yet others as brokers (Todros Abulafia, Abraham Bedersi). Oddly, Schirmann includes here Archbishop Pablo de Santa Maria, who started his life as Don Solomon Halevi. See Schirmann, "The Function of the Hebrew Poet," 239. Ross Brann writes that the Hebrew poets of the Party Kings era were "trained rabbinical scholars all." See his *The Experience of Judaism under the Orbit of Medieval Islam* (New York: Hagop Kevorkian Center for Near Eastern Studies, 1985), 15.

122 Brener, *Judah Halevi and His Circle*, 1–7; Schirmann, "The Function of the Hebrew Poet," 235–52; *EJ*, s.v. "Gabirol, Solomon ben Judah," by Shlomo Pines and Angel Saénz-Badillos (7:321–7); *EJ*, s.v. "Judah Halevi," by Daniel Lasker and Angel Saénz-Badillos (11:492–501); *EJ*, s.v. "Samuel Ha-Nagid," by A. M. Habermann (17:776–7). Solomon ibn Gabirol also composed a Bible commentary, or parts of one, that did not survive except in the citations of others. Scholars have theorized that Samuel ha-Nagid and possibly Judah Halevi may have composed exegeses, now lost as well. Judah Halevi's philosophical *Sefer ha-Kuzari* is also still read by Jewish students today.

In demonstrating how well synthesized the scholars' poetic and Andalusian selves were with their religious Jewish selves, Brener refers to an episode recorded by Joseph b. Judah ibn `Aknin, a contemporary of Judah Halevi. Ibn `Aknin reports about a particular garden wine-party, a "cultural artifact" adopted from the Spanish Muslims, where people drank wine and composed poetry, which they then recited. On this occasion, he reports, during the party Judah Halevi arose as if to recite the expected newly composed poem. Instead, he delivered a Talmudic *bon mot*. See Brener, *Judah Halevi and His Circle*, 78.

123 See Cohen, "The Best of Poetry," 34.

124 Brann, "Andalusian Hebrew Poetry," 101–2.

125 As in *BT Baba Metzi'a* 21b. For a discussion of this concept of the text speaking in human language and its use by the Talmudic sages, see Cohen, "The Best of Poetry," fnn. 104, 108. Cohen also discusses the idea that the *Zohar*, the medieval work that constitutes the main text of the kabbalistic approach to reading the Bible, rejects all comparisons between the Bible and human literature. Ibid., 24–38.

126 Uriel Simon, "The Spanish School of Biblical Interpretation," in *Moreshet Sepharad: The Sephardi Legacy*, 1:115. Scholars have noted that the Spanish approach appears to have been influenced by the approach of the earlier Babylonian Sa`adia Gaon (882–942). See Elizur, *Shirat ha-Ḥol*, 1:80.

127 Interestingly, while the Bible does contain poems and poetry, the rules of biblical poetry did not exert much influence over the Andalusian Hebrew poets. As discussed, they modeled their Hebrew poems after the Arabic. On the lack of influence of biblical poetry on Andalusian Hebrew poetry, see Ezra Fleischer, "Shirah `Ivrit be-Nusaḥ ha-Miqra be-Yimei ha-Beinayim," *Teudah* 7 (Tel Aviv: University Publication Projects, 1991), 204ff. Perhaps one explanation can be found in the *Kitāb al-muḥāḍara* of Moses ibn Ezra, his work on poetry and poetics. There Ibn Ezra maintains that the Bible contains very little poetry, with the exception of a few *rajāz*, a metric form that many ranked as below true poetry. On this, see Cohen, "The Best of Poetry," 15–57; Scheindlin, "Rabbi Moshe Ibn Ezra on the Legitimacy of Poetry," 101–15.

128 Mirsky, "Hebrew Literary Creation," 1:153; Simon, "The Spanish School," 1:117.

129 On Abū `Abbās, see Suzanne Pinckney Stetkeyvich, "Intoxication and Immortality: Wine and Associated Imagery in al-Ma`arrī's *Garden*," in *Homoeroticism in Classical Arabic Literature*, 213. For al-Ṭabarī's poetic references, see throughout his *Ta'rīkh al-rusul wa-al-mulūk* (Leiden: E. J. Brill, 1879–1901). In some later editions of al-Ṭabarī's work, formatting of the materials makes the poems stand out quite clearly. See for example al-Ṭabarī, *Ta'rīkh al-rusul wa-al-mulūk*, ed. Muḥammad Abū al-Faḍl Ibrāhīm (Cairo: Dār al-ma`ārif, 1960–77).

130 Simon, "The Spanish School," 1:115–36.

131 For more on al-Kanzi, see Uriel Simon, "The Contribution of R. Isaac b. Samuel al-Kanzi to the Spanish School of Biblical Interpretation," *JJS* 34:2 (1983), 171–8.

132 Isaac ibn Ghayyat's pupils include Moses ibn Ezra, Joseph ibn Sahl, and Joseph ibn Ẓaddik. Ibn Ghayyat wrote a commentary to the Talmud, legal works, responsa, and *piyyutim* (religious poetry). See *EJ*, s.v. "Ibn Ghayyat," by Angel Saénz-Badillos, 9:676–7.

Significantly, the later prolific poet Immanuel of Rome (*c.* 1261 to after 1328), who lived in Christian Spain but whose works reflect Muslim Spain, also wrote a work of biblical exegesis covering most of the books of the Bible. Walfish notes, "In his own estimation, Immanuel surpassed all his predecessors in revealing the mysteries of the biblical text." Subsequent generations did not agree with Immanuel's self-appraisal and so did not preserve his works. See Barry Dov Walfish, *Esther in Medieval Garb: Jewish Interpretation of the Book of Esther in the Middle Ages* (Albany: SUNY Press, 1993), 217. Later Spanish exegetes busied themselves only slightly with the linguistic questions that concerned their predecessors, focusing instead on theoretical problems. See Avraham Grossman, "Biblical Exegesis in Spain During the 13th–15th Centuries," in *Moreshet Sepharad: The Sephardi Legacy*, 1:137–46.

133 See *Princeton Encyclopedia of Poetry and Poetics*, ed. Alex Preminger, Frank J. Warnke, and O. B. Hardison, Jr. (Princeton, NJ: Princeton University Press, 1974), s.v. "New Criticism," 567.

134 A similar notion appears in Pagis, *Hebrew Poetry*, chapter 3.

135 Aviva Doron, "The Poet's Attitude in the Hebrew Poetry of Spain: Between Convention and Allusion," in *Jewish Studies at the Turn of the 20th Century*, ed. Borás and Sáenz-Badillos, I:392–7.

136 See *Shirat ha-Ḥol ve-Torat ha-Shir*, 35ff and 46–50.
137 See Alice Jardine, s.v. "Intertextuality," in Thomas A. Sebeok, ed., *Encyclopedic Dictionary of Semiotics* (Berlin: Mouton de Gruyter, 1986), 1:387. For more on Kristeva's work on intertextuality, see Julia Kristeva, *Desire in Language: A Semiotic Approach to Literature and Art*, ed. Leon S. Roudiez, trans. Thomas Gora, Alice Jardine, and Leon S. Roudiez (New York: Columbia University Press, 1980).
138 Daniel Boyarin, *Intertextuality and the Reading of Midrash* (Indianapolis: Indiana University Press, 1990), 14.
139 Norman Calder, "Tafsīr from Ṭabarī to Ibn Kathīr: Problems in the Description of a Genre, Illustrated with Reference to the Story of Abraham," in *Approaches to the Qur'an*, ed. G. R. Hawting and Abdul-Kader Shareef (London and New York: Routledge, 1993), 105.
140 As cited by Jardine in "Intertextuality," 1:388.
141 Ḥaviva Ishay, "Teqst ke-Interteqst: Shirei Ahava `Ivri'im ve-Safrut ha-`Ahava ha-`Aravit be-Yimei ha-Beinayim," *Te`udah: Meḥqarim ba-Safrut ha-`Ivrit be-Yimei ha-Beinayim*, 19, ed. Tova Rosen and Avner Holzman (Tel Aviv: Tel Aviv University, 2003), 59. While I did not find Ishay's final conclusions in the article quite convincing, her articulation of her intertextual approach remains compelling.
142 As Ishay herself points out, this understanding of the role of the reader was articulated earlier by Roland Barthes. See Ishay, "Teqst ke-Interteqst," 57.
143 Brann, "How Can My Heart Be in the East?," 366.
144 Elizur likewise points to Ibn Ezra's and Qimḥi's commentaries as appropriate sources for information on trends in Jewish exegesis in Muslim Spain. See Elizur, *Shirat ha-Ḥol*, 1:232ff.
145 See, for example, Elizur, *Shirat ha-Ḥol*, 3:215ff; Pagis, *Ḥiddush u-Masoret*.
146 For example, Arie Schippers divides between the secular poets and the religious scholars, declaring, "Poets are the representatives of the secular world, and are thus the natural counterparts to *faqīhs* [jurists], *ṣūfīs* [mystics], rabbis, and other pious and devote [*sic*] men, representing the opposite pole of society." Schippers, "Humorous Approach of the Divine," 121. As is apparent from the arguments and evidence included here, such an analysis did not hold true for medieval Andalusia. In Muslim Spain, jurists and rabbis wrote not only secular poetry, but secular poetry that incorporated religious themes and terms and imagery. Schippers references Ibn Sahl as the prime example of such a secular–religious divide, writing that "like many other Arab poets, religion did not seem to play a major role in Ibn Sahl's life." The numerous references to the Bible, Qur'ān, and *ḥadīth* that litter Ibn Sahl's poetry make such a statement puzzling (see above, nn. 77 and 115).
147 See Yellin, *Torat ha-Shir ha-Sefaradit*, 118; Pagis, *Ḥiddush u-Masoret*, 70.
148 Neal Kozodoy, "Reading Medieval Hebrew Love Poetry," *AJS Review* 2 (1977): 115.
149 Brann, "Andalusian Hebrew Poetry," 102.
150 Stetkeyvich, "Intoxication and Immortality," 213. Al-Qāḍī also notes the importance of paying attention to the ways in which the Qur'ān was modified in poetry as well as to why it was modified the way it was. See al-Qāḍī, 162.
151 For more on the relationship between Ibn Zaydūn and Wallāda, see Salma Khadra Jayyusi, "Andalusī Poetry: The Golden Period," in *The Legacy of Muslim Spain*, 343–51; Nykl, *Hispano-Arabic Poetry*, 106–21.
152 See Ezra Fleischer, "Le-Qorot R. Yehuda Halevi bi-Ne`urav ve-Raishit Qesharav `im R. Moshe ibn Ezra," *Kiryat Sefer* 61 (1986–7): 893–910. The article concerns the authorship of the poem ליל מחשבות לב אעירה, previously thought to have been written by Moses ibn Ezra to Judah Halevi; Fleischer maintains the true author is Joseph ibn Tzaddiq. See Stern, "Ḥiquei muwashshaḥot," 166–86. For the poem, see Yonah David, ed., *Shirei Yosef ibn Tzaddiq* (New York: American Academy for Jewish Research, 1982), 36–8.

153 See "הגנבת וגם כחשת דברי" by Solomon ibn Gabirol in his *Shirei ha-Ḥol*, ed. Brody and Schirmann, 124 (#199); also Solomon ibn Gabirol, *Shirei ha-Ḥol le-Rabbi Shelomo ibn Gabirol*, ed. Dov Jarden (Jerusalem, 5735 [1975]), 263 (#126). In a sly spin on the matter, Ibn Gabirol uses language and sentence structure that recall Elijah's chastising King Ahab for first sinfully killing Nabot the Jezreelite and then "inheriting" the latter's vineyard from him; says Elijah, "הֲרָצַחְתָּ וְגַם-יָרָשְׁתָּ" (1 K. 21:19). In so doing, Ibn Gabirol subtly yet threateningly reminds his plagiarist of the punishment God promised to Ahab for his actions: dogs will lick his blood and God will cut down all the male members of his household (vv. 19–22). Jarden does not mention this in his notes to the poem, pointing out only that the vocabulary of the opening phrase reflects Lev. 19:11 (לֹא תִּגְנֹבוּ וְלֹא-תְכַחֲשׁוּ, "You shall not steal, or defraud"). This playing with the language and the biblical text is also not evident in Cole's translation in *Selected Poems of Solomon ibn Gabirol*, 82.

154 As discussed in S. M. Stern's "Two Medieval Hebrew Poems Explained from Arabic," *Sefarad* 10 (1950): 325–38. Stern reports that A. Ehrlich maintains that Judah Halevi admits in his poem to not having solved Abū `Omar's riddle. Stern disagrees, insisting that Judah did solve it. In another case, Stern shows that a short two-line poem by Samuel ha-Nagid makes little sense unless one recognizes that it alludes to a particular Arabic method of reckoning, known as "reckoning by fingers." In a more recent study, Ross Brann has shown that Judah Halevi's famed "My Heart Is in the East" (ליבי במזרח) poem may be an intertextual reference to and even subversion of the Arabic motif of east vs. west. See his "How Can My Heart Be in the East?," 365–79. An Arabic example of this same motif can be found in Ibn Ḥazm's *Ṭawq al-ḥamāma*. See Pétrof, 95 (Arberry, 195; Nykl, 146).

155 For a discussion of several Hebrew poets and the Arabic *kharjas* that appear in their Hebrew poems, see Stern, "Ḥiquei muwashshaḥot," 166–86; Scheindlin, "Hebrew Poetry in Medieval Iberia," 39–60; Monroe and Swiatlo, "Ninety-Three Arabic Ḥarġas in Hebrew Muwaššaḥs," 141–64. See n. 16 above.

156 Stern appears to have followed Brody and Schirmann in attributing authorship of this poem to Moses ibn Ezra. Ezra Fleischer rejects this attribution, maintaining that other evidence indicates the author to be Joseph ibn Tzaddiq. See n. 154 and Stern, "Ḥiquei muwashshaḥot."

S. A. Bonebakker records and discusses the different Arabic terms used to express imitation/stealing/inspiration/borrowing, in his "Ancient Arabic Poetry and Plagiarism: A Terminological Labyrinth," *Quaderni di Studi Arabi* 15 (1997): 65–92. See also von Grunebaum, "The Concept of Plagiarism in Arabic Theory," 234–53; Monroe, "Hispano-Arabic Poetry During the Caliphate of Cordoba," 125–54. See also n. 71 above.

157 Brener, *Judah Halevi and His Circle*, ch. 1. Carmi brings a different poem by Judah Halevi, בי הצבי בי אדוני (*bi ha-tzvi bi adoni*), in which the *kharja* is in Arabic. See Carmi, ed., *The Penguin Book of Hebrew Verse*, 344–5. An example by Moses ibn Ezra appears in Scheindlin, *Wine, Women and Death*, 102–3 and in Schirmann, *Toledot ha-Shirah ha-`Ivrit be-Sefarad ha-Muslemit*, 1:214 (סוד ליבי ומצפוני, *sod libi u-matzpuni*). An example by Samuel ha-Nagid can be found in Scheindlin, *Wine, Women and Death*, 106–7 and in Schirmann, *Toledot ha-Shirah ha-`Ivrit be-Sefarad u-ve-Provans*, 1:153 (אש אהבים נשקה, *esh ahavim nishqah*). For more Hebrew poems with Arabic *kharjas*, see Monroe and Swiatlo, "Ninety-Three Arabic Ḥarġas in Hebrew Muwaššaḥs," 141–64.

158 In one such case, Judah Halevi turns a homoerotic Arabic poem by al-Mutanabbī into a hetero-erotic Hebrew poem. See Schirman, *Ha-Shirah ha-`Ivrit be-Sefarad u-ve-Provans*, 2:446 [#180b]. In another, Halevi incorporates a scandalous poem of his contemporary Ibn Shuhayd (regarding a woman whom Ibn Shuhayd describes in a lascivious manner) into a poem on the departure of a certain Yitzḥaq. See

Schippers, "The Hebrew Poets of Christian Spain," 521–9. Another of Halevi's poems, מאז מעון אהבה הייתי (*me'az me`on ahavah hayiti*), appears to be a translation of a secular love poem by the Muslim Abū al-Shayṣ al-Khazā`ī (eighth century) which Judah Halevi applies to the love of God. See Yisra'el Levin, "Biqashti et she-Ahava Nafshi," *Hasifrut* 2 (1971–2): 116–49; Fleischer, "Le-Qorot R. Yehuda Halevi be-Ne`urav." According to Norman Roth, only five of Judah Halevi's translations have survived. See Roth, "Jewish Reactions," 73. Such translations fall under the category of poetic techniques known as *mu`āraḍa*, imitation, in which poets imitate the rhyme and meter of a particular poem and attempt to surpass it in beauty. See *EI*[2], s.v. "mu`āraḍa," by Arie Schippers (7:261). See also nn. 71 and 156.

159 Kozodoy, "Reading," 117.

160 Levin notes this literary mixing of categories in his discussion of the influence of secular love poetry on religious Hebrew poetry in Spain. The boundary lines between the categories of love poetry and religious poetry, he writes, were often blurred in terms of language and expression. See Levin, "Biqashti et she-Ahava Nafshi," 297. Indeed, the Hebrew poets famously and consistently use human terminology, human expressions of love and yearning, in writing of the desire for closeness to God in the *piyyutim* of this period.

Such literary use of human sexuality for religious purposes appears much earlier, in the classical rabbinic explanation of the inclusion of the erotically charged Song of Songs in the canon of the Hebrew Bible. See above, 8. The idea that it was included to stand as a metaphor for God's love and yearning for Israel, and vice versa, has become so deeply ingrained in the Jewish tradition that some religious "translations" of the Song of Songs present only the metaphoric reading. For example, Mesorah Publications translates Song of Songs 4:5 שְׁנֵי שָׁדַיִךְ כִּשְׁנֵי עֳפָרִים תְּאוֹמֵי צְבִיָּה הָרוֹעִים בַּשּׁוֹשַׁנִּים ("Your two breasts are like two fawns that are twins of a gazelle, which feed among the lilies") as "Moses and Aaron, your two sustainers, are like two fawns, twins of the gazelle, who graze their sheep in rose-like bounty." In *Song of Songs: An Allegorical Translation Based upon Rashi with a Commentary Anthologized from Talmudic, Midrashic, and Rabbinic Sources (Artscroll Tanach Series)* (New York: Mesorah Publications Ltd, 1977–96).

Part I

Outsiders as lovers

2 "He has slain me like Uriah": Ibn Mar Shaul's unexpected love triangle

Sometime in the tenth century, a Jewish resident of Muslim Spain, the pious and highly regarded Hebrew grammarian, poet, and scholar of the Bible by the name of Isaac b. Mar Shaul, sat down and composed what appears to have been the very first post-biblical homoerotic Hebrew poem. Reflecting the time and place in which he lived, Ibn Mar Shaul naturally and effortlessly culled from the two worlds from whose atmosphere he simultaneously drew air. Ibn Mar Shaul's poem followed the familiar and well-loved themes, motifs, structure, imagery, rhyme-scheme, and meter of Arabic poetry, the dominant literary style of the day in Andalusia. And yet, the poem was pure Hebrew, each and every word drawn from biblical Hebrew alone. Moreover, while the poem followed the conventions of Arabic love poetry, no typical images drawn from Arab folklore and history made an appearance. Instead, as liturgical poets before him had done, Ibn Mar Shaul peppered his homoerotic secular love poem with references from the Bible.[1]

Surprisingly to the modern mind, Ibn Mar Shaul's Arabic-based Hebrew secular love poem did not incite cries of outrage on the part of his scholar-contemporaries, his pious students, or the learned rabbinic circles in which he moved. Instead, it launched an era of fused Andalusian secular Hebrew poems; many of these were works by rabbinic scholars that combined the literary and aesthetic values and forms of Arabic poetry with language and references drawn from Hebrew and the Bible.[2] Beginning with Ibn Mar Shaul, we find that the very same men who composed works of biblical exegesis, analyses of biblical Hebrew, studies on Jewish theology and theosophy, and liturgical poems yearning for God, simultaneously authored wine-songs extolling the virtues of drink and love poems yearning for the kiss and touch of the beloved girl or boy.[3]

But what was the purpose of this very first homoerotic biblically infused Hebrew love poem? Why did it provoke little outrage among the pious Jews of Lucena? Noting the close adherence of this Hebrew poem with the conventions of Andalusian Arabic poetry, Ezra Fleischer has proposed that perhaps Ibn Mar Shaul composed the poem for the express purpose of teaching his students the rules of both Hebrew grammar and Arabic poetics.[4] Indeed, Ibn Mar Shaul's student, the famed grammarian Jonah ibn Janaḥ (*c.* 990–*c.* 1050), notes that Ibn Mar Shaul often used his own poetic compositions as tools with which he taught his students Hebrew grammar as well as the rules, rhythms, and motifs of Arabic poetry.[5] And in fact, the earliest mention of Ibn Mar Shaul's innovative homoerotic Hebrew poem appears in Ibn Janaḥ's great work on Hebrew grammar, the *Kitāb al-luma`* (*Sefer ha-Riqmah*).[6]

Despite the poem's overwhelming adherence to the poetic conventions of the day, one cannot help but notice that it deviates from the mass of secular Hebrew poetry that it spawned in one important way. Namely, in describing the boy beloved and the lover's desire for him, Ibn Mar Shaul employs a biblical reference to 2 Samuel 11, to a particularly subversive end. A close analysis of Ibn Mar Shaul's homoerotic poem reveals that the poet rejects the common understanding of the biblical Uriah the Hittite as an innocent and pious soldier in King David's army, a cuckolded victim of David's adultery and murderous planning. Instead, through his poem, Ibn Mar Shaul presents an alternate reading of the biblical text, portraying Uriah as the typical lover, lusting so much for his male beloved (King David) that he eventually dies from his unrealized passions.

On Isaac Ibn Mar Shaul

Who was this man who changed the face of Andalusian Hebrew poetry? One of the more prolific but now lesser known of the Spanish Jewish intellectuals, Isaac ibn Mar Shaul was born in the southern Spanish town of Lucena at the end of the tenth century. In its early years, Lucena had been inhabited exclusively by Jews, whom one tradition credits with having founded the city.[7] Although Lucena's Jews were among the richest and most well integrated of the area, the city's greatest claim to fame was not financial but academic. At the beginning of the eleventh century, Lucena boasted an impressive roster of prominent scholars, including the philosopher/biblical commentator/liturgical poet Isaac ibn Ghayyat (1038–89), who taught at and eventually headed the yeshiva in Lucena. Moses ibn Ezra, Abraham ibn Ezra, Judah Halevi, and Joseph ibn Sahl were all active in the city at some point in the course of their careers.

Since he was born and raised in an environment overflowing with intellectual fertility, Isaac ibn Mar Shaul's wide-spanning scholarly creativity was early awakened. A devotee of biblical Hebrew, Ibn Mar Shaul grew to be a highly respected Hebrew grammarian, rivaling the famed Isaac ibn Gikatilla in grammatical expertise.[8] His students included the eminent Hebrew grammarian and philologist Jonah ibn Janaḥ, who refers to his teacher and quotes from him not infrequently in his own *Sefer ha-Riqmah.*[9] In addition to referring to his teacher's pedagogy and quoting lines of his poetry, Ibn Janaḥ also relates nuggets of personal information about Ibn Mar Shaul. We learn from Ibn Janaḥ that his teacher so strongly emphasized the need to understand every word of the Holy Tongue that when Ibn Mar Shaul realized he did not understand one of the phrases in Psalm 143, he broke off his nightly habit of reciting the psalm before bed.[10]

Not surprisingly, Ibn Mar Shaul's love of and devotion to the Hebrew language led him to non-grammatical study and production as well as grammatical activities. According to evidence found in the writings of both Ibn Janaḥ and Abraham ibn Ezra (*c.* 1089–1164), Ibn Mar Shaul wrote a commentary on the

Bible, or at least parts of one, though none of it has survived.[11] He also composed synagogue poetry (*piyyutim*) for different occasions and holidays. Some of these appeared in holiday prayer books not only in Spain, but in the later Jewish communities of Greece, Rome, Provence, and even as far off as India. Although he was known to be a prolific composer of such poetry and an innovator and trendsetter in the field, only fragments of his work have survived to the modern period.[12]

In addition to these religious uses of Hebrew, Ibn Mar Shaul's piety did not prevent him from engaging in another creative field, the writing of secular Hebrew poetry on the Andalusian Arabic poetic model. The homoerotic Hebrew poem mentioned earlier was not Ibn Mar Shaul's only secular composition. Rather, here too he excelled, with his secular poems traveling far beyond the confines of his home town of Lucena, as far off as Egypt. As mentioned earlier, Ibn Mar Shaul's secular Hebrew compositions so closely paralleled the motifs and themes of Andalusian Arabic poetics that he often used his poetic compositions as teaching tools. As Ibn Janaḥ reports, Ibn Mar Shaul taught his students Hebrew grammar, and the rules, rhythms, and motifs of Arabic poetry through his own secular Hebrew poems.[13]

All this wide-ranging literary creativity would have been enough to render Ibn Mar Shaul one of the most famous of the early Spanish Hebrew poets. In the modern period, however, Ibn Mar Shaul's claim to fame among many readers of medieval secular Hebrew poetry derives from one particular poetic innovation. While Ibn Mar Shaul may not have been the first to write secular Hebrew poems in Andalusia,[14] he was the first to introduce into secular Hebrew Andalusian poetry the idea of the male beloved of the male lover, a literary topos so common among Arabic poems.[15]

The poem

Over the years, a number of versions of Ibn Mar Shaul's poem have come to light. The earliest mention appears in Ibn Janaḥ's important work on Hebrew grammar, *Kitāb al-luma`* (*Sefer ha-Riqmah*), where Ibn Janaḥ cites only one line of his teacher's poem, line 5. The most complete version appears in Ḥaim [Jefim] Schirmann's *Shirim Ḥadashim min ha-Genizah* [New Hebrew Poems from the Genizah], based on a manuscript found in the Taylor-Schechter Genizah collection. Ezra Fleischer subsequently located another Taylor-Schechter manuscript, one that corrected two points and filled in a void in the Schirmann version.[16]

While this earliest of secular Hebrew homoerotic poetry appears not to have concerned Ibn Mar Shaul's immediate contemporaries, it has caused a measure of controversy among the modern researchers in the field. Some scholars found themselves uncomfortable with the notion that devout Jews would have composed homosexual poems of desire, given the uncompromising biblical prohibition against homosexuality in Leviticus 18:22 and 20:13;[17] thus, these scholars attempted to present this early poem (and the homoerotic poems that followed it) as an ode to a *female* beloved, translating the clearly male pronouns and verbs as if they were the feminine. Yosef Tobi, for example, maintains that Ibn Mar

Shaul's use of the צבי (*tzvi*, male deer) as a symbol for the male beloved in his love poems should be understood as symbolizing a beloved but platonic male friend, and nothing more.[18] Others, such as Schirmann and Norman Roth, reject such attempts at hetero-icizing the poems. They note that the Hebrew poets were perfectly capable of differentiating between male and female terminology when they wanted to, as Ibn Mar Shaul does here. Additionally, in Ibn Mar Shaul's ground-breaking homoerotic poem, *all* the people referred to in the poem to whom the beloved is compared are clearly male. [19] Similarly, Raymond Scheindlin raised the possibility that Ibn Mar Shaul's use of male imagery for the beloved here intends to reflect the hetero-erotic perspective of a female lover as narrator, as is common in Portuguese *cantigas de amigo*. He then discounts this possibility, noting that the narrator's comparing himself to a biblical male character (Uriah) "might almost have been devised specifically to block this route of escape."[20]

Basing himself on Schirmann's edition, Norman Roth translated the entire poem into English.[21] Roth's translation appears below, supplemented by a translation of the missing words supplied by Fleischer's manuscript and modified at points to more literally reflect the Hebrew:

1. צבי חשוק באספמיא   יצרו רב עליליה
2. והמשילו והשליטו   עלי כל [חי] וכל חיה.
3. יפה תואר כירח   עלי קומה יפהפיה,
4. ותלתליו כארגמן   עלי רקה פניניה.
5. כמו יוסף [בצור]תו   ובשער- אדוניה,
6. [יפה] עין כבן-ישי   הרגני כאוריה,
7. וגם השיק בכליותי[22]   ולבי אש פנימיה,
8. בעברו בי עזבני   חסר לבב ותושיה
9. בכו עמי, בנות יענה   וכל איה וכל דיה!
10. אהוב נפשי קטלני-   הזה משפט פליליה?
11. ש[פטני ולא ריח]ם   עלי ליבי ולא חיה[23]
12. ונפשי לו מאד חולה   וגם תועה והומיה
13. ומדבריו עלי לבי   כמו מטר עלי ציה.
14. דלני מבאר [שחת]   ואל ארד לתחתיה!

1. Gazelle desired in Spain
Wondrously formed,
2. Given rule and dominion
Over every little thing;
3. Lovely of form like the moon
With beautiful stature:
4. Curls of purple[24]
Upon a shining temple,[25]
5. Like Joseph in his form
Like Adonijah[26] in his hair.
6. Lovely of eyes like David,
He has slain me like Uriah.

7. He has enflamed my passions
   And consumed my heart with fire.
8. In passing me by, he has left me
   without understanding and wisdom.[27]
9. Weep with me every ostrich
   And every hawk and falcon!
10. The beloved of my soul has slain me –
    Is this a just sentence?
11. He judged me without mercy for my
    heart and has not allowed me to live.[28]
12. Because of him my soul is sick
    Perplexed and yearning.
13. His speech upon my heart
    Is like dew upon a parched land.
14. Draw me from the pit of destruction
    That I go not down to its nethermost part![29]

Poetic topoi and Ibn Mar Shaul

Most of this beautiful poem strikes us as unproblematic and not out of the ordinary, in line with the rules and conventions of poetic language and symbolism common in medieval Spain. The beloved appears without a name but with the Hebrew epithet typically used for unnamed male beloveds, צבי (*tzvi*), a male gazelle.[30] As usual, the poet gives us little to no information regarding the personality of the beloved to explain his love for him. Instead, the beloved's beauty alone is described, and in conventional terms rather than using person-specific imagery. After all, these poems were not so much expressions of personal experiences as homages to beauty as an idea and ideal.[31] As Scheindlin has noted, love receives poetic form in Andalusia "on behalf of a communal ideal" and not because of individual experience.[32] Thus the beloved's face, like those of most male beauties of this genre, reminds the viewer of the splendor and luster of the moon (l. 3). His forehead shines brightly like a pearl, and is contrasted with his typically dark curly hair (l. 4).[33] The rest of his body inspires aesthetic appreciation as well; he is "wondrously formed" (l. 1) and he is appreciably tall (l. 3).[34] All in all, Ibn Mar Shaul's beloved displays all the shared but handsome characteristics expected from the impersonalized male gazelle.

The paradigmatic description of the beloved's handsomeness causes a paradigmatic reaction on the part of the lover: Consumed by desire, the lover feels himself to be on fire, scorched and parched by the heat of his emotions. As the lover reports, the beautiful beloved "has enflamed my passions and consumed my heart with fire" (l. 7). As is typical for the lover, Andalusian and earlier, this passionate aching for the object of his affection leaves him in a state of bewildering sickness. "Because of him my soul is sick," he writes, "perplexed, and yearning" (l. 12). Andalusian poetry for the most part did not view love as an enjoyable emotion or state-of-being. For the poets writing in both Hebrew and

Arabic, influenced by the generations of Arabic poetry that came before them, love was an incurable illness or madness, a painful sickness for which people nonetheless longed.

Lovesickness not only caused excruciating burning in the lover, but was often a fatal disease in which only the lover's incessant suffering and eventual death proved the seriousness of his emotions. If a lover claimed to be dying of love, but was healthy enough to actually utter the words that pointed this out, he was thought to be faking his claims of lovesickness (and hence his emotions and devotion).[35] So, too, here Ibn Mar Shaul's lover speaks of dying from love for his gazelle. "The beloved of my soul has slain me," he writes in one such example (l. 10). And in what appears to be an attempt to avoid accusations of faking the seriousness of his condition, he insists here that he is already dead, languishing in the pit of destruction (באר שחת, *be'er shaḥat*) (l. 14).[36]

Another typical motif of love poetry that appears in Ibn Mar Shaul's poem concerns the responsibility of the beloved for the torment of his lover, the trope of the cruel beloved. Poetic beloveds were not innocents admired from afar, ignorant of the affection or suffering of their devotees. Rather, the poets frequently complained of the cruelty of the gazelles who *knowingly* taunted and teased them, gracing them with warmth one day and callously yanking away affection the next. Ibn Mar Shaul's gazelle exhibits precisely such heartless behavior. On some days, notes the lover, the beloved speaks with him; when he does, his attentions are as life-giving as "dew upon a parched land" (l. 13). Yet, the beloved's attentions and kindnesses are inconsistent. Though he has "rule and dominion over every little thing" (l. 2), he chooses to harm rather than to charm the very one who loves him most. Although the beloved has enflamed the lover's passions, setting his heart ablaze, the beloved cruelly, and typically, ignores him. Instead of basking in shared intimacy, the lover finds himself alone and abandoned, sighing, "In passing me by, he has left me without understanding and wisdom" (l. 8). Indeed, the beloved cares little, if at all, for the lover's yearning for him; instead, "he has judged me without mercy for my heart" (l. 11), an unjust and undeserved sentence, emphasizes the lover. Cruel beloved that he is, he pitilessly chooses to send his lover to death. Instead of raising him up to life, the beloved purposely sends the lover down to the pit of destruction. "The beloved of my soul has slain me" (l. 10), cries the lover. This is an intentional killing, not the result of an accident or of unconscious neglect.

Even the appeal to ostriches, hawks, and falcons (l. 9) lies within the realm of conventional poetic motifs. Earlier Arabic *qaṣīda*s and later Arabic and Hebrew poems of other types frequently present the speaker as turning to desert animals, requesting that they join him in his lamentation. The appeal to the animals of the desert serves to intensify the distress and suffering of the speaker. Utilizing this motif, our lover cries out in l. 9, "Weep with me, every ostrich and every hawk and falcon," seemingly seeking company in his hour of lonely yearning.[37]

Importantly, Ibn Mar Shaul's feathered audience consists not only of three different types of biblical birds, but of birds prohibited for consumption in the Bible.[38] Two of these, the hawk and falcon, are birds of prey. Their appearance in our poem at this juncture points readers to envision a somewhat macabre scene: Ibn Mar Shaul's lover finds himself dying of love, alone, with not one but two types of birds of prey circling over head, waiting for him to die. Since they are his only company, the lover appeals to them for comfort and empathy. Although the third bird – the ostrich – is neither a bird of prey nor capable of flight, its appearance in the bird triumvirate likewise supports this morbid scenario. In the Bible, the ostrich, בת-יענה (*bat ya'anah*), is seen as a voracious bird.[39] The Bible thus employs the ostrich as a negative symbol, suggesting wailing, loneliness, desolation, and living among the ruins.[40] The appearance of the ostrich in our poem brings this same sense of wailing, loneliness, and desolation to Ibn Mar Shaul's lover, dying alone while birds of prey circle overhead.[41]

Allusion (*remez/remizah*)

Although the greatest רמז (*remez*/allusion) user of Hebrew Spain appears to have been Solomon ibn Gabirol (*c.* 1020–*c.*1057), Ibn Mar Shaul's poem holds its own in this realm.[42] In fleshing out the gazelle's pulchritude, the lover detours from standard poetic imagery to compare his beloved to the most familiar characteristics of well-recognized biblical young male attractiveness. Even here, the biblical paradigms of beauty to which our lover matches his beloved engender little surprise. Each fits the accepted traditions of the period's poetry, while simultaneously expanding our understanding of the poem's gazelle.

The Joseph allusion: youthful beauty

The first biblical allusion appears about one-third of the way through the poem, at the end of the section describing the physical qualities of the object of the narrator's affection. "כיוסף בצורתו" (*ke-Yosef be-tzurato*) writes Ibn Mar Shaul in line 5a; in form the gazelle resembles Joseph, the exemplar of youthful biblical beauty in the Jewish tradition. After all, the Bible famously describes Joseph's good looks with a double-dose of phrasing; Genesis 39:6 paints Joseph as not only blessed by God and trusted by Potiphar, his employer, but as both "יפה תואר" (*yefeh to'ar*), beautiful of description, and "יפה מראה" (*yefeh mar'eh*), beautiful to behold, or good-looking. When, in the next verse, the wife of Potiphar "lifts up her eyes" to find herself inappropriately but uncontrollably attracted to her handsome enslaved employee, we have almost expected this to happen.[43]

In comparing his beloved to the double-described Joseph, the lover not only tells us that the beloved was extremely aesthetically pleasing, but describes what kind of beauty this was. For significantly, only one other character in the Bible receives such a two-fold description of beauty: Rachel, Joseph's mother. Says Genesis 29:17 of Rachel, "וְרָחֵל הָיְתָה יְפַת-תֹּאַר וִיפַת מַרְאֶה" (*ve-Raḥel hayta yefat to'ar ve-yifat mar'eh*), "and Rachel was beautiful of description and beautiful to behold." Based on the similarity of the unique doubled-language used for this mother–son pair, classical rabbinic interpreters understood that Joseph's good looks were not only reminiscent of his mother's,[44] but also that his handsomeness was that of a somewhat soft and feminine youth. While the phrase יפה תואר (*yefeh to'ar*) describes the beauty of numerous women in the Bible, Joseph remains the only *male* so designated.[45] And indeed, a few lines earlier in our poem, the lover utilizes this very phrase to speak of his young boy beloved's good looks. Writing of his *tzvi* that he is "יפה תואר כירח" (*yefeh to'ar ke-yare'aḥ*), "lovely of form as the moon," Ibn Mar Shaul hints again to the youthful, even feminine, comeliness that his beloved shares with the youthful Joseph, the beauty that so aroused the wife of Potiphar.

David allusion: eyes that charm

Ibn Mar Shaul's beloved reminds the lover not only of Joseph, but also of a slightly later biblical prototype of youthful male beauty: David. Early on in the David-saga, the Bible points to comeliness as one of David's key attributes. When King Saul first receives word of the youthful David's existence, he hears his servant reporting, "Behold, I have seen a son of Jesse the Bethlehemite, who knows how to play, and is a fine warrior man, and a man of war, and prudent in speech, and *a handsome person* [איש תואר, *ish to'ar*, literally, a man of description], and the Lord is with him" (1 Sam. 16:18). In describing David's physical beauty, the Bible uses a phrase (איש תואר, *ish to'ar*) reminiscent of that used to describe his handsome forefather Joseph (יפה תואר, *yefeh to'ar*).

So great was David's physical attractiveness that it was recognized by both Israelite supporter and Philistine enemy alike. When David later approaches the Philistine warrior Goliath to fight him in a one-on-one battle, the Philistine takes one look at the young challenger and, offended by what he sees, begins a verbal tirade against his opponent; as Goliath points out disparagingly, the Israelites had sent forth not their best fighter, but a youth ("נַעַר," *na`ar*), stick-wielding, red-headed, and good-looking ("יְפֵה מַרְאֶה," *yefeh mar'eh*) (1 Sam. 17:42). Goliath's disdainful assessment of David's handsome appearance implies that David was not simply good-looking, but good-looking in a feminine way. After all, the Bible notably places in Goliath's mouth the same phrase ("יְפֵה מַרְאֶה," *yefeh mar'eh*) for David as that which the Bible used to describe both the foremother Rachel and her handsome young son, Joseph.[46]

Yet David's most striking element of beauty was not his overall loveliness but one particular physical feature, and it is to this feature that Ibn Mar Shaul's lover draws our attention. "יפה-עין כבן ישי" (*yefeh `ayin ke-ven Yishai*) praises the lover in line 5b, comparing the beloved's eyes to the beautiful eyes of the son of Jesse (i.e., David). According to the narrator of 1 Samuel, David was, in fact, blessed with particularly striking eyes. Early on in the David cycle, God sends the prophet Samuel to Bethlehem to find the son of Jesse who will replace Saul as the next king of Israel (1 Sam. 16). One by one, Jesse passes seven of his eight sons before the prophet. Though some are tall and royal-looking, God chooses none of them. Instead, He chastises Samuel for judging them by their external appearance. In the end, God chooses David, the youngest and possibly smallest of the group, and the one whom Jesse had overlooked.[47] Despite God's earlier instructions to

Samuel not to look at a man's outward appearance as a measure of his quality (1 Sam. 16:7), Scripture then immediately describes David's physical being, saying, "and he was ruddy, with beautiful eyes (יְפֵה עֵינַיִם, *yefeh 'einayim*), and good-looking, and the Lord said 'Arise, anoint him for this is he' "[48] (1 Sam. 16:12). Although many males are described in Scripture as good-looking, no one else receives this particular compliment regarding his eyes.[49] David alone serves as the biblical paradigm of beautiful eyes. As such, David's eyes stand as the fitting referent used by Ibn Mar Shaul's lover in describing the eyes, a typical poetic element of beauty, of his beloved and handsome boy.[50]

Adonijah allusion: Adonijah?

While the gazelle resembles David in the magnificence of his eyes, his hair calls to mind yet another biblical male character. According to the poetic lover, his beloved's hair is both curly (תלתליו, *taltalav*) and, in true poetic fashion, dark, so dark it seems almost purple (ארגמן, *argaman*) [l. 4].[51] This reminds the lover of the hair of David's son Adonijah, as he says: "like Adonijah in his hair" (l. 5b). Now, the Bible informs us in no uncertain terms that Adonijah was indeed a man of impressive physical beauty. In 1 Kings 1:6, we read of him "וְגַם הוּא טוֹב תֹּאַר מְאֹד" (*ve-gam hu tov to'ar me'od*), "he was also a very handsome man." However, a problem immediately arises here. The biblical verse speaks of Adonijah as possessing an overall beauty (*tov to'ar*, good of description), not as possessing any one specifically handsome characteristic. Yet Ibn Mar Shaul's poetic reference clearly compares his beloved's *hair* to Adonijah's, a characteristic for which Adonijah is not particularly known in the Bible.

Indeed, for any listener or reader familiar with the Bible, it appears clear that Ibn Mar Shaul here intended to recall not Adonijah but Absalom, Adonjiah's legendarily coiffed elder brother.[52] Like his father, David, and his younger brother, Absalom too was a particularly all-around fine specimen of male splendor. Notes the Bible, "in all Israel there was none so much praised as Absalom for his beauty; from the sole of his foot to the crown of his head there was no blemish in him" (2 Sam. 14:25). However, unlike his brother Adonijah, Absalom's beauty was not restricted to mere generalities. Rather, like his handsome-eyed father, Absalom possessed a specific characteristic that drew people's attention: Absalom's hair was so thick, lustrous, and heavy that Absalom needed to shave it off once a year, and when he did so, its annual weight reached 200 shekels (2 Sam. 14:26). Unfortunately for Absalom, his legendary enviable mane proved famously to be his undoing. After a battle in which Absalom rebelled against his king-father in an attempt to usurp him, Absalom raced away on a mule (2 Sam. 18). Galloping through the trees, his wondrous locks streaming around him, Absalom appears to have misjudged the height at which he rode. Suddenly, he found himself dangling in midair, caught by his hair in the branches of an oak. Joab, David's military chief, came upon Absalom hanging helplessly from his hair and shot three darts into Absalom's heart. Ten of Joab's young arms-bearers then surrounded the wounded prince and struck him until he died (2 Sam. 18:9–15), quelling the rebellion but angering the king for murdering his beloved son (2 Sam. 19:1). Given this story, it seems obvious that of the two beautiful sons of David, it is Absalom and not Adonijah who should have appeared in l. 5b.

However, even this surprising use of the incorrect brother stands in line with the conventions of Andalusian poetry. According to Ibn Janaḥ, Ibn Mar Shaul's student, his master did not err in his choice of biblical brother and, he insists, one should not hypercorrect the poem to read "Absalom" or even "אח אדוניה" (*aḥ Adoniah*, the brother of Adonijah), as some have done. Rather, asserts Ibn Janaḥ, the poet's intentional use of Adonijah resulted from two professional concerns. One involved the poem's rhyme scheme. In Hebrew, the lines end with *–iya*, and "Absalom" simply does not fit the rhyme. The second reason for the appearance of Adonijah arose from a form of professional poetic playing with the materials or audience. According to Ibn Janaḥ, Ibn Mar Shaul purposely utilized the "wrong" brother in accordance with the common Arabic custom of name-changing, a form of metonymy in which the "wrong" name is used while intending to call to mind the "correct" name. Thus, Ibn Mar Shaul inserted the name Adonijah when his audience was expecting his brother Absalom, as a playful way of interacting with his audience.[53]

Uriah allusion: love and death

Like the three earlier male allusions, the final biblical personality allusion also fits the conventions of love poetry. But while the first three represent conventions of physical beauty, our final biblical allusion addresses the beloved's behavior. Employing the image of the stereotypical cruel, uncaring, dangerous, even murderous beloved, Ibn Mar Shaul writes of his gazelle, "he has slain me like Uriah" (l. 6). Readers familiar with the biblical accounts of David's rule cannot help but immediately recall the disturbing account to which this refers. According to 2 Samuel 11, King David deliberately ordered the death of one of his devoted and innocent soldiers, Uriah the Hittite. It is to David's killing of Uriah that the lover here compares his beloved's calculatedly callous and cruel treatment of him. What's more, since the biblical Uriah was guilty of no blame or sin or any action that would have earned him such an end, David's lethal treatment of Uriah was particularly cruel and pitiless.[54] This, too, becomes an important part of Ibn Mar Shaul's allusion. Lovers frequently portrayed themselves as innocent of any wrongdoing, suffering cruel torment and frequently death at the hands of their cruel beloveds. In comparing himself to the unjustly murdered Uriah, our lover here stresses this point.[55]

The awkwardness of Uriah

Although the Uriah reference thus fits well with the poetic motifs, it is precisely this almost clichéd comparison between the dying lover and Uriah the Hittite that strikes the reader as the least stereotypical and most highly problematic of all the imagery in our homoerotic poem.[56] Most prominently, while the biblical David is sometimes said by modern readers to have been involved in a homosexual relationship, his partner in this is not ever Uriah. Rather, the one male character with whom David famously bonds is his close friend Jonathan, the son of King Saul. In eulogizing Jonathan at his death at the hands of the Philistines, David cries, "I grieve for you, my brother Jonathan. You were most dear to me. Your love was wonderful to me more than the love of women" (2 Sam. 1:26). Those who maintain that David and Jonathan are romantically linked, rather than simply close friends, base themselves largely on this verse. [57] David utters no such words of affection, or *any* words of affection, for Uriah. Indeed, as far as one can tell from the Bible, David appears to acknowledge Uriah's existence only peripherally; for David, Uriah is little more than one of his thirty-seven hero-soldiers,[58] and the one who has the bad luck to have been the husband of a strikingly beautiful woman.

Just as Uriah's life was not bound up in a homosexual relationship with David in the Bible, so too Uriah's death there has nothing to do with homosexual love of David, despite the implications of Ibn Mar Shaul's poem. Uriah first appears on the biblical scene in 2 Samuel 11 as the soldier-husband of the rooftop bathing beauty Bathsheba, with whom David conducts an affair while Uriah fights the king's campaigns far from home. David's adulterous dallying with Bathsheba in her husband's absence ends in a problematic pregnancy. In an attempt to conceal his cuckolding behavior, David hastens to call Uriah home from the battle, ostensibly to report to him on the war's progress, and then sends Uriah to his home. David's plan rests on his asumption that Uriah will return to his wife, dally with her himself, and then logically assume that *he* fathered his wife's child. Much to David's chagrin, however, Uriah turns out to be a most loyal soldier and a man of great empathy. Unwilling to indulge himself while his commander and platoon remain in the field, Uriah chooses instead to camp out in the palace doorway with the other royal guards. Thwarted but not defeated, David hatches plan B: He sends Uriah to the front line so that he will die in battle. When this happens as planned, David marries the unfortunate (and pregnant) war widow.

Let us be sure to understand the issue clearly and in depth. In the Bible, David, the supposedly pious Israelite king handpicked by God (1 Sam. 16:7), sneaks around having an affair with a married woman who he knows is married (2 Sam. 11:2–3) and impregnates her. Rather than admit his sin and repent, David attempts to hide his crime through scheming and manipulation. When that doesn't work, he kills the husband in an attempt to save face. David's Hittite soldier, on the other hand, remains the picture of nobility, chivalry, loyalty, and bravery. Even though he is not himself an Israelite, he serves most faithfully in David's army, and identifies with the suffering of the army, while David their king, who sent them out to war in the first place, spends his time in sexual conquest of his soldier's wife.[59]

The two Hebrew words of line 6b of Ibn Mar Shaul's poem ("הרגני כאוריה," "He has slain me like Uriah") turn this picture of patriotism, chivalry, and loyalty completely on its head. In these two simple words, Ibn Mar Shaul's poem rejects all of Uriah's patriotic claims and loyalty-infused justifications and inverts the traditional reading of the biblical narrative. Ibn Mar Shaul's poem instead implies that Uriah avoids going home, not out of loyalty, duty, and honor, as he claims. Rather, Uriah avoids going home because nothing there, not even his beautiful wife, holds any interest for him. He does not choose to stay at the king's palace out of martial loyalty, patriotism, or respect for God's Ark and covenant with Israel, as he claims. Rather, like the poetic lover yearning for his handsome Joseph/Absalom/David-like beloved, Uriah insists on remaining in David's house because *Uriah is in love with David.* And like the cruel poetic beloved who returns his lover's passion by cruelly destroying him, David repays Uriah for his love by slaying him, "הרגני כאוריה" (*haragani ke-Uriah*).

Problems in 2 Samuel 11: Uriah is not what he appears to be

But from where does Ibn Mar Shaul draw such an idea? Is this literally poetic license or is Ibn Mar Shaul's poem reacting to something in the text itself, something that cries out to readers "דרשני" (*darsheini*, "explicate me")? If we return to the text of 2 Samuel 11, we see, through the light shined on the scriptural account by the poem, subtle textual problems that *do* call for such exegesis.

Namely, in 2 Samuel 11, Uriah the Hittite makes a number of less than believable declarations, which he follows up with strange behavior. In the first place, Uriah claims to so identify with the suffering of the Ark of God, Israel, and Judah, that he refuses to return home (v. 11). Such a declaration is somewhat difficult to fathom. After all, what soldier on campaign would refuse a permitted mid-war one-night visit with his notably beautiful wife (v. 2 "and the woman was *very* beautiful," "וְהָאִשָּׁה טוֹבַת מַרְאֶה מְאֹד," *ve-ha-ishah tovat mar'eh me'od*), a woman so striking that her bathing at twilight ("וַיְהִי לְעֵת הָעֶרֶב," *va-yehi le-`et ha-`erev*), a time of day at which it is notoriously difficult to see well, attracts the attention of the king himself, a man not at a loss for female company[60] *and* standing a distance away? Is Uriah made of stone? Uriah's self-control in the face of an opportunity to visit with his beautiful wife appears even more impressive when we recall that David forbade his soldiers from engaging in sexual congress while away on military campaigns (1 Sam. 21:5–6). Given this restriction, one would imagine that Uriah's desire to get home might be all the more compounded. The strangeness of his refusal to visit her while she is so close by and permitted to him stands out even more. Further perplexingly, not only to the reader but to David as well, Uriah refuses the opportunity to visit with his wife not once but three nights in a row (2 Sam. 11:9, 12–13)!

A non-homosexually oriented way of explaining Uriah's refusal to go home is to assume that Uriah knew what had transpired between the king and Bathsheba. Understandably irritated by their cavorting together while he was away at war, Uriah refused to participate in the king's attempted cover-up. However, such a reading runs up against a number of problems. Most obviously, Uriah was away from home on campaign when the David–Bathsheba affair occurred and thus was not likely to have heard about the palace intrigues unless someone specifically told him. The biblical text does not give any indication that this occurred. Rather, according to 2 Samuel 11, Uriah is sent from the battlefield straight to David. Additionally, although David had many wives and concubines, he is not known in the Bible for his behaving adulterously or inappropriately with women in general. There is little reason to assume that Uriah, having come directly home from battle, might have suspected his king of such a thing.[61]

The peculiarity of Uriah's refusal to go home becomes even more emphasized when we note the language used here by David. David does not simply *suggest* that Uriah visit his wife for the night, but, acting as king and commander-in-chief David officially *commands* Uriah to do so. Note the imperative form of the verbs in verse 8 as David instructs Uriah, "רֵד לְבֵיתְךָ וּרְחַץ רַגְלֶיךָ," (*reid le-veitkha u-reḥatz raglekha*), "Go down to your house and bathe your feet/legs." Given the muddle David found himself in, David's command concerned not only where he wanted Uriah to go, but also what he wanted Uriah to do when he got there. Translators have noted that David here employed a euphemism in which "feet/legs" refer not to one's actual feet/legs but to the genitals.[62] Thus, David commanded Uriah not only to go home, but to wash himself of the impurity of war and have sexual relations with his wife. Yet despite this royal command and despite being accompanied by a royal retinue bearing food and gifts for his household (v. 8), Uriah refuses to comply. Instead, Uriah quietly defies the royal order and retires to the entrance of the palace with the palace servants, rather than returning to his house to bask in the comfort of his home and to canoodle with his stunning wife (v. 9).

The geographic locations mentioned in the account add to the sense that it is Uriah's reluctance to leave David's side which stands behind his refusal to return home to his wife. According to verse 9, Uriah spends the first night in the doorway of the king's house, "וַיִּשְׁכַּב אוּרִיָּה פֶּתַח בֵּית הַמֶּלֶךְ" (*va-yishkav Uriah petaḥ beit ha-melekh*), refusing to go home to his own house ("וְלֹא יָרַד אֶל בֵּיתוֹ," *ve-lo yarad el beito*). In verse 13, Uriah repeats this behavior, once again returning to his sleeping-place among his lord David's servants ("וַיֵּצֵא בָעֶרֶב לִשְׁכַּב בְּמִשְׁכָּבוֹ עִם עַבְדֵי אֲדֹנָיו," *va-yetze ba-`erev lishkav be-mishkavo `im `avdei adonav*), rather than returning to his own home ("וְאֶל בֵּיתוֹ לֹא יָרָד," *ve-el beito lo yarad*). In verse 12, we find a different description of place. After David discovers that his loyal soldier did not head home as commanded, and why, David says to him, "Stay here today as well, and tomorrow I will send you back." So, verse 12 informs us, Uriah stayed in Jerusalem that day, and the next ("וַיֵּשֶׁב אוּרִיָּה בִירוּשָׁלַם בַּיּוֹם הַהוּא וּמִמָּחֳרָת," *va-yeshev Uriah be-Yerushalayim ba-yom ha-hu u-mi-maḥorat*).[63] The verse does not say that Uriah stayed in the palace, or its entrance, which is where he had been until now and to where he returns after dinner the next night. Rather, the verse tells us a seemingly extraneous piece of information, the name of the city Uriah is in. Why? People come and go from David's presence throughout the chapter, from distances near (Bathsheba's house) and far (the messenger from the battlefield, v. 22), with no mention of the city. Yet here, where we find Uriah staying in the same place, the text oddly includes the city name, rather than the actual place (the palace) in which Uriah finds himself. What could the verse possibly add by shifting the designation of Uriah's location from the palace to "in Jerusalem"? A hint can be found in the account's opening verse (2 Sam. 12:1). There the Bible reports that while David sends Joab and the army, and all of Israel, to battle the Ammonites in Rabbah, David himself "tarried in Jerusalem" ("וְדָוִד יוֹשֵׁב בִּירוּשָׁלָֽם," *ve-David yoshev be-Yerushalayim*). The biblical mention of the city name here stresses the fact that David remained a safe distance away from the battle in Ammon to which he sent his people. It is this distance from the war that appears to allow David, safely in Jerusalem, to engage in the very non-military pursuit of the wife of a soldier whom he has sent out of town on campaign. In recording that Uriah too now stays in Jerusalem (v. 12), the verses set up a parallel to David.[64] Just as David's tarrying "in Jerusalem" resulted in an illicit sexual affair with a nearby beauty, so too, the language hints, perhaps Uriah tarries "in Jerusalem" in the hopes of engaging in an illicit sexual encounter with a nearby beauty.

The possibility that Uriah was in love with David, as Ibn Mar Shaul's poem implies and as "in Jerusalem" may hint, appears also in Uriah's next set of behaviors, which contrast suspiciously with his protestations against luxury and indulgence. Initially, Uriah adamantly insists that he could not possibly eat and drink while his compatriots are out fighting (v. 11). However, when David subsequently invites him to dinner, Uriah not only eats but drinks so copiously that he becomes drunk (v. 13)! Even in this impressionable and suggestible state, Uriah impressively refrains from going home to sleep with his wife,[65] choosing instead to sleep again with his master's officers in the entry to the king's house. In other words, what Uriah should have done at home – eating and drinking with his beloved wife – he first protests against doing, declaring it wholly inappropriate. Then, with little convincing, he does exactly that, this time with his real beloved, David.

The text hints further to a transference of Uriah's emotions from his wife to his king with the subtle choice of words formed off of the root שכב (*shakhav*, to lie down), whose sexually charged noun and verb forms litter this biblical account. In describing the early goings-on between David and Bathsheba, the narrator writes (v. 4): "So David sent messengers to get her, and she came to him, וַיִּשְׁכַּב עִמָּהּ (*va-yishkav `ima*, he lay with her) ... and she went home."[66] Lest we think too naively of what went on, that they were just innocently "lying" there together, in the very next verse Bathsheba informs David she has become pregnant. Uriah employs the same euphemistic terminology in later *refusing* to spend the night with the very same woman. Says Uriah to David, "Shall I then go to my house, to eat and to drink and לִשְׁכַּב עִם-אִשְׁתִּי (*lishkav `im ishti*, to lie down with my woman)?" In describing Uriah's behavior after dining with David, the text uses the same verb-phrase once more, noting that Uriah went to "לִשְׁכַּב בְּמִשְׁכָּבוֹ" (*lishkav be-mishkavo*, to lie down on his bed) with the king's guards, but that he did not go down to his house (v. 13).[67] The language used here echoes David's earlier sexual interactions with Uriah's wife; as 2 Samuel 11:2 relates, when evening fell David arose from מִשְׁכָּבוֹ (*mishkavo*) only to lie right down again with Bathsheba (וַיִּשְׁכַּב עִמָּהּ, *va-yishkav 'ima*, v. 4).

Readers familiar with the Bible cannot avoid recalling that perhaps the most famous, or infamous, sexualized usage of the term משכב (*mishkav*) appears in biblical discussions of homosexual male sexual activity. In prohibiting male–male sexual relations, Leviticus 18:22 writes, "You shall not lie with a male מִשְׁכְּבֵי אִשָּׁה (*mishkevei ishah*, the layings of a woman); it is a תּוֹעֵבָה (*to`evah*)."[68] The phrase appears again in Leviticus 20:13, where a punishment is added: "A man who lies with a male as one lies with a woman מִשְׁכְּבֵי אִשָּׁה (*mishkevei ishah*), they have done a תּוֹעֵבָה (*to`evah*), both of them, they shall surely be put to death, their blood shall be upon them." In echoing the vocabulary choice of Leviticus 18 and 20, the language of 2 Samuel 11 subtly hints that Uriah longed to do exactly that which the Leviticus verses prohibited. Uriah longed to lay down מִשְׁכְּבֵי אִשָּׁה (*mishkevei ishah*) on his משכב (*mishkav*) in David's palace. Unable to do so, both because the Law prohibits it and because David appears to be completely unaware and uninterested, Uriah replaced his female partner (Bathsheba) with King David as best as he could. Instead of joining his wife in their bed for sex, משכב (*mishkav*), he chooses to spend the night בְּמִשְׁכָּבוֹ (*be-mishkavo*) in a bed in the king's palace with sexual thoughts and hopes on his mind.

Other textual hints and puzzling behavior on Uriah's part further support the reading of Uriah as romantically oriented toward his king, as hinted in Ibn Mar Shaul's poem. We recall that Uriah's primary claim for refusing David's offer of a vacation from the military hinged on Uriah's participation in and identification with Israelite life. "The Ark and Israel and Judah remain in booths, and my lord Joab and the servants of my lord are camping in the open field; shall I then go to my house, to eat and to drink, and to lie with my wife?" he asks incredulously (v. 11). In other words, he claims, if they suffer, he too, as part of them, must suffer. Not only is this empathy and patriotism exemplary, it is the opposite of the self-indulgent behavior of the Israelite king who is the audience of such words. However, something here sounds possibly disingenuous. Let us note the very first item of concern for Uriah: the Ark. This is none other than the Ark of the Covenant, the resting place of the Two Tablets of the Law, which accompanied the Israelites in battle when they fought. Uriah's primary concern here does not involve his friends, or his brothers-in-arms, or his commander. Rather, the Ark – the symbol of Israel's unique covenant with God – stands at the head of the list for a man who is, importantly, *not* an Israelite and thus not part of the very covenant with God symbolized by the Ark with which Uriah so identifies. From the start of the story to its end, Uriah is identified by the narrator over and over as a Hittite.[69] This implies that Uriah never officially or completely joined the Israelite religion he recalls here with such devotion.[70] Similarly, when Uriah appears elsewhere in the Bible, in the lists of David's "mighty men" (2 Sam. 23:39; 1 Chron. 11:41) or in God's later castigation of David's behavior in the entire affair (1 Kgs. 15:5), he likewise appears with the designation Hittite.[71] Additionally, three times the Bible refers to Bathsheba by both Uriah's name *and* ethnic/national designation, calling her "the wife of Uriah the Hittite."[72] Given this consistent non-Israelite identification, Uriah's claim of devotion to David's God and David's people sounds overstated.

In comparing the dying lover to the slain Uriah, Ibn Mar Shaul's poem presents an alternate understanding: Uriah's refusal to go home has little to do with his stated patriotic excuse. Rather, in placing the words "He has slain me like Uriah" in the mouth of the lover, the poem indicates that we ought to understand that Uriah viewed David in poetic *`ishq* fashion, as the beautiful but cruel beloved. Like the beloved, David caused Uriah to pine with love for him, ultimately killing Uriah for and with Uriah's passionate devotion, as cruel beloveds are wont to do.

Thus we see that with two short words in Hebrew, הרגני כאוריה (*haragani ke-Uriah*), Ibn Mar Shaul's poem turns the traditional understanding of the biblical account on its head and subtly hints at a new and somewhat sacrilegious reading of the biblical text. As we have seen, the more common reading of the Uriah–David relationship depicted in this biblical narrative presents them as cuckold-and-adulterer; they are linked not by a direct relationship with one another, but by each man's separate romantic/sexual relationship with Bathsheba, the woman in the middle. Uriah is perceived as he attempts to depict himself, as the paradigm of honor and virtue. In the poetic rendering, however, Ibn Mar Shaul's verses unravel that picture. In comparing the lover's death at the hands of his beloved to Uriah's death at the hands of David, the poem subtly calls our attention to otherwise unnoticed irregularities of both biblical content and biblical language. In so doing, Ibn Mar Shaul's poem brings to light an entirely new picture of the Hittite Davidic loyalist of 2 Samuel 11. Through this lens, we find Uriah as rejected homosexual lover, fatally in love with a man who is in love, not with him, but with his wife. In other words, what was a simple homosexual love poem, with two words is transformed into a midrashic exegesis on an otherwise somewhat problematic biblical section.

Classical and medieval exegesis on David and Uriah

Having established that Ibn Mar Shaul's poem reads the biblical Uriah subversively as yearning for David, one would be wise to ask the question: Is Ibn Mar Shaul's poem's suggested interpretation of 2 Samuel 11 and presentation of Uriah as lovesick for David his own innovation? Or, are there midrashic accounts, exegetical readings, which similarly presented Uriah's behavior and claims in a homoerotic light?

Classical rabbinic exegesis

Although midrashic explanations and commentaries on the David–Bathsheba–Uriah cycle abound, few to none share the perspective of Ibn Mar Shaul's poem. Indeed, quite the opposite is true. While Ibn Mar Shaul's poem subtly presents Uriah as a besotted but innocent victim of a cruel male beloved, traditional commentaries on the biblical account make no mention of this. Instead, they blame Uriah for his own unfortunate end and work to exonerate David from all culpability for his role in either the killing or the adultery that leads to it.

Interestingly, this attempted inversion, or even expunging, of the biblical record begins in the Bible itself. In rerecording David's life and history, 1 Chronicles very obviously omits altogether any mention of Uriah the Hittite as well as any record of David's adulterous interactions with Uriah's wife. Instead 1 Chronicles 3:5 innocently and simply records that four sons were born to David and Bathsheba in Jerusalem, one of whom was Solomon (the future king).[73] The adultery- and killing-laced background for this marital union merits no mention here. As far as 1 Chronicles is concerned, nothing out of the ordinary whatsoever took place regarding David and Bathsheba's marriage.[74]

Talmudic traditions follow suit, attempting to lessen David's guilt for the death of Uriah not through omission, as in the Bible, but by blaming Uriah himself. In *BT Shabbat* 56a and *BT Qiddushin* 43a, rabbinic scholars declare Uriah guilty of treason, a crime punishable by death. After all, they note, he refused to obey David's direct order to go home ("רֵד לְבֵיתְךָ," v. 8). Thus, according to this opinion, David's subsequent killing of his soldier was *not* a cover-up for his own sinful actions. Instead, David engaged in a somewhat justified punishment for the man's rebellious behavior.[75]

Other rabbinic commentators attempted to exonerate David not from the killing of Uriah but from the sin of adultery which caused David's messy state of affairs in the first place. In *BT Shabbat* 56a, R. Samuel bar Naḥmani quotes R. Nathan, who devised a complicated and legally controversial acquittal of David of sin: R. Nathan (and R. Samuel) insisted that all soldiers in David's army wrote bills of divorce for their wives before they went out to war. In case they went missing while on campaign, their wives would then be divorced retroactively to that moment and would be permitted to remarry.[76] Thus, when Uriah died, Bathsheba was considered retroactively divorced to the moment at which Uriah had written her the bill of divorce. In other words, Uriah's death ensured post facto that when David lay with Bathsheba, she was not actually a married woman.[77] No adultery took place.

Other sources admit that David engaged in inappropriate behavior, but mitigate his responsibility by insisting that it was God's will. In *BT Sanhedrin* 107a, David complains before God that the Jewish prayers include the line, "God of Abraham, God of Isaac, and God of Jacob," but not "God of David." God answers that the forefathers had been tested by Him and had prevailed and so earned themselves a place in the blessing. Hearing this, David demands that he too be tested, confident that he too will prevail. God acquiesces to the demand and even informs David that He will test him regarding adultery. Almost immediately after hearing this, the king took notice of the bathing Bathsheba and, in a quick turnaround, seemingly lost his wits and committed adultery, just as God had forewarned. Rava maintains that David then told God that he could have suppressed his lust had he wanted to. He did not do so, however, in order that people not say that the servant (David) had triumphed over the Master (God, who had decreed that David's name not be included in the blessing). In the same exonerative discussion, Rava taught that Bathsheba had been predestined to be David's wife during the six days of Creation. David was aware of this fact and so felt justified in bedding her when he did. David's sin thus was not that he "took her" to himself. Rather, he erred in that he did so a smidge too early, while she was still married to Uriah.[78] And, in *BT Avodah Zarah* 4b–5a, R. Joḥanan insists that God Himself predestined David to perform this "sin" to teach the power of penance to those who sin and then hesitate about the effectiveness of repenting. Just as David "sinned," repented, and was forgiven, so too all others.

Medieval Spanish exegesis

Unlike their classical rabbinic forebears, medieval Spanish exegetes were not opposed to blaming David for his sinning behavior in both bedding the married Bathsheba and then having her husband killed in a cover-up. This medieval acknowledgment of David's culpability comes as little surprise to those familiar with the Andalusian philosophy of biblical commentary. The Spanish school of biblical exegesis moved away from earlier generations' *derash* approach (homiletic or applied interpretation) to the Bible. Instead, the Spanish school emphasized the *peshat*, simple or contextual, reading of the biblical text. In light of the Bible's own repeated admission that David sinned (especially in 1 Kgs. 15:5), the Spanish exegetes found it difficult to argue for his innocence as the classical rabbinic texts so strenuously had.[79]

Although we would do best to compare Ibn Mar Shaul's poem with his own exegetical text in analyzing the matter, none of Ibn Mar Shaul's exegetical compositions have survived to the modern day. Fortunately, the works of three other key Spanish-school exegetes have survived, and these provide good information regarding material that would have been found among the Spanish exegetes. These are the commentaries of Rabbi David Qimḥi (1160–1235), Don Isaac Abrabanel (1437–1508) and Abraham ibn Ezra (1089–1164). As we shall see, like the Bible and Ibn Mar Shaul's poetic rendition, none exonerates David for his behavior. By the same token, none reads the Uriah–David relationship as one based on passionate romance, as Ibn Mar Shaul's poem seems to do.

Although not raised in Spain proper, Qimḥi's commentaries generally reflect the scholarly ideals and principles of Jewish Spain. Thus, despite his having been born in Narbonne, Provence, scholarly consensus includes Qimḥi as a member of the Spanish school of exegesis. He was the son and pupil of R. Joseph Qimḥi (1105–70), a grammarian, poet, exegete, and translator who had escaped from Spain to Provence with the persecutions of the Muslim Almohad government that had invaded Spain in 1146. With R. Joseph's death, his eldest son R. Moses Qimḥi (*c.* 1127–*c.* 1190), likewise a prominent Spanish grammarian and exegete, continued to raise and educate young David. The Qimḥis were not alone in continuing the Spanish customs and educational philosophies. The Provence Jewish community was known to have been heavily under the influence of the Spanish-Jewish community and their ethos.[80]

Under the Spanish influence of his father, brother, and community, David Qimḥi grew to become a well-respected philosopher and Hebrew grammarian whose biblical commentary was based equally on the principles of Hebrew grammar and of rationality. Although he included rabbinic *derash* interpretations in his commentary, he pointed this out when he did so. Otherwise, Qimḥi generally followed the Spanish custom of holding fast to the literal and contextual meaning of Scripture. Both his Spanish inclination toward *peshat* and his sometime incorporation of *derash* can be seen in his discussion of David's admittedly adulterous behavior in the Bathsheba–Uriah account.

In his commentary on 2 Samuel 11:4, "Now she [Bathsheba] was purifying herself," Qimḥi records two different explanations. Primarily, notes Qimḥi, this phrase comes to teach that David violated only the commandment against sex with another man's wife. He did not violate the commandment against sexual intercourse with a woman impure from her menstrual cycle. As a secondary explanation, and as a secondary explanation only, Qimḥi notes that "our rabbis" taught that since *BT Ketubbot* 9b maintains that all of David's soldiers issued conditional divorces to their wives before going out to war, Bathsheba was considered divorced retroactively. As a divorcee, she was permitted to David.[81] Apparently unsatisfied with the contortions of this explanation, which goes against the text's plain meaning, Qimḥi retreats from this rabbinic *derash* in his commentary a few verses later, on 2 Samuel 12:24. There he returns to his initial recognition of David's adultery as emphasized by the Bible itself. Qimḥi explains that while Uriah lived, the text referred to Bathsheba consistently as his wife, which she was. She appears without the title "wife of Uriah the Hittite" only after his death, or in events unconnected with her having been his wife.[82]

Like Qimḥi, Don Isaac Abrabanel (1437–1508) is not, strictly speaking, a Jewish scholar from Muslim Spain. Rather Abrabanel belongs to the ranks of Jewish scholars from Christian Spain, having spent the first forty-five years of his life in Portugal, and moving to Castille nine years before Ferdinand and Isabella expelled the Jews in 1492. However, like Qimḥi's, Abrabanel's Bible commentary reflects the *peshat*-focused methodology of the exegetes of Muslim Spain. Indeed, while Abrabanel did incorporate some midrashic materials into his exegesis, he insisted on *peshat* as the superior methodology.[83]

Where Qimḥi insists on David's culpability with a measure of subtleness, Abrabanel declares David a sinner on five counts, with no excuses or attempts at smoothing over David's abhorrent misdeeds. According to Abrabanel, in the first place, David sinned in conducting an adulterous affair with another man's wife, a deed made even ranker by that man being David's loyal fighter.[84] David compounded this sin with his attempts to trick Uriah into thinking the child was his, thereby denying his (David's) own seed. David's third offense concerned his having subsequently arranged for the death of the completely innocent Uriah. David then added to this evil by arranging for Uriah to die at the hands of the Ammonites, a Canaanite people whom Abrabanel calls here "enemies of God." What's more, other innocent men died as a result of that arranged battle (see 2 Sam. 11:17, 24). Finally, in quite an unseemly manner, David rushed to marry the grieving widow before the end of the obligatory ninety-day waiting period after the death of a husband. Regarding the rabbinic *derash* attempts to lighten David's culpability by claiming his soldiers had issued writs of divorce or he had not actually slept with Bathsheba, Abrabanel disparagingly writes, "These are the ways of *derash* and I will not respond to them." After all, he points out, the Bible states clearly that David sinned, more than once, and David himself admits to it. Unable to contain himself, Abrabanel thunders, "My mind cannot suffer to reduce David's sins, and I will not deny the simple truth (האמת הפשוט, *ha-emet ha-pashut*) of it!"[85] Rather, he notes, David sinned greatly, admitted all of it, repented fully, and accepted his punishment.

Of the three medieval exegetes, Abraham ibn Ezra alone hails from Muslim Spain proper and appears to have received his education there. Born in Tudela, he moved around Muslim Spain, from Cordoba to Seville, eventually wandering into Christian kingdoms and North African countries. Although not a professional rabbi or *dayyan* (judge) or religious scholar, he remains one of the most important biblical exegetes of both medieval Spain and the Jewish tradition. A man of impressive scholarly skills and knowledge, Abraham ibn Ezra was a poet, *payyetan*, grammarian, and translator who also wrote works on philosophy, astronomy and astrology. He was close with the Spanish philosopher-rabbi and poet Judah Halevi, whose daughter appears to have married Ibn Ezra's son Isaac. Sources indicate that Ibn Ezra composed religious and secular poems in both Hebrew and Arabic, though only the Hebrew have survived. He also composed scientific texts and works of biblical exegesis in both languages, though again, only the Hebrew products remain. As an exegete, Ibn Ezra insists on a *peshat* approach formed from strict adherence to philology and rational plausibility, and based on natural and psychological truths. While he does not reject midrashic interpretations of the narrative portions of the Bible, he insists that they be grounded in the text of the Bible itself if they are to be accepted.[86]

In his commentary to Psalm 32:1, Ibn Ezra notes that there appears to be a contradiction in the Bible; at points David appears to present himself as perfectly pious[87] and yet here in Psalm 32, he admits to having sinned. As David writes in verse 1, "Happy is he whose transgression is forgiven, whose sin is covered."[88] Indeed, notes Ibn Ezra, this is not the only Psalm in which David admits to having transgressed. In rectifying this contradiction, Ibn Ezra explains that in truth David did not sin against God; in that realm, his heart was whole. He did, however, sin against other people. In particular, insists Ibn Ezra, he sinned in the matter of Bathsheba, although he does not specify what the sin was.[89]

Although Ibn Ezra does not shy away from admitting that David sinned in some way, later on in his commentary he does attempt to mitigate the evil of David's actions somewhat. Commenting on Psalm 51:16, Ibn Ezra writes that David was not a true murderer, for he did not actually command anyone outright to kill Uriah. Rather, what David was guilty of was having had an "evil thought": he commanded Joab only to place Uriah in harm's way on the battlefield. Since he was thus not directly responsible for Uriah's death, he did not earn for himself capital punishment.[90]

In comparing Ibn Mar Shaul's poem to the roughly contemporaneous Spanish biblical commentaries, we can see that Ibn Mar Shaul's poem simultaneously reflected and departed from the exegetical vogue of the day. On the one hand, in comparing the unjustly killed lover to the slain Uriah, Ibn Mar Shaul's poem reflects Qimḥi's and Abrabanel's refusal to exonerate David from his cruel and unjust killing of his Hittite soldier. At the same time, Ibn Mar Shaul's exegetic comparison departs from the writings of Qimḥi and Abrabanel, which make no mention of any romantic feeling whatsoever on the part of Uriah. The Spanish scholars, like all the commentaries that preceded them, saw desire between David and Bathsheba only. Ibn Mar Shaul's poem stands alone in implying that the arrows of desire stretched also from Uriah to his king.

Conclusion

Ibn Mar Shaul's poem's homoerotic implications regarding the biblical Uriah, embedded in the two words הרגני כאוריה (*haragani ke-Uriah*), bear little in common with both the earlier and the contemporary commentaries on the events of 2 Samuel 11. Instead, as best as we can tell today, Ibn Mar Shaul's poem presents a unique reading of the goings-on hinted at in the language and behavior in the biblical text.

That Ibn Mar Shaul's secular lust poem both draws from the accounts of the Bible and presents a subtle and suggestive rereading of a biblical account should not prove as startling as it may seem at first glance. After all, Ibn Mar Shaul served not only as secular and liturgical poet but also as a biblical scholar/commentator who penned works of biblical exegesis, although they did not survive to the modern era. Additionally, Ibn Mar Shaul was one of the earliest and foremost of the Hebrew grammarians. His sensitivity to the structure of biblical Hebrew, its grammar and vocabulary, and his insistence on the importance of understanding biblical Hebrew and the text of the Bible was extraordinary.[91] What's more, we know from his students that Ibn Mar Shaul did not shy away from using his secular Hebrew poetry as a teaching tool.

In including David's killing of Uriah among the biblical *remizot* describing the male beloved, Ibn Mar Shaul's lover does far more than simply bring his male beloved in line with the poetic motif of the cruel, often lethal, beloved. In using what had been known heretofore as a clearly nonromantic biblical couple in a romantic and sexualized context, Ibn Mar Shaul's poem forces its readers to return to, reread, and reconsider the biblical text from which it derives (2 Sam. 11). And when we do, we realize that the biblical account of Uriah is not quite as clear as it would seem. Indeed, ambiguities of language and suspicious behavior litter the account. It appears that Uriah's odd and contradictory conduct and the text's sexually inflected vocabulary may have suggested to our top-notch grammarian and master of biblical Hebrew, either consciously or subconsciously, that another motivating factor lay behind Uriah's loyal façade: Uriah was hopelessly and, sadly, fatally in passionate love (*`ishq*) with the beautiful man who ruled over him but who did not return his affections. Apparently alone in such a subversive and sacrilegious interpretation, Ibn Mar Shaul embedded this analysis in his love poem, whose themes his biblical reading so resembled. In so doing, he uses a secular homoerotic love poem to point to an uncommon exegesis of a biblical text, and simultaneously uses a biblical text to bring to life an otherwise too typical Andalusian love poem.

Notes

1 The pre-Andalusian liturgical Hebrew poets utilized biblical citations in a much different fashion than did the Spanish poets. See Ezra Fleischer, *Shirat ha-Qodesh ha-`Ivrit be-Yimei ha-Beinayim* (Jerusalem: Magnes Press, 2007), 103–4; Israel Levin, *Shirah Araguha Yedei Ra`ayon* (Lod: Machon Haberman le-Meḥqarei Safrut, 2009).

2 Scholars credit Dunash ibn Labrat (920–90) with having been the first to introduce Arabic forms and meter into Hebrew poetry, a move not lauded by many scholars of his time, who accused Dunash of perverting Hebrew. Dunash appears to have restricted himself largely to liturgical poems or poems expressing religious sentiment and yearning for God. Scholars have noted that even among Dunash's secular poems, one does not find poems of desire using the thematic conventions of the Arabic poems.

Dunash's wife authored the earliest secular Hebrew love poem to have survived to modern times. In her poem she mourns the imminent absence of her husband as he sets off on a journey. Dunash compiled a response in kind. Both poems can be found in Fleischer, "`Al Dunash ben Labrat," 5:189ff. Peter Cole provides an English translation in his *Selected Poems of Solomon Ibn Gabirol* (Princeton and Oxford: Princeton University Press, 2001), 7. Fleischer points out that Dunash's wife's poem does not fit the genre of "typical" love poetry in that it is far too personal. See Fleischer's commentary in Ḥaim [Jefim] Schirmann, *Toledot ha-Shirah ha-`Ivrit be-Sefarad ha-Muslemit*, ed. Ezra Fleischer (Jerusalem: Magnes Press, 1995), 146, fn. 15. As noted above, Dunash's response likewise does not fit the "typical" model. Indeed, Yosef Tobi says of Dunash that he "expurgated the love element from his courtly poems." See Tobi, *Between Hebrew and Arabic Poetry*, 125.

While Dunash introduced the Arabic forms into Hebrew liturgical poetry, Ibn Mar Shaul's innovation lay in his utilizing the Arabic forms to write typical secular love poetry.

3 See a listing of such clergy-poets in Schirmann, "The Function of the Hebrew Poet." To be sure, Andalusian secular poetry included not only wine and love poems, but also praise poems, lamentation poems, poems of complaint and contemplation, boasting and scorn, and personal poems. We are concerned here with the love poems, the works that appear to contrast the most with the religious identity of their authors.

4 See Fleischer's comment in Schirmann, *Toledot ha-Shirah ha-`Ivrit be-Sefarad ha-Muslemit*, 146, n. 15. Fleischer's proposal results from his negative perspective on the existence of a Jewish court culture in Lucena at the time. Since Fleischer doubts the existence of a Lucenan Jewish court, he theorizes that Ibn Mar Shaul's poem was likely composed and sent to Cordoba for the courtiers to use there. If not, he says, then presumably the poem was written for didactic purposes.

5 Schirmann, *Toledot ha-Shirah ha-`Ivrit be-Sefarad ha-Muslemit*, 144–6, and 146, fn. 15.

6 Jonah ibn Janaḥ, *Sefer ha-Riqmah* (Frankfurt: [s.n.], 5616 [1856]), 179.

7 Lucena lies in the province of Cordoba, 72 km southeast of the city of Cordoba. See *EJ*, s.v. "Lucena," by Haim Beinart (13:247–8). Abraham ibn Daud (1110–80, Toledo) claimed that the city was founded as a result of Nebuchadnezzar's exile of the Jews from their homeland. The Jewish "character" of the city was mentioned also by Arabic sources, most notably the twelfth-century Muslim geographer al-Idrīsī (1100–63), who recorded that while Muslims lived in the outer, unprotected parts of the city, the Jews lived in its fortified section. According to Schirmann, from the second half of the tenth century until the mid-twelfth century, Lucena was also known as the center of Jewish legal study for the Jews of Spain. Some of the most noted names in Spanish Jewish halakhic circles, such as Isaac ibn Ghayyat, Isaac Alfasi, and Joseph ben

Meir ibn Migash, established houses of study (*batei midrash*) there, which drew devoted students. Many of the Spanish Hebrew poets received their Jewish education in Lucena's *yeshivot*. Among them were Moses ibn Ezra, Joseph ibn Sahl, Joseph ibn Tzaddiq, and possibly Judah Halevi. During the Muslim attack against the Jews of Granada in 1066, in which Joseph ha-Nagid was killed, his wife and son escaped to Lucena, where they were taken in by Ibn Ghayyat, then the head of Lucena's academy. After the Almohad attack on Lucena in *c.* 1148, the town more or less disappeared from Jewish history and sources. See Brener, *Judah Halevi and His Circle*, 45; Schirmann, *Toledot ha-Shirah ha-`Ivrit be-Sefarad ha-Muslemit*, 144–50; idem, "Yitzḥaq ben Mar Sha'ul," in *Sefer Assaf*, ed. M. D. Cassuto, Joseph Klausner, and Yehoshua Gutmann (Jerusalem: Mossad Harav Kook, 1953), 496–500; Schirmann, *Ha-Shirah ha-`Ivrit be-Sefarad u-ve-Provans*, 1:1:49–52.

8 Isaac ibn Gikatilla was the student of Menaḥem ibn Saruq, not to be confused with the slightly later grammarian and poet Moses ben Samuel ha-Cohen Gikatilla, or the kabbalist Joseph ben Abraham Gikatilla (1248–*c.* 1235). On Joseph's kabbalistic teachings, see below, n. 78.

9 Ezra Fleischer, "Ḥadashot be-Yitzirato shel R. Yitzḥaq bar Levi (Ibn Mar Sha'ul)," in *Meḥqerei Lashon Mugashim le-Ze'ev Ben-Haim be-Hagi`o le-Saivah*, ed. M. Bar-Asher, A. Dotan, D. Tenna, and D. Ben `Ami (Jerusalem: Y. L. Magnes, 1983), 425; Schirmann, *Shirim Ḥadashim min ha-Genizah*, 157–8; idem, *Toledot ha-Shirah ha-`Ivrit be-Sefarad ha-Muslemit*, 144–5.

10 Schirmann, "Yitzḥaq ben Mar Sha'ul," 502.

11 Ibid.; Simon, "The Spanish School," 1:118.

12 Fleischer, "Ḥadashot," 425–50; Schirman, *Shirim Ḥadashim*, 157–8; idem, *Toledot ha-Shirah ha-`Ivrit be-Sefarad ha-Muslemit*, 144–50; in his "Yitzḥaq ben Mar Sha'ul," Schirmann records the poem fragments (pp. 507ff).

13 The poem under discussion in this chapter is the only complete secular poem of Ibn Mar Shaul's that has survived to the modern period. Fragments of other secular poems appear scattered throughout in Ibn Janaḥ's text. See Schirmann, *Toledot ha-Shirah ha-`Ivrit be-Sefarad ha-Muslemit*, 144–6, esp. fnn. 7 and 16, and *Shirim Ḥadashim* [New Hebrew Poems], 157.

14 Ibn Mar Shaul's contemporary, Isaac ibn Khalfun, likewise composed secular Hebrew poetry on the Arabic model and was among the first to earn his living this way. Ibn Khalfun appears to have composed largely, though not exclusively, praise poetry, lauding paying patrons. On Ibn Khalfun, see Ann Brener, *Isaac ibn Khalfun: A Wandering Poet of the Eleventh Century* (Leiden: E. J. Brill, 2003); Cole, *The Dream of the Poem*, 35, Mirsky, ed., *Shirei Yitzḥaq ibn Khalfon*; Ḥaim [Jefim] Schirmann, "Yitzḥaq ibn Khalfun," *Tarbiz* 7 (1936): 291–318. In another article, Schirmann writes that Moses ibn Ezra implied that Ibn Khalfun was the first Hebrew poet to earn his livelihood from poetry. Schirmann adds that other professional poets probably appeared in the preceding generation. However, he names no specifics. See Schirmann, "The Function of the Hebrew Poet," 235–52.

One of Ibn Khalfun's more well-known non-praise poems is a humorous four-line love poem in which the lover skips along merrily to visit his beloved at her home only to find his visit thwarted by the presence of all her male family members. See Mirsky, ed., *Shirei Yitzḥaq ibn Khalfon*, 63 and Schirmann, *Toledot ha-Shirah ha-`Ivrit be-Sefarad ha-Muslemit*, 181.

15 Schirmann, "Yitzḥaq ben Mar Sha'ul," 503–4. See also Roth, "Deal Gently."

16 See Fleischer, "Ḥadashot," 450. Schirmann's rendition, cited below with Fleischer's emendations, appears in Jefim [Ḥaim] Schirmann, *New Hebrew Poems from the Genizah* [*Shirim Ḥadashim min ha-Genizah*] (Jerusalem: The Israel Academy of Sciences and Humanities, 1965), 158. Reproduced by permission. Menahem Zulay found a seven-line fragment in an Oxford manuscript (no. 2878/19), apparently copied by a very poor copyist who changed the voice to third person in some verses and switched the

order of the lines so that they made little sense (or became bad poetry). See Menahem Zulay, *Eretz Yisrael u-Fiyyuteiha: Meḥqarim be-Fiyyutei ha-Genizah*, ed. Ephraim Ḥazan (Jerusalem: Magnes Press, 1995), 578; Elizur, *Shirat ha-Ḥol*, 1:130–2. The seven-line poem appears also in Schirmann, "Yitzḥaq ben Mar Shaul," 513.

17 Scheindlin has suggested that the Hebrew poetic usage of the masculine gender was intended to create an atmosphere of "indefinite sexuality" rather than referring to maleness specifically. The beloved is a *type* of beauty, unrelated to gender specifics. In the thousands of lines of descriptive love poetry, he writes, hardly any specific details appear denoting maleness, except for the mention of the beard (when mentioned in the first place). Often, a reader can detect the gender of the beloved only through the grammatical phrasings, and not through any physical description. See Scheindlin, "A Miniature Anthology," 113–15. Importantly, Scheindlin does *not* take this genderless interpretive stance regarding the Ibn Mar Shaul poem under discussion, which he understands as clearly homoerotic, as noted at the end of the paragraph above.

18 Tobi maintains that the same is true in the praise poems of Ibn Mar Shaul's contemporary, Ibn Khalfun. See Tobi, *Shirat ha-Ḥol*, 4:57. On Ibn Khalfun, see n. 14, above.

19 Yehuda Ratzaby, "*Ha-Ahavah be-Shirat R. Shemuel ha-Nagid*," *Tarbiz* 39 (1969), fn. 25. See also Schirmann, "The Ephebe"; Roth, "The Care and Feeding of Gazelles," 95–118; idem, "Deal Gently"; idem, "Fawn of My Delights," 157–72; idem, "My Beloved Is Like a Gazelle."

20 Scheindlin, *Wine, Women and Death*, 87–8.

21 Roth, "Deal Gently," 31. A more lyrical translation by Scheindlin appears in his *Wine, Women and Death*, 87. Since Scheindlin's translation is incomplete, ending with line 6, I have used Roth's. Peter Cole has translated this poem as well, in his *Dreams of the Poem*, 28–9.

22 Schirmann's original reads כליותי (*kilyotai*). Based on the Taylor-Schechter manuscript, Fleischer emended it to the current form, which makes better grammatical sense in Hebrew. See Fleischer, "Ḥadashot," 450. See also Elizur, *Shirat ha-Ḥol*, 1:130–4.

23 Schirmann's version here reads: "ש ... ולא ריחם / עלי כל חי וכל חיה" (*sh ... ve-lo riḥem / `alei kol ḥai ve-kol ḥayya*). Based on the Taylor-Schechter manuscript, Fleischer emended it to the current reading: ש [... ולא ריח]ם / עלי לבי ולא חיה (*sh ... [ve-lo riḥem] / `alei libi ve-lo ḥiyya*). Fleischer here changes the words in the second half of the sentence and re-vocalizes the last word; he changes it from a noun (*ḥayya*, animal) to a *pi`el* (causative) verb (*ḥiyya*, he caused me to live). Thus, Schirmann's phrase reads: [*sh*] ... he has not had mercy / on all living things and all creatures. Fleischer's emended version reads: [*sh*] ... he has not mercy / on my heart and has not allowed me to live (as translated above). Although Elizur maintains that Fleischer's discovery fills in the missing first word of this line, שפטני (*shefatani*), a word that fits logically, thematically, and with the meter, I could not locate that point in his article. See Elizur, *Shirat ha-Ḥol*, 1:134; Fleischer, "Ḥadashot," 450.

24 In Biblical Hebrew, ארגמן (*argaman*) indicates a hue of purple bordering on violet. See *BDB*, 71, s.v. "ארגמן." If Ibn Mar Shaul is using the word in accordance with its biblical meaning, he thus intends that the beloved's hair is a hue of black so dark that it borders on purple. However, as Elizur notes (1:133), Ibn Mar Shaul's use of ארגמן (*argaman*) to indicate dark hair here strikes the student of Andalusian poetry as somewhat unusual. The medieval Hebrew dictionaries list the meaning of the word *argaman* as red, not dark brown/black/purple. See for example, Jonah ibn Janaḥ, *Sefer ha-Shorashim: hu ha-ḥeleq ha-sheni mi-maḥberet ha-diqduq* (Berlin: H. Itzkowski, 1896), 54, s.v. "argaman." The medieval poets more frequently use the word תכלת (*tekhelet*, violet-purple) to indicate dark hair; *argaman* appears in the poems as the color for lips and blushing cheeks (somewhat like crimson). See for example "לחיו כארגמן וכתכלת שערו"

(*leḥyo khe-argaman ve-khi-tekhelet se`aro*) in Moses ibn Ezra, *Shirei ha-Ḥol*, ed. Ḥaim Brody (Berlin: Schocken, 5695 [*c*. 1935]), 1:351 (הקדיר לבבי, *Hiqdir levavi*). Given this, we ought to picture the beloved here as light or red-haired. Indeed, Cole (*Dream of the Poem*, 28) renders the phrase: "his curly hair is crimson."

However, if so, the poem deviates from the poetic conventions of the period; although light hair eventually came into fashion, it did not enter the poetic corpus as a commonly used motif until the eleventh century. In fact, the eleventh-century Ibn Ḥazm launches a poetic and prose defense against those who criticize him for his attraction to light hair, an aesthetic preference still considered to have been an oddity or even a perversion of beauty in his day. Therefore, it strikes me as more likely that we are to envision the beloved here as bearing purpley-black dark hair that contrasts with a light face. In his translation, Raymond Scheindlin supports such a reading, translating ותלתליו כארגמן (*ve-taltalav ke-argaman*) as "Locks of Royal Blue." See his "A Miniature Anthology," 114. On the Spanish interpretation of biblical Hebrew words, see Elizur, 1:216–38; Norman Roth, "Seeing the Bible through a Poet's Eyes: Some Difficult Biblical Words Interpreted by Moses ibn Ezra," *Hebrew Studies* 23 (1982): 111–14. On the rise to popularity of light hair and examples of poems in which it appears in both Hebrew and Arabic, see Judah Halevi in Schirmann, *Ha-Shirah ha-`Ivrit be-Sefarad u-ve-Provans*, 1:438 and the English translation by Scheindlin in his *Wine, Women and Death*, 119; Abū Muḥammad `Alī ibn Ḥazm al-Andalusī, *Ṭauḳ al-ḥamâma*, ed. D. K. Pétrof (St. Pétersbourg-Leide: E. J. Brill, 1914), 77–80; English version: Nykl, trans., *A Book Containing the Risāla*, 38–41, and Arberry, trans., *The Ring of the Dove*, 60–4; Pérès, *La Poésie andalouse*, 402; Scheindlin, *Wine, Women and Death*, 118–21.

25 רקה פניניה (*raqah peniniyah*): Elizur explains this as a "red cheek" (1:131). She explains that in medieval Spain, the Hebrew word for pearl, פנינה (*peninah*) or פניניה (*peniniyah*), referred to both a white gem and a blazingly red gem (as in Lam. 4:7). Taking פניניה (*peniniyah*) here as red, and רקה (*raqah*) as cheek, she understands the description of the beloved as indicating light hair cascading over a reddish cheek. See Elizur, 1:222–6. Like Roth's translation above, Scheindlin's translation once again disagrees with Elizur. Reading רקה פניניה (*raqah peniniyah*) in accordance with the other meanings of both words, Scheindlin renders the phrase into English as "a brow of pearl." In other words, where Elizur sees light hair flowing over blushing red cheeks, Scheindlin sees dark hair tumbling over a white face. Roth's slightly more vague translation, "a shining temple," gives us little clue as to skin color but supports Scheindlin's contention that the body part under discussion here is the temple, rather than the cheek. An Arabic example in which pearl indicates whiteness rather than redness appears in a *ghazal* by Ibn `Abd Rabbihi (Cordoba, 860–940) which he recited in the presence of the great poet al-Mutanabbī (915–65): "... I never saw nor heard of a pearl like him / becoming a red coral by bashful blush." As cited by Monroe, "Hispano-Arabic Poetry During the Caliphate of Cordoba," 134–5, n. 28. The Arabic can be found in Yāqūt b. `Abdallāh al-Ḥamawī, *Kitāb irshād al-arīb ilā ma`rifat al-adīb*, ed. D. S. Margoliouth, Gibb Memorial Series (Leiden: E. J. Brill, 1909), 2:71. Cole, *The Dream of the Poem*, translates the full line as: "his curly hair is crimson against his cheeks of pearl," agreeing partially with both Elizur and Scheindlin.

Since the poetic conventions championed the bright whiteness of the face, and Ibn Mar Shaul earlier compared his beloved to the shining moon (l. 3a), I tend more toward Scheindlin's (and Roth's) reading here.

26 An in-depth discussion of this reference appears below.

27 I have here altered Roth's translation of 8a ("Because of him I have been left") to more accurately reflect the culpability of the beloved indicated by the Hebrew.

28 This line does not appear in Roth's translation, which relied on Schirmann's text. See above, n. 23.

29 Roth translated this as "that I not go down to hell." Since the "pit of destruction" (באר שחת, *be'er shaḥat*) is only part of hell, and since the Hebrew has לתחתיה (*le-taḥtiyah*, to its bottom), "its nethermost part" is more appropriate here.

30 Scholarly consensus notes that the Hebrew epithet for the male beloved צבי (*tzvi*, male gazelle) takes the place of the Arabic صبي (*ṣabī*, young boy), whose sound it imitates. The use of *tzvi* to refer to the boy beloved would likely not have sounded odd to the Hebrew ear, even to one unfamiliar with Arabic poetry and poetic motifs, because of a well-known verse in Song of Songs. In 2:9, we find "דּוֹמֶה דוֹדִי לִצְבִי" (*domeh dodi le-tzvi*), "my beloved resembles a male gazelle." Both "beloved" (*dod*) and "gazelle" (*tzvi*) are grammatically masculine nouns. As Wright and Rowson point out, the fawn "commonly symbolizes a prophetically beautiful male youth." See J. W. Wright, and Everett K. Rowson, eds, *Homoeroticism in Classical Arabic Literature* (New York: Columbia University Press, 1997), xiii. See also Allony, "Ha-Tzvi ve-ha-Gamal," 16–43; Elizur, 2:80–1.

31 Ladislav Drozdík takes this idea to an extreme, stating, "The Western image of the poet as a creative subject with deep emotional experience finds no parallel in classical Arabic poetry." See his "Erotic Imagery in Classical Arabic Poetry," *Asian and African Studies (Bratislava)* 6:1 (1997): 22. Dan Pagis more moderately wrote that the genre of love poetry hovered between the conventional and the personal as poets played with stock situations, characters, and descriptions to express particularized emotions. See his *Hebrew Poetry*, 48–54.

32 Scheindlin, "A Miniature Anthology," 106.

33 See nn. 24, 25 and Schippers, *Spanish Hebrew Poetry*, 176–8.

34 The Hebrew translates literally to "on top of a beautiful stature." One could argue (as I personally would be pleased to) that short is a height that is just as lovely as tall. Indeed, not all readers of the poem understood the line as speaking of the beloved's height, but of the loveliness of his body in general. Thus Scheindlin renders the phrase as "Atop a handsome form." Roth, however, reads this as height, presumably in line with the poetic topos that compares beloveds to tall palm trees.

35 In "Ibn Gabirol's Religious Poetry and Sufi Poetry," Scheindlin cites a poem that appears in a Ṣūfī collection of secular love poems. According to Scheindlin, Sarī al-Saqaṭī quotes an Arabic poem attributed to an unnamed woman who disbelieves her lover's claims of love: "When I claimed to love, she said, 'You lie!' / For if so, why do I see your limbs covered [with flesh]? / It's only love when your skin sticks to your gut, / When you are too deaf to answer when someone calls, / When you wither so that love leaves you nothing / but an eye with which to weep or confide." See *Sefarad* 54:1 (1994): 113–14. The Arabic can be found in Abū Naṣr `Abdāllah b. `Ali al-Sarrāj (d. 988), *Kitāb al-luma` fī al-taṣawwuf*, ed. R. A. Nicholson (Leiden: E. J. Brill, 1914), 251. Scheindlin notes that an anecdote cited by Abū al-Ṭayyib Muḥammad ibn Isḥāq al-Waššā attributes the poem to an unnamed woman, who addressed these verses to al-`Abbās b. al-Aḥnaf. See Scheindlin, fn. 11.

The cross-confessional strength of this trope and similarity in phrasing can be seen from even a quick comparison of the Arabic and Hebrew poems. For example, al-Mutanabbī (915–65, Kūfa) and Moses ibn Ezra write that they have grown so thin that others perceive their existence only when they speak. Similarly, Solomon ibn Gabirol writes that eyes cannot perceive his emaciated frame, only thoughts. Naṣr b. Aḥmad, aka al-Khubza'aruzzī (Basra, d. 938) and Judah ibn Shabbetay (b. *c.* 1188, Toledo or Burgos) both insist that they have withered away so much from love that if they fell into someone's eye, the person wouldn't even feel it (Ibn Shabbetay claims that not even an ant would feel it, if he fell into her eye). For the Arabic of Naṣr b. Ahmad, see Abū Hilāl al-`Askarī, *Dīwān al-ma`ānī* [The Book of Poetic Themes] (Cairo: Maktabat al-qudsī, 1352 H. [*c.* 1933], 272. For the Arabic of al-Mutanabbī and the Hebrew of Moses ibn Ezra, Solomon ibn Gabirol, and Judah ibn Shabbetay, see Pagis, *Shirat ha-Ḥol*, 109. For more on Naṣr b. Aḥmad, see *EI*[2], s.v. "Al-Khubza'aruzzī," by Charles Pellat (5:43), and for al-Mutanabbī, s.v. "Al-Mutanabbī," by R. Blachère and Charles Pellat (7:769–72). See also Ibn Gabirol, *Shirei ha-Ḥol*, 173–4. In his *Spanish Hebrew Poetry* (169–70), Schippers presents English translations of some of these and more Hebrew and Arabic poems in which the poet writes of wasting away for love. An example in Arabic and English from Ibn Quzmān of Cordoba (d. 1160) appears in Monroe, *Hispano-Arabic Poetry: A Student Anthology*, 274–5.

36 Medieval dictionaries understood the word שחת (*shaḥat*) to indicate the grave. See, for example, R. David Qimḥi, *Sefer ha-Shorashim* [*Radicum Liber sive Hebraeum Bibliorum Lexicon*], ed. Jo. H. R. Biesenthal and F. Lebrecht (Berolini, 1847; reprint Jerusalem, 1967), s.v. "שוח" (p. 375). Since the poem speaks of various levels of such a pit, I maintain that one ought to read the phrase באר שחת (*be'er shaḥat*) in keeping with its biblical usage. According to the Bible, the afterworld consists of more than one realm in the underground domain known as שאול, *she'ol*. One of these is called the "pit of destruction," באר שחת (*be'er shaḥat*). It appears that the further down one goes, the more dead one is or the worse it gets. The term באר שחת (*be'er shaḥat*) appears only once in the Bible, in Ps. 55:24.

37 *Qaṣīda* examples in which an appeal to or association with birds and desert animals stresses the speaker's mourning appear in Samuel ha-Nagid's *Diwan Shemuel ha-Nagid. Ben Tehillim*, ed. Dov Jarden (Jerusalem: Hebrew Union College, 5726 [1966]), #23 (כבודי מדאגה), line 13; #48 (הכל היום נסיעה), line 4; and in Moses ibn Ezra's *Shirei ha-Ḥol*, ed. Brody, 1:11 (#9, line 38). In one touching example by a poetess, the Granadan Jewish Qasmuna (twelfth century), writing in Arabic, appeals to and compares herself in her loneliness to a female gazelle grazing alone in a meadow. See Nichols, "The Arabic Verses of Qasmuna bint Isma'il ibn Bagdalah," 155–8.

38 Lev. 11:14, 16; Deut. 14:13, 15.

39 According to *BDB*, s.v. יען, this may have resulted from the name of the bird being derived from the Hebrew root יען (*y'an*), which indicates greed.

40 Mic. 1:8; Job 30:29; Isa. 13:21, 34:13.

41 *BDB* (s.v. אוה) suggests that the word איה (*aya*, hawk/falcon) probably derives from the onomatopoeic exclamation אוי (*oy*), a howling, which it presumably makes. This further supports my contention that Ibn Mar Shaul's choice of his bird-audience intends to conjure a desolate and grief-filled vision.

42 For more on *remez*, as well as the other category of biblical references in Hebrew Andalusian poetry, see Chapter 1, pp. 11ff.

43 According to the fifth-century *Midrash Tanḥuma*, Potiphar's wife's attraction to Joseph was not natural, but a punishment from God: When Joseph realized how high up in Potiphar's house he had reached, he began indulging in food and drink and curling his hair, and he thanked God for allowing him to forget his father's house. Seeing this, God said, "Your father mourns for you, wearing sackcloth and ashes and you are indulging in food, drink, and hair products? Because of this, your mistress will yearn to bed you and will afflict you." See *Midrash Tanḥuma* (Jerusalem: Levin-Epstein, 1979), *Vayeshev*, 8. A slightly different version of this *midrash* appears in the fifth-century *Genesis Rabbah*, 87:3. See *Midrash Rabbah Bereishit*, ed. J. Theodor and Ch. Albeck (Berlin, 1903–36; reprint, Jerusalem: Wahrmann, 1965). See also below, Chapter 7, n. 28.

44 See *Midrash Tanḥuma*, *Vayeshev* 8 and *Genesis Rabbah*, 87:3 (as in n. 43, above). Abraham ibn Ezra seems to be the only medieval commentator on the passage who notes the similarity of language used to describe both Rachel and Joseph. He does little with it, however, other than point it out, writing of Joseph's beauty only: "Like his mother." See the commentary of Abraham ibn Ezra on Gen. 39:11 in *Miqra'ot Gedolot: Bereishit* (Jerusalem: Mechon ha-Ma'or, 1990).

45 Women so described: Sarah (Gen. 12:11); Rachel (Gen. 29:17); Tamar, daughter of Absalom (2 Sam. 14:27); Esther (Esther 2:7); Abigail (1 Sam. 25:3); and the female captive of war (Deut. 21:11). A somewhat odd usage appears in Gen. 41:18 when Pharaoh recounts to Joseph his dream in which seven skinny cows ate seven healthy cows. He describes the healthy cows as "בְּרִיאוֹת בָּשָׂר וִיפֹת תֹּאַר" (*beriot basar ve-yefot to'ar*, healthy in flesh and good-looking). Perhaps since cows are female, this is not as odd a usage as it first appears.

46 The early biblical exegetes also picked up on the implication of feminine beauty in Goliath's words. According to *Leviticus Rabbah* 21:2 (fifth–sixth century), Goliath felt more than just contempt for David. R. Yudan suggests that Goliath's disparaging comments regarding David's beauty indicate that Goliath actually found himself attracted to the handsome shepherd and desired him. In *Midrash Vayiqra Rabbah*, ed. Mordecai Margulies (New York and Jerusalem: Jewish Theological Seminary of America, 1993), 2:470; also, *Midrasch Samuel*, ed. Solomon Buber (Krakau: 1893), 108 [21:1]. Fascinatingly, see also Henry E. Adams, Lester W. Wright, Jr., and Bethany A. Lohr, "Is Homophobia Associated with Homosexual Arousal?," *Journal of Abnormal Psychology* 105:3 (1996): 440–5. See also Chapter 4, n. 26.

47 In 1 Sam. 16:11, David's father refers to him as הַקָּטָן (*ha-qatan*), which could indicate both his position in the roster of his brothers as well as his size relative to them. According to *BDB* (s.v. קטן), the word *qatan* means small, young, or unimportant. It is not quite clear from the Bible which meaning Jesse intended in 1 Sam. 16:11. Although 1 Sam. 16 attributes to Jesse *eight* sons, with David "הַקָּטָן," seemingly the youngest, 1 Chron. 2:15 calls David the *seventh* son of Jesse, which would make him the next-to-last. Further perplexingly, the verse does not list or name an eighth. 1 Chron. 27:18 later refers to a man named Elihu as "David's brother" but that name appears in neither earlier listing. Some have therefore posited that Elihu was the youngest, while David was one older, the seventh, but smaller.

48 The entire phrase reads: "וְהוּא אַדְמוֹנִי עִם יְפֵה עֵינַיִם וְטוֹב רֹאִי" (*ve-hu admoni `im yefeh `einayim ve-tov ro'ee*). Somewhat misleadingly, *JPS* offers "He was ruddy-cheeked, bright-eyed and handsome." The Hebrew does not mention David's cheeks specifically as the source of redness and, in the case of Esau, the same epithet, אדמוני (*admoni*, reddish), clearly refers to his hair as well as his complexion (Gen. 25:25). *JPS* does note that the meaning of the Hebrew is uncertain here. See *The Hebrew Bible* (Philadelphia: Jewish Publication Society, 1917). Editorial commentary in *The New Oxford Annotated Bible* notes that אַדְמוֹנִי (*admoni*, "ruddy") in 1 Sam. 16:12 refers to both a reddish complexion and reddish hair, as in the Esau case. See Michael Coogan, ed., *The New Oxford Annotated Bible*, 3rd edn (Oxford: Oxford University Press, 2001). The fifth-century *Genesis Rabbah* 63:8 likewise understood David to have red hair; R. Abba bar Kahana says that David's hair was as red as if he had killed someone (i.e., he had stained himself with blood in so doing) and the prophet Samuel was therefore quite alarmed when he first laid eyes on him.

49 Praise of beautiful eyes does appear in Song of Songs 1:15 and 4:1, where we find the somewhat odd metaphor, "Behold you are beautiful, your eyes are like dove's eyes." This differs from the description used for David; while Song of Songs declares that the beloved is beautiful, the text of Samuel maintains that David's *eyes* are beautiful. Scholars have puzzled over the strange metaphor of a dove's eyes, which are not that fetching in reality. The editorial commentary on this verse in *The New Oxford Annotated Bible* explains the expression as a description not of a visual image, but of behavior/emotion, i.e., "bashful and full of desire." Why doves' eyes indicate bashfulness and lust, I do not know.

50 Both Arabic and Hebrew poems frequently refer to the dangerousness of the beloved's beautiful eyes, which spear and shoot arrows at the lover and the like. See Schippers, *Spanish Hebrew Poetry*, 153, 173–6. An example composed by Sa`d al-Dīn Muḥammad

(the son of the mystic Ibn al-`Arabī, 1165–1240) appears in Franz Rosenthal, "Male and Female: Described and Compared," in *Homoeroticism in Classical Arabic Literature*, ed. J. W. Wright and Everett K. Rowson (New York: Columbia University Press, 1997), 24–54. See also the homoerotic poem of the Muslim jurist and *ḥadīth* transmitter Abū al-Ḥusayn Sirāj b. `Abd al-Mālik b. Sirāj (Cordoba, d. 1114) in Abū al-Ḥasan `Alī b. Mūsā b. Sa`īd al-Andalusī, *Rāyāt al-mubarrizīn wa-ghāyāt al-mumayyazīn*, ed. Muḥammad Riḍwān al-Dāya (Dimashq: Dār Ṭalās, 1987), 128–9. An English translation can be found in Bellamy and Steiner, *Banners of the Champions*, 197. Al-Mu`tamid, the poetry-writing ruler of Seville (1040–95), wrote of a boy named Sayf (Sword), whose eyes cut like knives. See *Dīwān al-Mu`tamid ibn `Abbād*, ed. Badawī and al-Majīd, 67. Nykl includes a translation of this in his *Hispano-Arabic Poetry*, 143. According to Nykl, al-Mu`tamid received this boy as a gift from al-Ma`mūn of Toledo, sometime before 1075.

Peter Cole's translation of Ibn Mar Shaul's poem assigns the responsibility for the lover's death to his beloved's eyes in particular: "his eyes like Ben Yishai's / kill me like Uriah." See *Dream of the Poem*, 28 (lines 11–12).

51 See n. 24.

52 Allony points out that Schirmann did *not* think it so obvious. Instead, Schirmann understood the reference to Adonijah's hair as indicating the hair of the beard, which could have just as easily referred to Adonijah as Absalom (the beard status of neither one appears in the Bible). Allony disagreed with Schirmann, insisting that it was more likely that the entire poem referred to a beardless boy, the غلام امرد (*ghulām amrad*) so rampant in Arabic poetry. See Allony, "Ha-Tzvi ve-ha-Gamal," 35, and Schirmann, "The Ephebe," 59. I agree with Allony. After all, the previous two biblical allusions refer to Joseph and David in their *youthful* dewy beauty, presumably a stage in which the beard has yet to make an appearance. Additionally, beardedness was not a commonly celebrated poetic topos. The arrival of a boy's beard usually signaled the *end* of the boy's beauty and desirability. See Roth, "Fawn," 157; Rowson, "The Categorization of Gender," 58. Furthermore, of all the men in the Bible, why would Ibn Mar Shaul hold up Adonijah, whose facial hair status remains unknown, as the paragon of beautiful beardedness? The Bible singles out only one man as bearded: Aaron. Psalm 133:2 compares the beauty of brothers dwelling together to "the precious ointment upon the head, that runs down upon the beard, Aaron's beard, that runs down to the hem of his garments" ("כַּשֶּׁמֶן הַטּוֹב עַל הָרֹאשׁ יֹרֵד עַל הַזָּקָן זְקַן אַהֲרֹן שֶׁיֹּרֵד עַל פִּי מִדּוֹתָיו"). Interestingly, Aaron's beard appears in the Qur'ān as well, in 20:94.

53 See Schirmann, "Yitzḥaq ben Mar Sha'ul," 502; Roth, "Deal Gently," p. 31, n. 5. Against Ibn Janaḥ's instructions, Scheindlin switches to Absalom in his translation due to metrical concerns. See *Wine, Women and Death*, 186, fn. 16.

In theory, it is possible that Ibn Mar Shaul's use of Adonijah derived from a now-lost *midrash* or exegetical stream attempting to explain 1 Kgs. 1:5–6: "וַאֲדֹנִיָּה בֶן חַגִּית מִתְנַשֵּׂא לֵאמֹר אֲנִי אֶמְלֹךְ ... וְגַם הוּא טוֹב תֹּאַר מְאֹד וְאֹתוֹ יָלְדָה אַחֲרֵי אַבְשָׁלוֹם" (*ve-Adoniya ben Ḥaggit mitnase lemor ani emlokh ... ve-gam hu tov to'ar me'od ve-oto yalda aḥarei Avshalom*), "Now Adonijah the son of Ḥaggit exalted himself saying, 'I will be king,' ... and he [Adonijah] too was a very handsome man, and she gave birth to him after Absalom." Two problems are immediately apparent in these verses and call for explication. First, since the text here speaks only of Adonijah, why the use of the word וְגַם (*ve-gam*), "too" in v. 6? In addition to whom or to what? Second, Adonijah's mother is Ḥaggit, as mentioned in v. 5; Absalom is the son of Ma`acah (2 Sam. 3:3). Thus, "she," Ḥaggit, did *not* give birth to Adonijah after giving birth to Absalom, as the verses imply, but after *Ma`acah* (unmentioned here) gave birth to Absalom. In *BT Baba Batra* 109b, R. Jose bar Ḥanina provides an explanation for the strange formulation of verse 6: In rebelling against David, Adonijah mimicked Absalom's behavior, and thus the two brothers appear here together. R. David Qimḥi explains this a bit further, saying that the phrase "and he too was a very handsome man" intends to call to mind Absalom's beauty, which Adonijah resembled. In the cases of both brothers, their beauty made them prideful and led them to think they were fit to rule in their father's stead and rebel against him. See R. David Qimḥi, *Sefer Redak* (Lemberg: Pessel Balaban, 1878), on 1 Kgs. 1:6. Although Ibn Janaḥ makes no mention of any *midrash* or exegesis indicating that Adonijah's beauty resembled that of Absalom specifically regarding hair, one should not completely discount the possibility that Ibn Mar Shaul either knew of one or was constructing one here.

54 This was noted by the biblical text and characters as well. A more in-depth discussion of this biblical account follows.

55 That our lover feels himself blameless, undeserving of the treatment his brutal beloved has inflicted upon him, appears further on in the poem as well. In l. 10, he cries out in anguish, "The beloved of my soul has slain me – is this a just sentence?" The idea of an unjust death sentence once again recalls Uriah's death at David's hands.

56 Commenting on this poem, Ratzaby notes that, despite its Arabic flavor and imagery, the poem's use of biblical imagery makes it uniquely "Jewish." Interestingly, he then speaks only of the images used to describe the beloved's beauty (David, Adonijah, Joseph). Uriah appears as an allusion to the beloved's cruelty, and not his beauty; Ratzaby does not address the Uriah image. See Ratzaby, "Ha-Ahavah be-Shirat R. Shemuel ha-Nagid," 140–1.

57 The other oft-cited biblical "hint" to David's homosexual relationship with Jonathan appears in 1 Sam. 20, after King Saul, suspicious of the young musician-fighter whom his son so favors, threatens to put David to death. David and Jonathan decide that David must go into hiding, and at their parting, "they kissed each other and wept with each other; David wept the longer" (v. 41). Aside from these two verses, the biblical depictions of the emotional bond between the two men describe only Jonathan's feelings toward David. See 1 Sam. 18:1, 3; 1 Sam. 19:1; 1 Sam. 20:17; 1 Sam. 20:30–4 (Saul's suspicions). One MS version of *Pirkei Avot* (Ethics of Our Fathers) likewise attributes the lion's share of the emotion to Jonathan. There we read, "Every love which is dependent on something, when the thing ceases to exist, the love ceases to exist; and love which is not dependent on a thing, such a love never ceases to exist. What love is dependent on a thing? This is the love of Amnon for Tamar. And love which is not dependent on anything? This is the love of Jonathan for David." See *Mishna Codex Parma [De Rossi 138]* (Jerusalem: Kedem Publishers, 1970), 232. The "love of Amnon for Tamar" will be discussed in Chapter 6.

58 2 Sam. 23:8ff and 1 Chron. 11:10ff record thirty-seven "mighty men" (הַגִּבֹּרִים אֲשֶׁר לְדָוִד, *ha-gibborim asher le-David*), seemingly David's bravest fighters. The Bible does not include much detail about David's relationship or interactions with any one of them in particular.

59 The narrative voice of the Bible here notes this irony. 2 Sam. 11:1 writes, "At the turn of the year, the season when the *kings* go to battle, David sent Joab with his officers and all Israel with him and they devastated Ammon and besieged Rabbah; *but David* (וְדָוִד, *ve-David*) stayed in Jerusalem" (italics added). David's sexually self-indulgent behavior appears even more unseemly when one recalls that David's standing orders for his soldiers included prohibiting sexual congress while on campaign (1 Sam. 21:5–6).

60 According to the Bible, David had a total of eight named wives, a number of unnamed wives, and a number of concubines in a harem. Seven of the named wives (Michal, Aḥinoam, Abigail, Ma`acah, Ḥagit, Abital, and Eglah) married him either before or while he ruled in Ḥebron (2 Sam. 3:1–5; 1 Chron. 3:1–4; Michal appears in a detailed account in 1 Sam. 19; Abigail and Aḥinoam in a detailed account in 1 Sam. 25). The Bathsheba incident occurred after David moved his kingdom from Ḥebron to Jerusalem. When David married Bathsheba in 2 Sam. 11:27, she became the eighth of the named

wives. According to 2 Sam. 13:16, David married other women and amassed concubines during his Jerusalem period as well, though we do not know which of these, if any, predated the Bathsheba incident.

61 Indeed, in the somewhat similar case of Abigail the wife of Nabal, David waits till Nabal dies before making any overtures toward her. When he does so, it is with the honorable offer of marriage. See 1 Sam. 25.

62 Commentary in *The New Oxford Annotated Bible* on our verse refers the reader to similar usages in Isa. 6:2 and 7:20.

63 The exact number and order of the days as recorded in verses 12–13 are somewhat difficult to calculate. In the Hebrew it appears as if Uriah spends two days in Jerusalem and David invites him to dinner on the third day. The *JPS* translation follows this timeline. The *New Revised Standard Version* [*NRSV*] translation of the Bible understands the last word of v. 12, וּמִמָּחֳרָת (*u-mi-maḥorat*, "And on the next day") as leading off the sentence found in v. 13. Thus, the *NRSV* reads: "[v.12] ... So Uriah remained in Jerusalem that day. On the next day, [v. 13] David invited him to eat and drink ..." Thus, according to the *NRSV*, Uriah spent only one day "in Jerusalem" before returning to sleep in the servants' quarters. *The New Oxford Annotated Bible* uses the *NRSV* as its text.

64 Note that it is not only the word "Jerusalem" that repeats here. Verse 1 records "וְדָוִד יוֹשֵׁב בִּירוּשָׁלָֽם," *ve-David yoshev be-Yerushalayim* (and David remained [sat] in Jerusalem). Verse 12 uses the same verb to record "וַיֵּשֶׁב אוּרִיָּה בִירוּשָׁלַ֖ם," *va-yeshev Uriah be-Yerushalayim* (and Uriah remained [sat] in Jerusalem).

65 I intend here both meanings of the phrase "to sleep with."

66 לשכב עם (*lishkav` im*), or לשכב את (*lishkav et*) (as in Gen. 34:2) appears frequently in the Bible as the term for sexual congress. It is not, however, the only way to describe such an act in biblical Hebrew. The Bible also employs the slightly more visually explicit verb "לבוא אל" (*lavo el*, to come into, as in Gen. 38:2). Most euphemistically, we find the verb "to know," לדעת (*la-da`at*), as in Gen. 4:1. The frequent appearance of the root שכב (*shakhav*) and this root only in this account clearly indicates an intentional play on the word.

67 משכב (*mishkav)* literally translates to "a place of laying down" and hence translators have chosen the word "bed" or "couch" to describe where David got up from and where Uriah went down to when he finished his meal. I am not arguing with the translation. I do mean to point out that the biblical narrative insists on employing here the double-entendre that is משכב (*mishkav*) to describe the place where Uriah lay down to sleep or rest at David's, instead of a more neutral word. After all, biblical Hebrew utilizes other words for "to lie down" and for "bed/couch," that are not sexually charged. See for example the root לון (*lun*), as in Gen. 32:22; for מיטה (*mittah*, bed), see for example Gen. 47:31; for ספות (*sappot*, couches), see for example 2 Sam. 17:28. Significantly, none of these appears here.

68 Traditionally, translators have provided "abomination" for the word *to`evah.* What exactly the biblical Hebrew word means is not clear. The Bible considers a variety of things *to`evah.* Among them: the Egyptian perspective on Hebrews and Israelites breaking bread together (Gen. 43:32); idol worship (Deut. 17:26); a man remarrying his ex-wife after she has married and divorced another man (Deut. 24:4); eating certain animals (Deut. 14:3ff); the sacrifices of evil men (Prov. 21:27); and, not-commanded sacrifices (Isa. 1:13). Confusingly, translators have used "abomination" as the translation of other Hebrew words as well, such as שקץ (*sheqetz*) in Leviticus 11:11, etc.

69 Significantly, Hittites were a Canaanite people with whom the Israelites were commanded not to intermarry or strike covenants, as in Deut. 7:1–11 and 20:17. This sets an additional question mark over Bathsheba's marriage to Uriah, Bathsheba's identity, and David's permitting Uriah to serve in his army. At the same time, cordial interactions between the Israelites and Hittites go far back. Abraham buys the burial cave of

Machpela from Ephron the Hittite (Gen. 23:2); Esau marries three Hittite women, Judith, Basmat, and Ada (Gen. 26:4, 36:2); Rebecca tries to prevent Jacob from similar Hittite marital unions by sending him to her brother Laban (Gen. 27:46). In later years, the Hittites were known as a group of Canaanites whom the Israelites did not succeed in destroying completely during the conquest of the Land of Israel. In Solomon's time, they paid a levy of slave labor to Israel (1 Kgs. 9:20ff). Solomon himself took after his ancestral uncle Esau, as we see in 1 Kgs. 11:1 which reports that Solomon particularly loved "foreign" women, including Hittites. Interestingly, the Bible reports that among David's close companions, and possibly fighters, was another Hittite, Aḥimelech, mentioned in 1 Sam. 26:6 (but not mentioned in the listings of David's mighty men).

Interestingly, Uriah's Hittite designation appears in those segments of the narrative in which the narrator or other characters speak about him. When he himself acts or speaks, he appears as simply "Uriah."

70 Apparently puzzled by this same problem, R. David Qimḥi (Radaq, 1160–1235) writes, "It's possible that he was a convert, or an Israelite, and they called him 'Hittite' because he lived among the Children of Ḥet, as was the case with Itai the Gitti" (in 2 Sam. 15). Qimḥi avoids committing to this theory, however, preferring to let it remain in the realm of conjecture. See his *Sefer Redak*, 36 (on 2 Sam. 11:3). Others have suggested that Uriah was an Israelite, noting that the name "Uriah" is a Hebrew monotheistic name meaning "God is my light" or "God is light." Abraham Malamat discounts this, explaining that the biblical "Uriah" was simply the Hebraicized version of the Hittite "*ewir*" or "*ewar*," an epithet meaning "overlord," "ruler," or "king." Malamat thus suggests that Uriah may have been one of the pre-Davidic Hittite rulers of Jerusalem. See his "David and Uriah: The Consolidation of Power in Jerusalem by the Israelites," in *"An Experienced Scribe Who Neglects Nothing": Ancient Near Eastern Studies in Honor of Jacob Klein*, ed. Yitschak Sefati *et al.* (Bethesda, MD: CDL Press, 2005), 742–5. Uriah (Yong-Hwan) Kim supports the notion of Uriah's non-Israelite identity by pointing out that the text identifies Bathsheba not only as the wife of Uriah, but also as the daughter of Eliam, presumably the son of Aḥitophel, an Israelite "mighty man" (in 2 Sam. 23:34). That her Israelite father's name appears here as well, he notes, emphasizes the non-Israelite status of her husband. See his "Uriah the Hittite: A (Con)Text of Struggle for Identity," *Semeia* 90–1 (2002): 69–85. J. D'ror Chankin-Gould *et al.* disagree, maintaining that the name Aḥitophel is *not* an Israelite name; the insertion of the ending *tophel* ("insignificant"), like *boshet* ("shame"), was the book of Samuel's editor's attempt at excising pagan names from the text. Bathsheba's father's name, they claim, was likely Aḥiba`al (My brother is Ba`al), and hence he too was not an Israelite. See J. D'ror Chankin-Gould, Derek Hutchinson, David Hilton Jackson, Tyler D. Mayfield, Leah Rediger Schulte, Tammi J. Schneider, and E. Winkelman, "The Sanctified 'Adulteress' and her Circumstantial Clause: Bathsheba's Bath and Self-Consecration in 2 Samuel 11," *Journal for the Study of the Old Testament* 32:2 (March 2008): 339–52.

71 2 Sam. 23:8ff and 1 Chron. 11:41.

72 2 Sam. 11:3; 2 Sam. 12:10, 15.

73 1 Chronicles 3:5 lists her name as "Bat-Shu`a (בַּת-שׁוּעַ) the daughter of Ammiel." 2 Samuel 12 records the mother of Solomon as "Bathsheba the daughter of Eliam" (who we know from earlier in the chapter is the one-time wife of Uriah the Hittite). Scholars attribute the difference in name to variant textual spellings and maintain that this is in fact the same woman.

74 Interestingly, the Qur'ān also omits this episode entirely. The only hint to the Uriah–Bathsheba account appears in Q 38:22–6, a retelling of the prophet Nathan's parable of the sheep (in 2 Sam. 12). In the Qur'ān, the parable appears completely devoid of context, with no mention of Nathan. It appears as an actual event that took place rather

than as a pedagogic parable. Since prophets in Islam are understood to be sinless, the omission of David's adultery does not strike us as surprising. Indeed, the twelfth-century Baghdadi preacher Ibn al-Jawzī uses this "ridiculous" Bible story as "proof" that the Israelite traditions are unreliable. See Marc S. Bernstein, *Stories of Joseph: Narrative Migration between Judaism and Islam* (Detroit: Wayne State University, 2006), 37; Hava Lazarus-Yafeh, "Self-Criticism in Jewish and Islamic Traditions," in *Judaism and Islam: Boundaries, Communication and Interaction*, ed. B. H. Hary, J. L. Hayes, and F. Astren (Leiden: E. J. Brill, 2000), 308.

Although the episode is absent from the Qur'ān, it reappears in the Islamic exegetical texts. See below, n. 79.

75 According to the Tosafists (medieval commentators on the Talmud), the medieval scholars disagreed as to the precise act of treason. While Rashi (R. Solomon Yitzḥaqi, 1040–1105) maintains that Uriah treasonously refused David's order to go home, Rashi's son-in-law, R. Meir, determined that Uriah's disloyalty lay in his referring to Joab as "his master" while standing before the king. Rashi's grandson, R. Tam, hung Uriah's treason on an ever slighter slight, attributing it to Uriah's having mentioned Joab's name before King David's while speaking to David. See the Tosafot commentary on *BT Shabbat* 56a and *BT Qiddushin* 43a. Eliezer Segal maintains that understanding even trivial disrespect of the throne as treason appears to have been a uniquely Babylonian stance. See Eliezer Segal, *The Babylonian Esther Midrash: A Critical Commentary* (Atlanta: Scholars Press, 1994), 2:193ff.

76 See also *BT Ketubbot* 9a–b and *BT Baba Metzia* 59a. See the *mishnah* in *BT Gittin* 72a ff on exactly such a conditional divorce and the Talmudic commentary to it.

77 These legal contortions attempted to solve difficulties that ensue from the fact that in Jewish law a man divorces but a woman is divorced. If a man disappears, and there is no witness or evidence proving he has died, the woman is considered still married to him (an *agunah*, a "chained" woman). She may not remarry, for her husband might reappear one day, an event that would render the remarried woman and her new husband adulterers and any children produced from their union to be bastards. R. Nathan's retroactive-divorce solution attempts to solve for this. But the retroactivity is legally problematic: While her husband is alive but away, is the woman divorced or married? David takes advantage of this loophole. A variant, with the same ultimate point regarding treason as a capital crime, appears in *Genesis Rabbah* 32:1.

78 The later Spanish kabbalist Joseph ibn Abraham Gikatilla (1248–1325) expands upon this interpretation, teaching that David ought to have married Bathsheba before Uriah did, since she was David's true "soul mate." However, David did not deserve her at the earlier date because his evil inclination was too strong and drove him to commit blameworthy acts. Since the evil inclination was introduced into humanity through the sin of Adam and Eve, David's inability to marry Bathsheba straightaway was a direct result of that event. Ibn Gikatilla connects the two accounts further by noting that part of Adam's sin was that he ate the fruit of Eden before it was ripe, before the third year after which fruits are permitted (known as *`orlah*, the "foreskin" years, in Lev. 19:23). Similarly, David consummated his relationship with Bathsheba while she was not yet permitted to him, in the realm of the foreskin (*reshut ha-`orlah*), still married to Uriah (who, as a non-Israelite, possibly had a foreskin himself). In killing Uriah and marrying Bathsheba, David attempted to remove the Uriah barrier and theurgically repent for Adam's sin by reuniting with his other half and thus reuniting *Malkhut* and *Yesod*, the two Sefirot (mystical emanations of God's personality) that had been torn apart by Adam's sin. For Ibn Gikatillah's Hebrew text, English translation, and commentary, see Charles Mopsik, *Sex of the Soul: The Vicissitudes of Sexual Differences in the Kabbalah* (Los Angeles: Cherub Press, 2005), ch. 7.

79 The text of 2 Sam. 11 does not conceal David's actions from its readers. Similarly, 2 Sam. 12 hides neither God's nor Nathan's subsequent displeasure nor God's punishment of

David. 1 Kgs. 15:5 records explicitly, "David did what was right in the sight of the Lord, and did not turn aside from anything that He commanded him all the days of his life, except in the matter of Uriah the Hittite."

Although not the subject of the current work, this raises an interesting question. If the biblical text is so clear (and it is) and God too blames David (and He does), why *do* the classical rabbinic texts work so hard to redeem David from his sins in this episode? Sandra Shimoff discusses this matter at length in her "David and Bathsheba: The Political Function of Rabbinic Aggadah," *Journal for the Study of Judaism* 24:2 (1993): 246–56.

80 See *EJ*, s.v. "Provence," by Bernhard Blumenkranz and Alexander Shapiro (16:636–9).

81 See this discussion above, pp. 65–6.

82 See Qimḥi, *Sefer Redak* on those verses.

83 See *EJ*, s.v. "Abrabanel, Isaac ben Judah," by Tzvi Avineri *et al.* (1:276–9).

84 In support of this point, that the act was made even worse because Uriah served under David, Abrabanel writes, "After all, you have seen what went on in Spain in the days of Don Rodrigo [Roderic, the last Visigothic king of Spain, d. 711 or 712], when because he slept with the daughter of the chief Giuliano [Julian, a count or vassal under Roderic] who sat in Sivta [Ceuta], [he] brought all the Ishmaelites from across the sea and they took and conquered all of Spain, as revenge against that king who bedded his daughter." This idea that the Muslim conquest of Spain resulted from a fight between Roderic and Julian dates back to Ibn `Abd al-Ḥakam's ninth-century history *Futuḥ Miṣr wa-al-maghreb wa-al-Andalus.* See John Harris Jones, ed. and trans., *Ibn Abd-el-Hakem's History of the Conquest of Spain* (Göttingen: W. F. Kaestner, 1858), 18–22, Arabic 1–2. The Arabic lists Roderic's name as Ladrīq and Julian as Balyān. These appear to be orthographic errors, which Jones transcribes in English as Roderic and Julian.

85 Don Isaac Abrabanel, *Perush `al Nevi'im Rishonim* (Jerusalem: Hotza'at Sefarim Torah ve-Da`at, 5715 [1955]), on 2 Sam. 11. Note his play on the word פשוט (*pashut*, simple) to indicate the superiority of the *peshat* approach over that of *derash.*

86 For more on Ibn Ezra and his methodology, see *EJ*, s.v. "Ibn Ezra, Abraham ben Meir," by Uriel Simon and Raphael Jospe (9:665–72); Uriel Simon, "Interpreting the Interpreter," in *Rabbi Abraham ibn Ezra: Studies in the Writings of a Twelfth Century Polymath*, ed. Isadore Twersky and Jay Harris (Cambridge, MA: Harvard University Center for Jewish Studies, 1993), 281–96; and idem, "R. Avraham Ibn Ezra—Bein ha-Mefaresh le-Qor'av," in *Proceedings of the Ninth World Congress of Jewish Studies. Panel Sessions: Bible Studies and the Ancient Near East* (Jerusalem: Magnes Press, 1988), 23–42.

87 Ibn Ezra points to claims of piety in Psalms 16:10 and 86:2.

88 Jewish tradition has long understood the Psalms to have been composed by King David, the musician-king. For more on this, see *EJ*, "Psalms, Book of," by Nahum Sarna, Louis Isaac Rabinowitz, Godfrey Edmond Silverman, Bathja Bayer, and Avigdor Herzog (16:663–83).

89 See Ibn Ezra's commentary in *Miqra'ot Gedolot. Sefer Tehillim* (Jerusalem: Miqra'ot Gedolot Yerushalayim-Lublin, 1963), Psalm 51:2.

90 Ibn Ezra's claim is bolstered by noting that the idea that David deserved the death penalty for Uriah's killing makes no appearance in 2 Sam. 11–12. Interestingly, Ibn Ezra does not understand that David committed adultery with Bathsheba. Commenting on Ps. 51:2, Ibn Ezra writes, "I have already explained regarding the matter of Bathsheba, that she was not truly a married woman." I have been unable to find any evidence of the existence of such an explanation in Ibn Ezra's extant commentaries. His commentary on 2 Sam. itself either never existed or did not survive to modernity; we therefore have no way of pinpointing Ibn Ezra's reasoning on the matter. In his modern commentary to 2 Sam., Yaaqov Medan offers an interpretation that may reflect

Ibn Ezra's thought. Medan suggests that Uriah's refusal to go home might be seen as proof of the fact that he had divorced his wife. David called him home from battle precisely in order to see if the separation of the couple was complete. When Uriah refused to go home, David had his answer. Medan also notes that Nathan's later accusation against David (2 Sam. 12:9) does not charge him with adultery but with marrying Uriah's wife after arranging for Uriah's death. If David *had* committed adultery with Bathsheba, maintains Medan, the two would not subsequently have been permitted to marry one another (*BT Sotah* 27b–28a forbids an adulterous woman from subsequently marrying her partner in crime). That they did marry suggests that Uriah had divorced Bathsheba earlier. See Medan, *David u-Vat-Sheva': ha-ḥeṭ ha-'onesh veha-tiḳun* (Alon Shevut: Yeshivat Har-`Etzyon, 5762 [2001/2]), 16. Medan's reading of Nathan's accusation strikes me as somewhat forced. Nathan's words could also be understood as castigating David for exactly this: bedding Bathsheba while she was married to another and then marrying her, a violation of the law on two counts. After all, marrying a widow whose widowhood you have arranged may be bad behavior but it does not violate biblical or Jewish law.

91 We recall here that Ibn Mar Shaul ceased reciting a bedtime Psalm when he realized he could not parse the meaning of one of its words.

3 The gazelle and the golden calf: reading the footprints in the sand

If Uriah seems an unlikely hero to make an appearance as a biblical referent in a secular Hebrew love poem, an even more unlikely scriptural hero appears in an Arabic love poem of roughly the same period. In verses extolling the wondrous nature of a particular male beloved, the Muslim jurist-poet Abū Muḥammad `Ali b. Muḥammad b. Sa`id b. Ḥazm al-Andalusī equates the besotted lover to a mysterious Qur'ānic character named al-Sāmirī.

Like Ibn Mar Shaul's use of Uriah, Ibn Ḥazm's use of al-Sāmirī in his love poem ranks as highly unusual. Neither the biblical Uriah nor the Qur'ānic al-Sāmirī is traditionally linked with romance, love, or even with any close relationships with other people. Indeed, as with the biblical Uriah, al-Sāmirī plays a relatively minor role in the narrative of the Qur'ān.[1] Additionally, just as the Bible reveals little about David's soldier, the Qur'ān does not tell readers much about al-Sāmirī – from where he hails, what his nationality is, how he reached his position, or the source of his motivation. What we do know about this mysterious Qur'ānic character makes the comparison between him and a lover in a poem by a jurist-poet even more startling: according to Muslim tradition, al-Sāmirī created the golden calf and led the Israelites astray from their worship of God and into the heinous sin of idolatry.

Like Ibn Mar Shaul's Uriah poem, Ibn Ḥazm's al-Sāmirī poem sends his readers a message that strikes deeper than the surface of the work. However, Ibn Ḥāzm's incorporation of Scripture differs in one very significant way. Ibn Mar Shaul appears to use his secular love poem as a surprising site for a new and somewhat subversive reading of a sacred text. Ibn Ḥazm, by contrast, uses the sacred text in his poem to teach readers a somewhat subversive lesson about secular love.

On Ibn Ḥazm

Given the intellectual and cultural fertility of medieval Islamic Spain, it should not surprise us that one of the most prominent love poets of tenth- to eleventh-century Andalusia was also one of the outstanding Muslim theologians of his day, Abū Muḥammad `Alī b. Aḥmad b. Ḥazm (994–1064). Born in the city of Cordoba to a wealthy and learned family, Ibn Ḥazm was trained in all the arts important to a well-educated medieval Spanish Muslim. He studied not only

Arabic grammar, literature, lexicography, and rhetoric, but also *ḥadīth*, theology, and *fiqh* (Islamic jurisprudence).[2] As a result, Ibn Ḥazm grew to be an illustrious theologian, educator, Muslim legal authority, and poet. He wrote treatises on Islamic law, on *ḥadīth*, and even on other religious traditions, though the latter were mostly attacks against these faiths.[3] Though he had been raised in the Medinian-centered Mālikī school of Islamic law, the dominant school of Spanish Islam, Ibn Ḥazm adopted the more text-emphasizing Shāfi'īsm for a while.[4] Ultimately he rejected Shāfi'īsm as well, joining the more recently founded Ẓāhirī school, one which emphasized focusing on the manifest, non-esoteric, meaning of the Qur'ān. Eventually, Ibn Ḥazm rose to become the head of the Andalusian Ẓāhirī school and one of the foremost Ẓāhirī theologians of his age.[5]

Sometime between the ages of 26 and 30, Ibn Ḥazm composed the work for which he is most well known in the modern era, a thirty-chapter treatise on human love known as *Ṭawq al-ḥamāma, The Dove's Neck-Ring*. In this work, which combines poetry and prose, Ibn Ḥazm discusses the nature, causes, and root principles of love, the blameworthy and praiseworthy aspects of love and of the behaviors in which lovers engage, and the misfortunes that sometimes befall lovers. Ibn Ḥazm considered himself particularly qualified to write such a treatise, not only because of his strong intellectual and religious education. Rather, having been raised till the age of 14 in the women's quarters of his family home, he recognized that he had become quite familiar with the ins and outs of women's society and with their inner lives. Significantly, he attributed to these women his grounding in the fields of Qur'ān, poetry, and composition – all important elements for a theologian-poet.[6]

Interestingly, while Ibn Ḥazm remains one of the foremost Andalusian love theorists, and the *Ṭawq* one of the foremost Andalusian works on love, the original idea to compose such a work did not come from Ibn Ḥazm himself. Nor was its undertaking solely an intellectual exercise. Ibn Ḥazm writes that he began composing the *Ṭawq* at the request of a friend,[7] a request that coincided with a particularly dark period in Ibn Ḥazm's life. The Umayyad government in Cordoba, with whom Ibn Ḥazm had sided against the `Āmirids, had been overthrown in 1021. As Ibn Ḥazm relates on the final page of the treatise, his friend's appeal to write a work on love found him forcibly removed from his home, exiled from his homeland, and depleted of his riches. He agreed to the literary request partially to divert himself from his own heartache.[8] After all, notes Ibn Ḥazm, there is a *ḥadīth* that recommends that people whose hearts are overcome with grief distract themselves in things that may appear vain.[9] To any who, despite this teaching, may still accuse him of having written something too frivolous, or contrary to his religious views and correct religious practice, he assures them that he has done nothing untoward and inappropriate.[10]

Poem

Among the most defining and pleasing characteristics of Ibn Ḥazm's *Ṭawq* is that he illustrates his philosophical claims regarding love with poems that he himself wrote. Many of these compositions are beautiful, witty, and well-crafted works of art, pieces that home in on human psychology and behavior with an emotional intelligence of a man far older and more experienced than Ibn Ḥazm was at the *Ṭawq*'s composition. Importantly for the casual reader and the scholar alike, Ibn Ḥazm accompanies the poems in the *Ṭawq* with an explanation of what specific personal circumstances (when relevant) led him to compose it.

For the most part, Ibn Ḥazm's poems in the *Ṭawq* do not vary widely from the tropes of love poetry.[11] Indeed, his treatise and its supporting poetry set the very standard for many of the secular-love motifs. In some poems, however, Ibn Ḥazm deviates from the accepted poetic tropes and does so in quite unexpected ways. In these, our theologian and jurist-poet nonchalantly yet somewhat sacrilegiously compares the very profane love of one human for another to an episode or to characters in the sacred Qur'ān.

One particularly puzzling and Qur'ānically oriented poem of this type appears in Ibn Ḥazm's section in the *Ṭawq* entitled "On Contentment" (القنوع, *al-qunū*'). In this chapter, Ibn Ḥazm sensitively notes that when circumstances prevent lovers from physical proximity with one another, they often search for some item belonging to the missing dear one. Proximity to some element that once belonged to the beloved brings temporary comfort to the lonely sufferer. "To comport oneself thus," explains Ibn Ḥazm, "distracts the soul, occupies one's hopes, renews one's aspirations, and provides a certain measure of relief."[12] In support of this observation, Ibn Ḥazm refers to an actual case in which such a thing occurred. A friend told him, he relates, that the poet Sulaymān b. Aḥmad knew a man by the name of Ibn Sahl al-Ḥājib,[13] a man of supreme physical handsomeness. Sulaymān b. Aḥmad reported that he crossed paths with this Ibn Sahl a number of times in Sicily. One such time, he watched as the lovely Ibn Sahl crossed through a garden, followed, unbeknownst to him, by the intense gaze of a woman. After Ibn Sahl had gone far enough away, the woman followed in his just-abandoned footsteps, stopping at each one to kiss the imprint left behind.

Inspired by the image of the woman who bent forward to "kiss and caress the earth in which there was the trace of his feet,"[14] Ibn Ḥazm composed a poem:[15]

يلمونني في موطئ خفّه جفّا ولو علموا عاد الذى لام يحسد
فيأهل أرض لا تجود سحابها خذوا بوصاتي تستقلوا وتحمدوا
خذوا من تراب فيه موضع وطئه وأضمن أنّ المحل عنكم يبعّد
فكلّ تراب واكع فيه رجله فذاك صعيد طيّب ليس يجحد
كذلك فعل السامري وقد بدا لعينيه من جبريل أثر ممجّد
فصيّر جوف العجل من ذلك الثرى فقام له منه خوار ممدّد

According to Nykl's English translation:[16]

[1a] They criticize me harshly[17] on account of the traces of his feet:
[1b] If they knew, the one who blamed me would become envious of me!
[2a] Oh people of the land where the clouds are not liberal with water,
[2b] Take my advice and you will become free, and you will be thankful:

[3a] Take some of the dust on which his footprints are impressed,
[3b] And I guarantee that drought will be far removed from you,
[4a] For every bit of dust upon which his foot has tread
[4b] Is good soil, it cannot be denied!

[5a] Thus did the Sāmirī when there appeared
[5b] To his eyes the glorious footprint of Gabriel,
[6a] And he put some of that earth inside the calf,
[6b] And there came from him out of it a prolonged bleating.

Ibn Ḥazm then adds an additional stanza, preceded by the introductory phrase "And I say." Here the poet turns to the beloved himself, proclaiming:

لقد بوركت أرضٌ بها انت قاطنٌ   وبورك من فيها وحلّ بها السعد
فأحجارها درٌّ وسعدانها وردٌ   وأمواهها شهدٌ وتربتها ندٌّ

[7a] Blessed is the land in which you are dwelling,
[7b] And blessed are those who dwell in it, and happiness has descended upon it!
[8a] Hence its stones are pearls, and its thistles roses,
[8b] And its waters are honey, and its dust ambergris!

Tropes

In all its basic conventions, this poem differs little from the motifs expected of Andalusian love poems.[18] Despite any connection to reality or to actual people, love poems were rarely personalized compositions in which the beloved and lover appeared as identifiable individuals.[19] Instead, both appeared as prototypes. Scheindlin has noted that love receives poetic form in Andalusia "on behalf of a communal ideal," not because of individual experience.[20] Poetic conventions of language, structure, and motif dominated classical Arabic love poetry.

In line with these conventions, Ibn Ḥazm presents a completely unidentifiable beloved. On the most basic level, Ibn Ḥazm's beloved remains unnamed. From the very first line and throughout the poem, we find only the pronoun "he" to refer to the beloved.[21] What's more, the mooning narrator mentions neither his dear one's age nor status in life, his likes, his dislikes, personality quirks, nor any of his behaviors. We do not know if the beloved is sarcastic or gentle, miserly or giving, kind or cruel. In truth, we know so little personal data about the youth that we cannot understand *why* the lover has fallen under the spell of this particular beloved, only that he has. In this, Ibn Ḥazm's poem reflects the poetic standard of his age.

Although we ought not to be surprised by the namelessness of Ibn Ḥazm's beloved, Ibn Ḥazm's omission of any further identifying marks does prove somewhat puzzling. *`Ishq* poems frequently described the beloved's physical appearance, in much detail and using stereotypical imagery. However, we find none of this in Ibn Ḥazm's poem; instead it remains devoid of the expected formulaic depictions of the beloved's beauty. We hear nothing of the light of his face against the darkness of his hair, of the slenderness of his fingers and the slimness of his hips. We cannot picture the rosy blush of his cheeks or his enchanting eyes as they capture and subdue the lover.[22]

We soon realize, however, that Ibn Ḥazm purposely omitted these motifs because the beloved's beauty was of little concern here. Instead, the poem focuses on yet another major poetic trope: the yearning of the separated lovers for one another and the effect of such longing on the lover.[23] Andalusian love poems, after all, were based on the earlier `Udhrite ideal of the separated lovers suffering from unactualized love.[24] For the Andalusians, a fulfilled relationship provided little meat for a poem. Instead, love poems speak of mythic loves that once were but will not be again, or of almost-but-not-actually realized moments of union. In such situations, the separation leaves the lover craving some sort of closeness to the beloved.[25] It is this theme of separation and yearning that takes center-stage in Ibn Ḥazm's poem. So strong beats this yearning within our lover that he turns to substitutes with which to comfort himself. Unable, it seems, to locate a more classic item, such as a piece of clothing, lock of hair, used toothpick, or even already-chewed gum belonging to his beloved,[26] the lover finds himself reduced to following in the beloved's now empty footsteps, gathering up the dirt that had once come into contact with his glorious feet.[27] Indeed, this separation and the reaction it causes the lover (i.e., his seeking contentment) is the very cause for the poem's composition. It is not surprising then that it plays such a central role, almost to the exclusion of all else, in our poem.

While the lover's dirt-gathering may seem excessive, such behavior fits well with the trope of lovesickness or love-madness. Andalusian love-poets believed that true passionate love caused the frustrated lover to suffer both physical and mental imbalances. In this they followed the literary scholar and Mu`tazilī theologian al-Jāḥiẓ (d. 869). In his *Risāla fī al-`ishq wa-al-nisā'* ("Essay on Passionate Love and on Women"), al-Jāḥiẓ wrote, "*`Ishq* (passionate love) is that which causes a man to wander aimlessly about in a rapture, or die heartsick upon his bed."[28] Of these two options, Ibn Ḥazm's lover here demonstrates the former reaction. He wanders about the world, enraptured, gathering up dirt only because it once came into contact with the bottoms of the feet of one with whom he was enthralled.[29]

Another typical poetic element appears in the reaction of the lover's companions to his dust-gathering behavior. Wine and love poetry often made use of an audience of *nadīm*s, friends or drinking companions, to whom the poet turned for advice or support. Often, the lover received an undesired and opposite reaction from them. Frequently, these friends simply irritated the lover with their "continuous harping," as Raymond Scheindlin phrases it, on his improper and dangerous conduct.[30] We find here, as expected, that the lover's friends do not stand idly by as the lover describes and reacts to his new infatuation. Rather, they inject themselves into the scene to criticize him and attempt thereby to dissuade the lover from his self-destructive path (l. 1a). From their perspective, after all, they see a formerly sane man following along, loonily, in empty footsteps where someone has already passed and is no more. They reproach and criticize him strongly, not only for having succumbed to such a state, it seems, but also for continuing to revel in his love-induced illness.[31] Thus, his continuing in this plagued state becomes, to his friends, an act of willful stupidity and insanity from which they unsuccessfully attempt to dissuade him.

The lover's claim that his friends' criticism would disappear if only they had seen his beloved for themselves (l. 1b) may have also been a poetic trope. We find a similar claim in a Hebrew poem by the slightly later Judah al-Ḥarizi (*c.* 1166–1225).[32] In his *Taḥkemoni*, al-Ḥarizi includes a poem which he attributes to an unnamed Babylonian man (איש מבני עדינה, *ish mi-bnei `Adina*) who, he explains, wrote a poem full of impurity and lust. According to al-Ḥarizi, the man wrote:

If only the son of Amram had seen my beloved's face,	לו שר בנו-עמרם פני דודי
Flushed from having drunk wine,	מתאדמים העת שתות שכר
And the beauty of his curls, and the glory of his handsomeness,	ויפי קוצותיו והוד יפיו
He would not have ruled in his Torah: "and with a male."[33]	לא חק בתורתו "ואת זכר."[34]

Like Ibn Ḥazm's lover who declared his lover magical and possessing superhuman powers of soil rejuvenation (ll. 3–4), al-Ḥarizi's perverse Babylonian "poet" insists that his male beloved too stands head and shoulders above all others – though here the beloved's magnificent quality rests clearly in his looks. Like Ibn Ḥazm's narrator-lover, al-Ḥarizi's "Babylonian" appeals to an external (though imagined) audience; he insists that even Moses ("the son of Amram") would have fallen under his beloved's spell, had he only seen this male beauty for himself. Had that occurred, writes the Babylonian, Moses certainly would never have included in the Bible the Leviticus 18:22 injunction against sexual activity between two males, "Do not lie with a man as one lies with a woman; that is detestable."[35] So, too, Ibn Ḥazm's lover insists that if his critical friends had known his beloved for themselves, they would cease their criticism and envy him his passion instead (l. 1a–b).

Even the appearance of a male beloved in a poem by as pious a religious authority figure as Ibn Ḥazm is almost to be expected. In the first place, Arabic poetry was rife with expressions of male–male physical love.[36] In some cases, scholars suggest, poets utilized male pronouns to protect a female beloved, about whom it would have been considered "indiscreet" to compose such passionate verse.[37] Others have suggested that the use of the male pronoun served to neuter the players, and thereby the poem; in so doing, poets emphasized not actual, personal love between two people, but love as a de-gendered idea and ideal.[38] In the vast majority of situations, however, as scholars have noted, this was not the case; a male pronoun, especially in Arabic poetry, indicated a male beloved.

Ibn Ḥazm's use of the motif of the male beloved, an acceptable and widespread trope, thus fits well with the conventions of the day. Indeed, as Louis Crompton explains, Ibn Ḥazm makes no distinction between heterosexual and homosexual love in the *Ṭawq*. Rather, he sees love as an inborn disposition that one cannot control. For Ibn Ḥazm, all love is psychologically the same, no matter the status or gender of either partner. In this, Ibn Ḥazm departs from the Aristotelian Greek concept of love, which describes male–male love and male–female love as two different, though related, phenomena. Ibn Ḥazm, says Crompton, seems oblivious to any distinction,[39] and we see one clear example of this tendency here.[40]

The trope that doesn't fit:

The lover as al-Sāmirī

But all is not as well as it seems in our poem. In the final stanza we find an unusual and atypical element; here Ibn Ḥazm shockingly compares his infatuated lover to the Qur'ānic character al-Sāmirī. More startlingly, in so doing he compares his male beloved to the archangel Jibrīl (Gabriel). In explaining the lover's seemingly bizarre instructions to his audience to gather the dust of his beloved's footprints, Ibn Ḥazm's lover declares, "Thus did the Sāmirī when there appeared / to his eyes the glorious footprint of Gabriel, / and he put some of that earth inside the calf, / and there came from him out of it a prolonged bleating" (ll. 5–6). This usage of the holy Qur'ān in a secular love poem strikes us as wholly out of sync with secular love motifs. After all, Andalusian Arabic poets were largely "representatives" of the secular world, the natural foils for the pious men who served as religious functionaries in society.[41] Their secular poetry often lauded values that formed the very antithesis of those championed both in the Qur'ān and by the religious authorities, most prominent among them the joys of wine-drinking and sexual embrace with both boys and girls. As a jurist, Ibn Ḥazm's adoption of this secular motif might seem surprising on its own; his subsequent utilization of a Qur'ānic image in support of his quite irreligious subject strikes the reader as even more outrageous. And when we understand better the precise nature of the sacred account so utilized, our bewilderment becomes compounded.

Al-Sāmirī in the Qur'ān

The character of al-Sāmirī and the incident to which Ibn Ḥazm's poem refers in lines 9–12 will ring familiar to any reader with a grounding in the Qur'ān and in pre-Islamic Muslim sacred history.[42] According to Q 20:80–97, soon after the release of the Children of Israel from their slavery in Egypt, Mūsā (Moses) goes up a mountain to speak with Allāh. While there, Allāh informs him that He has tested the Children of Israel in Mūsā's absence and found them lacking; says Allāh, they have allowed themselves to be led astray by a character identified as "al-Sāmirī" (v. 85). Mūsā angrily hurries back down the mountain, demanding of his people an explanation for such disloyalty to both himself and Allāh (v. 86). The Children of Israel demur at first, claiming they have broken no promises, but then they explain: They were unable to carry the weight of all the ornaments they had been carrying[43] and so they threw them into the fire as al-Sāmirī had suggested. They explain further that al-Sāmirī then brought out of the fire a calf (made of the metals), which began to low, and he (al-Sāmirī) declared:[44] "This is your God and the God of Moses!"[45] Hearing this, Mūsā turns to interrogate his brother Hārūn (Aaron), who had been in charge of the people in Mūsā's absence. Worriedly, Hārūn explains that he did not stop the people from following al-Sāmirī because he feared Mūsā would then accuse him of causing a division among the people and of disobeying Mūsā's direct instructions to keep the people unified. Hārūn's explanation appears to satisfy Mūsā, who then promptly turns to al-Sāmirī and demands that he explain his behavior.[46] Replies al-Sāmirī simply, "I saw what they did not see. So I took a handful from the footprint of the messenger (الرسول, *al-rasūl*) and threw it; thus did my soul suggest to me" (v. 96).[47] Not appeased by such an explanation, Mūsā banishes al-Sāmirī (v. 97, "Get thee gone!") and declares that, as his punishment, al-Sāmirī will forever more be cut off from human contact ("but thy punishment will be that thou wilt say, 'touch not' [لا مساس, *lā misāsa*]").[48] Additionally, al-Sāmirī will receive "a promise that will not fail," a punishment from which he will not be able to conceal himself.[49]

The Qur'ānic al-Sāmirī vs. the poetic

As if the Qur'ānic account here recounted were not puzzling enough, especially regarding its ambiguities, when we compare this Qur'ānic section to the rendition that appears in Ibn Ḥazm's poem, we notice that the two do not actually match up on all points. Most significantly and obviously, Ibn Ḥazm's poem deviates from the Qur'ānic text, adding material that does not appear in the scriptural version.

The poetic departure from the scriptural text concerns the identity of the owner of the miraculous footprint. While Ibn Ḥazm's poem designates Gabriel as the source (l. 5), the Qur'ānic account makes no mention of Jibrīl whatsoever. Rather, according to the Qur'ān, al-Sāmirī says that he took dust from the footsteps of an unnamed messenger, الرسول (*al-rasūl*).[50] In fact, given the context of chapter 20, one would be justified in understanding the term as referring to Mūsā. After all, Mūsī is *the* messenger, the *rasūl*, who serves as the star of this scriptural account, performing miracles in Egypt, leading the Children of Israel through the sea, speaking directly with Allāh, and revealing the true religion to his people. Furthermore, he has just recently walked up a mountain in the middle of the desert, presumably thereby leaving imprints in the dust behind him.[51] However, Ibn Ḥazm's poem understands the term to refer to someone else entirely, a male he identifies only as Jibrīl.

The poem and the Qur'ānic narrative differ also regarding the process involved in creating the calf. While the Qur'ān credits al-Sāmirī with both creating and animating the cow, although the verses remain fairly ambiguous as to how exactly this occurred, the poem attributes to him only animation. In Q 20:87–8, the Children of Israel relate that they threw their too-heavy ornaments into the fire as *suggested by al-Sāmirī*. He then mysteriously "brought out the image of a calf (فأخرج لهم عجلا جسدًا له, *fa-akhraja lahum `ijlan jasadan lahu*)" which made cow-noises (خوار, *khuwārun*).[52] When Mūsā confronts al-Sāmirī and asks him to explain himself, the Israelite leader receives a vague reply. Says al-Sāmirī cryptically (v. 96), "I saw what they did not see. So I took a handful from the footprint of the messenger and threw it; thus did my soul suggest to me." He does not explain what he saw that others missed, why he merited extra vision, where he threw the dust, what he threw it into, at what point in the process he threw it, why his "soul" thought this would be a good idea, or how any of this connected to a spontaneously mooing calf. Ibn Ḥazm's poem, by contrast, states the matter somewhat more clearly: al-Sāmirī saw Jibrīl's footprints and, recognizing this as special (l. 5b, "there appeared to his eyes the glorious footprint of Gabriel"), he gathered dust from the print. He then put some of that dust into the calf which, according to the poem, already existed (l. 6a). Because of the dust's extraordinary origin/nature, the unanimated cow in which the dust was placed miraculously began mooing.

But from where did Ibn Ḥazm get such expansions of the Qur'ānic account? After all, as a future Ẓāhirī, a proponent of the school that emphasized a literal reading of the Qur'ānic text, Ibn Ḥazm ought to have been one of the last to depart from the text's plain meaning. In adding the character Jibrīl and a pre-existing cow into which al-Sāmirī throws dust, neither of whom appears in the Qur'ān, Ibn Ḥazm clearly departs from the literal reading.

In an attempt to locate the source for these extra-Qur`ānic details, we must turn to the Islamic traditions and exegesis. After all, although Ẓāhirīs took a literalist approach to the Qur'ānic text, they did not reject either the *ḥadīth* accounts or the *sunna*, important tools in understanding the lacuna-filled text of the Qur'ān. Moreover, while *ḥadīth* traditions impacted secular Arabic poetry little in the early years, from the ninth century onward *ḥadīth* influence increased not only in the poetic sphere, but in all areas of Arabic writing.[53] And so it is to the texts of Islamic exegesis that we now turn.

Al-Sāmirī and Islamic exegesis

The classical Islamic commentaries vary little in their explanations or expansions of the Qur'ānic account of the golden calf that mooed. Importantly, as we shall see, Ibn Ḥazm's poetic reference appears to draw more from these materials than it does from the Qur'ān alone. The lion's share of our sources will be drawn from the works of two of the most authoritative scholars of extra-Qur'ānic materials. These are the Qur`ānic commentary and the history of the world by the Qur'ānic exegete and exegetical compiler Muḥammad b. Jarīr al-Ṭabarī (838–923), and the collection of extra-Qur'ānic narratives by the trusted and respected compiler of *qiṣaṣ al-anbiyā'* (Stories of the Prophets), Aḥmad ibn Muḥammad al-Tha`labī (d. *c.* 1035), a contemporary of Ibn Ḥazm's.[54] When relevant, these will be supplemented by materials from the biography of Muḥammad (known as the *sīra*) by Ibn Isḥāq (d. 767), from the *tafsīr* (Qur'ān commentary) of `Abdallāh b. `Umar al-Bayḍāwī (d. 1286),[55] from the *qiṣaṣ al-anbiyā'* of Muḥammad b. `Abdallāh al-Kisā'ī (eleventh century),[56] and from the *qiṣas* collection of the Andalusian Ibn Muṭarrif al-Ṭarafī (Cordoba, d. 1032).[57]

According to the Islamic traditions, when the Children of Israel were poised to leave Egypt, they borrowed "ornaments," jewelry, from their Egyptian slave-masters.[58] When Allāh subsequently destroyed Fir'awn (Pharaoh) and his people, the ornaments remained in the hands of their former slaves, who took the items with them when they departed Egypt. When the Children of Israel reached the desert, Mūsā ascended the Mount to speak with Allāh. Hārūn, who was left in charge, informed the Children of Israel that the ornamental jewelry in their possession constituted "spoils," ill-gotten gains, and was therefore not permitted to them. So they dug a pit and buried the tainted precious metals in it and waited for Mūsā to return and issue a ruling on what to do with the load.[59] While some traditions maintain that the ornaments remained buried at this point, others relate that Harūn set them on fire right away.[60] While this was taking place, a man named al-Sāmirī noticed that the angel Jibrīl had ridden into the encampment of the Children of Israel on his horse. According to al-Suddī (d. *c.* 754), this occurred when Jibrīl arrived to take Mūsā to the mountain to see Allāh.[61] Now this horse was no ordinary steed but the "horse of life," a title she had earned due to her instrumental role in helping the Children of Israel as they escaped from Fir'awn and crossed the sea. According to traditions, when the Egyptians were pursuing the Children of Israel, Jibrīl's horse plunged straight into the water and Fir'awn's horses, smelling her (for she was in heat), followed her in. Jibrīl and his horse emerged unscathed but Fir'awn's horses and horsemen did not.[62] When the angel and his magnificent mount later entered the Israelite encampment in the desert, no one noticed them, perhaps because they were too busy otherwise, with the problem of the ornaments. Or, rather, only al-Sāmirī did and he alone recognized the supernatural status and power of both the angel and his horse.[63] So al-Sāmirī reached forward and gathered some of the dust that had touched the extraordinary horse's feet when it walked on the ground leaving behind its hoof prints.

The Islamic tradition presents a number of explanations for how the cow then came into being and came to life. Although all connect the cow's animation to al-Sāmirī's use of what Ibn Ḥazm characterizes as "glorious" (ممجّد, *mumajjad*) dust, they disagree as to the details regarding the timing and extent of al-Sāmirī's involvement. One view maintains that al-Sāmirī used the collected dust to create a cow where there previously was none. According to this view, al-Sāmirī brought the dust he had collected to the pile of melting jewelry and threw it in.[64] The miraculous dust mixed with the molten metals and, with no further explanation, a cow formed from the melting mass.[65] As soon as it exited the fire, it made a lowing sound. As in the Qur'ān, al-Sāmirī then declared to the assembled Children of Israel, "Behold your god and the god of Mūsā!" Amazed by what they had just witnessed, they began worshiping the calf as their god.[66]

Others credit al-Sāmirī with an even more active role. Here too al-Sāmirī throws the dust into the burning flames, but now he himself issues the order for the cow's formation. Standing before the pyre, al-Sāmirī cried out, "Become a calf of flesh that lows!" And so it did. He then presented the mooing cow to the Children of Israel and Qur'ānically declared, "Behold your god and the god of Mūsā!" Convinced, they began worshiping it.[67]

Another version places even more fault at al-Sāmirī's feet, but at the same time delays his dust-throwing until after the cow had already arisen. These exegetes explain that al-Sāmirī, and not the more commonly accepted Harūn, informed the people that the Egyptian ornaments constituted "spoils" and were thereby forbidden to them. He instructed them to throw the precious metals into a specially prepared pyre. After allowing the fire to burn for three days, he fashioned a cow out of the now melted metals and let it cool. Armed with a golden calf, al-Sāmirī took dust which he had collected earlier from the footprints of Jibrīl's miracle horse and threw it into the hollow metal animal. The calf then miraculously crouched to the ground and lowed once.[68]

A divergent chain delays al-Sāmirī's life-giving dust-throwing until after the cow has already been formed from the fire. According to the exegetes who put forth this version, after the Children of Israel threw their jewelry into the fire, a cow miraculously arose out of the metal mass. Noting this, al-Sāmirī took the handful of dust which he had collected from the footsteps of Jibrīl's horse and threw it into the animal-shaped mass of metal. Hit by the dust, the metal cow then bent forward and issued a moo sound.[69]

As such a survey of the materials shows, Ibn Ḥazm's poem derives its version of the al-Sāmirī account not from the Qur'ān directly but from the corpus of classical exegesis. While the Qur'ān states ambiguously that al-Sāmirī gathered the dust of the *rasūl* (messenger), both the exegetical materials and the poem identify this as the angel Jibrīl. Although the Qur'ān does not explain what al-Sāmirī claimed to have seen or to have understood that caused him to gather the dust together, the exegetical materials and the poem relate that al-Sāmirī recognized the extraordinary visitor as extraordinary, as an angel, and wanted a sustained connection to him. And, where the Qur'ān provides only a vague description of how exactly al-Sāmirī used the dust to create the mooing calf, the exegetical materials provide two slightly different options, one of which appears clearly in Ibn Ḥazm's poem. Ibn Ḥazm writes, "and he [al-Sāmirī] put some of that earth inside the calf, and there came for him out of it a prolonged bleating!" This reflects the exegetical report in which al-Sāmirī waited until after the metal cow had already come into existence and then threw the Jibrīlite dust into the metal animal itself, whereupon it issued cow noises.[70]

Implications of the al-Sāmirī reference

The appearance of a reference to Qur'ānic characters and to an account that appears both in the Qur'ān and in the numerous commentaries to the Qur'ān initially strikes us as highly unusual for a secular love poem, especially one that sings the praises of a homosexual beloved. A more in-depth analysis reveals that Ibn Ḥazm's use of these exegetically inflected scriptural elements operates on three distinct levels, none of them truly sacrilegious. On the most obvious level, Ibn Ḥazm employs the al-Sāmirī–Jibrīl legend for its correspondence to the tropes of love poetry. More significantly, Ibn Ḥazm utilizes the Qur'ānic account to simultaneously denigrate and ultimately elevate his poetic tale of passionate love.

Al-Sāmirī as the lover

On the literary level, many of the motifs typical of a good love story/poem appear also in the account of al-Sāmirī, a fact that explains its appearance in Ibn Ḥazm's otherwise secular homoerotic love poem. Al-Sāmirī, in the role of the active lover, finds himself drawn to an individual with whom he yearns for a union he cannot attain. We should note also that, according to Islamic tradition, al-Sāmirī and Jibrīl did not "meet" here (at the site of the dust-gathering) for the first time but, like many a love-couple (including the one in Ibn Ḥazm's poem), had a preexisting relationship that had been cut off. According to the Islamic tradition, Jibrīl had served as al-Sāmirī's nanny or foster parent. The narratives relate that when the Egyptian Fir'awn threatened to kill the Israelite boys, the Israelite mothers hid their young sons in caves and Allāh appointed angels to care for them. Jibrīl was charged with tending to al-Sāmirī, which he did most tenderly.[71] Now, years later, al-Sāmirī once more glimpses Jibrīl, whom he cannot contact, and yearns to be reunited with him. But like the poetic beloved, Jibrīl takes no notice of al-Sāmirī or his yearnings for him. Thus, in typical poetic fashion, our "lover" (al-Sāmirī) must content himself instead with something belonging to the absent object of his affection. Finding nothing but the earth touched by his feet, or by those of his horse, al-Sāmirī-as-lover settles for that and gathers it up to himself. What's more, like the typical poetic lover, al-Sāmirī alone recognizes the magnificence of the object of his affection (Q 20:96, "I saw what they did not see"). Moreover, he is convinced, as the poetic lovers are, that others would appreciate and benefit from his beloved, if only they too would come to know him. While the lover publicizes his beloved in verse, al-Sāmirī uses the dust to demonstrate Jibrīl's power by thereby creating a mooing golden calf and bringing it to the masses (Q 20:88, "This is your God and the God of Moses!"). And despite the criticism of their "friends" – in poetry, those who criticize the lover for his unreturned affection and in the Jibrīl–Sāmirī account, Mūsā and Allāh – both the lover and al-Sāmirī persist in their devotion until it overcomes each of them in time. For the poetic lover, his devotion leads to his suffering for love, often suffering to the point of isolating insanity; for al-Sāmirī, his devotion results in his ejection from the community and his eternal untouchability.

Al-Sāmirī as criticism of **`ishq**

Let us not understand, however, that Ibn Ḥazm's allusion to the al-Sāmirī–Jibrīl account rests only in its fitting the tropes of Andalusian love poetry. After all, while Ibn Ḥazm excelled as a talented composer of love poems, he was also a highly educated and extremely knowledgeable scholar of Islam, a theologian, and an exegete himself. His inclusion of a particular Qur'ānic reference in his decidedly secular, even sacrilegious, poem thus bears deeper consideration. Indeed, Arie Schippers has noted that Qur'ānic quotations and allusions appearing in secular Arabic poetry often served as an "anti-text within a text." Explains Schippers, "When a Koranic passage is inserted, additional solemnity, or, in the case of obscenities, humor, has been conveyed."[72] In our case, the Qur'ānic allusion to al-Sāmirī adds both "solemnity" and "humor" and serves as an "anti-text within a text," transmitting a moral message regarding proper behavior. It does so, however, by utilizing a surprising, and thereby titillating, scriptural example.

Ibn Ḥazm could not have failed to notice one particularly disturbing and important fact in the scriptural and *ḥadīth* accounts that cries out *against* the motifs of love poetry. Namely, al-Sāmirī is the *villain*, the "enemy of God,"[73] in all the Qur'ānic and exegetical texts in which he appears. In his adoration of Jibrīl, al-Sāmirī seduces the Children of Israel *away* from the worship of Allāh, and leads them to pagan idol worship, Islam's most grievous sin. When questioned by Mūsā regarding this egregious violation of monotheism, al-Sāmirī replies glibly, "Thus did my soul suggest to me" (Q 20:96). Mūsā remains neither impressed nor fooled by such a claim; after all, Islam teaches that one should follow Allāh's law, not the desires of one's own soul. So Mūsā imposes upon al-Sāmirī the aforementioned three-fold punishment related in Q 20:97: Al-Sāmirī is expelled from the community, no one will ever touch him again, and a great punishment "that will not fail" will befall him on the Day of Judgment.[74] A villain who draws people *away* from a relationship with the Divine strikes us as a perplexing and wholly inappropriate scriptural referent for the loyal lover in a poem, especially one by a pious theologian and religious leader such as Ibn Ḥazm.

Yet we soon realize that Ibn Ḥazm's utilization of such a well-known "enemy of God" as his hero is intentional; in so doing, Ibn Ḥazm embeds an implicit critique of the type of amatory love that his poem appears superficially to extol. In comparing the dust-gathering lover to the infamous dust-gathering idolater, Ibn Ḥazm implies that, like al-Sāmirī, the lover too behaves wildly incorrectly, perhaps even heretically. After all, al-Sāmirī sins by setting up worship of the cow as an idol. He not only worships something other than Allāh but, even more wickedly, leads others to follow him in his iniquity. So, too, the lover worships something other than Allāh: his beloved. Like al-Sāmirī, the lover too tempts others to follow him. Unabashedly, he appeals to the "people of the land where clouds are not liberal with water" (l. 3) and insists that if they follow his advice, in his awestruck treatment of his beloved's footprints, "you will become free, and you will be thankful" (l. 4). He attributes to his beloved, and not to Allāh, the power to bring rain and redeem the people from their suffering. Both al-Sāmirī and the lover thereby commit the ultimate sin in Islam, *shirk*, ascribing partners to Allāh, maintaining that others besides Him are worthy of worship.[75] Indeed, so serious a desecration of Islam is this that the Qur'ān twice states that Allāh pardons all sins except that of *shirk*.[76] In comparing his passion-soaked lover to such an idolatrous character, the jurist-poet Ibn Ḥazm appears to want his readers to see them as similarly problematic.

Further indication that Ibn Ḥazm employs al-Sāmirī here as a repudiation of all-encompassing, worshipful, amorous love comes from the theological writings of Ibn Ḥazm himself. In his works on Ẓāhirī doctrine, Ibn Ḥazm emphasizes the principle of the absolute oneness of Allāh. Ibn Ḥazm insists that Allāh stands as unique, not only in His power and glory but specifically with regard to His ability to harness and employ the power of creation.[77] Allāh alone creates life and living things. In his poem, both al-Sāmirī and the lover clearly violate this central principle. Both attribute miraculous powers of creation, reserved for Allāh alone, to someone else. Al-Sāmirī sees the dust of Jibrīl's (or his horse's) footprints and believes they possess generative powers.[78] Similarly sacrilegiously, the lover insists that wherever his beloved has trod, the dirt has become blessed; having touched the miraculous feet of his beloved, the dust has obtained regenerative capabilities. It enables the water-deprived earth to miraculously bloom again, even without the rainfall that normally derives from and depends on Allāh Himself. Thus he attributes to his beloved's feet the miraculous powers of creation that ought to be Allāh's alone.

Ibn Ḥazm expresses further censure of the lover's too-worshipful attachment to the object of his affection by drawing a parallel with al-Sāmirī's undesirable fate as well. As earlier noted, the Qur'ān speaks of two temporal punishments to which Mūsā sentences al-Sāmirī in chapter 20; both of these plague Ibn Ḥazm's lover as well. Rejecting al-Sāmirī's attempted justification for his actions, Mūsā cries out, "Get thee gone!" (v. 96). With this, Mūsā unceremoniously expels al-Sāmirī from the community, condemning him to a life of exile from his people. Ibn Ḥazm's lover's condition mirrors this first punishment quite nicely. Like the punished al-Sāmirī, Ibn Ḥazm's lover finds himself alone, alone in his belief in his beloved's magnificence, alone in his willingness to die for love of his dear one, the recipient of blame rather than of sympathy from those around him. "Men criticize me unjustly," the lover claims, emphasizing that he stands alone in the recognition, valuation, and adoration of his beloved. Even though he may physically live within his community, in his isolation and solitude he finds himself metaphorically on the outskirts of his society, like al-Sāmirī.

The second of the punishments that Mūsā imposes on al-Sāmirī likewise appears reflected in the lover's condition, i.e., the inability to unite physically with the object of one's affection. After first ejecting al-Sāmirī from the community, Mūsā ensures that rather than find his place in another human society, al-Sāmirī will forever more be condemned to live without any human interaction whatsoever. Each time someone attempts to come close, Mūsā thunders, al-Sāmirī will be condemned to cry out "*la misāsa*!" ("Touch not!") and, in so doing, push any potential confidants far away.[79] The poetic lover finds himself in precisely such a situation. He desires physical union with his beloved. Instead, he finds himself able to touch only an intermediate item (dirt) that has touched his beloved. He, like the untouchable al-Sāmirī, may not touch the one person whom he longs most to touch.

In matching the lover's situation with the first two of al-Sāmirī's punishments, Ibn Ḥazm seems to have intended to call to mind, to warn of, the third as well. We recall that Allāh's penalty for al-Sāmirī's idolatry reaches into the afterworld. According to Mūsā, al-Sāmirī receives a promise from Allāh that "will not fail" (v. 97). The verses that follow this sentence (20:99–104) imply that this refers to Allāh's promise to enact a severe and exacting punishment on the Day of Judgment. In constructing the parallel between the poetic lover and the scriptural sinner, Ibn Ḥazm hints that if the lover does not desist from his al-Sāmirī-like behavior, he too will face a similar fate on this day. Guilty of the same sin as al-Sāmirī, venerating other than Allāh, the lover earns for himself the same harsh retribution at the end of days, intimates Ibn Ḥazm.

Under normal poetic conditions, the lover's misery and affliction are understood as a badge of honor, as proof of his depth of sentiment, and as praise of his commitment to proper Andalusian values. Ibn Ḥazm himself writes that love and the sufferings for love were a "delightful condition and a disease yearned for." One with immunity from such a disease, he writes, longs to become infected and one already infected eschews being cured.[80] However, in setting up a parallel between the lover's suffering and al-Sāmirī's punishment, Ibn Ḥazm accentuates the lover's *sinfulness*, not his heroism. Ibn Ḥazm thereby turns the motif of the suffering lover completely on its head, moving from commendation of such behavior to chastisement and castigation.

Al-Sāmirī as elevation of `ishq

Yet this negative view of romantic love cannot be the final message Ibn Ḥazm sends in his inclusion of the al-Sāmirī account here. After all, in his introduction to the poem and in his prose description of the event that inspired it Ibn Ḥazm does not indicate any problem with the tricks played by lovers struggling for contentment when physically separated. Nor does he, throughout the *Ṭawq* or in any other of his writings, take issue with lovers, even those devoted to the point of obsession. Instead, he maintains that this adoration of the dear one is the natural, acceptable state of affairs. As he writes in our chapter, "I never saw two (persons) passionately in love with each other but they were giving one another locks of hair ..."[81] Indeed passionate love, he teaches, results when the heart recognizes the reunion of the parts of the soul separated in this world; and, hearts are in the hand of God.[82] What's more, in the beginning of the chapter "On Contentment" in the *Ṭawq*, he practically requires such obsessive love, saying, "A lover who is prevented from union must seek contentment in what he finds."[83] Even when the items passed back and forth strike us as somewhat unpalatable, such as already-chewed gum, Ibn Ḥazm expresses neither distaste nor criticism, as would be expected if he intended a condemnation of such lovers in general and the poem's lover specifically. Instead, he seems particularly impressed by the depth of love displayed by such gifts and, in particular, by the footprint-kissing woman in Sulaymān b. Aḥmad's account, the woman whom he used as positive inspiration for his verse.

More significantly, however, despite the analysis above, one cannot fail to notice that the al-Sāmirī–poetic lover parallel simply does not work on its most basic level. Namely, while a poetic lover, and our poem's lover, *is* romantically involved with the beloved, al-Sāmirī and Jibrīl do not ever appear as romantically linked, neither in the Qur'ān nor in any exegetical text. Nowhere in these texts does al-Sāmirī express even the hint of a desire to serve as Jibrīl's lover. Indeed, the Qur'ān leaves Jibrīl out of the cryptic account of the sin of the calf altogether. Instead, the Qur'ān refers only to an unnamed *rasūl* (messenger) who mysteriously left footprints in the dust in the Israelite camp, footprints from which al-Sāmirī inexplicably saw fit to gather dirt. It is the exegetical texts that introduce Jibrīl into the affair. And they too present an entirely unromantic vision of the man–angel relationship, stating simply that al-Sāmirī saw the angel Jibrīl approach, and recognized him as an angel and his horse as an angel's horse.[84] No amour or amorous leanings make themselves apparent here at all.

So why does Ibn Ḥazm employ this particularly unromantic duo in his clearly eros-driven love poem? Not only is it an extremely religiously problematic image in its use of an idolater, but in employing a non-lover pair, it also does not correspond to the poem's content or context. Surely the religious scholar Ibn Ḥazm could have found a more fitting scriptural or extra-scriptural image to utilize in his poem celebrating passionate lovers! That Ibn Ḥazm, jurist and theologian of the highest order, insists on such an obviously mismatched parallel for his homosexual love poem, brings us to reconsider the parallel itself and its details, to find the "anti-text within the text."

When we reassess Ibn Ḥazm's poem, we find that Ibn Ḥazm allegorizes a scriptural account, not to disparage *`ishq* (as it seemed beforehand) but to send a *positive* message about human love and lust. In comparing human passion to the decidedly asexual al-Sāmirī–Jibrīl account, Ibn Ḥazm raises *`ishq* out of the realm of physical, earthly lust and up to a more spiritual realm. In his incorporation of a sacred image, Ibn Ḥazm bestows on human passion a metaphysical, almost holy, sense. He does not denigrate human love and desire, as it might have seemed at first, but uses his poem and Scripture to elevate and sacralize *`ishq*.

After all, one should not overlook one very important and significant fact about the character known as Jibrīl; namely, he is not a human being. Like the angel Gabriel in Judaism and Christianity,[85] the Islamic Jibrīl is an angel, a celestial attendant of God and an intermediary between heaven and earth. Even more, Gabriel/Jibrīl belongs to the class of archangels, those chief or principal angels charged with the most important of functions. Among these, Jibrīl serves as the angel in charge of revelation, the divinely appointed messenger who brings Allāh's words to Muḥammad.[86] As such, despite all of al-Sāmirī's subsequent idolatrous actions, his initial reaction to having seen Jibrīl is actually quite on-target and religiously perceptive; he has seen an angel, a messenger of God, a being normally reserved for interactions with God's prophets. Al-Sāmirī thus *correctly* understands that he has been privileged to glimpse a holy sight, and one that no one else but he either noticed or appreciated. Furthermore, having recognized that he has seen an angel and his miraculous "horse of life," al-Sāmirī reacts not wholly inappropriately in gathering up the holiness-tinged footprint dust. Instead, he *correctly* understands that a sacred being does not pass through the world without somehow altering the mundane, profane, artifacts with which it has come into contact. After all, the dust touched by this miraculous creature *did* have transformative powers of creation; as the Qur'ān itself tells us, the footprint dust left behind miraculously manufactured and gave breath to an animal where before there was none.

In setting up a parallel between his beloved and the angel Jibrīl, Ibn Ḥazm's lover thereby removes the beloved from the realm of the flesh-and-blood human. He is not simply a human male, as observers might have thought, says the lover; and the lover does not lust for him in a physical, earthly way. Although critics might think that the lover loves the beloved because of his fleshy self alone, with the poetic parallel the lover-narrator implies that this is not the case. Indeed, as noted earlier, the poem omits any reference to the physical characteristics of the beloved. The poem focuses instead on the miraculous effect the beloved has on his environment. It is not his physical aspect that so enthralls the lover, but, stresses the lover, the beloved is Jibrīl-like: angelic, pure, untouched, and unsullied, a servant of God. Like al-Sāmirī who correctly identified the angelic nature of Jibrīl when he appeared, says the lover, I recognize and am enamored of the beloved's true nature, his miraculous God-given powers of healing and blessing.

In similar fashion, the lover's traipsing after his beloved's footprints should not be understood as the act of an insane person stricken with lust/love. Instead, like al-Sāmirī's honest adoration of the angelic Jibrīl, the lover's behavior reflects the actions of an honest admirer of something divinely touched and divinely sent. After all, it is not al-Sāmirī's reaction to Jibrīl and recognition of his powers that proves problematic and idolatrous in the Qur'ān and the exegetical materials. The problem lies in al-Sāmirī's subsequently having declared (Q 20:88), "This is your God and the god of Moses!" to the Israelites and their resulting idolatry. Importantly, while Ibn Ḥazm's lover recognizes and publicizes his beloved's unique and sacred nature, he never makes this sinful move. The lover never outright attributes divinity to his beloved, but keeps him in the realm of the miraculous. Perhaps to avoid a reader mistakenly associating the lover with such unacceptable sinfulness, Ibn Ḥazm avoids mentioning this most problematic part of the al-Sāmirī account altogether. His use of the account ends with the appearance and mooing of the cow, *before* al-Sāmirī utters his sinful, *shirk*-filled, statement.

Thus we see that Ibn Ḥazm uses a controversial scriptural image in his secular love poem in an unusual way. Unlike the mystics, he does not compare the sacred and the profane to express a difficult-to-conceptualize (sacred) love in human (profane) terms. Rather, he employs the sacred *in service* of the profane. Ibn Ḥazm here uses Scripture to sacralize an otherwise entirely secular love. In so doing, he takes a legally prohibited love, one between a man and his male lover, and elevates it to a level of spiritual sanctity.

Ibn `Arabī and al-Sāmirī

Interestingly, Ibn Ḥazm was not the only Muslim theologian to employ the al-Sāmirī account as a positive rather than a negative instructional tale. Ṣūfīs, the mystical members of the Islamic community, agreed with him. According to Ṣūfī readings of the Qur'ānic account, al-Sāmirī did *not* sin in his creating the golden calf out of the footprint dust. Rather, in his construction of the animal, al-Sāmirī involved himself in performing God's work. After all, teaches Sufism, God must be worshiped in every form.[87]

This idea developed in the work of the Andalusian mystical poet and philosopher Muḥyī al-Dīn ibn `Arabī (1165–1240). In Ibn `Arabī's reading of the Qur'ān's account, al-Sāmirī had been blessed with a divine vision in which he glimpsed one of the four angels who carried the throne of God. These angels were known to take four different forms: man, lion, eagle, and bull.[88] According to Ibn `Arabī, in the Qur'ānic account of the golden calf, al-Sāmirī spotted the angel who took the form of a bull (Jibrīl). Al-Sāmirī mistakenly thought he would then be able to recognize Mūsā's god in the bull and, for this reason, he created a bull from Jibrīl's dust.[89] According to this reading, al-Sāmirī did not intentionally commit the sin of *shirk*, as taught in the classical exegetical texts. Rather, his fault lay in his prematurely analyzing an incomplete spiritual experience; in so doing, he problematically attempted to anticipate divine acts.[90] His intent and goal, however, were pure and Allāh-oriented.

Thus, like Ibn Ḥazm, Ibn `Arabī considered the al-Sāmirī image appropriate for love poetry. In the latter half of his illustrious collection of mystical poems, the *Tarjumān al-ashwāq*, Ibn `Arabī includes a number of love poems dedicated to God, but phrased in secular terminology.[91] The al-Sāmirī image appears in the midst of poem #30, in which Ibn `Arabī employs numerous stereotypical images from Arabic `Udhrite and later secular love poetry to describe the human's yearning for union with God. There Ibn `Arabī writes (l. 32): "سامري الوقت قلبي كلما أبصر الآثار يبغى المذهب," "My heart is the Sāmirī of its age: whenever it sees the footprints, it desires the gilded one."[92] To understand this line, we must remember that Ibn `Arabī understood that the Qur'ānic al-Sāmirī experienced a divine vision in which he caught a glimpse of the bull-shaped angel (Jibrīl) charged with carrying the throne of Allāh. Taking note of its footprints, al-Sāmirī then sought to call Allāh forth – in Ibn `Arabī's interpretation – by forming a golden calf from the dust of the angel's footsteps. So, too, the mystic's heart, writes Ibn `Arabī. When the mystic's heart glimpses something that it recognizes as divinely touched, it moves forward, searching for the divine essence behind that thing. In comparing the mystic's search to al-Sāmirī's vision, Ibn `Arabī thus does not denigrate the mystic. Rather, in understanding al-Sāmirī as an honest seeker after Allāh and in using that image in his poem, he justifies and praises the mystical seeker of union with his Lord.

Admittedly, there is an important difference between Ibn Ḥazm's usage and that of Ibn `Arabī. Ibn Ḥazm utilizes the account in a secular poem concerning human *`ishq*; Ibn `Arabī incorporates the narrative into a mystical religious poem describing the human desire for God. Nonetheless, Ibn `Arabī's poem remains significant for our discussion. In employing a sacrilegious scriptural account/character in a mystical poem, Ibn `Arabī demonstrates that a Muslim theologian's comparison of a lover to al-Sāmirī does not necessitate a denigration of the emotion or person to whom he is compared. Instead, there are cases in which al-Sāmirī appears to describe and emphasize the elevated sacred state of a human's urge to unite with Allāh. In comparing the poetic lover's recognition of his beloved to al-Sāmirī's recognition of Jibrīl, Ibn Ḥazm similarly redeems al-Sāmirī from the role of complete villain and sees in him a more virtuous seeker of love.

Summary

References to Qur'ānic storylines and characters do not abound in Andalusian Arabic love poetry; for the most part, the composers of Andalusian Arabic secular poetry were themselves representatives of the secular world. However, in the poem analyzed here, we see the Ẓāhirī theologian and jurist Ibn Ḥazm unabashedly combining the two, uniting tropes of secular lust poetry with characters and themes drawn from Muslim Scripture and scriptural exegesis. While we are initially taken aback by such a combination, we soon realize that this engagement in two such seemingly different milieus does not pose as great a conflict with Ẓāhirī theology as one might think. Indeed, since the Ẓāhirīs could find no injunction in either the Qur'ān or the *sunna* against passionate love, they did not shy away from engaging in scholarship, or even poetry, on the topic.[93]

Yet Ibn Ḥazm's al-Sāmirī-centered *`ishq* poem presents the audience with more than simply a Ẓāhirī literary exercise in combining, masterfully so, two seemingly disparate worlds. After all, the lover here not only compares himself, in following worshipfully after the trace of his absent beloved and gathering up the remnants of his footsteps, to al-Sāmirī's gathering up the dust from the footprints of Jibrīl. Rather, he compares his very human boy-beloved to an archangel, the celestial messenger in charge of transmitting divine revelation. Furthermore, the lover attributes to his beloved the same miraculous characteristics that Jibrīl possesses. Dust touched by Allāh's angel miraculously brought an inanimate metal cow mooingly to life; so too, the lover contends, dust touched by the feet of his extraordinary beloved will bring to life earth that has been parched by drought. In incorporating the Islamic religious texts regarding the mysterious "villain" al-Sāmirī into his secular *`ishq* poem, Ibn Ḥazm presents readers with a subversive yet sublime message about the nature and power of romantic human love. It is, his lover affirms, miraculous, transformative, sacred, and somewhat divine.

Notes

1 In fact, although the story of the creation of the golden calf appears twice in the Qur'ān (ch. 20 and ch. 7), al-Sāmirī appears in only one telling (ch. 20). This will be discussed at greater length below.

2 *EI*[2], s.v. "Ibn Hazm, Abu Muhammad Ali," by R. Arnaldez (3:791).

3 Ibn Ḥazm's "attack" on Judaism, *Iẓhār tabdīl al-yahūd wa-al-naṣāra*, is really a textual criticism of Jewish Scripture written for Muslims, although he does use typically anti-Jewish language, calling the Jews "dirty," "vile," the worst liars, and a villainous breed. Ibn Ḥazm also composed a scathing and anti-Semitic response to a polemical work against the Qur'ān, which he believed was composed by the Jewish scholar, poet, and Granadan vizier Samuel ha-Nagid, with whom Ibn Ḥazm had earlier (as early as 1013) been friends and disputation-partners. Sarah Stroumsa has shown that the polemical work attributed to Samuel ha-Nagid by Ibn Ḥazm was not actually composed by him, but was a collection of quotations from the *Kitāb al-dāmigh* by the Muslim heretic Ibn al-Rāwandī (ninth century). It appears that Ibn Ḥazm drew the polemical quotations from a previous Arabic refutation of Ibn al-Rāwandī's work which, according to scholars, Ibn Ḥazm had not actually read through. See Brann, *Power in the Portrayal*, 54–90. Moshe Perlmann, "Eleventh Century Andalusian Authors on the Jews of Granada," *Proceedings of the American Academy for Jewish Research* 18 (1948–9): 269–90; idem, "The Medieval Polemics between Islam and Judaism," in *Religion in a Religious Age*, ed. S. D. Goitein (Cambridge, MA: Association for Jewish Studies, 1974), 103–38; Roth, "Muslim Knowledge"; idem, "Some Aspects of Muslim–Jewish Relations in Spain," II:179–214; Sarah Stroumsa, "From Muslim Heresy to Jewish–Muslim Polemics: Ibn al-Rāwandī's *Kitāb al-Dāmigh*," *JAOS* 107:4 (Oct.–Dec. 1987): 767–72. Camilla Adang has posited that Ibn Ḥazm's information and arguments on Jews and Judaism were provided by Karaites. See her *Muslim Writers on Judaism and the Hebrew Bible: From Ibn Rabban to Ibn Hazm* (Leiden, New York, and Köln: E. J. Brill, 1996), 94–109. For Ibn Ḥazm's criticism on the authenticity of Jewish Scripture, see Adang, *Muslim Writers*, 237–55.

4 Sunnī Islam consists of four schools of Islamic law, between which Muslims may shift back and forth. With few major theological distinctions between the schools, the differences mostly appear in the schools' philosophy for determining Islamic law and the particulars of the laws that result. The Mālikī school relies on a combination of *ra'y* (opinion) and *naṣṣ* (textual precedent) and considers the customs of the people of Medina (*'amal*) as legally significant, having descended from Muḥammad and his Companions (in the Mālikī view). The Shāfi'ī school relies more heavily on *naṣṣ*, along with *qiyās* (analogical reasoning), and generally rejects the Mālikī emphasis on Medinan practices. For more on these schools, see the entries under their names in the *EI*[2].

5 Ẓāhirism arose in the ninth to tenth centuries, largely as a reaction to a perceived intellectualizing of the Sunnī theologians. In the legal sphere, Ẓāhirism attempted to remove any trace of apparent subjectivity from *fiqh* (Islamic jurisprudence). Relatedly, Ẓāhirism maintained that the most appropriate way to read the Qur'ān and *ḥadīth* was as literally as possible. Ẓāhirīs thus derived law from the *ẓāhir* (literal) text, without the tools of casuistry or personal interpretation to help them. For more on the Ẓāhiri school, see Ignaz Goldziher, *The Ẓāhiris, Their Doctrine and Their History* (Leiden: E. J. Brill, 1971); *EI*[2], s.v. "al-Ẓāhiriyya," by Abdel-Magid Turki (11:394–6); Mazalaoui, "I Follow the Religion of Love," 126.

6 While Ibn Ḥazm credits women with the intellectual capacity both to understand and to teach the important religious sciences, he simultaneously maintains that they think about little aside from matchmaking and marriage, the tasks for which they were born. He attributes this to the fact that while men are divided in their interests, women have little else to occupy their minds and so they drift into the "paths of idleness" more quickly. See Ibn Ḥazm, *Ṭauḳ al-ḥamâma*, ed. Pétrof, 46–7. English translations: *A Book Containing the Risāla*, trans. Nykl, 71–2; and *The Ring of the Dove*, trans. Arberry, 100. See also Lois A. Giffin, "Ibn Hazm and the *Ṭawq al-ḥamāma*," in *The Legacy of Muslim Spain*, ed. Salma Khadra Jayyusi (Leiden: E. J. Brill, 1992), 421.

7 This friend may have been the Cordoban Abū `Amr b. Shuhayd (992–1035), an accomplished secular poet famous for his *mujūn* poetry (poems dealing with the perverse and impious). Ibn Shuhayd composed a system of literary theory based on the doctrine of *i`jāz al-Qur'ān* (the perfection of the Qur'ān in terms of Arabic language and literary excellence). He also maintained that poets received creative inspiration from a supernatural "genie"; the best poet was he who was then able to improvise well, since the soul was then in direct contact with the spiritual world. See Monroe, "Hispano-Arabic Poetry During the Caliphate of Cordoba," 138–42. Despite Ibn Shuhayd's celebration of the religiously immoral and his living out a hedonistic lifestyle, his two closest friends were the theologian Ibn Ḥazm and the *qāḍī* of Cordoba, Ibn Ḍakwān. See James Dickie, "Ibn Ŝuhayd: A Biographical and Critical Study," *Al-Andalus* 29 (1964): 247–52. See also Sells, "Love," 138ff. One particularly *mūjūn* poem by Ibn Shuhayd describes the narrator "creeping" up on a drunken youth and having his way with him while the boy remains in an unconscious drunken stupor. See Nykl, *Hispano-Arabic Poetry*, 104. For the Arabic, see Abū al-Ḥasan `Alī b. Mūsā ibn Sa`īd al-Andalusī, *Rāyāt al-mubarrizīn wa-ghāyāt al-mumayyazīn*, ed. Muḥammad Riḍwān al-Dāya (Dimashq: Dār Ṭalās, 1987), 124–5. An earlier example appears in a poem by Abū Nuwās. See Chapter 4, p. 127, and n. 45. For more on the "creeping" (*dabīb*) phenomenon, see Roth, "Deal Gently." See also Chapter 7, n. 58, Chapter 6, n. 43, and Chapter 8, n. 10.

8 More about Ibn Ḥazm's exile from Cordoba because of his loyalty to the Umayyads appears in Chapter 5, which discusses a poem about loyalty and faithfulness.

9 See *Ṭauḳ*, 3–4 (Nykl, 2–3; Arberry, 17). For more on Ibn Ḥazm's biography, see also Chejne, *Muslim Spain*, 251–2; Watt and Cachia, *A History of Islamic Spain*, 131ff.

10 *Ṭauḳ*, 144 (Nykl, 219; Arberry, 281–2). Ibn Ḥazm's declaration of piety was not simply an attempt at self-preservation. Rather, as Everett K. Rowson notes, "Even the most respectable and 'sanctimonious' individual was expected to compose *mūjūn* (profligacy) or stories depicting the most outrageous behavior, even attributing it to himself." See his "The Categorization of Gender," 52.

11 Ibn Ḥazm does include a chapter on those attracted to characteristics most others would find distasteful (anti-tropes?). This happens, he explains, when one falls in love with a person with such a characteristic early on in life; the beloved's look imprints upon the lover's brain (or heart). He admits that such a thing occurred to him when, as a youth, he fell madly in love with a blonde slave girl who served his family. Although standards of beauty dictated that black hair was desirable, and blonde was unappealing, "from that time on I never liked girls with black hair, even though it were more beautiful than the sun, and were the image of beauty itself." See Nykl, 39–41 (*Ṭauḳ*, 25–7; Arberry, 61).

12 Arberry, 183. Nykl's translation of this line (p. 135) is awkward and uncomfortable so I have employed Arberry's here. The Arabic original can be found in *Ṭauḳ*, 89.

13 According to Nykl (p. 139), "*al-ḥājib*" indicates the man's profession, "chamberlain" of the island of Sicily. Arberry (p. 186) leaves untranslated a part of the man's name.

14 Arberry more poetically translates this phrase as "embracing with her lips the traces of his feet upon the ground." See Arberry, 186.

15 *Ṭauḳ*, 90–1.

16 Nykl, 139–40. Nykl does not include the line numbers in his text. I have included them so that readers can see the hemistich form of the original Arabic. While Arberry's translation is more musical and poetic than Nykl's translation, Nykl's remains more wedded to the Arabic original. I have therefore chosen Nykl's translation here. For Arberry's translation, see his *The Ring of the Dove*, 186–7.

17 Both Nykl and Arberry translate the Arabic word "يلومونني" (*yalūmūnanī*), as "they blame me." Nykl writes "they blame me wrongly" while Arberry uses "they blame me cruelly." The variation may be traced back to a difference in the manuscripts used. In a good number of manuscripts, the first line reads: يلمونني في موطئ خفّه خطّا (*yalūmūnanī*

fī mawṭi' khuffihi khaṭṭan). In others, the final word of the phrase does not appear or, as in the rendition used by Pétrof (90), is written "جفا" (*jaffan*, roughly, harshly, with loathing). See also *Ṭawq al-ḥamāma*, ed. Nizār Wajīh Fallūh (Sidon and Beirut: al-Maktaba al-`aṣriyya, 1422/2001), 175, n. 1. Although both translations are misleading for the modern English reader, Nykl's is particularly problematic. In writing "they blame me wrongly," Nykl allows for the understanding that the lover claims that he did not do what "they" accuse him of. The rest of the poem clearly indicates that this is not the case; the poem's narrator admits that he *did* do it. It is the blame, he states, which is unjustified. The better translation appears to be as I have rendered it above: "They criticize me harshly."

18 For an overview of these motifs, see Schippers, *Spanish Hebrew Poetry*, 145–54; and Monroe, "Hispano-Arabic Poetry During the Caliphate of Cordoba," 152, n. 54. Schippers refers readers to two works on the themes of Arabic love poetry. They are: Ibn Abī `Awn (d. 934), *al-Tashbīhāt*, ed. Muḥammad `Abd al-Mu`īd Khān (London, 1950) and Ibn al-Kattānī (d. 1029), *Kitāb al-tashbīhāt*, ed. Iḥsān `Abbās (Beyrouth, 1968).

19 Ladislav Drozdík takes this idea to an extreme, stating, "The Western image of the poet as a creative subject with deep emotional experience finds no parallel in classical Arabic poetry." See his "Erotic Imagery," 22. Dan Pagis more moderately writes that the genre of love poetry hovered between the conventional and the personal as poets played with stock situations, characters, and description to express particularized emotions. See his *Hebrew Poetry*, 48–54.

20 Scheindlin, "A Miniature Anthology," 106.

21 Although most beloveds remained nameless, not all did. However, when a name did appear in a poem, it was frequently for a negative reason. As James Monroe explains, often a poet named his beloved in order to embarrass, annoy, or insult the beloved and the beloved's family. For example, `Abd al-Raḥmān, son of the Umayyad poet Ḥassān b. Thābit al-Khazrajī (d. 649) wrote love poems about Ramla, the daughter of the caliph Mu`āwiya, simply "to annoy her father and family." Monroe brings further examples in which, under caliphal order, poets were instructed to refrain from composing poems in which the caliphs' daughters and womenfolk were identifiable. He also discusses a poem written by Ibn Quzmān (*c.* 1078–1160, Cordoba) in which the poet identifies a boy by naming the boy's father, with the sole intent of annoying the elder man. See his "The Striptease that was Blamed on Abū Bakr's Naughty Son," 94–139. Ibn Ḥazm himself writes that he has named only those who can be named without thereby harming them in some fashion. See *Ṭauḳ*, 3 (Nykl, 3; Arberry, 17).

22 All these tropes can be found in Schippers, *Spanish Hebrew Poetry*, See n. 18 above.

23 Ibn Ḥazm's poem is unconcerned with *any* aspect other than separation and seeking contentment. Ibn Ḥazm states so quite clearly in the introduction to the chapter in which this poem appears and in his explanation of the background for this particular poem. For the same reason, Ibn Ḥazm also has little to say regarding the cause for the separation of the lovers (usually attributable to the cruel behavior of the beloved, another well-used Andalusian motif); the cause here remains beside the point. Ibn Ḥazm's poem focuses on what the lovers do subsequently to ease their pain. See n. 26 below.

24 See Baneth, "Ha-Shirah ha-`Aravit ha-Qeduma," 23–7; Bürgel, "Love, Lust and Longing," 91–6; Schippers, *Spanish Hebrew Poetry*, 145.

25 Here lies an important difference between the yearning of `Udhrite poems and that of Andalusian verse. `Udhrite couples frequently owed their distance from one another to fate or to the beloved's family. The most famous pre-Islamic example of this remains Layla and Qays (aka Majnūn Layla), whose separation was intentionally orchestrated by Layla's family. The separation of Andalusian couples, by contrast, often arose from the beloved's refusal to meet with the lover, in full knowledge of the torment this would cause. See Khairallah, *Love, Madness and Poetry*. Ibn Ḥazm's lover does not

assign the blame for the separation to anyone in particular in his poem. Like the physical appearance of the beloved, this too is beside the point for him. He dwells only in the moment here.

26 According to Ibn Ḥazm, lovers use all of these things in attempting to ease the pain of separation. See *Ṭauḳ*, 90 (Nykl, 139; Arberry, 185–6). An earlier poetic example of separated lovers exchanging trinkets appears in a Hebrew poem by the wife of the Hebrew poet Dunash ibn Labrat (920–90), the first to introduce Arabic meter into Hebrew poetry. In her poem, Dunash's wife writes touchingly of a gazelle and her beloved, poised at the moment of parting, exchanging cloaks and jewelry (she gives him her bracelet while he gives her his ring) in order that they not forget one another during their separation. See Fleischer, " 'Al Dunash ben Labrat," 5:189–202.

27 In another poem on separated lovers, Ibn Ḥazm's lover can find no material item with which to console himself. Instead, he comforts himself with the knowledge that he and the boy live in the same age, that the same sun that rises over him every morning shines on his dear one as well. Thus every new day presents another opportunity for "touching" something that the beloved has "touched." See *Ṭauḳ*, 93–4 (Arberry, 193–5; Nykl, 143–4). See also Chapter 7, n. 6.

An image closely resembling the woman's kissing the dust of the footprints of the beloved appears in a Hebrew poem by Ibn Ḥazm's Jewish contemporary and one-time friend, Samuel ha-Nagid (993–1056). He writes: "אשוט כהלך עלי גבעת לבונה ואדביק את לחיי אלי מדרך הליכיכי" (I wander like one roaming over a hill of frankincense, and I secure my cheeks to the imprint of your footsteps). In an earlier Arabic poem, by the `Udhrite Umayyad poet Quthayyir b. `Abd al-Raḥmān (d. 723), the lover advises his companions to touch, rather than kiss, the dust of the earth where his beloved `Azza had dismounted from her camel: "ومسا ترابًا كان قد مسّ جلدها وبيتًا وظلّا حيث باتت وظلّت." In our poem, Ibn Ḥazm likewise writes of touching, rather than kissing, the dust. Neither Quthayyir nor Samuel ha-Nagid associates the footprints with the angel Gabriel/Jibrīl, as in Ibn Ḥazm's poem. See Samuel ha-Nagid, *Diwan Shemuel ha-Nagid. Ben Tehillim*, 299 (#167) and Sāmī al-Dahhān, *al-Ghazal* (Cairo: Dār al-ma`ārif, 1964), 1:55. Al-Dahhān explains the background for this poem: `Azza had been married off to another man, and had moved to Egypt with him, with Quthayyir following. One year, after they had been separated for some time, Quthayyir either went on ḥajj or traveled to a certain place, as did `Azza, by coincidence. Her husband sent her to buy clarified butter and she wandered around the different tents looking for some. Eventually, she entered Quthayyir's tent, not knowing it was his. Quthayyir was then sharpening some arrows and when she entered, he cut himself, presumably due to the surprise at seeing her in his tent suddenly. She wiped off his blood, inspiring him to recite this poem. For more on Quthayyir and `Azza, see *EI*[2], s.v. "Kuthayyir b. `Abd al-Raḥmān," by Iḥsān `Abbās (5:551–3).

28 As in Lois A. Giffin, "Love Poetry and Love Theory in Medieval Arabic Literature," in *Arabic Poetry: Theory and Development*, ed. G. E. von Grunebaum (Wiesbaden: Otto Harrassowitz, 1973), 115. Arabic original in al-Jāḥiẓ, *Rasā'il al-Jāḥiẓ* (Miṣr: Maktabat al-khānjī, 1399/1979), 3:139. The tenth-century Arabic scholar of poetry and poets Dāwūd al-Iṣfahānī (897–967) traces this definition as far back as Plato, whom he quotes as having said, "I do not know what love (*hawā*) is except that I know it to be a divine madness, which cannot be either approved or blamed." See Nykl, *Hispano-Arabic Poetry*, 123. Interestingly, the opposite concept of love championed by the Muslim theologian and philosopher Ibn Sīnā (Avicenna, 980–1037) in his *Risāla fī al-`ishq* does not seem to have taken hold in Spain. Ibn Sīnā maintained that human–human love ennobled the human soul and contributed to its ascent to the divine. A discussion of this appears in G. E. von Grunebaum, "Avicenna's *Risāla fī al-`Ishq* and Courtly Love," *JNES* 11:4 (Oct. 1952): 233–8.

29 For an example of *`ishq*-induced insanity and illness, see Chapter 2, n. 35.

30 The narrator's in-poem "audience" could have served another role as well: protectors of the beloved, protectors who thereby threaten the narrator. See Scheindlin, "A Miniature Anthology," 122.

31 Ibn Ḥazm writes elsewhere of friends "blaming" a lover, criticizing him, for what appears to them to be inappropriate behavior. In one such poem, the lover earned the criticism for having fallen in love with a blonde girl, a hair color not acceptable in the Andalusian system. See *Ṭauk*, 25–7 (Nykl, 41; Arberry, 61–4), and above, n. 11.
An example of an address to a criticizing audience that echoes our poem quite closely appears in the collection of Andalusian Arabic poetry by Ibn Sa`īd al-Andalusī. There, the poet Abū `Alī al-Ḥusayn al-Nashshār (Valencia, twelfth century) writes, "Oh you who reproach me for my infatuation with Yaḥyā, when can I hope for release from loving him? ..." See Ibn Sa`īd al-Andalusī, *Rāyāt al-mubarrizīn*, 213. English translation from Bellamy and Steiner, *Banners of the Champions*, 60.

32 For more on al-Ḥarizi and his inclusion among the poets of Islamic Andalusia, see Decter, *Iberian Jewish Literature*, 126ff; Judah al-Harizi, *The Book of the Taḥkemoni: Jewish Tales from Medieval Spain*, translated, explicated, and annotated by David Simha Segal (London: Littman Library of Jewish Civilization, 2001), 402–4; idem, *Taḥkemoni*, ed. Y. Toporovsky (Tel Aviv: Hotza'at Maḥbarot le-Sifrut, 5712 [1952]), 418; Pagis, *Ḥiddush u-Masoret*, 72–3.

33 Entertaining – though inaccurate – English versions can be found in David Simha Segal's translation, 402–4. Segal renders our poem: "Had Moses seen my neighbor's cheeks / none other can surpass / He had not writ in his Torah / "Do not covet thy neighbor's ass." Problematically, the last line refers to a completely different biblical verse (Ex. 20:17, where "ass" refers to a donkey, not a human's rear end) than that cited in the Hebrew (Lev. 18:22, discussed above).

34 *Taḥkemoni*, 418. In his version, Dan Pagis includes a slight variation on the second line which drops the word העת (*ha-`et*, while) to read: "מתאדמים שתות שכר" (*mit'admim shetot shechar*, flushing red drinking wine). See his *Ḥiddush u-Masoret*, 72. In the *Taḥkemoni*, al-Ḥarizi follows this poem with ten rebuttals said to have been composed by ten outraged listeners.

35 In the Hebrew, al-Ḥarizi's poem ends with the first two words of Leviticus 18:22: ואת זכר לא תשכב משכבי אישה תועבה הוא (*ve-et zakhar lo tishkav mishkevei ishah to`evah hi*). Literally but lumpily translated, this would read: "And with a male you shall not lie down the lyings of a woman; this is an abomination/detestable."

36 Schirmann, "The Ephebe"; Wright, Jr., "Masculine Allusion," 1–23; Pellat, "Liwāṭ," 157; Roth, "Fawn," 157–72; idem, "The Care and Feeding of Gazelles," 95–118; idem, "Religious Constraints"; Rowson, "The Categorization of Gender," 50–79.

37 Crompton, "Male Love and Islamic Law," 153; Elizur, *Shirat ha-Ḥol*, 2:82; Ratzaby, "Ha-Ahavah be-Shirat R. Shemuel ha-Nagid," 146, esp. fn. 35; Pellat, "Liwāt," 157; Roth, "Fawn," 157–72; Schirmann, "The Ephebe," 56.

38 Scheindlin, "A Miniature Anthology," 113–15; idem, *Wine, Women and Death*, 87–8. See also Roth, "The Care and Feeding of Gazelles," 95–118; Pellat, "Liwāt," 157.

39 Crompton, "Male Love and Islamic Law," 144–9. In a very amusing essay entitled "Boasting Match over Maids and Youths," the earlier theologian al-Jāḥiẓ presents an imagined debate between opponents arguing the merits and demerits of sexual intercourse with males vs. females. Interestingly, the debate focuses not on any overarching philosophical or religious issues, but concentrates largely on practicalities; for example, the beauty of boys lasts for ten years, at most, before they reach puberty and become men (i.e., no longer beautiful). The beauty of a female, by contrast, lasts for at least forty years. On the other hand, when one purchases a female slave, one must wait before having sex with her in order to determine whether she is already pregnant or not; no such waiting is required when one purchases a boy slave. Indeed,

one never worries about pregnancy with boys. See William M. Hutchins, trans., *Nine Essays of al-Jahiz* (New York: Peter Lang, 1989), 139–66.

40 As Ibn Ḥazm notes, his poem is based on an actual event in which the protagonists were a male–female couple. Thus, it is possible that Ibn Ḥazm's poem is meant to depict the female lover's perspective as she aches for a male beloved, the actual situation that inspired the poem. The Arabic grammar here helps little; the narrator does not describe himself, and all of the verbs attributed to the narrator are in the first person present tense (which is the same for the male and female voice). Nonetheless, I am fairly unconvinced that this poem presents the female as narrator. In the first place, Ibn Ḥazm rarely, if ever, writes from the female perspective. Secondly, female protagonists do not consult male advisors who attempt to convince them to "snap out of it" (as in line 1). Relatedly, there would be little problem with a female having fallen for a male lover. And finally, Ibn Ḥazm compares the couple to the al-Sāmirī–Jibrīl relationship, in which both actors are male.

41 Schippers, "Humorous Approach of the Divine," 121. The same was not true for the Hebrew poets, the vast majority of whom filled religious roles as well.

42 By "pre-Islamic Muslim sacred history," I mean the sacred monotheistic history before the revelation to Muḥammad of the religion known as Islam, i.e., the accounts of the Children of Israel as they appear in the Qur'ān and in the *ḥadīth*.

43 Presumably the Israelites brought this jewelry from Egypt. See Exodus 12:35–6. The sin of the golden calf appears in the Bible in Exodus 32.

44 The Qur'ān (v. 88) uses the plural form فقالوا ("and they said," not "he said"). The simplest explanation for the plural would place this statement in the mouths of the Children of Israel, who had participated in and witnessed the event. Commentators largely appear to have thought this an incorrect understanding and, ignoring the plural, place the declaration in al-Sāmirī's mouth only. Infrequently, a commentator will suggest that the Children of Israel themselves uttered these words. See Muḥammad b. Jarīr al-Ṭabarī, *Jāmi` al-bayān `an ta'wīl āy al-qur'ān* (Beirut: Dār al-fikr, 1988), v. 9 (16): 199–200. In his translation of the Qur`ān, Abdullah Yusuf Ali explains that the plural refers to al-Sāmirī and his "partisans," but was accepted by the people as a whole and so the statement was attributed to them. See Abdullah Yusuf Ali, trans., *The Holy Qur-an: Text, Translation and Commentary* (Lahore, Pakistan: 1946), vol. 2, on Q 20:88.

45 The full text of v. 88 in English reads: "This is your God and the god of Moses but he has forgotten." Muslim exegetes divide into two camps regarding the subject of the phrase "he has forgotten." Some maintain this was uttered by the Qur'ān's narrative voice and refers to al-Sāmirī, who forgot all he learned under Mūsā (i.e., Islam). Others place the words in al-Sāmirī's mouth and explain that al-Sāmirī tried thereby to convince the Children of Israel that Mūsā was still up on the mountain because he had forgotten about them, or had gotten lost (forgotten the way), or that Mūsā had forgotten God. See al-Ṭabarī, *Jāmi` al-bayān*, 9 (16): 200–1.

Based on this verse, A. S. Yahuda asserts that the Qur'ānic legend of al-Sāmirī and the calf entered the Islamic canon when a Jewish informant related the biblical story of King Jeroboam of Israel (I Kgs. 12:28–9) to Muḥammad. According to I Kings 12, Jeroboam, in an effort to fortify his rule against the kingdom of Judea (home of the Temple), erected two calves of gold, placed one in Bethel and one in Dan and declared to his subjects, "Behold your gods, O Israel, who brought you up out of the land of Egypt." The Qur'ānic al-Sāmirī reflects Jeroboam both in deed and in words. In his telling, states Yahuda, the Jewish narrator referred to Jeroboam as "al-Sāmirī" because Jeroboam was crowned in Shechem (I Kgs. 12:1), the Samaritan sacred center in Muḥammad's day. Yahuda maintains that Muḥammad later unintentionally combined this story of Jeroboam with the account of the golden calf in the desert in Exodus 32. See Yahuda, "A Contribution to Qur'ān and Ḥadīth Interpretation," in

Ignace Goldziher Memorial, Volume I, ed. S. Löwinger and J. Somogyi (Budapest, 1948), 286–90.

An interesting biblical connection between a calf-idol and Samaria (not noted by Yahuda) appears in Hosea 8:5–6. There we read: "(5) He [God] rejects your calf, Samaria! I am furious with them! Will they never be capable of purity? (6) For it was Israel's doing. It was only made by a joiner, it is not a god. No, the calf of Samaria shall be reduced to splinters." *JPS Hebrew–English Tanakh* (Philadelphia: Jewish Publication Society, 1999). Unless otherwise noted, English translations of the Hebrew Bible in this chapter will follow this translation.

Jeroboam's words to the Israelites in the Land of Israel ("Behold your gods ...") reflect Aaron's when he built the original golden calf for their ancestors in the desert, "These are your gods, O Israel, who brought you up out of the land of Egypt" (Ex. 32:4). This is likely an intentional biblical intertextual reference, intended to hint/warn the Bible's readers that just as Aaron's calf-building ended badly for the Israelites, so too will Jeroboam's.

Heinrich Speyer and Uri Rubin have suggested parallels between the al-Sāmirī episode and the biblical Zimri of Num. 25:1–8. See Rudi Paret, *Der Koran: Kommentar und Konkordanz* (Stuttgart, 1971), 335; Uri Rubin, "Traditions in Transformation: The Ark of the Covenant and the golden calf in Biblical and Islamic Historiography," *Oriens* 36 (2001): 196–214.

46 The midrashic *Deuteronomy Rabbah* (*c.* 450–800) relates a similar story regarding Aaron's attempt at self-justification: having miscalculated, the Children of Israel thought that Moses was delayed in descending the mountain and would not be returning to them. And so the people stormed a meeting of the seventy Elders of Israel and demanded a new god. Ḥur, Aaron's grandson, rebuked them harshly, and they, in turn, killed him. They then turned on Aaron, threatening his life too. Attempting to buy some time until Moses' return and to appease his attackers while preventing them from sinning at the same time, Aaron asked the womenfolk for their jewelry. He later explained to Moses that he figured that since the women were more pious than the men, they would not easily acquiesce to this request. Aaron's plan might have succeeded, for the women did as he suspected and brought nothing forward. However, the men stepped in and brought forth their own precious metals. See, among others, *Deuteronomy Rabbah*, 15:21 in *Midrash Rabbah ha-Mevo'ar* (Jerusalem: Mekhon ha-Midrash ha-Mevo'ar, 5744–[1983–]), *Devarim*. Basing himself on the use of the word يكفون (*yakufūn*, they cleaved), Rubin suggests that the version in ch. 7 of the Qur'ān was based on the incident of Ba`al Pe`or in Num. 25:1–8, in which the Israelites cleaved to (נצמדים, *nitzmadim*) idol worship. See Rubin, "Traditions in Transformation," 201.

47 Overzealously, Ali comments (n. 2621), "This answer of the Sāmirī is a fine example of unblushing effrontery, careful evasion of issues, and invented falsehoods." Ali assumes al-Sāmirī lied in his explanation; in other words, according to Ali, al-Sāmirī saw nothing special but claimed, falsely, to have glimpsed something that the mass of the people there did not. That al-Sāmirī claims that he alone saw the angel (as we shall see below) only compounds the ludicrousness of the claim, he maintains. Unlike Ali, the Islamic traditions themselves accept the truthfulness of al-Sāmirī's claim of having seen an angel whom no one else spied. Only one tradition, suspicious for its lack of a chain of transmission (*isnād*), takes a position somewhat resembling Ali's. According to al-Ṭabarī, "some scholars" maintain that one should understand al-Sāmirī's "I saw what they did not see" as indicating that no one but he knew that he had thrown dust into the pyre (rather than that he saw something special). *Jāmi` al-bayān*, 9 (16): 205–6.

48 For an analysis of the phrase "*lā misāsa*" and its implications for al-Sāmirī's identity, see Ignaz Goldziher, "*Lā misāsa*," *Revue Africaine* 52 (1908), 23–5. See also below, n. 79.

49 The phrase remains as vague in the Arabic as in the English. The context of the narrative helps somewhat in deciphering the meaning. The verses that precede and follow our account concern the surety of the punishments of the Day of Judgment. Here, too, Allāh promises that without fail He will punish al-Sāmirī on the Day of Judgment. See also al-Ṭabarī, *Jāmiʿ al-bayān,* 9 (16): 206–8.

Interestingly, al-Sāmirī's punishment recalls a line from the Hebrew Bible's book of Lamentations. There the author blames the sinning prophets and priests of Jerusalem for having caused the destruction of the city. According to Lamentations 4:13–14, these two groups shed the blood of the just (דַּם צַדִּיקִים, *dam ẓaddiqim*) and then wandered blindly through the streets, so defiled by the blood they had just shed that none could touch their garments. Verse 15 then relates: " 'Away! Unclean!' people shouted at them, 'Away! Away! Touch not!' So they wandered and wandered again; For the nations had resolved: 'They shall stay here no longer' " (סוּרוּ טָמֵא קָרְאוּ לָמוֹ סוּרוּ סוּרוּ אַל תִּגָּעוּ כִּי נָצוּ גַּם נָעוּ אָמְרוּ בַּגּוֹיִם לֹא יוֹסִפוּ לָגוּר). Like al-Sāmirī, the prophets and priests were declared untouchable ("Touch not!") and were exiled ("Away!" and "They shall stay here no longer!"). Other than that both have sinned, I am unsure as to what link there is between al-Sāmirī's building a golden calf in the desert and the much later murderous priests/prophets of the First Temple period that should result in similar punishments. Even more befuddlingly, according to the Hebrew Bible only menstrual blood renders a body impure. Other spilled blood does not; while a dead body transmits ritual impurity, one does not need to come into physical contact with its blood or with it to be "infected" by impurity (see Num. 19). Thus Lamentations' exhortation against the priests/prophets remains enigmatic. What's more, the Lamentations' charges of exile and "Touch-not" come not from God or a prophet (as they do in the Qur'ān) but from some anonymous "people."

Another version of this account appears in Q 7:148–54, though with less detail and without any reference to al-Sāmirī. According to Ismail Albayrak, this absence of information derives from chapter 7's main concern: the insistence of the Israelites on sinning, despite Allāh's warning. See his "The Qur'ānic Narratives of the Golden Calf Episode," *Journal of Qur'ānic Studies* 3:1 (2001): 63. Chapter 7 relates simply that the "people of Moses" made a calf out of their ornaments, in the prophet's absence. It seemed to low (moo) and so they sinningly took it for worship. When they saw that they had erred, they repented. In this rendition, Mūsā reacts far more aggressively to his brother, seizing Hārūn by his hair and dragging him on the ground. The bedraggled Hārūn cries out that the people overcame him and threatened to kill him.

50 20:96: "فقبضت قبضة من أثر الرسول" (*fa-qabaḍutu qubḍata min athar al-rasūl*).

51 In the notes to his translation of the Qur'ān (n. 2621 in ch. 20), Abdullah Yusuf Ali proposes that al-Sāmirī might have intended to mislead Mūsā into just such an understanding. Ali suggests that perhaps al-Sāmirī hoped that a little flattery would convince Mūsā to forgive him for having constructed a pagan idol and leading the Children of Israel astray in worshiping it. And so, al-Sāmirī obsequiously claimed to have treated Mūsā's footprints as something unique and possibly supernatural, gathering up the dust Mūsā left when he walked by. No such interpretation appears in the classical commentaries surveyed here.

52 This vague reference to a cow mysteriously arising from a fire reflects Aaron's words to Moses in Exodus 32: 2–5. The narrative relates that Aaron collected the earrings from the people and fashioned them with a graving tool into the form of a calf (without any mention of a smelting fire). In v. 24, Aaron describes the situation somewhat differently to Moses. He reports that he collected the gold from the people and "I cast it into the fire, and there came out this calf." In reporting the matter this way, Aaron distances himself from active culpability by almost bewilderedly blaming the fire.

53 Zubaidi, "The Impact of the Qur'ān," 340–2.

54 Al-Ṭabarī wrote a *tafsīr* (commentary) of the Qur'ān known as *Jāmi` al-bayān `an ta'wīl āy al-qur'ān.* He also wrote a "History of Prophets and Kings" (*Ta'rīkh al-rusul wa-al-mulūk*), which used much *ḥadīth* and *tafsīr* materials. Both compendia are used here. Although al-Tha`labī too wrote a Qur`ān commentary, it did not survive to modern times. We draw here instead from his compendium of extra-Qur'ānic narrative expansions known as the *Qiṣaṣ al-anbiyā'* (Stories of the Prophets). Both of his works appear to have been well respected by classical Muslim scholars, despite a later suspicion of *qiṣaṣ* materials. For more on al-Tha`labī and this genre of Muslim literature, see Shari L. Lowin, *The Making of a Forefather: Abraham in Islamic and Jewish Exegetical Narratives* (Leiden: E. J. Brill, 2006).

55 Born in Fars, al-Bayḍāwī, of the Shāfi`ī school, became known for his scholarship and eventually served as chief *qāḍī* (religious judge) in Shirāz. He authored several theological works, works on law, jurisprudence, and grammar, and a Qur'ān exegesis, *Anwār al-tanzīl wa-asrār al-ta'wīl*, which was mainly a summary of the *tafsīr* of the Mu`tazilī scholar al-Zamakhsharī (1075–1144). For more, see $EI^2$, s.v. "Al-Bayḍāwī, `Abd Allah," by J. Robson (1:1129).

56 Of all the commentators here, al-Kisā'ī is considered the least "reliable"; his work appears intended for a popular rather than scholarly audience and the overall impression of the work is that al-Kisā'ī relied more on his memory or imagination than on written sources. He also adopted stories of Jewish origin which other authors did not accept, or know of, and did so freely. Al-Kisā'ī's work remains relevant since despite the official objection to his work, his materials can be detected as having seeped through to many different corpii. For more on al-Kisā'ī, see EI^2, s.v. "al-Kisā'ī, Ṣāḥib Ḳiṣaṣ al-Anbiyā'," by T. Nagel (5:176).

57 Al-Ṭarafī's *qiṣaṣ* deviates little from other works of the same genre and appears to rely largely on al-Ṭabarī's *tafsīr* and Isḥāq ibn Bishr's *Mubtada' al-dunyā wa-qiṣaṣ al-anbiyā'*. For more on al-Ṭarafī, see Roberto Tottoli, "The Qiṣaṣ al-anbiyā' of Ibn Muṭarrif al-Ṭarafī (d. 454/1062): Stories of the Prophets from al-Andalus," *al-Qantara* 19 (1998): 131–60.

58 Muḥammad b. Jarīr al-Ṭabarī, *Ta'rīkh al-rusul wa-l-mulūk* (Leiden: E. J. Brill, 1879–1901), 1:478. In his *tafsīr*, al-Ṭabarī includes multiple opinions as to what these "ornaments" included. Some said it included jewelry, while others insisted vehemently that no precious metals were involved. This latter stance poses a problem: If the ornaments were *not* metal, out of what was the golden calf formed? The scholars do not address this problem. See *Jāmi` al-bayān*, 9 (16): 198–9; Aḥmad b. Muḥammad al-Tha`labī, *Qiṣaṣ al-anbiyā' al-musamma `arā'is al-majālis* (Miṣr: Sharikat maktabat wa-maṭba`at Muṣṭafā al-Bābī al-Ḥalabī wa-awlādihī, 1374/1954), 209. According to al-Ṭabarī (*Ta'rīkh*, 1:486), Mūsā instructed them, on Allāh's command, to borrow these items. Al-Tha`labī adds that they did so on the pretext of needing to attend a festival. As noted above (n. 43), Ex. 12:35–6 relates that Moses commanded the Israelites to borrow jewels of silver and gold from the Egyptians, as per God's instructions in Exodus 11:1–3.

59 Al-Ṭabarī, *Ta'rīkh*, 1:489; *Jāmi` al-bayān*, 9 (16): 200; al-Tha`labī, 209.

60 Al-Ṭabarī, *Ta'rīkh*, 1:492–3; *Jāmi` al-bayān*, 9 (16): 205; al-Tha`labī, 209.

61 Al-Ṭabarī, *Ta'rīkh*, 1:489.

62 Al-Ṭabarī, *Ta'rīkh*, 1:489; al-Tha`labī, 208; al-Kisā'ī, in Isaac Eisenberg, *Vita Prophetarum auctore Muḥammad ben Abdallah al-Kisa'i* (Lugduni-Batavorum: E. J. Brill, 1923), 218–19. A similar account appears in Ibn Isḥāq's biography of Muḥammad (*sīra*). This work exists today only in a form shortened and heavily edited by Ibn Isḥāq's student Ibn Hishām (d. 827 or 833). It also appears in citations of other scholars, most notably al-Ṭabarī. Gordon D. Newby "recreated" the first part of Ibn Isḥaq's three-part work, *Kitāb al-mubtada'*, the section tracing from the creation of the world to the beginning of pre-Islamic Arabian history. This portion had been deleted by Ibn

Isḥāq's student, Ibn Hishām. See Gordon D. Newby, *The Making of the Last Prophet: A Reconstruction of the Earliest Biography of Muhammad* (Columbia: University of South Carolina Press, 1989), 132. On the problems with Newby's methodology, see Lawrence Conrad, "Recovering Lost Texts: Some Methodological Issues," *JAOS* 113 (1993): 258–63.

63 According to al-Bayḍāwī, al-Sāmirī recognized both Jibrīl and his horse from an earlier time in his life. Fearing Fir`awn's decree (Q 28:4), al-Sāmirī's mother had disposed of him shortly after his birth and Jibrīl cared for him till he grew up. See `Abdallāh b. `Umar al-Bayḍāwī, *Tafsīr al-Bayḍāwī* (Beirut: Dār al-kutub al-`ilmiyya, 1988), 2:56 (Q 20:96). See also the Andalusian al-Ṭarafī in Roberto Tottoli, ed., *The Stories of the Prophets by Ibn Muṭarrif al-Ṭarafī* (Berlin: Klaus Schwarz Verlag, 2003), 153–4. Al-Ṭarafī records another tradition that maintains that al-Sāmirī was not of the Children of Israel but joined with them and feigned Islam while continuing to worship cows in his heart. For an in-depth discussion of the Islamic explanations of al-Sāmirī's name, identity, where he came from, and how he recognized the angel Jibrīl, see Lowin, *The Making of a Forefather*, ch. 3.

64 Some exegetes note that al-Sāmirī asked Hārūn for permission to throw in what he held in his hand. Harūn, thinking that al-Sāmirī held more Egyptian jewelry in his closed fist, acquiesced. See al-Tha`labī, 209.

65 The logical problem here stands out: Why did horse-footprint dust create a calf and not a horse? The classical *ḥadīth* accounts do not emphasize this point. The choice of calf as idol posed a puzzle for the midrashic traditions as well, some of which did attempt to account for it. According to the eleventh-century *Midrash Leqaḥ Tov*, the Israelites saw the Ministering Angels helping them at the crossing of the sea and afterward saw their footprints, which resembled cow footprints (according to Ezek. 1:7, the angels of Ezekiel's vision had calves' feet). When later they requested that Aaron build them a new god, they thus requested it be in the form of a calf, reminiscent of this moment of salvific glory and power. And thus Aaron did, creating the calf out of the condensed earth from the ground. See Toviyahu ben Eliezer, *Midrash Leqaḥ Tov ha-Mekhuneh Pesiqta Zutarta `al Ḥamisha Ḥumshei Torah*, vol. 2, ed. S. Buber (Vilna: Ram, 5640 [1880]), on Ex. 32:4.

66 See al-Ṭabarī, *Ta'rīkh*, 1:492–3; al-Tha`labī, 209. In *Jāmi` al-bayān*, 9 (16): 205, al-Ṭabarī records this tradition with a particularly weak *isnād*, ending in Ibn `Abbās.

67 This explanation appears to derive from a close reading of Q 20:88, which attributes causality to al-Sāmirī himself: "Then *he* brought out for them the image of a calf" (emphasis mine). A similar explanation appears in al-Bayḍāwī, 2:56 (Q 20:96).

68 Al-Tha`labī, 209; and al-Kisā'ī, 219. Al-Tha`labī cites al-Suddī's opinion that the cow kept lowing and even walked about. See also al-Ṭabarī, *Ta'rīkh*, 1:493–4; *Jāmi` al-bayān*, 9 (16): 200, 205–6; and al-Ṭarafī, 154. A tradition from Mujāhid maintains that the cow did not actually moo. Rather, the air flowing through the hollow metal caused a lowing-like sound, which the Children of Israel mistook for a miraculous moo noise. See *Jāmi` al-bayān*, 9 (16): 205; al-Ṭarafī, 154–5. According to other accounts, Iblīs (Satan) caused the sound by taking up residence in the calf and blowing. Others maintain that al-Sāmirī set the rear end of the calf against a wall and placed a man on the other side of it, with his mouth at the level of the calf's rear, which had a hole in it. When the man blew through a hole in the wall, and into the cow's behind, it lowed. See al-Tha`labī, 209. A similar rendition appears in the earlier *tafsīr* of Ibn Abī Ḥātim (d. *c.* 713) who explains that the cow did not actually come to life and moo; the sound resulted from air entering into the empty metal vessel through a hole in its rear and issuing forth from its mouth. See `Abd al-Raḥmān ibn Abī Ḥātim, *Tafsīr al-Qur'ān al-`aẓīm*, ed. As`ad Muḥammad al-Ṭayyib (Riyad: Maktabat Nizār Muṣṭafā al-Bāz, 1997), V: 1568 (no. 8990). This is also cited in Uri Rubin, "Traditions in Transformation," 202.

Not surprisingly, some commentators found this whole line of thought uncomfortable. How could a human being command a cow to come into existence? How could footprint dust cause such a miraculous occurrence? Such powers of creation should belong to Allāh only! Thus we find in some of the commentaries that when Allāh informed Mūsā of the existence of the cow worshiped by the Children of Israel, Mūsā immediately asked the same question. Allāh replied that He Himself had breathed life into the hunk of metal. But, cried Mūsā, then You Yourself led them into temptation! See al-Ṭabarī, *Ta'rīkh*, 1:489, 490; *Jāmi` al-bayān*, 9 (16): 200. Al-Tha`labī tells the same story but adds that Allāh justified Himself, replying, "I saw into their hearts and merely made it easy for them to do what they already wished" (210). In al-Ṭabarī's works, Allāh remained silent. In *Exodus Rabbah* (eighth–tenth century), Moses expresses similar dismay at God's role in the sin, albeit His role is presented as more removed than Allāh's here. According to *Exodus Rabbah*, Moses defends the Israelites by pointing out to God that it was both irrational and unfair to blame them for paganism when He Himself told Moses they would sin against Him this way. See *Midrash Rabbah ha-Mevo'ar. Shemot*, 43:8.

69 Al-Ṭabarī, *Jāmi` al-bayān*, 9 (16): 200. In one tradition, the sources remain anonymous. Al-Ṭabarī includes another chain going back to Qatada (al-Ḥasan – `Abd al-Razzāq – Mu`mar – Qatada).

70 One wonders if Ibn Ḥazm's choice of an exegetical option was influenced by his having been a pious jurist, since the version he uses appears to be the slightly less sacrilegious one. In having the calf simply appear out of the fire, this rendition removes the active power of creation from a human (al-Sāmirī) and allows instead for the implication that Allāh Himself manufactured the calf.

71 Only Mūsā's escape from death appears in the Qur'ān. See Q 28:1–13. Al-Sāmirī's story appears only in the exegetical materials. For more on the various Islamic traditions regarding al-Sāmirī's rescue and his connection to Mūsā, see Lowin, *The Making of a Forefather*, 165–8.

72 Schippers, "Biblical and Koranic Quotations," xiii. Yellin mentions the phenomenon of Andalusian Arabic poets' utilization of the Qur'ān (and pre-Islamic Arabic materials) as well in his *Torat ha-Shir ha-Sefaradit*, 103.

73 Al-Ṭabarī, *Jāmi` al-bayān*, 9 (16): 200.

74 As noted above, n. 49.

75 Albayrak points out that al-Sāmirī's sacrilege appears even in the vocabulary he chooses when justifying his actions before Mūsā. Al-Sāmirī uses the term بصر (*baṣar*), meaning to see and, metaphorically, to think or know (Q 12:96: "I saw what they did not see"). The Qur'ān uses this same term a number of times in speaking of Allāh's knowledge of His creatures' thoughts and actions. Additionally, al-Sāmirī states that he took a قبضة (handful) from the footprint and from this created the calf. The Qur'ān employs this word, and derivatives of it, in describing Allāh's seizing the earth in His hand and performing creative actions. See Albayrak, "Qur'ānic Narratives," 64.

76 See Q 4:48, 116.

77 On Ibn Ḥazm's theological teachings, see Muḥammad Abū Zahrah, *Ibn Ḥazm, ḥayātuhu wa-`aṣruhu, ārā'uhu wa-fiqhuhu* (Cairo: Dār al-fikr al-`arabī, 1393/1954); Turki, 394–6 (in n. 5 above).

78 Some of the traditions surprisingly acknowledge these powers, but then mitigate them by reminding readers that Jibrīl is but a servant of Allāh Himself. Others insist Allāh alone created the calf and blew life into it. See n. 68.

79 Various scholars have attempted to puzzle out the source and meaning of the phrase *la misāsa*. Some, like Ignaz Goldziher, understood this as indicating that the Qur'ānic al-Sāmirī belonged to the Samaritans, whose purity laws prevented them from interacting freely with others. Just as the Qur'ān sees Jewish dietary laws as punishment for sin (Q 4:160), the Qur'ān here presents Samaritan purity laws as a punishment for

al-Sāmirī's actions. See *EI*[2], s.v. "al-Sāmirī," by Bernard Heller and Andrew Rippin (8:1046). For a fascinating discussion of the Muslim understanding of the intricacies of Jewish law as divine punishment, see Ze'ev Maghen, *After Hardship Cometh Ease: The Jews as Backdrop for Muslim Moderation* (Berlin and New York: Walter de Gruyter, 2006).

80 See *Ṭauḳ*, 11 (Nykl, 13; Arberry, 31). For samples of Arabic (and Hebrew) poems by other authors extolling suffering for love, see Schippers, *Spanish Hebrew Poetry*, 169–70. See also Monroe, *Hispano-Arabic Poetry: A Student Anthology*, 174, 274–5; and Scheindlin, "Ibn Gabirol's Religious and Sufi Poetry." In one example which plays with this trope of lovesickness, al-Mu`tamid, king of Seville, writes of wanting to remain ill (from some other illness) so that a particular beloved servant girl will continue to visit him. See *Dīwān al-Mu`tamid b. Abbād*, ed. Badawī and al-Majīd, 8. English translation from Nykl, *Hispano-Arabic Poetry*, 143.

81 Nykl, 139 (*Ṭauḳ*, 90; Arberry, 185).

82 *Ṭauḳ*, 6–7 (Nykl, 6–7; Arberry, 21–3).

83 Nykl, 137 (*Ṭauḳ*, 89; Arberry, 183).

84 When they do elaborate on the nature of the al-Sāmirī–Jibrīl relationship, they relate that the two resembled more parent and child, a decidedly un-*`ishq* filled bond. See above, p. 95.

85 While the Bible only hints at Gabriel's exact identity (see n. 86), the classical midrashic traditions state outright that he is one of the שרים של מעלה (*sarim shel ma`lah*, [angelic] servants of on high). See, for example, *BT Baba Batra* 75a, and the fifth-century *Genesis Rabbah*, ch. 78:1 in *Midrash Rabbah Bereishit*, ed. J. Theodor and Ch. Albeck (Berlin, 1903–36; reprint, Jerusalem: Wahrmann, 1965).

86 Jibrīl appears by name three times in the Qur'ān itself: 2:97 (as in charge of revelation), 2:98 (as an angel, possibly chief angel, along with Michael), and 66:4 (again, possibly a chief angel). He also appears numerous times in the *sīra* and *ḥadīth* literature. According to Islamic tradition, when he appears to humans, he generally appears as an ordinary man, well-built and strong, often wearing two green garments and a silk turban, and usually riding either a horse or a mule. See *EI*[2], s.v. "Djabrā'īl," by J. Pederson (2:362–4). The name "Gabriel" appears twice in the Bible, in the book of Daniel (8:15–19, 9:21–2). Both times the text describes him as looking like a man (כמראה גבר, *ke-mar'eh gever*, and איש, *ish*), and while the context indicates that he is not, in fact, a man, the text does not identify his true nature outright. In both cases Gabriel appears to Daniel to explain Daniel's vision to him.

87 In Juan R. I. Cole, "Individualism and the Spiritual Path in Shaykh Aḥmad al-Aḥsā'ī," in *Shi`ite Heritage: Essays on Classical and Modern Traditions*, ed. Lynda Clarke (Binghamton, NY: Global Publications/SUNY Binghamton, 2001): 347–8. Al-Aḥsā'ī (1753–1826), not a Ṣūfī himself, was not a supporter of this Ṣūfī stance. Ibn Ḥazm would have been particularly displeased to learn that he and the Ṣūfīs shared such an interpretation. As a committed Ẓāhirī opponent of *ta'wīl* (allegorical interpretation of Scripture), Ibn Ḥazm opposed the Ṣūfīs' exegetical methodology and the Ṣūfīs in general. See Goldziher, *The Ẓāhiris*, 123.

The Ṣūfī connection to al-Sāmirī has led opponents to accuse the Ṣūfīs of improperly following him. Critics have insisted that the ecstatic dance performed by some Ṣūfī groups as part of their meditation was invented and practiced by al-Sāmirī, who purposely made the movements promiscuous. The impious people who followed al-Sāmirī in his sinful worship of the golden calf danced this way around the statue, they say. See M. J. Kister, " 'Exert Yourselves, O Banū Arfida!': Some Notes on Entertainment in the Islamic Tradition," *JSAI* 23 (1999): 63.

88 The Ṣūfī vision of the throne of God and the four-faced angels reflect the vision of God's throne found in the book of Ezekiel 1. For more on this vision and its influence on the Jewish mystical tradition, see *EJ*, s.v. "Merkaba Mysticism," by Gershom Scholem, 14:66–7.

89 The Zohar, the thirteenth-century central text of mystical Judaism, similarly attributes to Gabriel the form of an ox. See *The Zohar*, trans. Harry Sperling and Maurice Simon (London: Soncino Press, 1931), 1:23b.

90 Michel Chodkiewicz, "The Endless Voyage," *Journal of the Muhyiddin Ibn Arabi Society* 19 (1996). See www.ibnarabisociety.org/articles/endlessvoyage.html. Accessed 23 Aug. 2012. Like Ibn `Arabī, midrashic texts allude to the tradition that the Israelites saw the four-faced angels of God's chariot at the crossing of the Red Sea, "corrupted" one of them, and sinned with the golden calf. See the ninth-century *Exodus Rabbah* 43:8 and n. 88 above.

91 The love poems of the *Tarjumān* have been the subject of some interpretive debate. While some see them as love poems disguised as mystical poems, others see them as mystical praises to God disguised as secular love poems.

92 Poem number 30 in Muḥyi'ddīn Ibn `Arabī, *The Tarjumán al-Ashwáq: A Collection of Mystical Odes by Muḥyi'ddín ibn al-'Arabí*, ed. and trans. Reynold A. Nicholson (London: Royal Asiatic Society, 1911), 33. Nicholson translates this somewhat awkwardly, and incomprehensibly, "My heart is the Sāmirī of the time: as often as it sees the footprints, it seeks the golden one that was turned to gold" (p. 111).

93 Mazalaoui, "I Follow the Religion of Love," 126.

Part II

Lovers and other liars

4 "His instruments are the instruments of Simeon and Levi": Ibn Gabirol and the silence of Jacob

Whereas Ibn Ḥazm employs the scriptural character of al-Sāmirī to speak of the beloved's divine-like power and nature, the Hebrew poem we turn to next alludes to Scripture for a decidedly more pessimistic view of the male beloved. Unlike his more upbeat Muslim contemporary, Solomon ibn Gabirol stresses not the positive aspects of his beloved's character, but the betraying nature of the adored one, and he uses Scripture to do so. In a short and somewhat difficult poem, Ibn Gabirol's lover compares his beloved's betrayal of him to the betrayal committed against the city of Shechem by Jacob's sons Simeon and Levi (Genesis 34). As with Ibn Mar Shaul's earlier Hebrew poem, which compared the beloved's treatment of the lover to David's murder of Uriah, Ibn Gabirol's verses, when analyzed, reveal a subversive reading of the biblical text embedded here. While the poem ostensibly criticizes Simeon and Levi for their treacherous attack on Shechem, hints in the meter, rhythm, and vocabulary of the poem point to a hidden critique of a less visible character in the biblical account. Namely, analysis of Ibn Gabirol's poem and its use of the scriptural referent reveal disapproval not for the actions of Simeon and Levi, but of the inaction of their father, Jacob.

Short biography of Ibn Gabirol

Brief and full of pain was the life of one of the most prolific and sublime of the Hebrew poets and philosophers of Muslim Andalusia, the famed Solomon ibn Gabirol, known in Arabic as Abu Ayyūb Yaḥyā ibn Sulaymān ibn Gabīrūl.[1] Born in Malaga *c.* 1021, Ibn Gabirol spent most of his life in the city of Saragossa, a center of Jewish and Arabic learning, to which his family had moved while he was yet a child and where he received an education in both spheres of knowledge in which the city excelled. When Ibn Gabirol was a teenager, his father, Judah, died, and the youth appears to have attached himself to the court of Yequtiel b. Yitzḥaq b. Ḥassan, a Jewish notable in Saragossa who became Ibn Gabirol's patron.[2] This close relationship ended with Yequtiel's death in 1039, an event mourned by Ibn Gabirol in more than one elegiac poem.[3] Ibn Gabirol remained in Saragossa until a short time after his mother died in 1045 and then made his way to Granada, where he attached himself to the court of Samuel ha-Nagid, the leader of the Granadan Jewish community and military chief of the Granadan ruler.[4] This relationship did not last long, however, and Ibn Gabirol soon found himself moving once more. Although the precise date of his death is somewhat disputed, the most reliable information places his death in Valencia in the year 1058, at less than 40 years of age.[5]

According to Ibn Gabirol's own description of himself in his poems, he was particularly short and unhandsome, two characteristics that led to his having endured a fair amount of teasing. From a young age he suffered from chronic pain, sometimes finding himself confined to bed, alone, for days on end. This unfortunate situation was either accompanied or caused by a nasty skin disease that modern scholars have theorized may have been skin tuberculosis.[6] Although Ibn Gabirol viewed his disease as a sort of "spiritual ransom" which he was fated to pay in exchange for living in the world, he wrote about it frequently in mocking and sarcastic terminology.[7] Given the aches and pains that he bore, it seems understandable that Ibn Gabirol was not always the pleasantest of men to be around. Moses ibn Ezra (*c.* 1055–*c.* 1135), in his famed treatise on poets and poetry, *Kitāb al-muḥāḍara wa-al-mudhākara*, notes that despite Ibn Gabirol's excellent and refined poetic style, he often erupted in bouts of irascibility brought on by his quick-triggered hot temper.[8] Indeed, Ibn Gabirol's skirmishes with influential men of his day were legendary and may have accounted for his falling out with Samuel ha-Nagid.

Although sickly, angry, and condemned to spend many hours against his will in the absence of human company, Ibn Gabirol early on proved himself a wordsmith of extreme beauty, depth, and sensitivity, composing poems in both the religious and secular realms. He wrote his earliest poems by no later than the age of 16 and important compositions by the age of 19.[9] Many of his secular poems were laudatory poems, praising his patrons and friends or grieving over their deaths. Others praised and described the beauty and power of nature, or of wisdom, or earthly love that drove the lover to distraction. A scholar of religion as well, Ibn Gabirol wrote mystical poetry and liturgical poems (*piyyutim*), many of which still appear in the prayer books of the Ashkenazi, Sephardi, and even Karaite communities.[10] His *piyyutim* and innovations as a *payyetan* (composer of liturgical poems) laid the foundations for the Andalusian style of *piyyutim* that grew up in his wake.

In addition to his works of poetry, Ibn Gabirol reported that he composed as many as twenty works of scholarship. Only two have survived to the modern period, both of them important works on philosophy, originally written in Arabic. Of the two, the more famous remains *Meqor Ḥayyim*, a Neoplatonic work on divinity and the Divine that manages to contain little that marks the work as specifically Jewish. Perhaps for this reason, the work was eventually rejected by Jewish thinkers and fell out of familiarity in Jewish circles.[11] The work rose to prominence among Christian philosophers, who knew it in its Latin translation as *Fons Vitae* and thought it to have been composed by a Christian or Muslim scholar named Avicebron or Avicebrol.[12] According to Moses ibn Ezra, Ibn Gabirol also composed works on physics and astronomy.[13] In addition to his philosophical, scientific, and poetic compositions, Ibn Gabirol was also known for his mastery of both the Written and Oral Torahs (i.e., the Hebrew Bible and Talmud).[14] Fragments of his biblical exegesis appear in the Bible commentaries of the slightly later Abraham ibn Ezra (1089–1164) and David Qimḥi (1160–1235), who cite them in his name.[15]

Possessing a fluid command of the biblical text, evident in both his exegesis and his religious poetry, Ibn Gabirol also became known as perhaps the greatest user of biblical רמז/רמיזה (*remizah/remez*) in medieval Spain. As noted, in רמז/רמיזה (*remizah/remez*), poets departed from the "regular" flow of the secular poem to hint at biblical events or personalities, without citing them directly. They then returned immediately to the content of the poem.[16] This type of poetic ornament depended not only on scriptural content, but also on the reader's familiarity with the Bible and its players, to make sense of the poetic verse. In a sense, רמז/רמיזה (*remizah/remez*) allowed the poet to play with both the scriptural text and the poem's audience, referring to the familiar sacred while turning it over and upside down in new and often surprising ways.[17] Though sickly, in pain, and generally veering toward anger, Ibn Gabirol nonetheless appears to have delighted in amusing his poems' audiences with innovative and often titillating incorporations of the biblical text, even in his secular lust poems, as we shall soon see.

Poem: הלנצח יעירני (*ha-Lanetzaḥ Ye`ireini*)

Scholars have theorized that because of his self-reported ugliness, repulsive illness,[18] and loneliness, Ibn Gabirol, who apparently never married, likely never experienced firsthand the charms of an adored favorite or the passion of falling in love with one who returned his ardor. Nonetheless, many are the poems of Ibn Gabirol in which he writes of precisely such emotions and ideas, of the allure of the male or female beloved, and of the power of the lover's desire for the object of his affection. In a sense, Ibn Gabirol's real-life suffering from unrealized love placed him solidly in the position of suffering-lover *extraordinaire*, a stance highly valued by Andalusian poetics; after all, it was assumed, a lover who did not suffer had no reason to write love poetry.

Exactly such a sentiment – that love is pain and the lover is one who suffers from passion – appears in a short, three-line poem by Ibn Gabirol, formulated in question-complaint form. This sentiment in and of itself should not strike us as unusual. What differentiates this poem from the mass of poems dealing with the suffering lover is Ibn Gabirol's masterful interweaving of numerous references, *remazim*, to unexpected biblical characters and storylines, both explicitly and subtly. Writes Ibn Gabirol:

הלנצח יעירני ולעד   יערער מוסדי חשק בשלוי
אשר פניו פני יוסף ביפיו   אבל כליו כלי שמעון ולוי
ולו נפשי לקחה לו אזי שב   לבקש עוד שאר נפשי בגוי[19]

[1a] Will he always awaken me and forever more
[1b] arouse the institutions of desire to agitate me in my tranquility?
[2a] For his face is like the face of Joseph in his beauty,
[2b] but his instruments are the instruments of Simeon and Levi.
[3a] If he were to take my soul to him, he would then return
[3b] to request the rest of my soul though I would thereby die.[20]

Ibn Gabirol's poem begins by speaking to its audience from the perspective of a lover tormented by his feelings for his beloved, which disrupt his serenity night after night, preventing him from sleeping. He then clarifies why he feels so beleaguered. His beloved, though beautiful, is also incredibly dangerous. In emphasizing these characteristics, Ibn Gabirol's lover notes that the beloved resembles the biblical Joseph in beauty and the biblical Simeon and Levi in harmfulness. As we will see, while Ibn Gabirol's use of these biblical brothers appears superficially as straightforward and obvious, a second glance at the phrase in which they appear, line 2, shows the line and the biblical comparison to be mysterious and full of hidden meaning.

Ibn Gabirol's poem and poetic tropes

Unrealized love and suffering for love

Little appears initially amiss in Ibn Gabirol's poem in terms of its conforming to the poetic styles and rules of the day; in truth, our poem fits the tropes of poetry in any number of ways. Most obviously, we find two lovers locked in an un-actualized relationship; rather than successfully spending time in one another's company, they find themselves separated by some unnamed obstacle, each alone in his own bed. To our lover, overcome with yearning and desire, the situation is nigh intolerable. Though he tries to rest, he finds no reprieve from his thoughts. Instead of a calming sleep washing over him, images of his absent beloved race through his mind and keep him from relaxing. Indeed, from the first two lines of the poem, one can easily picture the lover as he tosses and turns in bed, alone, while images of the beloved's face float above him, taunting him mercilessly and denying him the sweet oblivion of slumber.

Such love/lust-induced sleeplessness is not an invention of Ibn Gabirol's but was a hallmark of عشق (*`ishq*). As Ibn Gabirol's contemporary, the "authority" on love, Ibn Ḥazm noted, lovesickness was a disease that induced all sorts of torments. Most notable among them, explained Ibn Ḥazm, are a fondness for solitude and a tormenting sleeplessness.[21] Ibn Gabirol's lover, then, presents no deviation from type. Alone, unaccompanied by friends or advisors,[22] with only his thoughts for company, he cannot sleep, try as he might. Instead, his desire for his beloved boy awakens him every time he attempts to do so or manages to snag a few moments of calm (בשלוי, *be-shalvi*, l. 1b).

This obsessive love stands poised to result in a matter that is yet another poetic trope: the death of the lover at the hands of his beloved. It is not enough that our lover finds himself tortured by his heart and unable to rest his mind for a moment. Even eventual union with his beloved will provide no succor. Instead, moans the lover in line 3, "If he [the beloved] were to take my soul to him, he would certainly return to request the rest of my soul, though I would thereby die." In other words, even were the beloved to offer him union, this would not heal the lover from his suffering. Rather, the beloved's proposal would instead be met by the lover's death. According to Andalusian poetic dictates, if one feels oneself healthy and well, one could not possibly be in love; a true lover, such as the one in Ibn Gabirol's poem, suffers *to death.*[23]

The beautiful beloved

Other common poetic motifs likewise appear in Ibn Gabirol's poem, most obviously in the physical description of the beloved. The tropes regarding the external appearance of the beloved boys portrayed them as bearers of a youthful, dewy attractiveness. And this is precisely the depiction we find in Ibn Gabirol's poem. In line 2a, the beloved's physical appearance recalls that biblical paradigm of youthful male beauty, the forefather Joseph. Just as Ibn Mar Shaul's lover declared of his beloved, "like Joseph in his form (כיוסף בצורתו)," [24] Ibn Gabirol's lover recounts of his beloved that "His face is like the face of Joseph in his beauty." Readers of Genesis 39 will recall that after the young Joseph was attacked by his jealous older brothers, he was sold in Egypt as a slave in the house of Potiphar. Not long after his arrival, the wife of Potiphar took notice of their beautiful young servant, fell in lust with him, and attempted to entice him into lying with her. When the handsome Joseph would not be convinced or seduced, his mistress' lust for the beguiling servant drove her to physical aggression. Finding herself alone in the palace one day with Joseph, she grabbed at his clothes so powerfully that when Joseph ran from the room (and away from her) in refusal, his clothes remained behind him, in her tightly clenched fists. In describing the beauty that so ensnared the wife of Potiphar, Genesis 39:6 uses a phrase noteworthy for its rarity in the biblical text. Recounting the youth's eye-turning handsomeness, the Bible writes that he was יפה תואר ויפה מראה (*yefeh to'ar ve-yefeh mar'eh*), "of goodly description and goodly appearance."

Ibn Gabirol's reference to Joseph indicates that the beloved's beauty reflects more than just the trope of the youthful dewiness. Rather, as with Ibn Mar Shaul's beloved, Ibn Gabirol's beloved also radiates the typical Andalusian motif of feminized handsomeness. For Joseph is *not* the only biblical beauty to be so described. Rather, this exact doubled phrase appears in the Bible one other time: to describe Joseph's mother, Rachel. Genesis 29:16–17 relates that Laban had two daughters, an elder girl named Leah and a younger daughter named Rachel. While Leah had "soft eyes," Rachel was "יפת תואר ויפת מראה" (*yefat to'ar vi-yefat mar'eh*), "of goodly description and goodly appearance." That the biblical phrase indicates a particular type of beauty – feminine – becomes evident when we look more closely at the exact choice of words. Although the noun תואר (*to'ar*, description) appears with some frequency to describe both the Bible's handsome men and its fair women,[25] the noun מראה (*mar'eh*, appearance) is used to describe female beauty alone.[26] יפת מראה (*yefat mar'eh*) or טובת מראה (*tovat mar'eh*) ("of beautiful appearance" or "of goodly appearance") appears in the descriptions of Sarah, Rebecca, Rachel, Absalom's daughter Tamar, Bathsheba, Vashti, and Esther.[27] In describing Joseph with a term normally reserved for portraying womanly beauty, and with a doubled phrase that otherwise appears only to describe his mother, the biblical text implies that Joseph's handsomeness had a feminine quality to it.

In choosing the feminine Joseph as his image of beauty by alluding to the biblical phrasing of Genesis 39:6, Ibn Gabirol's lover relates that his beloved is a young, soft, feminized boy, in line with the Andalusian poetic tropes of male beauty. Scholars have long noted that the descriptions for Andalusian male and female beloveds so resemble one another that one sometimes has no way of detecting the gender of the lover's object of affection. When the poet omits any reference to gender-specific body parts (such as breasts or beard) and does not use gender-specific terminology, the poems can be read either homo- or hetero-erotically. In the case of boys, however, the first sign of true maleness often led to the lover's jilting his maturing beloved.[28]

The cruel beloved

Simeon and Levi and the attack on Shechem

Just as the first part of the description of the beloved, dealing with his physical aspect, sits squarely within the thematic parameters of Andalusian poetry of desire, so too the second part, a description of the beloved's actions, reflects the love/desire motifs. Writes Ibn Gabirol (l. 2), “אשר פניו פני יוסף ביפיו אבל כליו כלי שמעון ולוי,” “For his face is the face of Joseph in its beauty / But his instruments are the instruments of Simeon and Levi.” In comparing the beloved to the biblical weapon-wielding Simeon and Levi, the poet presents the beloved as the typical cruel and dangerous beloved.

The scriptural account to which Ibn Gabirol refers in this comparison stands as one of the more shocking tales of trauma and violence in the book of Genesis. Genesis 34 relates that Dinah, the daughter of Jacob, was raped by Shechem, a local prince of the nearby city bearing his name. After attacking and violating her, Shechem falls in love with Dinah, desires to marry her, and sends his father, Ḥamor, to ask for Dinah's hand in marriage from her brothers and father. Angered and dismayed by these events (v. 7), the circumcised sons of Jacob inform the Shechemites that they must circumcise themselves before any marital alliances might be made between them (v. 13). Pleased with such an answer, Ḥamor and Shechem convince the Shechemites to agree to the preconditions of the alliance, and every male in the city is circumcised. Then, on the third post-operative day, with the pain at its worst and all the males thereby incapacitated, two of the brothers, Simeon and Levi, take up their swords and launch a two-man attack against the city. They slay all the males, including Prince Shechem and his father, take their violated sister from Shechem's house, where she has been for the duration of the negotiations, and leave. The other sons of Jacob then step in and wholly plunder the town, taking everything of value as booty and turning the women and children into captives.[29]

Ibn Gabirol's poetic allusion to Simeon and Levi's violent and merciless assault on Shechem through his use of the term “instruments” (כלים) strikes the reader familiar with the Bible as a perfectly applicable *remez* (hinting) for describing the beloved's cruelty and dangerousness.[30] After all, Simeon and Levi's attack resulted not only in the deaths of Shechem (the rapist prince) and his father, Ḥamor, but also in the deaths of men *not* involved in their sister's rape. Indeed, Simeon and Levi appear to have indiscriminately slain every male in the city (v. 25). And, with the city thus undefended, the sons of Jacob continued the onslaught, despoiling the city completely and enslaving apparently innocent women and children (vv. 27–9). The episode presents an image of particularly cruel actors, a fitting referent for the cruel beloved.

The association between Simeon and Levi and menacing violence, in which they appear as bearers of threatening "instruments," accompanies Simeon and Levi through the book of Genesis. At the end of Jacob's life, Jacob gathers his sons to tell them what will ultimately become of them (Gen. 49). While most of the sons receive good news, Simeon and Levi do not fare well.[31] To Simeon and Levi, Jacob says,

> (6) Let not my person be included in their council,[32] let my being not be counted in their assembly. For when angry they slew men and when pleased they maimed oxen. (7) Cursed be their anger so fierce, and their wrath so relentless. I will divide them in Jacob, scatter them in Israel.

Although years have passed since the Shechem incident to which he alludes, Jacob does not refrain from raising the issue once again. At the end of his life and in his last speech to his brood, Jacob still sees his sons as violent attackers. His opposition to their behavior that day, when they undertook to viciously "slay men" and "maim oxen," remains as potent now as when they first took up their weapons. Then he said to Simeon and Levi, after their slaughter of the Shechemite males (Gen. 34:30), "You have brought trouble upon me, making me odious among the inhabitants of the land, the Canaanites and the Perizzites." At the end of his life he continues his disdain for their behavior that day, declaring, "Let not my being be counted in their assembly," distancing himself from Simeon and Levi and their aggressive use of their tools seemingly forever more.

Importantly, in his poem Ibn Gabirol applies the very same term to the cruel beloved as that used by Jacob to describe his sons' cruelty: instruments, כלים (*keilim*). As Jacob says at the beginning of his address to Simeon and Levi (49:5–6),

> (5) Simeon and Levi are brothers;[33] כְּלֵי חָמָס מְכֵרֹתֵיהֶם (*klei ḥamas mekheiroteihem*, instruments of *ḥamas*[34] are their weapons).[35]

The choice of the word "instruments" may seem insignificant at first, since the word כלים (*keilim*) is a general all-purpose word; it appears frequently in the Bible, either alone or in conjunction with another noun defining the type of instrument intended, to designate anything used as a utensil, vessel, implement or something carried.[36] Significantly, however, the word כלים (*keilim*) appears in association with Simeon and Levi only here, in Jacob's rebuke of the cruelty of their Shechemite assault (Gen. 49). In employing the same term for the beloved's behavior as that used by Jacob for Simeon and Levi's ruthlessness, Ibn Gabirol clearly (and successfully) intends the reader to recognize the trope of the beautiful but cruel and malicious beloved, on the model of Simeon and Levi.

Identity of the instruments

But what *are* these instruments used by our beloved, on the one hand, and by Simeon and Levi, on the other? Do they actually conform to the poetic tropes of meanness and danger? After all, the exact meaning of the term employed by Jacob in his condemnation of his sons in Genesis 49:5, כְּלֵי חָמָס מְכֵרֹתֵיהֶם (*klei ḥamas mekheiroteihem*), remains somewhat of a mystery. English translators, among others, have struggled to agree upon a definition.[37] The King James Version provides "instruments of cruelty are in their habitations."[38] The 1917 *JPS* translation of the Bible suggests "weapons of violence their kinship."[39] The updated *JPS* translation emends this, rendering the phrase "their weapons are the tools of lawlessness."[40]

The biblical context provides two possible explanations. On the most obvious level, one could logically read the "instruments" as swords. After all, the biblical account twice, in two consecutive verses, specifies the weapons used by Simeon and Levi in their attack and identifies them as swords. Records Genesis 34:25–6:

> (25) On the third day, when they [the Shechemites] were in pain, Simeon and Levi, two of Jacob's sons, brothers of Dinah, *took each his sword*, came upon the city unmolested, and slew all the males. (26) They put Ḥamor and his son Shechem *to the sword*, took Dinah out of Shechem's house, and went away.

Since the Bible records that Simeon and Levi came to the city armed with swords (v. 25), there seems little reason for the very next verse (v. 26) to mention again, by name, the weapons with which they then killed Ḥamor and Shechem. Yet it does. The repetition emphasizes the fact that their instruments of death were swords and swords *only*.[41] When Ibn Gabirol compares the lover's instruments to those borne by Simeon and Levi, he appears to instruct his readers to understand that, like the armed and dangerous forefathers, the beloved too carries a deathly dangerous sword.

Yet such an understanding of the term cannot be what Ibn Gabirol thought, or how he read the verse. For while the image of a sword-wielding youth may be the most obvious interpretation of the poem when read against the sword-wielding heroes of the biblical narrative, such an image makes little sense in the context of Andalusian poetry. Generally speaking, the beloved boys were not armed fighters; they were young boys, usually under the age of 14,[42] and often servants charged with the decidedly nonviolent task of pouring wine during poetry parties. A soldier, armed with a sword no less, stands as the antithesis of the soft and feminized boy who is the object of Andalusian poetic affection, especially one whose beauty recalls the decidedly nonviolent, youthful, and feminized Joseph (l. 2a).

Furthermore, if the poet intended the "instrument" of the beloved to refer to a sword, the comparison to Simeon and Levi's instruments seems too obvious. For then the poet, in effect, would be saying, "His swords are the swords of Simeon and Levi." Could there be a sword, an instrument of battle, which is *unlike* that of Simeon and Levi? A sword is an instrument of killing, of war, and remains so, unless beaten into a ploughshare or something else. One employs a sword to one main end – killing. In informing his readers that the beloved's swords resemble the swords of Simeon and Levi, Ibn Gabirol's lover tells us nothing new, interesting, or even poetic.[43]

A second possible interpretation requires us to read both the line of poetry and the biblical text with a slightly twisted sense of humor. In the biblical account of Genesis 34, Simeon and Levi successfully annihilated all of the Shechemite men only because their two-man attack constituted stage *two* of their dealing with the city. Stage one saw a negotiation in which the Shechemites agreed to circumcise themselves in return for intermarrying with Jacob's family and sharing in their fortune (vv. 14–25).[44] In stage two, Simeon and Levi entered the city full of recently circumcised men, now weakened and hurting, and slew them all before liberating their sister and bringing her home. In a certain sense then, Simeon and Levi's "instrument" was none other than the circumcised penises of the Shechemites. Only with them, or rather because of them, were Simeon and Levi able to single-handedly attack the city and put its residents to the sword.

Such reference to the penis as an "instrument," "tool," or "weapon" exists in the modern slang of many languages. Examples litter television, radio, film, and literature of all levels. Indeed, this militarized designation of the male genitalia is not new. It appears in the poems of one of the earliest influences on Andalusian love poetry, the famed Baghdadi poet Abū Nuwās (d. *c.* 813–15). In one particularly explicit poem, Abū Nuwās describes an aggressive sexual encounter with a sleeping boy, an interaction known in Arabic poetry as دبيب (*dabīb*), creeping. Writes Abū Nuwās: "I rose up and made for him, / Swaggering and erect, / Having prepared my ram for butting. / When I had fixed my lance in him, he woke / Like one prostrated by wounds."[45] Here Abū Nuwās names not one but two types of instruments of battle to refer to his genitals, the battering ram and lance.

If we read the poem's phrase in this fashion, with "instruments" referring to the beloved's penis, the words of Ibn Gabirol's lover take on a far more sexualized nuance. Says the lover now, my beloved appears as beautiful as the youthful, gentle, and innocent Joseph, who never harmed a soul. But do not be deceived; the youth knows how to use his "instrument," his penis. He is not the pliant and passive actor that he appears to be, the role that he, as the youthful Joseph-esque member of this relationship, ought to play.[46] Rather, instead of behaving as the *recipient* of my "affections," as he should, he wields his "instrument" as did Simeon and Levi their swords, aggressively, with intention to harm.

While such a reading clearly has its appealing points, it too ultimately proves unsatisfying. Most obviously, while poets often referred to their beloved's dangerous body parts in their descriptions of their beauty, they did so explicitly, naming both the body part itself and the weapon it resembled. Thus, eyes shoot arrows, hands and fingers slice like knives, and locks of hair curl around the beloved's face like biting snakes. In the case of beloved girls, breasts pierce like two lances ready to stab the one who dares come too close.[47] In the case of beloved boys, the first sprouting of the beard is said to resemble the sword sheath, both concealing a dangerous weapon.[48] In obvious contrast, Ibn Gabirol's poem only refers very generally to the beloved's danger zone, something the lover only vaguely designates as "instruments" (כליו, *keilav*). The comparison to the equally undefined "instruments of Simeon and Levi" does not much explain what the lover's instruments are.

One could theorize that perhaps Ibn Gabirol intended a well-known body part in his use of the word "instruments" and employed an Andalusian poetic code no longer known to us. After all, Hebrew and Arabic poets often employed code in their lust poetry. Thus, a lover's enjoying the nectar dripping from his beloved's rose was clearly understood as the poet's kissing his beloved's (red) mouth [the rose] and enjoying the taste of his/her saliva [nectar]. Or, when a lover finds himself tickled by the thorns in the beloved's rosebush, we understand that his young beloved's rosy-cheeked face has begun to sprout the first beard of puberty.[49] Significantly, however, the term "instrument" does not appear among these code words, tropes, or motifs in Andalusian poetry.

Instruments as betrayal

One soon realizes that the solution to our conundrum lies in understanding the instruments not as a physical item but as a behavior or personality trait. The true instrument that allowed Simeon and Levi to attack and defeat Shechem was not a weapon of war or a circumcised penis. Rather, their true tool was their guile, the dishonesty with which they deceived the Shechemites. As the Bible records, the brothers initially appear to accept Shechem's offer of uniting their two groups through marital bonds, adding only that the Shechemites must first circumcise themselves. However, the Bible instantly informs us that this stipulation, indeed their entire response to the Shechemites, was nothing more than a trick. As we read in Genesis 34:13, "Jacob's sons answered Shechem and his father Ḥamor, speaking with guile (בְּמִרְמָה, *be-mirmah*)." Instead of joining the Shechemites in kinship, Jacob's sons waited until the townspeople were weakened and defenseless, and then mercilessly attacked and slew them. Using the Shechemites' desire to join with the Children of Israel against them, the sons of Jacob betray the covenant they struck with them, a deceitful ruse they plotted from the very beginning.[50]

The phrase used by Jacob in his rebuke of Simeon and Levi in Genesis 49 likewise indicates that his sons' weapons were the instruments of betrayal. Turning to Simeon and Levi in Genesis 49:5, Jacob says, "Simeon and Levi are brothers; כְּלֵי חָמָס מְכֵרֹתֵיהֶם (*klei ḥamas mekheiroteihem*), the instruments of *ḥamas* are their weapons."[51] As noted earlier, translators have struggled to define the second half of this sentence, whose second word (חָמָס, *ḥamas*) bears an ambiguous meaning.[52] However, the most frequent and clearest biblical usages of this key word, חָמָס (*ḥamas*), link it to various sorts of trickery, duplicity, and violence caused by a betrayal of the truth, the manipulation of the truth, and the social contract that is thievery.[53] Significantly, classical rabbinic interpreters extended the definition of *ḥamas* to include also the betrayal of God that is idolatry.[54]

In attributing to the beloved these very same "tools of betrayal," Ibn Gabirol's lover accuses his beloved of behaving in precisely the same deceitful fashion. Though the beloved appears as beautiful, youthful, and innocent as Joseph, he manipulates his lover's desire for him, just as Simeon and Levi manipulated the Shechemites and their desire. Simeon and Levi's betrayal results in the death of the Shechemites; Ibn Gabirol's beloved's betrayal results in the death of the lover. As the lover writes of his duplicitous beloved (l. 3a–b), initially the beloved comes to take the lover's soul to him, seemingly lovingly (like Jacob's sons in accepting the Shechemite offer of unity). However, when he returns after a short absence, he does not do so to make good on his promise of love. Rather, like Simeon and Levi, who returned after an absence in order to kill the Shechemites and not marry them, the beloved comes to "request the rest of my soul though I thus die."

The particular vocabulary used by Ibn Gabirol in the rest of the poem further supports reading the "instruments" of the beloved and of Simeon and Levi as the betrayal specifically of one who offers a bond of love. In the first place, Ibn Gabirol's poem utilizes the language of marriage used in the Bible, where a man is said "to take to himself," לקחת לו (*laqaḥat lo*), a wife. Such phrasing appears in Genesis 34:16, when the brothers initially promised the Shechemites that they will intermarry with them, saying, "We will give our daughters to you וְאֶת בְּנֹתֵיכֶם נִקַּח לָנוּ (*ve-et benoteikhem niqaḥ lanu*), and your daughters we will take to ourselves." Ibn Gabirol's lover uses the same phrasing to speak of the beloved's behavior. He writes that initially the beloved "took her [my soul] to himself" (l. 3a); in Hebrew this is expressed with the phrase לקחה לו (*leqaḥah lo*), playing off of the biblical Hebrew term for marriage.[55]

This nonphysical understanding of the beloved's tool fits well within the framework of Andalusian poetic tropes. After all, the typical weapon of the beloved was his inconsistent, unfaithful, and betraying behavior, his cruel treatment of the one who loved him best. In a short and somewhat similar poem by Ibn Gabirol's one-time patron, Samuel ha-Nagid, we find this sentiment stated clearly and forcefully. Writes Samuel:

אלי, הפך נא לבב גוזל אשר גזל	נומי – וישיב לעפעפי מעט שינה
אהוב אשר בא באלתך ונתן לי	אהבת לבבו בלי אונס במתנה –
בגד וכן כל צבי בוגד, ועתה אם	תשא לחטאו, ואם אין – מחני נא![56]

Change, my God, the heart of that chick (*gozal*) that checked
My sleep, and make him give it back to me;
A fawn who swore by Your name to give
His love to me, a gift of his own free will,
And then betrayed me; lovers all betray.
Forgive his sin – or wipe me out, I pray.[57]

Here, too, we find a distressed lover, tossing and turning alone in bed, kept awake by his yearning for his beloved boy, whom he blames for his sleeplessness. Samuel ha-Nagid names outright the characteristic of the beloved that so harms him: betrayal. Says Samuel, although the beloved swore by God to love the poet/lover, he ultimately proved unfaithful. Indeed, he notes, such is the way of *all* boy-beloveds; they simply cannot be trusted, for they will all eventually prove untrue and treacherous.[58]

Problems with line 2b

While the imagery of the beautiful but deadly beloved, armed with instruments of deception, fits well with the tropes of Andalusian love poetry, something rings strange here in line 2. Although the words of line 2 point us to Simeon and Levi as the biblical allusion, the *structure* of the verse screams out an allusion to an entirely different referent. Says the lover about his beloved, "פניו פני יוסף ביפיו אבל כליו כלי שמעון ולוי" (*panav peni Yosef be-yofyo, aval keilav klei Shim`on ve-Levi*), "His face is the face of Joseph in his beauty, but his instruments are the instruments of Simeon and Levi." One familiar with the Hebrew Bible cannot help but hear the similarity to a line from an altogether different narrative, one that centers not around Jacob's sons and their actions, but on Jacob himself. In Genesis 27 the aged and blind patriarch Isaac famously declares of his son Jacob, "הַקֹּל קוֹל יַעֲקֹב וְהַיָּדַיִם יְדֵי עֵשָׂו" (*ha-qol qol Ya`aqov ve-ha-yadayim yedei `Esav*), "the voice is the voice of Jacob, but the hands are the hands of Esau." In both Genesis 27 and in our poem, we find the same distinctive and repetitive word pattern: noun–possessive noun–proper noun, noun–possessive noun–proper noun (voice–voice of–Jacob, hands–hands of–Esau: face–face of–Joseph [in beauty], instruments–instruments of–Simeon and Levi).

Let us return for a moment to the context of Genesis 27. According to this passage, at the end of his life, a blind Isaac desires to bless his elder, hunter son Esau and sends him out to hunt meat for him as a prelude to the blessing. Wanting Jacob to receive the blessing instead of her elder son, Esau, Isaac's wife Rebecca hatches an alternate plan; she slays goats from the family's own collection, cooks Isaac's favorite meal, and dresses the tent-dwelling Jacob in the hunter Esau's clothing, so that Jacob smells like his outdoorsy brother and will be able to deceive his father into giving him Esau's blessing. Jacob worries that his father might attempt to identify his son via touch, as the blind are wont to do, and that Isaac would then curse him rather than bless him. So Rebecca lays fur pelts over Jacob's smooth arms and neck in order that he feel like his hirsute twin. She then sends Jacob with the food into Isaac's tent. As soon as Jacob enters, the blind Isaac calls out, "Who are you, my son?" Replies Jacob, "I am Esau your firstborn; I have done as you have spoken" (v. 19). Surprised by the speed with which the meal has been caught and prepared, and seemingly suspicious, Isaac calls for his son to approach and reaches out to touch him. Feeling the Esau-like hairy arms but noting the voice of Jacob answering him, Isaac muses aloud (v. 22), "הַקֹּל קוֹל יַעֲקֹב וְהַיָּדַיִם יְדֵי עֵשָׂו" ("the voice is the voice of Jacob, but the hands are the hands of Esau"). Convinced that, despite the Jacobian voice, the man standing before him is the elder Esau, Isaac then blesses younger Jacob with the blessing of the firstborn. Deception completed, Jacob exits the tent just as the real Esau returns from the hunt.

Importantly, our poem's line mimics the phrase of Genesis 27 not only in structure but in content as well. As we can see, both the poem and the biblical narrative center round a case of identity fraud and betrayal by loved ones. The beloved and Jacob both present themselves as one thing while in reality they are another. Each presents himself at first as an honest and loyal participant in the relationship. The beloved presents himself as an innocent and loyal partner in a romantic relationship, showing his lover his Joseph-like face and taking the lover's soul to himself in love. Similarly, Jacob presents himself to his father as the obedient hunter-son (Esau) whom his father loves (Gen. 25:28).[59] Both ultimately prove false. The beloved turns out to betray his lover, taking his soul entirely, and thereby killing him, and the costumed son standing before Isaac turns out not to be the obedient elder son, Esau, but the deceptive younger son, Jacob.

Ibn Gabirol and criticism of Jacob

It cannot be a coincidence that Ibn Gabirol employs both the eminently identifiable linguistic structure and the theme of Jacob's deception of his father in a poem reproving the beloved for his manipulative and deceptive behavior. In utilizing the unique and highly recognizable sentence structure of Jacob's climactic deceptive moment in a poem about deception and fraud, Ibn Gabirol clearly means to bring our attention to this instance of Jacob as deceiver. Moreover, it appears he employs the Jacob–Esau verse/account as the implied backdrop to *criticize* Jacob on not one but two counts. Through the poem, we come to see the forefather as culpable, both for the fraud he committed against his father and his brother and for his subsequent hypocrisy in criticizing others for their deceptive behaviors.

This embedded criticism of Jacob arises from the parallels Ibn Gabirol draws between the inconstancy of the poem's beloved and the instruments of betrayal wielded by Simeon and Levi, moments of deception that Ibn Gabirol formulates linguistically to recall Jacob's duplicitous manipulation of his father. Two of the three elements here are presented in clearly critical terms. In the poem, the beloved's cruel and murderous behavior forms the very crux of the lover's complaint against him. Similarly, Jacob reproves his sons twice, in both Genesis 34 and Genesis 49, for their having intentionally violated the contract struck with the Shechemites. While the Bible never outright condemns Jacob for his deception of his father in Genesis 27, Ibn Gabirol's poem indicates that he did see the forefather's behavior as highly problematic. His use of the grammatical structure of Jacob's deception as the framework for the two other betrayals points us to the similarities among all three cases; all three episodes center on the betrayal of an innocent and undeserving loved one.[60] And, in linking Jacob's deception with two others that are clearly presented in a negative light, Ibn Gabirol subtly and surreptitiously insinuates that the behavior of the forefather was similarly blameworthy.

Ibn Gabirol's poetic references to the biblical episodes not only point to criticism of Jacob's betrayal of his father as a youth, but indict the forefather for subsequent hypocrisy as an adult. The more obvious source of this subtle charge rests in Ibn Gabirol's use of the word כלים (*keilim*), instruments. Significantly, this word comes not from the mouth of the Bible's narrator in Genesis 49:6 but belongs to Jacob himself in his harsh criticism of Simeon and Levi's betrayal of Shechem. However, Jacob's self-righteous condemnation of his sons' trickery strikes readers of the text as disingenuous. After all, Genesis 34 reveals that Jacob was present for his sons' deception-filled planning sessions from the onset.[61] Although he later claims to be innocent of and outraged by what his sons had wrought, he – the father of the group – was, in fact, present all along. Yet he did nothing to foil his sons' "guile"-filled plans. Instead, he remains silent, castigating them only after the deed has been completed and rebuking them at the *end* of his life (rather than during the planning stage), when he also disassociates himself from their actions. In employing Jacob's own word-choice in order to criticize the beloved for following Simeon and Levi's bad behavior, Ibn Gabirol points out the inherent hypocrisy of the forefather's condemnation.

Another element of Jacob's hypocrisy appears in Ibn Gabirol's usage of the structure of Isaac's description of Jacob in Genesis 27. As noted, Ibn Gabirol configures line 2 of his poem, in which the deceptions of the beloved and Simeon and Levi take place, to reflect the sentence structure used by Isaac in highlighting Jacob's fraud: "פניו פני יוסף ביפיו אבל כליו כלי שמעון ולוי" ("his face is like the face of Joseph in his beauty / but his instruments are the instruments of Simeon and Levi") reflects "הַקֹּל קוֹל יַעֲקֹב וְהַיָּדַיִם יְדֵי עֵשָׂו" ("the voice is the voice of Jacob but the hands are the hands of Esau"). Placing the reference to Jacob's castigation of his sons' betrayal in the format originally used to describe his own manipulation emphasizes his hypocrisy. Indeed, one cannot help but think that Jacob's sons might have easily learned the art of deception from none other than the father who practiced it before them. After all, of all the biblical forefathers, Jacob is the one known for manipulation of the truth, for trickery, for tendencies toward breaches of trust. In short order, he maneuvers his brother Esau out of his birthright (Gen. 25), tricks his father Isaac into giving him Esau's blessing (Gen. 27), and mysteriously manipulates his uncle Laban out of a good number of sheep (Gen. 30).[62] His brother Esau even notes that Jacob's name should have warned him of the man's character; having just lost his blessing to Jacob, Esau cries out (Gen. 27:36), "Was he, then, named Jacob that he might supplant me (וַיַּעְקְבֵנִי, *va-ya`qveini*) these two times? First he took away my birthright and now he has taken away my blessing!" In criticizing the beloved's lack of fidelity by employing the vocabulary of Jacob's castigation of his sons ("instruments") and melding it into the format of Jacob's own and most shocking manipulation (of his own father), Ibn Gabirol embeds an emphasis on and disapproval of Jacob himself.

One ought to note that just as it cannot be a coincidence that Ibn Gabirol employs the linguistic format of Genesis 27: 22, so it cannot be a coincidence that Ibn Gabirol chooses *not* to cite the very fitting content of the verse itself. Indeed, line 2 of Ibn Gabirol's poem could easily have read "His voice is the voice of Jacob but his hands are the hands of Esau" without losing much meaning. The message would have remained clear: Although the beloved's voice and perhaps his affect resemble the calm and soothing voice of the indoorsy young patriarch Jacob, the beloved's hands wreak violence and pain, like those of Jacob's hunter-twin, Esau.[63] Yet Ibn Gabirol changes the content, and thus the question arises: Why? As just noted, Genesis 27:22 famously speaks of the deception of a loved one and simultaneously sets up a distinction between innocence and violence, as does our poem. Rather than employ this fitting biblical verse, Ibn Gabirol only hints at it. For what reason?

While it may seem initially that the wording of Isaac's question in Genesis 27:22 fits well with the overall messages of the poem, it simply does not fit as well as the Simeon and Levi reference. After all, Ibn Gabirol's lover wants to tell his audience that while his beloved appears innocent, he is not only violent (as the hunter Esau presumably was) but is a deceptive con man. Esau, for all his faults, never appears in the Bible as deceptive, nor is this what Isaac's words say of him in Genesis 27:22. Isaac's characterization of his elder son is simply as one who is hairy, and it is this physical element of his brother that Jacob wants to imitate, not a behavioral characteristic. Thus, if Ibn Gabirol had formulated the line to read "הַקֹּל קוֹל יַעֲקֹב וְהַיָּדַיִם יְדֵי עֵשָׂו" ("the voice is the voice of Jacob but the hands are the hands of Esau"), we might misunderstand the lover as referring to a physical characteristic of his beloved.

The deep sense of betrayal that the poem's lover wishes to convey thus cannot be conjured up by referring to Isaac's musings about the physical differences between his twin sons. Instead, the lover needs to refer to another set of brothers, Simeon and Levi vs. Joseph. It is by using Jacob's accusation against his sons that the lover conveys the emotional violation he suffers at the hands of his disloyal beloved. For, like Simeon and Levi who breached an agreement regarding marital relations with the Shechemites, the beloved has transgressed the covenant of love that exists between lovers. And just as Simeon and Levi's betrayal resulted in the deaths of the men with whom they had struck this romantic contract, the beloved's betrayal results in the death of the lover (l. 3). This is not true of Jacob's deception of his father; Isaac, while horrified when he realizes that he has blessed the younger with the elder's blessing, continues life as normal, as does the violated Esau.

Classical midrashic and medieval absolution of Jacob as deceiver

But why embed such criticism of the forefather in a poem? And why do so in such a complex and subtle way? If Ibn Gabirol wanted to censure Jacob for his manipulation of his father, for his silence at the guise-filled planning of his sons against Shechem, and for his hypocrisy in reproaching them for it repeatedly as if he bore no responsibility, why not do so outright? And why not in a more acceptable context, such as a Bible commentary, rather than in a secular lust poem?

Classical rabbinic exoneration of Jacob

One possible answer to this question rests in classical rabbinic midrashic commentaries on the narrative of Genesis 27. The idea that forefather Jacob behaved in an intentionally deceptive manner, for which he was to be reproached, as highlighted by Ibn Gabirol's poem, was not well accepted among either the classical or medieval biblical exegetes. Indeed, the classical rabbinic commentaries strive to exonerate Jacob, despite what appears on the biblical page and despite Isaac's own claim of having been duped.[64] In the classical period, this midrashic exculpation of the forefather took a number of forms. Some denied Jacob's fabricating the truth, manipulating the biblical text to exonerate him. Others insisted upon criticizing Esau, thus insisting that Jacob's behavior represented the moral upper hand. Yet others maintained that Jacob's seemingly dishonest interaction with his father represented and was supported by the will of God.

Of the various midrashic treatments of Genesis 27:19, perhaps the most popular and longest enduring of interpretations is that which insists that, appearances notwithstanding, the forefather did not actually lie when he claimed to be his brother Esau. According to these midrashic texts, this fact becomes clear when we correctly punctuate the text. According to the fifth century *Midrash Tanḥuma*, one ought not read Jacob's statement "אָנֹכִי עֵשָׂו בְּכֹרֶךָ" (*anokhi `Esav bekhorkha*) as "I am Esau, your firstborn" – as the simple reading of the text indicates. Rather, one must repunctuate the sentence and read it as "I [am Jacob]; Esau [is] your firstborn."[65] Such an explanation is made possible by the fact that Hebrew has no real usable present-tense form of the verb "to be." Thus in Hebrew Jacob's response consists of three nouns in a row: אָנֹכִי, עֵשָׂו, בְּכֹרֶךָ (*anokhi, `Esav, bekhorkha*) I, Esau, your-firstborn. *Midrash Tanḥuma*'s reading relies on simply placing a semi-colon between the first and second nouns and turning each side into its own sentence. ("I; Esau your firstborn" becomes "It is I; Esau is your first-born.")

A similar re-punctuation and denial of Jacob's lie appears in the fifth-century *Genesis Rabbah* 65:18. There R. Levi likewise maintains that Jacob did not say, "It is I Esau, your firstborn." Rather, in responding to Isaac's "Who are you?" Jacob said, "I [who will in the future receive the Ten Commandments]. [But] Esau is your firstborn." This explanation hinges on Jacob's use of the formal and flowery first-person pronoun אנכי (*anokhi*) rather than the more common אני (*ani*). As R. Levi noticed, the same word, אנכי (*anokhi*), appears as the first word of the first of the Ten Commandments, "I am the Lord your God" (Ex. 20:2 and Deut. 5:6). Drawing a connection between the two appearances of this word, R. Levi explained that Jacob never intended to identify himself falsely as Esau. Rather, as his vocabulary choice reveals, Jacob aimed to reveal himself truthfully as the forefather of those who will receive the Ten Commandments.

Other exegetes attempted to exonerate Jacob from his lie by insisting on an alternate understanding of firstborn-ness. According to Genesis 25:24–6, the first of the twins to be born to Rebecca and Isaac was the ruddy and hairy Esau. Jacob exited only after him, holding on to the ankle of his twin. According to R. Jose ben Ḥalafta in *Genesis Rabbah* 63:8, one should not understand the order of their actual birth as the determining factor in establishing the "elder." Rather, Jacob was the first, thus deserving of the birthright, for the first "droplet" was Jacob's. In other words, because Jacob exited the womb second, we know that he was created of the sperm droplet that entered the womb first. After all, says R. Jose, when you drop precious stones into a thin-necked funnel, the one that exits first is not the one you dropped in first. Instead, the first one in exits last. Since Jacob exited second, maintains R. Jose, we know that he was created first, thus "elder," and correctly deserving of the blessing he sought.

Other classical rabbinic exegetes focused on the twins' personalities and behavior as cause for exonerating the forefather of the Jews from blame. Commenting on Genesis 25:27, *Genesis Rabbah* 63:10 teaches that the twins went to school together for the first thirteen years of their lives. There they both learned righteousness and religion. After the age of 13, Jacob alone continued on in the houses of study (בתי מדרשות, *batei midrashot*), studying God's word and worshiping Him. Esau went on to worship idols.[66] What's more, continues the midrash, Esau insisted on bringing others into his false worship. Jacob himself later used his loyalty to God in the face of his twin's idolatry to justify his actions in acquiring the better blessing. As *Genesis Rabbah* 65:15 reports, in preparing to "trick" Isaac into blessing him with the elder son's blessing, Jacob pointed out to Rebecca that while Esau was hairy, he himself was smooth-skinned. Noting Jacob's unusual terminology in Genesis 27:11, "וְאָנֹכִי אִישׁ חָלָק" (*ve-anokhi ish ḥalaq*, I am a smooth man), *Genesis Rabbah* 65:15 draws an analogy between Jacob's חָלָק (*ḥalaq*, smooth) and a similar-looking word in Deuteronomy 32:9. There Moses recites, "For the portion (חֵלֶק, *ḥeleq*) of the Lord is His people, Jacob the lot of His inheritance." According to this intertextual biblical play on words, in calling himself חָלָק (*ḥalaq*), Jacob reported that not only he was smooth-skinned but also that only he, and not his brother, had remained in God's camp (as His portion); Jacob's twin had turned to idolatry. In insisting on Jacob's righteousness and Esau's evilness, this line of commentary asserts that the ends (Jacob receiving the blessing) justified the means (Jacob deceiving his father and brother).

The classical exegetes accused Esau not only of false worship, clearly a reference to the religious practices of his descendants, but of immoral behavior as well, further pointing to Jacob's righteousness in ensuring by whatever means that he receive Isaac's blessing. *Genesis Rabbah* 65:10 understands that in calling Esau a hunter (Gen. 25:27), the Bible means to say that Esau "hunted" men with words; in courts of judgment, he refused to listen to the testimony of the accused, relying instead on intimidation and manipulation to elicit false confessions.[67] According to *Genesis Rabbah* 65:13, Esau tended toward thievery and intimidation of those weaker than he. As per his father's request, Esau went off to hunt food for the meal. However, he said to himself that if he did not find an animal, he would steal one or intimidate a shepherd to sell him a sheep at an unfairly reduced price. Now Esau's penchant for theft was recognized by Isaac. Because of this, says the midrash, Isaac went out of his way to remind Esau to take with him sharpened hunting tools (Gen. 27:3), items a hunter would not normally "forget," as a warning not to pilfer an animal but to hunt it legally. *Genesis Rabbah* 65:11 continues to heap evil on Esau's head. "Seven abominations were in Esau's heart," declaims the midrash. Yet when his father called for him, Esau said. "Here I am" (Gen. 27:1) as if he were innocent and righteous like Abraham and others who answer "*heneini*" ("Here I am") when God calls.[68]

Other classical rabbinic interpretations exonerate Jacob by concentrating on Isaac's blindness which, they maintained, resulted from Isaac's erroneously favoring the evil Esau over the righteous Jacob. According to R. Joshua b. Levi, while Rebecca understood that Jacob was the correct inheritor of the blessings, her husband did not. Instead, Isaac insisted on justifying the evil Esau, "עשו הרשע" (*`Esav ha-rasha*). Because of this lack of intellectual vision, Isaac ultimately lost his physical sight.[69] Similarly, according to *Tanḥuma*, Isaac knew of Esau's evil ways but allowed himself to be bribed with meat by his hunter son. Since "bribery blinds the eyes of the wise" (Deut. 16:19), Isaac lost his sight.[70] *BT Megillah* 28a takes Isaac's adoration of his evil son, whom he loved, one step further. According to R. Eliezer, Isaac gazed too often at the evil Esau. As R. Joḥanan teaches, one is prohibited from gazing at the image of an evil person. Because Isaac did not refrain, he lost his sight as a punishment.[71]

R. Ḥanina bar Papa, in *Genesis Rabbah* 65:8, sees the cause of Isaac's blindness not as punishment of Isaac, but as divine aid for Jacob in his manipulation of his father. In R. Ḥanina's understanding, God intentionally blinded Isaac in order to allow Jacob to come before him and take the blessings. In other words, while R. Ḥanina admits that Jacob deceived his father, he insists that this was a divinely mandated and divinely arranged deception. Jacob's "sin" was thus no sin after all.

Rabbinic insistence on God's role in facilitating and thus neutralizing the immorality of Jacob's "deception" appears in other formats as well. According to Genesis 27:30, Esau returned from the hunt split seconds after Jacob had received the blessing and had exited their father's tent. This suspiciously coincidental timing was noted by *Midrash Tanḥuma*. According to *Tanḥuma*, only divine intervention in Esau's usually expert and quick hunting provided Jacob (or, Rebecca) with the time needed to prepare food, put together his Esau-costume, and sit with Isaac while he ate and then blessed Jacob. *Tanḥuma* explains that Esau's normal hunting method consisted of his catching and binding one animal before going off to catch another. Each time he left in search of another animal, an angel would approach the one he had just bound and free it. This, says *Tanḥuma*, wasted enough of Esau's time to allow Jacob to successfully accomplish his task at their father's.[72] Similar insistence on divine help in tricking Isaac appears elsewhere in *Tanḥuma* as well. There the *midrash* notes that Jacob brought his father not only the food prepared by his mother, but also wine to drink (Gen. 27:25). Since the Bible does not record that Rebecca supplied Jacob with wine, puzzles the midrashic narrator, from where did he obtain the mind-fuzzing liquid? Answers *Tanḥuma*, the archangel Michael brought him of the wine of the Garden of Eden to present to his father.[73]

Other rabbinic explications similarly insist upon God's support of Jacob in his deception, although these do not point to outright participation on the part of the Divine (as contended by *Tanḥuma*). According to *Genesis Rabbah* 65:19, when Isaac asked Jacob to step forward so that he might feel him, panic overtook Jacob. His heart became as soft and weak as wax, and he wet himself. God called forth for him two angels, one at Jacob's left and one at his right. These two held Jacob upright by his elbows so that he would not faint. Thus divinely supported, Jacob was able to successfully fool his father.[74]

Other passages avoid addressing Jacob's actual behavior altogether, and focus instead on the Divine reaction to and support of the results. According to *Genesis Rabbah* 75:8, all the blessings with which Isaac blessed Jacob on earth, God blessed him with in heaven. In other words, God cared little for the method through which Jacob received Isaac's blessing; He not only supported the results, but echoed the blessing Jacob had obtained. In *Genesis Rabbah* 63:13, God's support for Jacob as the recipient of the blessing reaches back to the lentil episode of Genesis 25:29–34. There, Esau returns from hunting and, tired, asks Jacob for the lentil dish that sat before him. Jacob agreed but, he said, only if Esau were to sell him his birthright. "I am about to die; of what use is a birthright to me?" replied Esau (Gen. 25:32) and swore his birthright over to Jacob. He then "ate, drank, rose up, and went on his way" (Gen. 25:34). Says R. Kapra in *Genesis Rabbah* 63:13, Esau did not dine alone that evening. Rather, he invited over reckless men who mocked Jacob for valuing the birthright more than food. Replied God, since you so mocked the blessing of the birthright, I will follow through and ensure that Jacob does, in fact, receive it. And so Jacob, and not Esau, received Isaac's blessing later, in Genesis 27.

Exoneration of Jacob appears in the much earlier Aramaic *targum* texts as well. According to Genesis 27:35, when Esau came before his father to receive his blessing (after Isaac had already given it to Jacob), Isaac finally realized his error and cried out, "Your brother came with guile and took the blessing!" That Isaac meant to label the actions of his younger son a fraud is evident from his wording; Isaac here uses the Hebrew word for deception, מרמה (*mirmah*).[75] Despite the clear meaning of the Hebrew, the first-century *Targum Onqelos*, as well as the slightly later *Targum Pseudo-Jonathan* (second–third centuries), insist otherwise. They translate במרמה (*be-mirmah*) not as "with guile," but as "with wisdom," בחכמתא/בחכמא (*be-ḥokhmata/be-ḥokhma*). In so doing, the targumic texts shift any blame away from Jacob and reread his actions here in a completely positive, wise light.[76]

Medieval exoneration of Jacob

The medieval exegetes followed suit in attempting to absolve Jacob from any wrongdoing in his dealings with his father. For the medieval scholars, however, such a task was somewhat more complicated. The medieval school of biblical exegesis demanded attention to the plain reading of the words of the biblical text, *peshat*, rather than on *derashic* (homiletic) interpretations.[77] For the most part the medieval commentaries, therefore, had to admit that Jacob told an untruth to his father in Genesis 27:19. Yet in commentary after commentary, they insist that this was a righteous action, a "pious" act.

One iteration of this complex stance appears in the writings of the Spanish Abraham ibn Ezra (1089–1164). Ibn Ezra explains away the "guile" of which Isaac accused Jacob by pointing out that Jacob did not tell the truth. Jacob, Ibn Ezra states simply, lied. Yet Ibn Ezra pardons this behavior. Writes Ibn Ezra, some have said that prophets may not lie and, because of this, such commentators have gone through all sorts of contortions to reread Jacob's words as not lying. This, insists Ibn Ezra, is a claim without any basis in reality. Rather, one must understand more correctly that two types of prophets exist: those sent as messengers to deliver commandments, and those sent to predict the future.[78] Only the messenger-prophets are prohibited from lying at all. The predictor-prophets may, indeed sometimes might have to, say something that is not quite right (דבר שאיננו הוגן, *davar she-einneno hogen*).[79] In such cases, it does not harm them or their reputations to refer to them as prophets who told untruths; their lies were pious frauds. In Ibn Ezra's estimation Jacob's lie should not be considered a misdeed; Jacob was not a messenger-prophet and the untruth he told righted the course of history, giving him the blessing over Esau.

The Provençal Spanish-trained R. David Qimḥi (1160–1235) likewise recognizes Jacob's deception while clearing Jacob of wrongdoing. Unlike Ibn Ezra, Qimḥi maintains that the "guile" of Genesis 27:35 referred not to Jacob's words but to his deeds, for he made his hands hairy like his brother's. One should not be astonished, declares Qimḥi, that such a God-fearing and righteous man participated in such a charade. Jacob, explains Qimḥi, knew that he was more worthy of the blessing than his brother Esau and that God desired him to receive His blessing from Isaac. Jacob also knew that God would manipulate Isaac's spirit of prophecy to achieve that end. Jacob was thus not guilty of any sin. Indeed, says Qimḥi, even the Bible itself teaches that when righteous men switch truth for untruth, they do not thereby bring opprobrium down on their righteous heads. After all, God Himself commanded Samuel the prophet to tell an untruth (1 Sam. 16:2) and both Abraham and Isaac identified their wives as their sisters without censure or punishment. Indeed, since all three acted because of their fear of Heaven, none were called fabricators of the truth. So too Jacob, says Qimḥi. And, he adds exoneratingly, in Jacob's case he was simply obeying the commands of his mother Rebecca, who was herself a righteous prophet, and was following God's wishes.[80]

This dual attitude of recognizing the untruth of Jacob's words while attempting to purge him of any wrongdoing appears in the exegesis of the somewhat later Don Isaac Abrabanel (1437–1508).[81] On the one hand, Abrabanel refers to the attempts by some exegetes (namely the eleventh-century French R. Solomon Yitzḥaqi) to explain away the lies and deceit (שקר, *sheqer*, and כזב, *kezev*) of

Jacob's words as "forced" (נדחק, *nidḥaq*). At the same time, Abrabanel insists that Jacob did not actually lie in presenting himself as "Esau, your firstborn." When Esau willingly and of his own volition sold his birthright to Jacob (Gen. 25), he notes, Jacob became the elder and rightfully assumed Esau's title and position. Abrabanel adds that he is convinced (אין ספק אצלי, *ein safeq etzli*) that the mistake was Isaac's in understanding, not Jacob's in presenting. Isaac, he maintains, became confused as to which son was supposed to be standing before him. Therefore, he asked, "How did you so quickly find it, my son" (Gen. 27:20), as if he did not think that the son had gone hunting in the field. When Jacob answered, "The Lord your God granted me success," he meant that God sent his mother Rebecca to arrange the matter for him. But, says Abrabanel, Isaac did not understand him correctly and took Jacob's words at their most basic meaning, referring to success in the hunt.[82]

Ibn Gabirol's poem as response

While it would be ideal to look to the Bible commentary by Ibn Gabirol himself to see what his stance was on Jacob's behavior, we are not able to do so. Selections of his Bible exegesis have survived to the modern day, but only in citations that appear in the works of other medieval scholars (such as Abraham ibn Ezra, Solomon Parḥon, and R. David Qimḥi). Indeed, it is not clear if Ibn Gabirol wrote a commentary to the Bible in its entirety or only to specific sections. What can be detected from these citations is Ibn Gabirol's rationalistic approach to interpreting the Bible. Thus, in attempting to suss out Ibn Gabirol's stance on Jacob's behavior and his duping of his father, we are left only with the unusual and complex reference that he embeds in his homoerotic poem.

According to Ibn Gabirol's poem, Ibn Gabirol rejects the rabbinic machinations of exculpation of both the classical and the medieval texts. Like his medieval contemporaries in the Andalusian school of biblical interpretation who insisted on the plain meaning of the biblical text, Ibn Gabirol's poem recognizes the frauds enacted by both Jacob and his sons. As we have seen, Ibn Gabirol refers to the violent betrayal by the beloved as the "instruments" of Simeon and Levi, instruments of betrayal. And, Ibn Gabirol places both these acts of betrayal on the pattern of speech most closely associated with Jacob's own infamous deception in Genesis 25. The medieval exegetes attempt to lessen Jacob's culpability for his deceiving his beloved father. By playing with the language of the Bible, Ibn Gabirol's poem subtly publicizes his rather unpopular take, in which he not only recognizes the forefather's fraud but criticizes him for it rather than vindicates him. It is perhaps for this reason that Ibn Gabirol embeds his exegetical reading of the biblical text in a secular love poem rather than state it outright in exegetical format.

Ibn Gabirol's use of the secular poem as a place in which to embed unpopular biblical exegesis may have resulted from non-Jewish concerns as well. That is to say, the medieval Jewish admission of Jacob's culpability would have constituted a particularly problematic stance for Jews living in Islamic Spain.

Islam categorically denies any wrongdoing on the part of any figures it recognizes as prophets, Jacob among them. According to the Muslim understanding of the world, the men with whom God chose to speak are incapable of sinning, a state of being known as *`iṣma* (عصمة, infallibility). Indeed if one sinned, one would not be worthy of receiving God's word. Muslims therefore understood the Jewish admission of human faults on the part of these same prophets as evidence of Jewish manipulation and sacrilegious rewriting of the Divine text – an element of Islam's critique of Judaism. One example of this attitude can be found in the work of Ibn Gabirol's contemporary and one-time friend, Qur'ānic exegete, theologian, and poet Ibn Ḥazm. In his work examining the different religions, heresies, and sects of the world, Ibn Ḥazm points to Jacob's purported biblical deceptions in particular as one more proof of the Jews having falsified their Scriptures.[83] Indeed, writes Ibn Ḥazm commenting on Jacob's behavior in Genesis 27, even the good children among the pagans and the worst enemies of Allāh (كفار, *kuffār*, and اعداء, *a`dā'*) distance themselves from such deception and betrayal; how can we then accept that the prophet Jacob would have so behaved with his prophet father? Rather, Ibn Ḥazm insists, "This section [of the Bible] is composed of disgraces, and lies, and things that resemble fairy tales."[84]

Despite Islam's rejection of Jacob's culpability and its condemnation of the biblical text that speaks of Jacob in such unflattering terminology, Ibn Gabirol insists on accepting, emphasizing, and criticizing Jacob's fraud. However, it appears that perhaps because of the strong Muslim repudiation that might result from popularizing his perspective, Ibn Gabirol chose not to be forthcoming with such a stance. Instead, he embedded his analysis in a secular love poem written in biblical Hebrew where Muslims would be less likely to look for biblical exegesis, but where Jewish readers could not fail to notice it.

Notes

1 The Arabic version is how his name appears in Ibn Ezra, *Kitāb al-muḥāḍara*, 38a (70–1).

2 *EJ*, s.v. "Ibn Ḥasan, Jekuthiel ben Isaac," by J. H. Schirmann (9:679).

3 The cause of Yequtiel's death was execution. It appears he got caught up in court intrigues and ended up on the wrong side. See *EJ*, s.v. "Gabirol, Solomon ben Judah, Ibn," by Shelomo Pines and Angel Saénz-Badillos (7:321–7); Schippers, *Spanish Hebrew Poety*, 58; Cole, trans., *Selected Poems of Solomon Ibn Gabirol*, 3–4. According to Heinrich Graetz, Yequtiel held a position in the court of the Saragossan caliph Yaḥyā ibn al-Mundhir al-Muẓaffar similar to that held by Samuel ha-Nagid in Granada. When `Abdallah ibn Ḥakam murdered the caliph, he attacked members of the caliph's inner circle as well, Yequtiel among them. See Heinrich Graetz, *The History of the Jews*, vol. III (Philadelphia: Jewish Publication Society, 1902), 265–6.

4 Cole, *Selected Poems of Solomon Ibn Gabirol*, 3–4.

5 This date appears in Ṣā`id al-Andalusī, *Ṭabaqāt al-umam*, ed. Louis Cheikho (Beyrouth: Imprimerie Catholique, 1912), 89. See also Schippers, *Spanish Hebrew Poetry*, 56. Moses ibn Ezra states that Ibn Gabirol died in Valencia, where he was buried, when he was "thirty and a little" years of age. See Ibn Ezra, *Kitāb al-muḥāḍara*, 38a (70–1). Most scholars agree that this is an underestimation (or a confusion of facts) and put Ibn Gabirol's age at his death at closer to 40.

6 See Pines and Saénz-Badillos, 7:237ff (n. 3).

7 *Toledot ha-Shirah ha-`Ivrit be-Sefarad ha-Muslemit*, 267–8. The most famous poem of this sort, "הלא אצדק", appears in Ibn Gabirol, *Shirei ha-Ḥol*, ed. Jarden, 1:65–7 (#38). See below, n. 18.

8 The Judeo-Arabic reads: "*Kāna li-nafsihi al-ghaḍbiyya `ala `aqlihi sultān lā yamluk wa-shayṭān lā yamsik*" ("His angry spirit ruled over his intellect with a control that would not bend and as a satan that would not submit"). In Ibn Ezra, *Kitāb al-muḥāḍara*, 38a (70–1). The modern Israeli poet Yehuda Amichai (1924–2000) wrote of Ibn Gabirol, "Sometimes pus, sometimes poetry; always something is excreted, always pain." See *The Selected Poetry of Yehuda Amichai*, ed. and trans. Chana Bloch and Stephen Mitchell (Berkeley, Los Angeles, and London: University of California Press, 1996), 6; The Hebrew original appears in Yehuda Amichai, *Akhshav u-be-Yamim Aḥerim* (Israel, 1960), 31.

Interestingly, a *ḥadīth* commenting on the acceptability or unacceptability of composing profane poetry quotes Muḥammad as saying, "It is better for a man that his body be full of pus than that he be full of poems." See M. J. Kister, "*The Sīrah Literature*," in *The Cambridge History of Arabic Literature: Arabic Literature to the End of the Umayyad Period*, ed. A. F. L. Beeston, T. M. Johnstone, R. B. Serjeant, and G. R. Smith (Cambridge: Cambridge University Press, 1983), 358. Kister notes that when the Islamic attitude toward poetry later shifted to a more positive stance, this *ḥadīth* was emended to read, "It is better for a man that his body be full of pus than that he be full of poems *in which I was satirized*."

9 In his famed "אני השר" ("I am the Prince"), in which he boasts about his poetic skills, Ibn Gabirol states that he is but 16 years old. See *Shirei ha-Ḥol*, ed. Jarden, 1:225 (#109). According to Schirmann, Ibn Gabirol remains the only one of the Spanish Hebrew poets to state outright in a poem how young he was while writing. See Schirmann, *Toledot ha-Shirah ha-`Ivrit be-Sefarad ha-Muslemit*, 267–8. Moses ibn Ezra also takes note of Ibn Gabirol's youth, because of which, he writes, we ought to forgive him his frequent irate outbursts. *Kitāb al-muḥāḍara*, 37b–38a (70–1). Ibn Gabirol composed his didactic grammar poem *ha-`Anaq* at the age of 19. See *Shirei ha-Ḥol*, ed. Jarden, 375–83 (#225, #226).

10 See Pines and Saénz-Badillos, 7:235–45 (n. 3). Pines notes that Ibn Gabirol's religious and secular love poems differ from one another quite obviously, since Ibn Gabirol never describes love for God as a relationship between a lover and a beloved. The poems in which such imagery occurs are purely secular.

11 Elizur, *Shirat ha-Ḥol*, 1:100.

12 The identity of Avicebrol/Avicebron as Ibn Gabirol was revealed by the scholar Solomon Munk only in the nineteenth century when he discovered a manuscript of the thirteenth-century Shem Tov ibn Falaquera's Hebrew translations of Ibn Gabirol's original Arabic (which had been lost). He then compared the Hebrew to the Latin versions that had been attributed to the Muslim Avicebrol/Avicebron and discovered the author's true identity. See *EJ*, s.v. "Munk, Solomon," 14:615.

13 Ibn Ezra, *Kitāb al-muḥāḍara*, 37a (70–1).

14 Ibn Ezra uses the Arabic-Islamic terms שריעה (*shari`a*) and סנה (*sunna*). *Kitāb al-muḥāḍara*, 37b (70–1).

15 According to Pines and Saénz-Badillos (pp. 237–8) (n. 3), since an independent work of exegesis by Ibn Gabirol has not survived, scholars are unsure whether he composed a commentary to all of the Bible or just to particular portions.

16 Direct citations are known as שיבוץ (*shibbutz*, integration), which Ibn Gabirol also employs. For more on this and on similar "hinting" on the part of Arabic poets, see Chapter 1, pp. 99ff.

17 For more on *remizah/remez*, see Yellin, *Torat ha-Shir ha-Sefaradit*, 103–17; idem, *Kitvei David Yellin*, ed. Habermann, vol. 3, *Leḥeqer ha-Shirah ha-`Ivrit be-Sefarad*, 30–43; Brann, "Andalusian Hebrew Poetry," 3:112–14; Elizur, *Shirat ha-Ḥol*, 3:413ff.

18 In "הלא אצדק", Ibn Gabirol writes of his skin pustules as purple and oozing, among other things. See *Shirei ha-Ḥol*, ed. Jarden, 1:65–7 (#38).

19 Ibn Gabirol, *Shirei ha-Ḥol*, ed. Brody and Schirmann, 26 (#47). An Arabic heading, translated into Hebrew by the editors, assures readers that this is a love poem.

20 Translation mine. Since I am not a poet, I am more concerned with presenting an accurate translation of the original Hebrew while preserving the poem's readability, than in conveying the poem's poetic features into English. In the original Hebrew, the final words of the three lines all rhyme (*be-shalvi*, *ve-levi*, *be-gevi*). In the English I have presented, they almost rhyme (tranquility, Levi, die), if one uses one's poetic imagination.

21 See Ibn Ḥazm al-Andalusī, *Ṭauḳ al-ḥamâma*, ed. Pétrof, 14–15. English translation can be found in Arberry, *The Ring of the Dove*, 38. The Andalusian definition recalls that of al-Jāḥiẓ (*c.* 776–889) who wrote that *`ishq* "is a sickness that attacks the soul and spreads to the body by direct contagion, the soul being weakened by the violence done to the body and physical exhaustion being followed by [moral] weakness." See his *Kitāb al-qiyān* in Pellat, *The Life and Works of Jāḥiẓ*, 263.

22 Andalusian poets often turned to compatriots in their poems. See Chapter 3, p. 88. Here, Ibn Gabirol turns to no one.

23 Andalusian lovers, like those before them, often met their deaths through emaciation. See Naṣr ibn Aḥmad, al-Mutanabbī, and Ibn Gabirol's poems on this topic, Chapter 2, n. 35.

24 See Chapter 2.

25 For the male version, see the Adonjiah case, as noted above. For female versions, see Gen. 29:16 (Rachel), Deut. 21:11 (the beautiful captive of war), and Esther 2:7 (Esther).

26 The phrase יפה מראה (*yefeh mar'eh*) does appear in the context of one other male character: David. 1 Sam. 17:42 relates that when David approached Goliath, "the Philistine looked around, and saw David, and he disdained him for he was but a youth, and ruddy, and good-looking (יפה מראה, *yefeh mar'eh*)" (וַיַּבֵּט הַפְּלִשְׁתִּי וַיִּרְאֶה אֶת דָּוִד וַיִּבְזֵהוּ כִּי הָיָה נַעַר וְאַדְמֹנִי עִם יְפֵה מַרְאֶה). Although David's beauty is mentioned three other times in the Bible, only here is he described with a term otherwise reserved for women. It seems the narrative intends to imply that Goliath disdained David as a military challenge for he perceived him, on first glance, to be too young, ruddy (in other words, fresh-faced), and too much of a feminine pretty-boy to fight. No one else appears to have felt similarly about David's good looks. The other testaments to his handsomeness in the Bible describe him without this phrase, in solidly masculine terms. See also Chapter 2, p. 56 and n. 46.

27 In other words, the majority of biblical women whose beauty the text finds worthy of recording are portrayed as טובת/יפת מראה (*tovat/yefat mar'eh*). See Gen. 12:11 (Sarah), Gen. 24:16 (Rebecca), Gen. 26:7 (Rebecca), Gen. 29:17 (Rachel), 2 Sam. 11:3 (Bathsheba), 2 Sam. 14:27 (Tamar daughter of Absalom), Esther 1:11 (Vashti), Esther 2:7 (Esther). Still described as beautiful, but with other terminology, are Tamar, daughter of David (2 Sam. 13:1), Abishag the Shunammite (1 Kgs. 1:3, 4), and Abigail (1 Sam. 25:3).

28 See for example the poems of Abū Ja`far b. al-Ḥājj (Lorca, twelfth century), Abū Muḥammad Aḥmad b. `Abd Rabbīhī (Cordoba, 860–940), and Abū `Alī al-Ḥasan b. Rashīq al-Qayrawānī (Masila, 1000–64) in Ibn Sa`īd al-Andalusī, *Rāyāt al-mubarrizīn*, 202–3, 133–4, 249–51. English translations can be found in Bellamy and Steiner, *Banners of the Champions*, 64 (#62), 66–7 (#64–5). This tendency to abandon the bearded boy as a lover appears in earlier Greek poetry as well. As the fourth-century BCE Scythinos writes to his maturing boy beloved who has begun to sprout facial hair, "Get lost! Don't come near me! / Brambles interest me very little: / I want roses without thorns." As quoted by Marc Daniel in "Arab Civilization and Male Love," *Gay Sunshine* 32 (1977), trans. Winston Leyland; reprint in *Gay Roots: Twenty Years of Gay Sunshine*, ed. Winston Leyland (San Francisco: Gay Sunshine Press, 1991), 1:45.

29 The idea that the other brothers did not take part in the violence but did participate in the ultimate defeat and despoiling of the city appears in verses 27–9. Verse 26 relates that Simeon and Levi rescued Dinah and left. In the next verse, the Bible relates that the "sons of Jacob" came into the corpse-filled city and despoiled it, taking all that was in the houses, as well as the sheep, cattle, and asses, from both in the city itself and in the fields. They made captives of the women and children, and hauled off all the wealth of the city. Since Simeon and Levi had already left, it stands to reason that it is the *rest* of the "sons of Jacob" at work here.

30 See Chapter 1, pp. 11ff on *remez*.

31 Reuben, the eldest, receives a similarly negative pronouncement; Jacob is none too quick to forgive Reuben, it seems, for having bedded Jacob's concubine Bilhah in Gen. 35:22. In Gen. 49:3–4 Jacob informs Reuben that although he, as the firstborn, had exceeded his brothers in rank and in honor, he will excel no longer. Issachar receives somewhat unexplained perplexing news in vv. 14–15: a "strong-boned ass," he works hard but allows himself to become a "toiling serf" in order to enjoy the fat of the land.

32 One cannot discount the intentional biblical intertextual allusion to Gen. 34 here; the similarity between the word Jacob uses for "their council," סודם (*sodam*) and the place in which Simeon and Levi angrily slew men, where their wrath was relentless, סדום (Sodom), stands out. This is not the first time that Jacob castigates Simeon and Levi for their behavior at Shechem. See Gen. 34:30.

33 The *JPS* translation of the Bible renders the Hebrew אחים (*aḥim*) as "pair." I have included the more literal translation, "brothers."

34 This phrase is difficult to translate – a significant issue discussed below. For this reason, I have left it untranslated here. See discussion on pp. 128–9, and n. 37.

35 The translation of מכרות (*mekhorot*), like חמס (*ḥamas*), has proven befuddling to translators. *BDB* explains that the word is a hapax legomenon, occuring only in its plural form. The singular would be the feminine noun מכרה (*mekheira*), with the root כור (*kur*). *BDB* defines the word as "probably the name of a weapon," s.v. מכרה. Other translations have suggested that the word comes from the word מכורה (*mekhura*), not מכרה (*mekheira*), and means kinship or homeland. See nn. 38, 39, 40.

36 Among the many such couplings we find כלי שיר, *klei shir* (instruments of song), referring to musical instruments (Amos 6:5, 1 Chron. 15:16); כלי חמדה, *klei ḥemda* (utensils of delight/desire), designating precious objects (Naḥ. 2:10); כלי הרועים, *klei ha-ro'im* (the instruments of the shepherds), meaning a shepherd's bag (1 Sam. 17:40); כלי מלחמה, *klei milḥamah* (instruments of war), designating military arms (1 Sam. 8:12); and כלי הקודש, *klei ha-qodesh* (utensils of the Holy), referring to items used in the Temple/Tabernacle (Num. 4:15).

37 The translation trouble stems largely from the unclear usage of the key word חמס (*ḥamas*). *BDB* maintains that the term חמס (*ḥamas*) means to "treat violently or wrong." It goes on to say that not all the cases in which the word appears include actual physical harm. There are instances of ethical wrong, harsh treatment, "rude wickedness," injurious language, or "noisy, wild ruthlessness." *BDB* translates כלי חמס (*klei ḥamas*) as "instruments, weapons of violence," s.v. "חמס." I disagree with this translation for the reasons described further on in the discussion.

38 *Holy Bible. The New King James Version* (Nashville: Thomas Nelson Publishers, 1979), Gen, 49:5.

39 *The Hebrew Bible* (Philadelphia: Jewish Publication Society, 1917), Gen. 49:5.

40 *Tanakh: A New Translation of the Holy Scriptures* (Philadelphia, New York, and Jerusalem: Jewish Publication Society, 1985), Gen. 49:5.

41 Interestingly, the New Revised Standard Version (*NRSV*) translation of the Bible reflects such a reading. In a midrashesque translation of Gen. 49:5, the *NRSV* provides: "their swords are weapons of violence." I say "midrashesque" because the word "sword"

does not actually appear in the text of v. 5 itself. See *The New Revised Standard Version* in *The New Oxford Annotated Bible*, ed. Michael Coogan (Oxford: Oxford University Press, 2001).

42 European travel accounts indicate that these boys may have been as young as 9 or 10. The more common age appears to have been 14, the age at which pre-adult boyish attractiveness is said to be at its peak and just before the boy becomes a man. El-Rouayheb suggests that "fourteen" may also have been a standard rhetorical device that developed out of the comparison of the beloved's face to the shining moon, since the moon reaches its maximum luminosity on the 14th night of the lunar month. See El-Rouayheb, *Before Homosexuality*, 31.

43 More commonly, we find the beloved's eyes compared to swords. For Hebrew and Arabic examples of this, see Schippers, *Spanish Hebrew Poetry*, 173–6. Another popular trope compares the beloved girl's breasts to pointed swords. See `Abd al-`Azīz ibn Khayra, aka al-Munfatil (Granada, fl. eleventh century), in Ibn Sa`īd al-Andalusī, *Rāyāt al-mubarrizīn*, 155 [Bellamy and Steiner, *Banners of the Champions*, 174 (#163)]. Ibn Khayra is known to have composed a particularly obsequious poem in praise of Samuel ha-Nagid. Both this and the poem regarding the girl's breasts appear in *al-Dhakīra fī maḥāsin ahl al-jazīra*, a compendium of notable Iberians by Ibn Bassām al-Shantarīnī (d. 1147). For more on this work, see Brann, *Power in the Portrayal*, ch. 2.

A successful poetic comparison of a sword to something else appears in a poem by `Abdallāh ibn al-Ṭallā' (Mahdia, eleventh century). There the poet compares the pointy leaves of an artichoke to swords/spears guarding a virgin (the artichoke heart) in her tower. In *Rāyāt al-mubarrizīn*, 268–9 [Bellamy and Steiner, *Banners of the Champions*, 25 (#23)].

44 In their attempt to convince their compatriots to undergo the unpleasant operation in Gen. 34:22–3, Ḥamor and Shechem mention specifically the monetary gain to be made from an alliance with the Israelites: "But only on this condition will the men agree with us to dwell among us and be as one kindred: that all our males become circumcised as they are circumcised. Their cattle and substance and all their beasts will be ours, if only we agree to their terms, so that they will settle among us." For comparison, note that Jacob's sons had not mentioned outright any transfer of wealth, but spoke of a familial relationship, stating that once the Shechemites become circumcised "... we will give our daughters to you and take your daughters to ourselves; and we will dwell among you and become as one kindred" (v. 16).

45 See Wright Jr., "Masculine Allusion," 15. For more on Abū Nuwās, see Jamal Eddine Bencheikh, "Poetry of the East," in *The Different Aspects of Islamic Culture*, chief ed., Ekmeleddin İhsanoğlu, Volume 5: *Culture and Learning in Islam* (Paris: Unesco Publishing, 2003), 141–54. For an example of a "creeping" poem by the later Ibn Shuhayd (Cordoba, 992–1035), see Chapter 3, n. 7.

Interestingly, the Talmud speaks of something that sounds very much like *dabīb*. According to the Mishna in *Keritot* 1:1–2, in the case of homosexual acts committed by a man of legal age upon one asleep or upon a minor, the innocent party (the minor or the sleeping man) was not punished. See Kehati, ed., *Mishnayot Mevo'arot*.

46 Andalusian homoerotic relationships were *not* a meeting of two equal partners. Codes of sexual behavior allowed only for one adult male partner, who took the role of instigator and physical aggressor, and a younger, adolescent male partner, who served as passive recipient. While boys could be penetrated without losing their manliness since they (like women) were not (yet) men, an adult male who wished to be penetrated was considered mentally ill or defective (مأبون, *ma'būn*). See Rowson, "The Categorization of Gender," 64–8; Schirmann, "The Ephebe"; Wright, "Masculine Allusion," 14.

47 See for example `Abd al-`Azīz ibn Khayra of Granada (aka al-Munfatil, fl. eleventh century) who wrote of his beloved that her breasts, like spear points, served to guard

her "fruit" from being "plucked." See *Rāyāt al-mubarrizīn*, 155 [Bellamy and Steiner, *Banners of the Champions*, 174 (#163)]. See also n. 43 above and Elizur, *Shirat ha-Ḥol*, 2:77; Schippers, *Spanish Hebrew Poetry*, 153, 173–6, 178–9.

A nice example in which eyes are said to shoot arrows, which prove to be as effective as the arrows of the great warrior-king David, comes from Samuel ha-Nagid, *Diwan Shemuel ha-Nagid. Ben Tehillim*, 310 (#195). There the poet uses a play on language, comparing the arrow-shooting eyes (רובותיו, *rovotav*) to the multitudes (רבבוביו, *revivotav*) David famously kills in 1 Sam. 18:7. Similarly, `Umar b. `Umar of Cordoba (d. 1207) compares his beloved's eyes to swords, noting that she herself was the only one who did not fear her eyes, just as a sword does not frightens the bearer's heart. See *Rāyāt al-mubarrizīn*, 130–1 [Bellamy and Steiner, *Banners of the Champions*, 177 (#166)]. Similarly, al-Mu`tamid, caliph of Seville (r. 1069–91) names a boy with dangerous eyes Sayf (Sword). See Nykl, *Hispano-Arabic Poetry*, 143.

48 For example, the poems of Abū `Umar Aḥmad ibn `Abd Rabbīhi (Cordoba, 860–940) and Abū `Alī ibn Rashīq al-Qayrawānī (Masila, 1000–64), in *Rāyāt al-mubarrizīn*, 133–4, 249–51 [Bellamy and Steiner, *Banners of the Champions*, 66 (#64), 67 (#65)].

49 Schippers, *Spanish Hebrew Poetry*, 149–54, 178–80.

50 Note that while the poem presents Simeon and Levi alone as responsible for the injustice delivered to Shechem (as does Jacob in Gen. 49:5), Gen. 34:13 blames all of Jacob's sons together as having spoken "with guile." Furthermore, although Simeon and Levi alone attack the city, the rest of the brothers were not blameless in the affair. The text notes that after the massacre of the men-folk, the "sons of Jacob" descended on the city and completely despoiled it. One could read the discrepancy between Gen. 34 and 49 in two ways. There may initially have been a different plan of "guile," which Simeon and Levi, in their zeal for their sister, rejected and went on to attack the city alone; once they had begun, however, the rest of the brothers joined in. Or, this division of labor (attack/despoiling) was part and parcel of the original plan that Jacob, for reasons unclear, attributed wholly to the sword-wielding duo.

51 See above, nn. 35, 37, 41.

52 See above, n. 37.

53 Some examples of the use of the word חמס (*ḥamas*) include: Of a man who trickily leads others down false paths, Pr. 16:28–9 writes: "A shifty man (איש תהפוכות, *ish tahpukhot*) stirs up strife, and a querulous one alienates his friend. איש חמס (*ish ḥamas*) misleads his friend, making him take the wrong way." The psalmist in Ps. 27:12 entreats God, "Do not subject me to the will of my foes, for false witnesses (עדי שקר, *`edei sheqer*) and unjust accusers (יפח חמס, *yife'aḥ ḥamas*) have appeared against me." For a sense of a generalized manipulation of truth and righteousness, we find Gen. 6:11 accusing Noah's compatriots of filling the land with חמס (*ḥamas*). The surrounding verses (vv. 12–13) clarify: the earth had become corrupted (ותשחת, *va-tishaḥet*) because all flesh had corrupted its correct path on earth. Of *ḥamas* as violence resulting from the trickery of theft, Jeremiah thunders against Jerusalem, "As a well flows with water, so she flows with wickedness. חמס (*ḥamas*) and rapine (שד, *shod*) are heard in her" (Jer. 6:7).

54 See for example the fifth-century *Genesis Rabbah* 31:6. Other classical rabbinic exegetes understood *ḥamas* to indicate the betrayal of the social order that is stealing. See, for example, *Midrash Rabbah. Bereishit*, ed. Theodor and Albeck, 31:5; and *Numbers Rabbah* (*c.* eleventh to twelfth centuries), 11:1 in *Midrash Rabbah ha-Mevo'ar. Bamidbar*.

55 As in Gen. 24:4, where Abraham sends Eliezer to find a wife for his son Isaac, saying, "But to my country and to my homeland you shall go and take a wife for my son, for Isaac (וְלָקַחְתָּ אִשָּׁה לִבְנִי לְיִצְחָק, *ve-laqaḥta ishah li-vni le-Yitzḥaq*)." See also s.v. "לקח" in *BDB*.

56 Schirmann, *Ha-Shirah ha-`Ivrit be-Sefarad u-ve-Provans*, 1:155.

57 English translation by Roth in his "Deal Gently," 36. The Hebrew uses the phrase כל צבי בוגד (*kol tzvi boged*), meaning "every (male) gazelle betrays." For an interesting interpretation and analysis of this poem that emphasizes both the sexual innuendo and religious sentiment embedded in the verses, see Eddy Zemach and Tova Rosen-Moked, *Yetzirah Meḥukama: `Iyyun be-Shirei Shemuel ha-Nagid* (Jerusalem: Keter, 1983), ch. 16.

58 The last line of Samuel's poem presents a nicely subversive and sacrilegious use of a biblical referent, parroting Moses in Exodus 32:32. When Moses descends from Mount Sinai, having received the Ten Commandments, he finds the Israelites worshiping a golden calf. He calls to him those still loyal to God and charges them with smiting their sinning brethren, which they do, killing about 3,000 men. On the morrow, Moses returns to God to beg Him to forgive the Israelites. Says Moses, "וְעַתָּה אִם תִּשָּׂא חַטָּאתָם וְאִם אַיִן מְחֵנִי נָא מִסִּפְרְךָ אֲשֶׁר כָּתָבְתָּ," "Now, if you will forgive their sin [well and good]; but if not, erase me, please, from Your book which You have written." Says Samuel's lover of his male beloved, "ועתה אם תשא לחטאו, ואם אין – מחני נא!" (*ve-`ata im tisa le-ḥet'o ve-im ayin, meḥeini na*). Roth translates the line as "Forgive his sin or wipe me out, I pray." More closely translated, it reads: "Now, if you will forgive his sin [well and good], but if not, erase me please!"

59 "וַיֶּאֱהַב יִצְחָק אֶת-עֵשָׂו כִּי-צַיִד בְּפִיו וְרִבְקָה אֹהֶבֶת אֶת-יַעֲקֹב" ("Now Isaac loved Esau, because game was in his mouth and Rebecca loved Jacob"). *JPS* translates this difficult line as: "Isaac favored Esau because he had a taste for game but Rebekah favored Jacob." Note the verse's ambiguity as to which person had a taste for game, Isaac or Esau.

60 While the Shechemites were not actually "loved ones" of Simeon and Levi, as noted above, they had just entered into a marital relationship with the sons of Jacob by agreeing to "exchange" women in marriage.

61 In Gen. 34, Ḥamor and Shechem attempt to work out an agreement of intermarriage not with the brothers alone, but with Jacob as well. In fact, Ḥamor initially seeks out Jacob to speak with him, and finds him (v. 6). The biblical text provides no indication that Jacob then leaves the negotiating table, even after his sons return home. Indeed, after Ḥamor's speech, Shechem makes a personal appeal for Dinah's hand and, notes the Bible, addresses his words to Dinah's father *and* brothers (v. 11). When the biblical narrator notes in v. 13, that "Jacob's sons" – and not the family's patriarch – answer Shechem and Ḥamor *with guile*, one is hard-pressed to believe that Jacob was unaware of and uninvolved in the goings-on given that he had not gone anywhere.

62 The deception of Laban may have been somewhat justified. After first agreeing to pay Jacob's long-withheld back-wages by transferring to Jacob all the spotted and streaked sheep of his flock, Laban then runs off and hides all such sheep at a distance of three days' journey from Jacob, so that he could not be so paid. See Gen. 30.

63 The classical midrash explains that Isaac differentiated not between Esau's and Jacob's voices, but between their speech patterns and vocabulary choices. These served as indicators of their different personalities; Jacob was calm, innocent, and God-fearing while Esau was wild and heedless of the Lord. The *midrash* appears to have derived this explanation by noting the order of events in Gen. 27. According to the Bible, surprised by the speed with which his meal was supposedly caught and prepared, Isaac asked his costumed son (v. 20), "How is it that you have found it so quickly, my son?" Jacob replied, "Because the Lord your God sent me good speed." Only then does Isaac ask his son to step forward so that he may feel him to see whether he is, in fact, Esau. After feeling the hairy arms, Isaac utters his famous line, "The voice is the voice of Jacob but the hands are the hands of Esau." In other words, try as he might, the God-fearing Jacob proved unable to mimic his twin's irreligious nature and credited God with all of his successes. His father, identifying his hairy son by his arms, recognized this as an anomaly in Esau's speech patterns and was perplexed. See *Genesis Rabbah* 65:19, 65:21; and *Pirqei de-Rabbi Eliezer* (Jerusalem: Eshkol, 1973), ch. 32. The medieval Spanish Nahmanides (1194–1270) noted the impossibility that

the sage Isaac would not have recognized the difference between his sons' voices, since it is well known, he writes, that even sighted people can recognize their loved ones in the dark by listening to their voices. All the more so should the blind Isaac have been able to identify his sons by their voices. Instead, writes Nahmanides, Isaac must have meant that, despite Jacob's attempt to mimic Esau's voice, Isaac recognized Jacob's softer and more religious tone and his having mentioned God's name. See Nahmanides's commentary on Gen. 27:12 in Ḥaim Dov Chavel, ed., *Perushei ha-Torah le-Rabbeinu Moshe ben Naḥman (Ramban)* (Jerusalem: Mossad Harav Kook, 1969), 1:154.

64 In Gen. 27:35, Isaac says to Esau, "Your brother came with guile (בְּמִרְמָה, *be-mirmah*) and has taken away your blessing."

65 See *Midrash Tanḥuma*, ed. S. Buber (Vilna, 1885; reprint Jerusalem, 1964), *Toledot*, para. 10. *Tanḥuma* points out that we know Jacob never lied because the prophet Balaam said of him in Numbers 23:21, "No one has seen iniquity in Jacob" (לֹא-הִבִּיט אָוֶן בְּיַעֲקֹב, *lo hibit aven be-ya`aqov*).

66 The rabbis found hints to the initial shared education, followed by the sons' choosing different paths, in the wording of Gen. 25:27: וַיִּגְדְּלוּ הַנְּעָרִים וַיְהִי עֵשָׂו אִישׁ יֹדֵעַ צַיִד אִישׁ שָׂדֶה וְיַעֲקֹב אִישׁ תָּם יֹשֵׁב אֹהָלִים ("And the youths grew, and Esau became a cunning hunter, a man of the field, and Jacob was a quiet man, dwelling in tents").

67 This interpretation may have been sparked by seemingly extraneous information in the biblical text. Gen. 25:27 tells us that Esau grew to be both a "man of the field" (אִישׁ שָׂדֶה, *ish sadeh*) and a "skilled hunter" (אִישׁ יֹדֵעַ צַיִד, *ish yode`a tzayid*), a seeming repetition. In the midrashic reading of the Bible, one of these phrases must hint at some other form of hunting.

Like the fifth-century *Genesis Rabbah*, the eighth-century *Pirqei de-Rabbi Eliezer* maintains that Jacob studied Torah, while Esau, whose hands Isaac later recognized, engaged in bloodshed and in causing all sorts of other evil deaths, i.e., people-hunting. See *Pirqei de-Rabbi Eliezer*, ch. 32 (p. 237).

68 The abominations here vary, ranging from killing to sexual immorality. The fifth-century *Tanḥuma* (v. 1, *Toledot*, para. 8) cites this interpretation as well, but changes the abominations. According to one opinion brought in *Tanḥuma*, Esau (meaning, his descendants) was responsible for the destruction of seven different Temples to God. According to another opinion, seven times did Esau's descendants attack and kill different Israelite tribes.

69 *Genesis Rabbah* 65:6. This interpretation appears to hinge on and play with yet another seemingly extraneous biblical word. Gen. 27:1 relates that Isaac's eyes "grew dim from seeing" (וַתִּכְהֶיןָ עֵינָיו מֵרְאֹת, *va-tikhehena 'einav me-re'ot*). If we know his eyes "grew dim," why do we need the qualification "from seeing"? What else do eyes do but see? The midrashic explication understands the verse as hinting at two different types of vision-loss that affected Isaac, one physical and one intellectual.

70 *Tanḥuma*, *Toledot*, para. 8.

71 While R. Eliezer ben Azariah agrees that Isaac's blindness resulted from his favoring the evil Esau over the righteous Jacob, he maintains that the loss of sight was not a punishment from God, but a kindness. According to R. Eliezer, God knew that Esau was an unsavory character. He worried that Isaac would go to the marketplace and would hear men say, as he passed by, "That's the father of that evil one." So God blinded him, and he was forced to stay at home, safe from the insults caused by his son's evil reputation. See *Genesis Rabbah* 65:10.

A divergent school of thought maintained that Isaac knew quite well that Esau was wicked; he desired to bless Esau with the greater blessing in the hopes of preventing Esau from descending further into evil and hoped that the blessing might even lift Esau into righteousness. See, for example, *Tanḥuma*, *Toledot*, para. 14. Texts discussing and insisting on Jacob's righteousness permeate the classical midrashic corpus. In one interesting example, *Leviticus Rabbah* 36:4 insists that the entire world was created only because of Jacob's righteousness. What's more, Abraham, Jacob's grandfather, was saved from the fiery furnace of Chaldea, not due to his own righteousness, but because of his grandson's. Abraham knew this and, like Rebecca, preferred Jacob over Esau. See *Midrash Rabbah ha-Mevo'ar. Vayiqra*, v. 2.

72 *Tanḥuma*, *Toledot*, para. 10.

73 *Tanḥuma*, *Toledot*, para. 16.

74 *Genesis Rabbah* here ends with a citation from Isaiah 41:10, noting that God promises His servants, "Fear not, for I am with you, be not frightened, for I am your God; I strengthen and I help you, I uphold you with My victorious right hand." See also *Tanḥuma*, *Toledot*, para. 15.

75 *BDB* notes the primary meaning of מרמה (*mirmah*) as "deceit, treachery." S.v. "רמה."

76 Both *Targum Onqelos* and *Targum Pseudo-Jonathan* are found in *Miqra'ot Gedolot `al Ḥamisha Ḥumshei Torah* (Jerusalem: Pardes Publishers, 5715 [1955]). Following this line of interpretation, *Genesis Rabbah* 67:4 cites R. Joḥanan's explanation that Jacob did not come to his father in trickery, but armed with and because of the wisdom he had gleaned from studying the Torah (i.e., that he was the appropriate recipient of the blessing). See also *Genesis Rabbah* 80:8; *Tanḥuma*, *Toledot*, para. 24.

Significantly, the same shift from "guile" to "wisdom," from מרמה (*mirmah*) to חכמתא (*ḥokhmata*), appears in both targums' translations of Gen. 34:13, where Jacob's sons trick the Shechemites into circumcising themselves. There the targums report not that they "tricked" the Shechemites, but that they spoke to them "with wisdom." Following both the targumic examples and the midrashic exonerations of Jacob as above, *Genesis Rabbah* 80:8 turns the brothers' "trickery" into an act carried out under divine inspiration (רוח הקודש, *ruaḥ ha-qodesh*).

77 As discussed in Chapter 1, pp. 15–16.

78 Ibn Ezra's distinction here calls to mind the Muslim distinction between the رسول (*rasūl*) and the نبي (*nabī*). Both titles refer to prophets, men who receive direct revelation from God. Only the *rasūl*, however, has a Divine message of instruction to deliver to a particular community. According to Islam, both are infallible. See *EI*[2], s.v. "Rasūl," by A. J. Wensinck (8:454–5).

79 See Abraham ibn Ezra's commentary on Gen. 27:19 in Asher Weiser, ed., *Perushei ha-Torah le-Rabbeinu Avraham ibn Ezra* (Jerusalem: Mossad Harav Kook, 1976), 1:82.

80 See Qimḥi on Gen. 27:19 in Moshe Kamelher, ed., *Perushei R. David Qimḥi (Radaq) `al ha-Torah*: *Bereishit* (Jerusalem: Mossad Harav Kook, 1970), 145. *Genesis Rabbah* 65:15 notes that although Jacob obeyed his mother's commands, he did so with a heavy heart, stooped over, and crying, for he was loathe to deceive his father.

81 As noted in Chapter 2, although Abrabanel hailed from Christian Spain, his Bible commentary reflects the *peshat*-focused methodology of the exegetes of Muslim Spain.

82 Don Isaac Abrabanel, *Perush ha-Torah* (Jaffa, [*c.* 1954–5]), on Gen. 27:11. Like Qimḥi, Abrabanel also maintains that Rebecca was fulfilling God's intentions when dressing Jacob as Esau to get the elder's blessing.

83 For more on Muslim claims of Jewish manipulation and falsification of the Bible, see Lazarus-Yafeh, *Intertwined Worlds*; Adang, *Muslim Writers*; Shari Lowin, "Revision and Alteration," in *Encyclopaedia of the Qur'ān*, ed. Jane Dammen McAuliffe *et al.* (Leiden: E. J. Brill, 2004), 4:448–51; and David S. Powers, "Reading/Misreading One Another's Scriptures: Ibn Ḥazm's Refutation of Ibn Naghrella al-Yahūdī," in *Studies in Islamic and Judaic Traditions*, ed. William M. Brinner and Stephen D. Ricks (Atlanta, GA: Scholars Press, 1986), 109–22.

84 Abū Muḥammad `Alī b. Aḥmad b. Ḥazm, *Fiṣal fī al-milal wa-al-ahwā' wa-al-niḥal*, ed. Muḥammad Ibrāhīm Naṣr and `Abd al-Raḥmān `Umayrah (Beirut: Dār al-Jīl, 1985), 1:228.

5 The flames of love and the fire of Abraham: salvation through incineration

Around the time of the birth of Solomon ibn Gabirol in peaceful Malaga, the nearby city of Cordoba, capital of the liberal-minded Umayyad caliphate of the same name, found itself awash in turmoil. The Berber invasion and sack of the city in 1013 had defeated the religiously tolerant Umayyads and caused the city to begin to crumble.[1] Those who had actively and vocally served or otherwise supported the defeated rulers found it prudent to seek residence elsewhere. And so it was that the aforementioned Abū Muḥammad ʿAlī b. Aḥmad b. Ḥazm, Muslim theologian; scholar of *ḥadīth*, theology, and *fiqh*; poet; and master of Arabic grammar, literature, and lexicography uprooted himself from the beloved city of his birth and fled. Over the next six years, Ibn Ḥazm wandered about Andalusia, moving from city to city and in and out of prison on charges of political insubordination. When word reached him that an Umayyad claimant to the throne, al-Murtaḍā (ʿAbd al-Raḥmān IV), had raised an army to fight against the Berbers and redeem Cordoba, Ibn Ḥazm joined him as vizier and in his march to Granada. But success came to the Umayyads only in 1023, when the new caliph, al-Mustaẓhir (ʿAbd al-Raḥmān V), finally re-seized the city and the caliphate.[2] Rewarded for his loyalty, Ibn Ḥazm was once against appointed vizier, a position that ended a mere seven weeks later with the caliph's assassination and Ibn Ḥazm's imprisonment. Ibn Ḥazm's whereabouts over the four years post-incarceration are not known, but in 1027 he resurfaced in exile once again, this time in the Valencian city of Játiva. Disillusioned with politics, in need of diverting himself from his grief and loneliness, and in response to a request from a friend (possibly the Cordoban secular poet Abū ʿAmr b. Shuhayd, 992–1035), Ibn Ḥazm sat down to compose a work on poetry and poetics entitled *Ṭawq al-ḥamāma* (*The Dove's Neck Ring*).[3]

Among the numerous poems the very loyal Ibn Ḥazm composed and included in his poetic masterpiece are many that speak of the fidelity and/or betrayal practiced by lovers toward and against one another. Indeed, this popular and typical poetic theme can be found in an overwhelming number of his poems and verses.[4] One, in particular, will hold our attention for now. Like Ibn Gabirol's biblically tinged poem on the faithlessness of Simeon and Levi, Ibn Ḥazm's verse tantalizingly uses scriptural characters and exegetical storylines in the context of lovers' loyalty and duplicity.

Significantly, Ibn Ḥazm utilizes Scripture in his poem to a significantly different end than did Ibn Gabirol. Whereas Ibn Gabirol presents the poetic vision of human love as painful, Ibn Hazm presents human love as ultimately protective. Where Ibn Gabirol's composition speaks of a forefather's hypocrisy, Ibn Ḥazm's love poem recalls a forefather's fidelity and trustworthiness. And, most significantly, where Ibn Gabirol uses his verses on profane love as a vehicle for transmitting scriptural exegesis, Ibn Ḥazm takes the mirror stance, using Scripture in his poem to clarify and elevate profane love.

Ibn Ḥazm on oblivion

Roughly a fifth of the thirty chapters that make up the *Ṭawq* concern the various adversities confronting lovers who find themselves caught in the tight grip of *ʿishq* (عشق, passionate love). Slanderers, reproachers, and spies lurk around every corner, threatening the pair with exposure; lovers must endure separation, distance, and periodic emotional detachment; mockers take pleasure in scoffing at them; even their own bodies attack them, causing lovesickness that so physically debilitates them that were they "cast into the pupil of the eye of someone sleeping, / he would not wake up."[5]

Of the many such hardships faced by lovers and enumerated by Ibn Ḥazm, the most unfortunate circumstance occurs when the bond between the two comes to a final and inevitable conclusion. As Ibn Ḥazm writes, everything that has a beginning must also end, except, of course, for the delights of Paradise and the torments of Hell.[6] However, he notes, the severing of the bond of *ʿishq* can be caused by one of only two things: Either death comes to separate the two lovers or السلو (*al-sulūw*, oblivion/forgetting) does. Death, of course, needs no further explication. But oblivion, he explains, can be one of two types: natural or artificial/forced. In the case of natural forgetting, the heart of the lover becomes completely free, and the mind empties of all previously preoccupying thoughts of the beloved. One should not understand this to be an admirable or enviable turn-of-events. Rather, a man who can so manage to forget his beloved, Ibn Ḥazm asserts, possesses a shameful character; in forgetting, he has violated the sacrosanct bond of fidelity and love struck between himself and his beloved.[7] Andalusian principles of love, after all, demanded that a lover retain his loyalty for his beloved no matter the adversity involved. As the Cordoban poet Ibn Zaydūn (1003–70) once wrote: "Be proud – I'll bear with you; Delay – yet I'll endure; Exult – I'll grovel still; Run off – I will pursue; Speak – I shall hear for sure; Command – I'll do your will."[8]

While natural forgetting thus amounts to little more than betrayal, artificial forgetting, التّصبّر (*al-taṣabbur*)[9] presents a different case altogether. Here, explains Ibn Ḥazm, the lover *consciously wills* himself to forget his beloved. Whereas betrayal is unacceptable, consciously willed forgetting is not. But let us not think that a lover may engage in such behavior whenever he deems it to his liking. Rather, one may take such action only in response to a terrible calamity, one that has as its cause either some circumstance which "no self-respecting man could stomach" or some "turn of destiny against which resistance is vain."[10] For example, if the lover sees that the break between himself and his lover will stretch on indefinitely,[11] and that no indication of eventual restoration of the relationship is remotely evident, he may justifiably "force" himself to forget his beloved.[12]

Ibn Ḥazm's poem

It is in the context of this discussion of acceptable and unacceptable categories of self-preservation through forgetting that Ibn Ḥazm puts forth a one-line, one-sentence poem of particular power and intensity. Following two longer poems that deal with similar issues of betrayal and forgetting, this poetic one-liner is intended to demonstrate the benefits obtained by a lover who permissibly forces himself to forget a beloved. Writes Ibn Ḥazm:

كانت جهنّم في الحشى من حبّكم   فلقد أراها نار ابراهيما

Hell was in my bosom because of my love for you,
But now I see it as though it were Abraham's fire![13]

Ibn Ḥazm's lover here declares, quite succinctly, that forcing himself to forget his beloved has turned the pain of desire from hellish into a less-harmful or not harmful heat, akin to the famous flames that surrounded but did not burn the forefather Abraham.[14]

Readers familiar with Arabic will note that, in the second phrase, Ibn Ḥazm's poem employs the word حبّكم (*ḥubbikum*, my love for you [male plural]), the second-person masculine plural. In using this phrase, it seems as if the lover is addressing his words to a group of males rather than to one particular beloved. Such phrasing is rather unexpected. After all, Ibn Ḥazm himself relates that he has brought this poem as an example of the forced forgetting that a lover overcome with passionate desire, not friendship, engages in when attempting to save himself from the pain of separation from his beloved. In other words, this is not the case of a man isolated from his platonic friends, but one in which the relationship between two lovers who are partners in *`ishq* has come to an end. How then can we explain the use of the second-person masculine plural?

As we have seen in previous chapters, the appearance of a masculine beloved in Andalusian *`ishq* poetry is not cause for alarm. Indeed, many love poems in both Arabic and Hebrew address themselves to males. In many cases, the poet intended to refer to a male beloved, either actual or fictive, and in such cases the physical description, or inclusion of a male name, indicates as much. In other cases, the poem uses the male address but otherwise gives little indication regarding the gender of the object of desire. Because of this and because conventions of Andalusian modesty required that poets conceal the identities of their lovers, many scholars of both Arabic and Hebrew Andalusian poetry have contended that the masculine grammatical form should be understood as referring to a female beloved. One noteworthy example of the use of a male pronoun to refer to the female beloved appears among the poems of Ibn Zaydūn (1003–70), the one-time lover of Princess Wallāda of Cordoba. After Wallāda broke off their relationship and Ibn Zaydūn was forced to flee Cordoba, he composed one of the more famous Hispano-Arabic love poems, the *Nūnīyya*,[15] in her honor and in yearning for her. Lines 23–30 of the poem describe the beloved's physical appearance using masculine pronouns, though the recognized object was actually the female Wallāda. Thus we read (l. 26), "When *he* bends over, the pearls of the necklace weigh *him* down by reason of *his* having been brought up in luxury.[16] Other scholars posit that the masculine pronoun in *'ishq* poetry refers to neither a male nor female beloved but to a beloved of what Scheindlin terms "indefinite sexuality."[17] Basing himself on Jefim (Ḥaim) Schirmann's work, Dan Pagis argues with both these interpretations. He notes that Hebrew and Arabic poets often referred clearly and intentionally to *both* male and female as love partners.[18] For the purposes of the current discussion, the gender of the addressee matters little as long as we note that the use of the masculine does not prevent the poem from being recognized as a poem of *'ishq*.

The plural case presents a slightly greater challenge, on first glance. However, it is clear from the context in which the poem appears in the *Ṭawq* that the object of Ibn Ḥazm's poem is not a group of male lovers or platonic confidants. Rather, as a stated demonstration of the case of a lover who engages in forced forgetting to forget his beloved, the poem clearly intends a single person here. The plural usage thus appears to indicate the formal address, as in French where one uses the more formal "*vous*" in place of the familiar "*tu*." Indeed, in the *Nūnīyya*, Ibn Zaydūn frequently refers to his royal beloved Wallāda in the plural. One could also say that the plural form, indicated by the final "m" sound (the Arabic letter *mīm*), is meant to indicate emphasis over quantity. In this sense it resembles the word اللهم (*allāhumma*), the plural of الله (Allāh). Though plural in form, the word اللهم (*allāhumma*) does not indicate a plurality of gods.[19] Rather, it is a poetic form used in emphatic prayer and in emphatic entreaty of God. So, too, one might posit that Ibn Ḥazm uses *ḥubbikum* to emphasize the strength of the lover's ardor.

More significantly, Ibn Ḥazm may have utilized the plural form for its structural value relating specifically to its place in the poem itself. The plural *ḥubbikum* stands as an auditory match for the two words in the poem to which passion is compared: *jahannam* (Hell) and *nār Ibrāhīm* (Abraham's fire). Not only do all three end with the same emphatic "m" sound, but *ḥubbikum* is situated almost exactly equidistant from the other two words. Thus, the sounds of the words mirror and support the content of Ibn Ḥazm's verse: The passion that the lover feels for his beloved resembles, in concept, in form, and in rhyme, *both* Hell and Ibrāhīm's fire.

Ibn Ḥazm and the Andalusian tropes

Although our poem comes to only one line, a mere ten words in Arabic, it manages to include two of the most important tropes of Andalusian love poetry.

Namely, according to the poets, passionate love (عشق, *`ishq*) strikes the lover as a painful experience, not a state of pleasure or joy.[20] A lover who does not suffer for love cannot be considered a true lover.[21] Ibn Ḥazm himself explains quite in depth in the second chapter of the *Ṭawq* that a man in love does not glide through life with a cheery smile on his face and pleasant demeanor. Rather, a man truly afflicted with love will sport a brooding gaze and will express sudden confusion as well as abundant cheerfulness accompanied by deep depression, a preference for solitude, sleeplessness, and weeping. He will experience "a wasting away of the body not accompanied by any fever or ache preventing free activity and liberty of movement."[22] As we have seen, in this understanding of the torments of love, Andalusian *`ishq* followed the description presented by the earlier al-Jāḥiẓ (d. 868/9). Al-Jāḥiẓ wrote that passionate love is a "sickness that attacks the soul"[23] and then spreads to the body, resulting not only in moral weakness but in physical exhaustion.[24] It is a painful and incurable disease with which all desire to be infected and none strives to be cured.[25]

This state of passionate pain appears front and center in our one-line poem. Ibn Ḥazm's suffering lover opens the verse, moaning, "Hell was in my bosom because of my love for you." *`Ishq* does not wash over him like a warm embrace. It does not inspire him to dance barefoot through flowery meadows. It does not remind him of the taste of wine or chocolates. Rather, it thunders inside him intensely and fiercely. He feels nothing but pain, as if the tortures of Hell were raging in his chest.

In presenting the trope of *`ishq* as pain, Ibn Ḥazm utilizes yet another key Andalusian trope: *`ishq* as fire. According to the Andalusian poets, *`ishq* scalds and torches the lover from the inside like a fever does, leaving him scarred and suffering, as if he were the victim of an inferno.[26] Writes Ibn Ḥazm in an earlier chapter, its "conflagration truly bursts forth, its blaze waxes fierce, its flames leap up."[27] Indeed, in a longer poem discussing the signs of love, Ibn Ḥazm writes of the suffering lover, "The proof of pain [of love] is the fire which burns in the heart."[28] It is not surprising, therefore, that of all the elements to which Ibn Ḥazm's lover could have compared the pain caused by his passion, he *twice* chooses fire. Initially, "Hell was in my bosom," he declares of the burning sensation, the passion, roaring in his chest. But now it rages "as though it were Ibrāhīm's fire."

The fires of Ibn Ḥazm in the Qur'ān and Islamic exegesis

Not only does Ibn Ḥazm manage to include two of the more famous tropes of desire poetry (pain and fire) in this very brief poem, he atypically refers to two different Qur'ānic elements in so doing: جهنّم (*jahannam*, Hell)[29] and Ibrāhīm's fire. As already mentioned, many are the powerful and effective poems comparing the experience of *`ishq* to fire.[30] In the overwhelming majority of cases, the normal earthly element of fire struck the poets as a hot and painful enough image. They did not see a need to refer to flames of an unearthly provenance. In referring to both *jahannam* and Ibrāhīm's fire, Ibn Ḥazm deviates from the crowd.

Unlike the majority of the love poets, in this case Ibn Ḥazm seems to find "normal" fire to be lacking in intensity as a metaphor for passionate love. And so, he utilizes two far more "loaded" references for his lust poem, images derived from sacred Scripture.

That Ibn Ḥazm packs his pithy poem with not one but two references to the Qur'ān, at first glance fits in with a particular Andalusian artistic tendency noticed by Dan Pagis in his work on Andalusian Hebrew poetry. Pagis wrote that two of the conditions required by the Hebrew poets for a poem to be considered of value were brevity and "fine imagery."[31] Due to their fondness for both of these characteristics, the Hebrew poets developed a tendency to combine them, as Pagis puts it "cramming as many images as possible into a single line or verse."[32] This tendency, notes Pagis, was not invented by the Hebrew poets; rather, they adopted and adapted it from the poetry of the Arabic poets among whom they lived and wrote. Ibn Ḥazm's ten-word poem, which packs in two major scriptural references, presents itself as a particularly fine example of such Andalusian image-cramming.

Although Ibn Ḥazm likely "overstuffed" his poem in line with Andalusian poetic conventions, this fact does not free readers from a deeper analysis of the particular images Ibn Ḥazm chose for his image-overload. Again, while most Andalusian poets effortlessly compare a lover's suffering from the heat of his *`ishq* to one overcome by the scorching heat of a fire, few are the poets who identify the fire of passions with the fires of Islamic sacred Scripture. That Ibn Ḥazm not only does this but does it twice, in the course of ten words, surely indicates that he aimed to do more here than simply embellish his verse with lovely turns of phrase. To better understand both Ibn Ḥazm's poem and his use of Scripture, we turn to the Qur'ānic context of the images themselves.

Love is (Qur'ānic) Hell

On first read, the comparison between the fire of *`ishq* and the fires of *jahannam* appears self-evident. After all, that the Islamic Hell purports to be a nastily hot and painful place is by no means a secret. We can thus easily understand Ibn Ḥazm's comparison of *`ishq* to Hell as teaching simply that *`ishq*, like Hell, blazes and afflicts. Yet the Qur'ānic depiction of *jahannam* contains very detailed and specific features beyond just heat and pain. Familiarity with these features adds a deeper level to our understanding of Ibn Ḥazm's lover's painful experience of his passion.

Particularly dreadful and gruesome are the physical manifestations of Hell reported in the Qur'ān. In *jahannam* we find not only a deep pit out of which severe flames shoot, but also suffocating black smoke (Q 56:43), three columns of shadow that do not protect against the flames (Q 77:30–1), boiling water (Q 56:42), and poisonous hot wind (Q 52:27 and 56:42). The fire continuously roasts the skins of its denizens (Q 4:56); even worse, their garments are composed of fire (Q 22:19); Hell-dwellers must eat fire and drink boiling water (Q 2:174 and 6:70). If that were not torment enough, boiling water is poured on their heads

(Q 22:19), scalding them from both within and without. Mental torture accompanies the physical anguish of *jahannam*. For example, sinners will be able to see the fearful place from afar and will know that it is their destiny to fall into it. Nonetheless, they will be unable to prevent themselves from doing so (Q 18:53). Sinners will be irritatingly fettered together in Hell, cursing and blaming one another for their circumstances (Q 14:49, 7:38). Additionally, those destined for *jahannam* will know not only that the physical torments of Hell will last for eternity with no hope of abatement, but also that Allāh will not stand with them throughout this ordeal (20:74, 3:77, 40:10). A short prayer said to have been taught to the "common people" by Alī Zayn al-`Ābidīn, Muḥammad's great-grandson, highlights the Muslim recognition of the extreme pain of the fires of Hell as described in the Qur'ān. "I ask thee," pleads the Muslim before Allāh, "to have mercy on this delicate skin, this slender frame which cannot endure the heat of thy sun. How then will it endure the heat of thy Fire?"[33]

Familiarization with the particulars of Qur'ānic *jahannam* clarifies the message Ibn Ḥazm sends in equating his lover's passion to these particular flames, as opposed to those of a regular fire. We must first recall the context of our poem: a discussion of the extreme cases of suffering in response to which "forced oblivion" becomes acceptable. Ibn Ḥazm, like all Andalusian poets, understood *`ishq* to cause pain to the lover. Like them, he expected the lover to remain devoted to his beloved and bear this pain even when it burned like fire. However, in describing his passion here as akin to the exponentially worse fire of *jahannam*, Ibn Ḥazm's lover informs us that his suffering has exceeded the bounds of tolerable and foreseeable pain. As Ibn Ḥazm instructs in the introduction to the poem, one who engages in forced oblivion must have first experienced in his relationship with his beloved an appalling tragedy which, as Arberry translates, "no self-respecting man could stomach." Alternatively, the lover must have undergone devastation so great that a human cannot fight it or he must see no signs whatsoever of a renewed union with his longed-for beloved.[34] In describing *`ishq* here as a fire exponentially worse than that of an earthly blaze, as the punishing, torturous, and intolerable flames of Hell described in the Qur'ān, Ibn Ḥazm's lover informs his audience that his situation is of the exaggerated and severe circumstances that justify his engaging in forced oblivion.

Love is the Qur'ānic fire of Ibrāhīm

Ibn Ḥazm's second fire image, نار ابراهيم (*nār Ibrāhīm*, Ibrāhīm's fire), derives from Muslim Scripture as well. The incident to which this refers forms the final episode in a series told in the Qur'ān about the forefather Ibrāhīm's development from a child questioning the pagan religion of his parents into the earliest Semitic monotheistic prophet, the friend of Allāh (خليل الله, *khalīl Allāh*).[35] The account appears twice in the Qur'ān, in 21:51–71 and in 37:83–98.

According to Q 21:51–71, the more detailed of the two accounts, early in his life Ibrāhīm realized that the idol-worshiping religion of his father and his people constituted nothing but falsehood.[36] Armed with the truth of monotheism,

Ibrāhīm attempted to talk with his father and his people and convince them of the error of worshiping other than the Creator of the universe. Unfortunately, none of his efforts resulted in any change. Frustrated, Ibrāhīm threatened to "do something" (v. 57) to their idols when their backs were turned. And, indeed, when the people subsequently left him alone, Ibrāhīm stayed true to his word, smashing to pieces all of the idols except the biggest. When the people returned,[37] they found all their gods destroyed and, recalling that a "youth" named Ibrāhīm had earlier threatened the idols, they had him arrested and brought before them for an interrogation (vv. 59–61). Despite the evidence against him, Ibrāhīm denied any participation in the event; instead, he blamed the attack on the lone remaining idol, the biggest, and challenged his people to question the idol instead. When they pointed out that idols are unable to talk, Ibrāhīm cried out (vv. 66–7), "Why do you worship something apart from God that cannot profit or do you harm? Fie on you and those you worship besides God! Will you not understand?"[38] Unwilling to admit Ibrāhīm's truth, his people called to throw him into a fire and burn him (v. 68). Although the Qur'ān does not detail precisely what happened next, it does relate that Allāh suddenly stepped in, commanding the fire to "be cool and give safety to Ibrāhīm" (كُونِي بَرْدًا وَسَلَامًا عَلَى إِبْرَاهِيمَ, *kūnī bardan wa-salāman `ala Ibrāhīm*, v. 69). Although they had attempted to entrap him, says the Qur'ān, Allāh made them the greater losers, delivered Ibrāhīm and Lūt,[39] and brought these two to the land He had blessed for all the people (vv. 70–1).

Although few changes appear in the recounting of this episode in Q 37, a number of details important to the fleshing out of the story do surface there. According to this shorter version, in the midst of the pre-smashing religious disputation with his people, Ibrāhīm suddenly glances up at the stars, and then, turning back to his people, announces that he feels sick (vv. 88–9).[40] Perhaps alarmed by possible contagion, the people turn their backs on him and leave. Now alone, Ibrāhīm turns to the idols and attempts to engage them in conversation. Possibly noting the food offerings sitting untouched before them, he asks (vv. 91–2), "Will you not eat? What ails you that you speak not?"[41] Receiving no reply, he attacks them, smashing them with his right hand. Apparently hearing the commotion, the people hurry back to where they last saw Ibrāhīm, who, on seeing them approach, begins lecturing them again on the futility of idol worship ("Do you worship that which you yourselves have carved when Allāh has created you and what you made?" v. 96). In response, the people order a building to be built, from which they fling the patriarch into a red-hot fire. This appears not to work. Says the Qur'ān, though they had planned to ensnare him, Allāh made them the lowest, the most humiliated (v. 97).[42]

Ibrahim's fire in the **ḥadīth** *and Islamic exegesis*

Although the Qur'ānic narrative (as well as Ibn Ḥazm's poem) hinges on Allāh's command to the fire to "be cool and safe" for Ibrāhīm (21:69), the Qur'ān provides little elaboration as to what actually happened. Perhaps because of this gap in information, the Islamic exegetical texts explain and expound upon the miracle in a number of striking and different ways. Some exegetes, for example, point out that the command reached more than just the fire facing Allāh's friend; all fires, all over the world, no matter their source, became cool at that moment.[43] Moreover, on that day, no reptile/lizard had any fire in it, nor did any animal add to Ibrāhīm's fire.[44] Others note that the miracle applied not only to cooling the fire, but also to Allāh's ensuring that the cold was not too cool. Says Ibn `Abbās, if Allāh's command for coolness had not been followed by the command for safety (وسلاما, *wa-salāman*), the forefather would have died from cold.[45]

Some scholars understood that Allāh not only cooled the fire for Ibrāhīm but also created a veritable garden clubhouse for His friend in its place. Al-Suddī writes that when Ibrāhīm was catapulted into the furnace, the angels lifted him up by the arms. When they sat him down again, inside the fire, he found himself seated near a spring of water and surrounded by red roses and narcissi.[46] According to al-Tha`labī (d. 1036), sometime after King Namrūd (under whose command this episode took place) gave the order to throw Ibrāhīm into the furnace, the regent decided to check in on his enemy. Looking into the fire from above, a safe distance away, Namrūd saw the forefather sitting in a meadow while all around him the fire raged without touching him.[47]

Al-Ṭabarī (838–923) and others maintain that Allāh also provided the forefather with company in his "fire." They relate that when King Namrūd peered inside the fire he had constructed, he expected to see a man roasting to death. To his shock, when he peeked he saw that not only was the forefather alive and well, but that he was not alone. Sitting beside him was an angel, possibly the Angel of Shade, wiping the sweat from Ibrāhīm's brow.[48] According to Ibn `Asākir (1105–76), Ibrāhīm was accompanied by not one but two divinely sent guests; the angel Isrāfīl, he writes, sat on Ibrāhīm's right side and the angel Jibrīl sat on his left.[49] Similarly, but somewhat more ambiguously, the eleventh-century al-Kisā'ī records that Ibrāhīm was joined by two men of "extreme beauty" as he sat enthroned in the furnace.[50]

Allāh protected not only Ibrāhīm's physical well-being, but also his sartorial sensibilities. According to Ibn Isḥāq and others, Allāh sent the angel Jibrīl to sit with Ibrāhīm and to provide him with a silk shirt to wear.[51] Significantly, this new and delicate shirt was not damaged by the flames rising up around Ibrāhīm as he sat in his fiery garden. Indeed, the Islamic exegetes point out that when Ibrāhīm finally exited the fire, he did so by simply walking through the flames till he emerged on the other side, in perfect condition, with not even his garments singed.[52] So wonderful was Ibrāhīm's time spent in the fire that al-Minhāl b. `Umar records him as having said, "I have never experienced more pleasant days than the days I was in the fire."[53]

Ibrāhīm's fire as a poetic motif

As he does with the Qur'ānic image of Hell, Ibn Ḥazm employs the religious reference that is Ibrāhīm's fire to comment upon and elucidate the properties of *`ishq*. On a very basic level, in comparing his lover to this scriptural fire, Ibn Ḥazm simply reminds us that he speaks of a lover engaged in forced, rather than natural, oblivion. After all, Allāh *commanded* the fire to cool off for Ibrāhīm. In forced oblivion, the lover behaves similarly to Allāh, commanding his *`ishq* to weaken and decline in strength.

The comparison of *`ishq* to Ibrāhīm's fire also allows Ibn Ḥazm to *justify* the lover's engaging in forced oblivion. In the prose portion of the chapter "On Forgetting" (السلو, *al-sulūw*), Ibn Ḥazm notes that often people accuse a man engaged in forced oblivion of violating the principle of fidelity required of lovers; after all, the behavior of one *acting* as if he had forgotten his beloved differs little from that of one who truly has.[54] Ibn Ḥazm insists that, despite appearances, one who coerces himself to forget cannot be equated with one who comes upon oblivion naturally. He who attempts to force himself to erase his beloved from his mind and heart never truly succeeds in doing so. Instead, he "remains faithful to his covenant, as he gulps down the bitter draughts of patient endurance."[55] In declaring of his *`ishq*, "But now I see it as if it were Ibrāhīm's fire," Ibn Ḥazm's lover poetically underscores this principle. After all, in the case of Ibrāhīm, while the fire cools itself down in response to Allāh's command, it does not cease to exist. It continues to rage, blaze, and destroy as expected; it simply doesn't harm Ibrāhīm. In comparing his *`ishq* to this scriptural referent, our lover reveals that the same is true of his circumstance. Engaged in "conscious fortitude," he commands his passion to diminish and endeavors to force himself to forget his beloved. Despite his best efforts, however, his passion never truly abates. Rather, like the fire of Ibrāhīm the fires of his passion continue to blaze on. While "conscious fortitude" may seem to be an exercise in self-preservation, it is actually an act of self-delusion; almost against his will and despite all appearances, the lover remains loyal and eternally bonded to his beloved. Since he does not commit treason against his beloved by trying to force himself to forget, his engaging in forced oblivion is justifiable.

Ibn Ḥazm, Ibrāhīm's fire, and the sacralization of *`Ishq*

The Ibrāhīm allusion does more than simply fall in line with expected tropes of passion. Ibn Ḥazm's scriptural reference also sends a subliminal and somewhat subversive message about *`ishq*. Namely, in comparing passionate human desire to fires that were created by or otherwise touched by the hand of Allāh, Ibn Ḥazm insinuates that human love bears similar sacred characteristics and abilities. Passionate love can be as painful as the fire of divinely created Hell, notes Ibn Ḥazm's first hemistich, punishing and eternally torturing the lover with the ferocity with which Allāh punishes the residents of *jahannam*. But one should not be discouraged away from love, hints the poem. As the second hemistich reveals, the everlasting bond between two true lovers is ultimately as sacred as the bond between Allāh and Ibrāhīm, his beloved servant.[56]

A comparison between this poem and a longer one that Ibn Ḥazm includes in the same chapter highlights the message of sacredness embedded in our poem.

In the longer composition, Ibn Ḥazm's lover initially muses that, much to his surprise, he has successfully forgotten the beloved from whom he has been separated for far too long and with no hope of reunion or relief from his suffering. At the end of the poem, Ibn Ḥazm places one final telling stanza in the mouth of his "forgetting lover." Writes Ibn Ḥazm,

وأرى هواك كجمرةٍ   تحت الرّماد لها مدد

And I see desirous love for you as a live coal,
Burning underneath the ashes that feed it.[57]

Here Ibn Ḥazm states far more obviously what he hints at more subtly in the one-line Ibrāhīm fire poem: Though we may attempt to force ourselves to forget the beloved, forcing never works completely. The flames of passionate love may recede and the heat that burns in one's chest may cool off, but the fire never truly dies. It remains like a coal in one's soul, hidden under the ashes but burning all the while, waiting for the right moment, for some flammable material to draw near or, more simply, for a gust of air, and it will once again burst forth in a glorious blaze. Indeed, the very fact that a lover has thought such thoughts, or committed them to writing, testifies to the fact that the lover has not actually forgotten his beloved. For if he were not simply *acting* as if he had forgotten, but had truly freed his mind and his heart from all thoughts of the beloved, would he have been able to or cared to write a poem about the episode? Surely not. Like the ten-word poem that utilizes the Qur'ānic images of Hell and Ibrāhīm, here Ibn Ḥazm teaches that forced forgetting is not the same as true forgetting, and he once again justifies the lover who finds himself in need of employing such a tactic. That Ibn Ḥazm manages to express the same sentiment without utilizing a Qur'ānic referent emphasizes the fact that his inclusion of a sacred image in a poem on earthly love is not coincidental, but likely brings additional layers of meaning. In comparing the fires of passion to the divinely manipulated fire in which Ibrāhīm sat, Ibn Ḥazm embeds a message about the nature of human passion into his poem; as the poem's use of scriptural imagery indicates, human passion and desire are not to be disdained, but are sacred and divinely sanctioned.[58]

Problems with the fire of Ibrāhīm

Intriguingly, while the Ibrāhīm image works quite well on these fronts, on more close analysis we find that the narrative of Ibrāhīm's fire is actually quite an awkward image for our poem. Disturbingly, the Islamic account of Ibrāhīm in Namrūd's fire diverges from the situation of the Andalusian lover in two significant ways. On a very basic level, the poem and the scriptural account draw opposing pictures of the connection that links the two characters together in each text. More problematically, the poem and the scriptural materials ultimately present opposing messages regarding the value of continued loyalty in the face of insurmountable obstacles.

The more obvious of the two deviations between the scriptural account of Ibrāhīm and the poetic case in question concerns the very nature of the relationship between the actors. Namely, the poem presents two lovers separated by either unbearable catastrophe or infinite distance. In an attempt to save himself, the lover separates himself even further from his beloved, engaging in forced forgetting. The narrative of Ibrāhīm's fire presents the exact opposite relationship between its actors. Ibrāhīm and Allāh are not separated by catastrophe, distance, or willful forgetting. Indeed, they are not separated at all. Rather, the moment in which Ibrāhīm is tossed into the fire and Allāh commands it to cool off presents a moment of supreme *closeness*. Ibrāhīm finds himself hurtling toward the flames because, *unlike* the lover, he refuses to renounce, deny, or restrain his feelings for, his belief in, Allāh. In turn, Allāh Himself (and not an angel) steps in to save His beloved from incineration, intervenes in the workings of the world, and commands nature to turn against itself. Allāh's miraculous command to the fire thus bridges the expanse between the human actor and the divine. Unlike their poetic counterparts who are facing an unbridgeable chasm, the Qur'ānic characters have moved closer to, not further from, one another, forging a bond that is ever more intimate.

Even more significantly, this difference in relationship between the actors in the poem and those in the Qur'ānic narrative transmits opposing messages regarding the value of continued loyalty to an unresponsive beloved. Both the poem and the didactic context in which it sits teach that there are cases in which one *may* turn away from one's beloved. In such cases, but only in such cases, may one attempt to free oneself from one's loyalties through forced oblivion. In complete contrast, the Ibrāhīm account teaches Muslims to persist in their fidelity no matter the distance. For despite Ibrāhīm's not having had any direct contact with and encouragement from Allāh, the forefather persists in worshiping Him. So loyal is Ibrāhīm to Allāh that he persists in haranguing his people to follow Him. Even when they, as a result, catapult him into the air to land in a raging pyre, he refuses to recant. Instead, Ibrāhīm persists in his loyalty to Allāh.[59] Importantly, according to the Qur'ān, it is only in *response* to Ibrāhīm's unwillingness to forget Him that Allāh ultimately reveals Himself to him. Only because of Ibrāhīm's continued loyalty does Allāh intervene and force the flames to go against their essential nature. In other words, unlike the poetic fire, the Qur'ānic fire does not cool because Ibrāhīm attempts to save himself by forgetting the Divine, from whom he has heretofore heard nary a word. Rather, the cooled fire of Ibrāhīm results only from his *refusal* to forget, despite the lack of communication between them (till this point).

The fire of Moses

With these problems in mind, it strikes us as surprising that Ibn Ḥazm – master poet, theologian, and *ḥadīth* scholar – insists on employing the Ibrāhīm image here. Our wonder is compounded further when we recall that an equally or more appropriate scriptural fire image exists that Ibn Ḥazm could have employed in his poem, with fewer problems. This fire concerns the burning bush that materialized before the prophet Mūsā on the mountain in the valley of Ṭuwā.[60] This narrative, or references to it, appears at least six times in the Qur'ān, with varying degrees of detail. While some chapters speak of Mūsā encountering a fire from which Allāh speaks to him, only one mentions a fire that seems to spring forth from a tree while miraculously not harming the tree itself. And so, it is to this chapter that we now turn.

Mūsā's fire in the Qur'ān

According to chapter 28 of the Qur'ān, the account of Mūsā and the burning bush begins when, after having served his Midianite father-in-law for either eight or ten years,[61] Mūsā decides to leave Midian and travel with his family. While on the road, Mūsā spies a fire off in the distance, near "the mountain."[62] Thinking he might be able either to borrow an ember, or at least glean news from the people sitting around the flames, Mūsā heads off to investigate. When he reaches the fire, however, something odd transpires. Suddenly, he hears a voice calling to him from the right side of the valley, later identified as Ṭuwā,[63] from a tree sitting on blessed ground (v. 30). Identifying itself as Allāh, the Lord of the Worlds, the voice instructs Mūsā to throw down his staff. When he does so, the staff begins writhing as if it were a serpent, and Mūsā, fearing for his life, turns to flee. Allāh stops him, still speaking from the tree, and instructs Mūsā not to be afraid, for he is among those who are secure. After performing an additional miracle for Mūsā to use as credentials and proof of his messengership,[64] Allāh charges Mūsā with the mission to travel to Fir`awn (Pharaoh). There Mūsā will serve as Allāh's messenger in punishing Fir`awn and his people, who have grown rebellious and wicked.[65]

Mūsā's fire in Islamic traditions

Noting the many vague details of the Qur'ānic episode – (Where was the tree exactly? What was the relationship between it and the fire Mūsā had seen? What does it mean that the voice called out from the right?) – the exegetes provided narrative expansions intended to elucidate. According to Islamic traditions, Mūsā and his family were on their way back to Egypt from Midian to visit Mūsā's family in Egypt when they suddenly, and in accordance with Allāh's will, lost their way. Now, this took place in the winter, the season when the rains fall.[66] Cold, lost, and with kindling that had dried up,[67] Mūsā looked up and spotted a fire burning in the distance. Thinking he would ask the people to whom the fire belonged if they could help in locating the route to Egypt or, if not, that he might procure a burning coal with which to warm his family, Mūsā set off in the direction of the blaze. When he approached the fire, he realized that what he had seen from afar was, in actuality, a tree aflame. Frighteningly, no smoke arose from the blaze, and the tree, rather than being blackened and consumed, remained green. According to some commentators, as the flames grew more and more intense, the tree turned greener and greener.[68] Others maintain that angels surrounded it.[69] Miraculously, when Mūsā approached the bush, it retreated from him. When Mūsā then retreated, frightened by a mobile and flaming but uncharred and otherwise unaffected tree, it drew closer to him.[70] Mūsā then heard a voice emanating from the tree, identifying itself as Allāh. Immediately upon hearing Allāh's voice, Mūsā's fear receded.[71]

Mūsā and Ibrāhīm

A number of similarities between Ibrāhīm's fire and the Ṭuwā fire present themselves immediately. Most obviously, in both cases we find a blaze that appears initially as a searing, scorching conflagration capable of destroying that with which it comes into contact. And, in neither case does this occur. Ibrāhīm's fire should incinerate him but does not, and the Ṭuwā fire should reduce to ashes the tree in which it burns. Indeed, so convinced is Mūsā of the real danger of the fire he sees flaming in the tree that, according to the Muslim exegetes, he instinctively takes a step back to avoid getting hurt. And yet, like Ibrāhīm's fire, which did not burn the patriarch, the fire on the mountain does not consume the tree in which it burns. Instead of succumbing to the flames, the tree, like Ibrāhīm, remains alive and well, greener than ever, yet afire.

This refusal of both fires to obey their nature reflects a shared element of sacredness as well. Ibrāhīm's fire turned "cool and safe" in accordance with Allāh's command. In so doing, it served as hallowed servant of the Divine. The fire of Mūsā reveals an equally if not more sacred nature. The fire in the tree of Ṭuwā not only declined to burn the tree in which it lived, but, according to the Muslim exegetical explications of Q 28:30, the blaze served as the very medium through which Allāh spoke to Mūsā. In other words, the fiery tree in the valley of Ṭuwā briefly serves as a place in which Allāh Himself dwells. This was no regular fire, clearly, but a Divine and sacred conflagration!

Not only are the two fire images similar in these aspects, but on at least two points the fire of the burning bush presents an advantage over Ibrāhīm's fire as the appropriate parable for Ibn Ḥazm's poem. In the first place, the fire of Ibrāhīm is a fire that is external to the hero. The regent (Namrūd) and his people build the pyre and then launch the forefather into it. They do not set fire to him, using him as material to feed the flames, but build a stand-alone fire and only after it is raging do they toss him into it. By contrast, the flames of passion that burn in the lover, burn *in* the lover. The lover himself is the source of the fire, the material that feeds it and keeps it alive. Unlike Ibrāhīm who can be extracted from the fire without extinguishing it, the lover cannot be extracted from the flames of his own internal desire. So too the fire of Ṭūwā burns in the tree, which serves as the very material that feeds the flames. Like the lover, one cannot separate the tree from its fire without putting out the fire. The two elements are intertwined.

One can also not overlook the fact that the cause of Ibrāhīm's fire proves problematic as a parable for *'ishq* in a way that the Ṭuwā fire does not. From its very inception, Ibrāhīm's fire is intended to serve as an instrument of destruction.

According to both the Qur'ān and Islamic exegesis, it was a punishment levied against the patriarch for destroying his people's idols. No such retributional value accompanies either the fires of *`ishq* or of Ṭuwā. Unlike Ibrāhīm, neither the lover nor the tree commits any "sin" or wrongdoing that would call for a penalty. The lover has fallen in love with his beloved, behavior expected of a human being and not in violation of God's law. Ibn Ḥazm makes this point quite clearly in the *Ṭawq*, when he writes, "Love is neither disapproved by Religion nor prohibited by Law; for every heart is in God's hands."[72] As for the tree, it was simply going about its business being a tree before the fire took up residence there. Contrary to the case of Ibrāhīm, the fires that burn both the lover and the tree do not result from reprimand.

Given these facts, it seems clear that the scriptural image of the Ṭuwā fire could have been used to the same, if not better, effect than the Ibrāhīm scenario. "Hell was in my bosom because of my love for you, but now I see it as though it were Ṭuwā's fire!" the poetic lover could easily have proclaimed. Although at first *`ishq* burns within the lover like the flames of Hell, such a poem would teach, through forced oblivion it burns harmlessly like the fire burning in but not consuming the tree that Mūsā saw in the valley of Ṭuwā. Like the Ibrāhīm poem, the Ṭuwā poem would teach that forced oblivion ought not to be categorized as betrayal. For just as the fire of Ṭuwā continued to burn even after catching Mūsā's attention, so too the *`ishq* of forced oblivion never truly disappears from the lover's heart. Additionally, in comparing the lover's passionate fire for his beloved to the sacred fire from which Allāh spoke to Mūsā, Ibn Ḥazm would have successfully relayed the idea that human *`ishq* ought to be seen as a sacred element. Just as Allāh dwelled in the tree and its flames and spoke to Mūsā from within it, so too, such a comparison would teach, Allāh dwells, albeit figuratively, in the flames that burn within the chest of each and every noble and true lover.

Ibrāhīm and salvation

Given that the Ṭuwā fire thus poses a more appropriate scriptural comparison for the forced oblivion of Ibn Ḥazm's lover, it behooves us to reconsider Ibn Ḥazm's seemingly unsuitable choice for his love poem. As a theologian and jurist, Ibn Ḥazm would have been well aware of both Ibrāhīm's and Mūsā's fires, as well as of the exegetical narratives and commentaries on each. That he chooses Ibrāhīm's mismatched external fire for the lover's internal struggle must come to teach readers additional lessons regarding the fire of *`ishq* that Ṭuwā's fire was unable to transmit.

Indeed, deeper consideration of the materials reveals a significant difference between the two scriptural fires, one crucial for our understanding of what appears to be the poem's true message: *`ishq* as salvation. After all, one cannot overlook that Namrūd's fire, originally intended to punish and harm Ibrāhīm, instead saved his life. Significantly, Allāh commanded the flames to "be cool and safe for Ibrāhīm" rather than simply extinguishing them. In so doing, Allāh turned the very materials of Ibrāhīm's intended death into the keys to his deliverance. Mūsā's fire, by contrast, retains no such salvific power. No one's life is threatened by the flames, and no one is thereby saved. The fire of Ṭuwā instead serves to showcase Allāh's powers: He sets a tree ablaze but masterfully prevents that tree from being consumed. An impressive miracle? Yes. Salvific and redemptive? Not truly.

In using Ibrāhīm's model of fire rather than Mūsā's as the scriptural referent for *`ishq*, Ibn Ḥazm's poem teaches that human–human passion retains a protective power, one reminiscent of the flames that protected the patriarch. As the poem relates, at first the passion that raged inside the lover for his beloved appeared to him as hot, damaging, and punishing as the flames of Hell. It threatened to consume and destroy him. Finding himself embroiled in a situation in which no honorable man can be expected to remain, or perhaps finding himself indefinitely separated from the object of his affections with no hint of reunion, the lover engages in forced forgetting of his beloved. In so doing, he successfully tamps down the heat of his *`ishq* and saves himself from harm, just as Allāh saved Ibrāhīm from destruction in the pyre set by Namrūd. Indeed, just as Ibrāhīm's cooled-off fire was the very element that saved Ibrāhīm from death at the hands of his captors, so too the lover's now-tempered sacred passion becomes the very thing that saves him from ultimate annihilation. The fire of Ibrāhīm not only saves his life, it turns into a garden in which the patriarch flourishes. So, too, perhaps one ought to understand the lover as insisting that not only do the flames of *`ishq* actually save him but *`ishq* is what allows him to thrive; without it, a person would wither and life might not be worth living. The lover has come to realize, says the poem, that *`ishq* is not the punishment of the human condition, but it is our salvation.

Ibn Ḥazm vs. Ibn Maymūn: theologian vs. secular poet

Ibn Ḥazm was not the only Andalusian poet to employ the fire of Ibrāhīm in a secular poem on passionate love. A similar reference appears in a love poem by Abū Bakr b. Muḥammad b. Maymūn approximately a century after Ibn Ḥazm composed his masterful *Ṭawq*. Unlike Ibn Ḥazm, Ibn Maymūn was not a theologian or scholar of religion or of religious texts. A comparative look at these two poems and the ways in which they incorporate Ibrāhīm's fire into their verse emphasizes the unique usage our theologian makes of this sacred imagery in overlaying his secular erotica with tones of sacred redemption.

Short biography of Ibn Maymūn

Abū Bakr Muḥammad b. `Abdallāh b. Maymūn al-`Abdarī, known as Ibn Maymūn, began his career as a courtier, and perhaps a baron, in the royal court in twelfth-century Cordoba.[73] It was not long before he became a key member of the intellectual class of the city as well, rising to prominence, as did many of the intellectuals of his day, in the fields of both Arabic grammar and Arabic poetry, and earning himself fame for composing important works on poetics as well.[74] Though he appears to have originated in Cordoba, Ibn Maymūn left his hometown during the first major civil unrest that took place there, in the years between the fall of the Almoravid empire in Andalusia and the establishment of Almohad rule there (*c.* 1146). Seeking refuge from the turmoil, Ibn Maymūn fled to Marrakesh, where Almohad control was expanding and gaining strength. Ibn Maymūn prospered under the North African Almohads, serving as the teacher of the third Almohad ruler, al-Manṣūr (r. 1184–1199), whose father was considered to have been an Andalusian litterateur on par with the very best.[75] Ibn Maymūn appears to have been a religiously engaged man who occupied himself with the Qur'ān quite seriously. By the time he died in 1171, Ibn Maymūn was known as a man "full of knowledge," an accomplished *ḥāfiẓ* and possibly a Qur'ān reciter.[76] He remains best known for his accomplishments in the field of Arabic letters and for having composed works on grammar, such as *Sharḥ al-jumal*.[77]

Ibn Maymūn's secular poem and the use of Ibrāhīm's fire

According to the thirteenth-century historian of Arabic Andalusia Ibn al-Abbār,[78] Ibn Maymūn wrote not only commentary on poetry, but was also a poetic composer who was known to have penned numerous secular *ghazal* poems. That he later attempted to atone for these compositions by writing a similar number of ascetic poems does not diminish their poetic worth. Despite his personal negative take on his secular poetic activities, he appears on the roster of Andalusian poets of excellence included in Ibn Sa'īd's anthology, *Rāyāt al-mubarrizīn wa-ghāyāt al-mumayyazīn*. As an example of Ibn Maymūn's poetic skill, Ibn Sa'īd brings the following brief secular composition:

تقحّمت جاحم حرّ الضّلوع   كما خضت بحر دموع الحدق
أكنت الخليل؟ أكنت الكليم؟   أمنت الحريق؟ أمنت الغرق؟[79]

I rushed into Hell, the heat of my chest,
Just as I plunged into an ocean, of the tears of my irises.
Am I Abraham (*al-khalīl*)? Am I Moses (*al kalīm*)?[80]
Am I safe from burning? Am I safe from drowning?[81]

Ibrāhim's fire and the drowning of Mūsā

Ibn Maymūn's poem shares a number of elements common to the Andalusian poetic tropes found in Ibn Ḥazm's earlier Ibrāhīm poem. Most basically, both Ibn Maymūn's lover and Ibn Ḥazm's lover experience the love/lust that they feel for their beloved as painful, as a lover should. Indeed, Ibn Maymūn uses the same images of pain as used by Ibn Ḥazm a century earlier to express the hurt caused by *'ishq*; to both men, romantic passion strikes them as painfully as a raging fire located deep within their bodies.[82] Furthermore, like Ibn Ḥazm, Ibn Maymūn incorporates scriptural imagery, the very same in fact, to express the particularly awful pain of the heat of his passion. For both lovers, the fire burns so fiercely and so painfully, it feels to them akin to the fire of Hell. The difference between the two compositions lies only in the terminology. While Ibn Ḥazm employs the term جهنّم (*jahannam*, Gehenna), Ibn Maymūn utilizes the Qur'ānic synonym جحيم (*jaḥīm,* Hellfire).[83] Ibn Maymūn incorporates Ibn Ḥazm's second scriptural referent into his otherwise secular *'ishq* poem as well. "Am I *al-khalīl* ... Am I safe from burning?" the lover queries, comparing himself in his suffering to Ibrāhīm in the fiery furnace.[84]

However, aside from the similarity that the two poets compare their lovers' passion both to Hell and to Ibrāhīm's fire, the messages these images transmit do not resemble one another at all. Ibn Ḥazm's poem compares the fading ardor of a lover engaged in forced oblivion to the redemptive flames of Ibrāhīm's fire. To him, they are the same. Just as those cooled but not extinguished flames saved the forefather, says the poet-lover, so my forcibly reduced but not eradicated zeal for my beloved has saved me. Ibn Maymūn's poem, on the other hand, contrasts Ibrāhīm's cooled fire with *'ishq*. While Ibrāhīm's fire rescued him, Ibn Maymūn's lover declares, his passion does *not* cease to cause him harm. "Am I Abraham? Am I safe from burning?" asks Ibn Maymūn's lover. The question is, of course, rhetorical, as is the question regarding Mūsā ("Am I Moses? Am I safe from drowning?"). I am clearly not Ibrāhīm, implies the poet, and so I fully expect to die from my fiery lovesickness, in good poetic form. For Ibn Maymūn, the passion that a human lover feels for his beloved will only kill, and not save, him. It is not divine, it is not miraculous, and it is certainly not salvific.

The difference in Ibn Maymūn's poetic use of the Ibrāhīm fire image appears to be based on his alternate understanding of the nature of the scriptural fire itself. For Ibn Maymūn, the miracle of the Qur'ānic narrative rests not in the fire, but in the miraculous nature of the prophet himself. "Am I Abraham? Am I safe from burning?" queries the lover. Rather than comparing his passion to Ibrāhīm's flames, Ibn Maymūn's lover compares himself to the forefather. Unlike Ibn Ḥazm and the Qur'ān itself, Ibn Maymūn does not attribute to the fire itself any special qualities. Instead, in his presentation of the Qur'ānic account here, he emphasizes that it is the prophet himself whose special qualities enabled him to miraculously survive a blazing fire. Since the lover is an ordinary person, one not chosen by Allāh to be His mouthpiece and thus capable of sinning,[85] the lover can have no expectation that he too will miraculously be rescued by Allāh. For Ibn Maymūn, the fire of Ibrāhīm has no independent meaning. Ibn Ḥazm's lover makes no comparisons between himself and the forefather. Instead, he focuses entirely on drawing a parallel between the flames of human passion and those of the miraculous fire that obeyed Allāh's command.

As we can see, unlike the theologian and religious scholar Ibn Ḥazm, Ibn Maymūn does not employ sacred scriptural imagery to sacralize his earthly love. Nor does he employ scriptural images here to expand our understanding of the depth of true *'ishq*, as Ibn Ḥazm did regarding the truth of forced oblivion. Instead, Ibn Maymūn compares his lover to scriptural characters and imagery, before whom his human character falls short, to emphasize the pathos of the poem's lover. Unlike the theologian Ibn Ḥazm then, the non-theologian Ibn Maymūn writes a poem that tells us little new about either *'ishq* or Ibrāhīm.

Summary

Ibn Ḥazm's ten-word poem initially appears to be a simple love poem in which the poet employs the most common trope of Andalusian love poetry, presenting passionate love as a flaming, painful attack in the lover's chest. Even his usage of scriptural imagery at first seems to conform to type. Passionate love, proclaims Ibn Ḥazm's lover, burns like Hell, but with the application of some justified forced oblivion, one can reduce it to a more tolerable state of smoldering, like the cooled-off flames of Ibrāhīm.

Yet a closer look at this seemingly simple and seemingly conventional poem reveals that Ibn Ḥazm has once more employed scriptural imagery to a surprising end. Our theologian here utilizes the Qur'ānic narrative of Ibrāhīm to elevate mundane love in two different ways. On the one hand, in comparing his passion to a fire that has been touched by the Divine and which serves His will, Ibn Ḥazm endows his human *'ishq* with a sacred tinge. Unlike Ibn Maymūn, for whom human passion remains a human element, confined to the human realm, Ibn Ḥazm understands *'ishq* as holy, powerful, almost divine.

But that is not the only message regarding *'ishq* that Ibn Ḥazm sends by using the image of Ibrāhīm's fire. For if it were, he would have done better to compare the flames of love to the flames burning in the tree of Ṭuwā, the flames from within which Allāh called Mūsā to his mission. In positively comparing the passion of the lover for his missing beloved to the flames into which the forefather Ibrāhīm was thrown for failing to renounce his commitment to Allāh, Ibn Ḥazm turns a poetic trope on its head. Normally, passionate love is presented as a sickness, a desirable illness, but one so harmful that it eventually kills the lover who has been so infected. By contrast, in this poem, Ibn Ḥazm insists that such an understanding of love is mistaken. Instead, he suggests, we would do better to understand the true nature of *'ishq* as salvific. It acts not like the punishing infinite flames of Hell, but like the fire set by Ibrāhīm's enemies to punish him, which cooled off to save Ibrāhīm from the evil designs of his idolatrous people and their king. In forced oblivion, the lover's passion cools off, but does not disappear completely, thereby rescuing the lover from the worst of the fire that would otherwise consume him.

Notes

1 Some have suggested that Ibn Gabirol's family fled to Malaga from Cordoba as a result of this collapse of the Umayyad caliphate and the subsequent expulsion of Jews from the region. See Cole, *The Dream of the Poem*, 74.

2 Although al-Murtaḍa managed to wrest control and take the title of caliph for himself, he was murdered later that same year, while fleeing a battle in which his supporters had betrayed him. See *EI*^{2}, s.v. "'Abd al-Raḥmān," by E. Lévi-Provençal (1:84).

3 On Ibn Ḥazm, see *EI*^{2}, s.v. "Ibn Hazm, Abu Muhammad Ali," by R. Arnaldez (3:791). For more on Ibn Ḥazm, Ibn Shuhayd, and the writing of the *Ṭawq*, see Chapter 3. On Ibn Shuhayd, see esp. n. 7.

4 Ibn Ḥazm was not the only Andalusian to write of the betrayal of the lover. Both Jewish and Muslim poets employed this trope with almost depressing frequency. See Pagis, *Hebrew Poetry*, 13, 49; Roth, "My Beloved is Like a Gazelle."

5 As described by Naṣr b. Aḥmad, aka al-Khubza'arruzī. For the full poem in Arabic see Abū Hilāl al-`Askarī, *Dīwān al-ma`ānī* [The Book of Poetic Themes] (Cairo: Maktabat al-qudsī, 1352 H. [1933], 272. Other witty examples by both Arabic and Hebrew poets can be found in Schippers, *Spanish Hebrew Poetry*, 169–70 and above, Chapter 2, n. 35

6 See Ibn Ḥazm, *Ṭauḳ al-ḥamâma*, ed. Pétrof, 98; English translations: Arberry, trans., *The Ring of the Dove*, 202; and Nykl, trans., *A Book Containing the Risāla*, 152.

7 *Ṭauḳ*, 99 (Arberry, 202–3; Nykl, 153). Ibn Ḥazm allows for one exception: If a lover finds himself cuckolded, and thus betrayed by his beloved, the lover's deep-seated pride may truly and completely erase his feelings for his beloved from his heart and mind. Such a reaction, he writes, is not only understandable but justifiable. See *Ṭauḳ*, 105 (Arberry, 214; Nykl, 162).

8 As in A. J. Arberry, trans., *Moorish Poetry* (Cambridge: Cambridge University Press, 1953), 61. Ibn Zaydūn was, famously, the lover of Princess Wallāda, daughter of the caliph al-Mustakfī, and herself an accomplished poet. The Arabic appears in Ibn Sa`īd al-Andalusī, *Rāyāt al-mubarrizīn*, 122. Ibn Sa`īd states that Ibn Zaydūn's poem is better than a similar one written by al-Mutanabbī for Sayf al-Dawla (*c.* 915/16–968/9), ruler of northern Syria and founder of the Hamdanid dynasty. Al-Mutanabbī was Sayf al-Dawla's panegyrist, not lover. For more on Ibn Zaydūn, see *EI²*, "Ibn Zaydun," by G. Lecomte (3:973–4).

A similar declaration of fidelity to a missing beloved appears in a poem by the poetry-writing caliph of Seville, al-Mu`tamid (r. 1069–91). See *The Poems of Mu`tamid King of Seville*, trans. Smith, 45–6. On al-Mu`tamid, see also nn. 25 and 26, below.

9 *Ṭauḳ*, 99. Nykl and Arberry choose different terms to translate this phenomenon. Nykl (p. 153) calls it "acquired oblivion" while Arberry (p. 203) employs the phrase "conscious fortitude." Since the Arabic السلو (*al-sulūw*) indicates forgetting, I have chosen to follow Nykl's translation.

10 Arberry's phrasing, p. 203.

11 In discussing forced oblivion, Ibn Ḥazm does not differentiate between extensive distance caused by circumstances beyond the lovers' control or prolonged avoidance as practiced by the Andalusian beloved. Short avoidances, however, are to be tolerated.

12 *Ṭauḳ*, 101–2 (Arberry, 206; Nykl, 153). Ibn Ḥazm's teaching that a prolonged separation results in "acceptable" oblivion reflects the stance of the earlier al-Jāḥiẓ (d. 868/9). Al-Jāḥiẓ notes that "infrequency of meeting" inflames *`ishq* and separation "fans its flames" to the point of delirium. A prolonged separation, he cautions, causes *`ishq* gradually to fade and eventually die away. In Pellat, trans. and ed., *The Life and Works of Jāḥiẓ*, 264. Note the use of fire terminology in al-Jāḥiẓ's discussion of *`ishq*.

13 *Ṭauḳ*, 102 (Nykl, 157). Arberry (208) translates more rhymingly, though less accurately: "My bowels raged with your desire / As if engulfed in hellish fire: / Now I discover that I am / Immune to flames as Abraham."

14 This story appears in the Qur'ān, in chapters 21 and 37, and will be discussed in detail below.

15 So called because the entire poem rhymes in the letter *nūn*.

16 Italics mine. The full Arabic and English versions can be found in Monroe, *Hispano-Arabic Poetry: A Student Anthology*, 178–82. In a later article, Monroe writes that this line, complete with masculine pronouns, was meant to describe "the slenderness of the *lady's* waist." See Monroe, "Zajal and Muwashshaḥa," 399–400. Sieglinde Lug presents an in-depth analysis of the poem in "Toward a Definition of Excellence in Classical Arabic Poetry: An Analysis of Ibn Zaydūn's *Nūnīyya*," *JAOS*, 101:3 (1981): 331–45. She maintains that the physical description of the beloved in lines 25–30 reflects Wallāda's actual physical appearance.

17 See Scheindlin, "A Miniature Anthology," 110; Roth, "Fawn," 151–72; Pellat, "Liwāṭ," 157; Bellamy and Steiner, *Banners of the Champions*, xxix.

18 See Pagis, *Hebrew Poetry*, 64–6; Monroe, "The Striptease that was Blamed on Abū Bakr's Naughty Son," 94–139; Schirmann, "The Ephebe." On Ibn Ḥazm's use of both the male and female beloveds in his poetry, see Chapter 3, pp. 89ff.
19 s.v. "اله" in Edward William Lane, *An Arabic–English Lexicon*, vol. 1 (London and Edinburgh: Williams and Norgate, 1863).
20 According to Norman Roth, the chief purpose of both Arabic and Hebrew secular poetry was to express not the Joy of Love but the Pain of Love. See Roth, "My Beloved is Like a Gazelle," 148.
21 In the *Kitāb al-muwaššа*, we read a poem exemplifying this trope quite beautifully, one which incorporates the response of an unnamed woman to a claim of love offered up by al-`Abbās b. al-Aḥnaf. As al-`Abbās himself records: "When I claimed to love, she said 'You lie! / For if so, why do I see your limbs covered with flesh? / It's only love when your skin sticks to your gut, / When you are too deaf to answer when someone calls, / When you wither so that love leaves you nothing / But an eye with which to weep or confide." As cited by Scheindlin in his "Ibn Gabirol's Religious and Sufi Poetry," 113–14. The Arabic original appears in Abū al-Ṭayyib Muḥammad b. Iṣḥāq al-Waššā, *Kitāb al-muwašša*, ed. Rudolph E. Brünnow (Leiden: E. J. Brill, 1886), 50.
22 *Ṭauḳ*, 15 (Arberry, 38; Nykl, 19).
23 In Pellat, trans. and ed., *The Life and Works of Jāḥiẓ*, 263.
24 Ibid. As mentioned in Chapter 4, n. 21.
25 *Ṭauḳ*, 11 (Arberry, 31; Nykl, 13). The tenth-century scholar of poets and poetry Dāwūd al-Iṣfahānī (897–967) defined love similarly, calling lovesickness a "divine madness." Al-Iṣfahānī maintains that he learned this from Plato. See Nykl, *Hispano-Arabic Poetry*, 123. Taking this concept of lovesickness a little literally, al-Mu'tamid, the poet-king of Seville (r. 1069–91), once wrote of a man begging Allāh to allow him to remain in his sick-bed because his illness had brought a "fair gazelle" named Siḥr (Charm) to visit him. See Nykl, *Hispano-Arabic Poetry*, 143.
26 Examples include Abū Isḥāq al-Ḥuṣrī (d. 1061) in Ibn Sa`īd al-Andalusī, *Rāyāt al-mubarrizīn*, 259 [Bellamy and Steiner, *Banners of the Champions*, 13 (#11)]; al-Mu`tamid of Seville (1040–95), in *The Poems of Mu`tamid King of Seville*, 45–6, 47; Samuel ha-Nagid, *Diwan Shemuel ha-Nagid. Ben Tehillim*, 306–7 [#186, היא שלחה בינות], and 312 [#200, שור כי בנות ציון]. A longer poem, by Samuel ha-Nagid, ending with an Arabic *kharja*, similarly begins with a comparison between love and fire: "אש אהבים נשקה בי ואיך אתאפקה?" ("The fire of love has kissed me, how can I hold myself back?") See *Diwan Shemuel ha-Nagid. Ben Tehillim*, 314–15 [#202]. This metaphor extends to modern speech as well.
27 In "Signs of Love," *Ṭauḳ*, 13 (Arberry, p. 35; Nykl, 16).
28 See Nykl, *Hispano-Arabic Poetry*, 83. A slightly different wording, with the same meaning, appears in Arberry's translation of *The Dove's Neck Ring*, 44. The original Arabic appears on p. 18 in the *Ṭauḳ*.

One cannot help but recall that the biblical Song of Songs also compares the pain of love to fire's flames. In 8:1, the lover declares, "For love is as fierce as death, passion is mighty as Sheol. Its darts are darts of fire, a blazing flame." See *Tanakh: A New Translation of the Holy Scriptures*. The biblical word translated as "a blazing flame," שַׁלְהֶבֶתְיָה (*shalhevetya*), can also be read as "the flame of God." The idea that Ibn Ḥazm similarly saw human passion as of the flames of God will be discussed further on in the chapter.
29 The Arabic word *jahannam* may derive from the Hebrew גיהנום, Gehinnom, a contraction of גיא בן הינום (*Gei ben Hinnom*, i.e. the Valley of Hinnom), a valley that surrounds the ancient city of Jerusalem along its southern side, as indicated in Joshua 15:8. See *EI*[2], s.v. "djahannam," by L. Gardet (2:381–2). The association of evil with this valley appears to have derived from a combination of unfortunate circumstances. Garbage

from the walled city was burned there, surely causing a highly offensive stench. Additionally, Jeremiah 2:23 speaks of the worshiping of the pagan idol Moloch there, a practice that consisted of child sacrifice by fire (2 Kgs. 23:10; Jer. 7:31). Together, these facts conspired to turn the valley into the mouth of Hell, metaphorically if not literally. It seems possible that the association of Hell with a raging fire may derive from the two fires burning at this site.

30 Ibn Ḥazm himself uses this trope time and again, as in *Ṭauḳ*, 57, 62, 70 (Arberry, 120, 130, 145–6; Nykl, 88, 96, 107). In one particularly charming example, Ibn Ḥazm inverts the conventional simile and instead of comparing his passion to fire, he compares the twinkling lights in the night sky to the fiery tongues of the fire of his passion. See *Ṭauḳ*, 15 (Arberry 39; Nykl, 20).

31 The third condition concerned "appropriate theme."

32 See Pagis, *Hebrew Poetry*, 29–30.

33 In C. Padwick, *Muslim Devotions* (London: SPCK, 1961), 283. According to Padwick, this is the Shi`ī version of the prayer. The Sunnī version, to be recited on Tuesdays (according to `Abd al-Qādir al-Jilānī's teaching), differs little but begs Allāh for forgiveness rather than mercy. For more on Hell in Islam, see *EQ*, s.v. "Hell and Hellfire," by Rosalind W. Gwynne, 2:414–19. Gwynne notes the extra-Qur'ānic materials on Hell do not reduce the severity of punishments experienced by one condemned to its flames as described in the Qur'ān. Both Ibn Kathīr (d. 1373) and al-Ghazzālī (d. 1111), she writes, "describe the tortures of hell in disgusting detail."

34 *Ṭauḳ*, 99 and Arberry, 203 (Nykl, 153).

35 The Qur'ān refers to Ibrāhīm as Allāh's friend (خليل, *khalīl*) in Q 4:125: "Who can be better in religion than one who submits his whole self to God, does good, and follows the faith (*milla*) of Abraham, the true believer (*ḥanīfan*)? For God did take Abraham for a friend (*khalīlan*)." A similar relationship between God and Abraham appears in Isaiah 41:8, where God declares, "But you, Israel, my servant, Jacob, whom I have chosen, seed of Abraham, My friend." The Hebrew word that appears here as "friend," אֹהֲבִי (*ohavi*), literally means "he who loves me," which is different from the Arabic's "friend."

36 The Qur'ān indicates that Ibrāhīm had been guided to this realization by Allāh Himself. Since Islamic theology generally maintains that prophets are incapable of sinning (a condition known as عصمة, *`iṣma*), it follows that Allāh guided Ibrāhīm to the correct understanding of Him. Had Ibrāhīm not been guided, he might have followed his father and his people into idol-worship for a time, at least until he figured out the true nature of divinity—as he does in the midrashic versions of this account. In Islam, however, this would saddle Ibrāhīm with the most serious sin of شرك (*shirk*), associating with Allāh something that is not Allāh (i.e., false worship). To prevent this, Allāh intervened early in Ibrāhīm's life, guiding him along the correct path and preventing him from sinning. See below, n. 85. For more on this, see Lowin, *The Making of a Forefather*, ch. 2. For more on *`iṣma*, see *EI*$^2$, s.v. "`Iṣma," by E. Tyan (4:182–4) and *EQ*, s.v. "Impeccability," by Paul E. Walker (2:505–7).

37 The Qur'ān does not tell us here where they had gone, why, or where the idols had been located so that Ibrāhīm had unguarded access to them, which would seem an imprudent oversight on their part given Ibrāhīm's recent threat against the idols.

38 Similar narratives detailing the forefather's destruction of the idols, and his attempt to foist the blame on to the largest one, appear in pre-Islamic Jewish sources, such as the fifth-century *Genesis Rabbah* and the first-century BCE *Book of Jubilees*. For a more in-depth discussion of these, see Lowin, *The Making of a Forefather*, ch. 2.

39 According to the Qur'ān, Lūt (Lot) was the kinsman of Ibrāhīm and a prophet in his own right. He railed against the people of his city for their engaging in same-sex sexual relationships. When the city was overturned, he was saved. See, among others, Q 21:74.

40 Ibrāhīm's glancing at the stars here appears to be an intertextual reference to Q 6:76–80. There Ibrāhīm "discovers" Allāh by analyzing the behavior of the sun, moon, and stars, which some of his people worshiped as gods. Noting that each celestial orb sets, having been overcome by something greater than it (darkness covers the sun, for instance), Ibrāhīm realizes that none of these can be the true Lord. He rejects each in turn, ultimately recognizing Allāh as the creator of all. The Qur'ānic account hints that Ibrāhīm discovered monotheism on his own and simultaneously was guided to this belief by Allāh Himself. The Islamic exegetes comment upon and expand upon the Qur'ān's brief account and convoluted message. An in-depth discussion of these can be found in Lowin, *The Making of a Forefather*, 87–129. The forefather's contemplation of the heavens in his search for the true God appears in pre-Islamic Jewish midrashic sources as well. See Lowin, ibid.

41 The text does not tell us that Ibrāhīm and his people had been arguing while standing either in the idol-temple or before a set of idols. Ibrāhīm's addressing the idols here is the first indication in ch. 37 that they were present. Similarly, the text does not speak of anyone having brought the idols ritual food offerings. Ibrāhīm's words are our clue to this practice. The pre- and post-Qur'ānic midrashic sources, such as *Genesis Rabbah*, incorporate the food sacrifices into Abraham's discovery of the truth of monotheism. For more on this, see Lowin, *The Making of a Forefather*, ch. 3.

42 Interestingly, while ch. 21 informs readers that Allāh commanded the fire to be "cool and safe" for Ibrāhīm, ch. 37 does not mention this at all. Instead it ends the pericope with Allāh's statement (v. 97), "And they wished to ensnare him, but We made them the most humiliated." Unlike ch. 21, ch. 37 appears to expect the audience to fill in the missing information from what appears to have been common knowledge – that Allāh intervened and commanded the fire to turn cold.

While the story of Abraham in the fiery furnace of Chaldea does not appear in the Bible, it does appear frequently, and in many variations, in both canonical and non-canonical pre-Islamic midrashic texts. See, for example, *BT Pesaḥim* 118a and *BT Eruvin* 53a; *Midrash Rabbah Bereishit [Genesis Rabbah]*, 44:13; *Midrash Tanḥuma*, ed. Buber (1964), *Lekh Lekha*, para. 2; and *Chronicles of Jeraḥmeel or the Hebrew Bible Historiale*, trans. Moses Gaster, introduction by Haim Schwartzbaum (New York: KTAV, 1971), ch. 29. For an in-depth analysis of the relationship between the Muslim and Jewish versions of this narrative, see Lowin, *The Making of a Forefather*, ch. 4. A discussion of the relationship between Abraham's fire and the fire of Nebuchadnezzar in the biblical book of Daniel appears there as well.

43 Such behavior demonstrates fire's submission to Allāh's will, presenting an instructive model for human behavior. The reaction of the world's fires to a command meant for a specific one furthermore recalls a pre-Islamic *midrash* on the splitting of the sea in the third-century *Mekhilta* on *Beshalaḥ* (ch. 4). See Saul Horovitz and Israel Abraham Rabin, eds, *Mekhilta de-Rabi Yishma'el* [The Mekhilta of Rabbi Ishmael], 2nd edn (Jerusalem: Bamberger and Wahrmann, 1960), 104. Similarly, the fifth-century *Genesis Rabbah* 53:8 teaches that when Abraham's wife, Sara, was finally cured of her sterility and became pregnant, all the sterile women in the world became pregnant along with her.

44 Except for the gecko who attempted to blow his "fire" on the fire and add to it. The frog, however, tried to help Allāh by dipping herself in water and attempting to extinguish the flames. `Abd al-Razzāq al-Ṣan`ānī (744–827), *Tafsīr al-Qur'ān al-`aẓīm*, ed. Muṣṭafa Muslim Muḥammad (Riyad: Maktabat al-rushd, 1989), 2:24–5; Abū al-Ḥasan `Alī b. Ibrāhīm al-Qummī (d. *c.* 940), *Tafsīr al-Qummī* (Najaf: Matba`at al-Najaf, 1386–7 AH [*c.* 1967]), 2:73; `Ali b. al- Ḥasan b.`Asākir (1105–76), *Ta'rīkh madīnat Dimashq*, ed. `Umar ibn Gharāma al-`Amrawī (Beirut: Dār al-fikr, 1995), 6:185; Muḥamad Baqīr al-Majlisī (d. 1698), *Biḥār al-anwār* (Teheran: Dār al-kutub al-Islāmīyya, 1362–6 AH [1943–6]), 12:33. Muqātil, al-Ṭabarī (quoting Qatāda),

al-Tha`labī, and Ibn Kathīr omit the frog. See Muqātil ibn Sulaymān (*c.* 713–67), *Tafsīr Muqātil*, ed. `Abdallāh Maḥmūd Shiḥāta (Cairo: al-Ḥay'a al-Miṣriyya al-`āmma lil-kitāb, 1979–89), 3:613; al-Ṭabarī (838–923), *Jāmi` al-bayān*, 10 (17): 43–5; Aḥmad b. Muḥammad al-Tha`labī (d. 1036), *Qiṣaṣ al-anbiyā' al-musamma `arā'is al-majālis* (Miṣr: Muṣṭafā al-Bābī al-Ḥalabī wa-awlādihī, 1374/1954), 78; Abū al-Fidā' Ismā`īl b. Kathīr (d. 1373), *Tafsīr al-Qur'ā al-`aẓīm* (Beirut: Dār al-fikr, 1970), 5:352. Al-Qummī and al-Majlisī note that this fire outage lasted for three days.

45 Al-Ṭabarī, *Ta'rīkh*, 1:264; al-Tha`labī, 78.

46 Al-Tha`labī, 78; al-Bayḍāwī (d. 1286), *Tafsīr al-Bayḍāwī*, 2:74 (Q 21:69).

47 Al-Tha`labī, 78; according to al-Bayḍāwī, 2:74 (Q 21:69), the fire only singed his belt a smidge.

48 Isḥāq ibn Bishr, *Mubtada' al-dunyā wa-qiṣaṣ al-anbiyā'* (MS Huntington 388, Bodleian Library, Oxford University, Oxford), 168b; al-Ṭabarī, *Jāmi` al-bayān*, 10 (17): 44; idem, *Ta'rīkh*, 1:264; al-Tha`labī, 78; Ibn Kathīr (citing al-Suddī), *Tafsīr*, 5:352; al-Qummī, 2:73; al-Majlisī, 12:33, 42–3; Ibn `Asākir, 6:187; `Abd al-Raḥmān Jalāl al-Dīn al-Suyūṭī (d. 1505), *Al-Durr al-manthūr bi-l-tafsīr al-ma'thūr* (Cairo: al-Maṭba`a al-munīriyya, 1314 AH [1896/7]), 3:26. See also Ibn Isḥāq (d. 767) in Newby, *The Making of the Last Prophet*, 71.

49 Both of these are archangels in Islamic angelology. Jibrīl serves as the angel in charge of revelation. Isrāfīl appears as the angel who reads out divine decrees from the Tablet and transmits them to the angel to whose department they belong. Some traditions relate that three times each day and three times each night Isrāfīl looks into Hell and becomes so overcome with grief and violent crying that the earth stands in danger of becoming flooded by his tears. Islamic tradition identifies Isrāfīl with the unnamed angel in the Qur'ān who will appear on the Day of Judgment to rouse people from their graves by blowing a trumpet (as in 39:68). Interestingly, given the current discussion of the fire of Ibrāhīm, Isrāfīl's name derives from the Hebrew word for a particular type of angel known as a *seraf* (pl. *serafim*), meaning "Fiery One/s." For Isrāfīl, see *EI*², s.v. "Isrāfīl," by A. J. Wensinck (4:211); for Jibrīl, see *EI*², s.v. "Djabrā'īl," by J. Pederson (2:362–4).

50 See also Ibn Kathīr (citing Jubayr from al-Ḍaḥḥāk), *Tafsīr*, 5:352; Ibn `Asākir, 6:182; Muḥammad ibn `Abdallāh al-Kisā'ī in Eisenberg, *Vita Prophetarum*, 139.

51 Ibn Isḥāq, in Newby, 71; al-Tha`labī, 78.

52 Ibn Isḥāq, in Newby, 71; al-Ṭabarī, *Ta'rīkh*, 1:265 and *Jāmi` al-bayān*, 10 (17): 44; Ibn `Asākir, 6:187–8; al-Kisā'ī, 139, 148; al-Suyūṭī, 3:26.

53 Al-Tha`labī, 78.

54 Ibn Ḥazm points out that there is one universally effective way to tell the difference. One who is simply acting may make "a great show" of attacking his beloved, but he will not tolerate an attack made by another against the same person. *Ṭauḳ*, 99 (Arberry, 204; Nykl, 153).

55 As in Arberry's translation, 204. Arabic in *Ṭauḳ*, 99 (Nykl, 153).

56 This teaching regarding human love recalls that of the famed Muslim philosopher Ibn Sīnā (Avicenna, 980–1037). In his *Risāla fī al-`ishq*, Ibn Sīnā wrote that the love of one human for another contributes positively to the soul's ascent to the Divine; love turns the lower soul, the animalistic part of the soul, into something noble; only with an ennobled soul can one draw nearer to God. Von Grunebaum has pointed out that Ibn Ḥazm never once refers to the *Risāla* in his *Ṭawq*. It seems then that Ibn Ḥazm did not derive his stance on love from Avicenna but from the Ẓāhirī school of thought, of which he eventually became the leading proponent. A discussion of this appears in von Grunebaum, "Avicenna's *Risāla fī al-`Ishq*." See also above, Chapter 3, n. 28.

57 *Ṭauḳ,* p. 101. Arberry (208) translates this as: "And I suppose desire is like a coal / that feeds upon the fire still in my soul." Nykl (157) translates this more accurately but less poetically as: "And [I] believed love for you to be like burning coal spread under the ashes."

58 As we have seen, the Hebrew poets engage in such scriptural embellishments of their poetry all the time, using two poetic tropes known as *remez* and *shibbutz*. For a more in-depth discussion of these techniques, see above, Chapter 1; Brann, "Andalusian Hebrew Poetry," 3:112–14; Elizur, *Shirat ha-Ḥol*, 3:413ff, 351, 366–400; and Yellin, *Kitvei David Yellin*, 30–43. This "hinting" to Scripture was not unique to the Jews; Arab poets hinted to and incorporated elements from the Qur`ān and the literary history of Arabic poetry and poems. See Yellin, *Torat ha-Shir ha-Sefaradit*, 3:103–17. A discussion of this appears above, in Chapter 1, pp. 10ff.

59 This idea appears in the Islamic exegetical texts as well. Al-Tha`labī (77) writes that the "angel of waters" came to Ibrāhīm and offered to douse the fires for him. The "treasurer of winds" offered to cause the flames to fly off into the air. The archangel Jibrīl then came by and asked Ibrāhīm if he needed anything. Ibrāhīm rejected each in turn, insisting that he trusted in Allāh alone and would ask for help only from Him. It was in response to this statement, note the exegetes, that Allāh saved Ibrāhīm from the fire, commanding it to be cool and safe for him. According to al-Ṭabarī, Allāh commanded the angels to help Ibrāhīm, should he ask for them to do so. But Ibrāhīm called on Allāh alone and so, when the people pushed Ibrāhīm into the fire, Allāh Himself responded. See *Ta'rīkh*, 1:263.

60 This trope appears in poems penned by the Andalusian Hebrew poets as well. See for example Samuel ha-Nagid in his *Diwan Shemuel ha-Nagid. Ben Tehillim*, ed. Jarden, 312 (#200, שור כי בנות ציון). Although he does not employ the trope of the biblical burning bush or the midrashic fire of Abraham, Moses ibn Ezra writes of a beloved who manages to dwell inside the heart of the lover without becoming either consumed by the fire that rages there for him or drowned by the copious amount of the lover's tears. See Ibn Ezra, *Shirei ha-Ḥol*, 1:178 (#179). Samuel ha-Nagid also employs the image of the burning bush to describe red wine. See *Diwan Shemuel ha-Nagid. Ben Tehillim*, ed. Jarden, 289 (#142, חבלו בני עבים).

61 According to v. 27, the Midianite شيخ كبير (*shaykh kabīr*, v. 23) offered Mūsā one of his daughters as a wife if Mūsā would agree to work for him for eight years. If Mūsā agreed to complete the term in ten years, of his own accord, the Midianite added, it would be "a grace" to him [the father]. The Qur'ān does not detail which term Mūsā completed nor what one is supposed to learn from this conversation/offer. For a possible conflation of this story with the Jacob–Rachel–Leah story of Genesis 29, see Brannon M. Wheeler, *Moses in the Quran and Islamic Exegesis* (London and New York: RoutledgeCurzon, 2002), 37–63.

62 الطور, *al-ṭūr* (Q 28:29). The word generally means "the mountain." On two occasions in the Qur'ān it appears coupled with the word Sīnā'/Sīnīn (23:20; 95:2), meaning specifically Mount Sinai. Because of this, readers of the Qur'ān have generally understood the other eight appearances of the word, all associated with the wanderings of the Children of Israel in the desert, to indicate Mount Sinai as well. For more on *al-ṭūr* and Sinai in the Islamic tradition, see *EQ*, s.v. "Sinai," by Irfan Shahid (5:28–9); and, *EI*², s.v. "Al-Ṭūr," by E. Honigmann and C. E. Bosworth (10:663–5).

63 While chapter 20 of the Qur'ān leaves the valley unnamed, other Qur'ānic pericopes on Mūsā's call to serve as Allāh's messenger name it Ṭuwā (طوى). Cf. Q 20:12; 79:15–16. Some scholars have suggested that the enigmatic name Ṭuwā might be a misreading of the Syriac *ṭūr/ṭūrā* ("mountain"). Medieval Qur'ān commentators understood the name to mean something "twice done," meaning that the valley was twice blessed by Allāh's having called to Mūsā there. See *EQ*, s.v. "Ṭuwā," by William S. Brinner (5:395–6).

64 This second miracle required Mūsā to place his hand inside his cloak. When he withdrew it, his hand had turned white, without being ill or damaged. Cf. Exodus 4:6–8.

65 The Qur'ān refers to this first conversation between Mūsā and Allāh more than once, with differing levels of detail. Q 79:15ff and Q 26:10ff relate that Allāh called to Mūsā and charged him to go to Fir`awn, though neither rendition mentions either a

tree or a fire. Similarly, Q 19:51–3 relates that Allāh called to Mūsā "from the right side of the mountain" but omits any reference to a fire. Q 20:9ff and Q 27:7–14 relate that Mūsā encountered Allāh when he went searching for an ember or guidance at a fire he had seen from a distance, in the valley of Ṭuwā, but the passage makes no mention of a tree. Only chapter 28 mentions both fire and tree. Although it is not clear from the text of the Qur'ān (in chapter 28) that they are one and the same item, a tree on fire, the exegetical texts understand it as a given that they were.

For a comparison with the account of the burning bush as recorded in the Bible, see Exodus 3:2ff, and Chapter 8, n. 16, below.

66 Al-Ṭabarī, *Jāmi` al-bayān*, 9 (16): 141–3 and 11 (20): 70; al-Tha`labī (178) and al-Kisā'ī (209) add that not only was it raining that night, but Mūsā's wife was due to give birth at any moment.

67 Al-Ṭabarī, *Jāmi` al-bayān*, 9 (16): 142; *Ta'rīkh*, 1:465; al-Tha`labī, 178; al-Qummī, 2:139; al-Kisā'ī, 209; Ibn Isḥāq, in Newby, 125; Ibn `Asākir, 61:44.

68 This appears in Ibn `Asākir, 61:45–6 and al-Tha`labī, 178.

69 Interestingly, the commentators do not say whether Mūsā could see these angels. See Muqātil, 3:297; al-Ṣan`ānī, 2:67 (on Q 28:8); and al-Ṭabarī, *Jāmi` al-bayān*, 11 (19): 135. The presence of angels explains the Qur'ān's statement in 27:8, "Blessed is the one in the fire and the one [or, those] around it." Other sources explain that "the one around it" refers to Mūsā himself. Al-Ṭabarī cites an alternate explanation of Q 27:8 in which scholars maintain that what Mūsā saw was not actual fire (نار, *nār*) but a Divine light (نور, *nūr*), which he had perceived as fire from afar. See *Jāmi` al-bayān`*, 11 (19): 133–4, and *Ta'rīkh*, 1:463. See also al-Ṣan`anī, 2:67. In his commentary on the rendering of the episode in Q 28, Muqātil (3:343) maintains that this was a light shining from the Holy Land (الارض المقدسة, *al-arḍ al-muqqadasa*). Commenting on Q 20, Muqātil writes that Mūsā's attention was drawn to the fire, which gave off a great light, by the sound of the angels giving praise (تسبيح, *tasbīḥ*) to Allāh. Since Mūsā was frightened by the intensity of the light, Allāh sent the *sakīna* (a Divine presence of some sort, akin to the Jewish concept of the *shekhinah*) to calm him and speak with him. See Muqātil, 3:22.

70 Interestingly, the Qur'ān records that Mūsā retreated, frightened, not when he saw the blazing but living tree, but after his staff turned into a snake and started wriggling. See Q 28:31 and 27:10. See al-Ṭabarī, *Jāmi` al-bayān*, 9 (16): 143; al-Ṭabarī, *Ta'rīkh*, 1:465; al-Qummī, 2:140; Ibn Isḥāq, in Newby, 125.

71 See al-Tha`labī, 178–9; al-Ṭabarī, *Ta'rikh*, 1:465–6; al-Ṭabarī, *Jāmi` al-bayān*, 9 (16): 143, 11 (20): 71 and 11 (19): 134; Muqātil, 3:296.

Mūsā's experience at the fiery tree remains especially prominent and significant in Ṣūfī texts. This is discussed at length in Chapter 8.

72 He adds that many *rashīdūn* (rightly guided) caliphs as well as God-fearing imāms have themselves been lovers. *Ṭauḳ*, 6 (Arberry, 21–2; Nykl, 6).

73 So Emilio Garcia Gomez writes in his translation of Ibn Sa`īd's *Rāyāt al-mubarrizīn*, calling him "El magnate y cortesano." See Emilio García Gómez, *El Libro de las Banderas de los Campeones, de Ibn Sa`īd al-Maghribī* (Madrid: Instituto de Valencia de Don Juan, 1942), 190. The Arabic honorific applied to Ibn Maymūn by Ibn Sa`īd (p. 133), of which this is a translation/interpretation, is الرئيس الجليس (*al-ra'īs al-jalīs*).

74 According to Ibn Sa`īd, Ibn Maymūn composed a commentary on the famous *Maqāmāt* of al-Ḥarīrī (1052–1122). See Ibn Sa`īd, *Rāyāt al-mubarrizīn*, 133.

75 For more on al-Manṣūr, see EI^2, s.v. "Abū Yūsuf Ya`ḳūb b. Yūsuf b. `Abd al-Mu'min al-Manṣūr," by A. Huici Miranda (1:165–6).

76 This information appears in fn. 76, p. 133, of Ibn Sa`īd's *Rāyāt al-mubarrizīn*, where the modern editor, Muḥammad Riḍwān al-Dāya, cites the thirteenth-century historian Ibn al-Abbār. In the modern day, the word *ḥāfiẓ* generally refers to one who has memorized the Qur'ān in its entirety. In the medieval period, it also indicated one

who reached the highest rank as a *muḥaddith*, a transmitter of *ḥadīth*. The other confusing title applied to Ibn Maymūn by Ibn al-Abbār here, مجود (*mujawwid*), can indicate that Ibn Maymūn was either a Qur'ān reciter or an extremely careful and accurate scholar. Because of the ambiguity of the titles given to Ibn Maymūn in this source, one cannot tell whether Ibn al-Abbār considered Ibn Maymūn to have been a scholar of religion, in addition to a scholar of literature. Perhaps more tellingly, Ibn Sa`īd includes him among the Cordoban علماء اللغة (*`ulamā' al-lugha*), scholars of language, and not among the scholars of religion. He mentions him as the author of two works on Arabic grammar, but attributes to him no works of theology or exegesis.

77 This may actually have been a commentary on al-Zajjājī's *Kitāb al-jumal*, as indicated in the editor's fn. 76 in Ibn Sa`īd, *Rayāt al-mubarrizīn*, 133. See also EI^2, s.v. "Sharḥ," by Claude Gilliot (9:317).

78 His full name is Abū `Abdallāh Muḥammad b. `Abdallāh b. Abū Bakr b. `Abdallāh b. Abū Bakr al-Quḍā`ī al-Balansī (1199–1260). For more on Ibn al-Abbār, see Nykl, *Hispano-Arabic Poetry*, 332–3.

79 Ibn Sa`īd, *Rāyāt al-mubarrizīn*, 133.

80 The Arabic here uses code names for these men rather than their proper names: *al-khalīl* and *al-kalīm*. *Al-khalīl* refers to Ibrāhīm, the "friend" of Allāh, explained above in n. 35. *Al-kalīm* (الكليم) is the traditional Muslim epithet referring to Mūsā, meaning the "mouthpiece" or "interlocutor" of Allāh. The name derives from Qur'ānic passages in which Allāh speaks directly to Mūsā, an activity for which the Qur'ān uses a verb formed from the root كلم (*klm*), often used to mean word or speech. See Q 4:162, for example. The Qur'ān itself does not refer to Mūsā by this name. For more on this, see EI^2, s.v. "Mūsā," by D. B. Macdonald (7:639–40).

81 Arberry renders this somewhat poetically as: "I adventured fearlessly in love's flame that fired my breast / boldly plunged into the sea from my weeping eyes expressed. / Am I Father Abraham that such a blaze I could endure? Is it Moses that I am, that from drowning I am secure?" See Arberry, *Moorish Poetry*, 69. Arberry's first-person usage reflects the vocalization of the Arabic that appears in García Gómez's Arabic version of *Rāyāt al-mubarrizīn* (p. 190). In their translation, Bellamy and Steiner present Ibn Maymūn's lover as speaking to his beloved, rather than musing to himself: "You rushed into the blazing fire of my heart, / just as you plunged into the ocean of my tears. / Are you Abraham? Are you Moses? / Are you safe from burning? Safe from drowning?" In Bellamy and Steiner, *Banners of the Champions*, 199 (#188). The vocalized Arabic provided in the version of *Rāyāt al-mubarrizīn* edited by Muḥammad Riḍwān al-Dāya (p. 133) reflects this same second-person ("you") address. Given that the tropes of Andalusian poetry predominantly speak of a lover burned by his own passion or crying tears of frustration and/or fervor, I have elected to use the first-person rendition favored by García Gómez and Arberry. For the investigation of the significance of the Ibrāhīm image, the difference in addressee does not prove that significant.

82 Ibn Maymūn's poem also speaks of tears so copiously shed that they form a sea deep enough to drown a man. This, too, reflects a trope of love poetry, as noted, not surprisingly, by Ibn Ḥazm. In the *Ṭawq*'s chapter on "Signs of Love" (ch. 1), Ibn Ḥazm writes, "Weeping is a well-known sign of Love." He adds, however, that while some men are "ready weepers," whose "tear-ducts are always overflowing," others (such as himself) remain dry-eyed and unable to cry. See *Ṭauḳ*, 17 (Arberry, 42). Despite this personal admission, Ibn Ḥazm writes of the deluge caused by the tears of his passion in more than one poetic composition. See for example *Ṭauḳ*, 17, 34 (Arberry, 42–4, 78; Nykl, 22, 53). Like Ibn Maymūn, the earlier al-Mu`tamid of Seville (d. 1095), a rough contemporary of Ibn Ḥazm, also writes of both the burning and drowning natures of passion in a single poem. See *The Poems of Mu`tamid King of Seville*, 47.

The Bible also uses parables of fire and water to indicate the strength of passionate love. Song of Songs 8:6–7 declares: "[6] Let me be a seal upon your heart, like a seal upon your hand. For love is as fierce as death, Passion is mighty as Sheol. Its flames are flames of fire, a blazing flame. [7] Vast floods cannot quench love, nor can rivers drown it. If a man offered all his wealth for love, he would be laughed to scorn."

83 See, for example, Q 2:119. In his *Iḥyā' `ulūm al-dīn*, al-Ghazālī explains that the different names by which the Qur'ān refers to Hell indicate the different levels of Hell's architecture. Of the seven names/levels, *jahannam* sits at the top, while *al-jaḥīm* can be found second from bottom. See Gwynne, "Hell and Hellfire," 2:419 (n. 33 above). Only once does the term *jaḥīm* not serve as a synonym for *jahannam* in the Qur'ān; mysteriously, Q 37:97 uses the term to speak not of Hell, but of the fire into which Abraham was thrown. See Gwynne, "Hell and Hellfire," 2:414. Perhaps this Qur'ānic citation served as inspiration for Ibn Ḥazm's poem.

84 Ibn Maymūn also speaks of the lover's passion as causing him to drown in a sea of his own tears, which he compares to another scriptural image, the drowning of Moses. With this, Ibn Maymūn recalls the moment in which Mūsā's mother, under Allāh's inspiration, placed her infant son in an ark on the water in an attempt to avoid Fir`awn's decree demanding the death of the boy children of her people (Q 28:4ff). According to García Gómez (p. 190), Ibn Maymūn's reference to Mūsā's experience with water here refers to the crossing of the Red Sea. Such a reading strikes me as incorrect. After all, Mūsā was not the only one to cross the sea when the Israelites exited Egypt. The entire nation walked through with him. Furthermore, in the case of the crossing of the sea, Mūsā (and the Israelites) did not actually survive drowning, as it were. The sea split in half and they walked through on dry land (Q 26:63–8). In the case of the infant Mūsā on the river, he alone was thrown in, and he did in fact float on water, rather than drown in it. Thus, I maintain that Ibn Maymūn's poem here refers to Mūsā's infancy episode.

85 Prophets in Islam are blessed with عصمة (*`iṣma*), meaning they are incapable of sinning, a status that allows them to serve as receptacles for the holy words of the Divine. See above, n. 36.

Part III

Unsuitable love: family members as lovers

6 Poetic justice for the rape of Tamar: Ibn Gabirol's critique of David

Given that Solomon ibn Gabirol (*c.* 1021–*c.* 1058) was orphaned by his biological father at a young age, re-orphaned later by his patron Yequtiel ben Ḥassan, and never was a father himself (as far as we know), it is with particular interest that we turn to a love-and-lust poem in which Ibn Gabirol references biblical sons whose behaviors enrage their fathers. Our previous chapter on a Hebrew poem, "'His instruments are the instruments of Simeon and Levi': Ibn Gabirol and the silence of Jacob" (Chapter 4), discussed a similar instance of biblical fathers and sons in a love poem. There, the poetic composition, "הלנצח יעירני" (*ha-Lanetzaḥ ye`ireini*), hinged on a particularly gruesome account concerning the children of Jacob: the violent vengeance wrought by Simeon and Levi against the people of Shechem for the kidnapping and rape of Dinah, and Jacob's subsequent fury at their behavior. The current discussion concerns a Hebrew desire poem with a similarly harrowing *remez* (allusion) to a biblical family: the rape of Tamar, daughter of King David, by her half-brother Amnon, eldest son of King David (recorded in 2 Sam. 13). In this poem, the sexual violation of the family's daughter is the central focus of the *remez* rather than a side point, as it is in the Simeon and Levi poem, which focused on the brothers' reactions.

As with Ibn Gabirol's "הלנצח יעירני" (*ha-Lanetzaḥ ye`ireini*), the poem at hand, "אמנון אני" (*Amnon ani*), does more than marshal an unromantic biblical account into the service of love and poetry. As we shall see, while the poem references the biblical account, it also slyly turns it on its head. It renders the innocent bystanders of the Bible into criminal accomplices and turns a secretly-planned incestuous attack into a public declaration of intent. The poetic manipulation of the biblical account of 2 Samuel 13 leads readers to see in the scriptural text possible subtle disapproval of David for not taking a more active role in his children's lives. Against the traditional reading, the poem opens the window to seeing in the biblical formulation of the narrative an indictment of David, as well as of Absalom, for having known of Amnon's devious plans in advance but failing to combat them and protect Tamar. Like Ibn Gabirol's "הלנצח יעירני" (*ha-Lanetzaḥ ye`ireini*), his desire poem on Amnon and Tamar contains an embedded subversive exegesis of a biblical text.

"*Amnon ani*" by Ibn Gabirol

Among the many love and desire poems penned by Ibn Gabirol over the course of his short life, we find one that speaks with particular intensity and honesty, in the voice of a lovesick lover yearning for a particular maiden. According to the seventeenth-century anonymous editor of Ibn Gabirol's secular *dīwān*, this ranks as among the "most excellent and wonderful of his love poems."[1] Writes Ibn Gabirol,

אמנון אני חולה קראו אלי תמר   כי חושקה נפל ברשת וגם מכמר
רעי מיודעי אלי הביאוה   אחת שאלתי מכם אשר אומר:
קשרו עטרת על ראשה והכינו   עדיה ושימו על ידה בכוס חמר
תבוא ותשקני אולי תכבה אש   לבי אשר בלה בשרי אשר סמר.[2]

Rendering this poetically into English, Raymond Scheindlin translates:

Like Amnon sick am I, so call Tamar
And tell her one who loves her is snared by death.
Quick, friends, companions, bring her here to me.
The only thing I ask of you is this:
Adorn her head with jewels, bedeck her well,
And send along with her a cup of wine.
If she would pour for me she might put out
The burning pain wasting my throbbing flesh.[3]

Although Scheindlin's translation is powerful and poetic, it sometimes obscures elements of the original Hebrew important to our discussion. In such cases, the original Hebrew and alternate translations will be offered here.

2 Samuel 13 and the rape of Tamar

The element that stands out most prominently in this poem is the reference to the lovesick beloved using the names of two well-known biblical characters, Amnon and Tamar, whose story forms one of the more horrifying accounts in the Bible. Chapter 13 in 2 Samuel records the sordid account, in which Amnon, the eldest son of King David, falls in love with his beautiful half-sister Tamar.[4] Tormented by his passions, Amnon falls sick. Since Tamar was a virgin, the text explains, it seemed to Amnon "wondrous" to do something to her.[5] Now Amnon had a cousin and friend named Jonadav, a very wise man, who noticed that something seemed to be amiss with the prince, as the days went by and Amnon seemed to be increasingly weak and losing weight.[6] So he entreated the prince to share with him the source of his unwellness. Upon hearing from Amnon that the prince had fallen in love with his own sister,[7] Jonadav suggests a plan. He advises Amnon to take to his bed and feign illness;[8] when the king, Amnon's father, comes to visit him, Amnon is to request that his sister Tamar come and feed him bread (לֶחֶם, *leḥem*). What's more, Jonadav advises, Amnon should ask David to instruct Tamar to prepare food (הַבִּרְיָה, *ha-biryah*) in front of his (Amnon's) eyes and serve it to him herself. And so it happens. David comes to visit his "ill" son, Amnon requests that Tamar come and prepare food for him as he watches, and David sends Tamar to Amnon's house to cook for his seemingly sick son.

Obedient daughter that she is, Tamar sets off to fulfill her father's commands. She arrives at her brother Amnon's house to find him lying down, much as her father had found him, and so she gets to work. While Amnon watches, Tamar takes the dough, kneads it, forms it into cakes and bakes them.[9] She then takes the pan and pours out the cakes for him. But Amnon, deviating from the plan, refuses to eat. Instead he orders all the attendants to withdraw and then tells Tamar to bring the food to him in his chamber, so that he may "eat from your hand" (v. 10). Tamar complies, and when she steps forward to serve her supposedly ailing brother, he suddenly grabs hold of her, saying (v. 11), "Come, lie with me, my sister." Tamar refuses, and embarks upon a particularly eloquent plea to save herself. "Do not, my brother," she begins (v. 12), appealing to his sense of justice and morality, "do not force me, for this is not done in Israel. Do not do this detestable thing [הַנְּבָלָה הַזֹּאת, *ha-nevalah ha-zot*]."[10] Apparently seeing no change in Amnon, she then attempts to jolt her brother-attacker out of his lust-soaked stupor by appealing to him on an emotional level. She draws attention first to her own pathos and then appeals to his. "And I," she cries (v. 13), "where will I carry my shame? And you will be as one of the witless detestable men (הַנְּבָלִים, *ha-nevalim*) in Israel."[11] But still, her words fall on deaf ears. In desperation, she makes a suggestion seemingly constructed to buy her time. "Now speak to the king," she says, referring to their father, "he will not withhold me from you."[12] But to no avail. Amnon refuses to listen to her, overpowers her, and rapes her. Hatred for his once-beloved sister overcomes Amnon now that the deed has been done and, in an appalling scene of humiliation, he orders Tamar to leave his house.[13] She entreats him to refrain from this second evil, which she perceives as worse than the first,[14] but he once again turns a deaf ear to her pleas. Maliciously, he orders a servant boy to forcibly remove the princess from the premises and lock the door behind her.[15] Violated, humiliated, and left in the street, Tamar puts dust on her head, rips her striped coat, the very one worn by all the royal virgins (says the narrator), puts her hand against her head, and walks off howling (v. 19).

Ibn Gabirol and the classical tropes of *`ishq/ḥesheq* poetry

Before discussing what can only be described as a particularly repellent choice of a biblical episode to use in a love poem, we ought to note that in many ways Ibn Gabirol's poem employs various elements typical of medieval love poetry. Like our previous poems, "*Amnon ani*" uses as its starting point the typical scenario in which a romantic couple has been separated from one another's company, leaving the lover yearning for union. Against this stereotypical backdrop, Ibn

Gabirol unsurprisingly incorporates additional tropes, that of lovesickness, the fire of love, the cause of love's disease functioning as its cure, and the trope of the assembled company.

Lovesickness

Of all the poetic tropes that appear in our poem, the most obvious here concerns the narrator-lover's descent into illness. Like so many lovers before him, our lover finds himself experiencing such passion for his beloved that he is stricken with lovesickness. "Amnon, I am, sick," he declares in the opening line. If the mention of the name Amnon were not a clear enough hint to convey the cause and type of sickness he suffers from, our lover explains further: "Call to me Tamar," he cries (l. 1b), "כי חושקה נפל ברשת וגם מכמר," "for the one who desires her has fallen into a net, nay into a snare." While Scheindlin translates this snare as the snare of death ("And tell her the one who loves her is snared by death"), the poet himself does not actually mention death. Rather, the line proclaims that the one who desires his beloved finds himself entangled in a net or snare.[16] In other words, like the biblical Amnon infatuated with his sister, the lover is besotted with his own Tamar and finds himself caught up in the net that is his love for her, i.e., lovesickness.

Love, pain, and fire

The physical way in which our lovesick lover experiences the passion he feels for his beloved stands in line with the Andalusian definitions as well. We recall that, according to Ibn Ḥazm, real love (عشق, *`ishq*) consists of two elements: It is incredibly painful, and the pain is that of a fire that burns in one's heart.[17] Both these ideals appear in Ibn Gabirol's lover's description of his passion. In the final line of the poem our poet muses hopefully, "תבוא ותשקני אולי תכבה אש לבי אשר בלה בשרי אשר סמר." Scheindlin translates this as, "If she would pour for me, she might put out the burning pain wasting my throbbing flesh." While such a translation is wonderfully poetic, it obscures the explicit fire image apparent in the Hebrew. A more literal translation reveals the image: "If she would come and pour for me, she might extinguish *the fire in my heart* which is wasting my flesh, which is throbbing." The Hebrew makes clear that *fire* causes the pain that harms the lover and that these flames reside specifically in his heart. As we expect of *`ishq*, Ibn Gabirol's lover suffers from flames of love that scald and torch him from the inside, traveling from his heart through the rest of his body, causing it to pulse with an unpleasant and dangerous heat. According to Eddy Zemach, the difficult syntax of this final line demonstrates the lover's emotional state, overcome as he is with passion that burns and excites him simultaneously. Just as the words and the syntax fall over themselves, the lover too falls over himself, continuously seeking respite from the pain, but never finding it.[18]

Passion as cause and cure

In an interesting twist, our poetic hero perceives his beloved to be not only the cause of his illness, the instigator and object of his lovesickness, but also the cure for it. This we see in that rather than calling for distance between himself and the cause of his pain (i.e., his beloved), he invites it closer to him. "Quick, friends, companions," he calls out (l. 3), "bring her here to me!" He then continues, in Scheindlin's translation, "If she would pour for me, she might put out the burning pain wasting my throbbing flesh."[19] Although he sees her as the very cause of his pain, the one on whose account he finds himself dangerously ensnared and suffering, he understands that union with her serves as the cure for his trauma.

The idea that the beloved serves as both the root of and remedy for one's lovesickness was not an invention of Ibn Gabirol's, but constitutes a well-used trope of Andalusian poems of desire.[20] In Ibn Ḥazm's treatise on love and love poetry, the *Ṭawq al-ḥamāma*, Ibn Ḥazm writes that love "is an incurable disease and in it there is remedy against it."[21] In other words, love is a disease that contains its own cure, since the beloved both causes the pain of love and has within her (or him) the power to save the lover from it. So entrenched was this idea that we find it even earlier, in the work of the poet and Ẓāhirī theologian Ibn Dāwūd al-Iṣfahānī (868–909/10). In his classical medieval anthology of love poetry, al-Iṣfahānī rails against this particular poetic trope for an entire chapter, decrying it as a practical absurdity, since one could never hope to successfully cure the pain of love with love. Despite al-Iṣfahānī's critique, we find the trope in Arabic love poetry and its later inheritor, Andalusian love poetry.[22]

Nadīm*s and friends*

Another trope of love poetry that appears in Ibn Gabirol's poem concerns the "friends, companions" ("רעי מיודעי") addressed in line 2. As noted in the discussion of Ibn Ḥazm's poetic use of al-Sāmirī imagery in Chapter 3, a love poem's narrator frequently turned to or mentioned an assembled company, present or imagined.[23] This conceit may have reflected a reality in the Andalusian court: the actual presence of *nadīm*s, close companions with whom one celebrated at the wine-drinking parties where much poetry was composed.[24] Poetically speaking, this group of "friends" often consisted of the beloved's protectors, who posed a danger to the lover. At other times, the group was made up of friends of the lover. In the latter case, the lover sometimes appealed to them to advise or aid him in his tumultuous state.[25] Indeed, this is precisely the use we find in our present case. Here, the lover turns to his friends for help in easing his pain, requesting that they bring him Tamar, the object of his affection. He asks them not only to arrange for her visit, but also to dress her up in beautiful clothes and jewelry and send her along with a decanter of wine in her hand (ll. 2–3). Sick as he is, he cannot arrange for her visit on his own. In line with the poetic tropes, he instead turns to his companions to aid him in alleviating his pain and rectifying the situation.

Ibn Gabirol's poem plays with the classical tropes

Not only does Ibn Gabirol masterfully employ many of the expected poetic motifs and images in this poem, he demonstrates his poetic prowess further by simultaneously playing with them. Here Ibn Gabirol deftly turns two of the more predictable and anticipated tropes, the *sāqī* and the invitation poem, inside out. In so doing, he both uses and amends them in pleasing and sometimes surprising ways.

The sāqī

The first reworked trope to appear in the poem takes the form of one of the classic images found in both wine and love poetry: the wine-pouring youth, known as the *sāqī*. While the appearance of a *sāqī* in a poem often indicated that the poem was a wine poem and not a love poem, scholars of Andalusian poetry have pointed out that frequently the lines between wine poetry and love poetry bled into one another. The blurring of lines was such that often one cannot immediately tell to which category a poem rightly belongs. In one typical example, R. Moses ibn Ezra (1055–*c.* 1135–40) opens a love poem by announcing, "The desire of my heart and the darling of my eye – a fawn (*`ofer*) at my side, and a cup in my right hand."[26] This conflation of images (and thus genres) is almost to be expected. After all, at heart both groups of poems concerned themselves with the spirit of desire to the point of obsession. What's more, desire often struck a man when he found himself surrounded by fragrant gardens, plied with wine and other alcoholic drink, served by youthful male and female beauties, the *sāqīs*.[27] Arabic and Hebrew lovers often found themselves lusting after these attractive fresh-faced wine pourers and composed numerous love poems that either were dedicated to or concerned them.[28]

In line with this trope, Ibn Gabirol's lover clearly places his beloved in the role of *sāqīyya*. He asks his friends to ensure that she arrive equipped with wine in her hand, saying (l. 3b) "שימו על ידה בכוס חמר" (*simu `al yadah be-kos ḥamar*). In the final line of the poem he confirms this *sāqīyya* image, instructing his beloved explicitly that she is to arrive with the wine in hand, ready "to pour for me." Significantly, in requesting that his friends place the cup in the beloved's hand specifically (על ידה, *`al yadah*), Ibn Gabirol employs not only the imagery of wine poetry but also the very language typical of the genre. Hebrew formulaic depictions of the wine-pourer describe the wine appearing מידי (*mi-yedei*, by the hands of) or בידי (*bi-yedei*, from the hands of) the *sāqī*; Arabic poems frequently employ the Arabic equivalent, بكفّ (*bi-kaff*) or من كفّ (*min kaff*).[29] Thus, Ibn Gabirol's lover uses both the imagery and vocabulary of wine poetry and presents his beloved in the typical posture of the *sāqīyya*, leaning over the lover with wine jug in hand, pouring him wine.

Very atypically, however, our lover does *not* find himself falling in love/lust with the wine-pourer he has met at a wine-party, as we would expect of a love poem involving, or to, a *sāqīyya*. He does not describe the charms of one who circles the room, delicately and coquettishly pouring spirits and seducing him with her movements and her flirtations. Rather, our lover is "prestricken" by sickness; he has fallen into the net of love *before* the beloved *sāqīyya* even appears. It is in this already weakened and homebound state that he calls for his friends to send his beloved dressed up like a wine-pourer. In so doing, he turns the woman who is *already* his beloved into a *sāqīyya*, rather than the other way around.[30]

Invitation

Another wine-poem form that Ibn Gabirol simultaneously includes and distorts in his love poem concerns the lover's statement "קראו אלי" (*qir'u eilai*), "Call her to me." One category of poems prevalent among the Andalusian poets was known as "invitation poems." Addressed to the guest himself, these served as actual invitations to a drinking party, a common and well-loved feature of Spanish-Muslim court society. A. R. Nykl has pointed out that Rafī al-Dawla, son of the Almerian caliph al-Mu'taṣim b. Ṣumādiḥ (d. 1091), famously and frequently issued such poetic invitations to his royal drinking fests.[31] Parties and poetic invitations appeared in the Jewish milieu as well. Judah Halevi (1075–1141), a contemporary of Rafī al-Dawla, used this form in a party summons to Ibn Ghayyat (1038–89). Similarly, Moses ibn Ezra sent such poetic invitations to any number of invitees for various drinking sessions, often referencing the months of the year in which such gatherings were favored.[32] In charging his friends "קראו אלי" (*qir'u eilai*), "Call her to me," Ibn Gabirol's lover clearly intends his poem to serve as an invitation to "Tamar" to join him at a drinking party. Indeed, he subsequently sends his friends to retrieve her and bring her to his home, where she is to arrive dressed up in party clothes and prepared for an alcohol-imbued experience.

Yet even the least careful reader will note two deviations here from the classical format. In the first place, rather than invite her to a prepared party, as we would expect from this motif, Ibn Gabirol's lover asks Tamar herself to supply the spirits. If Tamar refuses the invitation, one surmises, no party will take place. It is thus not a true wine-party invitation, but a call to a private evening for two, veiled as a wine-party. What's more, while poetic invitations were normally addressed to the guest himself, Ibn Gabirol's poem addresses everyone *but* Tamar. Although she is clearly the intended invitee, the poetic invitation refuses to appeal to her straight-on. Instead, the invitation addresses the lover's friends, asking *them* to bring her, but not clearly inviting them along.[33]

The *remez* that doesn't fit: rape as erotica

The many lovely ways in which Ibn Gabirol's poem deftly and ingeniously both fits in with and plays with the tropes of love and wine poetry, however, cannot explain away one persistent troubling fact: Ibn Gabirol has chosen perhaps the vilest biblical *remez* possible for use in a love poem. After all, Amnon and Tamar are not a romantic couple, but siblings! And, the biblical account in which they appear does not present a tale of romantic love. Instead, 2 Samuel 13 clearly and unapologetically depicts an incestuous rape scene in which Amnon manipulates, overpowers, attacks, and rapes his sister as she cries out against him, and then he discards her like a piece of trash. Is *this* the twosome, and the moment, that the biblical scholar and master poet Ibn Gabirol chooses as the scriptural *remez* with which to compare his lovers?

The seemingly inappropriate nature of Ibn Gabirol's choice of *remez* has not gone unnoticed by scholars in the field. The least bothered by this particular *remez* appears to be Shulamit Elizur. In her analysis of the poem, Elizur instructs readers not to attribute too much significance to Ibn Gabirol's choice of biblical referent here. She cautions that in dealing with רמיזה (*remizah*) one must take from the scriptural context only that which is relevant and that which seems likely ("הדברים המתקבלים על הדעת", *ha-devarim ha-mitqablim `al ha-da`at*).[34] In our case, she writes, Ibn Gabirol employs "Amnon" as a metaphor for the illness and suffering of the lover (i.e., lovesickness) and the name "Tamar" to indicate a woman of beautiful appearance, the motifs so important to the medieval poets. "However," she continues forcefully, "it is impossible under any circumstances to apply to the poem any additional details from the scriptural account of Amnon and Tamar through any of these hints (*remizot*)."[35] Thus, while the biblical story ends in the rape of Tamar by Amnon, one should not consider at all that the use of "Amnon" and "Tamar" in the verses indicates an attempt at rape, or any such act, in the poem. After all, this element (the rape), Elizur insists, stands completely at odds with the conventions of love poetry, and thus outside the range of the poem.[36] Instead, one should understand Ibn Gabirol's poetic use of 2 Samuel 13 as caused only by its reflecting the poetic elements of the lovesick lover and Tamar-like beauty.[37]

Eddy Zemach takes the opposite stance, understanding Ibn Gabirol's use of the biblical *remez* here as consisting of far more extensive elements than only the idea of Amnon as lovesick lover. According to Zemach, the poetic lover's request that Tamar bring him wine not only intends readers to think of the rape, but points beyond the immediate context to the murder of Amnon by Absalom later in the chapter. There the biblical narrative relates that two years after the rape Absalom throws a sheep-shearing party to which he invites all of the king's sons, including Amnon, whom Absalom hates (2 Sam. 13:22). Unbeknownst to Amnon, Absalom had commanded his servants to wait until Amnon is drunk, until his "heart is merry with wine" (v. 28), and then kill him. And so they do. According to Zemach, by using the word "wine," the poem unites Amnon's eroticized biblical meal served by Tamar, at which there was no wine, with Amnon's later meal hosted and served by Absalom, which hinged on it. In linking these two meals, Zemach maintains, the poem warns its audience about the danger of erotic fulfillment. Just as Amnon's attainment of his erotic wish (sex with his sister Tamar) led to his death (murdered in revenge by Absalom), so the lover's yearning for realization of his sexual desire with his beloved will result in his death as well.[38]

Raymond Scheindlin's analysis of the poem takes a middle stance between Elizur and Zemach. On the one hand, like Elizur, Scheindlin understands Ibn Gabirol's choice of the Amnon and Tamar *remez* as a reflection of Ibn Gabirol's conformity to the values of the day. He notes that the biblical account contains many of the standard elements of secular love poetry, which must surely have pleased the poetic side of Ibn Gabirol. These include a lovesick lover whose passion affects his physical being, a beautiful and beloved maiden, a wine-party, friends who serve as advisors, etc. The horror of the biblical story's outcome probably attracted him to it as well, Scheindlin adds. Indeed, writes Scheindlin, Ibn Gabirol likely uses this incident despite its ugliness because "this is a rare erotic biblical story involving members of the courtly class," a class for which Ibn Gabirol was a most vocal member.[39]

On the other hand, like Zemach, Scheindlin sees Ibn Gabirol's use of the biblical *remez* as incorporating, rather than ignoring, the rape and doing so to send a message of warning to the poem's readers. After all, one cannot deny that the story of Amnon's rape of Tamar is not actually an "erotic" tale, as Scheindlin terms it, nor does the Bible present it as such. Rather, the Bible presents a brutal, humiliating, and tragic attack by a brother against his sister. As such, Scheindlin explains that the poem also serves as a dark commentary on the vagaries of love; it is, he writes, "an ironic piece with a point to make."[40] In other words, when it comes to love, observes the poem, people tend to exhibit a Groucho Marx-like attitude: once you get what you want and have sought, you disdain it. Ibn Gabirol's poem thus employs the Amnon and Tamar account as a cautionary tale. Despite the poetic insistence on the permanence of true *`ishq*, it warns, love rules a body as a fickle master.[41] It enflames you with its passions as it did Amnon, and just as quickly, after you have obeyed all love's directives and have finally obtained your beloved, it abandons you completely, just as it did Amnon post-coitus with Tamar. Learn from the Bible, hints the poem, and when it comes to love and passion be very careful of what you wish for.[42]

The poem inverts the Bible

Zemach's and Scheindlin's readings of Ibn Gabirol's troubling love-poem *remez* hinge on the similarities between Ibn Gabirol's poem and the biblical account on which it is based.[43] There is yet a third reading, one based not on the texts' similarities, but on a close examination of the points of difference. Importantly, Ibn Gabirol does not simply copy the scriptural account into his poem. Rather, he skillfully and subtly alters many of the very same biblical details that he so masterfully employs. Significantly, in doing so, Ibn Gabirol's poem turns the biblical story inside out: details that serve as elements of concealment in the biblical text are reconfigured by Ibn Gabirol's poem so as to reveal. In other words, by subtly shifting certain details, the poem changes the biblical Amnon's deviously and secretly planned sexual attack into the lover's clear and public invitation to a sexual romp.

Amnon's silent suffering vs. the lover's public pronouncement

The most obvious biblical element of secrecy which Ibn Gabirol transforms into an element of public knowledge concerns the very basic premise of both texts: Each man finds himself so overcome with emotion for his beloved that he falls ill with lovesickness. Yet while Amnon endeavors to hide his suffering even from those closest to him, Ibn Gabirol's lover embraces the opposite tactic, bringing his feelings for his beloved straight into the public realm.

That the biblical Amnon chooses to conceal his passion for his sister from those around him and suffer in silence becomes evident from the words of his close friend and confidant, his cousin Jonadav. Noting the prince's health deteriorating over a period of time, but unable to detect any obvious cause, Jonadav questions him one day, saying, (v. 4) "Why are you so weak (דל),[44] oh son of the King, morning after morning? Will you not tell me?" Jonadav's insistent comment illustrates that Amnon had been suffering for long enough ("morning after morning") that he had become noticeably ill. And he had been suffering silently; Amnon reveals his feelings *only* in response to Jonadav's pressing him on the matter ("Will you not tell me?"). What's more, even while revealing the cause of his illness, Amnon attempts to continue to conceal the absolute truth of his condition. "Tamar, the sister of my brother Absalom, do I love," he says, striving to distance himself from the full incestuous nature of his feelings by craftily removing his own sibling tie to Tamar from the equation.[45] Similarly, in reporting to Jonadav, Amnon omits the cause of his "love" for his sister, Tamar's beauty and virginity, revealed to readers in verse 2. In so doing, Amnon obscures from Jonadav important elements of the truth of the situation.[46]

Unlike Amnon, the poetic lover makes no attempts whatsoever at concealment. Instead, he reveals the cause of his illness without having been asked and announces it to all within hearing range. In the opening two lines he simply proclaims aloud that he is like Amnon, sick with emotion for a beautiful woman. That he announces these sentiments not to an empty room or to a discreet advisor, but to an assembled company, appears in the second hemistich of the first line. He requests that the object of his affection be brought before him, by declaring in the plural form (l. 1a), "קראו אלי" (*qir'u eilai*), "[You all] Call to me!"[47] In the following line the lover confirms that he is speaking to an actual audience, one made up of a *group* of comrades and advisors. "Friends, companions ("רעי, מיודעי," *re`ai, meyuda`ai*)," he proclaims. The plural form of address remains consistent throughout the poem, indicating the presence of the audience for the duration of the lover's instructions. To *them* does he express his wish ("אחת שאלתי מכם," *aḥat she'elati mikem*, "One thing I ask from you [plural]," l. 2b); *they* are to set a crown on her head (plural, קשרו, *qishru*); *they* are to dress her up (plural, הכינו, *hakhinu*); *they* are to place a cup of wine in her hand (plural, שימו, *simu*), and *they* are to bring her to him (plural, אלי הביאוה, *eilai havi'uha*). While the biblical Amnon initially keeps quiet, ultimately confiding only in one person (Jonadav), our poetic lover takes the opposite stance, engaging in the medieval equivalent of proclaiming his passions for his beloved from a baseball-field scoreboard.

Love vs. desire

The second poetic deviation from the biblical narrative concerns the wording used to describe the emotion each hero harbors for his beloved. Once again the poem incorporates an element from the biblical account only to invert it. The biblical presentation of Amnon's feelings as "love" serves to obscure Amnon's true state. The poem, by contrast, states quite clearly and in no uncertain terms that the lover *desires* his beloved.

At first glance, the biblical Amnon's emotional situation appears clearly and obviously stated: He is a man in love. Indeed, no fewer than four times do we find words formed from the Hebrew root "to love" (אהב, *ahb*) to describe his feelings for his sister. The narrative begins with precisely such a statement, informing us that Absalom the son of David had a beautiful sister named Tamar "וַיֶּאֱהָבֶהָ אַמְנוֹן בֶּן-דָּוִד," "And Amnon the son of David loved her" (v. 1). A short while later the verb appears again: in response to Jonadav's question as to what was bothering him, Amnon answers (v. 4), "אֶת-תָּמָר אֲחוֹת אַבְשָׁלֹם אָחִי אֲנִי אֹהֵב" ("Tamar, the sister of Absalom my brother, do I love"). After the rape has taken place, the narrator once more confirms that Amnon had earlier loved his sister, stating (v. 15), "וַיִּשְׂנָאֶהָ אַמְנוֹן שִׂנְאָה גְּדוֹלָה מְאֹד כִּי גְדוֹלָה הַשִּׂנְאָה אֲשֶׁר שְׂנֵאָהּ מֵאַהֲבָה אֲשֶׁר אֲהֵבָהּ", "And Amnon hated her with a great hatred, for the hatred with which he hated her was greater than the *love* with which he had *loved* her."

While such consistent repetition of Amnon's emotional state would seem to present the case as a clear instance of romantic love, other biblical language puts this assumption into question, indicating that this claim may be little more than a cover-up of Amnon's true feelings – lust. For while 2 Samuel 13:1 tells us that Amnon fell in love with his sister, it also tells us *why* he loved her: Tamar was beautiful. As verse 1 relates, "וּלְאַבְשָׁלוֹם בֶּן-דָּוִד אָחוֹת יָפָה וּשְׁמָהּ תָּמָר וַיֶּאֱהָבֶהָ אַמְנוֹן בֶּן-דָּוִד" ("Absalom the son of David had a beautiful sister and her name was Tamar; Amnon the son of David loved her"). We hear nothing of Tamar's personality, of any character, wisdom, or moral fiber that leads her brother to develop feelings for her. Rather, her external appearance alone caused him to "love" her, a reason more associated not with love but with physical desire.

The subsequent verses continue to undermine Amnon's claim of love and to hint at desire as the true emotion he feels for Tamar. In response to Jonadav's question concerning the cause of Amnon's decreasing health, Amnon tells Jonadav in verse 4 that he has fallen in *love* with Tamar. However, verse 2 had earlier reported that Amnon's illness is caused not by his love for Tamar but "כִּי בְתוּלָה הִיא," "because she is a virgin."[48] Significantly, the very next clause in verse 2 states, "וַיִּפָּלֵא בְּעֵינֵי אַמְנוֹן לַעֲשׂוֹת לָהּ מְאוּמָה," "Amnon found it wondrous to do something to Tamar." The proximity of these clauses to one another in verse 2 leads us to understand that Amnon's "wonder" hinged on her virgin status.[49] In other words, while Amnon claims to be in love with his sister in verse 4, verse 2 indicates that his true motivation was not love, but sexual arousal caused by his sister's beauty (v. 1) and virginity (v. 2). Amnon's claiming otherwise appears to be an intentional cover for the truth.

By contrast, although Ibn Gabirol's lover declares himself to be like Amnon ("אמנון אני," *Amnon ani*), he does not use Amnon's befuddling language of love. Instead, the lover records his emotion clearly and straightforwardly as desire. Despite Scheindlin's poetic inclusion of love in his translation ("Tell her one who *loves* her is snared by death," l. 2), in the strictest sense "love" remains conspicuously absent from the Hebrew poem. The poet refers to himself more bluntly as "חשקה" (*ḥoshqah*), the one who *desires* her.[50] He very obviously does *not* refer to himself as חולה אהבה (*ḥoleh ahavah*), "lovesick," a phrase well used in the Song of Songs[51] and in other Hebrew *`ishq*-poems. For the lover, what has overtaken him is חשק (*ḥesheq*, desire), that feeling of sexual attraction and need that is not necessarily based on an emotional connection, on אהבה (*ahavah*, love). In truth, many of the poems speak of "desire" and "lust" rather than "love," and the biblical חשק (*ḥesheq*) frequently carries with it the sense of "love."[52] However, in comparing himself to the four-time marked "love"-soaked Amnon, but using the word חשק (*ḥesheq*) rather than אהבה (*ahavah*), Ibn Gabirol's lover emphasizes the difference between the two terms. He purposely employs the term for desire over love, and thereby clearly reveals his more sexually focused, rather than spiritually romantic, emotions and intentions.

Curative cooking vs. libidinous latkes

Ibn Gabirol's shifting the biblical Amnon's attempts at secrecy into the lover's public declaration of intent can be seen also in the food-centered plans enacted by both men as part of their scheming to unite with their Tamars. Here, too, Ibn Gabirol incorporates an element of the biblical story only to subtly transform it to fit his poetic ends. Both Amnon and the lover request provisions of the beloveds, provisions that they both insist will ease their ailments when served by the beloved herself. In the biblical text, Amnon requests that Tamar "make a couple of cakes in my sight, וְאֶבְרֶה מִיָּדָהּ (*va-evreh mi-yadah*)" (v. 6). The phrase וְאֶבְרֶה מִיָּדָהּ generally appears in translation as "and I will eat from her hand"; the plainest meaning of the root ברה (*brh*) means either to eat or feed. Importantly, however, the root also indicates the act of eating or feeding that intends to fatten one up.[53] The noun בריה (*biryah*) refers to a food intended to put meat on one's skinny bones.[54] Now Amnon, we recall, had become ill because of his passion for his sister, a weakening and thinning that his cousin Jonadav had noticed. In his request וְאֶבְרֶה (*va-evreh*), Amnon thus asks not only to eat from Tamar's hand, but to be fattened up, cured, by a particular type of food she will make and then feed to him.[55] Our lover's request reflects Amnon's quite closely. In lines 2–3 of the poem, the lover instructs his friends to bring Tamar to him, as Amnon had requested of David to send him his Tamar. And, like Amnon, the lover directs the friends to ensure that Tamar provide him with nourishment. "Send along with her a cup of wine," he instructs (l. 3). The lover understands this liquid to be more than a simple intoxicant or thirst-quencher. Instead, he sees it as possessing medicinal powers capable of curing him of his illness, on par with the curative בריה (*biryah*) that Amnon requests of his sister. What's more, like Amnon, the lover links the food's therapeutic powers to its method of presentation. For Amnon, the בריה (*biryah*) must be prepared and served by his sister; for the lover, the wine must be brought and served by the beloved herself. When she pours it out for him, he says in the final line of the poem, she will thereby extinguish the punishing flames coursing through his flesh and cure him of his suffering.

Although the general thrust of the food-centered appeals resemble one another, the objective behind them differs wildly. Amnon uses his food request to conceal the truth of his health status and his intentions; the lover uses his to reveal the same. In the first place, we recall that after hearing of Amnon's infatuation with his sister, Jonadav advises the prince to *feign illness*. As part of this fake illness, this cover for Amnon's true state, Jonadav advises Amnon to request both the regular לֶחֶם (*leḥem*, bread) and the medicinal הַבִּרְיָה (*ha-biryah*) of his sister. Yet Amnon is not actually ill, but pretending. As Jonadav says in verse 5, "שְׁכַב עַל מִשְׁכָּבְךָ וְהִתְחָל" ("Lay down on your bed and feign sickness"). The request for medicinal food serves as yet another layer of cover. Interestingly, in attempting to follow Jonadav's instructions, Amnon almost exposes the truth. Speaking to his father, Amnon requests that Tamar cook not הַבִּרְיָה (*ha-biryah*) but that she תְּלַבֵּב שְׁתֵּי לְבִבוֹת (*telabev shetai levivot*), prepare two tellingly named "heart-shaped" or "libido" cakes.[56] Almost immediately Amnon recovers his wits, perhaps having heard what came out of his mouth, and in the next phrase he returns to Jonadav's sexually neutral, medical, and thus deceitful terminology, saying "וְאֶבְרֶה מִיָּדָהּ" (*va-evreh mi-yadah*), "and I will be cured by eating from her hand."[57] Thus we see that the food that Amnon requests to cure his fake sickness serves as a cover for his true state and his true desire. The food itself does not interest him at all, and indeed he never does consent to eating it (v. 9). After all, he is not ill but lovesick, and thus only union with Tamar will truly cure him, no matter what he deceitfully claims.

In complete contrast, the lover unabashedly uses food to reveal, in no uncertain terms, both the true romantic nature of his illness and his intentions toward the object of his desire. The lover asks that his beloved appear before him, not with a cold compress or a plain piece of toast as befits an ill man, but with a ready cup full of intoxicating wine (l. 3b, "שימו על ידה בכוס חמר").[58] Lest we somehow misunderstand the lover's intentions and imagine for a moment that the wine is either for her or is a watered-down drink with no particular significance attached, our lover states plainly what role these spirits are to play: "If she would pour for me she might put out the burning pain wasting my throbbing flesh." They are a remedy for his illness, a cure for the pain that rages in his heart and causes his flesh to throb. In so declaring, the lover reveals the nature of his illness quite plainly. This is not a man overcome with a fever caused by virus or infection. Rather, the erotic overtones of the line reveal quite clearly that his body pulses with the heat of desire and that he believes this pain can be relieved only by drinking intoxicating wine served from the hand of his beloved herself.

In addition, one cannot fail to note the risqué double-entendre embedded, none too deeply, in this final line. The immediate context, a request for the beloved to arrive with a glass of wine in hand, indicates that we ought to read the word

תשקני as Scheindlin does: *tashqeini*, "she will pour for me." However, without the vowels one could also read the word as *tishaqeini*, "she will kiss me." In Song of Songs 1:2, we find this verbal form in a verse that weaves together wine and love. Sighs the female lover in Song of Songs 1:2, "Let him kiss me (יִשָּׁקֵנִי, *yishaqeini*) with the kisses of his mouth, for your love is better than wine." One could posit that Ibn Gabirol had this biblical text in mind when composing the poem's final line. One could thus also read the line as: "If she would come and *kiss* me, she would put out the burning pain wasting my throbbing flesh."[59] Unlike Amnon who attempts to obscure his desire for his sister by hiding behind curative food-items, our lover spares no opportunity to reveal his yearning for his beloved, using even his call for a beverage to do so.

The clothes make the woman

The final use and deviation of significance concerns the attire worn by the beloveds. Both the biblical narrative and our poem describe the beloved girl as dressed in royal clothing. In the Bible, just before Amnon's servant complies with Amnon's post-rape command to eject Tamar from his house and bolt the door behind her, the narrator breaks into the narrative to state (v. 18), "And she had on a striped coat (כְּתֹנֶת פַּסִּים, *ketonet passim*), for such cloaks did the virgin daughters of the king wear."[60] The narrator thus reminds his readers that Tamar was not a common woman whom Amnon attacked and whom he was about to humiliate further; rather, as her clothes indicated, she was a royal virgin princess. Ibn Gabirol's poem uses the beloved's clothing to indicate her noble status as well. The lover directs his companions not only to dress his beloved before sending her to him, but to dress her up *like a princess*. She is to be dressed in jewels (עדיה, *`edyah*, l. 3b) like a woman of means and stature. Even more, she is to be given an item associated specifically with the imperial class: "קשרו עטרת על ראשה" (*qishru `ateret `al roshah*, l. 3a), cries the lover, "tie a *crown* upon her head!"[61]

While *both* women are described as dressed in clothing from the royal social class, only the biblical Tamar's royal clothing emphasizes the secrecy of the ruse planned and perpetrated against her. Tamar, after all, appeared before Amnon dressed not simply in the garments worn by princesses, but in the garments worn by *virgin* princesses. In other words, innocent of her brother's plans, she arrives at Amnon's house in her virgin clothes. She intends to leave that way as well, as a royal virgin wearing the garments appropriate for her title, for she brings no extra clothing to change into once she has destroyed the garments in the aftermath of the rape. One presumes that had Tamar known how fetching Amnon found her virginity (2 Sam. 13:2), she would not have worn clothing that so flashed it before him. In wearing her traditional virgin-princess-cloak, which she then mournfully destroys, Tamar demonstrates that she knew little regarding her brother's intentions that day.

The clothing of the poem's beloved, by contrast, displays no such presumed ignorance of the lover's intentions. The lover requests not only that his beloved arrive wearing a crown, but also that his friends "prepare her with ornaments"

(l. 2). Ibn Gabirol here uses the word עדיה (*`edyah*) from the root עדה (*`dh*), a root that appears fairly frequently in the Bible, meaning to adorn or decorate.[62] In a number of instances, words formed from this root appear connected either to brides on their wedding day or virgins attaining sexual maturity.[63] It seems then that the biblical עדיים (*`adayim*) refers to decorations with which marriage-age and marriage-minded maidens adorned themselves either to attract male sexual attention or at the ceremony that marked their transition into sexually active beings (i.e., their weddings). Ibn Gabirol's use of this particular word emphasizes the blatant sexual tension weaving through the poem; the lust-drenched lover asks that his beloved appear before him not simply well-dressed, for a party, but adorned with decorations associated with turning a virgin into a non-virgin.[64]

The somewhat strange grammatical phrasing used by the poem's lover in making this request furthers the contention of obvious sexual innuendo and intent through couture. Technically speaking, the lover does not request that his companions actually "decorate" the beloved with jewels/ornaments.[65] Rather, he instructs them to "prepare" her ornaments ("הכינו עדיה," *hakhinu `edyah*). "Her ornaments" can be understood not as the decorations that she will wear, but as body parts that she already owns. In other words, the lover instructs his friends not only to put a crown on the head of his beloved but to prepare her physical female ornaments, perhaps using oil and perfumes in anticipation of a night of passion with her lover.[66] Either way, whether he requests that she wear decorations associated with weddings or prepare her own body, in describing the beloved's clothing by using a term associated with preparing for sexual activity, the lover reveals his sexual intentions for the evening.

Thus we see that contrary to Elizur's cautionary analysis, our poem utilizes more of the biblical account of 2 Samuel 13 than the image of the lovesick lover and the beautiful female beloved. Rather, the poem borrows a host of biblical elements that it then both employs and tweaks. In so doing, the poem turns the story of a concealed desire and covert plan for sexual fulfillment into a well-disclosed passion accompanied by an explicitly stated strategy for realization.

Ibn Gabirol's poem as biblical exegesis

Yet all of this begs the question: Why? Why use an infamous tale of rape only to turn it into an open invitation to a party? Was Ibn Gabirol simply attempting to reduce reader repulsion as a response to his use of an infamous incestuous rapist as pining lover? Given Ibn Gabirol's expert control of both the Bible and biblical exegesis, one finds such an idea difficult to accept.

Ibn Gabirol's simultaneous use of the biblical account in such an odd context instead demands that we look more closely at the text of 2 Samuel 13. When we do, we see that the changes made by Ibn Gabirol's poem both highlight certain problems in the biblical text and solve for them. In other words, Ibn Gabirol's poem functions as a subtle exegesis of an otherwise problematic scriptural text. The traditional reading of Amnon's biblical attack against his sister places the blame squarely on Amnon's and Jonadav's conniving shoulders and presents

David and Absalom as innocent dupes. Ibn Gabirol's poem leads us to see holes in the logic of the biblical text that suggest otherwise as to David's and Absalom's involvement. Like the informed audience of Ibn Gabirol's poem to whom they are compared, these two biblical characters, those closest to both Tamar and Amnon, were, in fact, aware of both Amnon's passion for Tamar and, perhaps, his sinister plan for its realization.

Absalom

Perhaps the most obvious of the biblical difficulties that cries out for elucidation in the text of 2 Samuel 13 concerns Absalom's behavior upon meeting his sister after the rape. As we recall, cruelly and unceremoniously ejected from her rapist-brother's house, Tamar rips her cloak, pours ashes on her head, and roams the streets screaming. Her full-brother Absalom, who had not been present in the story at all to this point, suddenly appears out of nowhere: 2 Samuel 13 records, "(19) And she [Tamar] went forth, crying aloud as she went. (20) And Absalom said to her ..." And Absalom said to her? Where did he come from? How did he find her, wandering the streets as she was? Was he there all along?

If Absalom's sudden presence were not puzzling enough, the words he utters strike us as even more strange. Apropos of almost nothing, Absalom immediately remarks (v. 20), "Has Amnon your brother been with you?" While the Bible appears to present this as if it were the natural thing to ask, readers are left puzzled. How does Absalom know that this is what might have happened? According to 2 Samuel 13:1–5, both Amnon's passion for his sister and his planning to draw close to her occurred behind closed doors, with Jonadav his only advisor. So how does *Absalom* know? Tamar's screaming in the streets likely provided no hint; her cries, we are told, constituted a wordless cry of anguish ("וַתֵּלֶךְ הָלוֹךְ וְזָעָקָה", v. 19).[67] Confoundingly, when Absalom comes upon his sister wailing and wandering the streets in ripped clothes and with ashes on her head, he does not ask the most logical and expected question: "What happened?!?!" Instead, he somehow already knows not only that she had been sexually assaulted,[68] but that it was Amnon who had done so!

Even more troubling is Absalom's word-choice to describe what he thinks has happened. He does not use the traditional biblical language of rape or assault, the language used both by Tamar in imploring Amnon to cease and desist his attack and by the narrative itself in describing Amnon's forceful violence. In begging Amnon to repent of his plan, Tamar entreats her brother (v. 12), "Do not, my brother, do not *force* me (אַל תְּעַנֵּנִי, *al te-`anneini*)." The narrator subsequently reports that Amnon, refusing to listen to her, overpowers her and "וַיְעַנֶּהָ וַיִּשְׁכַּב אֹתָהּ" (*va-ye-`anneha va-yishkav otah*, v. 14), "he forced her and lay with her." Absalom does not utilize either phrase used by the narrator (and Tamar) here, "שכב" (*shachav*, lit., lay [someone])[69] or "עינה" (*`innah*, humiliate).[70] Instead, he asks (v. 20), "הַאֲמִינוֹן אָחִיךְ הָיָה עִמָּךְ" (*ha-Aminon aḥikh haya `imakh*), "Has Amnon your brother *been with* you?" Despite his sister's torn cloak, inconsolable wailing, and posture of mourning, Absalom strangely utilizes euphemistic language more appropriate for consensual sexual union. Even more strange, in verse 22 the narrator informs us that Absalom *knew* that Amnon had raped their sister, that she had not lain with him of her own will. Absalom hated Amnon and refused to speak with him ever again, records the narrator, "עַל-דְּבַר אֲשֶׁר עִנָּה אֵת תָּמָר אֲחֹתוֹ," because of the fact that Amnon had forced, raped (*`innah*), his sister Tamar.

Absalom's subsequent behavior ranks as even more disturbing, especially to the modern reader. One would expect that Absalom, having figured out that his sister had just been brutally raped, and by their brother no less, would have grabbed Tamar and rushed straight to their father-king David, demanding Amnon's punishment. Instead, before Tamar can utter even a word in response to Absalom's opening question, Absalom issues a barrage of directives encouraging inaction. Says Absalom (v. 20), "And now my sister, hold your silence, he is your brother, do not take this thing to heart." Hold your silence? For what reason? And what does the fact that Amnon is Tamar's brother have to do with it? If anything, their sibling connection poses more of a reason for Tamar (and Absalom) to present the issue before the king and demand justice. After all, Amnon has committed both rape and incest, *two* crimes. Additionally, why should Tamar "not take this thing to heart"? She has just been attacked and raped by her own brother! Rather than rage with her against her violation, Absalom oddly and disturbingly appears to belittle Tamar's suffering.[71]

In moving Amnon's desire from the private sphere to the public, through the lover's public declaration of his desire for his beloved (l. 1b כי חושקה, *ki ḥoshqah*), Ibn Gabirol's poetic rewriting of the biblical account provides Absalom's mystifying words and behavior with a measure of intelligibility. After all, if Absalom *knew* that Amnon had harbored feelings for their sister and had asked that she visit him at home, Absalom would have known easily where to find her. One is not hard pressed to believe that Absalom's quick presence after Tamar's ejection from Amnon's house may have been due to his loitering there out of concern for Tamar, concern sparked by his knowing that Amnon desired her.[72] Absalom's leaping to Amnon as the cause of Tamar's ripped virgin-cloak, a signal of the sexual assault, likewise makes sense if one understands that Absalom had prior knowledge of his brother's predilection for their sister. Indeed, his puzzling use of euphemistic language reveals Absalom's foreknowledge of Amnon's feelings: 2 Samuel 13:1–4 relates that Amnon was besotted with his sister to the point of weakness and illness. If Absalom knew this, and Ibn Gabirol's Amnon-esque lover's publicized declaration of his condition suggests that Absalom (and others) did, Absalom might justifiably have thought his brother in no position to force Tamar into submission. Perhaps Absalom thought that Amnon somehow managed to convince Tamar to submit, rather than physically and violently forcing her to do so.[73] Seeing her ripped virgin-cloak, Absalom figured Tamar had "been with" and was not assaulted by their weakened brother.

Prior knowledge of Amnon's passion and resulting weakened state, and the conjecture that Amnon may not have attacked his sister but seduced her, may also explain Absalom's seemingly outrageous and incomprehensible call for Tamar's silence. Amnon is your brother, he reminds her, and if he did manage to convince you to "be" with him, you are then both guilty of incest; it would be best for you, as well as for him, to remain silent about what you have done.

Absalom's counseling silence may also be attributable to a measure of self-interest on his part. If Absalom did have foreknowledge of Amnon's dangerous passion for Tamar, and yet did nothing to protect her, Absalom, her brother-protector, bears a measure of responsibility for what happened to her. That Tamar spends the rest of her days "desolate" in Absalom's house, rather than in her father's house as we would expect of an unmarried woman in the ancient world, indicates that Absalom recognizes his role as protector of his sister. Knowing that he failed to protect her from Amnon's desire, Absalom now encourages her silence to allow him to "make good" on his failure, which he does later by killing Amnon. In having the Amnon-lover confess both his passion and his plans before an assembled company (l. 1 "Like Amnon sick am I, so call to me Tamar and tell her ..."), Ibn Gabirol's poem implies that others, including Absalom, were aware of what passion burned in Amnon's heart and that he harbored a plan to realize his desires.

David

Absalom is not the only custodial man in Tamar's life whose befuddling biblical behavior Ibn Gabirol's love poem first highlights and then clarifies. As the Bible recounts, Amnon's feigning ill successfully triggers a sick-bed visit by his father, King David. At David's arrival, he finds his son lying in bed, an unusual appeal on his lips. Says Amnon to the king (v. 6), "תָּבוֹא-נָא תָמָר אֲחוֹתִי וּתְלַבֵּב לְעֵינַי שְׁתֵּי לְבִבוֹת וְאֶבְרֶה מִיָּדָהּ", "Let my sister Tamar come please, and prepare a couple of cakes (*levivot*) before my eyes, and I will be healed by eating from her hand."[74] In ten brief Hebrew words, Amnon makes four different but interlinked requests. He asks that 1) Tamar come to him and 2) prepare food for him, 3) while he watches and 4) that she feed it to him herself. Although David complies with the request, he reduces it from four parts to two. To Tamar, David says only, (v. 7), "לְכִי נָא בֵּית אַמְנוֹן אָחִיךְ וַעֲשִׂי-לוֹ הַבִּרְיָה," "Go please to the house of Amnon your brother and prepare the food (*ha-biryah*) for him." Why so tersely stated? The odd brusqueness of David's words become more obvious when we note that Amnon's four-part request appears three times in the space of four verses, each time in all its detail and almost word for word.[75] This is true even of the iteration that describes Tamar's complying with the request. The text could easily have simply stated, "so Tamar did what David commanded her." Instead we find a three-verse-long detailing of each move Tamar made (vv. 8–10). Only David's phrasing deviates from the four-part format. What significance is there in this?

When seen through the glasses of Ibn Gabirol's poem, in which the audience hears clearly the lover's announced desire and intentions, the unexplained changes David makes to Amnon's four-part plea become more understandable. The poem hints that, like the lover's informed audience, David heard what it was that Amnon was saying, even though Amnon thought he did not say it outright. In other words, David astutely detected the sexual nature of his son's innocently presented request. For David's abbreviated version of Amnon's words clearly aims at thwarting Amnon's desire and intentions and rendering him harmless to Tamar. In the first place, David sends Tamar to Amnon's *house*, rather than to Amnon. While this change may not seem significant at first glance, the change in destination reduces the face-to-face interactions between Amnon and Tamar. Under no royal or paternally commanded obligation to approach her brother, Tamar can simply enter the kitchen, cook, and leave. Additionally, whereas Amnon asks for the sexually charged לביבות (*levivot*) using a sexually charged verb (ותלבב, *va-telabev*), David instead directs Tamar, in asexual language (עשי, *`asi*), to make for Amnon the asexual and medicinal food, הבריה (*ha-biryah*). Furthermore, David omits entirely Amnon's sexualized voyeuristic request to watch while Tamar works.[76] And finally, David excludes Amnon's appeal for his sister to serve him up-close and personally, a move Amnon clearly intended only to bring his sister within arm's reach. Instead, David simply tells Tamar to prepare the food ("וַעֲשִׂי לוֹ הַבִּרְיָה," *ve-`asi lo ha-biryah*, v. 7). Presumably she is then free to return to her own quarters. In altering each and every item of Amnon's suspicious request, David indicates to the readers that he, like the lover's audience in Ibn Gabirol's poem, heard the sexualized intentions in Amnon's words. [77]

Jonadav

An additional biblical peculiarity that Ibn Gabirol's poetic formulation first highlights and then resolves concerns the presentation of Jonadav and his role in the events. On its face, 2 Samuel 13 presents Jonadav as at least partially, if not largely, responsible for Amnon's crime; it is Jonadav who advises a despondent Amnon to play sick; it is Jonadav who counsels Amnon to request of David that the king send Tamar to him; and it is Jonadav who provides Amnon with the script according to which he was to request that Tamar cook for and serve him; it is thus Jonadav who enables Amnon's access and proximity to the object of his desire (v. 5). At the same time, in introducing Jonadav in our narrative, 2 Samuel 13:3 calls him "אִישׁ חָכָם מְאֹד" (*ish ḥakham me'od*), a very wise man, employing a biblical term (חָכָם, *ḥakham*) generally used to refer to wisdom in the positive sense.[78] Additionally, no blame or punishment is ever leveled at Jonadav for his supposed masterminding of Tamar's rape. He is not reprimanded either by David or from Heaven. Indeed, when next we meet Jonadav, he is serving as wise and close counsel to David himself (2 Sam. 13:32–4). And so we are left confused. Should we understand the biblical presentation of Jonadav as an evil mastermind or as an innocent and wise man caught up in another's evil insanity?

According to the explication embedded in Ibn Gabirol's poem, no such uncertainty is warranted; instead, with one Hebrew word, the poem clears Jonadav of guilt. In line 2a, the lover calls out to an assembled company and charges them with bringing his beloved to him. There he says, "רעי, מיודעי, אלי הביאוה" (*re`ai, meyuda`ai, eilai havi'uha*), "Friends, Companions, bring her here to me." As we know, lovers in Andalusian poetry frequently turned to companions and counselors for help. That Ibn Gabirol's lover does so here does not in and of itself rank as particularly significant. What *does* catch our attention are the terms Ibn Gabirol utilizes in formulating this common trope; the lover calls to both מיודעי (*meyuda`ai*), my advisors, and רעי (*re`ai*), my friends. This may initially strike readers as a terminological overkill; however, to an audience familiar with the text of 2 Samuel 13, the allusion to Jonadav appears clear and strong. After all, the biblical description of Jonadav in 2 Samuel 13:3 reads: "Amnon had a friend (רֵעַ, *re`a*) whose name was Jonadav, the son of Shim`ah, the brother of David"). Although the two men were paternal first cousins, the biblical narrator somewhat jarringly presents Jonadav primarily as the prince's extremely close friend, his רע (*re`a*).[79] Such a description would not necessarily be of interest were it not for the fact that it occurs in a narrative that hinges on and emphasizes family relationships. The biblical narrative goes out of its way here to ensure we understand Jonadav's primary role as Amnon's friend, rather than as his cousin.

In alluding to Jonadav with the רע (*re`a*) *remez*, the poem suggests a new understanding of the role Jonadav plays in the biblical account. While the biblical Jonadav appears to act as Amnon's advisor, the רעים (*re`im*) of the poem are *recipients* of the lover's commands: "רעי (*re`ai*)," he charges them in l. 2, "bring her here to me!" He then provides them with a list of demands that they are to fulfill, saying, "the only thing *I* ask of *you* is this" (l. 2b). This unexpected shift from the active biblical רע (*re`a*) to the passive poetic רעים (*re`im*) leads us to return to the biblical depiction of Jonadav. When we do, we find indications in the Bible that Jonadav may not have been as responsible for the rape as he initially appears. In the first place, while Amnon uses sexually laden terminology to refer to the food he wants from Tamar and to the actions he wants her to perform (וּתְלַבֵּב לְעֵינַי שְׁתֵּי לְבִבוֹת *va-telabev le-`einai shetai levivot*, v. 8), Jonadav used sexually neutral terminology. According to v. 5, Jonadav advised Amnon to request of David, "תָּבֹא נָא תָמָר אֲחוֹתִי וְתַבְרֵנִי לֶחֶם וְעָשְׂתָה לְעֵינַי אֶת-הַבִּרְיָה," "Let Tamar my sister come and make for me, medicinally, bread (*ve-tavreini leḥem*) and make (*ve-`astah*) the medicinal food (*ha-biryah*) before my eyes." Furthermore, Jonadav never counseled Amnon to refuse to eat, to dismiss all the attendants, and then to move Tamar to the back room where he could realize his desires. Jonadav, naively perhaps, seemed to think that having Tamar in close proximity and watching her prepare his food would be enough to cure Amnon of his debilitating desire. It is Amnon who took it to the next level on his own. The sequence of events beginning with Amnon's refusal to eat what Tamar had prepared was concocted entirely by Amnon; it was not discussed first with Jonadav. In turning the biblical רע (*re`a*) into the poem's passive רעים (*re`im*), the poem suggests that Jonadav did not intentionally orchestrate Amnon's secret assault of Tamar nor did he necessarily know about it beforehand.

Classical and medieval exegesis

Once we allow for the idea that Ibn Gabirol's poem serves also as a subtle exegesis of a problem-laden biblical text, encouraging us to see the lover's public announcement in the biblical Amnon's purported secrecy, we must return to the question of why. Why would Ibn Gabirol, a masterful scholar of the Bible and Oral Torah and composer of works of biblical exegesis,[80] choose a secular *'ishq* poem as the site for biblical commentary? Indeed a poem whose final line speaks of a man's desire for his beloved to extinguish the fire of his burning throbbing flesh (l. 4) hardly seems the most appropriate vehicle for commentary on sacred Scripture.

A look into the traditional rabbinic exegesis concerning 2 Samuel 13 sheds light on the issue. Classical and medieval Jewish exegetes went out of their way to remove Absalom and David from any measure of involvement with Amnon's rape of Tamar. Instead, they heaped opprobrium on Jonadav alone. Ibn Gabirol's poetic exoneration of Jonadav and his insinuation that Absalom and David may have known in advance of both Amnon's desire and his intentions would have proved a particularly unpopular and problematic stance.

Rabbinic exoneration of Absalom

Despite the obvious strangeness of Absalom's reactions to Tamar in 2 Samuel 13, the classical Jewish sources that have survived do not address the issue. Unlike the modern reader, these exegetes appear to have been untroubled by Absalom's sudden appearance on the scene, by his seeming omniscient knowledge of what had happened to Tamar and with whom, or by his insistence on her silence. Perhaps Absalom's behavior somehow struck them as sensible, so they do not comment on it.

Unlike their classical rabbinic forebears, the medieval interpreters did find Absalom's behavior unsettling. However, the only matter that appears to have warranted their commenting concerns Absalom's instructions to Tamar in verse 20, "Now my sister, hold your silence, he is your brother, do not take this thing to heart." Rabbi Levi ben Gershom (Gersonides, 1288–1344) and Don Isaac Abrabanel (1437–1508) appear as puzzled as modern readers by Absalom's having united two such seeming non sequiturs, "hold your silence" and "he is your brother." They explain: Absalom meant that precisely *because* Amnon was her brother, it was not fitting to publicize his act and thus shame him.[81] While Gersonides appears satisfied with this, Abrabanel expresses a measure of continuing discomfort at Absalom's quieting his sister. Abrabanel adds that Absalom's behavior here, hushing Tamar and bringing her into his home, was part of the Divine plan for the death of Amnon. Each time Absalom entered and exited his home, he passed by his beautiful sister sitting humiliated and unmarried, שוממה (*shomema*);[82] this increased his desire for revenge against Amnon until he acted on it. Whether Absalom knew or should have known in advance what lurked in Amnon's heart, the medieval exegetes do not say.

Rabbinic exoneration of David

As with Absalom, the classical rabbinic sources do not concern themselves with any possible foreknowledge of Amnon's situation on David's part. Instead, the classical sources concern themselves mainly with discussing David's actions *after* the rape, as they do with Absalom. According to *Ecclesiastes Rabbah* (*c.* eighth century), the most disturbing element of David's behavior in 2 Samuel 13 concerns his lax attitude in punishing Amnon, or, more accurately, his not punishing Amnon. Speaking in Solomon's voice, *Ecclesiastes Rabbah* says, if David my father had become angry with Amnon [and, presumably, had punished him], it would have been better for Amnon than what Amnon received from God; had David punished Amnon, perhaps Absalom would not have subsequently taken justice into his own hands and killed his brother for violating their sister.[83] In other words, *Ecclesiastes Rabbah* criticizes David, not for knowing of Amnon's desires and remaining silent, but for hearing about the heinous action perpetrated by his son against his daughter and still remaining silent.[84]

An alternate midrashic stream strives to remove David further from an association with *any* aspect of his son's misdeeds. In *BT Megillah* 25a–b we find a somewhat bewildering discussion of what portions of the Bible one may read aloud and/or translate into Aramaic during synagogue services.[85] Apparently attempting to protect the honor of David or the House of David, the second-century *mishnah* there states, "The act of David and Amnon is read aloud but not translated." In other words, though one may read that portion of the Bible aloud in Hebrew, one may not translate it into a language more comprehensible to the common listener. The sixth-century Talmudic commentary on that *mishnah* extends the protection, teaching that the act of David and Amnon "is neither read aloud nor translated." Confusingly, the Talmud on the same page notes that although we might have (erroneously) thought to protect David's honor by not reading narratives in which his children commit immoral acts, the "act of Amnon and Tamar" is both read *and* translated.[86] Faced with three such different rulings regarding publicizing the story of Amnon's rape of Tamar, the Talmud explains: Where Amnon appears as "Amnon son of David," one reads but does not translate, but when he appears as "Amnon" only, one reads and translates. Although Amnon's actions do not necessarily reflect upon David's behavior and impugn his honor, one should nonetheless refrain from associating David outright with his sinning son. Thus, one may translate the story of Amnon's rape of his sister into the vernacular, but only those parts that do not identify him as David's son. David thus remains completely disassociated from any involvement in his son's actions.[87]

Other classical rabbinic sources absolve David from any responsibility for or association with Amnon's attack on his sister by attributing the unfolding of events to the unstoppable hand of the Divine. According to the sixth-century *BT Yoma* 22b, Amnon's rape of Tamar constituted one part of a four-fold payment David unknowingly called down upon himself as punishment for his adultery with Bathsheba, the wife of Uriah (2 Sam. 11).[88] In identifying the rape of Tamar as part of David's payment for his adultery, the Talmud presents Tamar's rape as unavoidable, decreed from on high, fated by God.[89] Whether David knew of Amnon's passion and plan thus becomes irrelevant.

The medieval Spanish-trained R. David Qimḥi (1160–1235), R. Levi ben Gershon (Gersonides, 1288–1344), and Don Isaac Abrabanel (1437–1508) similarly exonerate David from having any foreknowledge regarding Tamar's violation, though they do not consider it as part of a "four-fold" payment prophesied by David against himself. According to Qimḥi, the rape of Tamar and subsequent killing of Amnon were part of the Divine's punishment for David's sexual misconduct with Bathsheba and killing of Uriah as prophesied against David by Nathan that "the sword will never depart from your house" (2 Sam. 12:10).[90] Although Gersonides and Abrabanel do not cite Nathan's prophecy, they agree that Amnon's rape of Tamar resulted from David's killing of Uriah in order to take Uriah's wife.[91] The rape, they teach, like Absalom's later bedding of his father's concubines in public (2 Sam. 16:15–23), constituted part of God's punishment of David for his own earlier sexual immorality.[92] As with the Talmud, for these medieval commentators, Amnon's rape of Tamar was preordained by God. Thus the issue of David's foreknowledge becomes both unlikely and irrelevant.

Rabbinic condemnation of Jonadav

Just as the rabbinic reading of Absalom's and David's connection to Amnon's inner workings disagrees with that insinuated by Ibn Gabirol's love poem, so too the rabbinic understanding of Jonadav's role stands completely at odds with the reading of Jonadav implied by Ibn Gabirol's poem. While Ibn Gabirol's choice of language (רע, *re'a*) hints to Jonadav's passive rather than active role in Tamar's rape, the rabbinic texts see Jonadav as the "fall guy," laying the blame for Tamar's violation almost entirely at Jonadav's feet. The earliest version of this appears in the second-to-third-century Aramaic translation, the *Targum Jonathan* (*TJon*), to the book of Samuel. In translating the biblical title attributed to Jonadav in verse 3, רע (*re'a*), *TJon* uses the term שושבינא (*shoshvina*). Importantly, שושבינא (*shoshvina*) is the technical Aramaic term for the "best man," the friend of the groom who leads the bride to him.[93] In employing this particular term, rather than the more neutral Aramaic term for friend, חברא (*ḥavra*), *TJon* charges Jonadav with having literally brought Tamar to Amnon for sexual consummation, as one brings the bride before the groom.

The sixth-century *BT Sanhedrin* 21a continues in the *Targum*'s footsteps, endowing Jonadav with the lion's share of culpability for Amnon's actions. Commenting on 2 Samuel 13:3's description of Jonadav as "אִישׁ חָכָם מְאֹד" (*ish ḥakham me'od*), "a very wise man," Rav Yehuda said in the name of Rav, "איש חכם לרעה" (*ish ḥakham le-ra'ah*), a man with wisdom for evil.[94] Although the Bible generally does not employ the word "חכם" (*ḥakham*) in speaking of evil wisdom, Rav here disagrees. Jonadav's plans, he insists, are *not* to be read as neutral but as oriented toward evil. According to this perspective, the sexual violation of Tamar appears to have been part of Jonadav's original plans.[95]

This negative take on Jonadav's personality appears with little dissension among the later medieval Spanish and Spanish-trained exegetes as well. Qimḥi continues to cite the brief Talmudic teaching on Jonadav's evil genius, stating outright that Jonadav's wisdom was as a master of subterfuge and that he was the one who gave Amnon the idea for the ruse that brought Tamar to him.[96]

Gersonides and Abrabanel explain this in somewhat more detail. Amnon, they write, knew that what he desired of Tamar was wrong and thus, the Bible reports, "it seemed difficult for him to do anything to her" (וַיִּפָּלֵא בְּעֵינֵי אַמְנוֹן לַעֲשׂוֹת לָהּ מְאוּמָה, 2 Sam. 13:2).[97] In other words, Amnon's own moral conscience prevented him from acting on his desires. However, when he heard Jonadav's advice, which coincided with his own wishes, Amnon gave himself permission to act accordingly. Had Jonadav not counseled Amnon as he did, Amnon would have held back from sinning. One should thus be very wary, warns Gersonides, of the counsel of evil advisors.[98]

Ibn Gabirol vs. rabbinic exegetic exoneration

In the face of the classical and medieval exegesis clearing the male family members in 2 Samuel 13 of any and all prior knowledge in the assault against Tamar, Ibn Gabirol's poem comes to teach the opposite. By drawing a parallel between the audience before whom the poetic lover very clearly and very openly confesses his desires and those who circled the biblical Amnon (namely, Absalom and David), Ibn Gabirol's poem atypically asserts that the biblical characters knew of the dark passions that lurked in Amnon's heart. Although the biblical Amnon may have thought he was being sly and secretive about his desire for his sister, confiding only in Jonadav, the poem's shifting of the scenario from private to public domain indicates that the desire-drenched Amnon tipped his hand to all those with whom he came into contact. In other words, the peculiarities of Absalom's and David's behavior as recorded in the Bible point not to their tragic ignorance but to their knowledge. Ibn Gabirol's poem suggests that although Amnon thought he labored in secrecy, both Absalom and David harbored serious suspicions regarding Amnon's feelings for Tamar.

In allowing readers to see in Absalom and David a measure of foreknowledge of what was to befall Tamar, Ibn Gabirol's poetically suggested exegesis can be understood as charging them with the more serious crime of having been accessories. If David and Absalom knew of Amnon's dangerous passion for Tamar, as the poet's audience did, but neither took steps to prevent Amnon from acting on it, they bear a measure of guilt for what befell her. Even worse is the fact that both Absalom and David are the very men who ought to have worked hardest at defending Tamar. Absalom, after all, was her full brother, and David was both her father and her king. Yet neither of her protectors rose to the occasion in her defense, despite their seeming suspicions that evil and danger lurked on Tamar's horizon.

The problematic nature of such implied criticism of David becomes clear given the general rabbinic teaching regarding David's righteous nature. Although David's behavior throughout 2 Samuel frequently appears somewhat morally challenged, classical rabbinic and medieval teachings consistently avoided acknowledging it as such. After all, noted the rabbis, the Bible itself tells us more than once that David was beloved of God and followed His commands wholeheartedly. They recall that the Bible describes the actions and personality of David's great-grandson Abijam[99] by saying, "and his heart was not whole with the Lord his God, as the heart of David his father" (1 Kgs. 15:4).[100] David's righteousness becomes even clearer in the next verse. There the Bible records, "For David had done what was pleasing to the Lord and never turned throughout his life from all that He had commanded him, except in the matter of Uriah the Hittite" (1 Kgs. 15:5). Given this strongly worded scriptural statement, we find the medieval Spanish commentators, devotees of the *peshat* approach to the biblical text, willing to level criticism against the beloved poet-king for his behavior in 2 Samuel 11 only. As Abrabanel ultimately thundered in his commentary to the Bathsheba episode in 2 Samuel 11, "My mind cannot suffer to reduce David's sins and I will not deny the simple truth (האמת הפשוט, *ha-emet ha-pashut*) of it!"[101] However, due to the verse's insistence on David's innocence in all other affairs, the same *peshat*-based Abrabanel, like the earlier Qimḥi, refuses to take a similar stance regarding any of David's other possibly problematic actions. Despite David's lack of intervention in either preventing Tamar's rape or in punishing Amnon for it afterward, Abrabanel insists on the king's righteousness here.[102] In similar fashion Gersonides had earlier explained that 1 Kings 15:5, "testifies to the fact that in everything else that he [David] did, he did that which was right in God's eyes."[103] In other words, David sinned regarding Bathsheba and Bathsheba only. In all other interactions, David's behavior remained impeccable.

It should strike readers as no accident then that a poem in which Ibn Gabirol plays with both accepted poetic conventions and standard biblical elements stands as the very same poem that can be seen as playing with or against accepted rabbinic exegetic convention. In "*Amnon ani*," just as Ibn Gabirol simultaneously utilized and manipulated the poetic tropes, so he simultaneously employed and subtly altered the details of the biblical text. Thus what appears at first to have been a secret desire that led to a covertly hatched and covertly executed plan, Ibn Gabirol's publicly self-proclaiming poetic lover opens the door for us to see as a well-known yearning that may well have been preventable. In both obeying and breaking with the motifs, the masterful poet provided us with a poem that is indeed, as his anonymous seventeenth-century editor claimed, among "the most excellent and wonderful"[104] of love poems. In following and then altering the biblical text, the masterful exegetical scholar opened our eyes to a subtle and sacrilegious exegesis of otherwise puzzling biblical narrative interactions.

Notes

1 "ומן אג'ל תגאזלה ואעג'בה" (*wa-min ajal taghāzalihi wa-a`jabihi*). In Ibn Gabirol, *Shirei ha-Ḥol*, ed. Brody and Schirmann, 61 (#108).

In their earlier collection of Ibn Gabirol's secular poems, Bialik and Ravnitzky note that there is reason to doubt whether this poem was penned by Ibn Gabirol, although they do not state what that reason is. See *Shirei Shelomo ben Yehuda ibn Gabirol*, ed. Ḥ. N. Bialik and Y. Ḥ. Ravnitzky (Tel Aviv: Dvir, 1929), 14–15 (#15). Brody and Schirmann include the poem without any mention of suspicion in their critical version of Ibn Gabirol's *dīwān*. Their work was based on MS Shocken 37, the only complete manuscript version of Ibn Gabirol's *dīwān*, a text that had not yet been uncovered when Bialik and Ravnitzky labored over the materials. For more on the various manuscripts and published collections of Ibn Gabirol's poetry, see Elizur, *Shirat ha-Ḥol*, 1: 144–54 and 174–82.

2 Bialik and Ravnitzky include a slightly different final hemistich, copied from MS Adler 2954: "לבי אשר [חם] ובשרי אשר סמר," "[the fire of] my heart which is hot, and my flesh that throbs (*samar*)." According to Dov Jarden, the line should read "לבי אשר בלה שערי אשר סמר", "[the fire of] my heart which wears it [my heart] out and causes my hair (*se`ari*) to stand on edge (*samar*)." Jarden explains that the combination of סמר (*samar*) and שער (*se`ar*) appears in Job 4:15: "וְרוּחַ עַל פָּנַי יַחֲלֹף תְּסַמֵּר שַׂעֲרַת בְּשָׂרִי," "Then a spirit passed before my face, that made the hair of my flesh to stand up." See Ibn Gabirol, *Shirei ha-Ḥol*, ed. Jarden, 2:527 (#289). Brody and Schirmann point out in fn. 2 that Jarden's version is the one that appears in MS Shocken 37 (see above, n. 1). In the text, however, they include MS Adler's בשרי (*besari*, my flesh) rather than שערי (*se`ari*, my hair). While they do not explain this preference, it would appear that the more obvious eroticism of "בשרי אשר סמר" (*besari asher samar*, "my throbbing flesh," writes Raymond Scheindlin in his translation) struck them as more fitting to both the line and the theme of the poem. An example of the combination of בשר (*basar*, flesh) and סמר (*samar*, shudder/throb), without שער (*se`ar*, hair), appears in Ps. 119:120: "סָמַר מִפַּחְדְּךָ בְשָׂרִי" ("my flesh shudders in fear of You"). Although MS Adler includes the word חם (*ḥam*, hot), Brody and Schirmann use בלה (*balah*, to waste, wear out) but note that the unclear word could also be כלה (*kalah*, finished off). Scheindlin's translation follows; see n. 3.

3 Scheindlin, *Wine, Women and Death*, 111. Scheindlin's translation is based on the Hebrew version of the poem found in Schirmann's *Ha-Shirah ha-`Ivrit be-Sefarad u-ve-Provans*, 1:1, 214 (#5).

4 Amnon's mother was Aḥinoam the Jezreelite. The mother of Tamar and her full brother Absalom, who appears later in the scene, was Ma`acah the daughter of Talmai, king of Geshur. See 1 Chron. 3:1–3 and 2 Sam. 3:2–5. The Bible does not transmit much information on either Aḥinoam or Ma`acah or their relationships with David. Ma`acah appears only in the listings of David's sons (1 Chron. 3 and 2 Sam. 3). 1 Sam. 25:43 records that David married Aḥinoam either before or around the same time that he married Abigail, widow of Nabal the Carmelite (she became the mother of David's second son, 1 Chron. 3:1; 2 Sam. 3:3). Since in 2 Sam. 12:8 God says that He gave the wives of David's "master" to David, some have posited that Aḥinoam the Jezreelite was originally Saul's wife, Aḥinoam the daughter of Aḥimaatz (1 Sam. 14:50).

5 2 Sam. 13:2: "וַיֵּצֶר לְאַמְנוֹן לְהִתְחַלּוֹת בַּעֲבוּר תָּמָר אֲחֹתוֹ כִּי בְתוּלָה הִיא וַיִּפָּלֵא בְּעֵינֵי אַמְנוֹן לַעֲשׂוֹת לָהּ מְאוּמָה." Translators generally render this difficult verse as: "Amnon became so distraught because of his sister Tamar that he became sick, for she was a virgin and it seemed impossible to do anything to her." Reading וַיִּפָּלֵא (*va-yipale*) as "difficult," they explain that the royal virgins were probably kept under guard and thus Amnon could not gain access to Tamar, a theory put forth by earlier Jewish exegetes. See, for example, Qimḥi, *Sefer Redak*, on 2 Sam. 13:3.

Such a reading, however, does not solve the verse's difficulties. Only because she was a virgin could Amnon do nothing to her? Not because she was his sister, the reason mentioned in the verse as the cause of his descent into illness? Given the construction of verses 1 and 2, and since the root פלא (*pl'*) means "to be surpassing, extraordinary, wonderful," I suggest an alternate reading of the verses: Amnon fell in love with his beautiful sister and fell ill because he recognized the problematic incestuous nature of his feelings. Amnon's desire for his beautiful half-sister was compounded by the fact that she was a virgin, which he found particularly appealing (a not atypical fantasy); he thought it *wondrous*, otherworldly, possibly to the point of impossibility, to be able to do something (sexual) to her, precisely because she was a virgin. See *BDB*, s.v. פלא.

Using Akkadian and Ugaritic cognates, Gordon J. Wenham maintains that the biblical בתולה (*betulah*) does not indicate a virgin but rather a "girl of marriageable age," or "teenager" (many of whom, because of their youth, were *also* virgins). He argues unconvincingly that Amnon's desire for Tamar is caused by her youth (no virginity involved), and the coat she later wears and tears (vv. 18–19) is not a coat for royal virgins but for royal teens. See Gordon J. Wenham, "Betūlāh 'A Girl of Marriage Age,'" *Vetus Testamentum* 22 (1972): 326–48.

6 2 Sam. 13:4 records Jonadav's precisely worded question: "מַדּוּעַ אַתָּה כָּכָה דַּל בֶּן הַמֶּלֶךְ בַּבֹּקֶר בַּבֹּקֶר הֲלוֹא תַּגִּיד לִי." *JPS* translates this as "Why are you so dejected, O prince, morning after morning?" *NRSV* uses slightly different wording: "O son of the king, why are you so haggard morning after morning?" Both translations strike me as somewhat inexact. *BDB* defines דַּל as "low, weak, poor, thin," and in the case of Amnon, as the opposite of חזק (*ḥazek*), to be strong. Like later poetic lovesickness, it appears that Amnon's lovesickness had not only a psychological manifestation but also a physical one, causing him to lose weight and strength. *BDB*, s.v. דַּל.

7 In actuality, Amnon does not admit that he has fallen in love with his own sister. Instead he says, "אֶת-תָּמָר אֲחוֹת אַבְשָׁלֹם אָחִי אֲנִי אֹהֵב," "Tamar, the sister of my brother Absalom, do I love" as if she were not his sister too. This will be discussed more below.

8 Jonadav's advice is slightly puzzling. If Amnon is already sick enough to have drawn Jonadav's attention and concern, why does Amnon need to *feign* sickness? Perhaps Jonadav does not consider lovesickness to be a true ailment and thus he advises his cousin to pretend that he has a *real* disease.

9 The Bible refers to this food by different names. This will be discussed at length further on.

10 A review of the term נְבָלָה (*nevalah*) in the Bible reveals that the Bible uses the term to refer to three categories of sin. One indicates theft (Josh. 7:15); another indicates speaking foolishly or falsely (1 Sam. 25:25; Job 42:8; Isa. 9:16, 32:6); and, the largest category refers to sexual violations (Gen. 34:7; Deut. 22:21; Jer. 29:23; Judges 19:21–3; 20:9–10). Wenham, "Betūlāh 'A Girl of Marriage Age' " (342), maintains that sexual violation generally results in capital punishment. Bar-Efrat more correctly phrases this as "the culprit pays with his life," since not all of the cases in which sexual *nevalah* occurs result in trials in a court. See Shimon Bar-Efrat, "The Narrative of Amnon and Tamar" in his *Narrative Art in the Bible* (Sheffield: Almond Press, 1989), 262.

11 See n. 10.

12 Ironically, Tamar was correct on this point. David had not withheld her from Amnon; he had, wittingly or unwittingly, sent her straight to him.

Tamar's suggestion that David would allow his children to marry one another has spawned a host of scholarship attempting to understand the claim. After all, the Bible specifically prohibits any sibling marriage, half-siblings included (Lev. 18:9, 20:17; Deut. 27:22). Some scholars have therefore theorized that half-sibling marriage was permitted at the time nonetheless, either in Israel or in the royal court (Phoenicians and Egyptian pharaohs were noted for sibling marriage, after all). See, for example, William H. Propp, "Kinship in 2 Samuel 13," *Catholic Bible Quarterly* 55 (1993): 42–4. Pamela Tamarkin Reis maintains that Tamar's words indicate simply that she, "not a clever woman," thought that not only was sibling marriage legal, but that they, via intercourse, were now already married; according to Reis, Tamar's words here show that she does not want to be divorced. See Pamela Tamarkin Reis, "Cupidity and Stupidity: Woman's Agency and the 'Rape' of Tamar," *JNES* 25 (1997): 55. Reis's argument is unconvincing as is her characterization of Tamar as unclever. Tamar's attempt to talk her crazed and violently intentioned brother out of raping her is actually an intelligent and sensitive plea. One can clearly hear the increasingly desperate tone as Tamar attempts to save herself while realizing that her brother will not be reasoned with. The classical and medieval exegetes have an entirely different explanation of the matter than Reis does, discussed below.

13 J. P. Fokkelman has attempted to explain Amnon's almost instantaneous switch from love to hatred and ejection, calling Amnon an "uncouth egoist." Fokkelman suggests that since, as the victim of his attack, his sister serves as a witness to his disgusting nature, Amnon pushes her out the door. He locks the door behind her out of a panic that she might return sometime. Underneath this, writes Fokkelman, stands Amnon's fear of confrontation. See "II Sam. 13: 'Chips off the old block' (Scenes 8–9)," in his *Narrative Art and Poetry in the Books of Samuel*. Vol. 1 *King David* (Assen, The Netherlands: van Gorcum, 1981), 108. Fokkelman's interpretation echoes that of Don Isaac Abrabanel (1437–1508) in his *Perush `al Nevi`im Rishonim*, 2 Sam. 13:15. Other classical Jewish exegetes attribute Amnon's switch from love to hate to other causes, in some cases blaming Tamar herself. For example, in the Babylonian Talmud, R. Yitzḥaq teaches that during their sexual interaction one of Tamar's pubic hairs tied itself to Amnon's testicles and castrated him. This aroused his hatred for her. See *BT Sanhedrin* 21a.

14 Abrabanel maintains that she perceives this as worse because it entails her public humiliation. Bad as it was, the rape had occurred in private. With her ejection, her humiliation takes on greater, public, proportions. See Abrabanel's comments on 2 Sam. 13:19.

15 The harshness of Amnon's words and the disdain with which he refers to his once-beloved sister are particularly chilling. In v. 17, he says bitingly, "שִׁלְחוּ-נָא אֶת-זֹאת מֵעָלַי הַחוּצָה" (*shilḥu na et zot me-`alai ha-ḥutzah*), "Please send this away from me, outside." He uses the word "please" in commanding his servant (and, it seems the more formal plural form of the verb), but the word "this" to refer to his sister, a princess.

16 According to *BDB*, both רשת (*reshet*) and מכמר (*mikhmar*) are nets/snares used for entrapping animals. In the Bible, one uses a רשת (*reshet*) specifically to catch birds (as in Pr. 1:17). One uses a מכמר (*mikhmar*) to bring an animal to its fall (Is. 51:20). See s.v. "ירש" and "כמר", (III). Samuel ha-Nagid uses the term רשת (*reshet*) as a "snare of the heart." See Samuel ha-Nagid, *Diwan Shemuel ha-Nagid. Ben Mishle*, ed. Dov Jarden (Jerusalem: Hebrew Union College, 5743 [1983]), 397 (#1036).

17 In Ibn Ḥazm's chapter on the "Signs of Love," Ibn Ḥazm writes that love's "conflagration truly bursts forth, its blaze waxes fierce, its flames leap up." See Arberry, trans., *The Ring of the Dove*, 35; Arabic in Ibn Ḥazm, *Ṭauḳ al-ḥamâma*, ed. Pétrof, 13. This has been discussed in earlier chapters, esp. Chapter 5.

18 See Eddy Zemach, *Ke-Shoresh `Etz. Qeriah Ḥadasha be-Yud Dalet Shirei Ḥol shel Shelomo ben Gabirol* (Reḥavia and Tel Aviv: Hotza'at Sifri'at Po`alim, 1973), 139–40.

19 As just discussed above, Scheindlin's poetic sensitivity somewhat obscures the explicit fire image of the Hebrew. This has no negative effect on the current matter.

20 See Elizur's discussion on this topic, in her *Shirat ha-Ḥol*, 2:74–8.

21 Nykl, trans., *A Book Containing the Risāla*, 13. The Arabic appears in *Ṭauḳ*, 11. Perhaps the cure is not that effective, for Ibn Ḥazm goes on to discuss at length the notion that love is a disease without a cure, or a disease from which no sufferer desires to be cured.

22 See al-Iṣfahānī, *Kitāb al-zahra*, ed. A. R. Nykl with I. Tuqan (Chicago: University of Chicago Press, 1932), 290–336. Scheindlin points out that this trope hearkens back even further, to the earliest days of Arabic poetry, appearing in the works of that most famous author of *mujūn* (perversion) poetry, Abū Nuwās (d. *c.* 814). For example, in response to one who reproached him for falling ill after drinking to excess, he replied, "Leave off your blaming; / blame makes me rebel. / Cure me instead with that which made me ill." In other words, stop yelling at me and give me another drink, if you really wish to help me feel better. See Scheindlin, *Wine,*

Women and Death, 112. For more on Abū Nuwās, see Bencheikh, "Poetry of the East," 149–51; Jim Colville, trans., *Poems of Wine and Revelry: The Khamriyyat of Abu Nuwas* (London: Kegan Paul, 2005); Kennedy, *Abu Nuwas: A Genius of Poetry*; Meisami, "Arabic Mujūn Poetry," 8–30.

For an example of this same trope in a poem by Samuel ha-Nagid (993–1056), Ibn Gabirol's one-time patron, see his, *Diwan Shemuel ha-Nagid. Ben Tehillim*, 302 (#175, תרופה בפניה). An English translation appears in Roth, "The Care and Feeding of Gazelles," 102.

23 See Chapter 3, pp. 88ff.

24 For more on the *nadīm*, see Brener, *Judah Halevi and His Circle*, 59–61.

25 Scheindlin, "A Miniature Anthology," 122.

26 Schirmann, *Ha-Shirah ha-`Ivrit be-Sefard u-ve-Provans*, 1:2, 367–8 (#143). R. Judah Halevi (1075–1141) uses a similar phrase to begin a poem addressed to his mentor, Moses ibn Ezra. As the poem opens, the narrator writes that he finds himself standing with "כוס משמאל דוד מימין" (*kos mi-smol dod mi-yemin*), "a cup in my left hand, a beloved boy to my right." See Judah Halevi, *Diwan. Shirei ha-Ḥol*, ed. Ḥaim Brody (Berlin, 1901), 1:135.

27 Roth notes that the Persians often referred to the male *sāqī* as "the Turk" because the most desirable wine-serving boys, noted for their beauty and bravery, were thought to hail from Turkestan. See Roth, "The Care and Feeding of Gazelles," 100.

28 The conflation of wine and desire imagery resulting in poems dedicated to the *sāqī* has been noticed by, among others, Elizur, *Shirat ha-Ḥol*, 2:128–35; Roth, "Deal Gently"; Pagis, *Shirat ha-Ḥol*, ch. 10, entitled "Poems of Wine and Desire"; Schippers, *Spanish Hebrew Poetry*, 120–5; and Tobi, *Proximity and Distance*, 218.

We find this mixed trope as far back as Abū Nuwās, who often wrote of wine in sexual imagery and once compared the breaking open of a wine cask to the bleeding of a virgin bride on her wedding night. See Colville, *Poems of Wine and Revelry*, xi, 4. Abū Nuwās's influence reached both Muslim and Jewish Andalusian poets. On his influence on Samuel ha-Nagid, see Yehuda Ratzaby, "Shirat ha-yayin le-R. Shemuel ha-Nagid," in *Sefer H. M. Shapiro. Annual of the Bar-Ilan University Studies in Judaica and the Humanities*, ed. H. Z. Hirschberg *et al.* (Ramat Gan: Bar Ilan University, 1972), 423–74.

29 Schippers, *Spanish Hebrew Poetry*, 121–3. Zemach, "*Ke-Shoresh `Etz*," 137, unconvincingly asserts that the poem's phrase על ידה (*`al yadah*) derives from the biblical story of Rebecca; see below, n. 38.

30 A typical wine poem in which the poet describes falling for the female *sāqī* using *`ishq* terminology appears in Samuel ha-Nagid's *Diwan Shemuel ha-Nagid. Ben Tehillim*, 290 (#145, קח מצביה); and Schirmann, *Ha-Shirah ha-`Ivrit be-Sefarad u-ve-Provans*, 1/1: 167 (#17). In another poem by Ibn Gabirol, the lover first describes the beauty of the beloved maiden who sits with him, and then, in a twist on the motif, speaks of himself as crying because of a *lack* of available wine. See Schirmann, *Ha-Shirah ha-`Ivrit be-Sefarad u-ve-Provans*, 1:214 (#4) and in Brody and Schirmann, *Shirei ha-Ḥol le-Rabbi Shelomo ibn Gabirol*, 66 (#117). In a particularly snarky late example, al-Ḥarizi uses the terminology of love poetry to present the intoxicating effect of wine on the body. See al-Harizi, *Taḥkemoni*, ed. Toporovsky, 395.

31 Nykl, *Hispano-Arabic Poetry*, 185. Two others appear on pp. 145 and 173. Rafī al-Dawla's poetry can be found in Arabic in al-Fatḥ ibn Ḥāqān, *Maṭmaḥ al-anfus wa-masraḥ al-ta'annus fī mulaḥ ahl al-andalus*, ed. Muḥammad `Alī Šawābika (Beirut: Dār `ammār, 1983), 222–5.

32 Judah Halevi's poem to Ibn Ghayyat appears in his *Diwan. Shirei ha-Ḥol*, 1:174 (n. 115). An English translation appears in Brener, *Judah Halevi and His Circle*, 74. Other such invitation poems by Judah Halevi appear in his *Diwan. Shirei ha-Ḥol*, 2:243 (n. 23); an English translation can be found in Brener, 76. Invitation poems

by Moses ibn Ezra appear in his *Shirei ha-Ḥol*, 1:230 and 189 (n. 188). An English translation of the latter can be found in Brener, 75. Other Hebrew invitation poems appear in Schippers, *Spanish Hebrew Poetry*, 112 and in Elizur, *Shirat ha-Ḥol*, 2:15–19. For more on the phenomenon, see Pagis, *Shirat ha-Ḥol*, 258–9; Schippers, 107ff.

33 One might explain this anomaly by pointing out that the standards of modesty of the day might have prevented a man from issuing such an invitation directly to a woman. We recall that female beloveds were often spoken of and referred to as males because of modesty guidelines. Elizur notes that sometimes what looks like a homoerotic poem actually makes little sense unless we "translate" the beloved into a female. She brings two examples in which the breasts of the male beloved are praised, a clear indication that the object of desire should be understood as female. See Elizur, *Shirat ha-Ḥol*, 2:82. In like fashion, in Schirmann's notes to Moses ibn Ezra's "תאוות לבבי ומחמד עיני", a poem clearly addressed to a male beloved (עופר, *`ofer*, a male fawn), Schirmann suggests that the true gender of the beloved is female. He derives this interpretation from the poem's reference to Song of Songs 3:4 in line 13. See Schirmann, *Ha-Shirah ha-`Ivrit be-Sefarad u-ve-Provans*, 367–8. I am not sure I follow Schirmann's logic here; the beloved in that Song of Songs verse is male, not female. Perhaps Schirmann means that since Song of Songs' couple is heterosexual, the couple in the poem should also be understood as heterosexual even if they have reversed the roles of the characters in the biblical verse. In other words, if the poem's speaker/lover is male, then the beloved must be female (the opposite of the situation described in the Song of Songs verse).

It may be that Ibn Gabirol's besotted lover appealed to his beloved through a third party, in observance of the norms of poetic discreetness. However, such an explanation stands at odds with the rest of the poem, which does not seem much concerned about modesty. The lover makes little attempt to conceal his less than modest anticipations regarding the party's activities. Says he hopefully, "If she would pour for me, she might put out the burning pain wasting my throbbing flesh." This is a quite obvious and not so modest hint at the physical sensation ("throbbing") caused by unrealized/unconsummated male sexual arousal. "If she would pour for me," we can imagine the lovesick lover whispering, with a certain aroused glaze in his eye, "she might put out the burning pain *wasting my throbbing flesh*." A more risqué textual double-entendre is hidden in this line as well, discussed below.

34 Elizur, *Shirat ha-Ḥol*, 3:418.

35 Ibid.

36 The problematic nature of the Amnon–Tamar story was not overlooked in Andalusian Hebrew poetry. In a poem widely attributed to the Spanish Isaac ibn Ezra (*c.* 1109–mid-twelfth-century), son of Abraham ibn Ezra and son-in-law of R. Judah Halevi, the poet includes the Amnon–Tamar story as one of the many problematic biblical accounts that led to his apostasy from Judaism. The author's use of particular prepositions indicates that he read this episode as incest-rape. In referring to the problematic biblical episode in which Judah, mistaking his daughter-in-law for a prostitute, hires her for her services, as she had planned (Gen. 38), the poet uses the phrase "יהודה בא לתמר" (*Yehudah ba le-Tamar*), Judah came to Tamar. This was a consensual interaction. The next phrase, "and Amnon to his sister, a virgin," uses the same verb (בא, *ba*, came) but changes the preposition from ל (*le-*, to) to על (*`al*, on). With one small change, the poet switches the sense of the verb from consensual sex to forced sexual contact.

Fleischer and Schmelzer note that the poem appears in many manuscripts in which it is attributed to an anonymous author; an ascription to Isaac ibn Ezra appears in only one, a late manuscript found in the Cairo Genizah. Fleischer and Schmelzer therefore conclude that Isaac ibn Ezra's authorship of this poem should be considered wishful thinking. See Schirmann, *Toledot ha-Shirah ha-`Ivrit be-Sefarad ha-Notzerit*, 79; idem, *Ha-Shirah ha-`Ivrit be-Sefard u-ve-Provans*, #287; idem, *Shirim Ḥadashim*, 277–81; Menachem Schmelzer, ed., *Yitzḥaq ibn Avraham ibn Ezra. Shirim* (New York: Jewish Theological Seminary of America, 1981), appendix, 147; and Cole, *The Dream of the Poem*, 195. On Isaac ibn Ezra's conversion to Islam and reversion to Judaism, see Sarah Stroumsa, "On Jewish Intellectuals Who Converted in the Early Middle Ages," in *The Jews of Medieval Islam: Community, Society and Identity*, ed. Daniel Frank (Leiden: E. J. Brill, 1995), 189–91.

37 Among the many poems in which the name Tamar appears only in order to describe the beloved as a beautiful woman, one particularly apt example by Ibn Gabirol appears in Schirmann, *Ha-Shirah ha-`Ivrit be-Sefarad u-ve-Provans*, 1/1:214 (#4) and in Brody and Schirmann, *Shirei ha-Ḥol le-Rabbi Shelomo ibn Gabirol*, 66 (#117).

38 Zemach, *Ke-Shoresh `Etz*, 135–40. In similar vein Zemach claims that the poem's "על ידה" (*`al yadah*), lit. "on her hand," derives from and refers to the biblical account of the matriarch Rebecca, who brings Eliezer a jug of water, which she lowers from her hand to give him to drink ("וַתֹּרֶד כַּדָּהּ עַל-יָדָהּ וַתַּשְׁקֵהוּ," Gen. 24:18). Our poem, he maintains, purposely imitates the courtship of Isaac and Rebecca (through Eliezer) to emphasize that the courtship in our poem is not of the same type as Isaac and Rebecca's. It will result not in happiness (as theirs did), but in death, brought about by the jugs of wine served by Absalom to Amnon in revenge. See Zemach, *Ke-Shoresh `Etz*, 137. Given the overwhelming number of allusions to the biblical Tamar–Absalom narrative in the poem, this is not a most convincing interpretation of the phrase.

39 Scheindlin, *Wine, Women and Death*, 112. A measure of debate exists among the scholars as to whether a true "courtier" culture existed among the Jews of Andalusia. See Chapter 1, p. 15 and Chapter 2, n. 4.

40 Scheindlin, *Wine, Women and Death*, 124.

41 As previously noted, this fickleness is discussed at length by Ibn Ḥazm in *Ṭauḳ*, 99 (Arberry, 202–3; Nykl, 152–3).

42 The Baghdadi Muslim scholar al-Jāḥiẓ (781–869) wrote of a similar phenomenon. On the one hand, he noted, the "greatest of joys and most perfect of pleasures" is the lover's conquest and possession of the object of his affection. On the other hand, warned al-Jāḥiẓ, such "triumphant possession" of the beloved hastens the end of *`ishq*. See Pellat, trans. and ed., *The Life and Works of Jāḥiẓ*, 257 and 264.

43 Elizur's somewhat radical caution against over-reading the *remez* likewise derives from her recognition of the similarities that exist between the two texts.

44 On the translation of דל (*dal*), see n. 6.

45 Amnon's disingenuous phrasing in v. 4 ("the sister of my brother," not "my sister") might lead one to think that while Amnon and Absalom were paternal half-brothers, Absalom and Tamar were maternal half-siblings (insinuating that Tamar was not David's daughter). In other words, his phrasing indicates that Amnon and Tamar were not biologically related but shared a half-brother (Absalom). Indeed, the opening verse of the account seems to back up such an idea: 2 Sam. 13:1 reads: "וַיְהִי אַחֲרֵי-כֵן וּלְאַבְשָׁלוֹם בֶּן-דָּוִד אָחוֹת יָפָה וַיֶּאֱהָבֶהָ אַמְנוֹן בֶּן-דָּוִד וּשְׁמָהּ תָּמָר," "And it came to pass after this, that Absalom the son of David had a beautiful sister whose name was Tamar and Amnon, the son of David, loved her." The narrator does not refer to Amnon here as Tamar's brother. Additionally, Tamar is the only one of the three siblings not referred to in the verse as a child of David.

The narrative, however, has already given lie to Amnon's words. While 2 Sam. 13:1 presents an ambiguous biological relationship, the very next verse refers clearly to Tamar as Amnon's sister: "Amnon was so tormented that he made himself ill because of *his sister* Tamar," and 1 Chron. 3:9 confirms their sibling relationship. After listing the names of all of David's sons, the text concludes, "and Tamar was their sister" ("וְתָמָר אֲחוֹתָם," *ve-Tamar ahotam*). Since David's sons had different mothers, the only way Tamar could have been sister to all of them, including Amnon, is if she too were David's child. What's more, reference to a sibling relationship between Amnon and Tamar appears eleven to thirteen times over the course of the account in 2 Sam. 13 (depending on how one counts). Thus despite Amnon's attempts to present the matter as non-incestuous passion, the Bible informs us clearly that it was.

46 See n. 5.

47 The verb קרא (*qra*) can mean to call someone to someone or to announce, call out loud. The presence of the preposition אלי (*eilai*, "to me") indicates the former meaning, call her to me. Literally speaking, the Hebrew here does not include a clear sense of informing Tamar. This sense is, however, implied by the line's language and grammatical construction. Scheindlin poetically employs both senses of the word in his translation, "so call to me Tamar and tell her."

48 2 Sam. 13:2 "וַיֵּצֶר לְאַמְנוֹן לְהִתְחַלּוֹת בַּעֲבוּר תָּמָר אֲחֹתוֹ כִּי בְתוּלָה הִיא."

49 For this reading of the verse, see n. 5. The idea that Amnon desired Tamar *because* of her virginity appears also in the second-century *Mishnah Avot*, in the eighth- or ninth-century *Avot de-Rabbi Natan*, and in the exegesis of the medieval R. David Qimḥi. See *Massekhet Avot `im Perush Rashi*, ed. Moshe Alexander Zusha Kinstlicher (Bnei Berak, 5752 [1992]), ch. 5, *mishnah* 16; *Avoth de-Rabbi Nathan. Solomon Schechter Edition* [Hebrew] (New York and Jerusalem: Jewish Theological Seminary of America, 1997), ch. 40 (*nusḥa aleph*); and Qimḥi on 2 Sam. 13:3.

50 See below, n. 52.

51 For example, Song of Songs 2:5, 8:5.

52 The Bible frequently uses חשק (*ḥesheq*) to indicate love. However, it does indicate that the words are not exact synonyms. One example in which the difference between the two terms is illustrated can be found in another biblical tale of passion gone awry and resulting in rape: the rape of Dinah, the daughter of Jacob. According to Gen. 34:2, the Hivite prince Shechem sees Dinah, takes her, and forcibly lies with her (i.e., rapes her). Only *after* satiating his sexual desire does Shechem develop emotions for the woman he has just violated; Gen. 34:3 relates that *after* raping her, "his soul cleaved to Dinah the daughter of Jacob and he loved [*va-ye'ehav*] the lass" ("וַתִּדְבַּק נַפְשׁוֹ בְּדִינָה בַּת-יַעֲקֹב וַיֶּאֱהַב אֶת-הַנַּעֲרָ"). Shechem then sends his father to Jacob with a request for Dinah's hand in marriage. Ḥamor approaches Jacob and his sons and reports (v. 8), "שְׁכֶם בְּנִי חָשְׁקָה נַפְשׁוֹ בְּבִתְּכֶם תְּנוּ נָא אֹתָהּ לוֹ לְאִשָּׁה", "Shechem my son, his soul *desires* (*ḥashqa*) your daughter; please give her to him as a wife." Interestingly, although the text used the verb אהב (*ahav*), love, to describe Shechem's new feelings for Dinah in 34:3, Ḥamor uses the verb חשק (*ḥashaq*), desire (*ḥashqa nafsho be-vitchem*), in his conversation with Dinah's family. It seems Ḥamor may have been unaware of the change in Shechem's emotions; after all, to him Shechem had said only tersely and factually, "קַח-לִי אֶת-הַיַּלְדָּה הַזֹּאת לְאִשָּׁה" ("Get me this girl for a wife"). Ḥamor's words appear to reflect Shechem's initial state of being, his desire after having simply seen the girl walk by. One ought to note the significant fact that during the entire negotiation between the Canaanites and Jacob's sons, Dinah remains detained in the house of her kidnapper-rapist. Such conduct on Shechem's part reflects the behavior of one more overcome with desire, control, and possession, as his father's words reveal.

53 The adjectival form appears in Ezekiel 34:20: "הִנְנִי אָנִי וְשָׁפַטְתִּי בֵּין שֶׂה בִרְיָה וּבֵין שֶׂה רָזָה," "Behold, I will judge between the fat cattle (*seh viryah*) and the lean cattle."

54 *BDB* maintains that the root ברה (*brh*) is related to the root ברא (*br'*), meaning fat, or to be fat. In other words, one eats to fatten oneself up. S.v. "ברה" and "ברא." One should note also that, aside from our pericope, the verb ברה appears only two other times in Scripture, in 2 Sam. 3:35 and in 2 Sam. 12:17, both of which similarly describe scenarios in which eating is done as a remedy: 2 Sam. 3:35 reports that

David, having just returned from Abner's funeral and still mourning his friend, refuses to eat with the people who had come to eat the post-mourning meal with him, a meal that is intended to bring solace to the mourners. This appears in Hebrew as "וַיָּבֹא כָל-הָעָם לְהַבְרוֹת אֶת-דָּוִד לֶחֶם בְּעוֹד הַיּוֹם ..." (*va-yavo kol ha-`am le-havrot et David leḥem be-`od ha-yom*). In 2 Sam. 12:17, David, faced with the severe illness of his infant son, engages in fasting and throws himself on the ground in a penitential posture. The elders, worried for the king's health, attempt to lift him up and feed him but he refuses to eat with them. The text records this as "וְלֹא-בָרָא אִתָּם לָחֶם" (*ve-lo vara itam leḥem*). From these two passages we see that the verb was used to indicate eating done to treat an illness or to mark the end of a period of mourning marked by suffering.

In its noun form, the word בריה (*biryah*) is found in our account alone, and more than once. Each time, it appears with the definite marker, as הבריה (*ha-biryah*), *the* medicinal food (v. 5 and v. 7). Note that Jonadav tells Amnon to request two foods: the indefinitely marked לחם (*leḥem*, bread) and the definitely marked הבריה (*ha-biryah*). It appears that Jonadav means that Amnon should request both regular food and the more specific medicinal food.

55 In a lovely three-line homonym-riddled poem, Moses ibn Ezra employs the root ברה (*brh*) in the sense of food intended to cure one dying from lovesickness. See his *Shirei ha-Ḥol*, 1:344, no. 4. Use of the root ברא (*br'*) to indicate feeding someone in order to heal them appears in Moses ibn Ezra's previously mentioned "תאוות לבבי." In lines 6–7, the lover appeals to his beloved: "בוא הצבי קום והבריאני / מצוף שפתיך והשביעני" (*bo ha-tzvi qum ve-havri'eini / me-tzuf sefatekha ve-hasbi`eini*), "Come, my gazelle, arise and feed me (*havri'eini*) from the nectar of your lips, and thereby satiate me." See Schirmann, *Ha-Shirah ha-`Ivrit be-Sefard u-ve-Provans*, 1:2, 367–8 (#143). On other Hebrew (and Arabic) poems describing lovesickness as leading to physical thinness, see Chapter 2, n. 35.

56 The noun לביבות (*levivot*) and the accompanying verb ותלבב (*va-telabev*) appear only twice in the Bible, both in 2 Sam. 13. "Libido cakes" was suggested by Jonneke Bekkenkamp, as cited by Fokkelien van Dijk-Hemmes in "Tamar and the Limits of Patriarchy: Between Rape and Seduction (2 Sam 13 and Genesis 38)," in *Anti-Covenant: Counter-Reading Women's Lives in the Hebrew Bible*, ed. Mieke Bal (Sheffield: Almond Press, 1989), 140. The verbal form of the root appears in one other place in the Bible, a usage that supports reading 2 Sam. 13's use of the root with erotic/romantic underpinnings. In Song of Songs 4:9, the male lover declares to the female beloved (whom he calls his sister, an epithet not lost on us given the root's usage in the Amnon–Tamar context): "לִבַּבְתִּנִי אֲחֹתִי כַלָּה לִבַּבְתִּנִי באחד (בְּאַחַת) מֵעֵינַיִךְ בְּאַחַד עֲנָק מִצַּוְּרֹנָיִךְ," "You have ravished my heart (*libavtini*), my sister, my bride, you have ravished my heart (*libavtini*) with one of your eyes, with one bead of your necklace." *BDB* modestly suggests, "You have encouraged me ... ," a translation that fails to capture the romantic or sexual essence of the root לבב. See *BDB*, s.v. לבב.

57 The full request in Hebrew (v. 6) reads: "וַיֹּאמֶר אַמְנוֹן אֶל-הַמֶּלֶךְ תָּבוֹא-נָא תָּמָר אֲחֹתִי וּתְלַבֵּב לְעֵינַי שְׁתֵּי לְבִבוֹת וְאֶבְרֶה מִיָּדָהּ." Jonadav originally instructed Amnon (v. 5): "וְאָמַרְתָּ אֵלָיו תָּבֹא נָא תָמָר אֲחוֹתִי וְתַבְרֵנִי לֶחֶם וְעָשְׂתָה לְעֵינַי אֶת-הַבִּרְיָה לְמַעַן אֲשֶׁר אֶרְאֶה וְאָכַלְתִּי מִיָּדָהּ". Although Jonadav uses the neutral and common term לֶחֶם (*leḥem*, bread), the verb that accompanies it, וְתַבְרֵנִי (*ve-tavreini*), formed off of the ברה root (*brh*), indicates it too served as part of the medicinal feeding. In the next phrase, Jonadav uses the medicinal noun הַבִּרְיָה (*ha-biryah*) outright. As discussed above, n. 54.

58 The word חמר (*ḥemer*), a poetic word meaning wine, appears once in biblical Hebrew, in Deut. 32:14. Six attestations vocalized as *ḥamar* appear in the Aramaic portions of Ezra and Daniel (Ez. 6:9, 7:22; Dan. 5:1, 5:2, 5:4, 5:23). Ps. 75:9 uses the adverb form, "וְיַיִן חָמַר מָלֵא מֶסֶךְ וַיַּגֵּר מִזֶּה" ("There is a cup [in the Lord's hand] with foaming wine fully mixed; from this He pours"). The adverb form indicates something foaming,

fermented, boiled up. See *BDB*, s.v. חֲמַר. Since the biblical Hebrew *ḥemer* does not fit the poem's rhyme scheme (*mikhmar*, *omar*, *samar*), it appears that Ibn Gabirol used either the biblical Aramaic or a noun created from the biblical Hebrew verb in Ps. 75.

59 In conversation, Shulamit Elizur noted that the original pronunciation of the word, whether *tashqeini* or *tishaqeini*, would have been of little mystery since the poems were performed, recited before live audiences. However, Schirmann has noted that not all of the poems were publicized at on-the-spot oral competitions. Rather, poems were written down, often on nice paper, and sent around in their written format. See Schirmann, "The Function of the Hebrew Poet," 246. Thus it is possible that the play on words, visible in the written format only, is intentional. While I would like to believe that the reciter of the poem played around with his pronunciation and with his delivery so as to transmit both senses of the word, *tashqeini* and *tishaqeini*, we have no way of knowing this.

60 The term for Tamar's cloak, כְּתֹנֶת פַּסִּים (*ketonet passim*), appears in Gen. 37:3 to describe the garment Jacob gives to his son Joseph. If we are to understand the *ketonet* as indicating royal status, as it appears to in 2 Sam. 13, the ire experienced by Jacob's ten older sons when they saw the cloak he had given to their younger brother, and to him alone, becomes more understandable.

61 Ibn Gabirol here uses the constructive form (עטרת, *`ateret*) of the biblical Hebrew noun עטרה (*`atarah*); עטרת (*`ateret*) does not exist as an independent noun in biblical Hebrew. See *BDB*, s.v. עטר, 742–3. For other biblical uses of עטרת (*`ateret*) as crown, see, for example, Song 3:11; Ezek. 16:12, 21:31, 23:42; Zech. 6:11; Esther 8:15. After David defeated Rabbah in Ammon, 2 Sam. 12:30 reports, "וַיִּקַּח אֶת-עֲטֶרֶת-מַלְכָּם מֵעַל רֹאשׁוֹ וּמִשְׁקָלָהּ כִּכַּר זָהָב וְאֶבֶן יְקָרָה וַתְּהִי עַל-רֹאשׁ דָּוִד" ("And he took the crown [*`ateret*] of their king from his head – it weighed a talent of gold and in it were precious stones – and it was placed on David's head"). According to the *Anchor Bible*, while the Masoretic text (and others) presents the word as *malcām* (their king), other manuscripts have *melchom*, and "it has long been recognized that the correct reading is *milkōm*," the proper name of the Ammonite deity. Either way, the word *`ateret* signifies a crown. See P. Kyle McCarter, *The Anchor Bible. II Samuel* (Garden City, NY: Doubleday, 1984), 311.

62 *BDB*, s.v. "עדה."

63 See, for example, Jer. 2:32, 4:30; Ezek. 16:1–14; Isa. 49:18. Zemach maintains that since the appearance of עֶדְיָהּ (*`edyah*) in Jer. 2:32 links it with virginity ("הֲתִשְׁכַּח בְּתוּלָה עֶדְיָהּ," "Can a virgin forget her jewels?"), Ibn Gabirol's use of the word here links the beloved's virginity with Tamar's. See Zemach, *Ke-Shoresh `Etz*, 137. One should note that the phrase that immediately follows and parallels Jer. 2:32's "הֲתִשְׁכַּח בְּתוּלָה עֶדְיָהּ" concerns not virgins, but brides. The full phrase in Jer. 2:32 reads, "הֲתִשְׁכַּח בְּתוּלָה עֶדְיָהּ כַּלָּה קִשֻּׁרֶיהָ" ("Can a maiden/virgin forget her jewels, a bride her adornments?"). I maintain, therefore, that עֶדְיָהּ (*`edyah*) refers not to the jewels worn by any virgin, but to a virgin who, like a bride, has neared sexual maturity.

In one of Samuel ha-Nagid's secular poems, he too overlays the phrase עֶדְיָהּ (*`edyah*) with sexual connotations. The poem begins by comparing men in the world to clients of prostitutes. The world itself, says the poem, is like a harlot who adorns herself with her ornaments (*`edyah*) as a deception. See his *Diwan. Ben Qohelet*, ed. Dov Jarden (Jerusalem: Hebrew Union College, 5752 [1992]), 18 (#30). Similarly, Moses ibn Ezra utilizes the phrase in describing the earth dressing herself up in her finest to seduce the foolish with her beauty. See Ibn Ezra, *Shirei ha-Ḥol*, #84.

64 Precisely what both the lover and Amnon would like to do.

65 In the poems by Samuel ha-Nagid and Moses ibn Ezra mentioned above, the authors *do* use the same root for the verb and noun, תעד עדיה (*ta`ad `edyah*, she decorates herself with her decorations).

66 So do the women brought before Ahasuerus prepare themselves for their first night with him, spending six months with oil of myrrh and six months with perfumes and other ointments. See Esther 2:12.

67 According to *BT Sanhedrin* 21a, R. Yehoshua ben Qorḥa taught that Tamar's cries led to the creation of the law of "isolation" (יחוד, *yiḥud*), a law that forbids a legally adult man and woman from being alone together in a closed room unless they are siblings, married to one another, or parent–child. This is somewhat puzzling since Amnon and Tamar *are* brother and sister and thus, even according to the rules of יחוד (*yiḥud*), they would have been permitted to sit together in Amnon's back room.

68 It is possible that her ripped virgin-cloak provided a hint to the sexual assault. One should be aware, however, that cloak-ripping constitutes a traditional gesture of mourning the dead in the Bible, and as such is not necessarily related to mourning the loss of one's virginity. For example, David and all his servants rend their clothes upon hearing the rumor that Absalom has slain all of David's sons, in 2 Sam. 13:31.

69 The biblical Hebrew verb שכב (*shachav*), to lie down, also indicates sexual activity (*BDB*, s.v. שכב). Consensual sexual activity is usually partnered with the preposition עם (*'im*, with). When partnered with the direct object marker את (*et*), the phrase indicates an inappropriate (illegal or immoral) sexual action. See, for example: Gen. 26:10; 34:2, 7; 35:22; Lev. 15:24; Num. 5:19; 1 Sam. 2:22; and Ezek. 23:8. In the case of Tamar, in 2 Sam. 13:14, it indicates either that the actors were siblings and thus the sex illegal, or, more likely, that the action was done to, rather than with, Tamar. In other words, with את (*et*) here, the phrase indicates a sexual assault.

70 According to *BDB*, the verb ענה, in the *pi'el* form with a woman as the direct object, means to humiliate through cohabitation. Hence, the translators understand the verb to mean he forced her, raped her. See s.v. ענה.

71 Modern Bible scholars have attempted to explain Absalom's curious words. According to Fokkelman, Absalom believes that since Amnon is a prince, and much beloved by his father, bringing a case against him will likely have no result. See Fokkelman, 110–11, and Dominic Rudman, "Reliving the Rape of Tamar: Absalom's Revenge in 2 Samuel 13," *Old Testament Essays* 11:2 (1998): 335. However, the only son whom the Bible points out explicitly that David never reprimanded is not Amnon but Adonijah. See 1 Kings 1:5–6. Furthermore, if one compares David's reaction to Amnon's death (2 Sam. 13:31–9) with his reaction to Absalom's death (2 Sam. 19:1–5), it would appear that Absalom, and not Amnon, was their father's favorite. Indeed, David sends Amnon into Absalom's hands despite appearing to suspect that Absalom had evil intentions toward his elder brother (2 Sam. 13:23–7).

Others have insisted that by taking Tamar into his home and issuing these words of comfort, Absalom exhibited appropriate behavior, in line with that expected of him as her brother; this, they claim, constituted the only kindness Tamar experiences throughout the ordeal. See Bar-Efrat, "The Narrative of Amnon and Tamar," 245, 271; Mark Gray, "Amnon: A Chip off the Old Block? Rhetorical Strategy in 2 Samuel 13:7–15, the Rape of Tamar and the Humiliation of the Poor," *Journal for the Study of the Old Testament* 77 (1998): 43; Rudman, "Reliving the Rape of Tamar," 329–30; Phyllis Trible, "Tamar and the Royal Rape of Wisdom," in *Texts of Terror* (London: SCM Press, 1992), 51.

Jonadav later uses a similar phrase in attempting to comfort David after Absalom murders Amnon. Originally, a rumor had gone out saying that Absalom had killed all of the king's sons. When the correct information reaches the palace, that only Amnon was killed, Jonadav says, "וְעַתָּה אַל-יָשֵׂם אֲדֹנִי הַמֶּלֶךְ אֶל לִבּוֹ דָּבָר לֵאמֹר כָּל-בְּנֵי הַמֶּלֶךְ מֵתוּ כִּי-אִם אַמְנוֹן לְבַדּוֹ מֵת," "Now therefore let not my lord the king take the thing to his heart, to think that all the king's sons are dead for Amnon only is dead" (2 Sam. 13:33). This strikes me as no more comforting or logical a thing to say to David at the loss of his son than to Tamar at the violent loss of her virginity at the hands of her brother. Jonadav's use of the term seems to be a purposeful attempt to strike at David for not standing up for Tamar after the rape, and for allowing Absalom to advise her to not take the rape to heart and to keep quiet.

72 Male loitering out of concern for a female relative caught in sexually dangerous circumstances appears also in the Book of Esther. There, after Esther has been taken in to the king's harem as part of his round-up of all the kingdom's virgins in his search for a wife, her kinsman Mordecai sits himself down outside of the palace day after day, waiting to hear word from or about her. See Esther 2:11.

73 If this is the case, clearly Absalom grossly underestimated his brother.

74 See above for discussion of the use and translation of the word אברה (*evreh*) as used here.

75 The first appearance occurs in v. 5. There Jonadav advises Amnon that he speak to his father. In the next verse Amnon repeats each clause to David. The third iteration appears in the narrative's description of Tamar's resulting actions (vv. 8–9):

V. 5 Jonadav's advice to Amnon	*V. 6 Amnon Requests of David*	*VV. 8–9 Narrator's Report of Events*
Say to him [David], "Let my sister Tamar come, I pray thee, and	"Let my sister Tamar come, I pray thee, and	So Tamar went to the house of Amnon her brother, and he was lying down, and
prepare bread for me (ותבריני לחם, *ve-tavreini leḥem*) and let her prepare the food (הבריה, *ha-birya*)	prepare for me two cakes (ותלבב ... שתי לביבות, *u-telabev shetei levivot*)	she took the dough and kneaded it into cakes (ותלבב, *va-telabev*)
before my eyes so that I may look on,	before my eyes,	in front of his eyes, and cooked the cakes (לביבות, *levivot*).
and I will eat from her hand."	and I will be healed by eating from her hand (ואברה, *va-evreh*)."	She took the pan and set it out before him.

76 The nature of Amnon's request to watch becomes clearer when we bear in mind the oft-noted sensuality of food preparation and cooking. Nigella Lawson's British cooking show provides one example of this. According to Lynn Hirschberg of the *New York Times*, "Lawson's sexy roundness mixed with her speed-demon technique makes cooking dinner with Nigella look like a prelude to an orgy," http://www.nytimes.com/2001/11/18/magazine/hot-dish.html.

77 Jack M. Sasson has suggested that David actually may have been informed of the entire plan by Jonadav himself, to whom the king was close. After all, David's instructions to Tamar in v. 6 are a partial version of Jonadav's words to Amnon in v. 5. See Sasson's "Absalom's Daughter: An Essay in Vestige Historiography," in *The Land that I Will Show You: Essays on the History and Archaeology of the Ancient Near East in Honour of Maxwell Miller. Journal for the Study of the Old Testament, Supplement* 343, ed. J. Andrew Dearman and M. Patrick Graham (Sheffield: Sheffield Academic Press, 2001): 192.

78 For example, see the use of חכם (*ḥakham*) in Deut. 4:6, 32:6; 1 Kgs. 3:12; Pr. 10:6, 13:6, 15:20, 16:23 etc. Deut. 32:6 sets up נבל (*naval*), senseless, as the opposite of חכם (*ḥakham*), wise. Note that while 2 Sam. 13:3 calls Jonadav "אִישׁ חָכָם מְאֹד" (*ish ḥakham me'od*), Tamar twice uses the root נבל (*naval*) to refer to Amnon, whose

desire for his own sister does appear to be an idea without sense. Significantly, in the very next chapter, 2 Sam. 14:2 refers to the "wise woman of Tekoa" enlisted by Joab to help reconcile David with Absalom as "אִשָּׁה חֲכָמָה" (*ishah ḥakhama*). Wisdom that has evil connotations appears as ערמה (*`ormah*), as in Pr. 1:14 and others, and sometimes as מרמה (*mirmah*). A discussion of the latter term and of the rabbinic attempt to turn מרמה (*mirmah*) into a positive value appears in Chapter 4.

79 *BDB*, s.v. "רע."

80 Ibn Gabirol's exegesis has not survived in an independent tome, but as citations that appear in the works of scholars such as Abraham ibn Ezra (1089–1164) and R. David Qimḥi (1160–1235). Because of this, scholars are not certain whether Ibn Gabirol's exegesis addressed all portions of the Bible or only particular segments. See *EJ*, s.v. "Gabirol, Solomon ben Judah, Ibn," by Shelomo Pines (7:237–8).

81 Gersonides on 2 Sam. 13:20 and Abrabanel on 2 Sam. 13:1 (p. 351). It is not clear to me how this solves anything since it strikes me that precisely *because* Amnon was her brother that he deserves to be even more shamed for having raped her. For Gersonides, see his *Perushei Ralbag. Nevi'im Rishonim*, ed. Yaacov Leib Levi (Jerusalem: Mossad Harav Kook, 2008).

82 2 Sam. 13:20, "וַתֵּשֶׁב תָּמָר וְשֹׁמֵמָה בֵּית אַבְשָׁלוֹם אָחִיהָ" (*va-teshev Tamar ve-shomemah beit Avshalom aḥiha*). *BDB* lists the meaning of the root שמם (*šmm*) as "generally desolate, appalling or devastating" and translators have frequently understood the verse as describing Tamar's mental state. However, the Bible's usage indicates a functional understanding as more appropriate. The word שוממה/שומם (*shomem/shomemah*) appears five other times in the Bible, each time linking it with infertility (Isa. 49:8; 54:1; Lam. 1:4, 13, 16). A שֹׁמֵמָה (*shomemah*) appears to have been a woman who had not borne children. We ought therefore to understand that Tamar remains שֹׁמֵמָה (*shomemah*), an unmarried woman, condemned to living in her brother's house for the rest of her days, with no husband or family of her own.

A midrash found in the twelfth-century Italian *Midrash Sekhel Tov* supports this interpretation of שֹׁמֵמָה (*shomemah*). Gen. 47:19 records the words of the Egyptians who, depleted by famine, request from Joseph (the vizier) to buy the land from them in exchange for bread. They propose, "Why should we die before your eyes, both we and our land? Buy us and our land for bread, and we and our land will be bondmen unto Pharaoh; and give us seed, that we may live, and not die, and that the land be not desolate [וְהָאֲדָמָה לֹא תֵשָׁם, *ve-hadamah lo teisham*]"). Explaining the verse's last word, תֵשָׁם (*teisham*), *Sekhel Tov* writes: "In other words, so that the land will not be שממה (*shemmamah*), for land that is not worked resembles a widowed or abandoned woman, as it is written, 'And Tamar sat *shomemah*.'" Land that is שממה (*shemmamah*), he continues, resembles שדה הבור (*s'deh ha-bor*), a field *that is not seeded* (italics, mine). See Menaḥem ben Solomon, *Midrash Sekhel Tov `al Sefer Bereishit ve-Shemot*, ed. S. Buber (Berlin, 5660 [1899]), Gen. 47:19.

83 *Midrash Rabbah. Qohelet* [Ecclesiastes Rabbah], in *Midrash Rabbah ha-Mevo'ar*, 7:3:1. See also *Midrash Zuta. Qohelet*, ed. Shelomo Buber (Vilna, 5659 [1898]), ch. 7, #3. According to H. L. Strack and G. Stemberger, it is unknown whether this text is older than the eighth-century *Ecclesiastes Rabbah* or is an abridgement of it. See their *Introduction to the Talmud and Midrash* (Minneapolis: Fortress Press, 1992), 348. Gersonides later echoes this criticism in his commentary to 2 Sam. 8:18. Referencing Absalom's rebellion against David and his killing of Amnon, and also Adonijah's request to marry his father's concubine Abishag (1 Kgs. 2), Gersonides writes, "If the king had supervised his sons' education/morals/behavior (מוסר, *mussar*), this would not have happened to them." Note that Gersonides leaves out Amnon's rape of Tamar from the list of bad behaviors David might have prevented.

84 This criticism of David appears to derive from 2 Sam. 13:21, which relates that when David heard that his son had raped his daughter, he "became very wroth,"

"וַיִּחַר לוֹ מְאֹד" (*va-yiḥar lo me'od*). Yet David does nothing. David's inaction proves particularly surprising since the verb וַיִּחַר (*va-yiḥar*) appears numerous times in the Bible, each time followed by action of some sort on the part of the enraged person. See, for example, Gen. 30:2; 31:36; 39:19–20; Ex. 4:14; 32:19; Num. 11:1; 1 Sam. 11:16; 2 Sam. 6:7; Ps. 106:40, etc. On two occasions (Gen. 4:5 and 34:7), the action is slightly delayed, although it follows nonetheless. David alone reaches this level of powerful anger, anger that demands decisive action, yet none follows. This strikes the reader as strange, given the fact that the Bible and the Talmud both require punishment for one who engages in sexual intercourse with his sister (Lev. 18:9, 20:27; Deut. 27:22; *BT Yevamot* 22b and ff) as well as for one who rapes a virgin (Deut. 22:28–9). Amnon was guilty of *both* sins, yet David, king and administrator of justice, does nothing.

85 During the Talmudic period, Jews spoke Aramaic rather than biblical Hebrew. In order to understand the Bible when read aloud in synagogue, a "translator" repeated the text line by line in the Aramaic vernacular. This practice continues in some Yemenite communities, even in the modern day, when people no longer speak Aramaic as their mother tongue (or at all).

86 The fourth-century *Tosefta* to *BT Megillah* 25a–b (ch. 3, law 32) agrees. *Tosephta*, ed. M. S. Zuckermandel, with supplement by Saul Lieberman (Jerusalem: Wahrmann Books, 1970).

87 According to Maimonides in his legal code, the *Mishneh Torah*, when Amnon appears as "Amnon" one may read and translate, but when he appears as "Amnon son of David," one neither reads nor translates. See his *Mishneh Torah* (Jerusalem: Ḥ. Vagshal, 5744 [1984]), v. 1 (*Sefer Ahavah*), *Hilkhot Tefillah*, 12:12.

88 The other three parts of the "payment" likewise involve the fates of David's children: the death of the son born of David's adultery with Bathsheba (2 Sam. 12:15–19), the killing of Amnon by Absalom (2 Sam. 13:28–9), and the killing of Absalom by Joab (2 Sam. 18:9–17). The Talmud finds the source for this "four-fold payment" idea in 2 Sam. 12:16, David's ruling against a rich man accused of stealing a poor man's lamb: "And he shall restore the lamb fourfold." Since the case brought before David there was but a metaphor for David's own "stealing" of Bathsheba from Uriah, a metaphor crafted by Samuel, David's judgment of a "four-fold payment" was levied by God against David himself.

89 The obvious problem of the Talmudic discussion rests on the fact that four otherwise innocent human beings are forced to pay with their lives for David's sin, a deed in which they had absolutely no part and over which they had no control.

90 Qimḥi on 2 Sam. 13:15. The overarching rabbinic attitude toward David's righteousness can be summed up in a statement made about him in *BT Shabbat* 56a by R. Samuel bar Naḥmani, citing R. Jonathan: "Whoever says that David sinned is simply erring." The Talmud then gets into an argument about the viability of such a statement given that the Bible states explicitly that David sinned in the matter of Bathsheba and Uriah in 2 Sam. 12. While some rabbis attempt to exonerate David from even that sin, others maintain that the statement means to say, whoever says that David sinned *other* than in the Bathsheba incident is in error. James Diamond argues for an "ironic" reading of the many rabbinic texts classically understood to present David in the most righteous light possible. According to Diamond, the rabbis clearly wrote these texts with a heavy dose of irony, such that what appears to be a righteous reading of David is actually a scathing critique of the king and his behavior. See James A. Diamond, "King David of the Sages: Rabbinic Rehabilitation or Ironic Parody?" *Prooftexts* 27:3 (Fall 2007): 373–426.

91 Let us recall that David bedded Bathsheba *before* killing Uriah. He arranged to have Uriah killed in order to hide his sin by marrying the (Davidically impregnated) widow.

92 See Gersonides on 2 Sam. 12:7. In commenting on 2 Sam. 21:21, Gersonides adds that the "matter of Amnon" was caused by David's appointment of his sons to positions

of power during his own lifetime. Gersonides appears to mean here the death of Amnon, rather than Amnon's rape of Tamar; Amnon was the crown prince while Absalom was third in line for the crown. In killing Amnon, Absalom moved himself up the ladder, toward the seat of power.

Abrabanel adds punishments to the four normally recounted; he includes the death of the child that resulted from David's adultery with Bathsheba, the rape of Tamar, the killing of Amnon, Absalom's bedding of David's concubines (2 Sam. 16:22), Absalom's death at the hands of Joab (2 Sam. 18:14–15), and David's humiliation in having to run from a son who rebelled against him (i.e., Absalom, in 2 Sam. 15–18). See Abrabanel on 2 Sam. 13:20. Interestingly, Abrabanel also cites Qimḥi's theory of divine involvement, saying at the end, "And the thoughts of God are deep[ly mysterious]" ("ומחשבות השם עמקו").

93 Eveline van Staalduine-Sulman, *The Targum of Samuel* (Leiden, Boston, and Köln: E. J. Brill, 2002), 559.

94 The Talmud's comment appears based on a play on words on the title given to Jonadav in 2 Sam. 13:3; רֵעַ (*re'a*), meaning friend, is formed from the same consonants as רע (*ra'*), meaning evil.

95 This interpretation appears also in the somewhat later *Avot de-Rabbi Nathan* (*c.* 700–900) in warning against befriending evil people. See *Avoth de-Rabbi Nathan, Solomon Schechter Edition* [Hebrew] (New York and Jerusalem: Jewish Theological Seminary of America, 1997), version A, ch. 9 (p. 42). *TJon* translates literally: חכים (*ḥakim*).

96 Qimḥi on 2 Sam. 13:2.

97 For the various ways to read וַיִּפָּלֵא (*va-yipale*), see n. 5.

98 Abrabanel on 2 Sam. 13:1–9; Gersonides in his comments on 2 Sam. 13: 31. Abrabanel there refers to Jonadav as "יועץ בליעל" (*yo'etz beliya'al*, a good-for-nothing/evil advisor). Medieval Ashkenazi commentaries agreed with the Talmud and the Spanish exegetes. See *Midrash Sekhel Tov*, ch. 17; *Yalqut Shimoni 'al ha-Torah. Shemot* (thirteenth century, possibly Germany), ed. Dov Heiman and Yitzḥaq Shiloni (Jerusalem: Mossad Harav Kook, 1977), 42 (#169). This idea appears also in the first canto of a poem by the mid-eighteenth-century British poet Elizabeth Hands in *The Death of Amnon. A Poem* (Coventry: N. Rollason, 1789; reprint: London: Routledge, 1996), 29–31.

99 2 Chron. 13:2 renders his name as Abijah.

100 David was Abijam's great-grandfather (David→Solomon→Rehoboam→Abijam). There is no specific biblical Hebrew term for this relationship.

101 See his comments on 2 Sam. 11. Note his play on the word פשוט (*pashut*, simple) to indicate the superiority of the *peshat* approach over that of *derash*. On *peshat* vs. *derash*, see Chapter 1, pp. 15–16.

102 See Abrabanel's defense of David's behavior above, pp. 200–1. Abrabanel also attempts to exonerate David from not having punished Amnon as soon as he hears of the rape (2 Sam. 13:21). He points out that the punishment for incest with one's sister is כרת (*karet*), an undefined punishment issued by Heaven. An earthly court can inflict a punishment of lashes, but only if witnesses first warned the perpetrator not to act and then witnessed the event. In Amnon's case, the prince had dismissed all his attendants before seizing and attacking his sister (v. 9). Thus David, though king and head of the court, could not punish Amnon. Despite Abrabanel's justification of David's inaction, Abrabanel remained uncomfortable with the thought that David absented himself completely from the matter. Thus Abrabanel writes, "There is no doubt that he [David] rebuked him [Amnon] verbally, even if it is not mentioned in the text." See his comments to 2 Sam. 13:20. A similar rereading occurs in Elizabeth Hands's poem, *The Death of Amnon*, 29–31.

103 In his commentary to 1 Kings 15:5.

104 See Ibn Gabirol, *Shirei ha-Ḥol*, ed. Brody and Schirmann, 61 (#108); see above, n. 1.

7 The cloak of Joseph: Ibn Ḥazm and the therapeutic power of romantic love

Samuel ibn Gabirol was not the only Andalusian scholar-poet to incorporate seemingly problematic familial relationships from Scripture into his secular lust poetry. We find this phenomenon occurring also in a poem by his Muslim contemporary, our theologian-jurist-poet Ibn Ḥazm. Where Ibn Gabirol discomforts his readers by referring to the incestuous rape by a brother of his sister as a model for a romantic couple in his love poem, Ibn Ḥazm raises eyebrows by employing a father–son relationship in his. More specifically, the current discussion concerns a poem in which Ibn Ḥazm's narrator-lover compares the romantic and passionate love between himself and his beloved to the paternal–filial bond of love that the Muslim prophets Jacob and Joseph held for one another. While Ibn Gabirol utilizes an inappropriate family relationship in his lust poem, Ibn Ḥazm uses an otherwise innocent family relationship seemingly inappropriately.

As we have seen previously with Ibn Ḥazm's verses, his incorporation of a scriptural couple in a love poem presents readers with more than simply a surprising sacred image in the midst of an otherwise secular hymn to romantic love. Rather, as he did in his poetic integration of the Islamic accounts of al-Sāmirī and the dust of the golden calf, and of Ibrāhīm's stint in Namrūd's fiery furnace, here Ibn Ḥazm uses a scriptural image to teach his readers about the power of romantic love. In setting up his romantic lovers as a parallel to the father–son duo of Jacob and Joseph, Ibn Ḥazm once again champions the idea that romantic love is not to be criticized and censured. Even when the two partners are both males, as they are here, romantic love should be understood as pure, chaste, salvific, redemptive, even miraculous.

On contentment and a poem

Like Ibn Ḥazm's al-Sāmirī poem, which spoke of the lover consoling himself with the dust of his missing beloved's footprints, the poem under discussion can be found in the chapter on Contentment (القنوع, *al-qunū`*) in Ibn Ḥazm's treatise on love and lovers, the *Ṭawq al-ḥamāma*.[1] "On Contentment" discusses the behavior of lovers who, torn from the ones they love and prevented from nearness to them, seek contentment in alternate ways. As Ibn Ḥazm sensitively notes, lovers cannot live forever with the hole in their hearts caused by the absence of the beloved. Instead, they naturally and frequently seek to distract their souls from the pain of the situation, to provide themselves with a measure of relief, and to renew their hopes of union.[2] The most commonly recognized way for physically separated lovers to do this, he observes, is by their sending one another physical tokens. Indeed, asserts Ibn Ḥazm, he never saw any such separated couples who did not, at the very least, exchange perfumed, waxed, and beribboned locks of hair to serve as mementos of their love. So powerful is the desire to possess something that had once been in contact with the beloved, he adds, that such couples find themselves happily sending and receiving even already-chewed toothpicks and masticated gum.[3]

Proximity to even the smallest item that had once belonged to the beloved, notes Ibn Ḥazm, can "affect the soul in the most delightful way," bringing the lover contentment and relief.[4] Yet some poets take this notion to the extreme, he warns, writing of lovers who find contentment in recognizing that the same heavens spread out over both himself and his lover, or that the same earth supports them both, or that despite their separation, the two still live in the same time period. While Ibn Ḥazm proclaims that he himself composed a poem of this type, the likes of which no subsequent poet will ever be able to rival or excel in terms of artistic merit, he maintains that such verses have artistic value only.[5] Such sentiments, he avers, reflect nothing regarding the reality of the human condition and serve only to showcase the poet's verbal dexterity and fluency of expression.[6]

For Ibn Ḥazm, real lovers find contentment in actual contact with physical items, even small ones. Items that once belonged to the beloved, and not the intangible stars above, transmit the very essence of the yearned-for-beloved in his or her absence. These alone can provide the lover's soul with a great measure of comfort. Illustrating his point, Ibn Ḥazm writes that he composed the following poem that incorporates an example provided by God Himself:

لما منعت القرب من سيّدي ولجّ في هجري ولم ينصف
صرت بابصارى أثوابه او بعض ما قد مسّه اكتفي
كذاك يعقوب نبيّ الهدى اذ شقّه الحزن على يوسف
سمّ قميصًا جآء من عنده وكان مكفوفًا فمنه شفي[7]

[1a] When I was prevented from being near to my master
[1b] And he insisted on avoiding me and did not treat me justly,
[2a] I began to content myself with his dress,
[2b] Or was contented with something he had touched;
[3a] Thus Jacob, the prophet of true guidance,[8]
[3b] When the grief for Joseph caused him suffering,
[4a] Smelled the tunic which came from him,
[4b] And he was blind and from it got well.[9]

Andalusian tropes

Love and separation

The poem begins at the same starting point from which almost all عشق (*`ishq*, romantic love) poems begin: a bond of love unites two lovers. The depth of that love can be seen in the lover's somewhat unusual, but simultaneously stereotypical, reference to his beloved as "my master" (سيدّي, *sayyidī*, l. 1a). Lovers were well aware that the true stance of a lover was not one of arrogance and control, but of capitulation and meekness.[10] Raymond Scheindlin notes that this sense of submission and humility on the part of the Arabic and Hebrew Andalusian courtly lovers can be seen by opening any book of poetry at random.[11] The theologian, philosopher, and scholar of Arabic poetry al-Jāḥiẓ (*c.* 776/7–868/9, Basra) elucidates why this occurs. In his *Risāla fī al-`ishq wa-al-nisā'* (Essay on Passionate Love and Women), he explains that the source of the feeling of passionate love that afflicts lovers derives from its injuring the lover's manly sense of honor (مروءة, *murū'a*). Denied his manly masculinity, the lover is filled with a sense of submissiveness.[12] Not surprisingly then, while lovers frequently referred to their beloved as "friend," "adored one," or by a pet name such as "gazelle," our lover here chooses a title more reflective of this appropriate submissive attitude ("my master").

In further typical fashion, our poem speaks not of actualized love, with two happy and satisfied lovers, but, sadly and not unexpectedly, of a couple torn apart and unable to bridge the distance. Love poems almost never spoke of realized love, but of lovers mourning their physical alienation from one another and yearning, often without hope, for reunion.[13] Lois Anita Giffin points out that Muslim scholars were known to have debated whether sexual union (وصال, *wiṣāl*) with the beloved spoiled love by quenching the lover's desire or whether it inflamed love. The majority maintained that realizing one's desire did douse its flames; therefore, they taught, *`ishq* existed either only outside of marriage or before it, when union was not attainable.[14] Once union, وصال (*wiṣāl*), had been attained, a lover was left with no passionate material with which to inspire the muse of poetry.

Ibn Ḥazm's conformity to this trope of frustrated union appears immediately at the poem's opening. There the lover says unambiguously and typically (l. 1a), "[When] I was prevented from being near to my master" ("لمّا منعت القرب من سيدّي"). The subsequent lines flesh out this sense of separation. In depicting the lover as seeking comfort in the garments of his missing beloved, the poem emphasizes both the depth of the lover's feelings for his beloved and the physical distance that separates them and prevents them from union.

Cruel beloved

The sadistic behavior of the beloved in reaction to the forced separation from his lover likewise falls in line with the poetic tropes. While lovers often announce the anguish caused them either by their passion or by their separation from the beloved, or both, beloveds were famed for their pleasure in purposely increasing that suffering.[15] As al-Ṣabūnī (d. before 1240), the master poet of Seville, wrote of a cruel beloved, "Your reflection is easier to touch than you are; it treats me more kindly and is more faithful to its promises."[16] So we see in line 1b of Ibn Ḥazm's poem that the beloved boy does not work to bridge the distance between himself and his lover. Rather, as the lover moans in pain, the beloved remains hardhearted and insists on avoiding the one who so yearns for him. The beloved knowingly and purposely leaves his lover in a deplorable state, pining for even the smell of him, searching for it on something he has but touched. To make matters even worse, the beloved imposes this cruel treatment upon a completely innocent and undeserving victim, says the lover (l. 1b).

Love as suffering

The cruelty of the beloved often accompanied yet another trope, as it does here: the physical suffering caused to the lover by his passion for his missing and mean beloved. Although Ibn Ḥazm's lover does not mention his anguish outright, the flow of the poem leads us to see it quite clearly. We find the lover separated, against his will, from the one he yearns to be with, one he refers to as the "master" of his heart. Instead of both actors working to minimize the distance between them, his beloved knowingly engages in emotionally sadistic behavior that causes our lover pain and suffering. As he writes in line 1b, "he insisted on avoiding me and did not treat me justly." That he is suffering becomes clear from his comparing himself to the prophet Jacob. Just as Jacob's contact with Joseph's cloak brought him relief from suffering, from blindness, so too the lover's proximity to his beloved's clothes bring him relief from suffering. Lest we be fooled into believing that the lover's attempts will ultimately have the desired affect, in the opening to the chapter "On Contentment," in which our poem appears, Ibn Ḥazm warns us otherwise. Such attempts at self-consolation, he writes, remain within the sphere of an "illusion" or "distraction" for the soul;[17] although they divert one's attention from one's suffering, they are not a cure for it. Thus our lover, gazing at his beloved's clothes with high hopes of self-healing, still suffers.

Loyalty of the lover

Yet another well-known trope appears in the lover's insistence on remaining loyal to his beloved, despite both the unbridgeable distance between them and the latter's added cruelty. Lovers were expected to remain loyal and faithful to their beloved no matter what adversity and pain thereby presented itself to them. A lover who manages to "get over" his beloved was seen as a false lover, one whose emotions had been feigned from the beginning. A true lover, the Andalusians maintained, would never be able to "abandon" his beloved or his commitment to the beloved.[18] Reflecting this sentiment, Ibn Baqī, *muwashshaḥ* (multi-line strophic poems) poet of Cordoba/Toledo (d. 1145 or 1150), wrote, "If my tears should disappear, will people wink at each other and say: / 'He's already gotten over it' or 'He was never in love in the first place?' / Why don't they see my sighing as tears? But even when the turtle-dove cries, they say he sings."[19] To the Andalusians, the proof of real love lies in the lover's remaining faithful to his beloved even in the beloved's absence; if one but *appears* to be able to move on after the demise of a relationship, one might be accused of never having been in love in the first place, as Ibn Baqī's lover fears he might be.

In similar fashion, Ibn Ḥazm himself writes in his *Ṭawq* that a man who can manage to free himself from his bond to his beloved and forget him or her constitutes little more than a man of shameful character. In forgetting his beloved, he has violated the sacrosanct bond of fidelity and love.[20] Thus, not surprisingly, Ibn Ḥazm's lover here commits no such disgraceful act. Despite the distance between them, and despite the beloved's emotional brutality, our lover remains true and loyal. He does not abandon hope of union with his adored one and go off in search of a less problematic relationship. Rather, accepting the beloved's unkindness, he seeks contentment, not in the arms of another, but in something that same beloved has left behind.

Cause and cure

As in Ibn Gabirol's "*Amnon ani*" poem, discussed in the previous chapter, the final trope concerns the motif of love as cause and cure. Ibn Ḥazm himself writes, love "is an incurable disease and in it there is remedy against it."[21] The same element that brings about one's suffering constitutes the very element that has within it the power to save the lover from pain and destruction.[22] Thus while one's desire for one's beloved causes one much suffering and pain, one understands that the only cure for such an illness lies in union with the very same beloved.

This trope shines out clearly in our current poem. As the opening lines reveal, the beloved's absence and his insistence on enforcing the distance between them strikes the lover as an injustice through which he suffers ("When I was prevented from being near to my master / And he insisted on avoiding me and did not treat me justly, / I began to content myself with his dress ...). But while such behavior on the part of the beloved causes the lover's continued pain and suffering, the lover notes that only this same beloved can heal him. Ibn Ḥazm's lover does not look to content himself with drink, or seek solace in the arms of another.[23] He insists the only thing that can comfort him in his beloved's absence is something the beloved himself has once worn or touched ("I began to content myself with his dress, / Or was contented with something he had touched," l. 3a–b). Indeed so powerful is the healing power of the one who serves also as the cause of our lover's love-disease (*`ishq*), that the lover has only to *look* at the item for it to provide him with a sense of contentment. While Nykl's translation does not allow for us to see this, the original Arabic points clearly to this particular element: "صرت بابصاري اثوابه او بعض ما قد مسّه اكتفي" (*ṣirtu bi-abṣārī athwābahu aw ba`aḍa mā qad massahu aktafī*, I became content by my glancing at his clothes or at some of what he had touched). Arberry more accurately and poetically translates this as "Some garment wherein he had dressed / Something he had caressed – / To gaze on these, all else denied, / I was satisfied." Like the original Arabic, Arberry's translation emphasizes that the lover finds relief in simply gazing at the items his beloved has once touched.

"Like Jacob ..." – the lover and his scriptural referent

While the poetic tropes effectively transmit the poem's message of the suffering of the lover and his touching search for contentment, we soon see that the most powerful moment of Ibn Ḥazm's composition comes when the poet deviates from the secular motifs. In line 5 the lover transitions from the present tense, describing his own case and condition, to the Muslim sacred past, the scriptural case of Jacob and Joseph. As in the Hebrew poems, references to Scripture are not wholly without precedent in Andalusian Arabic poems and, to a certain extent, serve as a poetic trope.[24] And, as in the Hebrew poems, the Islamic references in the Arabic poems rely on and require the audience's familiarity with both the reference and its significance in the Islamic tradition in order to "work" and achieve the full effect. And so it is to the Qur'ānic narrative of Jacob and Joseph we now turn.

The story of Joseph in the Qur'ān[25]

The episode that forms the linchpin of Ibn Ḥazm's poem can be found in chapter 12 (*sūrat Yūsuf*) of the Qur'ān, the single longest-running narrative in the Muslim Scripture and the self-proclaimed "most beautiful of stories" ("احسن القصص" *aḥsan al-qiṣaṣ*, 12:3).[26] There we read of the trials and tribulations of Joseph, young son of the prophet Jacob, and his rise from obscurity to become the vizier of the land of Egypt. According to the Qur'ān, jealous of the favoritism their father Jacob showed their half-brother Joseph and his brother,[27] and declaring Jacob thereby to be suffering from a clearly wandering mind (v. 8), the rest of the sons of Jacob band together to rectify the situation and pull their father's love back in their direction. While one of the brothers suggests they slay Joseph, or at the very least exile him to some distant land, another advocates throwing him into a pit, where a passing caravan will likely find him and take him away (v. 9). The brothers then request of their father that he send Joseph with them to play, something it appears Jacob has not heretofore trusted them with. Faced with being parted from his beloved son for even an afternoon, Jacob initially balks at his sons' request. "Behold, it grieves me indeed to think that you might take him with you," Jacob says (v. 13), "for I dread lest the wolf devour him at a moment when you are heedless of him." Taken aback by Jacob's telescopic worry for only one of his sons, the brothers assure Jacob that if a wolf were brazen enough to attack while they were all present, not only Joseph but all of his sons would thereby perish. Such an argument appears to persuade Jacob, for the next verse relates that the brothers took Joseph with them and went off.

Away from Jacob, the brothers agree to enact their caravan-plan and throw Joseph into a deep well. They then return to Jacob at nightfall, weeping (v. 16). Now, despite their earlier assurances that a wolf would not attack only Joseph without also harming the rest of the group, the brothers claim that was exactly what had transpired. They had been racing one another, they explain to Jacob, and had charged Joseph with sitting with their things, and while they were thus preoccupied, a wolf came and devoured Joseph.[28] "But you will never believe us," they add sulkily and manipulatively, "even though we tell the truth" (v. 17). Before Jacob can react, the brothers produce Joseph's shirt, covered in false blood ("وَجَآؤُوا عَلى قَمِيصِهِ بِدَمٍ كَذِبٍ", *wa-jā'ū `alā qamīṣihi bi-damm kadhib*, v. 18). Despite the seemingly strong physical evidence, Jacob remains unconvinced of the truth of his sons' words and, though grieving, he says, "Your minds have made up a tale that may pass with you" (v. 18).[29]

At this pivotal point, the Qur'ānic narrative leaves Jacob and his sons to follow Joseph and his subsequent exploits in Egypt. We meet up with Joseph's brothers once again only some 40 verses later, after Joseph has been picked up by a caravan, sold to a man in Egypt, falsely accused of seducing and bedding the man's wife, imprisoned, successfully interpreted the dreams of the Egyptian king's imprisoned servants, successfully interpreted the king's own puzzling dream, acquitted of the charge lodged against him by his master's wife, and established as vizier in Egypt, in charge of the storehouses. When Jacob's sons reappear in the narrative, a famine has been raging in their home country, and the sons have traveled to Egypt in search of food. Now when they come before the Egyptian vizier, they do not recognize him as their brother Joseph (v. 58). He, however, recognizes them and, after providing them with food, he demands that the brothers return home and bring to him their brother who has stayed at home, one who has the same father as they do, but a different mother.[30] If they do not comply, they will receive no further grain. When the brothers return home and approach Jacob with this demand, he very reluctantly agrees to send his youngest son back with them. But when the brothers return to Egypt, tragedy strikes Jacob's family once again: the vizier hides his royal cup in the bag of this youngest brother, accuses him of theft, holds him hostage, and sends the rest of the brothers home.[31] Upon hearing of the loss of yet another son, Jacob accuses his sons of concocting still another story (v. 83). Jacob then declares, "How great is my grief for Joseph!" and, overcome, his "eyes become white with sorrow" (v. 84). Blinded by his grief, Jacob falls silent in melancholy.[32] Frustrated by their father's insistence on continuing to mourn for the long-gone Joseph, even in the face of newer problems, the brothers chastise him, saying (v. 85), "By Allah! You will never cease to remember Joseph until you reach the last extremity of illness or until you die!" But Jacob rejects his sons' complaint and, undaunted, sends them back to Egypt to enquire about both Joseph and "his brother" (v. 87). Reaching Egypt, the brothers note that they are once again low on funds and so they throw themselves on the vizier's mercy in their attempt to obtain food. Faced with his groveling brothers, Joseph reveals himself as their missing/sold brother. Now, apparently wanting to send word to Jacob that he is still alive or knowing somehow that Jacob has grown blind, Joseph sends the brothers with his shirt to their father. He instructs the messenger to place the shirt over Jacob's eyes, saying "he will come to see" (v. 93). Amazingly, as soon as the caravan leaves Egypt, Jacob announces that, although his sons may once again accuse him of being a fool, he most certainly has suddenly detected the scent of his son Joseph wafting toward him (v. 94). When the "bearer of good news" subsequently arrives and casts the shirt over Jacob's face, Jacob miraculously regains his sight; the family then travel en masse to Egypt, and father and son are joyfully reunited (vv. 96–100).[33]

The Islamic reference and the tropes of Andalusian poetry

Given our previous experience with Ibn Ḥazm's love poetry and its Qur'ānic references, we are not surprised to find that the Islamic account of Jacob and Joseph that he incorporates reflects many of the motifs so important to Andalusian love poetry. In fact, the scriptural referent in the poem's second half reflects and strengthens each of the poetic motifs that appear in the poem's first (Scripture-free) half. Specifically speaking, the Qur'ānic account of Jacob and Joseph includes the tropes of love hindered by an unavoidable separation, the continued loyalty of the lover in the face of continued adversity, the cruel beloved, and the trope of the cause of the lover's suffering functioning as its cure.

Further emphasis and development of each of these motifs emerge in the Islamic extra-scriptural renditions. Among those compendia relevant to our current conversation are the Qur'ān commentary and work on history by Muḥammad Jarīr al-Ṭabarī (838–923);[34] the compilations of extra-Qur'ānic narratives (*Qiṣaṣ al-`anbiyā'*, Stories of the Prophets) by Ibn Ḥazm's contemporary, Aḥmad ibn Muḥammad al-Tha`labī (d. *c.* 1035),[35] and by the later al-Kisā'ī (eleventh century)[36] and `Abdallah b. `Umar al-Bayḍāwī (d. 1286);[37] the biography (*sīra*) of Muḥammad by Ibn Isḥāq (d. 767);[38] and, the *qiṣaṣ* work of the Andalusian expert on Qur'ānic readings (*qirā'āt*), al-Ṭarafī (Cordoba, d. 1032).[39]

Love and separation

As is apparent from the review of the Qur'ānic account of Jacob and Joseph above, the similarities between the Islamic narrative and the situation described in Ibn Ḥazm's secular love poem can be seen in the basics of the storylines of both accounts. Namely, as in *`ishq* poetry in general and Ibn Ḥazm's poem here in particular, the scriptural story of Jacob and Joseph tells of two people bound together by special bonds of love. In this relationship, we find one partner – Jacob – playing the active role, akin to the lover, and one partner – Joseph – playing the passive role, akin to the beloved. This special bond of love, in which Jacob's heart attaches itself to his favorite child, Joseph, is presented at the scriptural narrative's onset. There, noting Jacob's reaction to Joseph's outrageous dream, in which the elements come to bow before him, Jacob's other sons enviously mutter to one another (Q 12:8), "Truly Joseph and his brother are more loved by our father than we are; but we are a goodly body!"[40] As the verse indicates, initially the brothers include Joseph's brother in Jacob's exaggerated affections. However, they realize that Jacob's love focuses a special lens on Joseph, that he is their father's super-favorite, and they react accordingly. In their jealousy, they conspire against Joseph only, plotting either to slay him or cast him out to a foreign land (v. 9). They request from their father that Joseph alone join them in the fields (v. 12), and ultimately they throw only Joseph into the pit and sell him away.

The sons' understanding that Jacob retains special affection for Joseph, and not his brother, becomes clearer in the Islamic exegetical texts that comment on and explain this passage. Al-Ṭabarī explains that the unique strength and power with which Jacob loved Joseph takes root the very moment Joseph was born. Jacob's other sons not only perceive this immediately, but they also see that Jacob grows exceedingly impatient whenever the young Joseph, and only Joseph, is absent. Because of his unique position in their father's affections, the brothers come to envy Joseph. And it is this envy, says al-Ṭabarī, that leads to their eventual ejection of Joseph from their midst.[41] Al-Tha`labī likewise notes that Jacob's special love for Joseph and his preferring Joseph over his other sons begins right from Joseph's birth. Each time a son was born to Jacob, al-Tha`labī explains, a new branch would sprout on a particular tree; Jacob would later cut that branch and give it to that son. Mystifyingly, no branch sprouted when Joseph was born. So Jacob prayed to Allāh to rectify the situation. In response to Jacob's prayers and much to his glee, the tree sprouted the requisite branch.[42] It appears that this miraculous response caused Jacob's love for Joseph to increase over the love Jacob felt for his other sons. Al-Ṭarafī and al-Bayḍāwī state, without specifying, that Joseph was dearer to Jacob than the rest of his sons "because of the tokens he saw in him." After Joseph reported his dream-visions to his father, says al-Bayḍāwī, Jacob's special love for Joseph intensified even more. Suddenly, Jacob found that he could not bear to be parted from Joseph. In response to this extra display of love for his young son, Jacob's other sons became more envious yet.[43]

Despite the intense bond of love that bound Jacob to Joseph, their time together did not last, an experience familiar to every Andalusian poetic couple. And, as in the case of separated couples, the physical alienation of Jacob from his beloved son is caused by elements other than his own doing. Unbeknownst to Jacob, his jealous sons plot to rid themselves of their pesky brother. Convincing their father that no harm will come to his dear Joseph, they take him out to the fields one day, grab him, and dump him into a pit. They then report to their father that a wolf devoured him, showing him Joseph's bloodied shirt as evidence. On the morrow they sell Joseph to a passing caravan who, in turn, sells him to a man in Egypt, thus setting off the extended period of separation that lasts for almost the entire remainder of the Qur'ānic chapter.[44] Like typical poetic lovers torn from one another by unnamed circumstances, and like the lovers of Ibn Ḥazm's poem, Jacob and Joseph thus find themselves cruelly separated from one another by events beyond their control and by a distance that they are unable to bridge.

Cruel beloved

An additional motif that appears both in the poem's first half and in our scriptural referent concerns Joseph's problematic behavior post-separation from his father. Although Joseph begins his traumatic adventure in chapter 12 as a captive and then a prisoner, he eventually rises to the position of vizier to the ruler of Egypt. Yet, like the cruel beloved who "insisted on avoiding" (l. 1b) the lover, thereby extending the distance between them and worsening the lover's suffering, Joseph makes no effort to contact his father even after his own rise to power. Instead, he allows his father to persist in suffering in his absence. What's more, instead of sending food to Jacob and his family during the years of famine, Joseph waits until his brothers travel to Egypt themselves. And then, rather than using the opportunity to send word to his surely worried father, Joseph cruelly begins toying with his brothers, accusing them of stealing, thereby causing his father further worry (12:58ff). Even more callously, Joseph forces his brothers to bring his full brother to him and then holds him hostage, causing his father even more anguish.[45] Like the poem's beloved who "insisted on avoiding me and did not treat me justly" (l. 1b), Joseph thereby plays the role of the cruel beloved to his father's yearning lover.

Suffering of the lover

Jacob's continued separation from his beloved and cruel Joseph causes our scriptural lover to suffer copiously, a typical motif. This we see both in Jacob's own testimony and in the words of his sons. Q 12:84 relates that after years of unending mourning for Joseph, Jacob learns that Joseph's full brother has now gone missing as well, detained by the Egyptian vizier. Turning away from his sons, an overcome Jacob cries out not for his second missing son, as the reader would expect, but for his already missing beloved. "How great is my grief for Joseph!" calls out Jacob. Jacob's sons are horrified by this telescoping of grief on Jacob's part. After all, Joseph is not the subject of the current tragedy. And so they exclaim in verse 85, "By God! Thou wilt never cease to remember Joseph till thou art broken in body and spirit or art dead!" Importantly, Jacob suffers not only emotional distress over his separation from Joseph. In true Andalusian fashion, his emotional state expresses itself in physical affliction. After learning that a second son has been detained in Egypt, Jacob not only falls further into grief for *Joseph* but, says the Qur'ān (12:84), "his eyes became white [blind] with sorrow and he fell into silent melancholy." Such physical distress was a common symptom, or result, of lovesickness. Love poems frequently tell of the lovesick lover unable to speak or move as a result of love-induced illness and weakness.[46] In many of these cases, the lover wastes away to the point that, as Ibn Quzmān wrote, "You would not see me / were it not that I still moan."[47] Jacob's affliction reflects these typical afflictions but with a twist. His mourning for his missing beloved results not in his becoming so ill that one can no longer see him, but in the loss of his own sense of sight. And, as just noted, in verse

85 Jacob's sons warn him that his incessant mourning will lead to even greater physical affliction, one likewise popular among the love-mourners in Andalusian poetry: death.

The idea that Jacob's suffering and eventual blindness were caused by his grief over Joseph's absence rather than by the more recent detainment of his second son appears in the Islamic exegetical texts as well.[48] Indeed, Joseph's name becomes so associated with causing grief and distress that some commentators make an etymological connection. Al-Tha`labī cites the teaching of Abū al-Qāsim al-Ḥabībī who explains that the Arabic name Yūsuf derives from the Arabic root اسف (*asf*), sorrow. Thus the name Yūsuf means "one who brings sorrow."[49]

Loyalty of the lover

The trope of the lover who remains loyal to his beloved in the face of all the pain and suffering appears in the poem's scriptural reference as well. Despite the time that has passed since Joseph's disappearance and the lack of indication that he will ever be reunited with Joseph, Jacob refuses to move on. He refuses to be comforted for the loss of his dear son and refuses to lavish his attentions on a substitute. Instead, though years have gone by,[50] Jacob's first reaction to hearing that Joseph's brother has been taken captive is not to mourn for the relevant son but for Joseph (v. 84), a reaction that greatly irritates his remaining sons (v. 85). Indeed, although the sons have made no mention of Joseph himself in their report, Jacob insists on bringing Joseph into the conversation. Sending his sons back to Egypt, Jacob says (v. 87), "O my sons! Go and enquire about Joseph and his brother, and never give up hope of Allah's soothing mercy." In remaining loyal and true to his missing beloved son Joseph, Jacob can be seen as reflecting the poetic motif of the true, long-suffering, and ever-loyal lover.[51]

Cause and cure

The final trope shared by both the poem's lover and our scriptural hero concerns the idea that love serves as both the cause of and cure for suffering. As noted above, the poem's lover sees his beloved in typical poetic fashion as the source of his pain (l. 1b, "he insisted on avoiding me and did not treat me justly"). Yet in his attempt to console himself by cozying up to something that reminds him of his beloved (l. 3b), the lover demonstrates that he also views his beloved as the only remedy for his illness.

Jacob, too, finds himself cured by the very person who stands as the cause of his suffering. As the Qur`ān relates, Jacob's love for Joseph causes his other sons' jealousy, which leads to their physically ousting Joseph from the family. It thus also leads to Jacob's incessant mourning for Joseph, and this causes Jacob's eventual blindness. As Ibn Ḥazm writes in his poem, "the grief for Joseph caused him [Jacob] suffering and he was blind," in other words, sorrow-induced blindness (l. 8). Joseph thus can be said to have served as the cause of Jacob's suffering. But Joseph also serves as the cure for Jacob's affliction, both in the Qur'ān and in the poem. When the Qur'ānic Joseph sends his tunic to his father and orders the "bearer of good news" to place it on his father's face, Jacob's grief-induced blindness miraculously disappears (v. 96). As Ibn Ḥazm writes (l. 4a–b), Jacob "smelled the tunic which came from him [Joseph] / and he [Jacob] was blind and from it got well."

While the Qur'ān attributes the cure for Jacob's blindness to the touch of Joseph's cloak upon his eyes, Ibn Ḥazm's poem here speaks of the *smell* of the tunic as medicinally healing. This perspective appears to have been influenced by exegetical readings of the Qur'ānic verses. The Qur'ān relates that Joseph's scent wafts toward Jacob as soon as the caravan departs Egypt (Q 12:94). According to the Islamic exegetical texts, the wind asked for and received permission from Allāh to bring the scent of Joseph to Jacob before the messenger arrived. So the wind shook out Joseph's shirt and carried that scent to his father.[52] Al-Tha`labī specifies that the shirt, created in Paradise, smelled of Paradise.[53] Ibn Ḥazm's poem combines the Qur'ān's verse with the exegetical explanation. The poem indicates that one ought to understand that when the messenger subsequently placed the shirt upon Jacob's face, he inhaled the scent that was known to be located there, and it was the scent that healed him.[54]

In some of the Islamic exegetical texts the interlocking of the cause and cure of Jacob's blindness appears even more sharply stated. These commentators note that just as Jacob's suffering was initiated by a shirt of Joseph's (Q 12:18), so it was subsequently cured by a shirt of Joseph's (Q 12:96). While the garment covered in blood kicked off Jacob's incessant mourning, the garment covered in Joseph's scent and aura cured Jacob of his grief-induced suffering. This cyclical fact was not lost on Joseph's brother Judah who, according to Qur'ān commentators, was the "bearer of good news" (v. 96) charged with bringing Joseph's shirt to their blind father. According to al-Suddī, when Joseph announced he was sending his shirt to Jacob, Judah stepped forward and said, "I was the one who brought the blood-soaked shirt to Jacob and told him that a wolf had eaten Joseph; today I will bring him this shirt and tell him that Joseph is alive, and I will gladden him as I had saddened him."[55] In other instances, the exegetes note that when Jacob saw Joseph's bloodied cloak and heard that his beloved son had been devoured, Jacob took the shirt and threw it over his face and wept until his face was stained by the shirt's blood.[56] Joseph's later throwing his shirt over Jacob's blind eyes to heal him thus reflects and undoes the very movement that had caused his sorrow in the first place.

Tropes added through use of the Qur`ānic allusion

Importantly, Ibn Ḥazm's reference to the Islamic narrative regarding Jacob and Joseph in the second half of his poem does more than simply support the tropes utilized in the first half. In poetically comparing the lover to Jacob and the beloved to Joseph, Ibn Ḥazm subtly incorporates two additional tropes into his verses. These concern the motif of the beautiful beloved and the concept of love as madness.

Joseph as the beautiful beloved

As we have seen time and again, while the love poems almost never describe the personality of the beloved, they almost always refer to the beloved's physical beauty. After all, Andalusian poems are not so much expressions of personal experiences and were possibly not even written with a real beloved in mind. Rather, they were intended as homages to beauty as an idea and ideal.[57] Interestingly, in the poem under discussion, while Ibn Ḥazm includes most of the other motifs so common in Andalusian love poetry, he deviates from the expected format and makes no mention of his beloved's physical appearance.

Or so it seems at first glance. When we consider the first half of the poem, we realize that Ibn Ḥazm's lover actually tells us quite a lot about the beloved's physical appearance and charms. In comparing his beloved to Joseph, Ibn Ḥazm indicates that, in true poetic fashion, his beloved possesses overwhelming and all-encompassing physical splendor.[58] After all, among the characteristics for which the prophet Joseph is legendary in the Islamic tradition, his beauty ranks high on the list. It is Joseph's loveliness that so enchants the wife of his Egyptian master, al-`Azīz, that despite both her higher rank and married status, she finds herself attempting to force him to bed her (12:22–9). When the Ladies of the City sneer at her for her infatuation with a lowly slave, the wife of al-`Azīz[59] slyly invites them to the palace for a banquet. Just as they raise their paring knives to the food, she calls Joseph to appear before the assembled company. Startled by the other-worldly beauty of the youth standing before them, the women accidentally slice their hands and exclaim (v. 31), "Allāh preserve us! No mortal is this! This is none other than a noble angel!"[60] Like the wife of al-`Azīz, the women find themselves captivated by the outstanding beauty of the boy, Joseph, who has appeared before them.

Joseph's beauty receives further praise in the extra-Qur'ānic texts. Al-Ṭabarī, al-Tha`labī, and al-Kisā'ī, to name but a few, note that along with his mother, Rachel, Joseph was more beautiful than any other human being.[61] Wahb ibn Munabbih taught more specifically that Allāh allotted ten measures of beauty to the world; Joseph received nine and the final measure of beauty was to be shared among the rest of mankind.[62] So often does the post-Qur'ānic Islamic literature refer to Joseph's extraordinary beauty, says Reuven Firestone, that it unintentionally somewhat mitigates the behavior of the wife of al-`Azīz; how can we blame her, he asks, given the powerful beauty that she found herself up against?[63] In incorporating Joseph into his poem in the role of beloved, Ibn Ḥazm presents his readers with the trope of the beautiful beloved par excellence.

The Joseph reference relates that the beloveds fit not only the requirement of overall comeliness, but also the specific tropes that spelled out the conventional forms a beloved's beauty was to take. For coincidentally or not, the Islamic sources describe Joseph's beauty in accordance with the very same standards. As noted earlier, in Andalusian poetry both boys and girls were praised for the whiteness of their faces, shining in the midst of their cascading black hair. This play on dark and light was often said to resemble the bright moon shining in the dark black sky.[64] Significantly, this very description appears time and again in the Islamic sources to describe Joseph's beauty. In one well-known *ḥadīth*, Muḥammad reports that while on his Night Journey and Ascension he met the prophet Joseph. Excitedly, the Companions questioned him as to what exactly the famously handsome prophet looked like. Replied Muḥammad, "Like the full moon at night."[65] In another *ḥadīth*, Abū Isḥāq b. `Abdallāh b. Abū Farwah relates that when Joseph would walk in the alleyways of Cairo, the radiance of his face would reflect from the walls around him "just as the light of the sun or the moon."[66] Al-Tha`labī relates that Joseph possessed a white birthmark between his eyes that "resembled the moon on the nights when it is full."[67] So common is this lunar description of Joseph that we find it appearing even in the words of the later Persian mystic and poet Jalāl al-Dīn al-Rūmī (1207–73). Speaking of his beloved, Rūmī writes, that he is "[a] strange Joseph, like the moon, who is reflected in a hundred wells."[68]

Other sources add more detailed descriptions of Joseph's incomparable beauty, many of which similarly fall exactly in line with the standard descriptions of attractiveness. Joseph's beauty, al-Tha`labī teaches, was like the light of the day, and his skin was white in color, a characteristic reminiscent of the white-faced beauties of Andalusian poetry. Furthermore, his face was handsome, his hair curly, and his nose curved;[69] he had large eyes, a flat belly, small navel, and strong arms, legs, and forearms. Like the later beloveds who resembled the tall palm tree, Joseph had good posture.[70] Like them, he too had a dark mole on his face that, in accordance with poetic standards, was said to have beautified it.[71] His eyelashes were like the feathers of eagles' wings. Like the teeth of the beloved, Joseph's teeth sparkled when he smiled, or glowed like pearls; light shone from his mouth when he spoke.[72] Al-Tha`labī's Cordoban contemporary, al-Ṭarafī, cites Ibn Kalbī's description of Joseph as a curly haired white man, with hulking arms and legs, a small navel, large eyes, and overall symmetrical physical constitution; he most resembled Adam in his appearance, and his face radiated light.[73] In comparing the beloved to such a well-known and oft-referred to Muslim standard of beauty, Ibn Ḥazm subtly provides his readers with this added trope.

Madness of Jacob

The second trope added by Ibn Ḥazm's reference to the Jacob–Joseph account concerns the trope of insanity that passion is said to bring to the lover. This connection between a lover's physical illness and his mental unwellness predates the Andalusian period of poetry. In his *Kitāb al-qiyān* (Book on Singing-Girls), al-Jāḥiẓ (*c.* 776/7–868/9) described *`ishq* as "a sickness that attacks the soul and spreads to the body by direct contagion."[74] In his *Risāla fī al-`ishq wa-al-nisā'* (Essay on Passionate Love and on Women), al-Jāḥiẓ expanded on this definition, adding that passionate love often so enflamed a man that it drove him to insane behavior and triggered erratic actions such as wandering "aimlessly about in a rapture."[75] The slightly later Arab scholar of poetry and poets Dāwūd al-Iṣfahānī

(897–967) more directly characterized the strength and effects of love on a person as a "divine madness."[76]

Ibn Ḥazm, like his predecessors, also understood the illness of *`ishq* to contain a psychological component. As he wrote, not only does one so afflicted not desire to be healed, a form of madness to be sure, but *`ishq* causes a man to see the world as an altered reality. Thus what one formerly disdained suddenly appears in his eyes as glamorous; even established temperaments and inborn dispositions become transformed.[77] In his chapter "The Signs of Love," Ibn Ḥazm describes the behaviors in which lovers engage as a host of erratic behaviors more attributable to one suffering from mental illness. These include brooding, sudden confusion and excitement, and manic-depressive-like mood swings. In support of his point, Ibn Ḥazm relates that once in Almeria, he was sitting with Mujāhid b. al-Ḥusayn al-Qayṣī in the shop of Ismā`īl b. Yūnus, a Jewish physician who was also an excellent physiognomist.[78] A man named Ḥātim was sitting in the corner of the shop, withdrawn. Pointing to Ḥātim, Mujāhid asked Ismā`īl to diagnose him. Ismā`īl looked at the man for a moment and then declared, "He is passionately in love (*`āshiq*)." Surprised at the doctor's correct diagnosis from afar, Mujāhid asked Ismā`īl how he knew. Ismā`īl explained that although the man appeared to all to be mentally disturbed, he, a doctor, was able to tell that the "extreme confusion" on Ḥātim's face was caused by love.[79]

In line with this understanding of love, in the Qur'ānic account of Jacob and Joseph we find people declaring Jacob's love for Joseph to constitute madness. From the very start, Jacob's sons maintain that his extraordinary love for Joseph has caused him to become afflicted with a form of mental illness. After noting Jacob's favoritism toward Joseph (and his brother), Jacob's sons remark (12:8), "إِنَّ أَبَانَا لَفِي ضَلاَلٍ مُّبِينٍ," "Really our father is obviously wandering (in his mind)!" Jacob appears to know that those around him believe his love for Joseph has caused a descent into madness. At the story's close, when Jacob smells the scent of Joseph wafting toward him as his son's caravan leaves Egypt, he proclaims (12:94), "I do indeed scent the presence of Joseph, nay think me not a dotard (لَوْلاَ أن تُفَنِّدُونِ)!" His words fall on deaf ears. In response to his declaration, those around him declare (v. 95), "By God! Truly thou art in thine old wandering mind (تَاللهِ إِنَّكَ لَفِي ضَلاَلِكَ القَدِيمِ)."[80] Although many years have passed, the charge of mental defect caused by love has not left Jacob. Even people other than his envious sons, people not personally invested in Jacob's psychological well-being, declare Jacob to be mentally incapacitated by his love for his beloved (Joseph). In referencing the Jacob–Joseph account, Ibn Ḥazm thus subtly includes the trope of love-induced insanity.

Jacob–Joseph as inappropriate scriptural reference

That a religious scholar such as Ibn Ḥazm composed a romantic poem that conforms to the tropes of secular love poetry fits well within the framework of Andalusian secular poetry. Scholars have shown that the secular poems written by religious figures play by the same rules as those written by secular, or a-religious, poets. They employ stock imagery, impersonalize love, and present chaste couples whose attempts to consummate the relationship are thwarted, leaving the lovers pining with lovesickness. Even the secular poets sometimes ornament their *`ishq* poems by incorporating scriptural narratives in which these same conventions can be detected. Thus Ibn Ḥazm's use of the Islamic Jacob–Joseph saga in his romantic poem does not prove out of the ordinary. This sacred account constitutes a touching and moving tale of love between two people, of the tragedy of their separation, of the pathos of yearning and suffering, and of the steps human beings take to content themselves in the absence of those they love. It is a perfect referent for an Andalusian poet.

And yet, despite all this, one cannot help but feel unsettled by Ibn Ḥazm's choice. For despite the sacred account's incorporating all the key motifs so important to and required by the Andalusian love poets, it is highly out of place in a romantic love poem. Most obviously, unlike the couple of our poem to whom they are compared, Jacob and Joseph are not romantically involved. They are, famously and significantly, father and son.[81] Despite the depth of their love, the strength of their bond, and the pain and yearning caused by their separation, the account of Jacob and his son Joseph cannot be seen as a tale of *`ishq*.

`Ishq *vs.* ḥubb

Muslim scholars have long distinguished between two categories of love, one which includes parental love of children, and one which must, by its very nature, exclude it. Al-Jāḥiẓ, the aforementioned ninth-century Mu`tazilī theologian and author of *Risāla fi al-`ishq wa-al-nisā'*, wrote of these two categories of emotions, with their disparate characteristics, as *ḥubb* (حبّ) and *`ishq*. *Ḥubb*, al-Jāḥiẓ wrote, denotes sentimental love and sentimental love only. This is the type of love used to describe how one loves (يحبّ, *yuḥibb*) God, or how God loves the believer, how a father loves (يحبّ, *yuḥibb*) his son, or a son loves his father, etc.[82] Al-Jāḥiẓ explains that while *ḥubb* constitutes the first stage of *`ishq*, it is not actually the same thing. As he writes, "[N]o one has ever known a man to fall sick and lose his reason out of *ḥubb* for his son or his country, *which is what this emotion is for*."[83] Conversely, he continues, we know of many who *have* died, after much suffering, from *'ishq*. This is not to say that one who finds himself separated from his son or country does not feel aching pangs at their parting. Al-Jāḥiẓ notes that one might experience even searing pain in such a case. Yet, that emotion should not be defined and categorized as *`ishq*. Love of one's child or of one's country remains in the category of sentimental love, *ḥubb*.

Even if one combines *ḥubb* with هوى (*hawā*, passion), the second stage of love, one will still not reach *`ishq*, insists al-Jāḥiẓ. A man in the grip of *hawā* may find himself under the sway of overpowering forces in the choice of the object of *hawā*, a state that resembles that of one in the grips of *`ishq*. Yet, this is still not the same emotion as *`ishq*. For unlike *`ishq*, *hawā* can be said not only of a lover, but also of religion, or one's love of country, or the like. When combined with sentimental love, the *ḥubb–hawā* combination can also be felt for a child, a friend, a country, even a type of clothing, carpet, or saddle-animal.[84] But it most certainly does not constitute that forceful pull a person feels for his romantic beloved.

`Ishq, al-Jāḥiẓ explains, requires that a third element be added to the mix: sexual attraction. According to al-Jāḥiẓ, this refers to the "natural attraction of men for women and women for men that is instinctive to the males and females of all animals."[85] The combination of sentimental love (*ḥubb*), passion (*hawā*), desire, and attraction, only this complete combination and nothing less, he declares, constitutes *`ishq*. Parent–child love lacks this romantic sense, this physical desire or sexual attraction. Thus, parent–child love, even one as strong as that between Jacob and Joseph, remains well outside the boundaries of *`ishq*.

This distinction between the romantic love that constitutes *`ishq* and the love between a parent and a child is maintained even by Ibn Ḥazm himself. In the prologue to the *Ṭawq*, Ibn Ḥazm engages in a long discussion of the nature and various types of love that exist between human beings. Only passionate love (*`ishq*), he writes, is "a reunion of parts of the souls, separated in this creation (world)."[86] Parent–child love, or, as Ibn Ḥazm terms it, "the love of kinship" or "of blood relatives," may be strong and it may be noble, but it does not constitute such a reunion.[87] Parent–child love, in Ibn Ḥazm's own determination, is not the same *stuff* as the love of two romantic partners. How then could Ibn Ḥazm use the Jacob–Joseph account, the story of the love of a father for his son, as the Qur'ānic image to which he compares the love of his romantic lovers in his poem?

The wife of al-`Azīz in the Qur'ān

Adding to our puzzlement at Ibn Ḥazm's problematic choice is the fact that in the very same Qur`ānic chapter where the narrative of Jacob and Joseph is found, we find a far better parallel that Ibn Ḥazm did *not* use. We speak here of the Qur'ān's account of the wife of al-`Azīz's attempted seduction of Joseph. Where the Qur'ānic and exegetical presentation of Jacob's love for Joseph remains in the realm of paternal love, the account of al-`Azīz's wife quite clearly presents a case of sexual romantic love, well in line with both al-Jāḥiẓ's and Ibn Ḥazm's definitions of *`ishq*.

Although this Qur'ānic narrative (Q 12:21ff) was mentioned earlier, in order to appreciate more fully the more fitting parallel it affords our poem, we return to it in more length. According to the Qur'ān, after the caravan of travelers pulled Joseph from the pit into which his brothers had thrown him, the travelers sell him to a certain man in Egypt, known as al-`Azīz.[88] Now it comes to pass after Joseph "attained his full manhood" (v. 22), that his owner's wife desires Joseph and wants to bed him. In a less than subtle move, she locks the doors upon them one day and says (v. 23), "Come unto me!" Despite the fact that Joseph desires her as well (v. 24), he will not be seduced; after all, not only is she married to his master, but Joseph is too righteous and pure to violate Allāh's law (vv. 23–4).

Joseph attempts to leave the room and she attempts to stop him from leaving and they race each other to the door, in their frenzy. Trying to prevent Joseph from escaping, the wife of al-`Azīz reaches out and grabs Joseph from behind as he runs from her, tearing his shirt. Seconds later, the door opens to reveal al-`Azīz himself standing there. Alarmed, the wife of al-`Azīz accuses Joseph of attacking her; Joseph protests his innocence. One of the members of the household notes that if the shirt is torn from the back, the truth stands with Joseph. And so it is. Al-`Azīz then chastises his wife, and charges her to beg forgiveness from Joseph. Now the "Ladies in the City" (v. 30) hear of the wife of al-`Azīz's passion for her slave and, gossiping about her, they accuse her of having lost her mind with love. Desirous of showing the women exactly what has so taken over her senses, the wife of al-`Azīz invites the women to a banquet she prepares for them, hands each a paring knife, and then summons Joseph. When he enters the room, the women find themselves so unmoored by his beauty that they cut their hands in shock, exclaiming (v. 31), "Allāh preserve us! No mortal is this! This is none other than a noble angel!" Thus the wife of al-`Azīz justifies her obsession and love-madness.

The wife of al-`Azīz and poetic tropes

As we can see, the Qur`ānic account of the wife of al-`Azīz contains all of the motifs of *`ishq* so important for an Andalusian love poem. In the first place, we find two lovers taken with one another in a passionate sense (Q 12:24). However, because they are mistress and servant, and she is already married, they are prevented from being together, as every good poetic couple is. When the wife of al-`Azīz finally does arrange for them to be alone together – reasoning, in good Andalusian fashion, that the cure for her love for him will be proximity to him – Joseph turns into the stereotypical cruel and heartless beloved, refusing to engage with her and racing to the door to abandon her. Joseph also plays the role of the prototypical beautiful beloved; when the Ladies of the City later catch sight of him, they declare that he must be an angel (12:31), so overwhelmingly handsome is he. Even the madness of love makes an appearance in the Qur'ānic account. Most obviously, the passion of the wife of al-`Azīz for Joseph leads her to such erratic and risky behavior as locking the two of them in a room together and then racing Joseph to the door, when al-`Azīz himself is standing on the other side (v. 25). Her less-than-sensible behavior is noted by the Ladies of the City, who assume she has lost her mind ("إِنَّا لَنَرَاهَا فِي ضَلَالٍ مُّبِينٍ", *inna la-narāhā fī ḍalāl mubīnin*, v. 30).[89]

*The wife of al-`Azīz and* **`ishq**

While the account of the wife of al-`Azīz and Joseph thus shares all the same love motifs as the Jacob–Joseph narrative, the former contains one key motif that the latter obviously and problematically lacks. Namely, the wife of al-`Aziz not only loves Joseph in a metaphysical sense, but desires him in a passionate sexual sense. As verse 24 clearly and unmistakably relates, "هَمَّتْ بِهِ" (*hammat bihi*), she desired him passionately.[90] Lest we think this is a case of one-sided infatuation, the verse quickly tells us otherwise: "وَهَمَّ بِهَا" (*wa-hamma bihā*), Joseph desired her passionately as well (v. 24). Unlike the case of Jacob and Joseph, here we have a clear case of a couple linked by passionate love and sexual desire. Here we find a clear-cut case of *`ishq*.

The extra-Qur'ānic commentaries on this episode likewise emphasize the *`ishq* nature of the account. In Q 12:20, the Ladies of the City gossip that the wife of al-`Azīz has fallen for her slave by saying "قَدْ شَغَفَهَا حُبًّا" (*qad shaghafahā ḥubban*, "he has inspired her with violent love," 12:30). Explicating this phrase, the early exegetes Mujāhid and al-Suddī` (seventh–eighth century) write: "Her love for Joseph reached the pericardium (شغاف, *shaghāf*) of her heart, entered beneath it, and overpowered it."[91] In a manner so typical of those afflicted with *`ishq*, love had pierced the wife of al-`Azīz in the heart and taken control of her, subjugating her. Others explain that love covered her completely or totally absorbed her.[92] Al-Bayḍāwī adds the element of the pain of *`ishq* to the wife of al-`Azīz's situation. He explains that the verb شغف (*shaghafa*) derives from a verb normally applied to a camel, meaning, "he smeared the beast with tar," thereby *causing the animal burning pain.*[93] Like the tarred animal which experiences a sense of burning, so the wife of al-`Azīz felt her love for Joseph as a pain burning in her heart. Ibn Waki` emphasizes the lunacy-inducing aspect of *`ishq*; one who is مشغوف (*mashghūf*), he writes, is the equivalent of one who is مجنون (*majnūn*), crazy or possessed by a spirit (*jinnī*).[94]

Lest one still misunderstand precisely what type of love burned inside the wife of al-`Azīz for Joseph, and inside him for her, the Islamic sources provide details. Al-Bayḍāwī says plainly that the Qur'ān's "هَمَّتْ بِهِ"/"وَهَمَّ بِهَا" (*hammat bihi/wa-hamma bihā*) signifies that the wife of al-`Azīz wanted sexual intercourse with Joseph and Joseph wanted the same of her.[95] Al-Ṭabarī cites a number of explicit, sexually charged possible scenarios. Either Joseph undid his belt and sat before her "as a circumciser sits" or he sat between her legs or he dropped his pants to his buttocks. Alternatively, the wife of al-`Azīz lay before him and he sat between her legs, or Joseph loosened her clothes as she lay before him, and/or he loosened his own, or he "sat with her as a man sits with his wife."[96] Al-Tha`labī, citing Ibn `Abbās, states that Joseph's desire grew so strong that he undid his waistband and stretched out beside the wife of al-`Azīz, just as an adulterous man does.[97] In all of these cases, sexual consummation is frustrated only at the last minute, as in the Qur'ān (12:24), when God miraculously intervenes to prevent Joseph from sinning.[98]

Indeed, so well affiliated with passionate love is the story of the wife of al-`Aziz that it formed the basis for numerous Ṣūfī love poems. As Islam's mystics, Ṣūfīs understood man to be in a constant state of yearning for immanent union with God (gnosis). Once a person had attained divine gnosis, he (or she) would have attained divine Love and knowledge. The narrative of Joseph and Zulaykha[99] (as al-`Azīz's wife is called in these texts) formed a fitting parallel for Ṣūfī writers; they saw a symbol of the Divine in the Qur'ān's portrayal of

Joseph as beautiful, righteous, and desired.[100] In similar fashion, Zulaykha's almost incessant and crazed yearnings for physical union with Joseph appeared to them to symbolize the Ṣūfī in his love of the Divine and quest for divine gnosis.[101]

So important was the story of Zulaykha's erotic urges for Joseph that the story served as the basis for at least two of the more enduring Persian epic poems, one by the Shī`ī al-Firdawsī (940–1020) and one by the Ṣūfī `Abd al-Raḥmān Jāmī (1414–92).[102] Interestingly, both poets shift elements found in the Qur'ānic Jacob account to the more obviously *`ishq*-infused Zulaykha. Both these epic poems relate that shortly after Joseph's release from jail and his appointment to be governor of the land, his former owner (Zulaykha's husband) dies. As a result, Zulaykha, who had never stopped longing for Joseph's love, suddenly finds herself with no money and no stature. Poor and pining, the formerly noble beauty loses her looks. Like Jacob in his mourning, her incessant yearning for Joseph results in the loss of her *eyesight*. Still desiring Joseph, she decides to build a hut by the wayside in order that she at least hear the sound of her beloved as he passes by. After much time passes in this manner, Zulaykha finally manages to gain admittance to Joseph's presence. But Joseph does not recognize the old, haggard, and ugly woman who stands before him. When she reveals her identity to him, Joseph finds himself moved with compassion for her and prays for the restoration of both her beauty and her eyesight. Just as Jacob's eyesight was restored thanks to Joseph, so, too, Zulaykha's returns to her, thanks to Joseph's prayers.[103] Newly rejuvenated in beauty, age, and sight, Zulaykha asks Joseph once again for union with her; in a surprising turn of events, this time he consents. They wed and she bears Joseph two sons. When Joseph eventually dies, Zulaykha falls into such sorrow at being "abandoned" once more by her beloved that she herself dies, but not before tearing her own eyes out, blinding herself once again.[104]

An embedded message deciphered

Given the existence of the account of the wife of al-`Azīz not only in the Qur`ān and in the extra-scriptural commentaries, but also in the popular and well-known corpus of Ṣūfī poetry, we are left to puzzle even more over Ibn Ḥazm's poetic choice. As we have seen, Jacob and Joseph remain steadfastly father and son, an inappropriate couple for a homosexually charged lust poem. By contrast, the Muslim accounts of the love, yearning, suffering, burning, and even blinding-then-healing of the wife of al-`Azīz provide a far more apt parallel in speaking of the power of and characteristics of *`ishq*. As a theologian, jurist, and scholar, Ibn Ḥazm would have been aware of the intricacies of both narratives. So why does Ibn Ḥazm insist on employing the Jacob–Joseph image as a metaphor, a particularly unseemly one, in his homoerotic lust poem?

When we reconsider Ibn Ḥazm's choice carefully, we realize that it is not actually as ill-fitting as it might seem. Andalusian tropes of love poetry were based on earlier Arab (`Udhrite) motifs in which the actualization of love is so frequently frustrated that such poetry is known as "pessimistic love poetry."[105]

In similar fashion, these unrealized love poems more often than not speak of such love as an ideal form, chaste and decorous. To what better image could one compare idealized romantic love than to the pure love between parent and child? In comparing the connection between the lover and beloved to that between Jacob and Joseph, Ibn Ḥazm raises an otherwise earthly, lustful love between a man and his beloved to a metaphysical level. Says Ibn Ḥazm's poetic lover: Do not imagine me as a pathetic, depraved person sniffing at the delicates of his absent beloved, as it might appear to you at first. Rather, picture me in your mind's eye as you would picture Jacob in his yearning for his son. Like Jacob's love, my love, he says, is the pure unadulterated love of a parent yearning for an absent child. My visual caress of my beloved's empty clothes is akin to the passion of a parent who cannot bring himself to move one item in his missing child's room, a parent who periodically caresses the child's bedspread for comfort and strength.

Had Ibn Ḥazm used the account of Zulaykha's love for her slave Joseph, this most important message about *`ishq* would have fallen by the wayside. After all, Zulaykha's love is the very opposite of chaste and decorous. In the first place, despite her royal status, she very unbecomingly chases her slave boy around the room, desperately grabs at his shirt until it tears, attempts to cover up her actions by lying, and then has him sent to jail. Additionally, in inviting the Ladies of the City to view Joseph, she herself explains that it is Joseph's overwhelming physical beauty, and seemingly little else, that has incited her lust for him. Through her invitation, the wife of al-`Azīz announces quite clearly that the only element that bonds her to Joseph is sexual attraction, and nothing more – no spiritual, emotional, or psychological ties make even the wisp of an appearance. In rejecting this scriptural example and choosing the narrative of Jacob–Joseph instead, Ibn Ḥazm more accurately transmits the sense of love as an ideal and chaste form.

But it is not just the sense of purity that differentiates Jacob's passion for Joseph from Zulaykha's. The account of Jacob's love for his son contains an even more important and critical message regarding *`ishq*, one critical to Ibn Ḥazm's poem but lacking from the account of the wife of al-`Azīz. Namely, the love that exists between scriptural father and son is miraculously healing. As Q 12:96 relates, Joseph's cloak cures Jacob of his sorrow-induced physical blindness. This element of the story was not incidental to Ibn Ḥazm; it is the very point of the scriptural reference in his poem. In comparing the lover's situation to that of Jacob–Joseph, the lover attributes the very same healing powers to *his* beloved. When he gazes on something his beloved has touched or worn, he finds himself miraculously healed of the sorrow and illness caused by his grieving for his absent beloved, as Jacob was.[106]

In comparing the beloved to Joseph and the lover to the healed Jacob, Ibn Ḥazm sends an additional message about the nature of human love: Its power is divine. Significantly, the Islamic sources relate that Joseph's cloak retained its powers from Allāh Himself. According to these sources, before Joseph's brothers lowered him into the well, they first stripped off his shirt.[107] Joseph called to them to return some clothing to him, pleading that they not leave him to die naked. The brothers callously refused, mockingly replying that if Joseph wanted something he should request it of the sun, moon, and stars of his dream.[108] Now when Abraham had been thrown into the fiery furnace prepared for him by the evil king Namrūd, relate the Islamic sources, he too was stripped naked. Allāh sent the angel Gabriel to him to dress him in a shirt. This was not just any shirt, but one made of the silk of Paradise. Abraham's son Isaac inherited this shirt when Abraham died, and Jacob inherited it from Isaac when Isaac died. Jacob later took the shirt and placed it in an amulet that he then hung around Joseph's neck.[109] When Joseph was thrown naked into the pit, an angel – some say Gabriel – came to him, took the shirt out of the amulet, and clothed Joseph in it. This shirt, made from the silk of Paradise, was the very garment that Joseph later sent to Jacob with instructions to place over his father's face. This divinely created and divinely provided shirt was the very one that healed Jacob of his blindness.[110] And it is this divinely created and provided shirt to which the lover compares his beloved's clothing. In so doing, the lover insinuates that his love, like that between Jacob and Joseph, is divinely sanctioned and protected. His beloved's healing powers derive not from some sort of black magic, but, like the power of Joseph's cloak, originate in Allāh himself.

We ought to note that the conceptualization of human love and passion as a powerful, divinely sanctioned, and redemptive element does not contradict classical Islamic teachings. Numerous *ḥadīth* deal with sexuality and sexual issues, and not necessarily in a condemnatory voice. One such oft-cited *ḥadīth*, transmitted by Muḥammad's wife `Ā'isha, relates that the ex-wife of Rifā`a al-Quraẓī once came to Muḥammad to complain. It seemed her new husband, `Abd al-Raḥmān b. al-Zubayr, was a man of unsatisfyingly small proportions, sexually speaking. In explaining what she meant, she held up the fringe of her garment as a visual aid.[111] Khālid b. Sa`īd, who was standing by the door, objected to such a frank discussion of sexuality and sexual behavior in front of the Prophet of Allāh. He cried out to Muḥammad's companion, "O Abū Bakr! Why do you not stop this lady from saying such things openly in front of Allāh's messenger?" Muḥammad, however, remained unfazed. Says the *ḥadīth*, "Allāh's messenger did nothing but smile." Then, turning to the woman, he gently ruled that she could not return to Rifā`a until she consummated her marriage with her current husband.[112]

Other traditions more brazenly link human sexual desire to religion. In one, a pure secret love for a human being is unproblematically compared to religious martyrdom; one who suffers and sacrifices himself in secret love for another resembles the martyr who dies because of his unwavering devotion to Allāh. More significantly, some Meccan contemporaries of Muḥammad reported that Muḥammad himself often spoke of his feelings for Allāh with the word *`ishq*, passionate romantic love.[113] In other words, the idea that one could speak of a man yearning for union with the sacred as one yearned for physical union with one's beloved struck the early traditionalists as completely within the realm of acceptable speech and consideration.

This religiously accepting approach toward human love and sexuality appears among the Andalusian scholars as well. Ibn Ḥazm himself writes, "Love is neither disapproved by religion nor prohibited by the Law." After all, he explains, every heart "is in God's hands."[114] He adds that many righteous caliphs and orthodox imams, some of whom he names, have been famous lovers. So, too, he writes, many respected pious men and experts/scholars of religious legal experts from the present and the past have composed love lyrics testifying to their passion, including `Ubayd Allah b. `Abd al-`Utba b. Mas`ūd, one of the famed Seven Jurists of Mecca.[115]

Summary

While Ibn Ḥazm's comparison of the passions of the lover and beloved to the father and son duo of Jacob and Joseph originally appeared awkward and misplaced, we now understand better the brilliance of such a move. Had Ibn Ḥazm employed the account of the wife of al-`Azīz's passion for her slave boy, an account that seems at first glance to be far more appropriate, his poem would not have sent any messages about the nature and character of earthly love. The parallel between the lover comforting himself by gazing at his absent beloved's things and the restoration of Jacob's sight by placing Joseph's shirt over his face enables Ibn Ḥazm to teach his readers a lesson about the power of human love. Namely, just as parent–child love is pure and unsullied, so too the passionate love between the lover and his beloved remains pure and unsullied. Just as the cloak of Joseph was miraculously healing of Jacob's blindness, so too the items touched by the beloved will miraculously heal the lover. In comparing his situation to that of the prophets Jacob and Joseph, the lover explains that just as the love between them was redemptive and salvific, so too the love between himself and his beloved is redemptive and salvific. And even more, as Jacob understood the situation to have been under the control of Allāh (Q 12:86), so too, implies Ibn Ḥazm's lover, our love is sanctioned and protected by the Divine.

Taken on its own, the message of the story of Joseph differs little from the messages of the other stories in the Qur'ān and of the Qur'ān in general. We find here lessons about Allāh's ultimate control of the universe, urgings to trust in the one God, and an emphasis on righteousness and good behavior under all circumstances. Indeed, Suzanne Pinckney Stetkeyvich has written that, within the context of the Qur'ān, the chapter of Joseph teaches that righteousness leads to salvation much as its other chapters do. Taken out of the Qur'ānic context, she notes, the homoerotic element of the story emerges.[116] In utilizing the Qur'ānic narrative in a secular love poem, Ibn Ḥazm has managed to combine the sacred text's two elements. On one hand, he lifts the account out of its sacred context and unabashedly applies it to a love poem that speaks of the passionate love between two men. Yet while he does so, Ibn Ḥazm simultaneously uses the Qur'ānic narrative for its religious message: like love of God, love of Man (His creation) is equally salvific and redemptive.

Notes

1 On the nature of the *Ṭawq* and the reasons for Ibn Ḥazm's writing it, see the discussion in Chapter 3, pp. 84–5 and Chapter 5, 149.
2 Ibn Ḥazm, *Ṭauḳ al-ḥamâma*, ed. Pétrof, 8; English translations: Arberry, trans., *The Ring of the Dove*, 183; Nykl, trans., *A Book Containing the Risāla*, 137.
3 *Ṭauḳ*, 90 (Arberry, 185; Nykl, 139). An earlier poetic example of separated lovers exchanging trinkets appears in a Hebrew poem by the wife of the Hebrew poet Dunash ibn Labrat (920–90), in which she writes touchingly of a doe and her beloved, poised at the moment of parting. In order that they not forget one another during their separation, she gives him her bracelet and he gives her his ring. They also exchange cloaks. See Fleischer, "*'Al Dunash ben Labrat*," 189–202. An English translation can be found in Cole, trans., *Selected Poems of Solomon Ibn Gabirol*, 7.
4 He writes that he was once astonished to see a man kissing the place of a wound he had received when his beloved stabbed him. When questioned about this odd behavior, the man explained that he found his wound dear to him, for it reminded him of his beloved. *Ṭauḳ*, 90 (Arberry, 185; Nykl, 138).
5 Boasting about one's poetic talent and skill appears to have been a well-established poetic characteristic. Ibn Wahbūn (d. *c.* 1087, Murcia) wrote in a poem that the famed and egotistical Iraqi poet al-Mutanabbī (915–65) "claimed to be a prophet because of pride in his poetry, but if he had known that you would recite it, he would have claimed to be a god." See Ibn Sa'īd al-Andalusī, *Rāyāt al-mubarrizīn*, 198–9. English translation from Bellamy and Steiner, *Banners of the Champions*, 93 (#87). Solomon ibn Gabirol (1021–58), at the age of 16, boasted of his own poetic skills: "I'm prince to the poem, my slave / I'm harp to the court musicians, / my song is a turban for viziers' heads, / a crown for kings in their kingdoms." Translation by Cole in his *Selected Poems of Solomon Ibn Gabirol*, 45. The Hebrew original appears in Ibn Gabirol, *Shirei Shelomo ben Yehuda ibn Gabirol*, 77 (#129) and in Ibn Gabirol, *Shirei ha-Ḥol*, ed. Jarden, 1:225 (#109).
6 *Ṭauḳ*, 93–4 (Arberry, 193–5; Nykl, 143–4). A modern take on the idea that people who love one another but are separated are comforted by reminding themselves that they live in the same age, under the same sun, etc., appears in the song "Somewhere Out There" by James Horner, Barry Mann, and Cynthia Weil, from the 1986 animated film, *An American Tail*. The film tells of Feivel Mousekewitz's immigration from Russia to America, where he becomes separated from his parents and his beloved sister Tanya. One night, missing one another terribly, the siblings sing of the bond between them and of their hope at being reunited. In the meantime, they comfort themselves by singing, "And even though I know how very far apart we are / It helps to think we might be wishing on the same bright star. / And when the night wind starts to sing a lonesome lullaby / It helps to think we're sleeping underneath the same big sky." Ibn Ḥazm would disagree; it doesn't help.
7 *Ṭauḳ*, 90–1.
8 Meaning, a prophet rightly guided by Allāh.
9 English translation by Nykl, 138–9. I have included the line numbers; they do not appear in Nykl's text.

Both Nykl's and Arberry's translations refer to the beloved in the feminine form: "mistress" (l. 1a), "she" (l. 1b), "her" (l. 2a–b). The Arabic, however, consistently presents the beloved in the masculine, e.g., "سيدي" (*sayyidī*, my master). I have altered Nykl's translation here to reflect the Arabic more accurately. Early scholars and translators often tried to avoid admitting that the religious poets of Islamic and Jewish Andalusia wrote poems to male beloveds, and were known to shift the beloved's gender in their translations. Sometimes the claim was made that the poet had intended a female beloved but used the male pronoun out of modesty concerns. See Pellat, "Liwāṭ," 157. Other scholars point out that such heterosexual rereadings of the poems are unnecessary. Raymond Scheindlin, for example, maintains that the use of the masculine gender was intended to create an atmosphere of indefinite sexuality, rather than maleness; the beloved, he notes, was the embodiment of the ideal of beauty rather than an actual person. Norman Roth takes the opposite stance, insisting that the use of the masculine gender did intend a masculine beloved. He points out that Andalusian love poetry was divided into two categories, *mujūniyyat* (love poems about girls or women) and *ghazāliyyāt* (love poems about boys). Similarly, Everett Rowson points readers to poems that hotly debated the comparative merits of males or females as sex partners, focusing on practical considerations (boys do not become pregnant, but sexual intercourse with females is less "messy") and further demonstrating that boy lovers, and poems to them, did exist. What's more, Rowson notes, the two categories were not understood to be mutually exclusive. The very same poet could and did write love poems to both females and males. See Bellamy and Steiner, *Banners of the Champions*, xxix; Roth, "Religious Constraints," 197; idem, "The Care and Feeding of Gazelles," 107; Rowson, "The Categorization of Gender," 58–9; Scheindlin, "A Miniature Anthology," 110; Schirmann, "The Ephebe," 56, 66. For more, see Chapter 2, pp. 51–2.

Schirmann also refers to H. Pérès's earlier insistence that not only did both Arabs and Jews compose poems in honor of the beautiful boy, but the boys themselves could have been either Muslim or Jewish, regardless of the religious identity of the poet. He quotes a poem by Ibn al-Zaqqāq (*c.* 1096–1134) in which the poet writes that his love for his Jewish "boyfriend" is so great that even though he is a Muslim, he has come to love the Sabbath. For Pérès, see Schirmann, "The Ephebe," 66. For Ibn al-Zaqqāq's *dīwān*, see Ibn al-Zaqqāq, *Dīwān*, ed. `Afifa Dairān (Beirut, 1964).

10 In the *Ṭawq*, Ibn Ḥazm devoted an entire chapter to "Submission." There he includes a poem that begins, "Submission in love is not odious / for in love the proud one humbles himself: / Do not be surprised at my docility in my condition / for before me al-Mustanṣir has suffered the same lot!" Nykl, 62. Pétrof (40) records the word translated here as al-Mustanṣir as المستبصر (*al-mustabṣir*, the one who seeks to see or understand something plainly); this makes little sense in this context ("قد ذل فيها قبلي المستبصر"). Perhaps because of this, Arberry (89–90) leaves out the caliph's name altogether in his translation: "Then do not marvel so at me / and my profound humility; / ere I was overthrown, this state / Proud Caliphs did humiliate." In his edition of the *Ṭawq*, Nizār Wajīh Fallāḥ corrects Pétrof's "المستبصر" to "المستنصر," al-Mustanṣir. In a footnote, Fallūḥ identifies him as al-Mustanṣir b. `Abd al-Raḥmān al-Nāṣir b. Muḥammad b. `Abdāllah (*c.* 914–76), also known as al-Ḥakam al-Mustanṣir, who inherited the Cordoban caliphate from his father at the latter's death in 961. Al-Mustanṣir was known for his erudition in religion, Arabic literature, and history, as well as for his affection for the *'ulama'* (Muslim religious scholars) and for his book-collecting. The caliph became infatuated with a Basque woman named Subḥ, whom he married and whose son (Hishām) he subsequently favored over all of his other sons. See Abū Muḥammad `Alī ibn Ḥazm al-Andalusī, *Ṭawq al-ḥamāma*, ed. Nizār Wajīh Fallūḥ (Sidon-Bayrūt: al-Maktaba al-`Aṣrīyya, 1422/2001), 102, fn. 3 and 47, fn. 1. Ibn Ḥazm mentions this love affair in the chapter on "The Nature of Love," in *Ṭauḳ*, 6 (Nykl, 6; Arberry, 22).

11 See Raymond Scheindlin, "Fawns of the Palace and Fawns of the Field," *Prooftexts* 6:3 (Sept. 1986): 194.

12 The lover's submissiveness extends not only to the beloved, but also to those surrounding him or her. Al-Jāḥiẓ's explanation appears in Giffin, "Love Poetry," 115.

13 Almost any Andalusian love poem, Arabic and Hebrew, will include this trope. Some particularly nice examples have been penned by Ibn Jākh of Badajoz (fl. 1042–68), the *qāḍī* and *faqīh* Abū Ḥafṣ `Umar b. `Umar of Cordoba (d. 1207), al-Mu`tamid, king of Seville (d. 1095), and the female poet Ḥamdah bt. Ziyād of Gaudix (fl. twelfth

century). These can be found in *Rāyāt al-mubarrizīn*, 97–8, 130–1, 46–9, 167–8 [Bellamy and Steiner, *Banners of the Champions*, 178 (#167), 177 (#166), 184 (#173), and 179 (#168)]. Ibn Ḥazm himself also wrote, "لئن أصحبت مرتحلًا بشخصي \ فقلبي عندكم ابدًا مقيم," "Though my body departs, my heart stays with you always." *Rāyāt al-mubarrizīn*, 118–19 [Bellamy and Steiner, *Banners of the Champions*, 185 (#174)]. Shulamit Elizur discusses this phenomenon in the context of Hebrew poems in *Shirat ha-Ḥol*, 2:74–8.

14 See Giffin, "Love Poetry," 123. Giffin adds that the Sunnī Ḥanbali jurist, philosopher, Qur`ān commentator, philosopher, philologist, and astronomer Ibn al-Qayyim al-Jawziyya (1292–1350) argued the opposite. According to Ibn al-Qayyim, true passion grows stronger and more delightful after lawful union. Only sinful union quenches *`ishq*. This opinion was not shared by the Andalusian poets.

15 As we have seen in previous chapters. A particularly good Hebrew example appears in Samuel ha-Nagid, *Diwan Shemuel ha-Nagid. Ben Tehillim*, 306 (#186), "היא שלחה בינות לחומי אש" ("She has sent a fire").

16 The entire poem can be found in *Rāyāt al-mubarrizīn*, 74 [Bellamy and Steiner, *Banners of the Champions*, 170 (#159)].

17 "وانّ في ذلك لمتعلّلًا للنفس" (*wa-inna fī dhālika lamuta`allilan lil-nafsi*), in *Ṭauḳ*, 89 (Arberry, 183; Nykl, 137).

18 As mentioned in Chapter 5 (p. 150), this sentiment is exemplified in a poem by Ibn Zaydūn (1003–70), lover of the princess Wallāda.

19 Bellamy and Steiner, *Banners of the Champions*, 171 (#160). The Arabic can be found in *Rāyāt al-mubarrizīn*, 136–8. The poet's full name appears there as Abū Bakr Yaḥyā b. Muḥammad b. `Abd al-Raḥmān al-Qaisī al-Qurṭubī. Ibn Baqī's use of the turtle-dove in this poem requires the reader to remember that turtle-doves are known both for their mournful voices and for their forming strong pair-bonds, making them emblems of devoted love. See the use of turtle-doves in Song of Songs 2:12.

20 *Ṭauḳ*, 99 (Arberry, 202–3; Nykl, 153). Ibn Ḥazm allows for one exception. If a lover finds himself cuckolded, his deep-seated pride may truly and completely erase his feelings for his beloved from his heart and mind. Such a reaction, he writes, is not only understandable but justifiable. See *Ṭauḳ*, 105 (Arberry, 214; Nykl, 162). See also Chapter 5, n. 7.

21 As phrased by Nykl, 13 (*Ṭauḳ*, 11; Arberry, 31).

22 For more on this trope, see Chapter 6, p. 183. See Elizur's discussion on this topic in 2:74–8. For an example of this same trope in a poem by Samuel ha-Nagid (993–1056), Ibn Ḥazm's contemporary, see Samuel ha-Nagid, *Diwan Shemuel ha-Nagid. Ben Tehillim*, 302 (#175, תרופה בפניה). An English translation appears in Roth, "The Care and Feeding of Gazelles," 102.

23 Eddy Zemach and Tova Rosen-Moked maintain that there *are* Andalusian poems that speak of this. See their analysis of Samuel ha-Nagid's poems, "שימה ימינך" ("Place your right hand") and "אמת כי צבי לוקט" ("It is true, a gazelle is gathering"), in their *Yetzirah Meḥukama*, 128–34. In both poems, Zemach and Rosen-Moked maintain that the lover has taken a second boyfriend and wants his permanent beloved to accept that fact. The poems can also be found in Samuel ha-Nagid's *dīwān*, *Diwan Shemuel ha-Nagid. Ben Tehillim*, 309 (#194) and 297 (#162). In a response article to Zemach and Rosen-Moked, Ezra Fleischer strongly disagrees with this reading. See Ezra Fleischer, "`Al Guf ha-Shir ve-Libo," *Moznayim* 57:3 (Elul 5743) [August 1983]: 56–7. In a poem by Samuel ha-Nagid found on the same page as שימה ימינך ("Place your right hand"), we read of the lover's refusal to betray his beloved this way. See *Diwan Shemuel ha-Nagid. Ben Tehillim*, 309 (#192, מה זה אשלם לדודי, "How shall I pay back my beloved").

24 See the two previous chapters on Ibn Ḥazm's poems. As David Yellin notes, "hinting" to Scripture was not unique to the Jews; Arab poets hinted to and incorporated

elements from the Qur`ān and the literary history of Arabic poetry and poems. See his *Torat ha-Shir ha-Sefaradit*, 103–17.

25 The biblical version of this same narrative runs from Gen. 37–50. The Qur'ān's version is not identical to the Bible's. For example, while the biblical Joseph dreams two dreams (Gen. 37), the Qur'ānic Joseph dreams only one. The biblical Jacob sends Joseph to join his brothers' shepherding activities and instructs him to report back to him. In the Qur'ān, Joseph joins his brothers only after they request that Jacob send Joseph with them to play. In the Qur'ān this forms part of their plot to do away with Joseph. In the Bible, it is a lucky happenstance for the resentful brothers.

26 According to al-Bayḍāwī (Fars, d. 1286), certain Muslim sects rejected the inclusion of chapter 12 in the Qur'ān on the grounds that the story was apocryphal. These were two branches of the Khārijīs: the Ajāridites and Maimūnians. See John Macdonald, "Joseph in the Qur'ān and Muslim Commentary," *Muslim World* 46 (1956): 113. On al-Bayḍāwī, see below, n. 37 and Chapter 3, n. 55. The Khārijī claim of chapter 12's apocryphalness puts v. 111, in which the Qur'ān declares its truthfulness, in a particularly complex light.

27 Meaning Joseph's full brother, son of the same mother as well as the same father (Jacob). While this brother is never referred to by name in the Qur'ān, the Islamic exegetical texts follow the biblical lead and refer to him as Benjamin.

28 In the Bible, the brothers avoid this lie by sending Joseph's blood-soaked cloak to Jacob with the message, "This we have found. Recognize, please, if it is the cloak of your son or not" (Gen. 37:32). Jacob himself supplies the missing information, that an evil but unidentified animal has mauled and eaten Joseph (v. 33).

The Qur'ānic identification of the animal as a wolf is likely related to a rabbinic exegetical text found in the fifth-century exegetical midrash, *Genesis Rabbah*. There the midrash writes that God sent Mrs. Potiphar to attack Joseph because Joseph had thanked God for sending him to Egypt and allowing him to thereby escape the evil eye of his brothers. In doing so, says the midrash, Joseph exhibited an exorbitant amount of insensitivity to his father's distress. Taking note, God said, "Layabout! By your life, I shall set the bear upon you!" And so we read (Gen. 39:7), "And it came to pass after these things that his master's wife cast her eyes upon Joseph." The Hebrew word for "bear" in this midrash is דוב (*dov*), an apparent play on words for the bad report, דיבה רעה (*dibbah ra`ah*), Joseph brings to his father about his brothers in Gen. 37:2. The Arabic word for "wolf" that appears in the Qur'ān and in the Islamic exegetical texts is الذِّئْب (*al-dhi'b*). Strictly speaking, the Hebrew cognate of the Arabic ذِئْب (*dhi'b*) is זאב (*ze'ev*), not דוב (*dov*). Nonetheless, one hears the auditory similarity between ذِئْب (*dhi'b*) and דוב (*dov*), which could have led to the switch to Arabic wolf from Hebrew bear. See *Midrash Rabbah Bereishit*, ed. Theodor and Albeck, v. 3, 87:4 and 84:7.

29 Unlike the Qur'ānic Jacob, the biblical Jacob exhibits no premonition of any danger. He subsequently believes that Joseph has been mauled to death by an animal, as his sons clearly intended him to (Gen. 37:33). He does not question his sons' claim, as his Qur'ānic counterpart does.

30 Meaning Benjamin, Joseph's full brother. See above, n. 27.

31 This differs from the biblical account. There, Joseph initially holds *Simeon*, the second born, hostage until the brothers return with Benjamin. A similar trick then ensues, in which Joseph hides his royal cup in Benjamin's bag and then accuses him of stealing it. However, the biblical Joseph does not jail Benjamin, as the Qur'ānic Joseph does. In the Bible, Judah steps forward to plead with the Egyptian vizier (Joseph) and begs to trade places with his accused brother. Joseph, no longer able to maintain his charade, reveals his true identity to his brothers and invites his family to move to Egypt. The biblical Jacob, unlike his Qur'ānic counterpart, knows nothing of the Benjamin-in-danger episode until after the danger has passed. See Genesis 42–5.

32 John Macdonald suggests that the Qur'ānic phrase "his eyes became white with mourning" may reflect a tradition found in the eleventh- to twelfth-century midrash *Sefer ha-Yashar* (*Miqqetz*) and in the Aramaic *targumim* (which he does not specify). There, Macdonald notes, when Jacob learns that Simeon has been held hostage in Egypt and that the brothers wish to bring Benjamin as well (Gen. 42), Jacob says to his sons, "You will bring down my gray hairs with sorrow to the grave." See Macdonald, "Joseph," 220; *Sepher hajaschar* (Berlin: Benjamin Harz, 1923), *Miqqetz*, 188. It is not clear why Macdonald looks to the post-Qur'ānic *Sefer ha-Yashar* for the influence of this phrase on the Qur'ān, especially since Genesis 42:38 relates the very same thing. Macdonald makes a more sound argument regarding Joseph's healing of his father's blindness. See n. 33.

33 Macdonald notes that in Gen. 46:4 God tells Jacob in a dream that "Joseph will place his hand upon your eyes." Although the Bible does not describe Jacob as blind or Joseph as having healed him, Macdonald suggests that this biblical verse may be the source for the Qur'ānic Jacob's blindness and subsequent healing. While this is an appealing idea, the connection between the Bible and the Qur'ān here would be stronger if one could point to a pre-Islamic midrashic reading of Gen. 46:6 that hints to blindness on Jacob's part. Additionally, if a biblical element can be said to have influenced the Qur'ānic motif of Jacob's blindness and Joseph's curing him, it seems more likely to be found in the story of Isaac. Gen. 27:1 relates that in his old age, Isaac went blind. Jacob (and his mother, Rachel) took advantage of this blindness to trick Isaac into giving Jacob the blessing of the elder Esau. When Jacob, dressed as Esau, entered his father's presence, Isaac was unsure which son stood before him; the man's voice sounded like Jacob's but his arms were hairy like Esau's. In v. 26, Isaac asks his unidentifiable son to step forward and then sniffs him. Recognizing the scent as that of the outdoorsy Esau, Isaac determines that the son before him is the "correct" one – Esau – and blesses him with the firstborn's blessing (vv. 27ff). Like the Qur'ānic Joseph, whose cloak and its scent restored his father's sight, the scent of Isaac's son allowed him to "see" his son, though in this case "sight" is metaphoric rather than physical. Isaac's "restored" sight also remains faulty, for he identifies the son as Esau when it is, in fact, Jacob.

34 Al-Ṭabarī, *Jāmi` al-bayān*; idem, *Ta'rīkh*.

35 Al-Tha`labī, *Qiṣaṣ*.

36 *Vita Prophetarum*, ed. Eisenberg. On al-Kisā'ī, see Chapter 3, n. 56.

37 See al-Bayḍāwī, *Tafsīr al-Bayḍāwī*, vol. 1. An English translation can be found in *Baidawī's Commentary on Sūrah 12 of the Qur'ān*, trans. A. F. L. Beeston (Oxford: Clarendon Press, 1963). On al-Bayḍāwī, see Chapter 3, n. 55.

38 Ibn Ishaq's biography of Muḥammad exists today only in a form shortened and heavily edited by his student Ibn Hishām (d. 827 or 833). The section from which this chapter's material derives was recreated by Newby, *The Making of the Last Prophet*. See Chapter 3, n. 62.

39 Tottoli, *The Stories of the Prophets*. For more on al-Ṭarafī, see Chapter 3, n. 57.

40 It appears they believe that since they outnumber Joseph and his brother, their father should either love them more or the same. This logic is not entirely clear to me. Alternatively, one could see this phrase as a threat. The brothers declare that Joseph and his brother are favored but, since they outnumber them, the larger group has the power and wherewithal to do something about it, to overpower Joseph and his brother. This reading gains a measure of support when we note that in the next verse the brothers plot to slay or exile Joseph and sell him to a passing caravan (12:19–20).

41 *Ta'rīkh*, 1:371–2.

42 Al-Tha`labī, 110.

43 Al-Ṭarafi, 97 (#258); al-Bayḍāwī, 477 (on v. 8). According to a tradition mentioned in Ibn Isḥāq (Newby, *The Making of the Last Prophet*, 103–4), in al-Ṭabari's *Ta'rīkh* (1:372), and in al-Ṭarafī (116–17), Jacob had entrusted his sister with temporary

custody of Joseph but, finding himself unable to spend even one more hour without his beloved son, he returned to claim him. Unfortunately for Jacob, his sister would not relinquish Joseph.

44 The classical Muslim commentators attempt to calculate exactly how much time Jacob spent separated from his beloved son. According to Mujāhid, the two spent thirty-four years apart; Ibn Jurayj estimates the separation at seventy-seven years while Yūnus ibn Ḥasan reckons seventy-three years, and al-Ḥasan insists on eighty years. Ibn Jurayj's calculation appears in al-Ṭabarī, *Jāmi` al-bayān*, 8 (13): 58 and *Ta'rīkh*, 1:378–9; al-Ḥasan and Mujāhid appear in al-Tha`labī, 114. Al-Ṭarafī (123, #326) cites an anonymous source saying forty years had passed between Joseph's dreams and their ultimate realization. Al-Ṭarafī cites also al-Ḥasan's reckoning of eighty years, adding that others say that Joseph was 17 years old when he was thrown into the pit, and lived twenty-three years after his reunion with his father, making him 120 years old at his death (123, #327). Similarly, al-Ṭabarī notes that "some of the people of the Tawrāh (Torah)" report that the Torah records that Joseph was 17 years old when he was sold and brought to Egypt; Joseph lived in al-`Aziz's house (i.e., the biblical Potiphar) for thirteen years before being made vizier; he was reunited with his father in Egypt twenty-two years after having been first taken away. See al-Ṭabarī, *Ta'rīkh*, 1:378–9.

45 It appears that al-Tha`labī and al-Kisā'ī were highly uncomfortable with such unfeeling behavior, so disrespectful on the part of Joseph regarding his loving father. Thus al-Tha`labī (140) cites a report from al-Fuḍayl b. `Iyād explaining that while in Egypt Joseph attempted to write a letter to his father every day; every day, the angel Gabriel would prevent him from doing so. In desperation, Joseph deposited the empty sheets in a storehouse, where they filled the place to capacity. Al-Kisā'ī (161–2) likewise insists that Joseph attempted to contact his father. He relates that while Joseph was waiting on the slave-dais to be sold, a Bedouin came upon him. Joseph asked the Bedouin to bring a message to his father, to tell Jacob that he was alive but being sold into slavery, and that he was grieving so greatly for his father that his tears washed away the mole that was on his right cheek. The Bedouin kept his promise to do so and Jacob, hearing word from his son, fell into a swoon. Other sources insist that Jacob knew all along that Joseph was alive without Joseph having to tell him. Al-Tha'labī (135), al-Ṭarafī (120, #316), and al-Bayḍāwī (44) record that Jacob saw the Angel of Death in a dream and asked him about Joseph; the Angel of Death informed him that Joseph yet lived. In another version, al-Tha`labī (136) relates that the Angel of Death told Jacob that Joseph would not die until God reunited them. That al-Tha`labi and al-Kisā'ī attempt to justify Joseph's behavior and the others attempt to lessen the inherent cruelty of remaining silent by adding material clearly not part of the Qur'ānic narrative emphasizes how cruel and problematic they perceived Joseph's treatment of his suffering father to have been. Al-Ṭabarī does not comment on the matter.

46 See Schippers, *Spanish Hebrew Poetry*, 168–70.

47 Monroe, *Hispano-Arabic Poetry: A Student Anthology*, 274–5. Permutations of the motif of wasting away to the point of invisibility appear in both Arabic and Hebrew, in poems by al-Mutanabbī, Kushājim, Naṣr ibn Aḥmad, Solomon ibn Gabirol, Moses ibn Ezra, Judah Halevi, and Ibn Shabbetay. These can be found in Schippers, *Spanish Hebrew Poetry*, 169–70, and Pagis, *Shirat ha-Ḥol*, 109.

48 See al-Tha`labī, 135; Newby, *The Making of the Last Prophet*, 111; al-Ṭabarī, *Ta'rīkh*, 1:404–9; idem, *Jāmi` al-bayān*, 8 (13): 57; al-Bayḍāwī, 495 (v. 95).

49 In al-Tha`labī, 108. Al-Tha`labī does note that the majority of Muslim scholars understand the name Yūsuf to be simply the Arabic version of the Hebrew Yosef, and thus not related to Arabic vocabulary or grammar.

In an unexpected twist, some of the exegetes attempt to explain the entire episode as Jacob's punishment for a wrong he had committed earlier. The misdeed is variously given as: Jacob refused to give food to a neighbor who asked for it; Jacob separated a slave girl from her family; or, Jacob slaughtered a calf in front of the birthing mother. The idea that Jacob committed an act for which he deserved punishment is not only completely absent from the Qur'ān, but flies in the face of the principle of prophetic *`iṣma* (sinlessness or inability to sin). Furthermore, while each act can be considered not "nice" or "generous," none violates any specific Islamic law (though the act may be considered *makrūh*, abhorrent). Perhaps for this reason the exegetes "allowed" Jacob to be guilty of such behavior. See al-Tha`labī, 116 and al-Kisā'ī, 157.

In a study of the principle of *`iṣma* in both Islam and Judaism, Moshe Zucker points out that the concept of prophetic infallibility did not originate with the rise of Islam but developed over time. He also notes that while the early rabbinic exegetes rejected any form of absolute prophetic sinlessness, the geonic exegetes reflected the stance of the Muslim Mu`tazilīs (the rationalist school) on the matter. Both groups claimed that while no such thing as *`iṣma* per se existed, prophets were nonetheless sinless. See Moshe Zucker, "Ha-Efshar she-Navi Yeḥeta? `Al Ba`ayat ``Isma' al-Anbiya`' ba-Islam u-va-Yahadut," *Tarbiz* 35 (1965): 149–73.

50 According to the exegetes, anywhere from twenty-two to eighty years have passed between Joseph's being thrown in the pit and reunification with his father. See n. 44.

51 See *Ṭauḳ*, باب الوفاء (*bāb al-wafā'*, Chapter on Fidelity), 72–7.

52 See al-Ṭabarī, *Ta'rīkh*, 1:407–9; *Jāmi` al-bayān*, 8 (13): 57–8 (Q 12:94); al-Bayḍāwī, 495 (Q 12:94).

53 Al-Tha`labī, 138.

54 Ibn Ḥazm's Jewish contemporary Samuel ha-Nagid employed the idea of the scent of the beloved's clothes as reviving in his "רעיה צבי מבור שבי התפתחי." See *Diwan Shemuel ha-Nagid. Ben Tehillim*, 297 (#161); and Schirmann, *Ha-Shirah ha-`Ivrit be-Sefarad u-ve-Provans*, 1:153 (#4).

55 Al-Ṭabarī, *Jāmi` al-bayān*, 8 (13): 63 (Q 12:95); *Ta'rīkh*, 1:409; al-Tha`labī, 138; al-Ṭarafī, 122 (#322).

56 Al-Bayḍāwī, 478–9 (Q 12:18); al-Tha`labī, 115; al-Ṭabarī citing al-Suddī, in his *Jāmi` al-bayān*, 7 (12): 162 (Q 12:16–17); al-Ṭarafī, 100 (#263).

57 Ladislav Drozdík takes this idea to an extreme, stating, "The Western image of the poet as a creative subject with deep emotional experience finds no parallel in classical Arabic poetry." See his "Erotic Imagery," 22. Dan Pagis more moderately wrote that the genre of love poetry hovers between the conventional and personal; poets play with stock situations, characters, and descriptions to express particularized emotions. See his *Hebrew Poetry*, 48–54. Scheindlin has noted that love receives poetic form in Andalusia "on behalf of a communal ideal" and not because of individual experience. See Scheindlin, "A Miniature Anthology," 106.

58 Ibn Ḥazm was not the only Andalusian poet to give life to his beloved's attractiveness by comparing him to Joseph. As discussed in Chapter 2, Ibn Mar Shaul compares his beautiful boy to Joseph in the earliest homoerotic Hebrew poem to come down to us. This trope appears also in an eros poem by an unknown author, who states: "His [physical] description was like the [physical] description of Joseph, whom women climbed over the wall to see / they praised him when he went out, they bowed before him and genuflected." In Schirmann, *Shirim Ḥadashim*, 2:463 (#228). A poem by Judah al-Ḥarizi echoes this sentiment when he writes, "He is a charming gazelle, the image of Joseph in his beauty." See al-Ḥarizi, *Taḥkemoni*, ed. Toporovsky, 395. In an interesting usage, Abū `Amr b. Shuhayd (d. 1034) writes in Arabic of a boy whose beauty was so great, that the Jews thought him to be Joseph. See Aḥmad ibn Muḥammad al-Maqqarī, *Nafḥ al-ṭīb, Analectes sur l'histoire et la littérature des Arabs d'Espagne*, ed. R. P. A. Dozy *et al.* (Leiden E. J. Brill, 1855–61), I, 98. Norman Roth translates this into English in his "Religious Constraints," 198. According to Monroe, Ibn Shuhayd was a close friend of Ibn Ḥazm. In Monroe, *Hispano-Arabic Poetry: A Student Anthology*, xiii. Ibn Shuhayd may have been the friend who

requested of Ibn Ḥazm that he compose the *Ṭawq*. For more on Ibn Shuhayd, see Chapter 3, n. 7.

59 The wife of al-`Azīz is not named in the text of the Qur'ān; hence, I have referred to her here as the Qur'ān does, as "the wife of al-`Azīz." See n. 88.

60 According to some Qur'ānic commentaries, so taken with his beauty were the women, that they began menstruating on the spot. For example, see al-Bayḍāwī, 482 (Q 12:31); al-Kisā'ī, 164–5. James Kugel investigates and analyzes the various Islamic and Jewish exegetical versions of the Assembly of the Ladies motif in depth in his *In Potiphar's House: The Interpretive Life of Biblical Texts* (San Francisco: Harper, 1990).

61 Al-Tha`labī, 108–9; al-Ṭabarī, *Ta'rīkh*, 1:371; al-Kisā'ī, 165. Al-Ṭarafī (104, #277) brings a *ḥadīth* tracing back to Muḥammad in which Muḥammad taught that Joseph and his mother were given two-thirds of the world's beauty, with the final third shared among the rest of mankind. Jewish traditions likewise draw the connection between Joseph's beauty and his mother's, and attribute to both of them a measure of beauty far above that of other humans. See Chapter 2, pp. 55ff.

62 Anas, as cited by al-Ṭabarī, reduces Joseph's share of the world's beauty to 50 percent. See al-Ṭabarī, *Ta'rīkh*, 1:371; al-Tha`labī, 109. The Babylonian Talmud in *Qiddushin* 49b uses the same formula to describe Jerusalem: "Ten measures of beauty descended to the world; Jerusalem took nine while the rest of the world shared the final one."

63 See "Yūsuf," *Encyclopaedia of Islam, Second Edition*. Brill Online, 2013. http://referenceworks.brillonline.com/entries/encyclopaedia-of-islam-2/yusuf-COM_1369.

64 See Schippers, *Spanish Hebrew Poetry*, 176–8. The twelfth-century Granadan poetess Nazhūn bint al-Qalā`ī once wrote of her beloved's beautiful face that "البدر يطلع في ازرته," "the full moon rises up from his collar." *Rāyāt al-mubarrizīn*, 160 [Bellamy and Steiner, *Banners of the Champions*, 92 (#86)]. Similarly, Ibn Idrīs of Murcia (1165–1202) claimed of his beautiful beloved, "بدرٌ لو انّ البدر قيل له اقترح املًا لقال اكون في هلالته!," "He is a full moon; if the moon above were given one wish, it would say, 'I would be one of his haloes.'" In *Rāyāt al-mubarrizīn*, 201 [Bellamy and Steiner, *Banners of the Champions*, 202 (#191)]. His contemporary Ibn Mālik (also of Murcia) more scandalously wrote, "وأهيف كالقمر الطّالع \ أبصرته في المسجد الجامع \ تقول من أبصره راكعًا \ كلّ المنى في سجدة الرّاكع," "I saw in the Friday mosque a slender youth, like the rising moon. / Whoever sees him bow in prayer says, 'All my desires are in his prostration as he bows.'" *Rāyāt al-mubarrizīn*, 197 [Bellamy and Steiner, *Banners of the Champions*, 192 (#181)]. Among the many Hebrew examples, see Samuel ha-Nagid, *Diwan Shemuel ha-Nagid. Ben Tehillim*, 309 (#193, אהי כופר); and Schirmann, *Ha-Shirah ha-`Ivrit be-Sefarad u-ve-Provans*, 168 (#19).

65 Al-Tha`labī, 108; Newby, *The Making of the Last Prophet*, 103; al-Kisā'ī, 165; al-Bayḍāwī, 472 (Q 12:31).

66 Al-Tha`labi, 109. According to al-Kisā'ī (161), the glimmer in his face was the light of prophecy; it was this that shone against the walls, filling the entire country with light.

67 Al-Tha`labī and al-Bayḍāwī explain elsewhere that this birthmark was a familial inheritance shared by Isaac, Sarah, and Jacob. See al-Tha`labī, 109, 138 and al-Bayḍāwī, 495 (on v. 90). Al-Kisā'ī recalls that Joseph's birthmark later proved to the brothers that he was their sibling because it was exactly like the one their father Jacob sported. See al-Kisā'ī, 175.

68 As cited by Annemarie Schimmel in her "Yūsuf in Mawlānā Rumi's Poetry," in *The Heritage of Sufism*, ed. Leonard Lewisohn (London and New York: Khaniqahi Nimatullahi Publications, 1992), 2:49.

69 Arabic descriptions of beautiful men, Muḥammad and Moses among them, often include a curved nose. See, for example, W. Montgomery Watt, *Muhammad: Prophet*

and Statesman (Oxford: Oxford University Press, 1961), 229. This is particularly interesting given anti-Semitic depictions of the Jew (cousin to the Arab) as hook-nosed. Jack G. Shaheen maintains that Hollywood movies depict Arabs, the bad guys, as hook-nosed as well. See his "Bad Arabs: How Hollywood Vilifies a People," *Annals of the American Academy of Political and Social Science* 588 (July 2003): 171–93.

70 As we have seen, this trope appears in the Hebrew poems as well: Ibn Mar Shaul refers to his beloved, whom he compares to Joseph in beauty, as tall. Ibn Gabirol playfully does this too, using doubled-language in his "כתמר את בקומתך," "Like Tamar are you in your height." "Tamar" can be read either as a woman's proper name or as the Hebrew word for a palm tree, a tall tree to which the beloved's height and suppleness were often compared. See Ibn Gabirol, *Shirei ha-Ḥol*, ed. Brody and Schirmann, 159 (#243) and idem, *Shirei ha-Ḥol*, ed. Jarden, 1:367 (#212).

71 Andalusian poets felt positively toward the mole. The eleventh-century Granadan `Abd al-`Azīz ibn Khayra (aka al-Munfatil) wrote, "There is a mole on Aḥmad's cheek, that enchants every free man to love / His cheek looks like a garden of roses where the gardener is an Abyssinian." Bellamy and Steiner, *Banners of the Champions*, 59 (#57). A somewhat more poetic translation appears in Erskine Lane, trans., *In Praise of Boys: Moorish Poems from al-Andalus* (San Francisco: Gay Sunshine Press, 1975), 19. Lane erroneously records the poet's name as `Abd al-`Azīz al-Habra. Other praise of moles appears in poems by al-Nashshār (twelfth century, Valencia) and Ibn Idrīs (1165–1202, Murcia). Arabic in *Rāyāt al-mubarrizīn*, 155–6. Al-Nashshār and Ibn Idrīs also wrote of the fetching nature of the boy beloved's mole. See *Rāyāt al-mubarrizīn*, 213, 201–2 [Bellamy and Steiner, *Banners of the Champions*, 60 (#58), 202 (#191)]. The maddening beauty of the mole can be found in later Ṣūfī descriptions of God as well. For example, in a poetic version of `Ayn al-Quḍāt's philosophical conception of "the face of God," we read, "Our intellect is maddened by the beauty of His cheek and mole, and from the wine of His love." See Carl W. Ernst, *Words of Ecstasy in Sufism* (Albany: State University of New York Press, 1985), 75–6. `Ayn al-Quḍāt was a Persian jurisconsult, mystic, philosopher, poet, and mathematician who was executed at the age of 33, in 1131.

72 Al-Tha`labī, 109. All the detail that al-Tha`labī supplies follows his opening claim that Joseph was so stunningly handsome that his beauty could not be described.

The comparison of teeth to pearls also appears as a poetic convention of beauty. In a poem by al-Muṣḥafī (aka Ja`far b. `Uthmān, d. 982), the court poet and vizier of the Cordoban caliph al-Ḥakam II (al-Mustanṣir), he writes: "She spoke to me and I said, 'Some pearls have fallen.' / And she looked down at her necklace to see if it had broken. / Then a smile lit up her face / and she showed me another string of pearls." See *Banners of the Champions*, 62 (#60). The Arabic appears in *Rāyāt al-mubarrizīn*, 117–18. See also Schippers on this trope, *Spanish Hebrew Poetry*, 153.

73 Al-Ṭarafī, 104 (#277).

74 In Pellat, *The Life and Works of Jāḥiẓ*, 263.

75 As cited in Giffin, "Love Poetry," 115. Arabic original in al-Jāḥiẓ, *Rasā'il al-Jāḥiẓ*, 3:139. Giffin notes that Shakespeare likewise understood madness and love to be connected. In *A Midsummer Night's Dream*, Theseus declares, "Lovers and madmen have such seething brains, / such shaping fantasies that apprehend / more than cool reason ever comprehends. / The lunatic, the lover and the poet / are of imagination all compact." See Act V, Scene I, ll. 4ff. William Shakespeare, *A Midsummer Night's Dream*, in *The Complete Works of William Shakespeare*, 3rd edition, ed. David Bevington (London and Glenview, IL: Scott, Foresman, and Company, 1980).

76 Al-Iṣfahānī traces this idea to Plato. See Nykl, *Hispano-Arabic Poetry*, 123.

77 *Ṭauḳ*, 11 (Arberry, 31; Nykl, 13).

78 This is Ismā`īl b. Yunūs al-A`war, whom Ibn Ḥazm mentions in his polemical writings against Judaism. There Ibn Ḥazm identifies Ismā`īl b. Yunūs with one of three forms of *dahriyya*, understood as religious relativist-agnosticism. See Brann, *Power in the Portraya*, 62–70.

79 *Ṭauḳ*, 18 (Arberry, 45; Nykl, 24–5).

80 In his notes to this verse, Abdallah Yusuf Ali places this sentence in the mouths of those people standing around Jacob; Jacob's sons, he points out, were not yet back from Egypt. He explains that Jacob's sons had successfully managed to convince the neighbors of Jacob's dotage. "Thus lies die hard, once they get a start," he warns. See Ali, *The Holy Qur-an*, 1:585, n. 1771.

81 Interestingly, we find a rabbinic exegetical stream that likewise appears to link romantic love with Jacob's love for Joseph. In explicating Song of Songs 8:6, "love is as strong as death, jealousy as cruel as the grave," a midrash in *Song of Songs Rabbah* explains: "Love that is as strong as death is the love of Jacob for Joseph, for it caused the murderous jealousy of his other sons toward Joseph." The Song of Songs, the erotically charged love poem between a male and female voice, clearly does not intend paternal love. Nonetheless, the midrash applies this verse to Jacob and Joseph. See *Midrash Rabbah ha-Mevo`ar. Shir ha-Shirim* (Jerusalem: Mechon ha-Midrash ha-Mevo`ar [1995]), 8:4 on Song of Songs 8:6.

82 Pellat, *The Life and Works of Jāḥiẓ*, 263.

83 Ibid. Emphasis mine.

84 Ibid.

85 Ibid. Such a definition appears not to recognize the sexual attraction between males, a situation in which Andalusian poetry so revels. In other essays, al-Jāḥiẓ himself wrote of the reasons one might prefer male lovers over female. See al-Jāḥiẓ, "Boasting Match over Maids and Youths," in *Nine Essays of al-Jahiz*, trans. William M. Hutchins (New York: Peter M. Lang, 1989), 139–66. It is possible that al-Jāḥiẓ's definition is purposely phrased this way to avoid a reader misunderstanding male–male love as platonic friendship. To transmit the unmistakable sense of sexual attraction, al-Jāḥiẓ resorted to heterosexual terminology, which would have been less likely to be confused with nonsexual love.

86 Nykl, 7 (*Ṭauḳ*, 7; Arberry, 23).

87 *Ṭauḳ*, 8 (Arberry, 25; Nykl, 9).

88 The Qur'ān first refers to the man who has purchased Joseph as al-`Azīz in Q 12:30. His wife is referred to simply as "the wife of al-`Aẓīz." The Islamic exegetical texts used here identify him also as Iṭfīr or Qiṭfīr, which Bernard Heller and Norman Stillman suggest may be an orthographic corruption of Fiṭfīr, the biblical Potiphar (Gen. 39). See *EI*[2], s.v. "Ḳiṭfīr," by B. Heller and N. Stillman (5:233–4). Al-Kisā'ī's designation, Quṭifār, sounds closest to the Hebrew and is orthographically more similar to the Arabic transcription of the Hebrew "Potiphar."

89 These are the same words, فِي ضَلَالٍ مُّبِينٍ (*fī ḍalālin mubīnin*, a clear error, or, straying from sanity) as used by Jacob's sons in accusing him of love-madness for Joseph in 12:8. The people who accuse Jacob of madness after he claims to sense Joseph's scent likewise use the word ضَلَال (*ḍalāl*).

90 M. Pickthall and A. Yusuf Ali both translate the word هَمَّتْ (*hammat*) as "desired" or "desired with passion." According to Lane, the root signifies a purposed or intended thing and the verbal form indicates an action that one desires or intends with strong determination to do. See Lane, *Arabic–English Lexicon*, vol. 2, s.v. "همم." Bell sanitizes the phrase somewhat, translating it as "she was fascinated with him and he was fascinated with her." See Muhammad Pickthall, *The Glorious Koran* (London: George Allen and Unwin, 1976); and Richard Bell, trans., *The Qur'ān* (Edinburgh: T & T Clark, 1937).

91 As in al-Ṭabarī, *Ta'rīkh*, 1:383–4; *Jāmi` al-bayān*, 7 (12): 197–8 (Q 12:30); al-Tha`labī, 121.

92 Al-Ṭabarī, *Jāmi` al-bayān*, 7 (12): 199–200 (Q 12:30); al-Ṭarafī, 105 (#280).
93 Al-Bayḍāwī, 482 (on v. 30).
94 Al-Ṭabarī, *Jāmi` al-bayān*, 7 (12): 199–200 (Q 12:30). Al-Kisā'ī, 162, writes that she was so astounded by Joseph's beauty, she fell passionately in love with him, "وشغفت بحبه" (*wa-shughifat bi-ḥubbihi*). He does not explain the origin of the verb شغف (*shaghaf*), although that this is sexual love and not platonic affection is clear.
95 ".قصدت مخالطته وقصد مخالطتها"
96 *Jāmī' al-bayān*, 7 (12): 183–5 (Q 12:24); al-Ṭarafī, 103. Al-Kisā'ī (163) records that she managed to untie seven knots on Joseph's trousers before Joseph came to his senses and raced out of the room.
97 Al-Tha`labī, 118–19. Ibn `Abbās, cited by al-Tha`labī here, attempts to mitigate Joseph's responsibility somewhat by adding that *al-shayṭān* (Satan) had jumped into the space between the two and, placing an arm around each of them, drew them together, causing a rise in Joseph's desire. More demurely, Jābir relates (citing al-Ḍaḥḥāk) that Joseph desired that the wife of al-`Azīz become his wife.
98 Joseph's desire for Potiphar's wife appears also in a discussion in the Babylonian Talmud of Gen. 39:11, which relates that Joseph came into the house one day "to do his work" when none of the other men were home. In *BT Sotah* 36b, R. Joḥanan (and Rav or Shemuel) says, Joseph had intended to have sexual intercourse with Mrs. Potiphar that day. He was prevented from doing so only at the last minute when a portrait of his father's face appeared before him through the window and lectured him. Immediately, says the Talmud, "his bow remained steady, his strong arms stayed limber" (quoting Gen. 49:24). Explains R. Joḥanan, Joseph's passion subsided, and he stuck his hands in the ground so that his seed came out into the ground from between his fingernails. See also *Genesis Rabbah* 87:7. The emergence of an image of Jacob's face, an image that prevents Joseph from sinning, appears also in the later Muslim exegetical texts. There Jacob is said to be biting his nails, perhaps echoing the rabbinic texts. See, for example, al-Ṭabarī, *Ta'rīkh*, 1:380; al-Kisā'ī, 163; Newby, *The Making of the Last Prophet*, 105; and al-Ṭarafī, 102. Al-Tha`labī (119) notes an additional report which cites a teaching of Ibn `Abbās: Jacob appeared and hit Joseph on the chest with his hand and "Joseph's desire left through his fingertips." Ibn `Abbās (d. 688) was widely considered by the Islamic sources to have acquired proficiency in "Israelite" traditions. See al-Ṭabarī, *Ta'rīkh*, 1:462.
99 As noted above, the Qur'ān does not provide the wife of al-`Azīz with a name. This did not prevent the Islamic exegetical sources from naming her. According to Marc Bernstein, the Arabic Islamic sources originally identified her as Ra`īl, a possible confusion with the name of Joseph's mother, Raḥīl. The name Zulaykha is of Persian origin, says Bernstein, and was picked up by later Arabic sources. The wife of al-`Azīz appears as "Zulaykha" in the writings of al-Firdawsī, al-Kisā'ī, and al-Bayḍāwī, who names her also Ra`īl. Later Jewish sources pick up the name Zulaykha from the Muslim sources. The earliest Hebrew example ("זליכה") appears in the *c.* thirteenth-century *Sefer ha-Yashar*, a work in which a number of Islamic motifs can be found. See *Sepher hajaschar*, 157–67; Bernstein, *Stories of Joseph*, 209. Al-Tha`labī (118) notes an additional possible rendition of her name: Bakkā bt. Fayūsh.
100 Schimmel points out that an alternative Ṣūfī poetic symbology places Joseph as the soul principle. We find this in the poetry of the Persian Ṣūfī "poet of love" Jalāl a-Dīn al-Rūmī, as well as in compositions by other Ṣūfī poets. According to these teachings, just as Joseph had to undergo trials and tribulations before reaching a position of honor and power in Egypt, and before reuniting with his family, so too the soul must undergo trials and tribulations before reaching union with God. See Schimmel, "Yūsuf in Mawlānā Rumi's Poetry," 48.

In Rūmī's poetry in particular, Joseph serves as a symbol of the beloved par excellence and sometimes appears to serve as a stand-in for Rūmī's own beloved spiritual master, Shams al-Dīn al-Tabrīzī. See Schimmel, "Yūsuf in Mawlānā Rumi's Poetry,"

57. Schimmel includes a number of Rūmī's poems in which Joseph appears as the yearned-for-beloved.

101 Schimmel, "Eros," 132.

102 Al-Firdawsī is more famously known as the author of the *Shānāma*, an epic poem hailed as the national epic of Iran. Because of the greater number of Arabic words that appear in the Yūsuf and Zulaykha poem than in the *Shānāma*, scholars have questioned the attribution to him as author of the former. See *EI*^{2}, s.v. "Firdawsi," by Cl. Huart and H. Massé (2:918–20).

103 The motif of Zulaykha's weeping-induced blindness and Joseph's miraculous restoration of her sight existed before the fifteenth-century Jāmī poem; it is alluded to in a poem by Rūmī two centuries earlier. See Schimmel, "Yūsuf in Mawlānā Rumi's Poetry," 50.

104 Abdulraḥmān Jāmī, *The Book of Joseph and Zuleikha*, trans. Alexander Rogers (London: David Nutt, 1892), 191–210, 217–18. The idea that Zulaykha and Joseph wed after the death of her husband appears in a more conservative form in the classical Muslim works as well. See al-Ṭabarī, *Ta'rīkh*, 1:392; al-Tha`labī, 128; al-Kisā'ī, 167–8; Newby, *The Making of the Last Prophet*, 108; al-Ṭarafī makes sure to point out first that the king of Egypt had converted his entire kingdom to Islam before he married Joseph to al-`Azīz's wife (called here "the wife of 'Itfīr"). Al-Ṭarafī, 111 (#294). The Muslim commentators surveyed here point out that after Joseph wed the former wife of al-`Azīz, he found her a virgin. She explained that despite her beauty and youth, her husband "did not approach women," which both caused and explains her crazed lust for the beautiful Joseph. This echoes Rav's statement in *BT Sotah* 13b, that Potiphar had originally purchased Joseph "for himself." The angel Gabriel then came and mutilated Potiphar's sexual organ before he could take any action. This rabbinic reading appears to have been based on Gen. 41:45's sudden reference to Potiphar as Poti-phera (פוטי פרע), a name the rabbis understood as derived from "mutilation" (פרע, *p-r-`*) and perhaps from Gen. 39:1's identifying Potiphar as Pharaoh's "סריס" (*saris*), a word the rabbis normally related to male castration. The Greek translations of the Bible likewise understood *saris* to refer to a castrated male. See Ross S. Kraemer, *When Aseneth Met Joseph* (New York and Oxford: Oxford University Press, 1998), 314; Kugel, *In Potiphar's House*, 75–6; Hayim Tadmor, "Was the Biblical *Sarīs* a Eunuch?," in *Solving Riddles and Untying Knots: Biblical, Epigraphic, and Semitic Studies in Honor of Jonas C. Greenfield*, ed. Seymour Gitin, Ziony Zevit, and Michael Sokoloff (Winona Lake, IN: Eisenbrauns, 1995), 317–25.

105 See Schippers, *Spanish Hebrew Poetry*, 145; Bürgel, "Love, Lust, and Longing," 91–3, 112; Baneth, "Ha-Shirah ha-`Aravit ha-Qeduma," 23–7. On the difference between `Udhrite and Andalusian separation, see Chapter 3, n. 25.

106 While Jacob's blindness was cured when his eyes were touched by Joseph's shirt, the lover finds succor in simply gazing at his beloved's clothes or at items he had once touched. We find such an idea in Rūmī as well. According to Rūmī, looking at the beauty of the beloved, immersing oneself in such a beatific vision, makes the lover oblivious to pain. This recalls the Ṣūfī phenomenon of *naẓar*, the practice of contemplating a beautiful pubescent boy who, in his beauty, was understood to serve as "witness" to the beauty of the Divine and of His creation. Rūmī's poems abound with allusions to Joseph as such a curative beauty. In this Joseph serves as the "manifestation of divine Beauty." See Schimmel, "Yūsuf in Mawlānā Rumi's Poetry," 53–5. On *naẓar*, see Rowson, "The Categorization of Gender," 62; Schimmel, "Eros," 131.

107 Al-Tha`labī, 113; al-Kisā'ī, 158–9; al-Ṭarafī, 99 (#265) and 121 (#319); and al-Bayḍāwī, 478 (on v. 15) and 495 (on v. 93). Al-Bayḍāwī (478, on v. 15) says they did so that they could smear it with blood and thereby deceive their father. Al-Bayḍawī also allows for the option that the shirt Joseph subsequently sent to Jacob was either

the shirt he was then wearing or the one that was in the amulet (as discussed below), but he is not certain. In another passage, al-Tha`labī maintains that Joseph's shirt, the one stripped off of him by his brothers, had been passed down from Adam, who had received it in the Garden of Eden. When the brothers brought it to Jacob after dipping it in animal blood, Jacob recognized it. See al-Tha`labī, 113. For more on Adam's garment, see Stephen D. Ricks, "The Garment of Adam in Jewish, Muslim, and Christian Tradition," in *Judaism and Islam: Boundaries, Communication and Interaction*, ed. B. H. Hary, J. L. Hayes, and F. Astren (Leiden: E. J. Brill, 2000), 203–25.

108 Q 12:4.

109 Ibid. According to al-Tha`labī (113) and al-Ṭarafī (121, #319), Jacob did so to protect Joseph from the Evil Eye.

110 According to al-Ḍaḥḥāk and al-Suddī, the shirt inherited from Abraham was woven in Paradise and had the scent of Paradise. When the shirt touched an ailing or afflicted person, that person would be restored to health. See al-Tha`labī, 138 and al-Ṭarafī, 121 (#319). Al-Kisā'ī (156–7) notes that Joseph inherited five miraculous items from Abraham: the turban of prophethood, the coat of friendship, the girdle of victory and contentment, the ring of prophethood, and the staff of light. The theme of the paradisiacal shirt that clothed Joseph in the pit and then healed Jacob's blindness appears to have taken hold in the Muslim popular imagination as well, for we find it in an anonymous Egyptian thirteenth- to fourteenth-century Arabic poetic rendition of the Joseph story. See *The Story of Joseph in Arabic Verse*, ed. and trans. R. Y. Ebied and M. J. L. Young (Leiden: E. J. Brill, 1975), lines 152ff and 419ff. This account appears in the medieval *Midrash `Asarah Harugei Malkhut*, also called *Midrash Eleh Ezkera*. See Adolph Jellinek, *Bet ha-Midrasch* (Jerusalem: Bamberger and Wahrmann, 1938), 6:19–20. For more on this midrash, see *EJ*, s.v. "Ten Martyrs, The," by Moses Hess (19:640–1).

111 One is given to understand from this that Rifā`a, her first husband, was apparently more well-endowed.

112 *Ṣaḥīḥ Bukhārī*, ed. and trans. Muḥammad Muhsin Khān (Bayrut: Dār al-`arabiyya, 1985), 7:459–60 (#684). According to Islamic law, once a man has fully divorced his wife, he may not remarry her until she has first married another and consummated that marriage. Jewish law rules exactly oppositely. A man may remarry his divorced wife only if she has not married another first (as in Deut. 24:1–4).

113 Yaris Eshots, "`Ishq," in *The Qur'an: An Encyclopedia*, ed. Oliver Leaman (Oxford: Routledge, 2006), 310–11.

114 *Ṭauḳ*, 6; Arberry, 21–2.

115 *Ṭauḳ*, 6 (Arberry, 23).

116 Stetkeyvich, "Intoxication and Immortality," 211. On the nonsexual themes of Q 12, see also Mustansir Mir, "The Qur'anic Story of Joseph: Plot, Themes, and Characters," *Muslim World* 76:1 (Jan. 1986): 1–15.

Part IV

The hermeneutics of desire

8 Surprise kisses and the burning bush: Ibn al-Milḥ and the metaphysics of passion

Ibn Ḥazm is not the only Muslim poet to have utilized sacred imagery in his secular verse on desire, and, specifically, to have compared passionate couples to scriptural characters and storylines. At around the same time during which Ibn Ḥazm was active in Cordoba and Játiva, a man in Silves by the name of Abū al-Qāsim Aḥmad b. Muḥammad b. al-Milḥ was similarly engaged in writing poetry and other forms of high-level literature. Whereas Ibn Ḥazm left behind many poems, Ibn al-Milḥ's oeuvre did not survive the years as well and not much of it remains. Yet in one of the eros poems that did survive, we see that Ibn al-Milḥ, like Ibn Ḥazm, not only utilized Qur'ānic imagery but, in doing so, sent important and moving messages about the spiritual power and significance of passionate human love.

On Ibn al-Milḥ

Not much remains known about Abū al-Qāsim Aḥmad b. Muḥammad b. al-Milḥ. According to Ibn Sa`īd, he lived in the eleventh century, in the city of Silves, and belonged to the circle of literary men there.[1] He was known as a remarkably talented writer, one of the most intellectually fertile and artistic poets of his set. He appears to have lived in a world in which poetry surrounded him. His father was Abū Bakr b. al-Milḥ, a companion (*nadīm*) of the ruler of Silves, Mu`taḍid b. `Abbād, who had ascended to the throne in 1042 on the death of his father. Mu`taḍid was himself a poet of some renown, writing of his love for wine-drinking, women, and various other pleasures.[2] In Abū Bakr b. Milḥ's capacity as a member of the court and of the ruler's entourage, he served as an "able-flatterer"[3] who practiced his art in highly valued verse. The father's poetic interest and skill was inherited by his son; Ibn al-Abbār notes that Ibn al-Milḥ and his father used to write reciprocal poems with one another, compositions which showcased considerable capacity for spontaneity and poetic talent on both of their parts.[4]

Initially, it might seem as if Ibn al-Milḥ's poetry should not be included as an example of love poetry written by religious scholars. After all, although Ibn al-Milḥ proved himself an eloquent and superior writer and poet, he was not a jurist, exegete, or religious philosopher. Ibn Sa`īd places him in the category of

"Notable Men" (أعيان, *a`yān*) and refers to him as an *adīb* (أديب), a term that refers to a man of letters rather than a religious scholar. This more "secular" or literary categorization of Ibn al-Milḥ appears also in the work of the thirteenth-century historian of Arabic Andalusia Ibn al-Abbār, who refers to Ibn al-Milḥ as an *adīb shā`ir* (أديب شاعر), a man of letters who (also) wrote poetry.[5]

However, despite these a-religious categorizations, we cannot dismiss Ibn al-Milḥ from the religious sphere so easily. According to Muḥammad Riḍwān al-Dāya, the modern editor of Ibn Sa`īd's *Rāyāt al-mubarrizīn*, notes in the margins of Ibn Sa`īd's text provide important supplemental information regarding Ibn al-Milḥ's religious involvement. According to these notes, Ibn al-Milḥ was not completely estranged from either practical religious observance or the religious intellectual sphere. Instead, Ibn al-Milḥ was known to be in charge of the prayers at the mosque in his city. Additionally, not infrequently Ibn al-Milḥ was charged with delivering the *khūṭba*, the religious sermon preached during the weekly Friday prayer sessions.[6] Thus, it appears that while Ibn al-Milḥ was known primarily for his literary prowess, he served also in a religious capacity. In addition to his literary skills, he had the religious education, knowledge, and authority needed in order to compose and deliver the learned weekly orations.

There is an additional reason for including Ibn al-Milḥ in the category of religious poets here. Just as Ibn al-Milḥ's world was infused with poetry, so too religion permeated his environment. According to Ibn Sa`īd, Ibn al-Milḥ's father was involved in religious life as well. Although Abū Bakr had been a companion or courtier of the pleasure-loving Mu`taḍid, he did not remain in this post for the duration of his life. At some point, Abu Bakr retired from court, became pious, and became the official *khaṭīb* (mosque preacher) of Silves.[7] In this capacity, he was known as particularly competent in religion and as a forceful orator.[8]

While one's father's religious position and level does not necessarily dictate that one's secular poetry is infused with religion, in the case of Ibn al-Milḥ's poem his father's situation does prove of importance. According to Ibn Sa`īd, the poem under discussion may actually have been written by the *nadīm*-turned-*khaṭīb* Abū Bakr b. al-Milḥ, and not the son under whose name Ibn Sa`īd records it. Either way, according to Ibn Sa`īd's compendium, whether the author of the poem was Ibn al-Milḥ son or Ibn al-Milḥ père, the author was not simply a secular writer with little religious background. Although neither man attained the stature or high level of learning we find with Ibn Ḥazm, both were poets of impressive poetic ability who tended toward religion and who had some measure of religious training and authority. Thus, while the poem at hand does not entail the sophisticated and complex use of Scripture and religious materials that Ibn Ḥazm's poems do, we can include it as of a similar type, and can detect similar elements at work.

The poem

Although Abū al-Qāsim b. al-Milḥ, or his father, composed many lines of poetic verse, according to Ibn Sa`īd the following constitutes the precious pearl (الفرائد, *al-farā'id*) of his poetic compositions. Ibn al-Milḥ writes:[9]

تعرضت من شفّني حبّه ببدء سلام شفاها
فجاد عليّ بتقبيلةٍ وقد كان أعرض عني وتاها
فكنت كموسى أتى للضياء ليقبس نارًا فناجى إلها

I faced off with the one whose love rendered me lean,
by orally greeting him first
He generously granted me a kiss, though he had been
avoiding me and haughty
I was like Mūsā when he approached the light, to take
fire and whispered to Allāh in secret conference

One sees immediately why Ibn Sa`īd referred to this poem as a precious gem. In three brief lines, Ibn al-Milḥ successfully captures and transmits the passion and surprised awe experienced by the lover who, after sustained alienation from the object of his passion, suddenly finds himself not only in physical proximity to him but engaging in passionate physical contact with him. Importantly, this physical interaction does not result from the lover having crept up on the beloved to engage him while he sleeps.[10] Instead, the beloved has initiated this physical contact, much to the lover's shock and pleasure. This surprise, says Ibn al-Milḥ, recalls that experienced, famously, by the prophet Mūsā when he thought he was going to obtain fire from a burning bush and instead spoke with Allāh there.

Ibn al-Milḥ and the poetic tropes

Many of the classic tropes of *`ishq* poetry make their appearance in this poem, as we would expect. Most basically, of course, the lover does not experience the passion of love and desire as enjoyable but as an affliction. It is a state of being that causes him physical harm, to the point that he finds himself losing weight and wasting away. As he writes, the love he bears for his beloved "has rendered him lean" (شفني حبّه, *shaffanī hubbuhu*).

Part of the reason for the lover's suffering from love can be found in the cruel behavior of the beloved boy, as is typical in such poetry. As we see, it is not simply that the two are separated from one another (another trope); rather, the beloved boy increases the pain of this distance by purposely avoiding the lover. The lover relates in line 2 that the beloved has been avoiding him. Making matters even worse, the poem hints that when they do get in close enough proximity to one another, the beloved will not deign to interact with the lover. Instead, he behaves arrogantly and holds himself aloof (وتاها, *wa-tāha*).[11]

Even the not entirely pure and chaste scenario – the lovers actually kiss in line 2 – fits in with the tropes of *`ishq* poetry. Although the `Udhrite poems on which the Andalusian forms were based focused on unconsummated desire, Andalusian poems frequently included moments of realization. Stolen kisses, remembered touches and caresses, warm embraces – the lovers of Andalusian poetry not only yearned to experience these for the first time with the objects of their affection, but in some cases either called to relive them or in fact relived them in their verses. Sometimes such phsyical contact consisted of kissing, and sometimes much more. For example, Ibn Abī Rawḥ (twelfth century, Algeciras) recalls a night he spent with his beloved on the banks of a river, where they embraced, "sipping the wine of kisses," and "picking the roses of modesty."[12] Ibn Sa`īd (1213–86) subtly tells of an affair in which he deflowered his beloved, robbing her of her "blush of beauty," much to his satisfaction.[13] His great uncle Abū Ja`far b. `Abd al-Malik b. Sa`īd (d. 1163) wrote of a garden that was happy watching people who, free from the eyes of the censors, embraced, enfolded among one another, and kissed each other's lips.[14] As we can see, Ibn al-Milḥ's description of a consummated kiss (l. 2) thus fits in with the tropes of Andalusian love poetry.

It is in the final line of the poem that we can see why Ibn Sa`īd considered this to be the precious gem of Ibn al-Milḥ's poetry. Here Ibn al-Milḥ incorporates into the poem a familiar Qur'ānic narrative: the story of Mūsā's theophany, his first explicit experience of Allāh. Significantly, Ibn al-Milḥ is not alone among the Andalusian poets in utilizing this scriptural moment in a poem of desire. His contemporary Samuel ha-Nagid, for example, similarly employed the image of the burning bush in his secular verses.[15] Approximately a century later, as discussed in Chapter 5, Ibn Maymūn used the image in an Arabic *`ishq* poem as well. What makes Ibn al-Milḥ's poem stand out is that he does not use the moment in an expected fashion; in other words, he does not compare the bush that burned without consuming its source to the flames of desire, or of beauty, as in Samuel ha-Nagid's and Ibn Maymūn's material. Ibn al-Milḥ focuses our attention not on the bush or the fire itself but, unexpectedly, on Mūsā's reaction to seeing such a miraculous thing.

Mūsā and the fire in the Qur'ān

The Qur'ān relates the account of Mūsā's first encounter with the Divine five times, with somewhat varying information in each version. Interestingly, the fire itself does not appear in all five tellings, though it is clearly alluded to in each one. In order to obtain a complete picture of the event, and its significance for understanding Ibn al-Milḥ's poem, one must read all the versions together.[16]

According to the Qur'ān in chapter 28, after Mūsā killed a man in Egypt, he ran to Midian to escape.[17] There he met and aided some female shepherds who were being abused, and who subsequently brought him home and asked their father to hire him (28:26). The father agreed to employ his daughters' savior on condition that Mūsā marry one of the daughters and serve him for a period of eight to ten years.[18] Mūsā agreed to the terms, married the man's daughter and served him as contracted. When the term was completed, Mūsā took his family and left his father-in-law's house, intending to return to Egypt. It was then that something miraculous happened. Lost and without fire, Mūsā spied a fire on a mountain in the distance. Assuming it had been lit and was tended to by people, he told his family to wait while he traveled to it. "I will bring you news from there, or a burning stick for you to warm yourselves," he said (28:29).[19] When he reached the fire, a voice suddenly called to him by name, from the right-hand side of the valley, from a tree (28:30). It identified itself as the voice of Allāh, the Lord of Worlds, and commanded him to take off his shoes, for he was in a sacred valley (20:11–12).[20] The voice of Allāh then informed Mūsā that he had been chosen to go to Fir`awn (Pharaoh) because Fir`awn had become arrogant.[21] He provided Mūsā with two signs of His power: he turned Mūsā's staff into a snake and then back to a staff, and turned Mūsā's hand white without harming it.[22]

In comparing the lover to Mūsā at this particular moment of divine revelation, Ibn al-Milḥ emphasizes the shock that the lover felt when his avoidant beloved suddenly underwent a change of heart and kissed him.[23] After all, Mūsā was not expecting to meet Allāh at this fire. Cold and lost, he was searching for human contact and help, not theophany. Just as Mūsā was not expecting Allāh when he approached the fire, the last thing that Ibn al-Milḥ's lover was expecting from his cruel beloved was physical affection. Indeed, as we see in line 1, the lover had geared himself up for a confrontation with his beloved. Worn out from his unconsummated and unreturned passion, and no longer willing to absorb the alienating and haughty treatment, the lover initiates a verbal interaction (شفيا), one that seems intended to force the beloved to react to him in some way. When the beloved responds with intimate physicality, kissing, the lover is as shocked as Mūsā was, he tells us.

Impressively, in the eight words of line 3, Ibn al-Milḥ manages to call to mind three different types of surprise, radiating out in three different directions. The first two surprises are those of Ibn al-Milḥ's lover and of Mūsā, as just discussed. But let us not forget the surprise of the audience reading or hearing these words for the first time. After all, Ibn al-Milḥ has here compared the surprise felt by a man when his male beloved kisses him to the surprise of one of the greatest prophets in Islam at the moment that he first encounters God. One would be hard pressed to imagine a more shocking and almost blasphemous comparison for a Muslim audience than that between homoerotic intimacy and divine revelation.

In addition to the fact that Ibn al-Milḥ's poem utilizes the narrative of Mūsā's theophany – one of the most spiritually charged of the Qur'ānic episodes – to such a sacrilegious end, we note that the poem also changes a significant element of the Qur'ānic account in its comparison. Namely, the poem maintains that when Mūsā approached the fire, فناجى الها (*fa-nāja illāhan*), he spoke to God.[24] Yet, this is not quite what takes place in the Qur'ān. There, in each of the five renditions of the account, it is Allāh, not Mūsā, who speaks at the fire. He calls Mūsā by name, introduces Himself, and begins showcasing His power, turning Mūsā's staff into a snake, then turning his hand white. Allāh informs Mūsā that he is to go to Fir`awn to rebuke him because Fir`awn has been sinning. While Mūsā does speak in two of the renditions, in Q 20 and Q 28, both times he simply responds to something Allāh said.[25]

Not only does Ibn al-Milḥ shift the initiative from Allāh to Mūsā, he uses the very vocabulary of the Qur'ān itself in doing so. According to Ibn al-Milḥ, Mūsā went toward the light to get fire for his family with no prior knowledge of what awaited him there, and once there فناجى الها (*fa-nāja illāhan*). This phrase, meaning he whispered to Allāh, or entrusted Allāh with a secret, or took Allāh into his confidence, is the very one used by the Qur'ān to describe Allāh's first interaction with Mūsā.[26] But in the Qur'ān, the phrase places Allāh as the subject of the action and Mūsā as the object. In Q 19:51, Allāh commands Muḥammad to relate to his people the story of Mūsā, a man specially chosen by Allāh to be both a messenger and a prophet. In the next verse, Allāh continues: "وَنَٰدَيْنَٰهُ مِن جَانِبِ ٱلطُّورِ ٱلْأَيْمَنِ وَقَرَّبْنَٰهُ نَجِيًّا," "We called to him from the right-hand side of the mountain and brought him close to Us, in secret communion (*najīyyan*)."[27] Ibn al-Milḥ retains the Qur'ān's vocabulary in his poem but attributes it to the opposite character. Instead of Allāh bringing Mūsā into communion with Him in a secret and intimate fashion, Ibn al-Milḥ's Mūsā initiates contact, the very same intimate contact, with the Deity (*fa-nāja illāhan*). In reversing the subject and object of the Qur'ān's phrase, Ibn al-Milḥ draws our attention to this moment even more acutely.

Mūsā's theophany and Islamic exegesis

Given this significant deviation from the text of the Qur'ān, one would do well to turn to the Islamic exegetical materials to see if Ibn al-Milḥ's presentation of the events finds grounding in a traditional explanation of the account. As in the analyses of Ibn Ḥazm's poems, the relevant materials come from the exegesis and history of Muḥammad b. Jarīr al-Ṭabarī (d. 923), from the collection of extra-Qur'ānic narratives by the respected compiler Aḥmad b. Muḥammad al-Tha`labī (d. 1036), from the reconstructed biography of Muḥammad by Ibn Isḥāq (d. 767), and from the *tafsīr* of `Abdallāh b. `Umar al-Bayḍāwī (d. 1286). These will be supplemented by the early commentary of Muqātil b. Sulaymān (713–67), the exegesis of al-Qummī (d. *c.* 940), the *qiṣaṣ al-anbiyā'* works of Muḥammad b. `Abdallāh al-Kisā'ī (eleventh century) and of the Andalusian Ibn Muṭarrif al-Ṭarafī (Cordoba, d. 1032), the history of Ibn `Asākir (1105–76), and from the *tafsīr* of Abū al-Fidā' Ismā`īl b. Kathīr (d. 1373).

Puzzlingly, the Islamic exegetes do not provide much commentary on the matter that would prove helpful for understanding Ibn al-Milḥ's poem more clearly. The classical sources concern themselves mostly with explaining the more practical problems of the story as it appears in Scripture. Namely, why was Mūsā looking for fire? Did he not have a fire-stick with him, as any traveler would have? And, why was fire so important at that particular juncture in his travels? What does the Qur'ān mean when it relates that Mūsā was looking for "guidance"? Guidance regarding what precisely?[28]

In answering these questions, the exegetes present a relatively united front. Mūsā, they relate, was looking for guidance because he had gotten lost along the way and no longer knew which direction to turn in order to get to Egypt. Additionally, it was winter, and nighttime, and some say it was raining heavily or snowing.[29] Others note that the situation was even more dire: Mūsā's wife was pregnant and her labor pains had begun.[30] Cold and in the dark, the family needed a flame in order to stay warm. So, Mūsā took out the fire-drill that he carried with him. But no matter how many times he struck it, nor how hard he tried, he could not coax a spark out of it, although it had been working on earlier occasions.[31] Seeing a fire in the distance, Mūsā logically assumed the flames had been kindled by human hands, and so he took himself over to the mountain in search of a burning ember for fire for his family and directions for the trip.

The sources relate relatively similar accounts regarding what happened when Mūsā reached the fire. As in the Qur'ān, according to the extra-scriptural materials Mūsā was not the first to react upon seeing the flames. Indeed, some report that he did not realize the unusual nature of the fire at all. Others maintain that he saw that the more brightly the flames burned, the more green the bush from which they arose became.[32] Even so, Mūsā did not initiate an interaction with the bush.[33] Instead, as he reached the area in his search for fire, the flaming bush made the first move; it drew back from him as he approached. Startled by the unusual sight of a moving (and flaming) shrub, Mūsā himself moved backwards, away from it, in great fear. When he then moved to leave the site entirely, the bush suddenly moved closer to him. Then, as in the Qur'ān, a voice began speaking to Mūsā and commanded him to remove his shoes.[34] The voice revealed itself to be the voice of Allāh who, as in the Qur'ān, brought Mūsā into His confidence by giving him the signs of His power and sending him on a mission to Fir`awn.

Mūsā's theophany and Ṣūfī thought

As is evident, Ibn al-Milḥ's presentation of the account of Mūsā's theophany veers from the details as told in both the Qur'ān and the *tafasīr*. In both groups of sacred texts, Allāh takes the initiative; by contrast, the poem indicates that Mūsā acted first. Yet we should not dismiss Ibn al-Milḥ as simply having made a mistake in his reading of the Qur'ān. Nor should we jump to the conclusion that he purposely altered the sacred narrative for poetry's sake. Rather, further examination shows that Ibn al-Milḥ's poetic presentation reflects a reading of the text found more commonly in Ṣūfī circles.

Most basically, Ibn al-Milḥ's comparison of the lover's desire for his beloved reflects the Ṣūfī yearning for union with Allāh and the Ṣūfī representation of such yearning which utilizes the terms and imagery of human intimacy. Although some Ṣūfīs demanded distance from sexuality and other entrapments of the material world in order to attain gnosis, many more understood human sexuality as a useful and important tool in the quest to achieve union with the Divine. Passionate human love, after all, is the most powerful of human emotions, the one through which two people fuse together. And, fusion with the Divine is what a mystic seeks above all. Thus, the twelfth-century mystic Rūzbiḥān Baqlī spoke of human love as "the ladder toward the love of the Merciful."[35] Working on this same understanding of the human experience, the famed Persian mystic Jalal al-Dīn Rūmī (d. 1273) filled his *Mathnawī* with sexualized tales and language, aimed at conveying mystical knowledge.[36] Annemarie Schimmel notes that Rūmī once explained himself by saying, "My dirty jokes are not dirty jokes, but instruction."[37] So well utilized was the imagery of human passion by Ṣūfī poets, that at times a reader can almost not tell if one is reading a lust poem or a religious poem.

The Ṣūfī use of the terminology of eroticism gives a new perspective on the most obviously sacrilegious element of Ibn al-Milḥ's words: his comparison of a prophetic experience of God to that of a human couple engaging in a passionate kiss. While non-mystics see kissing as an expression of sexual arousal and attraction, in Sufism the language of kissing was used as a "tender expression of divine grace and inspiration."[38] A kiss was seen as more than simply flesh on flesh; for the Ṣūfīs, kissing was seen as symbolizing an exchange of souls.[39] It was said that during the wee hours of the night, the loneliest part of the day, the soul received the kiss of grace from the Divine. Because of this image, the nightly prayers (*munājāt*) of the Ṣūfīs became a most favored practice, a time for intimate communion and union with the beloved divinity.[40]

Ibn al-Milḥ's comparison is made even more blasphemous by the homoeroticism in his poem, by the fact that the two people engaged in a passionate kiss which recalls the interaction of Allāh and Mūsā are both male. Yet Ṣūfī poems utilized just such homoerotic imagery in their pious paeans. For Ṣūfī poets, the beautiful male youth on the cusp of manhood (*c.* 14 years of age) served as testimony to the eternal beauty of the Divine.[41] Indeed, they were known to envision Allāḥ Himself in the form of a beardless youth, often wearing a cap awry. Although orthodox Muslim thinkers and authorities decried what they perceived to be a blasphemous anthropomorphism of an unembodied divinity, Ṣūfīs insisted that they had not fabricated this image; they noted that it is found in a *ḥadīth*. There Muḥammad reports that he saw Allāh as a beautiful youth with abundant hair, dressed in robes of gold, seated on a throne, and wearing a crown. Variant versions report that the youth was wearing a cap on his head, set askew.[42] Thus Ṣūfīs extolled the beauty of boys, as symbolic of Allāh, and in similar fashion they wrote of yearning for union with males, precisely as Ibn al-Milḥ's lover does.

Another moment of potential sacrilege in Ibn al-Milḥ's verse results from his setting up as a parallel of sorts to Allāh a beloved who is not only beautiful but cruel, thus implying cruelty on Allāh's part as well. Yet even this notion appears in Ṣūfī thought and poetry, where poets present the "beautiful boy" who stands for the Divine as hard-hearted and tormenting.[43] In her study of the Qur'ān commentary of the twelfth-century Persian mystic Rashīd al-Dīn Maybudī, Annabel Keeler explains that Ṣūfīs understood that before Allāh led one to gnosis, He first caused one to suffer difficulties, sometimes quite severe; only by suffering first could one truly experience the subsequent intensity of love in union with the Divine. Thus, in Maybudī's phrasing, Allāh first brings a seeker into a "field of perplexity" and makes him feel as if his head were a ball for the "polo-stick of affliction."[44]

Importantly, Ṣūfīs saw this harsh divine behavior in the Qur'ānic narrative of Mūsā at the fire, precisely as Ibn al-Milḥ's poem implies. In Maybudī's commentary on the Qur'ān, he explains that when Mūsā entered the wilderness in his trip toward Midian (in Q 28:22), he entered symbolically into this "field of perplexity" and hardship.[45] Maybudī insists that this was not a coincidental stumbling into difficulty. Rather, because Allāh desired to guide Mūsā to Him and connect with him, He first had to ensure Mūsā's suffering. Allāh thus commanded that the road become lost, that the clouds rain down cold rain, that Mūsā's family (including his pregnant wife) cry out in distress, and that the flints refuse to spark.[46] The idea that Allāh had manipulated the events, had caused Mūsā to lose his way or the fire-drill to go dry, appears in some of the traditional exegesis as well.[47] But the non-Ṣūfī reason for this elaboration of the Qur'ānic text differs from Maybudī's. The traditional exegetes were concerned with explaining difficulties in the Qur'ānic text (i.e., how could Mūsā, a seasoned traveler, suddenly get lost and why did he not bring fire-starting tools with him when he set out, etc.). They also wanted to show divine control over the universe, and over prophets' lives in particular. Thus, the exegetical elaborations teach that Mūsā did not just happen to stumble upon this miraculous fire and its charge of prophecy; rather, Allāh chose him in advance and purposely led him to it, and to his prophetic mission. Maybudī, however, sees this moment as significant for an additional reason; Allāh led Mūsā through hardship before leading him to union with Him. According to Maybudī, the flints themselves pointed this out to Mūsā. Frustrated by his inability to cause the flints to spark, Maybudī writes, Mūsā threw the flints away from himself in a pique. When he did so, they turned to him in explanation. Do not be angry with us, said the flints, we have more than enough fire in us but Allāh commanded that we give none to you; He arranged all of this hardship, they added, so that He could then lead you to Himself at the fire. There, as readers know, He then favored Mūsā with gnostic intimacy.[48]

Ṣūfīs and Mūsā's journey

Maybudī is not the only Ṣūfī to see parallels between the mystic's experience of the Divine and Mūsā's. For the Ṣūfīs generally, Mūsā served as a model they strove to emulate. After all, in the Qur'ān the Divine speaks with Mūsā directly, on more than one occasion, a fact that earns Mūsā the title *al-kalīm*, a designation that can be understood either as Allāh's "mouthpiece" or Allāh's "interlocutor."[49] This direct experience of Allāh, unmediated by any external agent or by an altered state of being, was exactly what the Ṣūfīs most desired for themselves. As mystics, they were much concerned with attaining an immanent experience of the Divine. Mūsā in his journey toward the fire at which such an experience took place became the model of the spiritual wayfarer. Paul Nwyia writes that early Ṣūfī exegetes taught that meditating on Mūsā's experiences would open a gateway for the mystic into a direct relationship with God, as Mūsā had experienced. Indeed, later Ṣūfīs came to regard Mūsā as the perfect mystic, one who was "called to enter into the mystery of God."[50]

One of the earliest of the mystical interpretations of Mūsā's story can be found in the *tafsīr* attributed to Ja`far al-Ṣādiq (d. 765), the sixth Shī`ī imam whom the Ṣūfīs valued as a great mystic.[51] As Annabel Keeler observed and explained,

Ja`far al-Ṣādiq understood Mūsā's own journey from Egypt to Midian and then from Midian to the mountain in the valley of Ṭuwā not simply as a historical fact but as symbolic of a spiritual journey which he was then undergoing.[52] Ja`afar al-Ṣādiq called his readers' attention to Q 28:22, which records that when Mūsā set out for Midian, he asked Allāh to guide him along the correct path. According to Ja`far al-Ṣādiq, this verse indicates that Mūsā was not simply asking for practical travel help but that he was orienting his heart toward the Divine in search of His spiritual guidance.[53] He progressed in his spiritual journey when he arrived at Midian's waters and found a group of men watering their flocks while preventing the female shepherds from doing so. Q 28:23–4 relates that Mūsā rose and aided them, watering their flocks for them. He then withdrew into the shade and prayed, "My Lord, I am in dire need of whatever good thing You may send me" (v. 24). For Ja`far al-Ṣādiq, this prayer presents Mūsā's declaration of his awareness of his own need, of his absolute dependence upon the Divine.[54] Indeed, Mūsā here refers to himself as فقيرٌ (*faqīr*), impoverished, a term used to refer to the Ṣūfī mendicant, a fact that perhaps inspired Ja`far's interpretation. Mūsā's progress continued when he left Midian and traveled with his family to Egypt, stopping finally at the mountain in the valley of Ṭuwā in search of fire. There Allāh commanded Mūsā to remove his shoes (Q 20:12). The classical exegetes maintain that this was because Mūsā's shoes were of donkey leather, an impure substance, and the land he stood on was holy.[55] Ja`far al-Ṣādiq, however, maintains that the command had nothing to do with practical ritual purity; instead, it symbolized the mystic's imperative to remove from his heart everything other than the Divine, Who then fills it instead.[56]

Ja`far al-Ṣādiq's understanding of the theophanic culmination of Mūsā's spiritual journey provides a framework for explaining Ibn al-Milḥ's poetic rewriting of the Qur'ān. According to Ja`far, the theophany that Mūsā experienced was possible only because Mūsā had undergone what Ṣūfīs call the state of *fanā'*, the annihilation of the self, commonly understood as the highest level on the mystic's journey. In this state, one successfully denies one's human consciousness, and one absents oneself so completely that all that remains is the Divine. Indeed, one exists only with and through the Divine. Ja`far al-Ṣādiq understood that at the moment at which Allāh spoke to Mūsā, Mūsā qua Mūsā was completely absent; he subsisted only through Allāh. A similar idea appears in Maybudī's twelfth-century *tafsīr*. Commenting on Q 67:1, Maybudī writes that hearing the name of God, "Allāh," automatically induces in the seeker the annihilation of the self (*fanā'*). Indeed, the one who hears this name pronounced becomes so effaced that not even his imagination remains. This, Maybudī writes, is what happened to Mūsā when Allāḥ spoke to him at the fire in Q 20:12 and introduced Himself to him. At that moment, Mūsā completely absented himself from himself and, having achieved *fanā'*, existed only for the Divine. The fire, he explains, was not simply a fire but symbolized the fire of *tawḥīd*, of unity with God.[57]

With this state of *fanā'* in mind, we are able to understand better Ibn al-Milḥ's seemingly odd attribution of action or speech to Mūsā, a complete contrast to the Qur'ān's depiction of the events. In the first place, when one has undergone such desired annihilation, one no longer truly exists. One has successfully removed what Maybudī calls "the veil of division" between one's self and the Other; all that remains once the person has united with the Divine is the Divine. This conflation of Allāh and Mūsā, in his role as the successfully effaced seeker, is reflected in Ibn al-Milḥ's choice of words. Instead of drawing two distinct portraits, one of Allāh and one of Mūsā, Ibn al-Milḥ blurs the line between them by attributing speech to the one who did not speak. Such Ṣūfī melding of an erased human personality with the Divine expressed in speech appears most famously in the story of Manṣūr al-Ḥallāj (858–922). According to legend, al-Ḥallāj once knocked on the door of his master Junayd and when the latter asked who was there, the ecstatic al-Ḥallāj replied, "*Anā al-ḥaqq*," I am the Absolute Truth, identifying himself in his annihilated state with one of the names of Allāh.[58] Ibn al-Milḥ conflates Mūsā and Allāh in his poem not only by assigning Allāh's actions to Mūsā but by using the very term with which the Qur'ān describes Allāh's actions. As previously noted, in Q 19:52 Allāh relates that when He called Mūsā to Him on the mountain, He قَرَّبْنَٰهُ نَجِيًّا (*qarrabnahu najīyyan*), "brought him close to Us in secret communion." Pointedly, in Ibn al-Milḥ's poem, Mūsā approached the light to get fire but then *he* whispered or conferred with God with precisely this terminology; فناجى الها (*fa-nāja illāhan*), writes Ibn al-Milḥ, turning the subject into the object and the object into the subject as they join together in communion.

The earlier Ja`far al-Ṣādiq likewise puts words in Mūsā's mouth despite Mūsā's silence in the Qur'ān. Tantalizingly for this reading of Ibn al-Milḥ's poem, Ja`far maintains that Mūsā verbalized an explanation to Allāh of his own state of *fanā'*. Commenting on Q 20:11–12, a Qur'ānic passage in which Mūsā never utters a word, Ja`far writes that Mūsā declared to Allāh that Allāh was the only thing that existed, that Mūsā existed only through Him, and that he bears only those attributes that Allāh bestows upon him, namely His own.[59] In other words, according to Ja`far al-Ṣādiq, not only had Mūsā successfully effaced himself and joined with the Divine at the fire but then he, not Allāh, declared his own success.

Ibn al-Milḥ's Ṣūfī-esque lack of differentiation between seeker and Sought accounts for another potentially odd turn of phrase in his poem. In the second line, Ibn al-Milḥ writes of the lover's surprise when the beloved replaces his standoffish treatment of the lover with kissing. The lover notes that the beloved فجاد علي بتقبيلةٍ (*fa-jāda alayya bi-taqabilatin*). Closely rendered, the phrase reads: he generously granted me kissing. But, who kissed whom?[60] The grammar of the sentence does not specify who kisses and who is kissed. And in not clarifying, the sentence sends an important message and relates a recognizable truth: when two lovers merge in passionate embrace, particularly in kissing, there is no real divide between actor and recipient. Both kiss and are kissed simultaneously. This resembles Mūsā's union with the Divine, in which Mūsā fused with his Creator to become one in intimacy with Him.

Summary

At the outset, Ibn al-Milḥ's poem of desire appears to function within the boundaries of the tropes of Andalusian poetry. It includes a yearning and loyal lover, a cruel beloved, and a surprising moment of physical union. Even the comparison of this secular moment of surprise to Scripture does not initially strike readers as problematic. After all, such scriptural incorporation constituted a favorite Andalusian method of playing with the audience/readership.

A closer look, however, reveals that the poet's presentation of the Qur'ānic account has deviated not from the motifs of poetry but from the sacred text itself, and in one very significant way. In using somewhat vague language, and attributing Qur'ānic verbs to Mūsā, Ibn al-Milḥ's poem suggests a shifting of the action from the deity to the prophet, a shift that implies a measure of initiative on the part of the human actor which is absent from the Qur'ān itself. This move is not reflected in any of the traditional exegetical materials which serve to explicate and expand upon the narratives of the Qur'ān.

Yet, Ibn al-Milḥ's presentation of the scriptural account here does not fall outside the bounds of Muslim thought entirely. Instead, a close reading shows that it reflects a Ṣūfī reading of the sacred text, of Mūsā's first experience of theophany in particular.[61] Ṣūfīs understood that Mūsā not only encountered the Divine at the fire of Ṭuwā, as in the Qur'ān, but united with Him there in mystical gnosis. In comparing the interaction between the lover and his beloved to that between the prophet and Allāh, Ibn al-Milḥ turns an intimate erotic encounter into a moment of mystical gnosis. In a sense, in so doing, the poem does the reverse of what Ṣūfī poetry does; while Ṣūfī poetry uses human passion as a model for the mystic's relationship with the Divine, Ibn al-Milḥ's poem uses the relationship with the Divine as a model for human relationships. He thus transforms the beloved from a pretty, young, cruel, object of desire into a source of revelation. As in the three poems by Ibn Ḥazm, Ibn al-Milḥ's poem uses a sacred image to sacralize human passion, moving desire out of the field of the physical and insisting on its spiritual nature and power.

Notes

1 Ibn Sa'īd al-Andalusī, *Rāyāt al-mubarrizīn*, 91.
2 See Nykl, *Hispano-Arabic Poetry*, 129–33. Nykl (p. 132) refers to the pleasures of the flesh in which Mu'taḍid engaged as the "pleasures of Venus."
3 Ibid., 133. Nykl brings a poem proving Ibn al-Milḥ's skill on the matter here.
4 See *Rāyāt al-mubarrizīn*, 91, n. 182.
5 As noted by the editor of Ibn Sa'īd's *Rāyāt al-mubarrizīn*, 91, n. 181.
6 Ibid.
7 Ibid., 91.
8 Ibid., 91, n. 182.
9 Ibid., 91. English translation, mine. Since the authorship of the poem is under dispute, I refer to the poet here as Ibn al-Milḥ, the name by which both father and son were known. When I mean to differentiate between the two, I use the man's *kunya* (nickname).

10 Such creeping up on sleeping beloveds, an activity known as دبيب (*dabīb*), was a recognized way of engaging them, in poetry if not in fact (though likely also in fact). See Chapter 3, n. 7, and Chapter 4, p. 127 and n. 45. The poem by Ibn Shuhayd mentioned below in n. 14 is one example of this practice.

11 The verb, from the root *tyh* (تيه), also means to get lost and wander about. This does not appear to be the meaning used here. Instead, the verb's indication of arrogant and haughty behavior, a boastful swaggering brag, seems more appropriate. Emilio García Gómez translates the phrase as "y se mostraba altanero." See García Gómez, *El Libro de las Banderas*, 159.

12 *Rāyāt al-mubarrizīn*, 84–5; English translation from Bellamy and Steiner, *Banners of the Champions*, 172 (#161).

13 *Rāyāt al-mubarrizin*, 178 [Bellamy and Steiner, *Banners of the Champions*, 173 (#162)]. Ibn Sa`īd says of his beloved that she came to him as a red rose and he left her as an oxeye daisy. In other words, she arrived to their encounter as a virgin but did not leave that way.

14 *Rāyāt al-mubarrizīn*, 162 [Bellamy and Steiner, *Banners of the Champions*, 175 (#164)]. For more on Abū Ja`far, see *Rāyāt al-mubarrizīn*, 170–1.

Ibn Sa`īd's compilation is full of poems with sentiments like this. A particularly vivid example comes from Ibn Shuhayd (Cordoba, 992–1035), who writes of sneaking up to his sleeping beloved boy after the night watchman had dozed off and then engaging in passionate kissing with him all night long. See *Rāyāt al-mubarrizīn*, 124–5 [Bellamy and Steiner, *Banners of the Champions*, 188 (#177)]. The Hebrew poets also frequently wrote of kissing, usually in an oblique fashion; rather than mentioning the act outright, they spoke of drinking in the nectar of the beloved's mouth or flower or the like. See Chapter 1, p. 7.

15 In one such example, Samuel ha-Nagid writes of the fire of beauty that rests in faces of the daughters of Zion when they look about themselves. This fire, a sacred fire, kills those who see them or get too close to them, much as the fire of the Tabernacle incinerated Nadab and Abihu, when they brought a foreign fire before the Lord without having been so authorized (Lev. 10:4). Though the fire of these girls' faces is thus clearly dangerous, Samuel calls it אש סנה (*esh sneh*), the fire of the burning bush. Like that fire, which did not harm its source (the bush), the fire of the faces of Zion's daughters does not harm its source (Zion's daughters). See Samuel ha-Nagid, *Diwan Shemuel ha-Nagid. Ben Tehillim*, 312 (#200). See also Chapter 5, n. 60. In another poem by Samuel ha-Nagid, a man enjoying a glass of red wine excitedly declares it to be like the אש סנה (*esh sneh*), aflame but without burning or melting the glass it sits in. Ibid., 289 (#142).

16 The five versions are: 19:51–3, 20:9–16, 27:7–12, 28:28–36, 79:15–19. Q 26:10–17 mentions the conversation between Mūsā and Allāh about Mūsā's mission to Egypt but gives the readers no sense that a miraculous event concerning fire had just taken place. Although this story was reviewed in Chapter 5 (especially, n. 66), since it is the basis of Ibn al-Milḥ's poem, it bears recounting here, in greater detail. This rendition will also emphasize different elements of the account, those more relevant to Ibn al-Milḥ's poem than those that were relevant for Ibn Ḥazm's in Chapter 5.

A similar episode appears in the Bible in Exodus 3, although the details differ. Most obviously, Moses and his family were not on their way to Egypt when he saw the burning bush. Rather, Moses was tending his father-in-law's sheep one day, still in Midian, when he took the sheep to graze on the edge of the desert, on Mt. Horeb. Suddenly, an angel appeared to him in the midst of the fire in the bush, which was not being consumed by the flames. Intrigued by this "great sight" and curious as to why the bush was not burning, Moses turned aside and moved closer to investigate further. At that point, God called out to him, by name.

17 Chapter 28 presents the longest sustained narrative of Mūsā's life, beginning with his birth and ending with his defeat of Qarūn (the biblical Koraḥ). It is the only rendition

to provide a full context for Mūsā's travels in Midian. It does not, however, explain the reason for or context in which Mūsā killed an Egyptian, nor do any of the other versions of the account.

18 The Qur'ān does not state why the old man strikes this somewhat strange deal nor which term Mūsā eventually fulfilled. This part of the account appears in Q 28 only. See Chapter 5, n. 61.

19 The word for "news" here is خبر (*khabr*). In Q 20:10, Mūsā notes more explicitly that they are lost, and not simply in need of traveler's updates: "Maybe I can bring you a flaming brand from it or find some guidance there." The Qur'ānic word for guidance here is هدى (*huda*). This is the same in the other versions of the account.

20 Q 20 is the only chapter to mention the removing of the shoes.

21 Allāh tells him this explicitly only in Q 28 and Q 20.

22 The shorter versions of this account, Q 19 and Q 79, do not mention these signs.

23 In Bellamy and Steiner's translation, the beloved allows the lover to kiss him. The Arabic seems to imply that the opposite has occurred, that the beloved bestows a kiss upon the lover (as I have translated). In truth, because of the grammar of the sentence, and the vocabulary chosen here, one could translate the phrase either way. See *Banners of the Champions*, 194 (#183). This will be discussed more at length below. See especially n. 60.

24 Bellamy and Steiner translate the phrase as "but then spoke to God in secret." See *Banners of the Champions*, 194 (#183). García Gómez translated similarly: "y tuvo un coloquio secreto con Dios." See *El Libro de las Banderas,* 158–9. The precise meaning of the verb is discussed further on in the paragraph.

25 In 20:17, Allāh asks Mūsā what is in his hand, and Mūsā replies that it is the stick he uses for work as a shepherd. In 28:39, after Allāh finishes telling Mūsā that He wants him to go to Fir`awn for he and his people are wicked, Mūsā points out that he had earlier killed an Egyptian and he fears that the Egyptians will kill him if he returns to the country. He also requests that Allāh send his brother Harūn (Aaron) with him as an aide. (Mūsā requests this in chapter 20 as well, but not in his first words to Allāh. See 20:25–35.) Mūsā's initial silence contrasts with the behavior of Moses in the Bible. In Exodus 3, Moses sees the fire, notes that it is strange, and announces that he is going to step closer to investigate further. Only after he does this does God speak to him from within the flames.

26 See Hans Wehr, *A Dictionary of Modern Written Arabic*, ed. J. Milton Cowan (Beirut: Librairie du Liban; London: Macdonald and Evans, 1980), s.v. نجا (نجو), form three. Lane does not attribute any meaning to the verb formed from this root that would make sense in this context (the definitions range from breaking wind, to feeling safe, to cleaning oneself after voiding one's bowels). He does include the form نجوى, which he defines as a "secret discourse between two parties," and the form نجيّ, which he defines as "a person, or persons, discoursing secretly, or telling secrets with one another." In Lane, *Arabic–English Lexicon*, vol. 2.

27 *The Qur'an: A New Translation by M. A. S. Abdel Haleem* (Oxford: Oxford University Press, 2004).

28 Other issues of concern were: What does it mean that the voice called Mūsā from the right side? What type of bush was it? How did the bush relate to the fire? See also the discussion in Chapter 5.

29 See Muqātil ibn Sulaymān, *Tafsīr Muqātil*, 3:22 (Q 20:9ff), 3:297 (Q 27:7), 3:343 (Q 28:29); al-Ṭabarī, *Jāmi` al-bayān*, 9 (16): 141–2 (on Q 20:9–10), 11 (19):133 (on Q 27:6–8), and 11 (20): 70 (on Q 28:29); idem, *Ta'rīkh*, 1:463; al-Tha`labī, *Qiṣaṣ*, 178; al-Kisā'ī, in Eisenberg, *Vita Prophetarum*, 209; Ibn Muṭarrif al-Ṭarafī, *The Stories of the Prophets*, intro. and notes by Tottoli, 139; Ibn Kathīr, *Tafsīr*, on Q 20:9–10 and 28:29–32. Al-Qummī maintains that heavy snow fell that night, and there were gusting winds, and darkness, and it was "hellish night." See al-Qummī, *Tafsīr al-Qummī*,

2:139 (Q 28:23–9). Ibn `Asākir notes that conditions were so terrible and the darkness so heavy, that it began to drive Mūsā a little mad. See Ibn `Asākir, *Ta'rīkh madīnat Dimashq*, 61:44.

30 See al-Kisā'ī, 209; al-Tha`labī, 178. Al-Bayḍawī maintains that Mūsā's wife had given birth that night. See al-Bayḍawī, *Tafsīr al-Bayḍawī*, on Q 20:10.

31 Ibn Isḥāq maintains that Allāh purposely caused the fire-drill's failure that night. See Ibn Isḥāq in Newby, 125. Similarly, al-Ṭarafi states that Allāh caused Mūsā to get lost (139). Other exegetes hint at this point, without stating it explicitly. See al-Ṭabarī, *Ta'rīkh*, 1:465; Ibn Isḥāq in Newby, 125.

32 As noted in Chapter 5 (n. 69), a few commentators maintain that angels surrounded the fire, but they do not specify if Mūsā could see them. See Muqātil, 3:297; al-Ṭabarī, *Jāmi` al-bayān*, 11 (19): 135 (Q 27:6–8); and `Abd al-Razzāq al-Ṣan`ānī (744–827), *Tafsīr al-Qur'ān al-`aẓīm*, 2:67 (Q 28:8). Muqātil says that he could hear them; Mūsā's attention was drawn to that fire by the sound of angels praising Allāh. See Muqātil, 3:343 (Q 20).

33 Al-Qummī, 2:140 (Q 28:23–9); al-Bayḍawī, on Q 20:11; al-Tha`labī, 178; Ibn `Asākir, 61:44–5. Ibn Kathīr notes that Mūsā stood mesmorized by the splendor of what he was seeing. See Ibn Kathīr on Q 27:8 and 28:30. Muqātil writes that he told his family to wait because he had seen a light or a fire, which was the fire of the Lord of Worlds (3:22 on Q 20:10), or of the Mighty Lord (3:297 on Q 27:7), or of the Holy Land (3:343 on Q 28:29).

34 Al-Ṭabarī, *Ta'rīkh*, 1:465–6; al-Ṭabarī, *Jāmi` al-bayān*, 9 (16): 143 (Q 20:11–12); al-Thal`abī, 178; al-Ṭarafī, 139, and Ibn Isḥāq, in Newby, 125. Al-Ṭabarī includes a number of reports in which Allāh first causes Mūsā to hear "the squeaking of a pen," i.e. Allāh writing His revelations in the Book. See *Jāmi` al-bayān*, 9 (16): 94–5 (Q 19:52–3).

35 Schimmel, "Eros," 133. For more on Baqlī, see Kristin Zahra Sands, *Ṣūfī Commentaries on the Qur'ān in Classical Islam* (London and New York: Routledge, 2006), 74–6.

36 This is discussed by Schimmel in "Eros," and at length by Mahdi Tourage in his *Rūmī and the Hermeneutics of Eroticism*, chapter 1. Tourage maintains that Rūmī was the only Persian mystic to employ the phallus as an esoteric symbol. In the Zohar and other texts, Jewish mysticism (known as *Kabbalah*) also understands human sexuality as an important tool for attaining gnosis and as an image with which to represent the human search for God. See for example Elliot Wolfson's studies, *Through a Speculum that Shines: Vision and Imagination in Medieval Jewish Mysticism* (Princeton, NJ: Princeton University Press, 1994); idem, *Circle in the Square: Studies in the Use of Gender in Kabbalistic Symbolism* (Albany: State University of New York Press, 1995). The Zohar describes Moses' high mystical state as Moses having had intercourse with the Shekhina (a feminine attribute of God), for he was her husband. See *EJ*, s.v. "Moses," section by Louis Jacobs (12:400–1).

37 Schimmel, "Eros," 121.

38 Ibid., 135.

39 The idea that one dies, exchanges one's soul with God, through a divine kiss can be found in the rabbinic exegetical materials as well. See the deaths of Moses, Aaron, and Miriam by God's kiss in *BT Baba Batra* 17a.

40 Schimmel, "Eros," 136. Annabel Keeler points out that the word *munājāt* derives from the same root, نجي (*njy*), used in Q 19:52 (noted above) to describe Allāh's taking Mūsā to him "in secret communion." See Annabel Keeler, *Sufi Hermeneutics: The Qur'an Commentary of Rashīd al-Dīn Maybudī* (Oxford and New York: Oxford University Press in association with the Institute for Ismaili Studies, 2006), 249. See discussion of *nāja/najīyyan* above, pp. 261–2.

41 Schimmel, "Eros," 131.

42 See Jim Wafer, "Muhammad and Male Homosexuality," in *Islamic Homosexualities: Culture, History and Literature*, ed. Stephen O. Murray and Will Roscoe (New York and London: New York University Press, 1997), 90. The orthodox authorities objected to this *ḥadīth* and rejected it as invalid. Ṣūfīs, however, referred to it often.
43 Schimmel, "Eros," 131–2.
44 Keeler, *Sufi Hermeneutics*, 251.
45 Ibid., 251–3. Mūsā was not the only Qur'ānic prophet to have experienced suffering as the precursor to divine love in the mystics' understanding; Ibn `Aṭā' al-Adamī (d. 922) wrote of Joseph that before Allāh allowed him to taste the "wine of intimacy," He first led him through a long journey in the "terrain of affliction." See ibid., 252.
46 Ibid., 254–5.
47 As already discussed above.
48 Keeler, *Sufi Hermeneutics*, 255.
49 See Chapter 5, n. 80.
50 As translated by Annabel Keeler, "Moses from a Muslim Perspective," in *Abraham's Children: Jews, Christians, and Muslims in Conversation*, ed. Norman Solomon, Richard Harries, and Tim Winter (New York: T & T Clark, 2005), 60. Keeler refers readers to Paul Nwyia, *Exégèse Coranique et Langue Mystique* (Beirut: Dar el-Machreq éditeurs, 1970), 83. One should not understand by this that Ṣūfīs elevated Mūsā over Muḥammad. They did not. Rather, they maintained that Mūsā served as a model for Muḥammad and his prophecy. As great as Mūsā was, Muḥammad was even greater.
51 Keeler points out that scholars are in doubt as to whether the attribution of this *tafsīr* to Ja`far is correct. She notes that Gerhard Böwering remained so doubtful that he referred to the author as "Pseudo-Ja`far al-Ṣādiq" and maintained that he lived 200 years after the Shī`ī imam, in the tenth century. See Keeler, "Moses from a Muslim Perspective," n. 22 and Böwering, "The Light Verse: Qur'ānic Text and Sufi Interpretation," *Oriens* 36 (2001): 135.
52 Keeler, "Moses from a Muslim Perspective," 60–1.
53 See Paul Nwyia, ed., *Le Tafsīr Mystique attribué a Ǧa`far Ṣadiq* (Beyrouth: Imprimerie Catholique, 1968), 216 (on Q 28:22). This idea is expressed by later Ṣūfīs as well. For example, Abū Ḥāmid Muḥammad al-Ghazzālī (d. 1111) maintains that Mūsā removed both shoes to signify his cutting off his attachment to both worlds, leaving him only with the Divine. See Keeler, *Sufi Hermeneutics*, 249.
54 See Nwyia, *Le Tafsir Mystique*, 216.
55 Muqātil, 3:22 (Q 20:12); al-Ṭabarī, *Jāmi` al-bayān*, 9 (16): 143–5 (Q 20:11–12); al-Tha`labī, 179; al-Ṭarafī, 140; Ibn Kathīr, 3:126 (on Q 20:12); al-Bayḍāwī (on Q 20:12) adds that removing one's shoes shows humility.
56 Nwyia, *Le Tafsir Mystique*, 209 (on Q 20:12).
57 Keeler, *Sufi Hermeneutics*, 257–9.
58 Despite al-Ḥallāj's intentions, he was executed for what was perceived to be an exceedingly blasphemous declaration. See Annemarie Schimmel, *Mystical Dimensions of Islam* (Chapel Hill: University of North Carolina Press, 1975), 62–77.
59 Nwyia, *Le Tafsir Mystique*, 209; Keeler discusses this in "Moses from a Muslim Perspective," 61.
60 Bellamy and Steiner, in *Banners of the Champion*, present the lover as the initiator of physical contact here, translating the phrase as "He generously allowed me to kiss him" (p. 194, #183). This interpretation draws strength from the fact that Andalusian poetic tropes generally insisted on a sexually active lover and a sexually receptive beloved (hence either a female or a young boy). Although both the active and passive roles in homosexual sexual activity were forbidden by Islamic law, medieval Islamic society (at least in literature) differentiated between the two roles. Everett Rowson has noted that a man's desire to be penetrated by another man was considered perverted and shameful; boys, however, since they were not yet men, could be penetrated without

losing their manliness, provided that they showed no pleasure at the act. See Rowson, "The Categorization of Gender," 64–6.

61 I do not intend to say here that this poem proves that Ibn al-Milḥ – either Abū al-Qāsim or Abū Bakr – was a Ṣūfī. Not much is known about father or son in the first place, let alone about their theological stances. A single poem, of uncertain authorship, certainly provides no real evidence in either direction. The most we can say is that some Ṣūfī ideas may have infiltrated the common squares in Andalusia, or in Silves in particular. My point here is much more specific. I maintain that this poem reflects a Ṣūfī-like attitude toward both human passion and intimacy, and toward the mystic's understanding of his relationship with the Divine.

Summary

Although it may be difficult to envision such a phenomenon in this day and age, among the famous composers of secular poetry in Muslim Spain were men who were not only themselves religious but also functioned as religious scholars and authorities. While serving as jurists, rabbis, imams, exegetes, religious philosophers, *khatībs*, liturgical poets, and religious communal leaders, they also composed verses extolling the beauty of nature, the delight of imbibing alcohol and sitting in gardens, the value of friendship and the pain of loss. Most startlingly, they wrote of love and desire, physical and powerful, hetero- and homoerotic, words that leap off the page and cross the centuries of time to grab hold of both our hearts and our guts.

In composing these works, the religious poets embraced and utilized the tropes and motifs of their time. As we have seen, beloveds are generally young, dark-haired and lovely, cruel and taunting, available and completely inaccessible. The lovers are left yearning, burning, and suffering from that most desired of illnesses, lovesickness. And, they followed the day's convention in incorporating sacred Scripture into their decidedly non-sacred poems of eros.

Earlier scholarship has maintained that such incorporation of the sacred into the profane served as a way of entertaining audiences and readers. Scholars have noted that Andalusian poets from all walks of society, writing in Arabic and Hebrew, loved to titillate their listeners. And little raises an amused eyebrow faster than the unexpected appearance of a character, or quote, or reference to a sacred text in a secular poem full of lust, love, and sexual innuendo.

Yet, if we see such references as simply poetic ornamentation or audience entertainment, we do the poems a disservice. After all, it can be no accident that the majority of such scriptural references occur in the poems of men who were themselves religious scholars of various types. As Neal Kozodoy has written of the Hebrew "courtier" poet, he was "bibliocentric at his spiritual core."[1] Indeed, Scripture and religion played a central role in both the private and intellectual lives of the Jewish and Muslim scholar-poets alike. It stands to reason that they could not completely abandon one part of their personality (religious scholar) while engaging the other part (secular love poet).

This study thus attempts to understand the scriptural allusions not as simple embellishment but as the multilayered and multifaceted religious signifiers that their audiences would have recognized. In this, I have engaged in an intertextual analysis, looking first to the scriptural source of the allusion used, to see the ways in which the poetic version both resembles and deviates from it. This comparison reveals an interesting "problem" common to the seven poems investigated here: none of the scriptural references in these *love* poems relates back to a narrative of *passionate love*. Instead, our lovers and their beloveds are compared to a father and son, a pious devotee of the Lord, an idolater and the object of his worship, an adulterous king and the general whom he cuckolds, two brothers intent on vengeance, a prophet and the Divine, and an incest-rapist. In order to gain insight into the scholar-poets' seemingly inappropriate use of these references, this study thus turned to the extra-scriptural traditions, both the classical and the contemporary, in which these characters and storylines appear.

Such analysis of the Arabic poems reveals that Ibn Ḥazm and Ibn al-Milḥ employed Scripture here in order to transmit a message about earthly human love. Namely, one should not categorize passionate human love, eros, as something belonging to the baser, sinful human tendencies. Instead, passionate love is like the salvific fire into which Ibrāhīm was thrown and from which he was rescued, like the life-giving footprints of the angel Jibrīl's miraculous horse, like Yusūf's Paradise-woven cloak which restored his father's sight, and like the divine communion experienced by Mūsā in the valley of Ṭuwā. In other words, the Arabic poems here use sacred imagery to justify the "profane" emotion and experience of human intimacy. Passionate love, we see here, is understood as miraculous, as holy, as prophetically mystical, and as redemptive.

In the Hebrew poems, we can see the opposite at work; allusions to the scriptural narratives in the eros poems of Ibn Mar Shaul and Ibn Gabirol serve as alternate interpretations of the biblical text. Uriah refuses to go home not because he is a loyal soldier but because he is in love with King David; Amnon's secret plot to "have" his sister was known and problematically ignored by the very men responsible for preventing its fulfillment; and Jacob's condemnation of Simeon and Levi's attack on the city of Shechem becomes a critique of his own inaction. Such readings of the Bible appear to be at odds with both the traditional and contemporaneous understanding of these accounts. In these somewhat radical analyses of Scripture, hiding in secular poems of desire, the poems of Ibn Mar Shaul and Ibn Gabirol reflect what Neal Kozodoy noted about the relationship between the Andalusian Hebrew poets and the Bible. It is, he wrote, an exegetical relationship, one in which "[p]art of a poem's indirect function might actually be thus to suggest new interpretations of the biblical text."[2] Somewhat ironically, while the medieval Jewish exegetes insisted on an approach to the Bible based on *peshat* (a simple plain reading), the poetic compositions of their contemporaries – which utilized the language, structure, and characters of the Bible – were anything but *pashut* (plain).[3]

The current study has concentrated on seven poems, written by four roughly contemporaneous poets. I do not presume that the use of scriptural allusions in eros poems as discussed here occurs across the board, in every case in which a scriptural allusion appears in an Andalusian poem of desire. In most cases, the

Muslim and Jewish poets incorporated Scripture in a fairly straightforward and indeed an ornamental manner. However, I maintain that the Hebrew poems analyzed here are not the only such compositions in which a biblical *remez* hints to an alternate reading of the sacred text.[4] Similarly, I suspect that Ibn Ḥazm and Ibn al-Milḥ are not the only two Muslim Arabic poets whose poems turn an experience of human love and desire into a sacred moment of salvation.

Such enfolding of exegesis and secular poetry is not entirely unforeseeable. After all, what differentiates poetry from other forms of verbal communication is precisely that it is composed of figurative language in need of interpretation.[5] The poets of Muslim Spain themselves encouraged this formula, insisting, as Moses ibn Ezra phrased it, "אטיב אלשער אכדבה" (*aṭyab al-shi'ir akdhabuhu*), the best of poetry is its deceitful, i.e., non-literal, part.[6] In analyzing the poems, we thus need not restrict ourselves to parsing them only in terms of their structure and syntax, engaging the scriptural language and phraseology for identification purposes alone. Instead, we are encouraged to investigate, with caution and care, what may lie beneath. As the Elizabethan poet, courtier, and soldier Sir Philip Sidney (1554–86) wrote, "There are many mysteries contained in Poetry, which of purpose were written darkly, lest by profane wits it should be abused."[7] It is my hope that this study has begun to unravel some of the mystery, without abusing the sanctity of either poem or Scripture.

Notes

1 Kozodoy, "Reading," 115.

2 Kozodoy, "Reading," 118. He calls this an incidental but significant benefit.
Poetry was not the only arena in which Jewish scholars of Iberia deviated from accepted readings of the Bible. In a study of Abraham ibn Ezra's commentary to the Song of Songs, David Wacks shows that Ibn Ezra's interpretation deviated from the traditional approach to the text, producing a commentary that might have been considered controversial to his contemporaries. Wacks sees in Ibn Ezra's work an "intertextual play linking biblical, exegetical, and poetic texts both sacred and secular." See David A. Wacks, "Between Secular and Sacred: Abraham ibn Ezra and the *Song of Songs*," in *Wine, Women and Song: Hebrew and Arabic Literature of Medieval Iberia*, ed. Michelle M. Hamilton, Sarah J. Portnoy, and David A. Wacks (Newark, DE: Juan de la Cuesta Hispanic Monographs, 2004), 47–58.

3 Dan Pagis brings a wonderful example of this in his commentary on a poem by Moses ibn Ezra in which the poet complains that as he grows older, his loneliness increases. Of the thirty-seven words of the poem, notes Pagis, only seven can be understood according to their plain (*peshat*) meaning. The other thirty are all metaphor on metaphor, and require one's focused attention and careful parsing in order to make the poem's meaning clear. See Pagis, *Shirat ha-Ḥol*, 35ff.

4 This claim derives from initial analysis of other select poems by Ibn Gabirol as well as by Samuel ha-Nagid, for future study.

5 In his early work on the Hebrew poetry and poetics of medieval Spain, Dan Pagis stresses this need. See his *Shirat ha-Ḥol*, 35ff and 46–50.

6 Rina Drory notes that in classical Arabic literature, the phrase appears as "احسن الشعر اكذبه" (*aḥsan al-shi'ir akdhabuhu*). See *Models and Contacts*, 5. See also Brann, *The Compunctious Poet*, 72ff. Brann notes, that the original source of this sentiment can be found in the *Metaphysics* of Aristotle. See ibid., 191, n. 63.

7 Cited by Morton W. Bloomfield in his "Allegory as Interpretation," *New Literary History* 3:2 (Winter, 1972): 306. Bloomfield himself wrote, "If a work of art is to have any meaning, it must in some sense be symbolic" (309).

Bibliography

'Abd al-Razzāq al-Ṣan'ānī, *Tafsīr al-Qur'ān al-'aẓīm*. Edited by Muṣṭafa Muslim Muḥammad. Riyad: Maktabat al-Rushd, 1989.

Abrabanel, Don Isaac. *Perush 'al Nevi'im Rishonim*. Jerusalem: Hotza'at Sefarim Torah va-Da'at, 5715 [1955].

—— *Perush ha-Tanakh*, 4 vols. Jaffa, 5714–5720 [1954–60].

—— *Perush ha-Torah*. Jaffa [1954–5].

Abrahams, Israel. *The Book of Delight and Other Papers*. New York: Arno Press, 1980.

Abramson, S., ed. *Kol Shirei Rabbi Shemuel ha-Nagid. Ben Mishle*. Tel Aviv, 1948.

Abū Zahrah, Muḥammad. *Ibn Ḥazm, ḥayātuhu wa-'aṣruhu, ārā'uhu wa-fiqhuhu*. Cairo: Dār al-fikr al-'arabī, 1393/1954.

Adams, Henry E., Lester W. Wright, Jr., and Bethany A. Lohr, "Is Homophobia Associated with Homosexual Arousal?," *Journal of Abnormal Psychology* 105:3 (1996): 440–5.

Adang, Camilla. *Muslim Writers on Judaism and the Hebrew Bible: From Ibn Rabban to Ibn Hazm*. Leiden, New York, and Köln: E. J. Brill, 1996.

Albayrak, Ismail. "The Qur'ānic Narratives of the Golden Calf Episode." *Journal of Qur'ānic Studies* 3:1 (2001): 47–69.

Ali, Abdullah Yusuf, trans. *The Holy Qur-an: Text, Translation and Commentary*. Lahore, Pakistan, 1946.

Ali, Ahmed, trans. *Al-Qur'ān: A Contemporary Translation*. Princeton, NJ: Princeton University Press, 1984.

Allony, Nehemiah. "The Reaction of Moses Ibn Ezra to 'Arabıyya." *Bulletin of the Institute of Jewish Studies* 3 (1975): 19–40.

Allony, Nehmiah. "Ha-Tzvi ve-ha-Gamal be-Shirat Sefarad." *Otzar Yehudei Sefarad* 4 (1961): 16–42.

Amichai, Yehuda. *Akhshav u-be-Yamim Aḥerim*. Israel, 1960.

Amīn, Uthmān, ed. *Iḥṣā' al-'ulūm*, 2nd edition. Cairo: Dār al-fikr al-'arabī, 1949.

Arberry, A. J., trans. *Moorish Poetry*. Cambridge: Cambridge University Press, 1953.

—— *The Ring of the Dove*. London: Luzac and Company, Ltd., 1953.

Al-'Askarī, Abū Hilāl. *Dīwān al-ma'ānī* [The Book of Poetic Themes]. Cairo: Maktabat al-qudsī, 1352 H. [1933].

Assis, Yom Tov. "Sexual Behavior in Mediaeval Hispano-Jewish Society." In *Jewish History: Essays in Honor of Chimen Abramsky*. Edited by Ada Rapoport-Alpert and Steven J. Zipperstein. London: Peter Halban, 1988.

Avoth de-Rabbi Nathan. Solomon Schechter Edition. New York and Jerusalem: Jewish Theological Seminary of America, 1997.

Babylonian Talmud. Vilna: Ram Publishers, 1927.

Baiḍawī's Commentary on Sūrah 12 of the Qur'ān. Translated by A. F. L. Beeston. Oxford: Clarendon Press, 1963.

Baneth, David Tzvi. "Ha-Shirah ha-`Aravit ha-Qeduma." In *Peraqim be-Toledot ha-`Aravim ve-ha-Islam.* Edited by Hava Lazarus-Yafeh. [Tel Aviv]: Hotza'at Reshafim, [1967].

—— "Ha-Shirah ve-ha-Proza ha-Omanutit ba-Tequfa ha-`Abbasit." In *Peraqim be-Toledot ha-'Aravim ve-ha-Islam.* Edited by Hava Lazarus-Yafeh. Tel Aviv: Hotza'at Reshafim, 1967.

Bar-Efrat, Shimon. *Narrative Art in the Bible.* Sheffield: Almond Press, 1989.

Bauer, Thomas and Angelika Neuwirth, eds. *Ghazal as World Literature I: Transformations of a Literary Genre.* Beirut: Ergon Verlag Würzburg in Kommission, 2005.

al-Bayḍāwī, `Abdallah b. `Umar. *Tafsīr al-Bayḍāwī.* Beirut: Dār al-kutub al-`ilmiyya, 1988.

Bell, Richard, trans. *The Qur`ān,* 2 vols. Edinburgh: T & T Clark, 1937.

Bellamy, James A. "The Impact of Islam on Early Arabic Poetry." In *Islam: Past Influence and Present Challenge.* Edited by Alford T. Welch and Pierre Cachia. Albany, NY: SUNY Press, 1979.

—— "Qasmuna the Poetess: Who was She?" *JAOS* 103 (1983): 423–4.

—— "Sex and Society in Islamic Popular Literature." In *Society and the Sexes in Medieval Islam.* Edited by Afaf Lutfi al-Sayyid Marsot. Malibu, CA: Undena Publications, 1979.

Bellamy, James A. and Patricia Owen Steiner. *The Banners of the Champions: An Anthology of Medieval Arabic Poetry from Andalusia and Beyond.* Madison, WI: The Hispanic Seminary of Medieval Studies, 1989.

Ben Solomon, Menaḥem. *Midrash Sekhel Tov `al Sefer Bereishit ve-Shemot.* Edited by S. Buber. Berlin, 5660 [1899].

Ben-Ze'ev, Judah Leib. *Shir 'Agavim.* Edited by G. Kressel. Tel Aviv, 5737 [1977].

Bencheikh, Jamel Eddine. "Poetry of the East." In *The Different Aspects of Islamic Culture,* Volume 5: *Culture and Learning in Islam.* Edited by Ekmeleddin İhsanoĝlu. Paris: Unesco Publishing, 2003.

Bernstein, Marc S. *Stories of Joseph: Narrative Migration between Judaism and Islam.* Detroit: Wayne State University, 2006.

Bernstein, Simon, ed. *Shirei Yehuda ha-Levi.* New York: Hotza'at Ogen, 1944.

Biale, David. *Eros and the Jews: From Biblical Israel to Contemporary America.* New York: Basic Books, 1992.

Bloch, Chana and Stephen Mitchell, eds and trans. *The Selected Poetry of Yehuda Amichai.* Berkeley, Los Angeles, and London: University of California Press, 1996.

Bloomfield, Morton W. "Allegory as Interpretation." *New Literary History* 3:2 (Winter 1972): 301–7.

Bonebakker, S. A. "Ancient Arabic Poetry and Plagiarism: A Terminological Labyrinth." *Quaderni di Studi Arabi* 15 (1997): 65–92.

—— "Religious Prejudice against Poetry in Early Islam." *Medievalia et Humanistica* 7 (1976): 77–99.

Borg, Gert. "The Divine in the Works of Umayya b. Abū al-Ṣalt." In *Representations of the Divine in Arabic Poetry.* Edited by Gert Borg and Ed de Moor. Amsterdam-Atlanta, GA: Rodopi, 2001.

Boudhiba, Abdelwahab. *Sexuality in Islam.* Translated by Alan Sheridan. London: Saqi Books, 2004.

Böwering, Gerhard. "The Light Verse: Qur'ānic Text and Sufi Interpretation." *Oriens* 36 (2001): 113–44.

Boyarin, Daniel. *Intertextuality and the Reading of Midrash*. Indianapolis: Indiana University Press, 1990.

Brann, Ross. "Andalusian Hebrew Poetry and the Hebrew Bible: Cultural Nationalism or Cultural Ambiguity?" In *Approaches to Judaism in Medieval Times*, vol. 3. Edited by David R. Blumenthal. Atlanta: Scholars Press, 1988.

—— "The Arabized Jews." In *The Literature of al-Andalus*. Edited by Maria Rosa Menocal, Raymond P. Scheindlin, and Michael Sells. Cambridge: Cambridge University Press, 2000.

—— *The Compunctious Poet: Cultural Ambiguity and Hebrew Poetry in Muslim Spain*. Baltimore: Johns Hopkins University Press, 1991.

—— "'How Can My Heart Be in the East?' Intertextual Irony in Judah Ha-Levi." In *Judaism and Islam: Boundaries, Communication, and Interaction*. Edited by B. H. Hary, J. L. Hayes, and F. Astren. Leiden: E. J. Brill, 2000.

—— *Power in the Portrayal: Representations of Jews and Muslims in Eleventh- and Twelfth-Century Islamic Spain*. Princeton and Oxford: Princeton University Press, 2002.

—— "Signs of Ambivalence in Islamic Spain: Arabic Representations of Samuel the Nagid." In *Ki Baruch Hu: Ancient Near Eastern, Biblical, and Judaic Studies in Honor of Baruch A. Levine*. Edited by Robert Chazan, William W. Hallo, and Lawrence Schiffman. Winona Lake, IN: Eisenbrauns, 1999.

Brener, Ann. *Isaac ibn Khalfun: A Wandering Poet of the Eleventh Century*. Leiden: E. J. Brill, 2003.

—— *Judah Halevi and His Circle of Hebrew Poets in Granada*. Leiden: E. J. Brill, 2005.

Brody, Ḥaim. "Moses ibn Ezra – Incidents in His Life." *JQR* 24 (1933): 309–20.

Brown, Francis, S. D. Driver, and Charles A., Briggs, eds. *A Hebrew and English Lexicon of the Old Testament*. Oxford: Clarendon Press, 1972.

Bürgel, J. C. "Luve, Lust, and Longing: Eroticism in Early Islam as Reflected in Literary Sources." In *Society and the Sexes in Medieval Islam* (Giorgio Della Vida Conference). Edited by Afaf Lufti al-Sayyid-Marsot. Malibu: Undena Publications, 1979.

Butrovic, Amila. "Ibn Quzman." In *The Literature of al-Andalus*. Edited by Maria Rosa Menocal, Raymond P. Scheindlin, and Michael Sells. Cambridge: Cambridge University Press, 2000.

Cachia, Pierre. "Andalusi Belles Lettres." In *The Legacy of Muslim Spain*. Edited by Salma Khadra Jayyusi. Leiden, Boston, New York, and Köln: E. J. Brill, 1992.

—— *Arabic Literature: An Overview*. London: RoutledgeCurzon, 2002.

Calder, Norman. "Tafsīr from Ṭabarī to Ibn Kathīr: Problems in the Description of a Genre, Illustrated with Reference to the Story of Abraham." In *Approaches to the Qur'an*. Edited by G. R. Hawting and Abdul-Kader Shareef. London and New York: Routledge, 1993.

Carmi, T., ed. and trans. *The Penguin Book of Hebrew Verse*. New York and London: Penguin Books, 1981.

Caro, R. Joseph. *Shulḥan Arukh, Oraḥ Hayyim* [Mif'al Shulḥan Arukh ha-Shalem]. Edited by Shamma Friedman. Jerusalem: Mif'al Shulḥan Arukh ha-Shalem, 5768 [2007].

Chankin-Gould, J. D'ror, *et al.* "The Sanctified 'Adulteress' and her Circumstantial Clause: Bathsheba's Bath and Self-Consecration in 2 Samuel 11." *Journal for the Study of the Old Testament* 32:2 (March 2008): 339–52.

Chavel, Ḥaim Dov, ed. *Perushei ha-Torah le-Rabbeinu Moshe ben Naḥman (Ramban)*. Jerusalem: Mossad Harav Kook, 1969.

Chejne, Anwar G. *Muslim Spain: Its History and Culture*. Minneapolis: University of Minnesota Press, 1974.

Chodkiewicz, Michel. "The Endless Voyage." *Journal of the Muhyiddin Ibn Arabi Society* 19 (1996).

Chronicles of Jeraḥmeel or the Hebrew Bible Historiale. Translated by Moses Gaster. Introduction by Haim Schwartzbaum. New York: KTAV, 1971.

Cohen, Gerson D. "The Song of Songs and the Jewish Religious Mentality." In *Studies in the Variety of Rabbinic Cultures*. Philadelphia: Jewish Publication Society, 1991.

Cohen, Mordechai Z. "The Best of Poetry: Literary Approaches to the Bible in the Spanish Peshat Tradition." *Torah U-Madda Journal* 6 (1995–6): 15–57.

—— *Three Approaches to Biblical Metaphor: From Ibn Ezra and Maimonides to David Kimhi*. Leiden: E. J. Brill, 2003.

Cohen, Tova. "Veils and Wiles: Poetry as Woman in Andalusian Hebrew Poetry." In *Israel and Ishmael*. Edited by Tudor Parfitt. Richmond, Surrey: Curzon Press, 2000.

Cole, Juan R. I. "Individualism and the Spiritual Path in Shaykh Aḥmad al-Aḥsā'ī." In *Shi`ite Heritage: Essays on Classical and Modern Traditions*. Edited by Lynda Clarke. Binghamton, NY: Global Publications/SUNY Binghamton, 2001.

Cole, Peter, trans. and ed. *The Dream of the Poem: Hebrew Poetry from Muslim and Christian Spain 950–1492*. Princeton: Princeton University Press, 2007.

—— trans. *Selected Poems of Solomon Ibn Gabirol*. Princeton and Oxford: Princeton University Press, 2001.

Colville, Jim, trans. *Poems of Wine and Revelry: The Khamriyyat of Abu Nuwas*. London: Kegan Paul, 2005.

Conrad, Lawrence. "Recovering Lost Texts: Some Methodological Issues." *JAOS* 113 (1993): 258–63.

Coogan, Michael, ed. *The New Oxford Annotated Bible*, 3rd edn. Oxford: Oxford University Press, 2001.

Coulson, Noel J. "Regulation of Sexual Behavior under Traditional Islamic Law." In *Society and the Sexes in Medieval Islam*. Edited by Afaf Lutfi al-Sayyid Marsot. Malibu, CA: Undena Publications, 1979.

Crompton, Louis. "Male Love and Islamic Law in Arab Spain." In *Islamic Homosexualities: Culture, History and Literature*. Edited by Stephen O. Murray and Will Roscoe. New York and London: New York University Press, 1997.

al-Dahhān, Sāmī. *Al-Ghazal*. Vol. 1. Cairo: Dār al-ma`ārif, 1964.

Daniel, Marc. "Arab Civilization and Male Love." Translated by Winston Leyland. *Gay Sunshine* 32 (1977); *Gay Roots: Twenty Years of Gay Sunshine*. Edited by Winston Leyland. San Francisco: Gay Sunshine Press, 1991.

Decter, Jonathan P. *Iberian Jewish Literature: Between al-Andalus and Christian Europe*. Bloomington and Indianapolis: Indiana University Press, 2007.

—— "The Rendering of Qur'ānic Quotations in Hebrew Translations of Islamic Texts." *JQR* 96 (2006): 336–58.

Deuteronomy Rabbah. See *Midrash Rabbah ha-Mevo'ar*.

Dickie, James. "Ibn Ŝuhayd: A Biographical and Critical Study." *Al-Andalus* 29 (1964): 247–52.

Dīwān Ibn Sahl al-Andalusī. Edited by Aḥmad Ḥusayn al-Qarnī. Egypt: al-Maktaba al-`arabiyya, 1926.

Dīwān al-Mu`tamid ibn `Abbād. Edited by Aḥmad Aḥmad Badawī and Ḥāmid `Abd al-Majīd. Cairo: Al-Maṭba`a al-āmīriyya, 1951.

Doron, Aviva. "New Trends in the Conception of Hebrew Poetry in the 13th and 14th Century in Spain in Relation to Spanish Literature." In *Encuentros and Desencuentros: Spanish Jewish Cultural Interaction Throughout History*. Tel Aviv: University Publication Projects, 2000.

—— "The Poet's Attitude in the Hebrew Poetry of Spain: Between Convention and Allusion." In *Jewish Studies at the Turn of the 20th Century Vol. 1*. Edited by Judit Targarona Borás and Angel Sáenz-Badillos. Leiden, Boston, and Köln: Brill, 1999.

Drory, Rina. *Models and Contacts: Arabic Literature and its Impact on Medieval Jewish Culture*. Leiden and Boston: E. J. Brill, 2000.

Drozdík, Ladislav. "Erotic Imagery in Classical Arabic Poetry." *Asian and African Studies (Bratislava)* 6:1 (1997): 21–44.

Ebied, R. Y. and M. J. L. Young, eds and trans. *The Story of Joseph in Arabic Verse*. Leiden: E. J. Brill, 1975.

Ecclesiastes Rabbah. See *Midrash Rabbah ha-Mevo'ar*.

Eisenberg, Isaac. *Vita Prophetarum auctore Muḥammad ben Abdallah al-Kisa'i*. Lugduni-Batavorum: E. J. Brill, 1923.

Elizur, Shulamit. *Shirat ha-Ḥol ha-'Ivrit be-Sefarad ha-Muslemit*. Ramat Aviv: The Open University, 2004.

El-Rouayheb, Khaled. *Before Homosexuality in the Arab-Islamic World 1500–1800*. Chicago: University of Chicago Press, 2005.

Encyclopedia of Homosexuality. Edited by Wayne R. Dynes. New York: Garland, 1990.

Encyclopedia of Islam. New Edition. Leiden: E. J. Brill, 1960 [i.e. 1954]–2009.

Encyclopedia Judaica. Detroit: Macmillan Reference in association with the Keter Publishing House, 2007.

Encyclopedia of Medieval Iberia. Edited by Michael Gerli. New York: Routledge, 2003.

Encyclopaedia of the Qur'ān. Edited by Jane Dammen McAuliffe. Leiden: E. J. Brill, 2001–6.

Encyclopedic Dictionary of Semiotics. Edited by Thomas A. Sebeok. Berlin: Mouton de Gruyter, 1986.

Ernst, Carl W. *Words of Ecstasy in Sufism*. Albany: State University of New York Press, 1985.

Eshots, Yaris. "`Ishq." In *The Qur'an: An Encyclopedia*. Edited by Oliver Leaman. Oxford: Routledge, 2006.

Exodus Rabbah. See *Midrash Rabbah ha-Mevo'ar*.

al-Fatḥ ibn Ḫāqān, *Maṭmaḥ al-anfus wa-masraḥ al-ta'annus fī mulaḥ ahl al-andalus*. Edited by Muḥammad `Alī Šawābika. Beirut: Dār `ammār, 1983.

Fierro, Maribel. "Alfonso X 'The Wise': The Last Almohad Caliph?" *Medieval Encounters* 15 (2009): 175–98.

Finkel, Joshua. "An Eleventh Century Source for the History of Jewish Scientists in Mohammedan Land (Ibn Ṣa`id)." *JQR* 17 (1927–8): 45–54.

Fleischer, Ezra. "`Al Dunash ben Labrat, ve-Ishto, u-Veno." In *Meḥqarei Yerushalayim be-Sifrut `Ivrit*. Edited by Dan Pagis. Jerusalem: Magnes Press, 5744 [1984].

—— "`Al Guf ha-Shir ve-Libo." *Moznayim* 57:3 (Elul 5743) [August 1983]: 56–7.

—— "Ḥadashot be-Yitzirato shel R. Yitzḥaq bar Levi (Ibn Mar Sha'ul)." In *Meḥqerei Lashon Mugashim le-Ze'ev Ben-Ḥaim be-Hagi'o le-Seivah*. Edited by M. Bar-Asher, A. Dotan, D. Tenna, and D. Ben `Ami. Jerusalem, Y. L. Magnes, 1983.

—— "Le-Qorot R. Yehuda Halevi be-Ne`urav ve-Raishit Qesharav `im R. Moshe ibn Ezra." *Kiryat Sefer* 61 (1986–7): 893–910.

—— "Shirah `Ivrit be-Nusaḥ ha-Miqra be-Yimei ha-Beinayim." *Teudah* 7 (1991): 201–48.

Fokkelman, J. P. "II Sam. 13: 'Chips off the old block' (Scenes 8–9)." In *Narrative Art and Poetry in the Books of Samuel*. Vol. 1 *King David*. Assen, The Netherlands: van Gorcum, 1981.

Gabrieli, Francesco. "Religious Poetry in Early Islam." In *Arabic Poetry: Theory and Development*, ed. G. E. von Grunebaum. Wiesbaden: Otto Harrassowitz, 1973.

Garcia-Arenal, Mercedes. "Jewish Converts to Islam in the Muslim West." In *IOS XVII*. Edited by Uri Rubin and David J. Wasserstein. Tel Aviv: Eisenbrauns, Inc., 1997.

García Gómez, Emilio. *El Libro de las Banderas de los Campeones, de Ibn Sa`īd al-Maghribī*. Madrid: Instituto de Valencia de Don Juan, 1942.

Gersonides. See Levi ben Gershom.

Giffin, Lois A. "Ibn Hazm and the *Ṭawq al-Ḥamāma*." In *The Legacy of Muslim Spain*. Edited by Salma Khadra Jayyusi. Leiden: E. J. Brill, 1992.

—— "Love Poetry and Love Theory in Medieval Arabic Literature." In *Arabic Poetry: Theory and Development*. Edited by G. E. von Grunebaum. Wiesbaden: Otto Harrassowitz, 1973.

Goitein, S. D. "A Jewish Addict to Sufism." *JQR* 64 (1954–5): 37–49.

Goldstein, Miriam. "Adaptations of the Arabic Qaṣīda in Andalusian Hebrew Poetry." In *Ben `Ever la-`Arav*. Edited by Yosef Tobi. Tel Aviv: Afikim Publishers, 2004.

Goldziher, Ignác. *A Short History of Classical Arabic Literature*. Translated by Joseph Desomogyi. Hildesheim: Georg Olms, 1966.

Goldziher, Ignaz. "*Lā misāsa*." *Revue Africaine* 52 (1908), 23–8.

—— *The Ẓāhiris, Their Doctrine and Their History*. Leiden: E. J. Brill, 1971.

Graetz, Heinrich. *The History of the Jews*, vol. III. Philadelphia: Jewish Publication Society, 1902.

Gray, Mark. "Amnon: A Chip off the Old Block? Rhetorical Strategy in 2 Samuel 13: 7–15, the Rape of Tamar and the Humiliation of the Poor." *Journal for the Study of the Old Testament* 77 (1998): 39–54.

Grossman, Avraham. "Biblical Exegesis in Spain During the 13th–15th Centuries." In *Moreshet Sepharad: The Sephardi Legacy*. Edited by Haim Beinart. Jerusalem: Magnes Press, Hebrew University, 1992.

Gully, Adrian. "Taḍmīn, 'Implication of Meaning' in Medieval Arabic." *JAOS* 113:3 (July–Sept. 1997): 466–80.

Halevi, Judah. *Diwan. Shirei ha-Ḥol*, 2, vols. Edited by Ḥaim Brody. Berlin: Ḥevrat Mekitze Nirdamim, 1901, 1909.

al-Ḥamawī, Yāqūt b. `Abdallāh. *Kitāb irshad al-arīb ilā ma`rifat al-adīb* (Gibb Memorial Series 2, no. 71). Edited by D. S. Margoliouth. Leiden: E. J. Brill, 1909.

Hamori, Andreas. "Examples of Convention in the Poetry of Abū Nuwās." *Studia Islamica* 30 (1969): 5–26.

Hands, Elizabeth. *The Death of Amnon. A Poem*. Coventry: N. Rollason, 1789. Reprint: London: Routledge, 1996.

al-Harizi, Judah. *The Book of the Taḥkemoni: Jewish Tales from Medieval Spain*. Translated, explicated, and annotated by David Simha Segal. London: Littman Library of Jewish Civilization, 2001.

—— *Taḥkemoni*. Edited by A. Kaminka. Warsaw, 1899.

—— *Taḥkemoni*. Edited by Y. Toporovsky. Tel Aviv: Hotza'at Maḥbarot le-Sifrut, 5712 [1952].

The Hebrew Bible. Philadelphia: Jewish Publication Society, 1917.

Heinrichs, Wolfhart. "Contacts between Scriptural Hermeneutics and Literary Theory in Islam: The Case of *majāz*." In *Zeitschrift für Geschichte der arabisch-Islamischen wissenschaften* 1 (1984): 253–84.

—— *The Hand of the Northwind: Opinions on Metaphor and the Early Meaning of isti'ara in Arabic Poetics*. Mainz: Deutsche Morgenländische Gesellschadt, 1977.

—— "*Isti`ārah* and *badī`* and their Terminological Relationship in Early Arabic Literary Criticism." In *Zeitschrift für Geschichte der arabisch-Islamischen wissenschaften* 1 (1984): 180–211.

Hillenbrand, Robert. " 'The Ornament of the World': Medieval Córdoba as a Cultural Center." In *The Legacy of Muslim Spain*. Edited by Salma Khadra Jayyusi. Leiden, New York, and Köln: E. J. Brill, 1992.

Holy Bible. The New King James Version. Nashville: Thomas Nelson Publishers, 1979.

Ibn Abī Ḥātim, `Abd al-Raḥmān. *Tafsīr al-Qur'ān al-`aẓīm*. Edited by As`ad Muḥammad al-Ṭayyib. Riyad: Maktabat Nizār Muṣṭafā al-Bāz, 1997.

Ibn al-`Arabī, Muḥyi'ddīn. *The Tarjumán al-Ashwáq: A Collection of Mystical Odes by Muḥyi'ddin ibn al-'Arabí*. Edited and translated by Reynold A. Nicholson. London: Royal Asiatic Society, 1911.

Ibn Asākir, `Ali b. al-Ḥasan. *Ta'rīkh madīnat Dimashq*. Edited by `Umar ibn Gharāma al-`Amrawī. Beirut: Dār al-fikr, 1995.

Ibn Bishr, Isḥāq. *Mubtada' al-dunyā wa-qiṣaṣ al-anbiyā'*. MS Huntington 388. Bodleian Library. Oxford University. Oxford, England.

Ibn Daud, Abraham. *Sefer ha-Qabbalah*. Critical Edition, Translation, and Notes by Gerson D. Cohen. Philadelphia: Jewish Publication Society, 1967.

Ibn Ezra, Moses. *Kitāb al-muḥāḍara wa-al-mudhākara. Liber Discussionis et Commemorationis*. Edited by A. S. Halkin. Jerusalem: Mekitze Nirdamim, 1975.

—— *Shirei ha-Ḥol*, vol. 1. Edited by Ḥaim Brody. Berlin: Hotza'at Schocken, 5695 [1935].

Ibn Gabirol, Solomon. *Shirei ha-Ḥol le-Rabbi Shelomo ibn Gabirol*. Edited by Ḥaim Brody and Ḥaim Schirmann. Jerusalem: Machon Schocken, 5735 [1974].

—— *Shirei ha-Ḥol le-Rabbi Shelomo ibn Gabirol*. Edited by Dov Jarden. Jerusalem, 1975.

—— *Shirei Shelomo ben Yehuda ibn Gabirol*. Edited by Ḥ. N. Bialik and Y. Ḥ. Ravnitzky. Tel Aviv: Dvir, 1929.

Ibn Ḥazm, Abū Muḥammad `Alī b. Aḥmad. *Fiṣal fī al-milal wa-al-ahwā' wa-al-niḥal*. Edited by Muḥammad Ibrāhīm Naṣr and `Abd al-Raḥmān `Umayrah. Beirut: Dār al-Jīl, 1985.

—— *Al-Taqrīb li-ḥadd al-manṭiq wa-al-madhkhal ilaihi*. Edited by Iḥsān `Abbās. Beirut, n.d.

Ibn Ḥazm al-Andalusī, Abū Muḥammad `Alī. *Ṭauḳ al-ḥamâma*. Edited by D. K. Pétrof. St. Pétersbourg-Leide: E. J. Brill, 1914.

—— *Ṭawq al-ḥamāma*. Edited by Nizār Wajīh Fallūḥ. Sidon-Bayrūt: al-Maktaba al-`Aṣrīyya, 1422/2001.

Ibn Janaḥ, Jonah. *Sefer ha-Riqmah*. Frankfurt: [s.n.], 5616 [1856].

—— *Sefer ha-Shorashim: hu ha-ḥeleq ha-sheni mi-maḥberet ha-diqduq*. Berlin: H. Itzkowski, 1896.

Ibn al-Jawzī. *Dhamm al-hawā*. Edited by Muṣṭafa `Abdelwāhid. Cairo, 1381/1962.

Ibn Kathīr, Abū al-Fidā' Ismā`īl. *Tafsīr al-Qur'ān al-`aẓīm*. Beirut: Dār al-fikr, 1970.

Ibn Sa`īd al-Andalusī, Abū al-Ḥasan `Alī b. Mūsā. *Rāyāt al-mubarrizīn wa-ghāyāt al-mumayyazīn*. Edited by Muḥammad Riḍwān al-Dāya. Dimashq: Dār Ṭalās, 1987.

Ibn Sa`īd, `Alī b. Mūsā. *Al-Mughrib fī ḥulā al-maghrib*. Edited by Ṣhawqi Ḍayf. Cairo: Dār al-ma`ārif, 1955–64.

`Īsā, Fawzī Sa`d. *Al-Shi`r al-andalusi fī`aṣr al-muwaḥḥidīn*. Beirut, 1991.

Al-Iṣfahānī, Ibn Dāwūd. *Kitāb al-zahra*. Edited by A. R. Nykl with I. Tuqan. Chicago: University of Chicago Press, 1932.

Ishay, Ḥaviva. "Mechaniqat ha-'Miqud' be-Shirei Ḥesheq shel Shelomo ibn Gabirol: ha-Mesamen ha-Miqra'i ba-Shir ke-`Adasha Memaqedet ba-Matzleima." *Revue Européenne des Études Hébraïques* (2001): 39–51.

—— "Teqst ke-Interteqst: Shirei Ahava `Ivriim ve-Safrut ha-Ahavah ha-`Aravit be-Yimei ha-Beinayim." In *Te`udah: Meḥqarim be-Safrut ha-`Ivrit be-Yimei ha-Beinayim*, 19, ed. Tova Rosen and Avner Holzman. Tel Aviv: Tel Aviv University, 2003.
al-Jāḥiẓ. "Boasting Match over Maids and Youths." In *Nine Essays of al-Jahiz*. Translated by William M. Hutchins. New York: Peter M. Lang, 1989.
—— *Kitāb al-qiyān*. See Pellat, *The Life and Works of Jāḥiẓ*.
—— *Rasā'il al-Jāḥiẓ*. Vol. 3. Miṣr: Maktabat al-khānjī, 1399/1979.
Jāmī, Abdulrahmān. *The Book of Joseph and Zuleikha*. Translated by Alexander Rogers. London: David Nutt, 1892.
Jastrow, Marcus. *Dictionary of the Targumim, Talmud Bavli, Yerushalmi, and Midrashic Literature*. New York: The Judaica Press, 1971.
Jayyusi, Salma Khadra. "Andalusī Poetry: the Golden Period." In *The Legacy of Muslim Spain*. Edited by Salma Khadra Jayyusi. Leiden, Boston, New York, and Köln: E. J. Brill, 1992.
Jewish Prince in Moslem Spain: Selected Poems of Samuel Ibn Nagrela. Introduced, translated, and notes by Leon J. Weinberger. Tuscaloosa: University of Alabama Press, 1973.
Jones, John Harris, ed. and trans. *Ibn Abd-el-Hakem's History of the Conquest of Spain*. Göttingen: W. F. Kaestner, 1858.
JPS Hebrew–English Tanakh. Philadelphia: Jewish Publication Society, 1999.
Kahana, David, ed. *Kovetz Ḥokhmat R. Abraham ibn Ezra*. Warsaw, 1894; reprint, Jerusalem: Hotza'at Kedem, 1971.
Kamelher, Moshe, ed. *Perushei R. David Qimḥi (Radaq) `al ha-Torah: Bereishit*. Jerusalem: Mossad Harav Kook, 1970.
Keeler, Annabel. "Moses from a Muslim Perspective." In *Abraham's Children: Jews, Christians, and Muslims in Conversation*. Edited by Norman Solomon, Richard Harries, and Tim Winter. New York: T & T Clark, 2005.
—— *Sufi Hermeneutics: The Qur'an Commentary of Rashīd al-Dīn Maybudī*. Oxford and New York: Oxford University Press in association with the Institute for Ismaili Studies, 2006.
Kehati, Pinḥas, ed. *Mishnayot Mevo'arot*, 7th edn. Jerusalem: Keter, 1976.
Kennedy, Philip. *Abu Nuwas: A Genius of Poetry*. Oxford: Oneworld Publications, 2005.
—— "Abū Nuwās, Samuel and Levi." In *Medieval and Modern Perspectives on Muslim–Jewish Relations*. Edited by Ronald Nettler. Luxembourg: Harwood Academic Publishers, 1995.
—— *The Wine Song in Classical Arabic Poetry: Abū Nuwās and the Literary Tradition*. Oxford: Clarendon Press, 1997.
Khairallah, As`ad E. *Love, Madness and Poetry: An Interpretation of the Magnun Legend*. Beirut: Orient-Institut der Deutschen Morgenländischen Gesellschaft, 1980.
Kim, Uriah (Yong-Hwan). "Uriah the Hittite: A (Con)Text of Struggle for Identity." *Semeia* 90–1 (2002): 69–85.
al-Kisā'ī. See Eisenberg.
Kister, M. J. " 'Exert Yourselves, O Banū Arfida!': Some Notes on Entertainment in the Islamic Tradition." *JSAI* 23 (1999): 53–78.
—— "*The Sīrah Literature*." In *The Cambridge History of Arabic Literature: Arabic Literature to the End of the Umayyad Period*. Edited by A. F. L. Beeston, T. M. Johnstone, R. B. Serjeant and G. R. Smith. Cambridge: Cambridge University Press, 1983.
Klausner, Joseph. *Historia shel ha-Sifrut ha-`Ivrit ha-Ḥadashah*. Jerusalem: Aḥiasaf, 5712–19 [1951–8].

Kozodoy, Neal. "Reading Medieval Hebrew Love Poetry." *AJS Review* 2 (1977): 111–29.

Kraemer, Ross S. *When Aseneth Met Joseph*. New York and Oxford: Oxford University Press, 1998.

Kristeva, Julia. *Desire in Language: A Semiotic Approach to Literature and Art*. Edited by Leon S. Roudiez. Translated by Thomas Gora, Alice Jardine, and Leon S. Roudiez. New York: Columbia University Press, 1980.

Kugel, James L. *The Idea of Biblical Poetry: Parallelism and Its History*. New Haven and London: Yale University Press, 1981.

—— *In Potiphar's House: The Interpretive Life of Biblical Texts*. San Francisco: Harper, 1990.

Kuntze, Simon. "Love and God: The Influence of the Ghazal on Mystic Poetry." In *Ghazal as World Literature*. Edited by Thomas Bauer and Angelika Neuwirth. Beirut: Ergon Verlag Würzburg in Kommission, 2005.

Lane, Edward William. *An Arabic–English Lexicon*, 2 vols. London and Edinburgh: Williams and Norgate, 1863, 1898.

Lane, Erskine, trans. *In Praise of Boys: Moorish Poems from al-Andalus*. San Francisco: Gay Sunshine Press, 1975.

Lazarus-Yafeh, Hava. *Intertwined Worlds: Medieval Islam and Bible Criticism*. Princeton, NJ: Princeton University Press, 1992.

—— ed. *Peraqim be-Toledot ha-'Aravim ve-ha-Islam*. Tel Aviv: Hotza'at Reshafim, 1967.

—— "Self-Criticism in Jewish and Islamic Traditions." In *Judaism and Islam: Boundaries, Communication and Interaction*. Edited by B. H. Hary, J. L. Hayes, and F. Astren. Leiden: E. J. Brill, 2000.

Leneman, Helen. "Reclaiming Jewish History: Homo-erotic Poetry of the Middle Ages." *Changing Men* 18 (Summer/Fall 1987): 22–3.

Levi ben Gershom. *Perushei Ralbag. Nevi'im Rishonim*. Edited by Yaacov Leib Levi. Jerusalem: Mossad Harav Kook, 2008.

Levin, Yisra'el. "Biqashti et she-Ahavah Nafshi." *Hasifrut* 2 (1971–2): 116–49.

Levin, Israel. *Shirah Araguha Yedei Ra'ayon*. Lod: Machon Haberman le-Meḥqarei Safrut: Hotza'at ha-Kibbutz ha-Me'uḥad, 2009.

Leviticus Rabbah. See Midrash Rabbah ha-Mevo'ar.

Lowin, Shari L. *The Making of a Forefather: Abraham in Islamic and Jewish Exegetical Narratives*. Leiden: E. J. Brill, 2006.

Lug, Sieglinde. "Toward a Definition of Excellence in Classical Arabic Poetry: An Analysis of Ibn Zaydūn's *Nūnīyya*." *JAOS* 101:3 (1981): 331–45.

Macdonald, John. "Joseph in the Qur'ān and Muslim Commentary." *Muslim World* 46 (1956): 113–31, 207–24.

Maghen, Ze'ev. *After Hardship Cometh Ease: The Jews as Backdrop for Muslim Moderation*. Berlin and New York: Walter de Gruyter, 2006.

Maimondes, Moses. *Mishneh Torah*. Jerusalem: Ḥ. Vagshal, 5744 [1984].

—— *Perush le-Massekhet Avot*. Edited by Mordechai Dov Rabinovitz. Jerusalem: Mossad Harav Kook, 5721/1961.

al-Majlisī, Muḥamad Baqīr. *Biḥār al-anwār*. Teheran: Dār al-kutub al-Islāmīyya, 1362–6 AH [1943–6].

Malachi, Zvi and Chana David, eds. *Meḥqarim be-Yetzirat Shelomo ibn Gabirol*. Tel Aviv: Machon Katz le-Ḥeqer ha-Sifrut ha-'Ivrit, Tel Aviv University, 1985.

Malamat, Abraham. "David and Uriah: The Consolidation of Power in Jerusalem by the Israelites." In *"An Experienced Scribe Who Neglects Nothing": Ancient Near Eastern*

Studies in Honor of Jacob Klein. Edited by Yitschak Sefati *et al.* Bethesda, MD: CDL Press, 2005.

al-Maqqarī, Aḥmad ibn Muḥammad. *Nafḥ al-ṭīb. Analectes sur l'histoire et la littérature des Arabs d'Espagne*. Edited by R. P. A. Dozy *et al.* Leiden: E. J. Brill, 1855–61.

—— *Nafḥ al-ṭīb min ghuṣn al-andalus al-raṭīb*. Edited by Iḥsān `Abbās. Beirut: Dār al-ṣādir, 1388 AH [1968].

Margalioth, Mordecai. *Hilkhot Hannagid*. Jerusalem: Louis M. and Minnie Epstein Fund of the American Academy for Jewish Research, 1962.

Margoliouth, D. S. "The Origins of Arabic Poetry." *Journal of the Royal Asiatic Society* (1925): 417–49.

Massekhet Avot `im Perush Rashi. Edited by Moshe Alexander Zusha Kinstlicher. Benei Berak, 5752 [1992].

Mazalaoui, Mahmoud A., " 'I Follow the Religion of Love': The Erotic Surrogate in the Arabic Tradition." In *Poetics of Love in the Middle Ages: Texts and Contexts*. Edited by Moshe Lazar and Norris J. Lacy. Fairfax, VA: George Mason University Press, 1989.

McCarter, P. Kyle. *The Anchor Bible. II Samuel*. Garden City, NY: Doubleday, 1984.

Medan, Yaaqov. *David u-Vat-Sheva': ha-ḥeṭ ha-'onesh yeha-tiḳun*. Alon Shevut: Yeshivat Har-`Etzyon, 5762 [2001/2].

Meisami, Julie Scott. "Arabic Mujūn Poetry: The Literary Dimension." In *Verse and the Fair Sex: Studies in Arabic Poetry and in the Representation of Women in Arabic Literature*. Edited by Frederick de Jong. Utrecht: M. Th. Houtsma Stichting, 1993.

Mekhilta de-Rabi Yishma'el. Edited by Saul Horovitz and Israel Abraham Rabin, 2nd edn. Jerusalem: Bamberger and Wahrmann, 1960.

Menahem b. Solomon b. Isaac. *Midrash Sekhel Tov `al Sefer Bereishit ve-Shemot*. Edited by Shelomo Buber. Berlin, 5660 [1899].

Menocal, Maria Rosa, Raymond P. Scheindlin and Michael Sells, eds. *The Literature of al-Andalus*. Cambridge: Cambridge University Press, 2000.

Midrash `Asarah Harugei Malkhut. In *Bet ha-Midrasch*. Vol. 6. Edited by Adolph Jellinek. Jerusalem: Bamberger and Wahrmann, 1938.

Midrash Leqaḥ Tov. See Toviyahu ben Eliezer.

Midrash Rabbah Bereishit. Edited by J. Theodor and Ch. Albeck. Berlin, 1903–36; reprint, Jerusalem: Wahrmann, 1965.

Midrash Rabbah ha-Mevo'ar. Jerusalem: Mechon ha-Midrash ha-Mevo'ar, 5744– [1983–].

Midrasch Samuel. Edited by S. Buber. Krakau, 1893.

Midrash Tanḥuma. Jerusalem: Levin-Epstein, 1979.

Midrash Tanḥuma. Edited by S. Buber. Vilna, 1885; reprint Jerusalem, 1964.

Midrash Vaykira Rabbah. Edited by Mordecai Margulies. New York and Jerusalem: The Jewish Theological Seminary of America, 1993.

Midrash Zuta. Qohelet. Edited by Shelomo Buber. Vilna, 5659 [1898].

Miqra'ot Gedolot: Bereishit. Jerusalem: Mechon ha-Ma'or, 1990.

Miqra'ot Gedolot `al Ḥamisha Ḥumshei Torah. Jerusalem: Pardes Publishers, 5715 [1955].

Miqra'ot Gedolot. Sefer Tehillim. Jerusalem: Miqra'ot Gedolot Yerushalayim-Lublin, 1963.

Mir, Mustansir. "The Qur'anic Story of Joseph: Plot, Themes, and Characters." *Muslim World* 76:1 (Jan. 1986): 1–15.

Mirsky, Aharon. "Hebrew Literary Creation." In *Moreshet Sepharad. The Sephardi Legacy*. Edited by Haim Beinart. Jerusalem: Magnes Press, 1992.

—— ed. *Shirei Yitzḥaq ibn Khalfon*. Jerusalem: Bialik Institute, 1961.

Mishna Codex Parma [De Rossi 138]. Jerusalem: Kedem Publishers, 1970.
Monroe, James T. *Hispano-Arabic Poetry: A Student Anthology*. Berkeley: University of California Press, 1974.
—— "Hispano-Arabic Poetry During the Caliphate of Cordoba." In *Arabic Poetry: Theory and Development*. Edited by G. E. von Grunebaum. Wiesbaden: Otto Harrassowitz, 1973.
—— "Kharjas in Arabic and Romance: Popular Poetry in Muslim Spain?" In *Islam: Past Influence and Present Challenge*. Edited by Alford T. Welch and Pierre Cachia. Albany, NY: SUNY Press, 1979.
—— "The Striptease that was Blamed on Abū Bakr's Naughty Son: Was Father Being Shamed or Was the Poet Having Fun? (Ibn Quzmān's Zajal no. 133)." In *Homoeroticism in Classical Arabic Literature*. Edited by J. W. Wright, Jr. and Everett K. Rowson. New York: Columbia University Press, 1997.
—— "Zajal and Muwashshaḥa: Hispano-Arabic Poetry and the Romance Tradition." In *The Legacy of Muslim Spain*. Edited by Salma Khadra Jayyusi. Leiden: E. J. Brill, 1992.
Monroe, James T. and David Swiatlo. "Ninety-Three Arabic Ḥarǧas in Hebrew Muwaššaḥs: Their Hispano-Romance Prosody and Thematic Features." *JAOS* 97:2 (Apr.–Jun., 1997): 141–64.
Mopsik, Charles. "The Secret of the Marriage of David and Batsheva (Chapter 7)." In *Sex of the Soul: The Vicissitudes of Sexual Differences in the Kabbalah*, edited by Daniel Abrams. Los Angeles: Cherub Press, 2005.
Muqātil ibn Sulaymān. *Tafsīr Muqātil*. Edited by `Abdallāh Maḥmūd Shiḥāta. Cairo: al-Ḥay'a al-Miṣriyya al-`āmma lil-kitāb, 1979–89.
ha-Nagid, Samuel. *Diwan Shemuel ha-Nagid. Ben Mishle*. Edited by Dov Jarden. Jerusalem: Hebrew Union College, 5743 [1983].
—— *Diwan Shemuel ha-Nagid. Ben Qohelet*. Edited by Dov Jarden. Jerusalem: Hebrew Union College, 5752 [1992].
—— *Diwan Shemuel ha-Nagid. Ben Tehillim*. Edited by Dov Jarden. Jerusalem: Hebrew Union College, 5726 [1966].
Nahmanides. See Chavel, Ḥaim Dov.
Newby, Gordon D. *The Making of the Last Prophet: A Reconstruction of the Earliest Biography of Muhammad*. Columbia: University of South Carolina Press, 1989.
Nichols, J. M. "The Arabic Verses of Qasmuna bint Ismail Ibn Bagdalalı." *International Journal for Middle East Studies* 13 (1981): 155–8.
Nicholson, Reynold A., trans. *The Tarjumán al-Ashwáq: A Collection of Mystical Odes by Muḥyi'ddín ibn al-'Arabí*. London: Royal Asiatic Society, 1911.
Numbers Rabbah. See *Midrash Rabbah ha-Mevo'ar*.
Nwyia, Paul. *Exégèse Coranique et Langue Mystique*. Beirut: Dar el-Machreq éditeurs, 1970.
—— ed. *Le Tafsīr Mystique attribué a Ǧa`far Ṣadiq*. Beyrouth: Imprimerie Catholique, 1968.
Nykl, A. R. trans. *A Book Containing the Risāla known as The Dove's Neck-Ring about Love and Lovers composed by Abū Muḥammad `Alī ibn Ḥazm al-Andalusī*. Paris: Libraire Orientaliste Paul Geuthner, 1931.
—— *Hispano-Arabic Poetry and its Relations with the Old Provençal Troubadours*. Baltimore: Johns Hopkins University Press, 1946.
—— ed. *Mukhtārāt min al-shi`r al-Andalusī*. Beirut: Dar al-`ilm lil-malāyīn, 1949.
Ouyang, Wen-Chin. *Literary Criticism in Medieval Arabic and Islamic Culture: The Making of a Tradition*. Edinburgh: Edinburgh University Press, 1997.

Padwick, C. *Muslim Devotions*. London: SPCK, 1961.

Pagis, Dan. "Ha-Meshorer ke-Navi ba-Shirah ha-`Ivrit bi-Yemei ha-Beinayim." In *Ha-Shir Davur al-`Ofanav*. Edited by Ezra Fleischer. Jerusalem: Magnes Press, 1993.

—— *Hebrew Poetry of the Middle Ages and the Renaissance*. Berkeley, Los Angeles, and Oxford: University of California Press, 1991.

—— *Ḥiddush u-Masoret be-Shirat ha-Ḥol ha-`Ivrit: Sefarad ve-Italia*. Jerusalem: Keter, 1976.

—— *Shirat ha-Ḥol ve-Torat ha-Shir le-Moshe ibn Ezra u-venei Doro*. Jerusalem: Mossad Bialik, 1970.

Paret, Rudi. *Der Koran: Kommentar und Konkordanz*. Stuttgart, 1971.

Pellat, Charles, trans. and ed. *The Life and Works of Jāḥiẓ*. Translated from French by D. M. Hawke. London: Routledge and Kegan Paul, 1969.

—— "Liwāṭ." In *Sexuality and Eroticism among Males in Moslem Societies*. Edited by Arno Schmitt and Jehoeda Sofer. New York, London, and Norwood (Australia): Haworth Press, 1992.

Pérès, Henri. *La Poésie andalouse en arabe classique au XIe siècle*. Paris: Adrien-Maisonneuve, 1953.

Perlmann, Moshe. "Eleventh Century Andalusian Authors on the Jews of Granada." *Proceedings of the American Academy for Jewish Research* 18 (1948–9): 269–90.

—— "The Medieval Polemics between Islam and Judaism." In *Religion in a Religious Age*. Edited by S. D. Goitein. Cambridge, MA: Association for Jewish Studies, 1974.

Pickthall, Muhammad. *The Glorious Koran*. London: George Allen and Unwin, 1976.

Pirqei de-Rabbi Eliezer. Jerusalem: Eshkol, 1973.

Powers, David S. "Reading/Misreading One Another's Scriptures: Ibn Ḥazm's Refutation of Ibn Naghrella al-Yahūdī." In *Studies in Islamic and Judaic Traditions*. Edited by William M. Brinner and Stephen D. Ricks. Atlanta, GA: Scholars Press, 1986.

Princeton Encyclopedia of Poetry and Poetics. Edited by Alex Preminger, Frank J. Warnke, and O. B. Hardison, Jr. Princeton, NJ: Princeton University Press, 1974.

Propp, William H. "Kinship in 2 Samuel 13." *Catholic Bible Quarterly* 55 (1993): 39–53.

al-Qāḍī, Wadād. "The Limitations of Qur'ānic Usage in Early Arabic Poetry: The Example of a Khārijite Poem." *Festschrift Ewald Wagner zum 65. Geburtstag*. Beirut, 1994.

Qimḥi, R. David ben Joseph. "Perush `al Sefer Shemuel." In *Miqra'ot Gedolot ha-Ma'or. Nevi'im u-Ketuvim*. Jerusalem: Mechon ha-Ma'or, 2001.

—— *Sefer HaShorashim*. [*Radicum Liber sive Hebraeum Bibliorum Lexicon*]. Edited by Jo. H. R. Biesenthal and F. Lebrecht. Berlin: F. Impresis G. Bethge, 1847; Reprint, Jerusalem, 1967.

—— *Sefer Redak*. Lemberg: Pessel Balaban, 1878.

Qohelet Rabbah. See *Midrash Rabbah ha-Mevo'ar*.

al-Qummī, Abū al-Ḥasan `Alī b. Ibrāhīm. *Tafsīr al-Qummī*. Najaf: Matba`at al-Najaf, 1386–7 AH [1967].

The Qur'an: A New Translation by M. A. S. Abdel Haleem. Oxford: Oxford University Press, 2004.

Ratzaby, Yehuda. "Ha-Ahavah be-Shirat R. Shemuel Ha-Nagid." *Tarbiz* 39 (1969): 137–69.

—— "Shirat ha-Yayin le-R. Shemuel ha-Nagid." In *Sefer H. M. Shapiro. Annual of the Bar-Ilan University Studies in Judaica and the Humanities*. Edited by H. Z. Hirschberg *et al.* Ramat Gan: Bar Ilan University, 1972.

Reis, Pamela Tamarkin. "Cupidity and Stupidity: Woman's Agency and the 'Rape' of Tamar." *JNES* 25 (1997): 43–60.

Ricks, Stephen D. "The Garment of Adam in Jewish, Muslim, and Christian Tradition." In *Judaism and Islam: Boundaries, Communication and Interaction*. Edited by B. H. Hary, J. L. Hayes, and Fred Astren. Leiden: E. J. Brill, 2000.
Rosen, Tova. *Unveiling Eve: Reading Gender in Medieval Hebrew Literature*. Philadelphia: University of Pennsylvania Press, 2003.
Rosenthal, Franz. "Fiction and Reality: Sources for the Role of Sex in Medieval Muslim Society." In *Society and the Sexes in Medieval Islam* (Giorgio Levi Della Vida Conference). Edited by Afaf Lufti al-Sayyid-Marsot. Malibu: Undena Publications, 1979.
—— "Male and Female: Described and Compared." In *Homoeroticism in Classical Arabic Literature*. Edited by J. W. Wright and Everett K. Rowson. New York: Columbia University Press, 1997.
Roth, Norman. "The Care and Feeding of Gazelles: Medieval Arabic and Hebrew Love Poetry." In *Poetics of Love in the Middle Ages: Texts and Contexts*. Edited by Moshe Lazar and Norris J. Lacy. Fairfax, VA: George Mason University Press, 1989.
—— "'Deal Gently with the Young Man': Love of Boys in Medieval Hebrew Poetry of Spain." *Speculum* 57:1 (1982): 20–51.
—— "'Fawn of My Delights': Boy-Love in Hebrew and Arabic Verse." In *Sex in the Middle Ages*. Edited by Joyce E. Salisbury. New York and London: Garland Publishing, 1991.
—— "Jewish and Muslim Physicians of `Ali ibn Tashufīn." *Korot* 10 (1993–4): 83–91.
—— "Jewish Reactions to the *`Arabiyya* and the Renaissance of Hebrew in Spain." *Journal of Semitic Studies* 28:1 (Spring 1983): 63–84.
—— "Maimonides on Hebrew Language and Poetry." *Hebrew Studies* 26:1 (1985): 93–101.
—— "Muslim Knowledge of the Hebrew Bible and Jewish Traditions in the Middle Ages." *Maghreb Review* 16:1–2 (1991): 74–83.
—— "'My Beloved is Like a Gazelle': Imagery of the Beloved Boy in Religious Hebrew Poetry." *Hebrew Annual Review* 8 (1984): 143–65.
—— "New Light on the Jews of Mozarabic Toledo." *AJS Review* 11:2 (Autumn 1986): 189–220.
—— "A Note on Research into Jewish Sexuality in the Medieval Period." In *Handbook of Medieval Sexuality*. Edited by Vern L. Bullough and James A. Brundage. New York and London: Garland Publishing, 1996.
—— "Polemic in Hebrew Religious Poetry of Mediaeval Spain." *Journal of Semitic Studies* 34:1 (Spring 1989): 153–77.
—— "Religious Constraints on Erotic Poetry among Muslims and Jews in al-Andalus." *Maghreb Review* 19:3–4 (1994): 194–205.
—— "A Research Note on Sexuality and Muslim Civilization." In *Handbook of Medieval Sexuality*. Edited by Vern L. Bullough and James A. Brundage. New York and London: Garland Publishing, 1996.
—— "Sacred and Secular in the Poetry of Ibn Gabirol." *Hebrew Studies* 20–1 (1979–80): 75–9.
—— "Satire and Debate in Two Famous Medieval Poems from al-Andalus: Love of Boys vs Girls, the Pen and other Themes." *The Maghreb Review* 4 (1979): 105–13.
—— "Seeing the Bible through a Poet's Eyes: Some Difficult Biblical Words Interpreted by Moses ibn Ezra." *Hebrew Studies* 23 (1982): 111–14.
—— "Some Aspects of Muslim–Jewish Relations in Spain." In *Estudios en Homenaje a Don Claudio Sanchez Albornoz en sus 90 años*. Edited by Maria del Carmen Carlé, Hilda Grassotti, and Germán Orduna. Buenos Aires: Instituto de Historia de España, 1983.

—— "The 'Wiles of Women' Motif in the Medieval Hebrew Literature of Spain." *Hebrew Annual Review* 2 (1978): 145–65.
Roth, Philip. *Operation Shylock*. London: J. Cape, 1993.
—— *Portnoy's Complaint*. Toronto, New York, and London: Bantam Books, 1970.
—— *Zuckerman Unbound*. London: J. Cape, 1981.
Rowson, Everett. "Arabic Poetics in Hebrew Poetry in the Golden Age." *Prooftexts* 16:1 (1996): 105–11.
—— "The Categorization of Gender and Sexual Irregularity in Medieval Arabic Vice Lists." In *Body Guards: The Cultural Politics of Gender Ambiguity*. Edited by Julia Epstein and Kristina Straub. New York and London: Routledge, 1991.
—— "The Effeminates of Early Medina." *JAOS* 111:4 (Oct.–Dec. 1991): 671–93.
Rubin, Uri. "Traditions in Transformation: The Ark of the Covenant and the Golden Calf in Biblical and Islamic Historiography." *Oriens* 36 (2001): 196–214.
Rudman, Dominic. "Reliving the Rape of Tamar: Absalom's Revenge in 2 Samuel 13." *Old Testament Essays* 11:2 (1998): 326–39.
Saḥīḥ al-Bukhārī, ed. and trans. Muḥammad Muhsin Khān. Bayrut: Dār al-`arabiyya, 1985.
Ṣā`id al-Andalusī. *Ṭabaqāt al-umam*. Edited by Louis Cheikho. Beyrouth: Imprimerie Catholique, 1912.
al-Sarrāj, Abū Naṣr `Abdāllah b. `Ali. *Kitāb al-luma` fī al-taṣawwuf*. Edited by R. A. Nicholson. Leiden: E. J. Brill, 1914.
Sasson, Jack M. "Absalom's Daughter: An Essay in Vestige Historiography." In *The Land that I will Show You: Essays on the History and Archaeology of the Ancient Near East in Honour of Maxwell Miller. Journal for the Study of the Old Testament, Supplement* 343 (2001).
Scheindlin, Raymond. "Fawns of the Palace and Fawns of the Field." *Prooftexts* 6:3 (Sept. 1986): 189–203.
—— *The Gazelle: Medieval Hebrew Poems on God, Israel, and the Soul*. New York and Oxford: Oxford University Press, 1991.
—— "Hebrew Poetry in Medieval Iberia." In *Convivencia: Jews, Muslims, and Christians in Medieval Spain*. Edited by Vivian B. Mann, Thomas F. Glick, and Jerrilynn D. Dodds. New York: George Braziller, Inc., 1992.
—— "The Hebrew Qasida in Spain." In *Qasida Poetry in Islamic Asia and Africa*. Edited by Stefan Sperl and Christopher Shackle. Leiden: Brill, 1996.
—— "Ibn Gabirol's Religious and Sufi Poetry." *Sefarad* 54:1 (1994): 109–42.
—— "The Influence of Muslim Arabic Cultural Elements on the Literature of the Hebrew Golden Age." *Conservative Judaism* 35:4 (1982): 63–72.
—— "The Jews of Muslim Spain." In *The Legacy of Muslim Spain*. Edited by Salma Khadra Jayyusi. Leiden: E. J. Brill, 1992.
—— "Merchants and Intellectuals, Rabbis and Poets: Judeo-Arabic Culture in the Golden Age of Islam." In *Cultures of the Jews: A New History*. Edited by David Biale. New York: Schocken Books, 2002.
—— "A Miniature Anthology of Medieval Hebrew Love Poems." *Prooftexts* 5:2 (1985): 105–35.
—— "Rabbi Moshe Ibn Ezra on the Legitimacy of Poetry." In *Medievalia et Humanistica*, 7. Edited by Paul Maurice Clogan. Cambridge: Cambridge University Press, 1976.
—— "Secular Hebrew Poetry in Fifteenth Century Spain." In *Crisis and Creativity in the Sephardic World, 1391–1648*. Edited by Benjamin R. Gampel. New York: Columbia University Press, 1997.

—— *Wine, Women and Death: Medieval Hebrew Poems on the Good Life*. Philadelphia: Jewish Publication Society, 1986.

Schild, Maarten. "Islam." In *Sexuality and Eroticism among Males in Moslem Societies*. Edited by Arno Schmitt and Jehoeda Sofer. New York, London, and Norwood (Australia): The Haworth Press, 1992.

Schimmel, Annemarie. *As Through a Veil: Mystical Poetry in Islam*. New York: Columbia University Press, 1982.

—— "Eros – Heavenly and not so Heavenly – in Sufi Literature and Life." In *Society and the Sexes in Medieval Islam* (Giorgio Levi Della Vida Conference). Edited by Afaf Lufti al-Sayyid-Marsot. Malibu: Undena Publications, 1979.

—— *Mystical Dimensions of Islam*. Chapel Hill: University of North Carolina Press, 1975.

—— "Yūsuf in Mawlānā Rumi's Poetry." In *The Heritage of Sufism*. Vol. II. *The Legacy of Mediaeval Persian Sufism*. Edited by Leonard Lewisohn. London and New York: Khaniqahi Nimatullahi Publications, 1992.

Schippers, Arie. "Biblical and Koranic Quotations in Hebrew and Arabic Andalusian Poetry." In *Ben `Ever le-`Arav*, vol. 2. Edited by Yosef Tobi and Yitzhak Avishur. Tel Aviv: Afikim Publishers, 2001.

—— "The Hebrew Poets of Christian Spain and the Arabic Literary Heritage." In *Jewish Studies at the Turn of the 20th Century*. Edited by Judit Targarona Borás and Angel Sáenz-Badillos. Boston, Leiden, and Köln: E. J. Brill, 1999.

—— "Humorous Approach of the Divine in the Poetry of Al-Andalus: The Case of Ibn Sahl." In *Representations of the Divine in Arabic Poetry*. Edited by Gert Borg and Ed de Moor. Amsterdam and Atlanta, GA: Rodopi, 2001.

—— "Nasīb and Ghazal in 11th and 12th Century Arabic and Hebrew Andalusian Poetry." In *Ghazal as World Literature*. Edited by Thomas Bauer and Angelika Neuwirth. Beirut: Ergon Verlag Würzburg in Kommission, 2005.

—— *Spanish Hebrew Poetry and the Arabic Literary Tradition: Arabic Themes in Hebrew Andalusian Poetry*. Leiden: E. J. Brill, 1994.

Schirmann, Ḥaim. *Ha-Shirah ha-`Ivrit be-Sefarad u-ve-Provans*. Jerusalem: Mossad Bialik, 1954.

—— *Shirim Ḥadashim min ha-Genizah* [New Hebrew Poems from the Genizah]. Jerusalem: ha-Akademya ha-Le'umit ha-Yisra'elit le-Mada`im, 5726 [1965].

—— *Toledot ha-Shirah ha-`Ivrit be-Sefarad ha-Muslemit*. Edited and notes by Ezra Fleischer. Jerusalem: Magnes Press, 1995.

—— *Toledot ha-Shirah ha-`Ivrit be-Sefarad ha-Notzerit u-ve-Drom Tzarefat*. Edited and notes by Ezra Fleischer. Jerusalem: Magnes Press, 1997.

—— "Yitzḥaq ben Mar Sha'ul, ha-Meshorer mi-Lucena." In *Sefer Assaf*. Edited by M. D. Cassuto, Joseph Klausner, and Yehoshua Gutmann. Jerusalem: Mossad Harav Kook, 1953.

Schirmann, Jefim. "The Ephebe in Medieval Hebrew Poetry." *Sefarad* 15 (1955): 55–68.

—— "The Function of the Hebrew Poet in Medieval Spain." *JSS* 16 (1954): 235–52.

—— *New Hebrew Poems from the Genizah*. Jerusalem: The Israel Academy of Sciences and Humanities, 1965.

—— "Yitzḥaq ibn Khalfun." *Tarbiz* 7 (1936): 291–318.

Schmelzer, Menahem, ed. *Yitzḥaq ibn Avraham ibn Ezra. Shirim*. New York: Jewish Theological Seminary of America, 1981.

Schmitt, Arno and Jehoeda Sofer. *Sexuality and Eroticism among Males in Moslem Societies*. New York, London, and Norwood (Australia): Haworth Press, 1991.

Segal, Eliezer. *The Babylonian Esther Midrash: A Critical Commentary*, 3 vols. Atlanta: Scholars Press, 1994.

Sells, Michael. "Love." In *The Literature of al-Andalus*. Edited by Maria Rosa Menocal, Raymond P. Scheindlin, and Michael Sells. Cambridge: Cambridge University Press, 2000.

Sepher hajaschar. Berlin: Benjamin Harz, 1923.

Shaheen, Jack G. "Bad Arabs: How Hollywood Vilifies a People." *Annals of the American Academy of Political and Social Science* 588 (July 2003): 171–93.

Shakespeare, William. *A Midsummer Night's Dream*. In *The Complete Works of William Shakespeare*, 3rd edition. Edited by David Bevington. London and Glenview, IL: Scott, Foresman, and Company, 1980.

Shimoff, Sandra. "David and Bathsheba: The Political Function of Rabbinic Aggadah." *Journal for the Study of Judaism* 24:2 (1993): 246–56.

Simon, Uriel. "The Contribution of R. Isaac b. Samuel al-Kanzi to the Spanish School of Biblical Interpretation," *JJS* 34:2 (1983): 171–8.

—— "Interpreting the Interpreter." In *Rabbi Abraham ibn Ezra: Studies in the Writings of a Twelfth Century Polymath*. Edited by Isadore Twersky and Jay Harris. Cambridge, MA: Harvard University Center for Jewish Studies, 1993.

—— "R. Avraham Ibn Ezra—Bein ha-Mefaresh le-Qor'av." In *Proceedings of the Ninth World Congress of Jewish Studies. Panel Sessions: Bible Studies and the Ancient Near East*. Jerusalem: Magnes Press, 1988.

—— "The Spanish School of Biblical Interpretation." In *Moreshet Sepharad: The Sephardi Legacy*. Edited by Haim Beinart. Jerusalem: Magnes Press, 1992.

Smith, Dulcie Lawrence, trans. *The Poems of al-Mu`tamid King of Seville*. London: John Murray, 1915.

Song of Songs: An Allegorical Translation Based upon Rashi with a Commentary Anthologized from Talmudic, Midrashic, and Rabbinic Sources (Artscroll Tanach Series). New York: Mesorah Publications Ltd, 1977–96.

Song of Songs Rabbah. See *Midrash Rabbah he-Mevo'ar*.

Sprachman, Paul. "Le beau garçon sans merci: The Homoerotic Tale in Arabic and Persian." In *Homoeroticism in Classical Arabic Literature*. Edited by J. W. Wright Jr. and Everett Rowson. New York: Columbia University Press, 1997.

Stern, S. M. "Arabic Poems by Spanish-Hebrew Poets." In *Romantica et Occidentalia: études dédiées à la memoire de Hiram Peri*. Edited by Moshe Lazar. Jerusalem: Magnes Press, 1963.

—— *Hispano-Arabic Strophic Poetry*. Edited by L. P. Harvey. Oxford: Clarendon Press, 1974.

—— "Ḥiquei Muwashshaḥot `Aravi'im be-Shirat Sefarad ha-`Ivrit." *Tarbiz* 18:3–4 (1957): 166–86.

—— "Muhammad and Joseph: A Study of Koranic Narrative." *JNES* 44 (1985): 193–204.

—— "Two Medieval Hebrew Poems Explained from Arabic." *Sefarad* 10 (1950): 325–38.

Stetkeyvich, Suzanne Pinckney. "Intoxication and Immortality: Wine and Associated Imagery in al-Ma`arrī's *Garden*." In *Homoeroticism in Classical Arabic Literature*. Edited by J. W. Wright Jr. and Everett K. Rowson. New York: New York University Press, 1997.

Strack, H. L. and G. Stemberger. *Introduction to the Talmud and Midrash*. Minneapolis: Fortress Press, 1992.

Stroumsa, Sarah. "From Muslim Heresy to Jewish–Muslim Polemics: Ibn al-Rāwandī's *Kitāb al-Dāmigh*," *JAOS* 107:4 (Oct.–Dec. 1987): 767–72.

—— "On Jewish Intellectuals Who Converted in the Early Middle Ages." In *The Jews of Medieval Islam: Community, Society and Identity*. Edited by Daniel Frank. Leiden: E. J. Brill, 1995.

al-Suyūṭī, `Abd al-Raḥmān Jalāl al-Dīn. *Al-Durr al-manthūr bi-l-tafsīr al-ma'thūr*. Cairo: al-Maṭba`a al-munīriyya, 1314 AH [1896/7].

al-Ṭabarī, Muḥammad ibn Jarīr. *Jāmi` al-bayān `an ta'wīl āy al-qu'rān*. Beirut: Dār al-fikr, 1988.

—— *Ta'rīkh al-rusul wa-l-mulūk*. Leiden: E. J. Brill, 1879–1901.

Tadmor, Hayim. "Was the Biblical *Sarīs* a Eunuch?" In *Solving Riddles and Untying Knots: Biblical, Epigraphic and Semitic Studies in Honor of Jonas C. Greenfield*. Edited by Seymour Gitin, Ziony Zevit, and Michael Sokoloff. Winona Lake, IN: Eisenbrauns, 1995.

Tanakh: A New Translation of the Holy Scriptures. Philadelphia, New York, and Jerusalem: Jewish Publication Society, 1985.

Targum Onqelos. See *Miqra'ot Gedolot `al Ḥamisha Ḥumshei Torah*.

Targum Pseudo-Jonathan. See *Miqra'ot Gedolot `al Ḥamisha Ḥumshei Torah*.

al-Tha`labī, Aḥmad b. Muḥammad. *Qiṣaṣ al-anbiyā' al-musamma `arā'is al-majālis*. Miṣr: Sharikat maktabat wa-maṭba`at Muṣṭafā al-Bābī al-Ḥalabī wa-awlādihī, 1374/1954.

Tibi, Amin T., trans. *The Tibyān: Memoirs of `Abd Allāh b. Buluggīn, Last Zīrid Amīr of Granada*. Leiden: E. J. Brill, 1986.

Tobi, Yosef. *Between Hebrew and Arabic Poetry: Studies in Spanish Medieval Hebrew Poetry*. Leiden, Boston: E. J. Brill, 2010.

—— *Proximity and Distance: Medieval Hebrew and Arabic Poetry*. E. J. Brill: Leiden and Boston, 2004.

—— "*Shirat ha-Ḥol ha-`Ivrit be-Sefarad ke-Shirah Ḥazranit – ha-Omnam*?" In *Ben `Ever le-`Arav*, Volume IV (*Prof. Amnon Shiloah Jubilee Volume*). Haifa: Center for the Study of Jewish Culture in Spain and Islamic Countries, 2008.

—— "The Reaction of Rav Sa`adia Gaon to Arabic Poetry and Poetics." *Hebrew Studies* 36 (1995): 35–53.

—— "Ha-Yesod ha-Dati be-Shirei ha-Milḥamah shel Shemuel ha-Nagid u-ve-Shirei ha-Shevaḥ ha-`Aravi'im bi-al-Andalus." *Te`udah-Meḥqarim ba-Safrut ha-`Ivrit be-Yimei ha-Beinayim* 19 (2003): 3–25.

Torat Ḥaim. Jerusalem: Mossad Harav Kook, 1987.

Tosephta. Edited by M. S. Zuckermandel, with supplement by Saul Lieberman. Jerusalem: Wahrmann Books, 1970.

Tottoli, Roberto. "The Qiṣaṣ al-anbiyā' of Ibn Muṭarrif al-Ṭarafī (d. 454/1062): Stories of the Prophets from al-Andalus." *al-Qantara* 19 (1998): 131–60.

—— *The Stories of the Prophets by Ibn Muṭarrif al-Ṭarafī*. Berlin: Klaus Schwarz Verlag, 2003.

Tourage, Mahdi. *Rūmī and the Hermeneutics of Eroticism*. Leiden and Boston: E. J. Brill, 2007.

Toviyahu ben Eliezer. *Midrash Leqaḥ Tov ha-Mekhuneh Pesiqta Zutarta `al Ḥamisha Ḥumshei Torah*. Vol. 2. Edited by S. Buber. Vilna: Ram, 5640 [1880].

Trible, Phyllis. *Texts of Terror*. London: SCM Press, 1992.

van Bekkum, Wout Jac. "Life and Work of a Thirteenth Century Poet: Rabbi Eli`azar Ben Ya`aqov ha-Bavli." In *Ben `Ever la-`Arav* v. 2. Edited by Yosef Tobi and Yitzhak Avishur. Tel Aviv: Afikim Publishers, 2001.

van Dijk-Hemmes, Fokkelien. "Tamar and the Limits of Patriarchy: Between Rape and Seduction (2 Sam 13 and Genesis 38)." In *Anti-Covenant: Counter-Reading Women's Lives in the Hebrew Bible*. Edited by Mieke Bal. Sheffield: Almond Press, 1989.

van Gelder, Geert Jan. "Forbidden Firebrands: Frivolous *Iqtibās* (Quotation from the Qur'ān) according to Medieval Arab Critics." *Quaderni di Studi Arabi* 20–1 (2002–3): 3–16.

—— "Mudrik al-Shaybānī's Poem on a Christian Boy: Bad Taste or Harmless Wit?" In *Representations of the Divine in Arabic Poetry*. Edited by Gert Borg and Ed de Moor. Amsterdam and Atlanta, GA: Rodopi, 2001.

van Staalduine-Sulman, Eveline. *The Targum of Samuel*. Leiden, Boston, and Köln: E. J. Brill, 2002.

von Grunebaum, G. E. "Avicenna's *Risāla fī al-`Ishq* and Courtly Love." *JNES* 11:4 (Oct. 1952): 233–8.

—— "The Concept of Plagiarism in Arabic Theory." *JNES* 3 (1944): 234–53.

—— "The Early Development of Islamic Religious Poetry." *JAOS* 60 (1940): 23–9.

Wacks, David A. "Between Secular and Sacred: Abraham ibn Ezra and the *Song of Songs*." In *Wine, Women and Song: Hebrew and Arabic Literature of Medieval Iberia*. Edited by Michelle M. Hamilton, Sarah J. Portnoy, and David A. Wacks. Newark, DE: Juan de la Cuesta Hispanic Monographs, 2004, 47–58.

Wafer, Jim. "Muhammad and Male Homosexuality." In *Islamic Homosexualities: Culture, History and Literature*. Edited by Stephen O. Murray and Will Roscoe. New York and London: New York University Press, 1997.

—— "Vision and Passion: The Symbolism of Male Love in Islamic Mystical Literature." In *Islamic Homosexualities: Culture, History and Literature*. Edited by Stephen O. Murray and Will Roscoe. New York and London: New York University Press, 1997.

Walfish, Barry Dov. *Esther in Medieval Garb: Jewish Interpretation of the Book of Esther in the Middle Ages*. Albany, NY: SUNY Press, 1993.

al-Waššā, Abū al-Ṭayyib Muḥammad b. Iṣḥāq, *Kitāb al-muwašša*. Edited by Rudolph E. Brünnow. Leiden: E. J. Brill, 1886.

Wasserstein, David J. "Jewish Élites in al-Andalus." In *The Jews of Medieval Islam: Community, Society, and Identity*. Edited by Daniel Frank. Leiden, New York, and Köln: E. J. Brill, 1995.

—— "The Language Situation in al-Andalus." In *The Formation of al-Andalus, Part 2: Language, Religion, Culture and the Sciences*. Edited by Lawrence I. Conrad. Ashgate: Variorum, 1998.

—— "The Muslims and the Golden Age of the Jews in al-Andalus." *IOS* 17. Edited by Uri Rubin and David J. Wasserstein. Tel Aviv: Eisenbrauns, Inc., 1997.

—— *The Rise and Fall of the Party Kings: Politics and Society in Islamic Spain 1002–1086*. Princeton: Princeton University Press, 1985.

Watt, W. Montgomery. *Muhammad: Prophet and Statesman*. Oxford: Oxford University Press, 1961.

Watt, W. Montgomery and Pierre Cachia. *A History of Islamic Spain*. Edinburgh: Edinburgh University Press, 1967.

Wehr, Hans. *A Dictionary of Modern Written Arabic*. Edited by J. Milton Cowan. Beirut: Librairie du Liban; London: Macdonald and Evans, 1980.

Weiser, Asher, ed. *Perushei ha-Torah le-Rabbeinu Avraham ibn Ezra*. Jerusalem: Mossad Harav Kook, 1976.

Wenham, Gordon J. "Betūlāh 'A Girl of Marriage Age.' " *Vetus Testamentum* 22 (1972): 326–48.

Wheeler, Brannon M. *Moses in the Quran and Islamic Exegesis*. London and New York: RoutledgeCurzon, 2002.

Wolfson, Elliot. *Circle in the Square: Studies in the Use of Gender in Kabbalistic Symbolism*. Albany: State University of New York Press, 1995.

—— *Through a Speculum that Shines: Vision and Imagination in Medieval Jewish Mysticism*. Princeton, NJ: Princeton University Press, 1994.

Wright, J. W., Jr. "Masculine Allusion and the Structure of Satire in Early `Abbāsid Poetry." In *Homoeroticism in Classical Arabic Literature*. Edited by J. W. Wright, Jr. and Everett K. Rowson. New York: Columbia University Press, 1997.

Yahuda, A. S. "A Contribution to Qur'ān and Ḥadīth Interpretation." In *Ignace Goldziher Memorial Volume* I. Edited by S. Löwinger and J. Somogyi. Budapest, 1948.

—— *'Ever ve-'Arav*. Hotza'at Ogen, [1946], 105–112.

Yalqut Shimoni `al ha-Torah. Shemot. Edited by Dov Heiman and Yitzḥaq Shiloni. Jerusalem: Mossad Harav Kook, 1977.

Yellin, David, ed. *Gan ha-Meshalim ve-ha-Ḥidot: Osef Shirei Todros ben Yehuda Abu al-`Afia*. Jerusalem, 5692–6 [1932–4].

—— *Leḥeqer ha-Shirah ha-'Ivrit be-Sefarad*. In *Kitvei David Yellin*, vol. 3. Edited by A. M. Habermann. Jerusalem: Reuben Mas, 5735 [1975].

—— *Torat ha-Shir ha-Sefaradit*, 2nd edition. Jerusalem: Magnes Press, 5732 [1972/3].

Zemach, Eddy. *Ke-Shoresh `Etz. Qeriah Ḥadasha be-Yud Dalet Shirei Ḥol shel Shelomo ben Gabirol*. Rehavia and Tel Aviv: Hotza'at Sifriat Poalim, 1973.

Zemach, Eddy and Tova Rosen-Moked. *Yetzirah Meḥukama: `Iyyun be-Shirei Shemuel ha-Nagid*. Jerusalem: Keter, 1983.

The Zohar. Translated by Harry Sperling and Maurice Simon. London: Soncino Press, 1931.

Zubaidi, A. M. "The Impact of the Qur'ān and Ḥadīth on Medieval Arabic Literature." In *The Cambridge History of Arabic Literature*, I: *Arabic Literature to the End of the Umayyad Period*. Edited by A. F. L. Beeston *et al.* Cambridge: Cambridge University Press, 1983.

Zucker, Moshe. "Ha-Efshar she-Navi Yeḥeta? `Al Ba`ayat ``Isma' al-Anbiya`' ba-Islam u-va-Yahadut." *Tarbiz* 35 (1965): 149–73.

Zulay, Menaḥem. *Eretz Yisrael u-Fiyyuteiha: Meḥqarim be-Fiyyutei ha-Genizah*. Edited by Ephraim Ḥazan. Jerusalem: Magnes Press, 1995.

Zwettler, Michael. "A Mantic Manifesto: The Sūra of 'The Poets' and the Qur'ānic Foundations of Prophetic Authority." In *Poetry and Prophecy: The Beginnings of a Literary Tradition*. Edited by James L. Kugel. Ithaca, NY and London: Cornell University Press, 1990. 75–120.

Index

Aaron *see* Hārūn
Abbasid caliphate 3, 6, 10, 27n32
ʿAbd al-Raḥmān I 3
ʿAbd al-Raḥmān III 3
al-ʿAbdarī *see* Ibn Maymūn
Abrabanel, Don Isaac 19, 67; on Absalom 199; on David 67–8, 82n84, 200–1, 203, 217n92, 217n102; on Jacob 138–9; on Jonadav 202, 217n98; on Tamar 206n14
Abraham: Eliezer and 145n55; and fiery furnace of Chaldea 148n71, 171n42, 239; as friend of God 170n35; monotheism, discovery of 171n41; shirt of Paradise and 239, 253n110
Abraham ibn Ezra 15, 68; commentary of 19, 35–36n85, 75n44, 148n79, 276n2; exegesis on David and Uriah 68–9; and Ibn Mar Shaul 17, 50, 66, 121; on Jacob 138
Absalom: Amnon and 186, 194–6, 202, 209–10n45, 213–14n71; beauty of 57–8, 77n53; as brother of Tamar 188–9, 194–6, 204n4, 205n7, 209n45; rabbinic exoneration of 199; and rape of Tamar 194–6; rebellion vs. David 215n83, 216n92
Abū ʿAbbās 16
Abū al-Qāsim Aḥmad b. Muḥammad b. al-Milḥ *see* Ibn al-Milḥ
Abū ʿAmr b. Shuhayd *see* Ibn Shuhayd
Abu Ayyūb Yaḥyā ibn Sulaymān ibn Gabīrūl *see* Ibn Gabirol, Solomon
Abū Bakr b. Milḥ 257–8
Abū Jaʿfar Muḥammad b. Jarīr al-Ṭabarī *see* al-Ṭabarī
Abulafia, Todros 15, 22n5, 22n6, 26n24, 29n48, 33n64, 36n88, 42n121
Abū Nuwās 34n69, 38n101, 39n102, 63n33, 104n7, 127, 206n22, 207n28, 244n45
Adonijah 57–8, 77–78n53, 77n52, 78n56, 213n71
adultery 24n15, 64–6, 67, 81n74, 82–83n90
ahava/*ḥoleh ahavah* 7, 190; *see also ḥubb*
Aḥimaatz 35–36n85, 204n4
ʿAli b. Muḥammad b. Saʿid b. Ḥazm al-Andalusī, Abū Muḥammad *see* Ibn Ḥazm
Alī Zayn al-ʿĀbidīn 155
allusions, explanation of use in poetry 2, 9, 10–11, 17, 96, 2; *see also iqtibās*; *remizot/remez*; *shibbutz*; *talmīḥ*
Almeria 3, 232
Almohads 4–5, 25n21, 25n22, 26n25, 66, 165
Almoravids 4, 25n21, 165
Amichai, Yehuda 141n8
ʿĀmirids 85
Ammonites 62, 67
Amnon: Absalom and 194–6, 209–10n45, 213–14n71; David and 196–7; food and 190–2; Ibn Gabirol's use of 186–7, 202–3, 208n36; Jonadav and 197–8, 205n6, 205n7, 205n8; lovesickness and 182, 189–90, 204n5, 205n6, 205n7, 210n49; rabbinic exoneration of 199, 202–3; rape of Tamar 180–1, 206n13; Tamar, biological relationship with 209–10n45, 213n67, 215n81
Andalusian love poetry: Hebrew and Islamic scriptural references in 9–10; history of 3–6; *iqtibās and talmīḥ* in 10–11; and medieval Spanish conventions 6–9; *shibbutz and remizah* in 11–13; tropes of 220–3; *see also* tropes

Index of complete poems cited (by title)

Printed in Great Britain
by Amazon

59261909R00188